THE ASSOCIATION FOR SCOTTISH LITERARY STUDIES
NUMBER THIRTY

SIR DAVID LYNDSAY
SELECTED POEMS

*

THE ASSOCIATION FOR SCOTTISH LITERARY STUDIES

The Association for Scottish Literary Studies aims to promote the study, teaching and writing of Scottish literature, and to further the study of the languages of Scotland.

To these ends, the ASLS publishes works of Scottish literature (of which this volume is an example), literary criticism and in-depth reviews of Scottish books in *Scottish Literary Journal* (to be re-launched as *Scottish Studies Review* in November 2000) and scholarly studies of language in *Scottish Language*. It also publishes *New Writing Scotland*, an annual anthology of new poetry, drama and short fiction, in Scots, English and Gaelic, by Scottish writers. ASLS has also prepared a range of teaching materials covering Scottish language and literature for use in schools.

All the above publications, except for the teaching materials, are available as a single 'package', in return for an annual subscription. Enquiries should be sent to: ASLS, c/o Department of Scottish History, University of Glasgow, 9 University Gardens, Glasgow G12 8QH, United Kingdom, telephone +44 (0)141 330 5309. The ASLS website is at this address: http://www.arts.gla.ac.uk/ScotLit/ASLS/

A list of Annual Volumes published by ASLS can be found at the end of this book.

THE ASSOCIATION FOR SCOTTISH LITERARY STUDIES
GENERAL EDITOR — LIAM McILVANNEY

SIR DAVID LYNDSAY
SELECTED POEMS

Edited by

Janet Hadley Williams

GLASGOW

2000

First published in Great Britain, 2000
by The Association for Scottish Literary Studies
c/o Department of Scottish History
University of Glasgow
9 University Gardens
Glasgow G12 8QH

A catalogue record for this book
is available from the British Library.

The Association for Scottish Literary Studies acknowledges
subsidy from the Scottish Arts Council towards
the publication of this book.

Printed and bound in Great Britain by The Cromwell Press, Trowbridge, Wilts

CONTENTS

ACKNOWLEDGEMENTS   vi
INTRODUCTION
    Sir David Lyndsay of the Mount, c.1486-1555   vii
    Lyndsay's Literary Inheritance   xiii
    'Myne mater': Lyndsay's own writing   xviii
    Lyndsay's Scots   xxi
    Editorial Approach   xxi

THE POEMS

1.	The Dreme	1
2.	The Complaynt of Schir David Lindesay	41
3.	The Testament and Complaynt of our Soverane Lordis Papyngo	58
4.	The Answer to the Kingis Flyting	98
5.	The Deploratioun of the Deith of Quene Magdalene	101
6.	The Justing betwix James Watsoun and Jhone Barbour	109
7.	The Tragedie of the Cardinall	112
8.	Squyer Meldrum	128
9.	The Testament of Squyer Meldrum	174
10.	Ane Dialog betwix Experience and ane Courteour (1-684)	183

NOTES   207
ABBREVIATIONS AND BIBLIOGRAPHY   329

ACKNOWLEDGEMENTS

I have received expert help from a variety of sources, not least the pioneering scholarship of Douglas Hamer, editor of the Scottish Text Society's four-volume critical edition of Lyndsay's works. Hamer had neither the enormous benefit of the *Dictionary of the Older Scottish Tongue*, nor the advice of its excellent staff. I am fortunate in being deeply indebted to both.

For assistance over many years I wish to thank the staff of the following institutions: Aberdeen University Library, the Bodleian Library, the British Library, Cambridge University Library, Edinburgh University Library, Glasgow University Library, the Huntington Library, California, St Andrews University Library, St John's College Library, Cambridge, Lambeth Palace Library, the National Library of Australia, the National Library of Scotland, and the Australian National University Library.

Many scholars gave me advice on specific aspects of Lyndsay's poems, or read my editions and notes. For their generous willingness to share their knowledge, I'm glad to thank Mrs Myrtle Anderson-Smith, Professor Dominic Baker-Smith, Professor Priscilla Bawcutt, Mr Charles Burnett, Dr Catherine van Buuren, Dr Ian Campbell, Dr Carol Edington, Dr Jonathan Glenn, Professor Luuk Houwen, Professor R.J. Lyall, Dr Emily Lyle, Mr J. Derrick McClure, Professor A.A. MacDonald, the late Professor C.A. Mayer and Mrs D. Mayer, Dr George Philp, Dr John Purser, Professor Felicity Riddy, Mrs C.G.W. Roads, Mrs Barbara Ross, Dr Margaret Sanderson, the late Dr Helena M. Shire, Professor Grant G. Simpson, Professor A.M. Stewart, Dr Andrea Thomas, and Mr Nigel Tranter.

I wish to thank the Association for Scottish Literary Studies for the commission to edit Lyndsay. The former General Editor of the series, Dr Douglas Mack, gave me great encouragement; the present General Editor, Dr Christopher MacLachlan, offered much wise advice.

I'm grateful beyond words to my family, especially my husband, for so much loving support.

INTRODUCTION

Sir David Lyndsay of the Mount, c.1486-1555

More details of Lyndsay's life survive than can be found for some other fifteenth- and sixteenth-century Scottish poets, such as Robert Henryson or William Dunbar, yet for many aspects of it no record remains.[1] Lyndsay's exact birthdate is unknown, but there is evidence for dating it c.1486, within the last years of James III's reign.[2] His mother's name is not known, although his grandmother may have been a daughter of James Ramsay, burgess of Cupar, and Elizabeth Balfour.[3] His father, also David, was a lesser landholder whose estates, granted by his feudal superior, Patrick, Lord Lindsay of the Byres, were in East Lothian and Fife.[4] Lyndsay, the eldest of five sons,[5] had inherited them in turn by 1524.[6]

Lyndsay knew Latin, which suggests that as a boy he attended a local grammar school,[7] but no records of this survive. There is, moreover, only equivocal evidence of his possible university study. A person of his name was admitted among graduates of St Salvator's College, St Andrews University, 1508-09,[8] but later, unlike Henryson or Dunbar, Lyndsay was not styled 'Maister' (indicating a graduate of four years' study). Study abroad is unlikely; Lyndsay's handwriting, to judge from the sole surviving example in a letter written in 1531,[9] shows no evidence of the italic influence suggestive of continental or continentally-influenced training.[10] This letter preserves the only known signature in holograph: 'Dauid Lyndsay'.

A 1508 reference mentions a 'Lyndesay' who had been attached to the stable of the short-lived infant Prince of Scotland and the Isles.[11] If this was the poet, as his later activities would suggest, his introduction to the lively household of James IV, and to some of the principal duties of heralds, was impressive, for these were the years of the internationally-known tournaments of the Black Lady.[12] At this court, too, was the cleric and court servitor, William Dunbar, then near the height of his career.[13] Lyndsay perhaps knew him, and is likely to have noted the easy intimacy of Dunbar's address to his patron, James IV, for his own poems to James V sometimes have a similar tone. Undoubtedly Lyndsay came to know Dunbar's compositions, as his later admiring reference (*Papyngo*, 17) confirms.

A hiatus in the treasury records obscures Lyndsay's next steps, but by 1511 he was receiving a royal pension of £40, and in 1512 was called 'ischar to the Prince',[14] who was James IV's third and only surviving son, James. Lyndsay's later claim to James V (*Complaynt*, 15-16) that he had 'enterit to thy majestie / The day of thy natyvitie' thus is plausible. Lyndsay, like other royal servants,[15] probably had diverse duties, but only one record reflects this, a payment on 12 October 1511 for 'ij elnis blew taffatis and vj quartaris ₃allow taffatis to be [serve as material for] ane play coit to Dauid Lindesay for the play playt in the King and Quenis presence in the Abbay'.[16] The Abbey venue associates the unknown production with a particular religious feast, such as St Michael's day, then just past (29 September), or possibly with the fanfare launch (12 October) of James IV's great warship, 'Michael'.[17]

By 1513 Lyndsay had purchased part of a tenement located 'on the south side of the High Street' of Edinburgh,[18] conveniently close to the royal residences. (Nearby, at St Giles, the provost was Gavin Douglas, at this date almost finished his translation of the *Aeneid*. His house, an entitlement of the church office, was just to the west of the church.)[19] By the year's end, however, James IV's defeat and death at the battle of Flodden had left Scotland with a king only fifteen months old. From 1514 to 1523, Lyndsay's old post became 'Kingis maister uschar'.[20] He now was closely involved, day and night, in James V's safekeeping,[21] and was the affectionate companion of the king's leisure hours ('quhen thow come frome the scule', *Complaynt*, 97). From his allusions in the *Dreme* (c.1526), Lyndsay seems to have used these hours for educational as well as recreational ends.[22]

In the upheaval after Governor Albany's departure in 1524, the king, aged twelve, was declared of age to rule, and a general parliamentary decree revoked all gifts and appointments made during the minority.[23] Lyndsay was not reinstated, but his claim that James V continued to 'pay me weill my pentioun' (*Complaynt*, 272) is verified in the royal accounts.[24] Lyndsay's Douglas connection—his marriage in the early 1520s to Janet Douglas, a 'semestair of the Kingis lynnyng claithis'—perhaps was useful during the period from June 1526, when Archibald Douglas, the Earl of Angus, had taken control of the government.[25] Nonetheless, after the king took personal control in 1528 Lyndsay was reinstated as king's familiar (though perhaps after a short delay); Janet Douglas also remained at court.[26] In the informal and positive *Complaynt* (1529), Lyndsay distances these years of instability. The tactics of former faction leaders become mini-dramas of greed, corruption, and deceit and, in their light, the pressing present needs for strong government and church reform are stressed.[27]

It is at this time (1529-30) that there are hints that Lyndsay also has the additional duties of a herald. He was a witness described as acting 'in nomine et ex parte Leonis armorum' when the heralds became patrons of a new chaplainry founded in St Michael's aisle, Falkirk;[28] and he was paid £15 for accompanying the servant of Henry Percy, Earl of Northumberland, on his return journey from Scotland.[29] By 1530, Lyndsay was officially 'herauldo'.[30] His yearly pension remained £40 with annual livery (clothing allowance), but he could now expect it to be increased by the occasional perquisites given to officers of arms during diplomatic missions. His *Testament...of the Papyngo*, written by November 1530, reflects the personal and political changes. Ambitious in style and aims, the poem looks forward to a flowering of the arts in Scotland under James V's adult rule and, in a 'Commonyng' of clerical birds, makes a witty yet urgent call for church reform that drew English attention to the poem.[31]

For Lyndsay, the 1530s were years of diplomatic travel, chiefly to initiate or renew various trading agreements and, less publicly, to further negotiations for a suitable spouse for James V. As Snowden Herald, Lyndsay went first to the Habsburg court in Brussels in 1531.[32] In the following years he was part of a series of diplomatic missions to France,[33] which culminated in James V's wedding journey of 1536. These were lengthy stays in France, of three to eight months, with travel sometimes via the English court (where he was called 'Lion King of Arms').[34] Lyndsay thus had many opportunities to observe cultural activities furth of Scotland. Little of his own writing, however, can be linked with certainty to these years. Probably it was in the period when marriage negotiations with France were underway but not concluded, and the king had just received another chivalric order[35] that James V exchanged with Lyndsay some poetic insults in high courtly style. The latter's *Answer...to the Kingis Flyting* alone survives. Lyndsay's poem has a camaraderie—in the choice of insults and compliments, recall of risky amorous adventures, and in the reticent allusions to the king's Scottish mistress and proposed French queen—that suggests a bachelor recipient.

As senior herald, Lyndsay had returned early from France to prepare for Edinburgh's formal welcome for the new queen, Madeleine de Valois, but the princess's death only months after her arrival in Scotland brought all to a sudden halt. Some aspects of the planned reception, such as the dramatic tableaux of 'disagysit folkis' (110), are mentioned by Lyndsay in his *Deploratioun of...Magdalene*, a poem of solemn state mourning. Very few further details of his plans are to be found elsewhere. The arrangements for the queen's funeral, noted sparingly in treasury accounts, were also Lyndsay's concern.[36]

More evidence survives of Lyndsay's involvement in the following year's welcome to Marie de Guise, James V's second wife. For her arrival in St Andrews in June, Lyndsay produced a pageant that recalled in part the entry of Margaret Tudor into Edinburgh in 1503.[37] The herald himself took the speaking role, offering the queen traditional exhortations to be virtuous and obedient.[38] Perhaps it was at this time, when the court was gathered at St Andrews, and celebratory jousting took place, that Lyndsay presented the lighthearted entertainment of the *Justing of...Watsoun and...Barbour*, in which two unlikely court servants are the 'campiounis'. His *Suplicatioun...in Contemptioun of Syde Taillis*, with its compliments to the queen, appears to be another entertainment for the enlarged court of James V and Marie de Guise.[39] Lyndsay organised the queen's formal entry into Edinburgh in July 1538. He conferred with the burgh leaders, and with the various tenement dwellers with frontage onto the High Street, whose 'rowmes' or spaces were needed as stations for the presentation of an unspecified tableaux series. Lyndsay himself was among those named 'to answer' for various sections of the route. He also advised all participants about the 'ordour and furnessing' to be carried out, and was consultant on the content of the welcoming oration, delivered in French by the King's Advocate, Henry Lauder.[40]

It is most unlikely that Lyndsay was not involved in the preparations for the queen's coronation (22 February 1540), but extant references close to the time of the coronation connect him with the visit of Henry VIII's envoy, Ralph Sadler, who had come to Scotland partly to persuade James V to follow his uncle's approach to religious reform.[41] Lyndsay, with Sir John Borthwick, Sir William Ogilvy, and Rothesay Herald, entertained him. Lyndsay acted in his official role—Sadler describes him as 'chief herauld to the king of Scots'[42]—but his known concern for church reform, and Borthwick's in the political aspects of Henrician-inspired change, possibly were considered by James V qualifications for the task.[43] The king certainly continued to show favour to the chief herald: in June he assigned to Lyndsay and his wife 1000 merks owed to him by Sir Walter Lundy.[44]

Between 1540 and 1542, Lyndsay's known activities seem connected once again to his herald's office. At home, he is recorded as a formal witness to various public proclamations.[45] A record of a mid-1541 diplomatic journey by an unnamed Snowden Herald—to John III in Portugal and perhaps also Charles V at Valladolid—possibly refers to further travels abroad for Lyndsay.[46] A letter sent to him by James V on 3 October 1542, which addresses the herald, for the first time, as 'knycht' as well as 'Lyoun King of Armes', and augments his pension 'for all the dayis of his life' by the annual gift of two chalders of oats for his horse,[47] suggests that Lyndsay had reached the peak of his

career as an officer of arms and king's familiar. His completion of a
heraldic record book is associated with this royal recognition.[48] The
armorial provides a splendid heraldic overview of the nobility of James
V's Scotland. In Lyndsay's brief accompanying comments, captions,
and short genealogical notes, the manuscript also reflects official
attitudes to many legal and historical issues of the day.[49]

In the early 1540s, Scotland's political and religious policies
were under intense challenge. Rapprochement with England was seen
by some, perhaps including Lyndsay (as his stance in the *Tragedie*
would argue), as the best way to preserve peace; but by others such
support was considered an attack on the established church. Strained
relations with England worsened into war, and James V did not long
survive the defeat of the Scottish forces at Solway Moss (24
November 1542). His death initiated another long minority, since his
daughter, Mary, was then only days old. Lyndsay had been among
those at the king's bedside (and thus later he could make forthright
poetic allusion to the Beaton's illegal behaviour there).[50] His role as
king's familiar had ended, but as Lyon King he was responsible for
funeral arrangements.[51] He continued to act in that office on behalf of
the then-anglophile regency government led by the Earl of Arran, in
the new year travelling to London to return the late king's collar,
garter, and statutes of the Order bestowed in 1535.[52]

One of the causes of instability during these years was the
reversal of Arran's initially supportive stand on church reform, and
with it the withdrawal of his earlier authorisation of the use of
Scripture 'in the vulgar toung'.[53] Lyndsay does not refer to the
countermand directly, but the change from a policy he endorsed
perhaps forced him to withdraw to the Mount.[54] Yet it seems equally
likely, since the herald was approaching his sixties, that the move was
set in natural train by the king's death.[55] There is evidence of
Lyndsay's presence in Fife, residence at the Mount, and role as
representative for Cupar, on several occasions during these years.[56]

It was as Lyon King that Lyndsay was in the thick of the siege
at St Andrews Castle that followed the murder of Cardinal Beaton in
1546. The committed reformers who had killed Beaton were local men
almost certainly known to Lyndsay.[57] They held the castle in
expectation of the arrival of English support, and with the added ad-
vantage of the governor's son as a hostage. Accompanied by 'one
trumpatt', Lyndsay made two official visits to negotiate with them,
and at the second was able to make progress on behalf of the govern-
ment.[58] Lyndsay wrote his *Tragedie of the Cardinall*, in which the
wraith of Beaton himself is narrator, in the following year. Its ironic
wordplays and more overt criticisms of the cardinal's policies perhaps
placed the poem with others seen as heretical or propagandistic by the

Scottish Dominican Provincial Council held in Edinburgh in 1549.[59] The more colourful, particularised note by the historian, Pitscottie, that the Council condemned and burned 'Schir Dawid Lyndsayis buike', is not confirmed, however, in the printed statutes.[60]

A further mission saw Lyndsay in Denmark by late 1548.[61] His tasks (a trade treaty and a request for assistance against English attack) were made more challenging because Denmark had become officially Protestant. It is not known whether Lyndsay's interest in Erasmian reform was in this setting as valuable as his skills in negotiation,[62] but he was more successful in arguing Scotland's case than was the envoy sent to put England's position at almost the same time. (He was the exiled Protestant Scot, Lyndsay's former colleague, Sir John Borthwick.)[63] Lyndsay's return was delayed, first by the wintry weather, and then by the wreck of his ship in icy February seas,[64] but his enforced extended stay in Denmark could not have been intellectually uncongenial.[65] The printing of a Danish translation of the Bible was then underway, sponsored by Christian III and directed by an expatriate Protestant Scot, John Macalpine.[66] Possibly Lyndsay was encouraged by this enterprise to begin work on *Ane Dialog*, in which he calls for the translation of the Scriptures into Scots, and offers something of an annotated substitute.[67]

After Denmark, heraldic duties abroad were taken on by the up-coming herald,[68] but Lyndsay made one more appearance at home as Lyon King, in January 1554-55 presiding over a Lyon Court trial of the messenger, William Crawar, for abuse of his office.[69] The lessened official workload coincides with Lyndsay's increased literary output, much of it with explicit Fife connections. One such is linked to his friend, William Meldrum of Cleish and Binns, who died in late 1550. Lyndsay wrote a *Historie* of Meldrum's life, appending a gently satiric *Testament*. These poems were perhaps for family or local circulation only, since there is no evidence of their publication during Lyndsay's lifetime or for some years after his death.

Two other works were for wider audiences. Advertised by a short play known as the *Cupar Banns*, Lyndsay's *Satyre of the Thrie Estaitis*, with jests apt for a Fife audience but vivid allusions appropriate to all aspects of Scottish society, was performed on the Castle Hill, Cupar, in June 1552.[70] Locals (including Lyndsay himself, it is often suggested) probably staged the play—extant records give no clue[71]—and the result evidently ensured that the work was not forgotten. On 13 August 1555, the *Thrie Estaitis* was performed again, with some revisions, this time on the new Greenside playfield in Edinburgh, before the regent, Marie de Guise.[72] In these same years, perhaps from 1549, Lyndsay worked with a scholar's care on his other major poem, *Ane Dialog...of the Miserabyll Estait of the Warld*.

First published in 1554, it attempted to fill the need Lyndsay saw for a text combining scriptural translation, religious history, and educative commentary. Attitudes towards the function and nature of poetry were changing, and continued to do so after 1560 under the influence of the newly-established kirk: this poem, in tune with the changing outlook, soon became Lyndsay's most popular work.[73] It was his last, for Lyndsay's death is cited in a charter dated 13 March 1555.[74]

Lyndsay's Literary Inheritance

Lyndsay was not ostentatiously learned—later critics have been more than usually divided about the extent of his scholarship[75]—but he had read and used many early works of technical, historical, and literary interest. Lyndsay might have encountered Sacrobosco's *Sphæra Mundi*, which he called the 'Speir' (*Dreme*, 639), as a text-book.[76] 'Plenius and worthy Tholomie' (*Dreme*, 748) he perhaps met similarly.[77] Later, he must have sought out others, such as the French adaptation of the fifth-century work by Orosius, published in 1509; the English translation by Walter Lynne of Carion's *Chronica* (1532), published in 1550; and the English translation by Thomas Langley of the near-contemporary Latin work, *De Inventoribus Rerum* (1528), by Polydore Vergil, published in 1546. They were only three of the several works on which he drew for *Ane Dialog*.

Classical literature, however, often had for Lyndsay a symbolic value rather than the strong influence of writing known in depth. His references to 'the ornat Ennius' and Hesiod, 'the perfyte poet soverane' (*Ane Dialog*, 226, 229-30), sharpen his contrast between the rhetorically brilliant work of the 'plesand poetis' they represented, and his own 'sad sentence' (210), but he perhaps chose these two simply because of their balancing origins—one from Rome, the other from Greece—for neither was well known at this time.[78] The most important aspect for Lyndsay of another illustrious classical group—of Aristotle, Plato, Virgil, and Cicero (*Ane Dialog*, 566-77)—was the fact that they wrote in 'thare most ornate toung maternall' (*Ane Dialog*, 569). By associating their names with this detail, Lyndsay used them to support his own argument for the use of the vernacular. Lyndsay derived other classical allusions from secondary sources. Those he made to 'Titus Levius', Homer, and Herodotus, for instance, he obtained from Carion. Ovid's *Amores*, II, vi (Corinna's lament for her parrot), perhaps gave some impetus to Lyndsay's composition of the *Testament of the Papyngo*, but this cannot be proved; later bird poems in English and Scots probably were more influential.[79] By contrast, Lyndsay appears to have read Lucan closely, with admiration for his apt descriptive phrases. For the striking comparison—of King Alexander's sweeping actions with the effect of 'thounder, or fyre-flaucht in the air' (*Ane Dialog*, 3662-63)—he acknowledged directly a debt to Lucan's *Pharsalia*.[80]

Lyndsay's general debt to French theatrical genres has been noted.[81] He was also aware of the French tradition of dream poetry, beginning with the *Roman de la Rose*, but this, too, seems an indirect influence, via Chaucer and others. The *Deploratioun*, however, offers a small amount of evidence that Lyndsay knew the work of his French contemporary, Clément Marot.[82]

Most familiar to Lyndsay was the poetry composed in his native language, which, like Dunbar, he called 'Inglis' (*Papyngo*, 24). Thus, in the *Papyngo*, Lyndsay cited the English writers, Chaucer, Gower, and Lydgate, as literary progenitors as well as writers of the highest ability (11-14), and he added, without national differentiation, the names of those Scots he considered to be the best of the following generations.

Allusions to Chaucer, Gower, and Lydgate had been made earlier by Douglas and Dunbar,[83] yet Lyndsay's reference in turn was no mere imitation. Lyndsay linked his own *Squyer Meldrum* (26-27), for example, to two works by Chaucer, *Troilus and Criseyde*, and the Jason and Medea story in the *Legend of Good Women*, to indicate that he would be concerned similarly with love and betrayal in a chivalrous context. *Squyer Meldrum* does not interact with these poems in the subtle ways in which Henryson's *Testament* and Chaucer's *Troilus* do so, but the connection illuminates the poem's structural patterning, and the way in which Meldrum and his lady are presented. It is difficult to be sure what other specific works of Chaucer Lyndsay knew. (Probably they included, mistakenly, Lydgate's *Complaint of the Black Knight*, since that poem had been published in Scotland, c.1508, with the title, *The Mayng or Disport of Chaucer*.)[84] Nonetheless, Chaucer's impact on Lyndsay's style, whether direct or indirect (through Lydgate, Henryson or Dunbar), is evident. It is found, for instance, in Lyndsay's occasional use of a distinctively Chaucerian expression (*Dreme*, 105; *Squyer Meldrum*, 991); in the practice (perhaps also learned from Gower's *Confessio Amantis*) of the unobtrusive rhetorical art of conversing in verse, most notably in the *Complaynt*; in the clerkly allusion to a particular book to build a useful introductory scaffolding, as in the *Tragedie*; or in the careful adoption of the elaborate nine-line *Anelida* 'complaint' stanza for the *Dreme*'s formal and counselling 'Exhortatioun'.

Of Lydgate's works Lyndsay possibly knew his *Troy Book* and the *Siege of Thebes* (*Dreme*, 42), but almost certainly the *Fall of Princes*, the popular translation (from a French intermediary) of

Boccaccio's *De Casibus Virorum Illustrium*, which Lyndsay
ostensibly cited at the beginning of his *Tragedie of the Cardinall*. He
also was aware of Lydgate's additional moralising envoys, and chose
to extend their function by introducing ironic undertones and a
dramatic presentation, thus allowing the fictional Beaton to speak his
for himself. Lyndsay also pointedly drew away from the stress on
Fortune as the agent of destruction, which till then had been central to
the *De Casibus* mode: when his 'Beaton' instead places blame before
those secular and religious leaders who had shirked their
responsibilities, the poem became politicised.

Lyndsay alluded to (and sometimes gave his assessment of)
many Scottish writers and their works, or to the central characters and
distinctive features of them. In the *Testament of the Papyngo*, for
instance, Lyndsay offered special praise for the writing of six earlier
poets: Quintyng, Mersar, Rowle, Henderson, Hay, and Holland (19).
So little survives of the compositions of the first three that the equal
weight Lyndsay gave to these writers—for he listed them together in a
single line—now seems inexplicable.[85] Their plight (and that of
Walter Kennedy, of whose poems only a handful survives) must act as
a reminder that much has been lost from the picture of Lyndsay's
literary inheritance. Yet it is still possible to understand something of
Lyndsay's attitude to the last three, in particular Robert Henryson, a
fellow layman among many poet-clerics.

In his *Dreme*, Lyndsay drew extensively upon Henryson's
Testament of Cresseid and *Orpheus and Eurydice*, as Denton Fox has
noted. These echoes are not simply imitative, but offer evidence of
some thoughtful readings. Lyndsay selects those details from
Henryson's portrait of Venus, for example, that assist his theme of
good kingship; thus her beneficent aspects, as 'lustie luffis quene', are
kept uppermost (*Dreme*, 404-18; *Test. Cresseid*, 217-38). In another
passage he alters the emphasis of Henryson's depiction of Hell, so that
the churchmen among its inhabitants are highlighted (*Dreme*, 169-82;
Orpheus, 310-44). Less known are Lyndsay's appreciative responses
within his own beast and bird tales, the *Complaint of Bagsche* (103ff)
and the *Testament of the Papyngo* (680-81), to the ironic comedy and
stylistic restraint of the *Fables*. There is Henrysonian influence, too,
in the sententious position Lyndsay takes in *Ane Dialog*, 'But sad sen-
tence should have ane sad indyte' (Prol. 210), which looks back to the
opening of the *Testament of Cresseid*. The two poets have compatible
views on social justice, similarly based on a thorough knowledge of
the Vulgate: both, for instance, quote the scriptural appeal to a God
who sleeps too long (*Ane Dialog*, 2701; *Thrie Estaitis*, 1160; *Fables*,
1295); and both speak for the rights of the weak and unprotected in so-
ciety (*Bagsche*, 179-80; *Fables*, 2761-62).

Lyndsay's allusion to Gilbert Hay among poets suggests that he knew the *Buik of King Alexander the Conquerour*, since Hay's other works, also possibly known to Lyndsay, were prose translations.[86] The central theme of Hay's *Buik*, good government, was the focus of much of Lyndsay's writing. In *Ane Dialog* he refers to the example of Alexander's rule among others more and less successful, adding what appears to be a direct reference to Hay's work: 'Geve thow at lenth wald reid his ryng.../ In Inglis toung, in his gret buke, Att lenth his lyfe thar thow may luke' (3652, 3654-55). The *Buik of King Alexander the Conquerour* is also a likely source for the comparison Lyndsay makes between Gaudefer's heroism against the odds, which Hay details (3652-928), and Meldrum's courage at his last uneven battle (*Meldrum*, 1280-82).

Richard Holland's *Buke of the Howlat*, an important source for Dunbar, also gave Lyndsay a witty precedent for the clerical-avian drama of his *Papyngo*.[87] Several more alliterative works were familiar to Lyndsay: he refers to 'Golibras' (*Meldrum*, 1315), of the fifteenth-century alliterative romance, *Golagros and Gawain*; and to the story of the 'Gyir Carling' (*Dreme*, 45), which is alliterative in its only surviving form.[88] Alliterative diction influenced Lyndsay's style in his own romance of *Squyer Meldrum* (as, for instance at 19, 111, 143, 152). The same poem reveals that non-alliterative romances, such as *Lancelot of the Laik* (1079) and *Eger and Gryme* (1318), as well as historical verse, also were known to Lyndsay. He took delight, in particular, in recalling Hary's *Wallace* in verbal echoes (such as those at 45, 55-56), and in modelling his account of Meldrum's sea battle en route to Scotland upon Wallace's encounter with the 'Rede Reffayr'.

William Dunbar's importance to Lyndsay is reflected in the perceptive assessment he made of the senior poet. Citing the *Goldyn Targe* in evidence, Lyndsay describes Dunbar as one 'quhilk language had at large' (*Papyngo*, 17). Undoubtedly, Lyndsay was influenced by Dunbar's ability to use his extensive vocabulary with great rhetorical freedom and flexibility. Lyndsay adopted, for example, the vigorously alliterative lists of servitor-scoundrels used by Dunbar (B9, B67; *Complaynt*, 361-63, *Papyngo*, 390-92); he re-used the expressions of Dunbar's petitionary openings (cf. B54 and *Bagsche*), and drew upon Dunbar's high-style passages of seasonal description (*Papyngo*, 101-12; *Ane Dialog*, 133-201). He addressed to James V the slightly impertinent comments, sometimes proverbially or colloquially expressed, that recall Dunbar's similar lines to James IV (B63; *Complaynt*, 103-04, 461-82), and he borrowed an occasional word perhaps coined by Dunbar—'duddroun' for instance—for his own use (*Answer*, 59). Yet even a casual glance at Lyndsay's poems is enough to show that they are not Dunbar imitations. As often as his lines

appear to parallel those by Dunbar, Lyndsay's writing seems to engage
in a more robust sense with examples of his senior colleague's
'language at large'.[89] He changes the emphasis, or finds different uses
for his Dunbarian material. Describing the moon, for instance,
Lyndsay notes that this sphere lacks all light except 'the reflex of
Phebus bemes brycht' (*Dreme*, 389-90). The appropriation of the very
similar lines in the *Goldyn Targe* (32-33) seems intentional, but in the
advice-to-princes context of his *Dreme*, Lyndsay uses Dunbar's clever
image of dazzling brightness didactically, to underline the fact that a
planet (or monarch) dependent solely on reflected light ultimately is
limited and weak. The concluding joke of Dunbar's *Schir, lat it neuer*
(B66), the king's promise to buy Dunbar clothing as rich as that of a
bishop's mule, also caught Lyndsay's imagination. He added a less
personally-directed bite to it in the *Papyngo*, where the bird transforms
the disciples, Peter and Paul, into courtiers, and impertinently claims
that their gifts at Yule were much less rich than the current trappings
of episcopal mules (*Papyngo*, 1050-52).

Yet it was to Gavin Douglas, author of the *Palice of Honour*,
creator of the 'trew translatioun' of Virgil's *Aeneid*, and more than
three other works, that Lyndsay gave highest honour among writers in
the vernacular, praising both his rhetorical skill and his learning.
Lyndsay knew the *Palice* and the *Eneados* well; possible verbal echoes
occur in several of his poems.[90] Many of these allusions belong to a
tradition common also to Dunbar and others, yet there are some that
show that Lyndsay had read Douglas's poems with great care and
appreciation. His praise of James I (*Papyngo*, 430-36), for instance, is
a thoughtful adaptation of Douglas's opening homage to Virgil.
Lyndsay retains Douglas's 'Gem of ingyne' and 'flude of eloquence'—
apt for a monarch who was reputedly a poet[91]—and keeps something
of the alliterative flow of Douglas's 'peirless perle, patroun of poetry',
although he partially replaces the latter with 'peirll of polycie / Well
of justice', to make far more fitting kingly epithets.

Lyndsay alluded to the opening line of the *Aeneid* to introduce
(and elevate) his own subject: 'Sa I intend, the best I can, / Descryve
the deidis and the man' (*Meldrum*, 35-36). That his echo was of
Douglas's translated version, 'The batalis and the man I wil discrive',
is a significant link between the two poets. Lyndsay found congenial
Douglas's desire as a translator to make more widely available that
'erst was bot with clerkis comprehend' ('Exclamatioun', 45). In *Ane
Dialog*, Lyndsay spoke similarly. In his own somewhat different
context, he echoed Douglas's re-application of Virgil's homage to
Jupiter ('Thus I beseik the, Lord...be of my muse / All other Iove and
Phebus I refus', X Prol. 150-52), when in traditional manner he re-
jected the pagan muses ('Beseikand the gret God to be my muse',

243). Lyndsay also replaced the earlier poet's preference for the 'gentill' reader with a new emphasis on the needs of the 'unlernit'. He did so not in an attacking spirit, but in an admiring attempt to continue and extend Douglas's role as a 'bridge...between the world of learning...and the world of vernacular poetry.'[92]

'Myne mater': Lyndsay's own writing

Lyndsay took the tradition of authorial modesty to mocking heights: from his own comments (*Complaynt*, 49; *Answer*, 15-16; *Ane Dialog*, 224), some of them more serious than others, Lyndsay claimed that he was neither a 'baird', the kind of lowly strolling-player that Dunbar so despised (B65, 17), nor a 'poeit', a term at this time often applied to the classical writers, or to those of outstanding rhetorical skill or pretensions to it. Of his poems, Lyndsay spoke neutrally of 'myne dyting', 'myne mater' (*Papyngo*, 64, 66; *Ane Dialog*, 297), or used the general term for something composed or in writing, 'indyte' (*Ane Dialog*, 246). For the action of composing, Lyndsay used the same word as a verb (*Answer*, 60; *Meldrum*, 32, *Ane Dialog*, 6109). Such self-effacement is somewhat deceptive; a differing evaluation of his role is quietly evident at other places. For example, Lyndsay presents himself in the manner of Chaucer and Henryson, seated in his 'oritore' or study (*Dreme*, 1031; *Tragedie*, 2), engaged in the clerkly activities of writing or reading. Like scholars Douglas and Skelton, he also cross-references his work, mentioning the *Dreme* within the lines of the *Complaynt* (99). In the later *Squyer Meldrum*, moreover, Lyndsay adds himself to the end of a list that begins with ancient poets and takes in later writers, including, explicitly, Chaucer (24), although his mock-modest excuse for doing so is subject-matter that is as 'nobill' as that of these poets (34).

Lyndsay followed earlier Scottish writers in the variety of genres he used, including the dream-poem, petitionary complaint, testament, beast tale, chivalric romance, dialogue, tragedy, mock tournament, formal lament and, in ironic tone, courtly love poem (*Thrie Estaitis*, 271-94). He was also continuing a well-established tradition when he sometimes used these genres as 'modal medleys.'[93] The *Testament of the Papyngo* is Lyndsay's outstanding example: therein, bird fable, *De Casibus* tragedy, *chanson d'aventure*, complaint, and testament, among other genres, interact in tragi-comic manner. Other poems, such as the *Answer to the Kingis Flyting*, which begins in flyting insult and cries for vengeance, progresses to admonitory counsel, and ends in extravagant compliment, repay close attention. Devotional verse, on the other hand, such as that composed by Holland (*Howlat*, 718-54),

Kennedy, and Dunbar in the Marian hymn tradition, was one category Lyndsay did not attempt (as far as is known), even in a less ornate form. (Perhaps a result of his status as layman, or of later censorship, this omission also could be linked to reservations about the highly-crafted, Latin-based nature of that poetic mode.)[94]

Lyndsay's metrical skill is considerable. Like others before him, he preserved a traditional decorum, matching the metre to the kind of poem he was writing. Thus, for example, he used the four-foot couplet for romance and informal complaint, rhyme royal for courtly lament or testament, and the elaborate Chaucerian nine-line stanza for the high-style 'exhortatioun'. Yet Lyndsay is distinctive among fellow poets in the extent of his use of stanzaic change within a single work. (This perhaps was derived from an interest in verse drama, where it was more common.)[95] In his most metrically varied non-dramatic work, *Ane Dialog*, Lyndsay used formal eight- and nine-line stanzas, rhyme royal, and tetrameter couplets, switching from one to another as a way of organising his material into sections of narrative and thematic argument or commentary. The metrical shifts also had visual usefulness in such a long work, perhaps contributing to the poem's later popularity as a text for private study, recital, or reading aloud in discrete portions. In other poems, Lyndsay used metrical transitions to signal changes in theme or viewpoint. Thus, in the *Papyngo*, Lyndsay's high-style prologue in the nine-line stanza (*aabaabbcc*), with the elevated theme of praise for vernacular poetry past and present, is separated from the poem that follows by the use there of the courtly yet flexible rhyme royal stanza, the distinction allowing Lyndsay's own narrative to become in part an example of the opening claims. The *Answer*'s colophonic concluding couplet and the *Dreme*'s final two-stress stanza have been called doggerel, yet each piece, metrically distinct from the poem proper, has a part to play, the couplet reinforcing Lyndsay's jocular stance of poetic inability, the stanza universalising the sombre king-directed counsel that has preceded it. The rhetorical display of the single thirteen-line alliterative stanza that opens the *Thrie Estaitis* also has a defined purpose, providing a superb attention-gathering verbal 'fanfare'. Even where Lyndsay used the same metre throughout a poem, there is evidence of a lively interest in the metrical aspect of composition: Lyndsay had noted, for instance, the five-stress couplet of Hay's *Buik*, possibly its earliest use in a work in Scots, and adopted it, with tongue in cheek, for his mock-heroic *Justing of Watsoun and Barbour*.

Lyndsay's stylistic range is wide: in the prologues of the *Dreme*, *Papyngo*, and *Ane Dialog*, for example, he wrote in the high style of which Dunbar and Douglas were masters, contributing his own examples of the refined diction (*impurpurit*, for instance) that was a feature of this style. Lyndsay also was at home in the reverse of this style—the comic verse in which colloquial and native diction was used for insults, flyting, cursing, mock heroic narrative, and parody. This is evident, for instance, in the conversation between the tailor's wife and the soutar's wife in the *Thrie Estaitis* (1319-33), with its alliterative vigour, and colloquial words or collocations—'kow-clink', 'get thair paiks'. The *Complaynt*'s interplay of oaths and colloquialisms with a more formal diction also attests to Lyndsay's skill. The *Justing*, *Syde Taillis* and the *Answer* also have some features of this low style, but the latter, replying to the king, deftly avoids the concentrated alliterative abuse of Dunbar's *Flyting*, or Rowle's *Cursing*.[96]

Much of Lyndsay's verse, however, is in the 'middle' style that accommodated elaborate narrative as well as counsel and instruction. Lyndsay enriched it at need; sometimes, for instance, by the addition of internal rhyme, as in the *Papyngo*'s final stanza (the traditional dismissal of the book). This middle style, based on the rhyme royal stanza, also allowed Lyndsay flexibility to develop extended metaphors and comparisons; to explain, for example, the heavenly contentment of the diverse 'glorifeit bodeis' in terms of the varying capacities of everyday measuring vessels—'crowat', 'pynte stope', 'quart', 'galloun pitschair', 'puntioun', 'tun' (*Ane Dialog*, 6176-95). Word-play of various kinds is another frequent feature of Lyndsay's style. His use, for example, of the word 'angelicall' in the opening line of the *Papyngo* aptly anticipates the poem's bird theme.[97] Its significance is stressed again in both the bird's testament-bequest of her 'voce angelycall' (1103), and in the final stanzas, where the flight of the bird's 'angell fedderis' (1160) lightly suggests her (and the poet's) link with the angelic hierarchy of divine messengers. Lyndsay also gives ironic senses to proverbial comparisons ('tygerris toung' and 'strang lyke an elephand', for instance, in the *Answer*, 4, 25). He wittily uses the transferred epithet, such as that describing Edinburgh's speech-makers in terms of their rhetorical skill (*Deploratioun*, 162, 'ornate oratouris').

Lyndsay's poetic interest in the social order continues a preoccupation of writers such as Henryson in the *Fables*, or Dunbar in the poems *Quhy will ʒe, merchantis*, B55 (in which he points to the loss of 'commone proffeitt' (4) for 'laik of reformatioun' (2)), *Fredome, honour and nobilnes*, B13, and *Doverrit with dreme*, B11. In the latter (as in B79, 41-52), there are attacks on the topics Lyndsay addresses—the pride, corrupt lifestyle, and neglect of preaching duties of churchmen (6-15), for example. Yet in Lyndsay's work there is also evidence of a desire to consider such 'non-poetic' issues with a new intensity, and to weave them together with poetic concerns. One of his most striking methods of doing so was a fruit of his dramatic expertise. In several poems Lyndsay experimented with the use of personae, presented either with Henrysonian touches of irony, as in *Bagsche*, or with the sharp satire of the *Papyngo*'s deathbed exchanges.[98] The use of the voice of the wraith of David Beaton, a real figure well known for his part in recent political and religious turmoil, took another step, which the *De Casibus* form cleverly disguised. Such inventiveness greatly appealed to English and Scottish writers from the 1550s onwards, its influence evident, for example, in Robert Sempill's poem on John Hamilton, *The Bischoppis Lyfe and Testament*, of 1571.[99] Lyndsay also engaged poetically with current issues by re-applying convention. In *Ane Dialog*, for instance, he gave new twists to the traditional apology for his book's inadequacies. His wish that his work should be directed to 'colyearis, cairtaris, and to cukis' resembles earlier mock-modest 'banishments', yet also differs from them. In this late poem, these members of society are Lyndsay's preferred audience, he makes plain. He addresses the 'gentyl redar' in the expected fashion, begging amendment of his text where necessary. Yet unlike his predecessors, he also puts to that reader, on behalf of the 'unlernit', some uncomfortably topical questions: 'Thocht every commoun may nocht be one clerk.../ Quhy suld of God the marvellous hevinly werk / Be hid frome thame?' (552-55).

Lyndsay's Scots

Lyndsay wrote in the vernacular language of Lowland Scotland, now called Early Middle Scots (1450-1550).[100] Neither authorial manuscripts nor many of the earliest printed editions of Lyndsay's poems are known to have survived, so it is difficult to identify with confidence those aspects of Lyndsay's Scots that are distinctive. There are East Central regionalisms in his writing, such as 'buller' (*Papyngo*, 95), which is still in use in Fife.[101] A detailed study of these, and of other characteristics of Lyndsay's Scots, such as the singular senses he gave to some words ('ladrone' for instance), or his use of anglicised forms, is yet to be made.[102] Given the interventionist editing of the later sixteenth-century printers on whose texts we now rely, such a study would require careful qualification.[103]

Editorial Approach

The *Selections* contains full texts of nine of Lyndsay's extant poems. A tenth, *Ane Dialog*, is represented by a long excerption, chosen to convey the thematic, structural, and metrical variety of the whole. (Of the remaining four, two are the unsubstantiated attributions, *Kitteis Confessioun* and *Peder Coffeis*;[104] the third and fourth are the *Complaint and Publict Confessioun of the Kingis Auld Hound, callit Bagsche*, c.1530-c.1542, and *Ane Suplicatioun...in Contempt of Syde Taillis*, c.1538-c.1540.)

The *Selections* is designed to introduce Lyndsay's writing to new readers, and to offer scholars freshly-edited texts and original research. For greater accessibility, texts are accompanied by an on-the-page gloss, but they remain as faithful as possible to the earliest or best exemplars, any variants used from other witnesses recorded in the Notes. The spelling is modernised conservatively: *з* is replaced by *y*; *y* by *th* (where the value requires); *i* by *j* (as in *Ianuarie* to *Januarie*), and *u* by *v* (as in *ouerdriue* to *overdrive*; *neuer* to *never*, although in some cases, such as *ovir* or *evir*, the metre indicates a monosyllabic pronunciation). Also in accord with present-day usage, *w* has been replaced by *v* (as in *wailзeand* to *vailyeand*); *v* by *u* (*vmquhyle* to *umquhyle*), and *w* by *u* (*Ewrope* to *Europe*, *wnto* to *unto*). *Off* has been modernised to *Of*, and abbreviations have been expanded. Capitalisation, italicisation, and punctuation follow present usage; line and stanza numbering are added.

As far as is possible, the poems are presented in chronological sequence. In several instances, however, precise composition dates cannot be established: no autograph manuscripts of Lyndsay's works exist, nor, in almost all cases, have the earliest printed editions survived. Poem titles are listed in full, as accurately as the varied bibliographic circumstances permit, near the beginning of the Notes. Where necessary, for ease of reference, carefully shortened forms are used at the head of relevant poem texts.

The Notes begin with brief discussions on the following topics: texts used and consulted; title; poetic form; date; and metre. Additional notes (such as that on *Ane Dialog*'s marginal material) are inserted at this point when required. A following Bibliography contains full references to all works cited in shortened form.

Notes to the Introduction

[1] Substantial studies are Hamer 1931-36: IV.ix-xl; Lyall 1989: xiv-xxii, and Edington 1994.

[2] Lyndsay was probably twenty-one by 19 October 1507, the date on which Patrick, Lord Lindsay of the Byres, made him the customary grant of the lands of Garmylton (now Garleton)-Alexander near Haddington, East Lothian; see Laing 1871: I.ix; Edington 1994: 11-12.

[3] Dickinson 1928: 167-69; Hamer 1931-36: IV.249 (note on James Ramsay); Lindsay 1938: 15; Hamer 1931-36: IV.284.

[4] HMC 1891: 141-43; Edington 1994: App. 2; *RMS*, II, no. 911; III, nos 1781, 2748.

[5]*RMS*, III, nos 2529, 2748.

[6]Hamer 1931-36: IV.250 (no. 47); *RMS*, III, no. 1781. Lyndsay's perspective in his poems reflects this. For Fife, see, for example, *Tragedie*, 215, 260-61; *Cupar Banns* (in Hamer 1931-36: II.10-32), 25-80; for East Lothian, see the knowing reference to Aberlady, *Complaynt*, 478-49.

[7]Durkan 1962: 151-54, 168; Durkan 1990: 123-24.

[8]Anderson 1926: 202-04.

[9]London, BL, MS Cotton Caligula B.I., fol. 313.

[10]Simpson 1977: 16-22.

[11]*ER*, XIII.127. A small piece of later evidence supports this servant's connection with the poet. In Paris for the 1536-37 royal wedding ceremonies, by then in the post of senior herald, Lyndsay was given responsibilities for the king's horses and saddlery; *TA*, VI.455, 456.

[12]See Fradenburg 1991: 225-55.

[13]Bawcutt 1992: 108-09; Baxter 1952: 142, 181-82.

[14]*TA*, IV.269, 441.

[15]See Bawcutt 1992: 49, 79, and compare the career of Sir James Inglis, who combined duties as James IV's clerk and Prince James's chaplain with participation in dramatic performances and the writing of literary compositions; see *Papyngo*, 40-41n.

[16]*TA*, IV.313.

[17]Macdougall 1989: 237-38.

[18]Wood 1941: I, ii.168.

[19]Bawcutt 1976: 8.

[20]*ER*, XIV.8-9, 127-28, 156-57, 220, 242, 409, 462; *ER*, XV.44; *TA*, V.112; *RSS*, I, no. 31; *TA*, V.37; *TA*, V.127, 196. (The 'master of houshald' of *TA*, V.160, probably is an error.)

[21]HMC 1904: 11-12.

[22]'Antique' tales, such as those Lyndsay mentions, of the great king Alexander, or of 'worthy Pompeyus' (*Dreme*, 35), were believed to teach proper behaviour, moral lessons, and provide edifying examples—in contrast, for instance, to the unmentioned, and morally more dubious romance of Lancelot. The prophecies Lyndsay also mentions (43) had a recognised place in such a scheme, especially in this time of political crisis, when their notions of coming order could be a means of 'confortand' the king, an objective to which Lyndsay alludes explicitly (46); Hadley Williams 1990: 155-66; Sutton and Visser-Fuchs 1997: 188-342.

[23]*APS*, II.286-87, 290.

[24]*ER*, XV.116, 229; *TA*, V.310, where payments cite Lyndsay as 'quondam [formerly]' usher to the king. A good account of the financial difficulties of the treasury during this period is Murray 1983: 45-49.

[25]Accounts between September 1518 and June 1522 are lost; from 1522 see *TA*, V.196 and *RSS*, I, no. 3570.

[26]*ER*, XV.395. Janet Douglas twice subsequently received gifts from the king: *RSS*, II, nos 998; 1889.

[27]Hadley Williams 1996b: 213-15.

[28]Protocol Book of James Meldrum 1520-33 (Edinburgh, SRO B30/1/1, fol. 110^v).

[29]*TA*, V.377.

[30]*ER*, XVI.12; *TA*, V.431-32.

[31]The poem was printed in London by John Byddell; see *Papyngo*, note on 'Text'.

[32]See *James V Letters*, 191; 193-94; 203-04; Hadley Williams, 'Of officiaris' (in press).

[33]*TA*, VI.44; *SP Henry VIII*, VII.385; Bapst 1889: 180 (Vienna, *Haus- Hof- und Staats Archiv*, Rep. P. fasc. c. 227, nos 7 and 9); Archives Nationales, Paris, J961[8], no. 105 (this was slightly more than £50 Scots); *James V Letters*, 226; *TA*, VI.46, 232; Archives Nationales, Paris, J961[8], no. 52.

[34]*L&P Henry VIII*, IX.151, 165, 178.

[35]The Scottish king had received the Order of the Golden Fleece from the Emperor in 1532; see *James V Letters*, 221-22.

[36]Innes 1978: 6. For the funeral Lyndsay was paid the traditional herald's 'pow' or 'poll' penny, of 'ane croune of wecht [a crown of full or standard weight]'; *TA*, VI.423.

[37]At the town gateway, Marie de Guise, similarly, was offered keys, hers to the 'haill of Scotland', Margaret Tudor's to the city of Edinburgh; see Pitscottie, I.378-79 and Leland 1774: IV.289; Kipling 1998: 263-64.

[38]Pitscottie, I.379.

[39]Lyndsay perhaps composed it during the following two years; as also his *Complaint and Publict Confessioun of...Bagsche*, but this, despite its topical references, is difficult to date with precision.

[40]Marwick, 1869-82: II.89-91; Hadley Williams, 'Lyndsay and Europe' (in press). The welcome Lyndsay devised made a favourable impression on the new queen, who wrote of it to her mother, the Duchess de Guise, but only the latter's pleasure at the news, a brief comment, has survived; see Wood 1923: 6.

[41]*SP Sadler*, I.46-49.

[42]*L&P Henry VIII*, XV.248.

[43]Such an interpretation is not at odds with James V's reported response to an interlude (which some critics argue was written by Lyndsay) that was performed earlier in the same year before English visitors. At its end, it was said, James V threatened to send to Henry VIII 'six of the proudest' of the degenerate Scots prelates portrayed. If so, it perhaps was a dramatic gesture, politically astute rather than expressive of any real change of commitment; see London, BL, MS Reg. 7. c. xvi, fols 136-139 (Sir William Eure to Thomas Cromwell), rpt Hamer 1931-36: II.1-6; Kantrowitz 1975: 11-27; Lyall 1978.

[44]*ADCP*, 488, 8 June 1540.

[45]*APS*, II.326, 369.

[46]*James V Letters*, 430-31, 437-38; Burnett 1996: 299.

[47]*RSS*, II, no. 4910.

[48]Edinburgh, NLS, Adv. MS 31.4.3; Laing 1822. It is now considered the earliest extant native Armorial Register; see Burnett 1996: 297-98; Hadley Williams, 'Lyndsay and Europe' (in press).

[49]See Hadley Williams 1996b: 223-26.

[50]Pitscottie, I.408; *Tragedie*, 120-23.

[51]*TA*, VIII.142, 143.

[52]*L&P Henry VIII*, XVIII, i.307; London, BL, Add. MS 33531, fol. 13.

[53]*APS*, II.415. Lyndsay's support for the availability of the scriptures in the vernacular is stated in *Ane Dialog*, 643-84.

[54]Edington 1994: 59-60. An incomplete record of a payment to him in August 1545, of £43 (*TA*, VIII.403), cautions against hasty conclusions about Lyndsay's loss of favour. As senior herald he appears to have received payments when appropriate, as on the completion of the Danish mission in 1549.

[55]Janet Douglas also disappears from court records from this time.

[56]*APS*, II.410, 411, 443, 446, 448, 456, 468, 469; *APS*, II.429, 441; *TA*, VII.275.

[57]See Sanderson 1986: 222-28.

[58]*SP Henry VIII*, V.581-82. Knox's assertion that Lyndsay later also gave unofficial 'counsall' to the Castilians to call upon Knox himself to preach (*Works*, I, 186) is not confirmed by other sources, nor is there evidence to support the argument (Edington 1994: 64) that Lyndsay made any further visits from the Mount.

[59]*Concilia Scotiae*, II.120.

[60]Pitscottie, II.141. See Hamer 1929: 11-14 for the arguments identifying the 'buike' as the *Tragedie*. An act of parliament of 1 February 1551 (*APS*, II.488-89) targets the printers of heretical 'bukis ballatis sangis blasphematiounis rymes or Tragedeis outher in latine or Inglis toung'.

[61]*TA*, IX.259; Christensen 1983: 67-69; Hadley Williams 1992: 101-03.

[62]See Cameron 1990: 168-71 for an overview of this aspect of Lyndsay's writing.

[63]See Christensen 1983: 68; Durkan 1982: 152-53.

[64]Christensen 1983: 69.

[65]See further, Edington 1994: 176-77.

[66]Macalpine, formerly a Dominican prior at Perth, was now professor of theology at Copenhagen; see further Bredahl Petersen 1937.

[67]At his eventual return in spring, Lyndsay received 100 French 'crounis of the sone' (£112 10s Scots) for his expenses; *TA*, IX.347.

[68]*TA*, X.84-85.

[69]Chalmers 1806: I.39; Burnett 1981: 181-82.

[70]George Bannatyne included the text of the *Cupar Banns* and lengthy excerpts from the play in his manuscript of 1568, fols 164[r]-168[r]; 168[r]-210[r]. For full discussions and texts, see Hamer 1931-36: IV.xxxiv-xxxvii, 125-240; II, and Lyall 1989.

[71]See *Cupar Banns*, 11, 17, 271-72; Mill 1927: 168.

[72]Marwick 1869-82: II.197, 198-99, 284; Mill 1927: 168.

[73]See Geddie 1912: 299-317 and Hamer 1931-36: IV.xlvi-liv for the history of Lyndsay's literary reputation.

[74]*RMS*, IV, no. 1006. No will survives, but a document disputing the disposition of Lyndsay's property reveals that he was in comfortable circumstances at the time of his death. (A separate study of the document is in preparation.) For the text, see Hamer 1931-36: IV.275-77.

[75]See, for example: Warton 1824: III.125, 134; Williams 1915: 170-71; Hamer 1931-36: IV.xxxviii ('a degree of scholarship not idly to be put aside'); Kinghorn 1970: 40.

[76]On the mathematics of the earthly sphere, the *Sphæra mundi* had appeared in numerous fifteenth and sixteenth-century editions. One was a text 'cum questionibus P. d'Ailly' (Paris 1515), in use at King's College, Aberdeen; see Macfarlane 1985: 369; Durkan and Ross 1961: 131, 150.

[77]Both were part of the university Arts syllabus; see Macfarlane 1985: 368-70.

[78]They were not mentioned by Chaucer or Douglas. Skelton cites them among other 'poetis laureat' in his *Garlande...of Laurell* (328, 347).

[79]See notes to the *Papyngo*, p. 238 (Form).

[80]See Bk x, 34-36. Lucan was highly regarded in the medieval-Renaissance period; cf. Chaucer, *HF*, 1498-1502, and Douglas, *Pal. Honour*, 900; *Eneados*, I, v.102n. Copies of the *Pharsalia* were owned by several sixteenth-century Scots including John Forman, possibly the schoolmaster of that name at Cupar in the 1540s, who owned a copy of the text printed at Louvain, c. 1475; see Durkan and Ross 1961: 98, also 60, 145, 159.

[81]See Lyall 1989: xxiii-xxvi.

[82]For details, see notes to the *Deploratioun*, pp. 260-66.

[83]See Dunbar, *Golden Targe* (B59), 253-68; Douglas, *Pal. Honour*, 919-21.

[84]See *CM*, 179-203.

[85]For the first three, see *Papyngo*, 19n.

[86]See *Papyngo*, 19n.

[87]The mock-'dolorous songes funerall' of the clerical birds in Skelton's later *Phyllyp Sparowe* perhaps also contributed.

[88]For the text, see *Bann. MS*, fols 136[v]-137[r].

[89]See further, Hadley Williams, 'Dunbar and His Immediate Heirs', forthcoming.

[90]See, for instance, *Dreme*, 232 and *Eneados* VI, vii.5; *Ane Dialog*, 243 and *Eneados*, X Prol. 150-52; *Ane Dialog*, 165 and *Pal. Honour*, 1844; *Ane Dialog*, 104 and *Pal. Honour*, 2161; *Papyngo*, 113-17, 126, *Ane Dialog*, 185 and *Pal. Honour*, 49-52, *Eneados*, XII, Prol. 73; *Ane Dialog*, 1451-54 and *Pal. Honour*, 348-49 ('swatterit').

[91]This also implies that David Lyndsay knew the *Kingis Quair*.

[92]See Bawcutt 1976: 95.

[93]See Aitken 1983: 26 for discussion of the use of 'different verse-kinds succeeding one another by abrupt transitions of style and often metre'.

[94]Lyndsay gave some attention to this issue in *Ane Dialog*, 2323-96.

[95]See further, McGavin 1993.

[96]*Bann. MS*, fols 104^v-107^r and *Maitl. Fol. MS*, no. xlvi.

[97]Dr Helena Shire noted this energetic epithet in an (unpublished) paper delivered at the Second International Conference on Scottish Language and Literature (Medieval and Renaissance), University of Strasbourg, 5-11 July 1978.

[98]See Hadley Williams 1989.

[99]Cranston 1891-93: no. 28.

[100]See Aitken 1985 (for a concise history of Scots), and Bawcutt 1996: 12-17 (for further details of late fifteenth-century Scots in context, discussion of orthography and grammar).

[101]See *CSD*, pp. xxxi-xxxv, and Mather and Speital 1975-86: II.154.

[102]See, however, Aitken 1983: 28-30.

[103]See Aitken 1983: 26-39; Aitken 1997: 3.

[104]*Kitteis Confessioun* first appeared in *The Warkis*, of 1568; see Hamer 1931-36: I.123. *Peder Coffeis, Bann. MS*, fol. 162, is there ascribed to 'linsdsay' in a later hand.

*

THE DREME

1

Rycht potent prince, of hie imperial blude,
Onto thy grace I traist it be weill knawin
My servyce done onto thy celsitude,
Quhilk nedis nocht at lenth for to be schawin.
And thocht my youthed now be neir over blawin,   5
Excerst in servyce of thyne excellence,
Hope hes me hecht ane gudlie recompence.

2

Quhen thow wes young, I bure the in myne arme
Full tenderlie, tyll thow begouth to gang
And in thy bed oft happit the full warme,   10
With lute in hand syne sweitlie to the sang.
Sumtyme in dansing, feiralie I flang,
And sumtyme playand fairsis on the flure,
And sumtyme on myne office takkand cure.

3

And sumtyme lyke ane feind transfegurate   15
And sumtyme lyke the greislie gaist of Gye,
In divers formis, oft tymes disfigurate,
And sumtyme dissagyist full plesandlye.
So, sen thy birth, I have continewalye
Bene occupyit, and aye to thy plesoure,   20
And sumtyme seware, coppare, and carvoure,

4

Thy purs maister and secreit thesaurare,
Thy ischare, aye sen thy natyvitie,
And of thy chalmer cheiffe cubiculare,

1 *imperial*: supreme
3 *celsitude*: majesty
4 *Quhilk*: Which
5 *thocht*: although; *youthed*: time of youth; *over blawin*: at an end
6 *Excerst*: Exercised
7 *hecht*: promised   8 *bure*: carried
9 *tyll*: until; *gang*: walk
10 *happit*: wrapped
11 *syne*: thereupon
12 *feiralie*: vigorously; *flang*: sprang
13 *fairsis*: short dramas; *flure*: floor
14 *office*: regular duties; *cure*: care

15 *transfegurate*: transformed
16 *greislie*: grisly; *gaist...Gye*: ghost of Guy   17 *disfigurate*: deformed
18 *dissagyist*: disguised   19 *sen*: since
21 *seware*: attendant at table; *coppare*: cupbearer; *carvoure*: carver
22 *purs maister*: purse keeper; *secreit thesaurare*: privy treasurer
23 *ischare*: usher [doorkeeper]; *natyvitie* birth
24 *chalmer*: bedroom; *cubiculare*: groom of the chamber

Quhilk, to this houre, hes keipit my lawtie.   25
Lovying be to the blyssit Trynitie
That sic ane wracheit worme hes maid so habyll
Tyll sic ane prince to be so aggreabill!
5
Bot now thou arte, be influence naturall,
Hie of ingyne and rycht inquisityve   30
Of antique storeis and dedis marciall.
More plesandlie the tyme for tyll overdryve
I have, at lenth, the storeis done discryve
Of Hectour, Arthour, and gentyll Julyus,
Of Alexander, and worthy Pompeyus,   35
6
Of Jasone and Media, all at lenth;
Of Hercules, the actis honorabyll,
And of Sampsone, the supernaturall strenth,
And of leill luffaris, storeis amiabyll.
And oft tymes have I fenyeit mony fabyll   40
Of Troylus, the sorrow and the joye,
And seigis all—of Tyir, Thebes, and Troye;
7
The Prophiseis of Rymour, Beid, and Marlyng
And of mony uther plesand storye
Of the Reid Etin, and the Gyir Carlyng,   45
Confortand the quhen that I sawe the sorye.
Now, with the supporte of the king of glorye,
I sall the schaw ane storye of the new,
The quhilk affore I never to the schew.
8
Bot humilie I beseik thyne excellence,   50
With ornate termes thocht I can nocht expres

25 *lawtie*: loyalty
26 *Lovying be*: Praises be
27 *sic*: such; *wracheit*: miserable; *maid...habyll*: has been found suitable
28 *Tyll*: To; *aggreabill*: pleasing
29 *influence naturall*: natural inclination
30 *ingyne*: intelligence
31 *antique*: old; *dedis marciall*: notable acts of war
32 *overdryve*: pass
33 *done discryve*: described
34 *gentyll*: well born; *Julyus*: Julius [Caesar]   38 *Sampsone*: Samson
39 *leill*: faithful; *luffaris*: lovers
40 *fenyeit*: imagined; *fabyll*: fable
42 *seigis*: sieges; *Tyir*: Tyre
43 *Rymour*: [Thomas the] Rhymer; *Beid*: Bede; *Marlyng*: Merlin
45 *Reid Etin*: Red Etin; *Gyir Carlyng*: Old Ogress
46 *Confortand*: Comforting; *sorye*: distressed
50 *humilie*: humbly; *beseik*: entreat,
51 *ornate termes*: ornamented language

This sempyll mater for laik of eloquence,
Yit nocht withstandyng all my besynes,
With hart and hand my mynd I sall adres
As I best can and moste compendious.   55
Now I begyn. The mater hapnit thus.

The Prolong
9

In to the calendis of Januarie,
Quhen fresche Phebus, be movyng circulair,
Frome Capricorne wes enterit in Aquarie,
With blastis that the branchis maid full bair.   60
The snaw and sleit perturbit all the air
And flemit Flora frome every bank and bus
Throuch supporte of the austeir Eolus.

10

Efter that I the lang wynteris nycht
Hade lyne walking in to my bed allone,   65
Throuch hevy thocht that no way sleip I mycht,
Remembryng of divers thyngis gone,
So up I rose and clethit me anone.
Be this, fair Tytane with his lemis lycht
Over all the land had spred his baner brycht.   70

11

With cloke and hude I dressit me belyve,
With dowbyll schone and myttanis on my handis.
Howbeit the air wes rycht penitratyve,
Yit fure I furth, lansing ovirthorte the landis
Towarte the see, to schorte me on the sandis,   75
Because unblomit was baith bank and braye.
And so as I was passing be the waye

---

53 *Yit*: Yet; *besynes*: diligence
54 *adres*: prepare
55 *compendious*: concise
57 *calendis*: first day [of the Roman month]   58 *circulair*: in a round
59 *Capricorne*: [planetary house of] Capricorn; *Aquarie*: Aquarius
60 *blastis*: blasts; *bair*: bare
61 *perturbit*: threw into disorder
62 *flemit*: banished; *Flora*: goddess of flowers; *bus*: bush
63 *austeir*: stern; *Eolus*: Aeolus
65 *lyne*: lain; *walking*: awake

66 *hevy thocht*: burdensome thought
68 *clethit*: dressed; *anone*: forthwith
69 *Be*: By; *Tytane*: Titan [the sun]; *lemis lycht*: rays of light
70 *baner*: banner
71 *hude*: hood; *belyve*: with haste
72 *dowbyll*: double thickness; *schone*: shoes; *myttanis*: mittens
73 *Howbeit*: Although; *penitratyve*: keen
74 *fure*: went; *furth*: forth; *lansing*: bounding; *ovirthort*: across
75 *see*: sea; *schorte*: shorten the time

12

I met dame Flora, in dule weid dissagysit,
Quhilk in to May wes dulce and delectabyll,
With stalwart stromes hir sweitnes wes surprisit.   80
Hir hevynlie hewis war turnit in to sabyll,
Quhilkis umquhyle war to luffaris amiabyll.
Fled frome the froste, the tender flouris I saw
Under dame Naturis mantyll, lurking law.

13

The small fowlis in flokkis saw I flee   85
To Nature, makand gret lamentatioun.
Thay lychtit doun besyde me on ane tree
(Of thare complaynt I hade compassioun),
And, with ane pieteous exclamatioun,
Thay said, 'Blyssit be somer with his flouris   90
And waryit be thow wynter with thy schouris!'

14

'Allace, Aurora!' the syllie larke can crye,
'Quhare hes thow left thy balmy lyquour sweit
That us rejosit, we mountyng in the skye?
Thy sylver droppis ar turnit in to sleit.   95
O fair Phebus, quhare is thy hoilsum heit?
Quhy tholis thou thy hevinlie plesand face
With mystie vapouris to be obscurit, allace?

15

Quhar art thou May, with June, thy syster schene,
Weill bordourit with dasyis of delyte?   100
And gentyll Julet, with thy mantyll grene,
Enamilit with rosis, reid and quhyte?
Now auld and cauld Janeuar, in dispyte,
Reiffis frome us all pastyme and plesoure.
Allace! Quhat gentyll hart may this indure?   105

---

78 *dule weid*: mourning dress
79 *in to*: in; *dulce*: pleasant; *delectabyll*:
   delightful
80 *stalwart*: severe; *stromes*: storms
81 *hevynlie hewis*: celestial tints; *sabyll*:
   black   82 *umquhyle*: formerly
84 *mantyll*: loose sleeveless cloak; *law*:
   low   85 *flee*: flie
87 *lychtit doun*: landed
91 *waryit*: cursed; *schouris* showers
92 *syllie*: simple; *can*: did

93 *balmy lyquour*: fragrant fluid
94 *mountyng*: flying upwards
95 *sylver droppis*: drops of dew
96 *hoilsum*: health-giving
97 *tholis*: allows
98 *mystie vapouris*: mist; *obscurit*:
   darkened
99 *schene*: fair   100 *dasyis*: daisies
101 *Julet*: July   102 *Enamilit*: Enamelled
103 *cauld*: cold   104 *Reiffis*: Steals

16

Oversylit ar, with cloudis odious,
The goldin skyis of the Orient,
Cheangeyng in sorrow our sang melodious,
Quhilk we had wount to sing with gude intent,
Resoundand to the hevinnis firmament.   110
Bot now our daye is cheangit in to nycht.'
With that thay rais and flew furth of my sycht.

17

Pensyve in hart, passing full soberlie
Onto the see, fordwart I fure anone.
The see was furth, the sand wes smoith and drye.   115
Than up and doun I musit myne alone
Tyll that I spyit ane lytill cave of stone,
Heych in ane craig. Upwart I did approche
But tarying, and clam up in the roche,

18

And purposit, for passing of the tyme,   120
Me to defende frome ociositie,
With pen and paper to regester in ryme
Sum mery mater of antiquitie.
Bot idelnes, ground of iniquitie,
Scho maid so dull my spretis me within   125
That I wyste nocht at quhat end to begin,

19

Bot satt styll in that cove, quhare I mycht se
The woltryng of the wallis, up and doun,
And this fals wardlis instabilytie
Unto that sey makkand comparisoun,   130
And of the wardlis wracheit variasoun
To thame that fixis all thare hole intent,
Considdryng quho moste had suld moste repent.

---

106 *Oversylit*: concealed
107 *Orient*: East
108 *Cheangeying*: Transforming; *sang*: song
109 *had wount*: were accustomed
110 *Resoundand*: Re-echoing; *firmament*: vault   112 *rais*: rose
114 *fordwart*: further on
115 *furth*: at low tide; *smoith*: smooth
116 *musit*: meditated silently; *myne alone*: on my own

118 *Heych*: High; *craig*: crag
119 *But*: Without; *clam*: climbed; *roche*: cliff   120 *purposit*: resolved
121 *defende*: protect; *ociositie*: idleness
122 *regester*: set down   124 *ground*: basis
125 *spretis*: spirits
126 *wyste*: knew
128 *woltryng*: rolling to and fro; *wallis*: waves   129 *wardlis*: world's
131 *variasoun*: changeability

20

So with my hude my hede I happit warme,
And in my cloke I fauldit boith my feit.   135
I thocht my corps with cauld suld tak no harme:
My mittanis held my handis weill in heit,
The skowland craig me coverit frome the sleit.
Thare styll I satt, my bonis for to rest,
Tyll Morpheus with sleip my spreit opprest.   140

21

So throw the boustious blastis of Eolus
And throw my walkyng on the nycht before,
And throuch the seis movying marvellous
Be Neptunus, with mony route and rore,
Constranit I was to sleip withouttin more.   145
And quhat I dremit, in conclusioun,
I sall yow tell ane marvellous visioun.

Finis.

Heir endis the Prolong.
And followis the Dreme.

22

Me thocht ane lady, of portratour perfyte,
Did salus me with benyng contynance.
And I, quhilk of hir presens had delyte,   150
Tyl hir agane maid humyl reverence
And hir demandit, savyng hir plesance,
Quhat wes hir name? Scho answerit courtesly,
'Dame Remembrance', scho said, 'callit am I,

23

Quhilk cummyng is for pastyme and plesoure   155
Of the, and for to beir the companye,
Because I se thy spreit, withoute mesoure,
So sore perturbit be malancolye,
Causyng thy corps to waxin cauld and drye.

135 *fauldit*: wrapped
136 *corps*: body; *tak*: take
138 *skowland*: forbidding
140 *spreit*: mind   141 *boustious*: violent
144 *route...rore*: loud noise and roars
145 *Constranit*: Compelled
148 *portratour*: appearance; *perfyte*: flawless

149 *salus*: greet; *benyng*: kindly; *contynance*: countenance
151 *humyl reverence*: humble deference
152 *savyng...plesance*: without offence to her wish   157 *mesoure*: moderation
158 *perturbit*: agitated; *malancolye*: depression
159 *waxin*: wax [astrol.], become

Tharefor get up, and gang anone with me.'   160
So war we boith, in twynkling of ane ee,
                            24
Doun throw the eird, in myddis of the centeir,
Or ever I wyste, in to the lawest hell.
In to that cairfull cove, quhen we did enter,
Yowtyng and yowlyng we hard, with mony yell.   165
In flame of fyre, rycht furious and fell,
Was cryand mony cairfull creature,
Blasphemand God, and waryand Nature.
                            25
Thare sawe we divers papis and empriouris,
Withoute recover, mony cairfull kyngis;   170
Thare sawe we mony wrangous conquerouris
Withouttin rycht, reiffaris of utheris ryngis.
The men of kirk lay boundin in to byngis:
Thare saw we mony cairfull cardinall,
And archebischopis in thare pontificall,   175
                            26
Proude and perverst prelattis out of nummer,
Priouris, abbottis, and fals flattrand freris.
To specifye thame all it wer ane cummer:
Regulare channonis, churle monkis, and Chartereris,
Curious clerkis and preistis seculeris.   180
Thare was sum part of ilk religioun
In haly kirk quhilk did abusioun.
                            27
Than I demandit dame Remembrance
The cause of thir prelattis punysioun.
Scho said, 'The cause of thare unhappy chance   185

160 *anone*: forthwith
162 *eird*: earth; *myddis*: the middle of
163 *or*: before; *wyste*: knew
164 *cairfull*: dismal
165 *yowtyng*: yelling; *yowlyng*: howling
168 *waryand*: cursing 169 *papis*: popes
170 *Withoute recover*: Without possibility
    or means of recovery
171 *wrangous*: wrongfully appointed
172 *rycht*: [just] claim; *reiffaris*: stealers
    [by force]; *ryngis*: kingdoms, power
173 *boundin...byngis*: bound in a heap

175 *pontificall*: vestments
176 *perverst*: wicked;
    out...nummer: past counting
177 *flattrand*: flattering; *freris*: friars
178 *ane cummer*: a hardship
179 *regular*: monastic; *churle*: churlish;
    Chartereris: Carthusians
180 *seculeris*: non-monastic
181 *ilk*: every; *religioun*: religious order
182 *did abusioun*: committed abuses
184 *punysioun*: punishment

Was covatyce, luste, and ambitioun,
The quhilk now garris thame want fruitioun
Of God and heir eternallie man dwell
In to this painefull, poysonit pytt of hell.

28

Als, thay did nocht instruct the ignorent,   190
Provocand thame to pennence, be precheing,
Bot servit wardlie prencis insolent
And war promovit be thare fenyeit flecheing,
Nocht for thare science, wysedome nor techeing.
Be symonie was thare promotioun,   195
More for deneris nor for devotioun.

29

And uther cause of the punysioun
Of thir unhappy prelattis imprudent:
Thay maid nocht equale distributioun
Of haly kirk, the patrimonie and rent,   200
Bot temporallie thay have it all mispent
Quhilkis suld have bene trypartit in to thre.
First, to uphauld the kirk in honestie;

30

The secunde part, to sustene thare aistatis;
The thrid part, to be gevin to the puris.   205
Bot thay dispone that geir all uther gaittis—
On cartis and dyce, on harllotrie and huris.
Thir catyvis tuke no compt of thair awin curis,
Thare kirkis rewin, thare ladyis clenely cled
And rychelye rewlit, boith at burde and bed.   210

31

Thare bastarde barnis proudely thay provydit,
The kirk geir larglye thay did on thame spende.

187 *garris*: makes; *want*: lack; *fruitioun*:
   enjoyment   188 *man*: must
191 *Provocand*: Urging
192 *servit*: served; *wardlie*: worldly;
   insolent: arrogant
193 *promovit*: advanced; *fenyeit*:
   deceitful; *flecheing*: insincere
   speeches   194 *science*: learning
195 *symonie*: simony
196 *deneris*: money [lit. silver pennies];
   nor: than
200 *patrimonie*: inheritance
201 *temporallie*: for material ends

204 *aistatis*: rank   205 *puris*: needy
206 *dispone*: distribute; *geir*: property;
   gaittis: directions
207 *cartis...dyce*: cards...dice;
   harllotrie...huris: loose living and
   prostitutes
208 *catyvis*: wretches; *compt*: account;
   awin: own; *curis*: spiritual charges
209 *rewin*: collapsed; *clenely*: neatly;
   cled: clothed
210 *rewlit*: ?arrayed; *burde*: table
211 *barnis*: children; *provydit*: made
   provision for 212 *larglye*: liberally

In thare difaltis thare subdetis wer misgydit
And comptit nocht thare God for tyll offend,
Quhilk gart tham want grace at thair letter end.'   215
Rewland that rowte, I sawe, in capis of bras,
Symone Magus and byschope Cayphas,

32

Byschope Annas and the tratour Judas,
Machomete, that propheit poysonabyll;
Choro, Dathan and Abirone thare was,   220
Heretykis we sawe unnumerabyll.
It wes ane sycht rycht wounderous lamentabyl
Quhow that thay lay in to tha flammis fletyng,
With cairfull cryis, girnyng and greityng.

33

Religious men wer punyste panefullie   225
For vaine glore, als for inobedience,
Brekand thare constitutionis wylfullie,
Nocht haiffand thare overmen in reverence.
To knaw thare Rewle thay maid no delygence;
Unleifsumlie thay usit propertie,   230
Passing the boundis of wylfull povertie.

34

Full sore wepyng, with vocis lamentabyll,
Thay cryit lowde, 'O Empriour Constantyne,
We may wyit thy possessioun poysonabyll
Of all our gret punysioun and pyne!   235
Quhowbeit thy purpose was tyll ane gude fyne,
Thow baneist frome us trew devotioun,
Haiffand sic ee tyll our promotioun.'

35

Than we beheld ane den full dolorous,
Quhare that prencis and lordis temporall,   240

213 *difaltis*: negligence; *subdetis*:
    parishioners
214 *comptit*: cared
215 *gart*: made; *letter*: latter
216 *rowte*: crowd; *capis...bras*:
    copes of brass
217 *Symone Magus*: Simon Magus;
    Cayphas: Caiaphas
219 *Machomete*: Mohammed;
    poysonabyll: corrupting
220 *Choro...Abirone*: Korah...Abiram

223 *fletyng*: floating
224 *girnyng*: snarling; *greityng*: weeping
227 *constitutionis*: regulations
228 *overmen*: superiors
229 *Rewle*: Rule, prescribed way of life
230 *Unleifsumlie*: Improperly
231 *wylfull*: voluntary
232 *vocis*: voices; *lamentabyll*: pitiable
234 *wyit*: lay blame on
235 *pyne*: suffering
236 *fyne*: purpose   238 *ee*: eye

War cruciate with panis regorous.
Bot to expreme thare panis in speciall,
It dois exceid all my memoriall;
Importabyll paine thay had, but confortyng,
Thare blude royall maid thame no supportyng.   245

36

Sum catyve kyngis, for creuell oppressioun,
And uther sum, for thare wrangus conquest,
War condampnit, thay and thare successioun.
Sum for publict adultrye, and incest;
Sum leit thare peple never leif in rest,   250
Delyting so in plesour sensuall.
Quharefor thare paine was thare perpetuall.

37

Thare was the cursit Empriour Nero,
Of everilk vice the horrabyll veschell.
Thare was Pharo, with divers prencis mo,   255
Oppressouris of the barnis of Israell;
Herode and mony mo than I can tell.
Ponce Pylat was thare, hangit be the hals,
With unjuste jugis, for thare sentence fals.

38

Dukis, merquessis, erlis, barronis, knychtis,   260
With thay prencis, wer punyst panefullie,
Partycipant thay wer of thare unrychtis.
Fordwarte we went and leit thir lordis lye
And sawe quhare ladyis, lamentabyllie,
Lyke wod lyonis, cairfullie cryand,   265
In flam of fyre rycht furiouslie fryand.

39

Emprices, quenis, and ladyis of honouris,
Mony duches and comptas full of cair;

---

241 *cruciate*: tormented; *regorous*:
  harsh
242 *expreme*: state; *in speciall*:
  specifically
243 *memoriall*: recollection
244 *Importabyll*: Unbearable; *but*:
  without   248 *condampnit*: damned
249 *publict*: open
250 *leit*: allowed; *leif*: live
254 *veschell*: vessel
255 *Pharo*: Pharaoh; *mo*: more

257 *Herode*: Herod Antipas
258 *Ponce Pylat*: Pontius Pilate;
  hals: neck   259 *jugis*: judges
260 *Dukis*: Dukes; *merquessis*:
  marquises   261 *thay*: those
262 *Partycipant*: Taking part; *of*: in the
  matter of; *unrychtis*: misdeeds
264 *lamentabyllie*: with lamentation
265 *wod*: mad; *lyonis*: lions
268 *duches*: duchesses; *comptas*:
  countesses

Thay peirsit myne hart, thay tender creaturis
So pynit in that pytt, full of dispare,   270
Plungit in paine, with mony reuthfull rair;
Sum for thare pryde, sum for adultrye,
Sum for thare tyisting men to lechorye;

40

Sum had bene creuell and malicius,
Sum for making of wrangous heretouris;   275
For to rehers thare lyffis vitious
It wer bot tarye to the auditouris.
Of lychorye thay wer the verray luris,
With thare provocatyve impudicitie
Brocht mony ane man to infelicitie.   280

41

Sum wemen, for thare pussillamytie,
Overset with schame, thay did thame never schryve
Of secreit synnis done in quietie.
And sum repentit never in thare lyve,
Quhairfor, but reuth tha ruffeis did thame ryve   285
Regoruslie, withoute compassioun.
Gret was thare dule and lamentatioun.

42

'That we wer maid!' thay cryit oft, 'Allace!
Thus tormentit with panis intollerabyll!
We mendit nocht, quhen we had tyme and space,   290
Bot tuke in eird our lustis delectabyll.
Quharfor with feindis, ugly and horrabyll,
We ar condampnit for ever more, allace,
Eternalie withouttin hope of grace.

43

Quhare is the meit and drynke delicious   295
With quhilk we fed our cairfull cariounis?
Gold, sylver, sylk, with peirlis precious,
Our ryches, rentis and our possessionis?

---

270 *pynit*: distressed
273 *tyisting*: enticement of
275 *wrangous*: wrongful; *heretouris*: heirs
276 *rehers*: repeat; *vitious*: wicked
277 *bot tarye*: only delay
278 *luris*: lures
279 *impudicitie*: shamelessness
280 *infelicitie*: unhappiness

281 *pussillamytie*: cowardice
282 *Overset*: Overcome; *schryve*: make
       confession   283 *quietie*: privacy
285 *tha*: those; *ruffeis*: fiends;
       ryve: tear apart
290 *mendit*: reformed
291 *delectabyll*: agreeable
296 *cariounis*: flesh

Withouttin hope of our remissionis,
Allace! Our panis ar insufferabyll　　　　　300
And our tormentis to compt innumirabyll!'

44

Than we beheld quhare mony ane thousand
Comoun peple laye flichtrand in the fyre.
Of everilk stait thare was ane bailfull band.
Thare mycht be sene mony sorrowfull syre,　　　　　305
Sum for invy sufferit, and sum for yre,
And sum for laik of restitutioun
Of wrangous geir, without remissioun.

45

Mansworne merchandis for thar wrangus winning,
Hurdaris of gold and commoun occararis,　　　　　310
Fals men of law in cautelis rycht cunning,
Theiffis, revaris, and publict oppressaris,
Sum part thair was of unleill lauboraris;
Craftismen thair saw we, out of nummer.
Of ilke stait to declare it wer ane cummer.　　　　　315

46

And als, langsum to me for tyll indyte
Of this presoun the panis in speciall
(The heit, the calde, the dolour, and dispyte),
Quharefor I speik of thame in generall.
That dully den, that furneis infernall,　　　　　320
Quhose reward is rew without remede,
Ever deyand and never to be dede;

47

Hounger and thrist in steid of meit and drynk,
And for thare clethyng, tadis and scorpionis!
That myrke mansioun is tapessit with stynk;　　　　　325
Thay se bot horrabyll visionis,

299 *remissionis*: pardon for sins
303 *flichtrand*: fluttering
304 *stait*: estate; *bailfull*: wretched
305 *syre*: man
306 *invy*: envy　　　307 *laik*: lack
309 *Mansworne*: Perjuring; *wrangus*:
　　wrongful
310 *Hurdaris*: Hoarders; *occararis*:
　　usurers　　　311 *cautelis*: stratagems
312 *publict*: open
313 *unleill*: disloyal; *lauboraris*: labourers

315 *cummer*: trouble
316 *als*: also; *langsum*: tedious; *tyll*: to;
　　indyte: put into words
317 *panis*: punishments
318 *dispyte*: contempt
320 *dully*: gloomy; *furneis*: furnace
321 *rew*: distress　　　322 *deyand*: dying
323 *thrist*: thirst　　　324 *tadis*: toads
325 *myrke*: dark; *mansioun*: abode;
　　tapessit: hung; *stynk*: stench

Thay heir bot scorne and derysionis
Of foule feindis and blasphemationis;
Thare feillyng is importabyll passionis;

48

For melody, miserabyll murnyng.   330
Thare is na solace, bot dolour infinyte
In bailfull beddis, bitterlye burnyng,
With sobbyng, syching, sorrow, and with syte.
Thare conscience thare hartis so did byte,
To heir thame flyte it was ane cace of cair,   335
So in dispyte, plungeit in to dispair.

49

A lytill above that dolorous doungeoun
We enterit in ane countre full of cair,
Quhare that we saw mony ane legioun
Greitand and gowland, with mony reuthful rair.   340
'Quhat place is this', quod I, 'of blys so bair?'
Scho answerit and said, 'Purgatorye,
Quhilk purgis saulis or thay cum to glorye.'

50

'I se no plesour heir, bot mekle paine;
Quharefor', said I, 'leif we this sorte in thrall;   345
I purpose never to cum heir agane.
Bot yit I do beleve and ever sall,
That the trew kirk can no waye erre at all.
Sic thyng to be, gret clerkis dois conclude,
Quhowbeit my hope standis most in Cristis blud.'   350

51

Abufe that, in the thrid presoun, anone
We enterit in ane place of perditione,
Quhare mony babbis war makand drery mone
Because thay wantit the fruitioun
Of God, quhilk was ane gret punytioun.   355

---

329 *feillyng*: physical sensation;
   importabyll: insupportable;
   passionis: suffering
330 *murnyng*: wailing
333 *syte*: sorrow
335 *flyte*: quarrel; *cace*: circumstance
340 *gowland*: howling; *reuthful rair*:
   pitiable cry   341 *bair*: destitute

343 *purgis*: cleanses; *saulis*: souls; *or*:
   before   344 *mekle*: much
348 *trew kirk*: true church
351 *presoun*: prison; *anone*: forthwith
352 *perditione*: eternal damnation
353 *babbis*: babies
354 *fruitioun*: enjoyment

Of baptisme thay wantit the ansenye.
Upwart we went and left that myrthles menye,
52
In tyll ane volt, abone that place of paine,
Unto the quhilk, but sudgeorne, we ascendit.
That was the Lymbe, in the quhilk did remaine　　　360
Our forefatheris, because Adam offendit,
Etand the fruit the quhilk was defendit.
Mony ane yeir thay dwelt in that doungeoun,
In myrknes and in desolatioun.
53
Than throuch the erth, of nature cauld and dry,　　　365
Glaid to eschaip those places parrelous,
We haistit us rycht wounder spedalye.
Yit we beheld the secretis marvellous,
The mynis of gold, and stonis precious,
Of sylver, and of everilk fyne mettell,　　　370
Quhilk to declare it wer over lang to dwell.
54
Up throuch the walter, schortlie we intendit,
Quhilk invirons the erth, withouttin doute;
Syne throw the air, schortlie we ascendit
His regionis throuch, behaldyng in and out,　　　375
Quhilk erth and walter closis round aboute;
Syne schortlie upwarte, throw the fyre we went,
Quhilk wes the hiest and hotest eliment.
55
Quhen we had all thir elimentis over past,
That is to saye, erth, walter, air and fyre,　　　380
Upwart we went, withouttin ony rest,
To se the hevynnis was our maist desyre;
Bot or we mycht wyn to the hevin impyre,
We behuffit to passe the way, full evin,
Up throuch the speris of the planetis sevin.　　　385

---

356 *ansenye*: sign
357 *menye*: multitude
358 *volt*: vault
359 *sudgeorne*: tarrying
360 *Lymbe*: Limbo
362 *defendit*: guarded
366 *parrelous*: perilous
370 *mettell*: metal　　372 *walter*: water

378 *hotest*: hottest; *eliment*: element
379 *thir*: these
383 *hevin impyre*: empyrean, highest
　　heaven
384 *behuffit*: were obliged; *full evin*:
　　precisely
385 *speris*: spheres; *sevin*: seven

56

First to the Mone, and vesyit all hir speir,
Quene of the see and bewtie of the nycht;
Of nature, wak and cauld and no thyng clere,
For of hir self scho hes none uther lycht
Bot the reflex of Phebus bemes brycht. 390
The twelf singnis scho passis rounde aboute
In aucht and twenty dayis, withouttin dout.

57

Than we ascendit to Mercurious,
Quhilk poetis callis god of eloquence;
Rycht doctourlyke, with termes delicious, 395
In arte exparte and full of sapience.
It wes plesour to pans on his prudence.
Payntours, poetis, ar subject to his cure,
And hote and dry he is, of his nature.

58

And als, as cunnyng astrologis sayis, 400
He dois compleit his cours naturallie,
In thre houndreth and aucht and thretty dayis.
Syne upwart we ascendit haistelye
To fair Venus, quhare scho rycht lustelie
Was set in to ane sett of sylver schene; 405
That fresche goddes, that lustie luffis quene.

59

Thay peirsit myne hart, hir blenkis amorous.
Quhowbeit that sumtyme scho is chengeabyll,
With countynance and cheir full dolorous,
Quhylummis rycht plesand, glaid and delectabyll; 410
Sumtyme constant, and sumtyme variabyll,
Yit hir bewtie, resplendand as the fyre,
Swagis the wraith of Mars, that god of yre.

386 *Mone*: Moon; *vesyit*: observed
387 *see*: sea
388 *wak*: weak; *clere*: bright
390 *reflex*: reflected light
391 *singnis*: signs [astrol.]
392 *aucht*: eight
393 *Mercurious*: Mercury
395 *doctourlyke*: learned; *delicious*: delightful
396 *exparte*: skilled
397 *pans*: reflect on
398 *subject to*: under; *cure*: care
399 *hote*: hot
400 *astrologis*: astronomers
405 *set*: seated; *sett*: [zodiacal] seat
407 *blenkis*: glances
408 *chengeabyll*: liable to change
409 *cheir*: expression
410 *Quhylummis*: Sometimes
413 *Swagis*: Assuages; *wraith*: wrath

60

This plesand planeit, geve I can rycht discrive,
Scho is baith hote and wak, of hir nature. 415
That is the cause scho is provocatyve
Tyll all thame that ar subject to hir cure,
To Venus werkis tyll that thay may indure.
Als, scho completis hir coursis naturall
In twelf monethis, withouttin ony fall. 420

61

Than past we to the speir of Phebus brycht,
That lusty lampe and lanterne of the hevin
And glader of the sterris, with his lycht,
And principall of all the planetis sevin;
And satt in myddis of thame all, full evin, 425
As roye royall, rollyng in his speir
Full plesandlie, in to his goldin cheir,

62

Quhose influence and vertew excellent
Gevis the lyfe tyll everilk erthlie thyng.
That prince, of everilk planeit precellent, 430
Dois foster flouris and garris heirbis spryng
Throuch the cauld eirth, and causis birdis syng.
And als, his regulare movyng in the hevin
Is juste, under the zodiack full evin.

63

435

For to discryve his diadame royall,
Bordourit aboute with stonis schyning brycht,
His goldin cairt, or throne imperiall,
The foure stedis that drawis it full rycht,
I leif to poetis because I have no slycht. 440
Bot of his nature he is hote and drye,
Completand in ane yeir his cours trewlie.

414 *geve*: if
416 *provocatyve*: excites lust
418 *Venus werkis*: Dalliance; *tyll that*:
  until; *indure*: last
420 *fall*: declension [astrol.]
422 *lusty*: bright
423 *glader*: gladdener; *sterris*: stars
424 *principall*: chief

426 *roye royall*: king kingly; *rollyng*:
  driving   427 *cheir*: chair
429 *Gevis*: Bestows
430 *precellent*: pre-eminent
431 *heirbis*: herbs
433 *regulare movyng*: recurring course
434 *juste*: exact   435 *diadame*: crown
437 *cairt*: chariot   438 *stedis*: horses
439 *slycht*: knack

64

Than up to Mars, in hye, we haistit us,
Wounder hote and dryer than the tunder;
His face flamand, as fyre rycht furious,
His bost and brag more aufull than the thunder,   445
Maid all the hevin most lyk to schaik in schonder.
Quha wald behauld his countnance and feir
Mycht call hym, weill, the god of men of weir.

65

With colour reid and luke malicious,
Rycht colerick of his complexioun;   450
Austeir, angrye, sweir, and seditious,
Principall cause of the distructioun
Of mony gude and nobyll regioun.
War nocht Venus his yre dois metigate,
This warld, of peace, wald be full desolate.   455

66

This god of greif, withouttin sudgeornyng,
In yeris twa his cours he doith compleit.
Than past we up quhare Jupiter, the kyng,
Satt in his speir, rycht amiabyll and sweit.
Complexionate with waknes and with heit,   460
That plesand prince, fair, dulce and delicate,
Provokis peace and banesis debait.

67

The auld poetis, be superstitioun,
Held Jupiter the father principall
Of all thare goddes, in conclusioun,   465
For his prerogatyvis in speciall,
Als be his vertew in to generall.
To auld Saturne he makis resistance
Quhen, in his malice, he walde wyrk vengeance.

442 *in hye*: quickly
443 *tunder*: tinder   444 *flamand*: flaming
445 *bost...brag*: vaunting...bragging
446 *in schonder*: apart
447 *feir*: bearing
448 *weill*: rightly; *weir*: war
450 *colerick*: choleric
451 *Austeir*: Severe; *sweir*: lazy;
    seditious: factious
454 *metigate*: moderate

456 *sudgeornyng*: resting
460 *Complexionate*: Constituted;
    waknes: weakness
461 *dulce*: agreeable; *delicate*: refined
462 *banesis*: exiles
463 *auld*: of classical antiquity; *be*: by
465 *conclusioun*: summary; *speciall*:
    particular
466 *prerogatyvis*: privileges

68

This Jupiter, withouttin sudgeornyng,   470
Passis throw all the twelf planetis, full evin,
In yeris twelf. And than, but tarying,
We past unto the hiest of the sevin,
Tyll Saturnus, quhilk trublis all the hevin.
With hevy cheir and cullour paill as leid,   475
In hym we sawe bot dolour to the deid;

69

And cauld and dry he is, of his nature.
Foule lyke ane oule, of evyll conditioun,
Rycht unplesand he is of portrature.
His intoxicat dispositioun,   480
It puttis all thyng to perditioun.
Ground of seiknes and malancolious,
Perverst and pure, baith fals and invyous,

70

His qualite I can nocht love, bot lack.
As for his movying naturallie, but weir,   485
About the singis of the zodiack,
He dois compleit his cours in thretty yeir.
And so we left hym in his frosty speir.
Upwarte we did ascend incontinent,
But rest, tyll we come to the firmament,   490

71

The quhilk was fixit full of sterris brycht,
Of figour round, rycht plesand and perfyte,
Quhose influence and rycht excellent lycht
And quhose nummer may nocht be put in wryte.
Yit cunnyng clerkis dois naturallye indyte   495
How that he dois compleit his cours, but weir,
In space of sevin and thretty thousand yeir.

---

475 *cullour*: complexion; *leid*: lead
476 *dolour...deid*: sorrow until death
478 *Foule*: Repulsive; *oule*: owl;
    conditioun: disposition
480 *intoxicat*: poisoned
481 *puttis*: brings; *perditioun*: ruin
482 *Ground*: Basis; *malancolious*:
    melancholy

483 *Perverst*: Evil; *pure*: mean;
    invyous: malicious
484 *love*: esteem; *lack*: censure
485 *but weir*: without doubt
486 *singis*: signs
489 *incontinent*: immediately
491 *fixit*: motionless; *sterris*: stars

72

Than the nynt speir and movare principall
Of all the laif we vesyit; all that hevin
Quhose daylie motioun is contyneuall, 500
Baith firmament and all the planetis sevin,
From est to west, garris thame torne full evin
In to the space of four and twenty houris.
Yit, be the myndis of the austronomouris,

73

The sevin planetis, in to thare proper speris, 505
Frome west to est thay move naturallie;
Sum swyft, sum slaw, as to thare kynde afferis,
As I have schawin afore, speciallie,
Quhose motioun causis contynewallie
Rycht melodious harmonie and sound, 510
And all throw movying of those planetis round.

74

Than montit we, with rycht fervent desyre,
Upthrow the hevin callit christallyne,
And so we enterit in the hevin impyre,
Quhilk to discryve, it passis myne ingyne, 515
Quhare God in to his holy throne devyne
Ryngis in to his glore inestimabyll,
With angellis cleir, quhilkis ar innumirabyll.

75

In ordouris nyne thir spretis glorious
Ar devydit, the quhilkis excellentlye 520
Makis lovying with sound melodious,
Syngand 'Sanctus!' rycht wounder ferventlye.
Thir ordouris nyne thay ar full plesandlye
Devydit in to ierarcheis three,
And thre ordouris in everilk ierarche. 525

76

The lawest ordoure ar of angelis brycht,
As messingeris send unto this law regioun;

498 *movare principall*: principal mover
499 *laif*: rest; *vesyit*: observed
502 *garris*: makes; *torne*: turn
507 *kynde*: nature; *afferis*: appertains
512 *fervent*: passionate
517 *Ryngis*: Rules   518 *cleir*: bright

519 *ordouris*: [angelic] orders; *spretis*: spirits
520 *devydit*: separated
521 *Makis lovying*: Gives praise
522 *Sanctus!*: Holy!
524 *ierarcheis*: hierarchies

The secund ordour, archangelis full of mycht;
Virtus, potestatis, principatis of renoun;
The saxt is callit dominatioun;   530
The sevint, thronus; the auchtin, cherubin;
The nynt and heast callit seraphin.

77

And nyxt, on to the blyssit Trynitie,
In his tryumphant throne imperiall,
Thre in tyll one and one substance in thre,   535
Quhose indivisabyll essens eternall
The rude ingyne of mankynd is to small
Tyll comprehend; quhose power infinyte
And devyne nature no creature can wryte;

78

So myne ingyne is nocht suffecient   540
For to treit of his heych devinitie.
All mortal men ar insufficient
Tyll considder thay thre, in unitie;
Sic subtell mater I man on neid lat be;
To study on my Creid it war full fair,   545
And lat doctouris of sic hie materis declare.

79

Than we beheld the blyste humanitie
Of Christe, sittand in to his sege royall,
At the rycht hand of the devynitie,
With ane excelland courte celestiall,   550
Quhose exersitioun, contynewall,
Was in lovyng thair prince with reverence,
And on this wyse thay kepit ordinance.

80

Nyxt to the throne, we saw the Quene of quenis,
Weill cumpanyit with ladyis of delyte.   555
Sweit was the sang of those blyssit virginnis:

---

528 *archangelis*: archangels
529 *Virtus*: Virtues; *potestatis*:
 powers; *principatis*: sovereignties,
 princes
530 *saxt*: sixth; *dominatioun*:
 dominations
531 *sevint*: seventh; *thronus*: thrones;
 auchtin: eighth; *cherubin*: cherubim
532 *heast*: highest; *seraphin*: seraphim

541 *treit*: discourse on; *devinitie*: divine
 nature
544 *subtell*: abstruse; *on neid*: of
 necessity; *lat*: leave
545 *Creid*: Creed
546 *doctouris*: scholars
547 *humanitie*: human form
551 *exersitioun*: occupation
553 *keipit ordinance*: kept good order
555 *cumpanyit*: associated

No mortall man thare solace may indyte.
The angellis brycht, in nummer infinyte,
Everilk ordour in thare awin degre,
War officiaris unto the deite;   560

81

Patriarkis and prophetis honorabyll,
Collaterall counsalouris in his consistorye;
Evangellistis, apostolis venerabyll,
War capitanis on to the kyng of glorye,
Quhilk, chiftane lyke, had woun the victorye.   565
Of that tryumphand courte celestiall
Sanct Peter was lufetenand generall.

82

The martyris war as nobyll stalwart knychtis,
Discomfatouris of creuell batellis thre
(The flesche, the warld, the feind and all his mychtis), 570
Confessouris, doctouris in divinitie,
As chapell clerkis on to his deite.
And last we sawe infinyte multytude
Makand servyce unto his celsitude,

83

Quhilkis be the hie devyne permissioun,   575
Filicitie thay had invariabyll,
And of his Godhed cleir cognitioun,
And compleit peace thay had, interminabyll;
Thare glore and honour was inseparabyll.
That plesand place, repleit of pulchritude,   580
Innumirabyll it was of magnitude.

84

Thare is plentie, of all plesouris perfyte:
Evident brychtnes but obscuritie,
Withouttin dolour, dulcore and delyte,

---

560 *deite*: deity
561 *Patriarkis*: Patriarchs
562 *Collaterall*: Attendant; *consistorye*:
    court
563 *Evangellistis*: Evangelists; *apostolis*:
    apostles
564 *capitanis*: military captains
565 *chiftane lyke*: like a commander;
    woun: won
567 *lufetenand*: second in command
568 *martyris*: martyrs

569 *Discomfatouris*: Conquerors; *batellis*:
    forces in battle-order
570 *mychtis*: power
571 *Confessouris*: Confessors of the faith
577 *Godhed*: Divine nature; *cognitioun*:
    knowledge
580 *repleit*: fully possessed of;
    pulchritude: beauty
581 *Innumirabyll*: Incalculable
583 *Evident*: Clear; *obscuritie*: darkness
584 *dulcore*: sweetness

Withouttin rancour, perfyte cheritie;   585
Withouttin hunger, sasiabilitie.
O happy ar those saulis predestinate
Quhen saule and body sall be glorificate!
                              85
Thir marvellous myrthis for to declare
Be arithmetik, thay ar innumirabyll;   590
The portratour of that palice preclare
By geomatre, it is inmesurabyl;
By rethorike, als inpronunciabyll.
Thare is none eiris may heir, nor eine may se,
Nor hart may thynk thare greit felycitie.   595
                              86
Quhare to sulde I presume for tyll indyte
The quhilk Sanct Paule, that doctour sapient,
Can nocht expres, nor in to paper wryte?
The hie excelland worke indeficient,
And perfyte plesoure, ever parmanent,   600
In presens of that mychtie kyng of glore
Quhilk was and is and sall be ever more.
                              87
At Remembrance humilye I did inquyre
Geve I mycht in that plesour styll remane.
Scho said, 'Aganis reasoun is thy desyre;   605
Quharefor, my freind, thow mon returne agane,
And for thy synnis, be pennance, suffer paine,
And thole the dede with creuell panis sore,
Or thow be ding to ryng with hym in glore.'
                              88
Than we returnit, sore aganis my wyll,   610
Doun throw the speris of the hevinnis cleir,
Hir commandiment behuffit I fulfyll.
With sorye hart, wyt ye, withouttin weir,

585 *cheritie*: love
587 *saulis predestinate*: souls
    preordained [by God to salvation]
588 *glorificate*: glorified
591 *portratour*: dimensions; *preclare*:
    splendid
592 *geomatre*: geometry;
    inmesurabyl: infinite

593 *rethorike*: rhetoric; *als*: also
594 *eiris*: ears; *eine*: eyes
597 *Sancte Paule*: St Paul
599 *indeficient*: unfailing
600 *parmanent*: enduring
608 *thole*: suffer; *the dede*: death
609 *Or*: Before; *ding*: worthy; *ryng*:
    reign   613 *wyt*: know

I wald full faine haif taryit thare all yeir.
Bot scho said to me, 'Thare is no remede.   615
Or thow remane heir, first thow mon be dede.'
                        89
Quod I, 'I pray yow hartfullye, madame,
Sen we have had sic contemplatioun
Of hevinlye plesouris, yit, or we passe hame,
Lat us have sum consideratioun   620
Of eirth, and of his situatioun.'
Scho answerit and said, 'That sall be done.'
So wer we boith brocht in the air full sone,
                        90
Quhare we mycht se the erth all at one sycht,
Bot lyke one moit, as it apperit to me,   625
In to the respect of the hevinnis brycht.
'I have marvell', quod I, 'quhow this may be?
The eirth semis of so small quantitie.
The leist sterne fixit in the firmament
Is more than all the eirth, be my jugment.'   630

                  The quantite of the Erth.
                        91
Scho sayis, 'Sonne, thow hes schawin the veritie.
The smallest sterne fixit in the firmament
In deid it is of greter quantytie
Than all the eirth, efter the intent
Of wyse and cunnyng clerkis sapient.'   635
'Quhat quantytie is than the eirth?' quod Ie.
'That sall I schaw', quod scho, 'to the schortlie,
                        92
Efter the myndis of the austronimouris
And, speciallie, the auctour of the *Speir*,
And uther divers gret phelosiphouris.   640
The quantytie of the erth circuleir
Is fyftie thousand liggis, withouttin weir,
Sevin houndreth and fyftie and no mo.
Devidyng aye ane lig in mylis two,

---

614 *full faine*: very willingly   629 *sterne*: star
625 *moit*: a minute speck   639 *auctour*: author
628 *quantitie*: dimensions   642 *liggis*: leagues

93

And everilk myle in aucht stagis devyde,   645
Ilk staige ane hundrith pais, twenty and fyve,
Ane pais, fyve fute, quha wald than rycht desyde;
Ane fute, four palmes, geve I can rycht discryve;
Ane palme, four inche, and quha sa wald belyve,
The circuit of the eirth, passe round aboute,   650
Man be considderit on this wyse, but doute.

94

Suppone that thare war none impediment
Bot that the eirth but perrell wer, and plane,
Syne, that the persoun wer rycht deligent
And yeid ilk day ten liggis in certane,   655
He mycht pas round aboute and cum agane
In four yeris saxtene oulkis and dayis two.
Go reid the auctour and thow sall fynd it so.'

Finis.

The devisioun of the Eirth.

95

Then certanlye scho tuke me be the hand
And said, 'My sone, cum on thy wayis with me.'   660
And so scho gart me cleirly understand
How that the eirth trypartit wes, in thre,
In Affrik, Europe, and Assie,
Efter the myndis of the cosmographouris,
That is to say, the wardlis discriptouris.   665

96

First, Asia contenis in the Orient
And is weill more than baith the uther twane;
Affrik and Europe, in the Occident,
And ar devydit be ane sey certane,
And that is callit the see Mediterane   670
Quhilk, at the strait of Marrok, hes entre,
That is betwix Spanye and Barbarie.

---

645 *stagis*: stages
647 *pais*: pace; *desyde*: determine
648 *palmes*: breadth of the human palm
649 *belyve*: accept as true
657 *oulkis*: weeks
659 *certanlye*: assuredly
663 *Affrik*: Africa; *Assie*: Asia

664 *Efter*: In accordance with
666 *contenis*: lies
667 *weill*: well; *twane*: two parts
668 *Occident*: West
670 *Mediterane*: Mediterranean
671 *Marrok*: Morocco
672 *Spanye*: Spain; *Barbarie*: Barbary

97

Towart the southwest lyis Affrica
And in the northwest, Europa doith stand
And all the est contenis Asia.   675
On this wyse is devydit the ferme land.
It war mekle to me to tak on hand
Thir regionis to declare in speciall,
Yit sall I schaw thare names in generall.

98

In mony divers famous regionis   680
Is devydit this part of Asia,
Weill planesit with cieteis, towris, and townis:
The gret Ynde and Mesopotamia,
Penthapolis, Egypt, and Seria,
Capadocia, Seres, and Armenye,   685
Babilone, Caldia, Perth, and Arabye;

99

Sedone, Judea, and Palestina,
Ever Sethea, Tyir, and Galelie,
Hiberia, Bactria, and Phelestina,
Hircanea, Compagena, and Samarie.   690
In lytill Asia standis Galathie,
Pamphilia, Isaria, and Leid,
Regia, Arathusa, Assiria, and Meid.

100

Secundlie we considderit Africa,
With mony fructfull famous regioun,   695
As Ethiope, and Tripolitana;
Zeuges, quhare standis the tryumphant toun
Of nobyll Cartage, that ciete of renoun;

---

675 *est*: east   676 *ferme land*: mainland
682 *planesit*: provided; *towris*: towers;
    townis: villages   683 *Ynde*: India
684 *Penthapolis*: Pentapolis; *Seria*: Syria
685 *Capadocia*: Cappadocia; *Armenye*:
    Armenia
686 *Babilone*: Babylonia; *Caldia*:
    Chaldea; *Perth*: Parthia; *Arabye*:
    Arabia
687 *Sedone*: Sidon; *Judea*: Judaea;
    Palestina: Palestine
688 *Sethea*: Scythia; *Tyir*: Tyre; *Galelie*:
    Galilee

689 *Hiberia*: Iberia; *Phelestina*: ?Ascalon
690 *Hircanea*: Hircania; *Compagena*:
    Comagene; *Samarie*: Samaria
691 *lytill Asia*: Asia Minor; *Galathie*:
    Galatia
692 *Pamphilia*: Pamphylia; *Isaria*:
    Isauria; *Leid*: Lydia
693 *Regia*: ?Rhagæa; *Arathusa*:
    ?Arachosia; *Meid*: Media
695 *fructfull*: fruitful
696 *Tripolitana*: ?Tripolitania
697 *Zeuges*: Zeugitania
698 *Cartage*: Carthage

Garamantes, Nadabar, Libia,
Getulia, and Maritania,   700
101
Futhensis, Numedie, and Thingetane,
Of Affrick thir ar the principall.
Than Europe we considderit, in certane,
Quhose regionis schortlie rehers I sall.
Foure principallis I fynd abone thame all,   705
Quhilkis ar Spanye, Italie, and France,
Quhose subregionis wer mekle tyll avance:
102
Nether Scithia, Trace, and Garmanie,
Thusia, Histria, and Panonia,
Denmark, Gotland, Grunland, and Almanie,   710
Pole, Hungarie, Boeme, Norica, Rethia,
Teutonia, and mony divers ma;
And was in foure devidit Italie:
Tuskane, Ethuria, Naiplis, and Champanye,
103
And subdevydit sindry uther wayis,   715
As Lumbardie, Veneis, and uther ma,
Calaber, Romanie, and Janewayis.
In Grece, Eperus, and Dalmatica,
Tessalie, Athica, and Illeria,
Achaya, Boetia, and Macedone,   720
Archadie, Pierie, and Lacedone.
104
And France we sawe, devydit in to thre:
Belgica, Rethia, and Aquitane,

699 *Garamantes*: Garamantia; *Nadabar*:
  ?Nababurum; *Libia*: Libya
700 *Getulia*: Gaetulia; *Maritania*:
  Mauritania
701 *Futhensis*: ?Fez; *Numedie*: Numidia;
  Thingetane: Tingitana
708 *Nether*: South; *Trace*: Thrace;
  Garmanie: Germany
709 *Thusia*: ?Thusis; *Histria*: Istria;
  Panonia: Pannonia
710 *Grunland*: ?Lapland
711 *Pole*: Poland; *Boeme*: Bohemia
714 *Tuskane*: Tuscany; *Ethuria*: Etruria;
  Naiplis: Naples; *Champanye*:
  Campania

716 *Lumbardie*: Lombardy; *Veneis*:
  Venice
717 *Calaber*: Calabria; *Romanie*:
  Rome; *Janewayis*: Genoa
718 *Grece*: Greece; *Eperus*: Epirus;
  Dalmatica: Dalmatia
719 *Tessalie*: Thessaly; *Athica*: Attica;
  Illeria: Illyria
720 *Achaya*: Achaia; *Boetia*: Bœotia;
  Macedone: Macedonia
721 *Archadie*: Arcadia; *Pierie*: Pieria;
  Lacedone: Lacedemonia
723 *Belgica*: Belgium

And subdevydit in Flanderis, Picardie,
Normandie, Gasconye, Burguinye, and Bretane, 725
And utheris divers Duchereis, in certane,
The quhilks wer to lang for to declare;
Quharefor, of thame as now I speik na mare.

105

In Spanye lyis Castelye and Arrogone,
Naverne, Galice, Portingall, and Garnat. 730
Than sawe we famous ylis, mony one,
Quhilks in the occiane sey was situate.
Thame to discryve my wyt wes desolate;
Of cosmographie I am nocht exparte,
For I did never study in that arte. 735

106

Yit I sall sum of thare names declare,
As Madagascar, Gardes, and Taprobane,
And utheris divers ylis, gude and fair,
Situate in to the sey Mediterrane,
As Syper, Candie, Corsica, and Sardane, 740
Crete, Abidos, Thoes, Cecilia,
Tapsone, Eolie, and mony uther ma.

107

Quho wald at lenth heir the discriptioun
Of everilk yle als weill as the ferme land,
And properteis of everilk regioun, 745
To study and to reid, man tak on hand,
And the attentike werkis understand,
Of Plenius and worthy Tholomie,
Quhilks war exparte in to cosmographie.

108

Thare sall thay fynd the names and properteis 750
Of every yle, and of ilke regioun.
Than I inquirit of eirthly Paradyce,

725 *Gasconye*: Gascony; *Burguinye*:
  Burgundy; *Bretane*: Brittany
726 *Duchereis*: Duchies [of France]
729 *Castelye*: Castile; *Arrogone*:
  Aragon
730 *Naverne*: Navarre; *Galice*: Galicia;
  Portingall: Portugal; *Garnat*:
  Granada 732 *occiane sey*: open sea
737 *Gardes*: Gades; *Taprobane*:
  ?Ceylon

740 *Syper*: Cyprus; *Candie*: ?Cauda;
  Sardane: Sardinia
741 *Abidos*: Abydos; *Thoes*: Chios;
  Cecilia: Sicily
742 *Tapsone*: Thapsus; *Eolie*: Eolian Is.
747 *attentike*: authentic
748 *Plenius*: Pliny; *Tholomie*: Ptolemy
752 *eirthly Paradise*: garden of Eden

Of the quhilk Adam tynt possessioun.
Than schew scho me the situatioun
Of that precelland place, full of delyte,   755
Quhose properteis wer lang for to indyte.

Of Paradice.
109
This Paradyce, of all plesouris repleit,
Situate I saw in to the Orient.
That glorius gairth of every flouris did fleit:
The lusty lillyis, the rosis redolent,   760
Fresche holesum fructis, indeficient;
Baith herbe and tree thare growis ever grene,
Throw vertew of the temperat air serene.
110
The sweit, hailsum, arromatyke odouris
Proceidyng frome the herbis medicinall,   765
The hevinlie hewis of the fragrant flouris;
It was ane sycht wounder celestiall.
The perfectioun to schaw in speciall,
And joyis of that regioun devyne,
Of mankynd it exceidis the ingyne.   770
111
And als, so hie in situatioun,
Surmountyng the myd regioun of the air,
Quhare no maner of perturbatioun
Of wodder may ascend so hie as thair,
Four fludis flowyng frome ane fontane fair,   775
As Tygris, Ganges, Euphrates, and Nyle,
Quhilk, in the est, transcurris mony ane myle.
112
The countre closit is aboute, full rycht,
With wallis hie of hote and birnyng fyre,
And straitly kepit be ane angell brycht,   780

753 *tynt*: lost   756 *properteis*: qualities
759 *gairth*: enclosed garden; *fleit*: abound
760 *lillyis*: lilies; *redolent*: fragrant
761 *fructis*: fruits; *indeficient*: unfailing
764 *hailsum*: wholesome
765 *Proceidyng*: Emanating; *medicinall*:
    curative
767 *sycht*: sight; *wounder*: wondrously

773 *perturbatioun*: disturbance
774 *wodder*: weather
775 *fludis*: rivers; *fontane*: natural
    spring   776 *Tygris*: Tigris; *Nyle*: Nile
777 *transcurris*: run across
778 *closit*: enclosed; *aboute*: in all
    directions
779 *wallis*: walls   780 *straitly*: strictly

Sen the departyng of Adam, our grandschyre,
Quhilk throw his cryme incurrit Goddis yre,
And of that place tynte the possessioun,
Baith frome hym self, and his successioun.

113

Quhen this lufesum lady Remembrance   785
All this foresaid had gart me understand,
I prayit hir of hir benevolence,
To schaw to me the countre of Scotland.
'Weill, sonne,' scho said, 'that sall I tak on hand.'
So suddanlie scho brocht me, in certane,   790
Evin juste abone the braid yle of Bertane,

114

Quhilk standis northwest in the occiane see
And devydit in famous regionis two:
The south part, Ingland, ane full ryche countre;
Scotland, be north, with mony ylis mo;   795
Be west Ingland, Yriland doith stand also,
Quhose properteis I wyll nocht tak on hand
To schaw at lenth, bot only of Scotland.

Of the realme of Scotland.

115

Quhilk, efter my sempyll intandiment,
And as Remembrance did to me report,   800
I sall declare the suith and verrayment
As I best can, and in to termes schort.
Quharfor effecteouslie I yow exhorte,
Quhowbeit my wrytting be nocht tyll avance,
Yit, quhare I faill, excuse myne ignorance.   805

116

Quhen that I had oversene this regioun,
The quhilk of nature is boith gude and fair,
I did propone ane lytill questioun,
Beseikand hir the sam for to declare,

781 *grandschyre*: forefather
782 *incurrit*: incurred
785 *lufesum*: lovely
787 *prayit*: asked earnestly
791 *Evin juste*: directly; *braid...Bertane*:
    broad isle of Britain
796 *Yriland*: Ireland

799 *sempyll*: simple; *intandiment*:
    understanding
801 *suith*: truth; *verrayment*: verity
802 *schort*: brief
803 *effecteouslie*: earnestly
804 *tyll avance*: to be praised
809 *sam*: same

'Quhat is the cause our boundis bene so bair?'   810
Quod I, 'Or quhate dois mufe our misere?
Or quhareof dois proceid our povertie?
                    117
For, throw the supporte of your hie prudence,
Of Scotland I persave the properteis,
And als considderis, be experience,   815
Of this countre the gret commoditeis.
First, the haboundance of fyschis in our seis,
And fructuall montanis for our bestiall,
And for our cornis, mony lusty vaill.
                    118
The ryche ryveris, plesand and proffitabyll;   820
The lustie loochis, with fysche of sindry kyndis;
Hountyng, halkyng, for nobyllis convenabyil,
Forrestis full of da, ra, hartis, and hyndis.
The fresche fontanis, quhose holesum cristel strandis
Refreschis so the fair flureist grene medis,   825
So laik we no thyng that to nature nedis.
                    119
Of every mettell we have the ryche mynis,
Baith gold, sylver, and stonis precious;
Howbeit we want the spyces and the wynis,
Or uther strange fructis delycious,   830
We have als gude, and more neidfull for us:
Meit, drynk, fyre, clathis, thar mycht be gart abound,
Quhilkis ellis is nocht in al the mapamound;
                    120
More fairer peple, nor of gretar ingyne,
Nor of more strenth, gret dedis tyll indure.   835
Quharefor, I pray yow that ye wald defyne
The principall cause quharefor we ar so pure,

810 *boundis*: lands
811 *mufe*: cause   812 *proceid*: originate
814 *persave*: observe
816 *commoditeis*: advantages
817 *haboundance*: copious supply
818 *fructuall*: fruitful; *montanis*:
    mountains; *bestiall*: domestic animals
819 *cornis*: grain crops; *vaill*: valley
821 *loochis*: lochs; *sindry*: sundry
822 *convenabyil*: appropriate

823 *da...hyndis*: doe, roe, stags...hinds
824 *fontanis*: natural springs; *cristel*:
    clear; *strandis*: streams
825 *flureist*: flowery; *medis*: meadows
826 *nedis*: is necessary
827 *mynis*: mines
831 *als*: as; *neidfull*: desirable
832 *gart abound*: caused to be plentiful
833 *ellis*: otherwise; *mapamound*: globe
837 *pure*: poor

For I marvell gretlie, I yow assure,
Considderand the peple and the ground,
That ryches suld nocht in this realme redound.'   840

121

'My sonne,' scho said, 'be my discretioun,
I sall mak answeir, as I understand.
I say to the, under confessioun,
The falt is nocht, I dar weill tak on hand,
Nother in to the peple nor the land.   845
As for the land, it lakis na uther thing,
Bot laubour and the pepyllis governyng.'

122

'Than quharein lyis our inprosperitie?'
Quod I, 'I pray yow hartfullie, madame,
Ye wald declare to me the veritie,   850
Or quho sall beir of our barrat the blame?
For be my treuth, to se I thynk gret schame,
So plesand peple, and so fair ane land,
And so few verteous dedis tane on hand.'

123

Quod scho, 'I sall efter my jugement,   855
Declare sum causis in to generall,
And in to termes schorte, schaw myne intent,
And syne transcend more in to speciall.
So this is myne conclusioun fynall:
Wantyng of justice, polycie, and peace,   860
Ar cause of thir unhappynes, allace!

124

It is deficill ryches tyll incres
Quhare polycie makith no residence,
And policey may never have entres
Bot quhare that justice dois delygence   865
To puneis quhare thare may be found offence.
Justice may nocht have dominatioun
Bot quhare peace makis habitatioun.'

---

840 *redound*: be plentiful
841 *discretioun*: judgement
844 *falt*: defect; *dar...hand*: dare to assert
845 *Nother*: Neither   847 *laubour*: work
851 *barrat*: distress   854 *tane*: taken
858 *transcend*: pass onward

860 *Wantyng*: The lack; *polycie*: good
     government
862 *deficill*: difficult; *incres*: increase
864 *entres*: entrance
865 *dois delygence*: is persistently
     applied   867 *dominatioun*: authority

125

'Quhat is the cause, that wald I understand,
That we sulde want justice and polycie   870
More than dois France, Italie, or Ingland?
Madame,' quod I, 'schaw me the veritie.
Sen we have lawis in this countre,
Quhy want we lawis exersitioun?   875
Quho suld put justice tyll exicutioun?

126

Quhare in dois stand our principall remeid?
Or quha may mak mendis of this myscheif?'
Quod scho, 'I fynd the falt in to the heid,
For thay in quhome dois ly our hole releif,
I fynd thame rute and grund of all our greif.   880
For quhen the heddis ar nocht delygent,
The membris man, on neid, be necligent.

127

So, I conclude, the causis principall
Of all the trubyll of this natioun
Ar in to prencis, in to speciall,   885
The quhilkis hes the gubernatioun,
And of the peple dominatioun;
Quhose contynewall exersitioun
Sulde be in justice exicutioun.

128

For quhen the sleuthful hird dois sloug and sleip,   890
Taking no cure in kepyng of his floke,
Quho wyll go sers amang sic heirdis scheip
May habyll fynd mony pure, scabbit crok,
And goyng wyll at large, withouttin lok.
Than lupis cumis, and Lowrance, in ane lyng,   895
And dois, but reuth, the sely scheip dounthryng.

874 *exersitioun*: exercising
875 *exicutioun*: execution
876 *remeid*: remedy
878 *heid*: ruler   880 *rute...grund*: source
881 *heddis*: rulers
882 *membris*: limbs; *man*: must; *on
    neid*: of necessity
886 *gubernatioun*: governing
890 *hird*: shepherd; *sloug*: move lazily

891 *floke*: flock   892 *sers*: search
893 *habyll*: possibly; *scabbit*: scabbed;
    crok: old ewe
894 *goyng*: going; *at large*: free,
    unhindered; *lok*: lock
895 *lupus*: wolf; *Lowrance*: Laurence;
    in...lyng: in a direct course
896 *reuth*: pity; *sely*: guileless;
    dounthryng: thrust down

129

Bot the gude hird, walkryfe and delygent,
Doith so that all his flokis ar rewlit rycht,
To quhose quhissill all ar obedient;
And geve the wolffis cumis, daye or nycht,   900
Thame to devore, than ar thay put to flycht,
Houndit and slane be thare weill dantit doggis.
So ar thay sure, baith yowis, lambis and hoggis.

130

So, I conclud, that throw the necligence
Of our infatuate heidis insolent,   905
Is cause of all this realmes indigence,
Quhilkis in justice hes nocht bene delygent,
Bot to gude counsall inobedient,
Havand small ee unto the comoun weill,
Bot to thare singulare proffect everilk deill.   910

131

For quhen thir wolffis, be oppressioun,
The pure peple but piete doith oppres,
Than sulde the prencis mak punisioun,
And cause tha rebauldis for to mak redres,
That ryches mycht, be policey, incres.   915
Bot rycht difficill is to mak remeid,
Quhen that the falt is so in to the heid.'

The Complaynt of the Comoun Weill of Scotland.

132

And thus, as we wer talking to and fro,
We saw a boustius berne cum ovir the bent,
But hors, on fute, als fast as he mycht go,   920
Quhose rayment wes all raggit, revin, and rent,
With visage leyne, as he had fastit Lent;
And fordwart fast his wayis he did advance
With ane rycht malancolious countynance,

---

897 *walkryfe*: wakeful
899 *quhissill*: whistle
903 *sure*: secure; *yowis*: ewes; *hoggis*: one-year-old sheep
905 *infatuate*: infatuated; *insolent*: arrogant
909 *Havand...ee*: Paying...heed; *comoun weill*: general welfare
910 *singular proffect*: exclusive profit; *deill*: bit   912 *piete*: compassion
914 *rebauldis*: rogues
919 *boustius*: rough; *berne*: man; *bent*: stretch of open ground
921 *rayment*: clothing; *raggit*: in tatters; *revin*: torn   922 *leyne*: lean; *as*: as if

133

With scrip on hip and pyikstaff in his hand,   925
As he had purposit to passe fra hame.
Quod I, 'Gude man, I wald faine understand,
Geve that ye plesit, to wyt quhat wer your name?'
Quod he, 'My sonne, of that I think gret schame,
Bot sen thow wald of my name have ane feill,   930
Forsuith thay call me "Jhone the Comoun Weill".'

134

'Schir Commoun Weill, quho hes yow so disgysit?'
Quod I, 'Or quhat makis yow so miserabyll?
I have marvell to se yow so supprysit,
The quhilk that I have sene so honorabyll.   935
To all the warld ye have bene proffitabyll,
And weill honorit in everilk natioun.
How happinnis, now, your tribulatioun?'

135

'Allace!' quod he. 'Thow seis how it dois stand
With me, and quhow I am disherisit   940
Of all my grace, and mon pas of Scotland
And go, afore quhare I was cherisit.
Remane I heir, I am bot perysit,
For thare is few to me that takis tent,
That garris me go so raggit, revin, and rent.   945

136

My tender freindis ar all put to the flycht,
For Polecey is fled agane in France,
My syster, Justice, almaist haith tynt hir sycht,
That scho can nocht hald evinly the ballance.
Plane Wrang is clene capitane of ordinance,   950
The quhilk debarris Laute and Reassoun,
And small remeid is found for Oppin Treassoun.

137

In to the south, allace, I was neir slane!
Over all the land I culd fynd no releiff,

---

925 *scrip*: small satchel
930 *have...feill*: wish to know
934 *supprysit*: injured
942 *afore*: before
943 *perysit*: dead   945 *revin*: torn
946 *tender*: dear; *put...flycht*: forced to flee

949 *ballance*: pair of scales
950 *clene*: absolute; *capitane*: captain; *ordinance*: ammunition
951 *debarris*: shuts out
952 *small remeid*: little redress

Almoist betwix the Mers and Lowmabane,   955
I culde nocht knaw ane leill man be ane theif.
To schaw thare reif, thift, murthour and mischeif,
And vecious workis, it wald infect the air,
And als langsum to me for tyll declair.

138

In to the Hieland I could fynd no remeid,   960
Bot suddantlie I wes put to exile.
Tha sweir swyngeoris, thay tuke of me non heid,
Nor amangs thame lat me remane ane quhyle.
Syklykin to the Oute Ylis, and in Argyle,
Unthrift, Sweirnes, Falset, Povertie, and Stryfe,   965
Pat Polacey in dainger of hir lyfe.

139

In the Law land I come to seik refuge,
And purposit thare to mak my residence.
Bot Singulare Proffect gart me soune disluge,
And did me gret injuris and offence,   970
And said to me, "Swyith, harlote, hy the hence!
And in this countre se thow tak no curis
So lang as my auctoritie induris".

140

And now I may mak no langer debait,
Nor I wate nocht quhome to I suld me mene.   975
For I have socht throw all the spirituall stait,
Quhilkis tuke na compt for to heir me complene.
Thare officiaris thay held me at disdane,
For Symonie, he rewlit all that rout,
And Covatyce, that carle, gart bar me oute.   980

141

Pryde haith chaist frome thame humilitie,
Devotioun is fled unto the freris;
Sensuale Plesour hes baneist Chaistitie,
Lordis of religioun thay go lyke seculeris,

---

955 *Mers*: Merse; *Lowmabane*:
    Lochmaben 960 *Hieland*: Highland
962 *sweir swyngeoris*: indolent rogues;
    heid: heed
964 *Syklykin*: Similarly; *Oute*: Outer
965 *Unthrift*: Wastefulness; *Falset*:
    Falsehood   966 *Pat*: Put
967 *Law land*: Lowland

969 *disluge*: remove
971 *Swyith...hence!*: Swiftly, villain, go
    quickly!
972 *tak...curis*: have no interest
975 *mene*: lament
980 *carle*: worthless fellow; *gart
    bar...oute*: had me excluded
984 *seculeris*: seculars

Taking more compt in tellyng thare deneris,   985
Nor thay do of thare constitutioun;
Thus ar thay blyndit be ambitioun.

142

Oure gentyll men ar all degenerat;
Liberalitie and Lawte, boith ar loste,
And Cowardyce with lordis is laureate,   990
And Knychtlie Curage turnit in brag and boste.
The civele weir misgydis everylk oist,
Thare is nocht ellis bot ilk man for hym self,
That garris me go thus baneist lyke ane elf,

143

Tharefor, adew. I may no langer tarye.'   995
'Fair weill,' quod I, 'and with Sanct Jhone to borrow.'
Bot wyt ye weill, my hart was wounder sarye,
Quhen Comoun Weill so sopit was in sorrow.
Yit efter the nycht cumis the glaid morrow.
'Quharefor, I pray yow, schaw me in certane   1000
Quhen that ye purpose for to cum agane?'

144

'That questioun, it sall be sone desydit,'
Quod he. 'Thare sall na Scot have confortyng
Of me tyll that I see the countre gydit
Be wysedome of ane gude auld prudent kyng,   1005
Quhilk sall delyte hym maist, abone all thyng,
To put justice tyll exicutioun,
And on strang tratouris mak puneisioun.

145

Als yit to the I say ane uther thyng.
I se rycht weill that proverbe is full trew: 1010
"Wo to the realme that hes ovir young ane king".'
With that, he turnit his bak and said adew.
Over firth and fell, rycht fast fra me he flew,
Quhose departyng to me was displesand.
With that Remembrance tuk me be the hand,   1015

---

985 *compt*: care; *tellyng*: reckoning   997 *sarye*: sore   998 *sopit*: steeped
989 *Lawte*: Loyalty   1002 *sone*: soon
990 *laureate*: pre-eminent   1008 *strang*: guilty
992 *oist*: military campaign 994 *elf*: spirit   1014 *displesand*: displeasing
996 *to borrow*: to pledge

146

And sone me thocht scho brocht me to the roche
And to the cove quhare I began to sleip.
With that, one schip did spedalye approche,
Full plesandlie saling apone the deip,
And syne did slake hir salis and gan to creip   1020
Towart the land, anent quhare that I lay;
Bot wyt ye weill, I gat ane fellown fraye!

147

All hir cannounis sche leit craik of at onis!
Down schuke the stremaris frome the topcastell.
Thay sparit nocht the poulder nor the stonis.   1025
Thay schot thare boltis and doun thar ankeris fell.
The marenaris thay did so youte and yell
That haistalie I stert out of my drame,
Half in ane fray, and spedalie past hame,

148

And lychtlie dynit, with lyste and appityte;   1030
Syne efter, past in tyll ane oritore
And tuke my pen, and thare began to wryte
All the visioun that I have schawin afore.
Schir, of my dreme, as now, thou gettis no more,
Bot I beseik God for to send the grace   1035
To rewle thy realme in unitie and peace.

Heir endis the Dreme.

And begynnis the Exhortatioun to the Kyngis Grace.

149

Schir, sen that God of his preordinance
Haith grantit the to have the governance
Of his peple, and create the one kyng,
Faill nocht to prent in thy remembrance   1040
That he wyll nocht excuse thyne ignorance,
Geve thow be rekles in thy governyng.
Quharefor, dres the, abone all uther thyng,

1020 *slake*: loosen; *creip*: move slowly
1021 *anent*: opposite
1022 *fellown fraye*: great fright
1023 *cannounis*: cannons; *leit...of*:
  caused to explode; *onis*: once
1024 *stremaris*: arrow-pointed pennons
1025 *poulder*: gunpowder; *stonis*: missiles

1026 *boltis*: short heavy arrows
1027 *marenaris*: mariners
1028 *stert*: started [involuntarily]
1030 *lyste*: pleasure 1031 *oritore*: study
1037 *preordinance*: power to preordain
1040 *prent*: print 1042 *rekles*: negligent
1043 *dres*: apply

Of his lawis to keip the observance
And thow schaip lang in ryaltie to ryng.   1045
                    150
Thank hym that hes commandit dame Nature
To prent the of so plesand portrature:
Hir gyftis may be cleirly on the knawin.
Tyll dame Fortune thow nedis no procurature,
For scho hes lairglie kyith on the hir cure: 1050
Hir gratytude sche hes on to the schawin.
And, sen that thow mon scheir as thow hes sawin,
Have all thy hope in God, thy creature,
And aske hym grace, that thow may be his awin.
                    151
And syne, considder thy vocatioun,   1055
That for to have the gubernatioun
Of this kynrik thou art predestinate.
Thou may weill wyt, be trew narratioun,
Quhat sorrow and quhat trubulatioun
Haith bene in this pure realme infortunate;   1060
Now conforte thame that hes bene desolate,
And of thy peple have compassioun,
Sen thow, be God, art so preordinate.
                    152
Tak manlie curage and leif thyne insolence,
And use counsale of nobyll dame Prudence.   1065
Founde the fermelie on Faith and Fortytude.
Drawe to thy courte Justice and Temporance,
And to thy Commoun Weill have attendance.
And also I beseik thy celsitude,
Hait vicious men, and lufe thame that ar gude,   1070
And ilke flattrer thow fleme frome thy presence,
And fals reporte out of thy courte exclude.

1045 *And*: If; *schaip*: plan
1047 *prent*: imprint
1048 *on*: in; *knawin*: seen
1049 *procurature*: accredited agent
1050 *lairglie*: abundantly; *kyith...cure*:
      devoted her careful attendance
1052 *scheir*: reap; *sawin*: sown
1053 *creature*: creator

1056 *gubernatioun*; governing
1057 *kynrik*: kingdom
1059 *trubulatioun*: misery
1064 *insolence*: unbridled conduct
1066 *Founde...fermelie*: Steadfastly base
      your conduct 1070 *vicious*: wicked
1071 *fleme*: exile

153

Do equale justice boith to gret and small,
And be exampyll to thy peple all,
Exersing verteous deidis honorabyll.   1075
Be nocht ane wrache, for oucht that may befall;
To that unhappy vice and thow be thrall,
Tyll all men thow sall be abhominabyll.
Kyngis nor knychtis ar never convenabyll
To rewle peple, be thay nocht lyberall: 1080
Was never yit na wrache to honour habyll.

154

And tak exempyll of the wracheit endyng
Quhilk maid Mydas of Trace, the mychtie king,
That to his goddes maid invocatioun,
Throw gredines, that all substanciall thing   1085
That ever he tuycheit suld turne, but tarying,
In to fyne gold. He gat his supplicatioun:
All that he tuychit, but delatioun,
Turnit in gold, boith meit, drynk, and clethyng,
And deit of hounger but recreatioun.   1090

155

Als, I beseik thy majestie serene,
Frome lychorie thow keip thy body clene.
Taist never that intoxicat poysoun.
Frome that unhappy sensuall syn, abstene
Tyll that thow get ane lusty plesand quene.   1095
Than tak thy plesour with my benesoun.
Tak tent how prydful Tarquyne tynt his croun
For the deforsyng of Lucres, the schene,
And was depryvit and baneist Romes toun.

156

And in dispyit of his lycherous levying,   1100
The Romanis wald be subject to no kyng
Mony lang yeir, as storyis doith recorde,
Tyll Julyus, throw verteous governyng

1076 *wrache*: miser
1077 *and...thrall*: if you are enslaved
1079 *convenabyll*: suitable
1083 *Mydas...Trace*: Midas of Thrace
1085 *substanciall*: material
1086 *tuycheit*: touched
1088 *delatioun*: delay

1090 *recreatioun*: nourishment
1092 *lychorie*: lechery
1097 *Tarquyne*: Tarquin
1098 *deforsyng*: raping; *Lucres*: Lucretia
1099 *depryvit*: deprived of office
1100 *dispyit*: contempt

And princelie curage, gane on thame to ryng,
And chosin of Romanis empriour and lord.   1105
Quharfor, my soverane, in to thy mynd remord
That vicious lyfe makis oft ane evyll endyng,
Without it be throw speciall grace restord.

157

And geve thow wald thy faime and honour grew,
Use counsall of thy prudent lordis trew,   1110
And se thow nocht presumpteouslie pretend
Thy awin perticulare weill for tyll ensew.
Wyrk with counsall, so sall thow never rew.
Remember of thy freindis the fatell end,
Quhilks to gude counsall wald not condiscend,   1115
Tyll bitter deith, allace, did thame persew.
Frome sic unhape, I pray God the defend.

158

And fynalie, remember thow mon dee,
And suddanlie pas of this mortall see,
And art nocht sicker of thy lyfe two houris,   1120
Sen thare is none frome that sentence may fle.
Kyng, quene, nor knycht, of lawe estait, nor hie,
Bot all mon thole of deith the bitter schouris.
Quhar bene thay gone, thir papis and empriouris?
Bene thay nocht dede? So sall it fair on the.   1125
Is no remeid, strenth, ryches, nor honouris.

159

And so, for conclusioun,
Mak our provisioun
To get the infusioun
            Of his hie grace,   1130
Quhilk bled with effusioun,
With scorne and derisioun,
And deit with confusioun,
            Confirmand our peace.
            Amen.

1106 *remord*: ponder
1109 *grew*: flourish
1111 *presumpteouslie*: arrogantly;
    pretend: seek
1112 *perticulare*: individual; *ensew*:
    follow
1115 *condiscend*: acquiesce

1117 *unhape*: ill fate
1119 *mortall see*: transitorily-held throne
1120 *sicker*: certain
1123 *schouris*: showers
1125 *fair on*: happen to
1131 *with effusioun*: pouring forth

THE COMPLAYNT
OF SCHIR DAVID LINDESAY

Schir, I beseik thyne excellence,
Heir my complaynt with pacience.
My dolent hart dois me constrane
Of my infortune to complane,
Quhowbeit I stand in gret dowtance   5
Quhome I sall wyte of my myschance:
Quhidder Saturnis creueltie,
Ryngand in my natyvitie,
Be bad aspect, quhilk wyrkis vengeance,
Or utheris hevinlye influence;   10
Or geve I be predestinate
In courte to be infortunate,
Quhilk hes so lang in servyce bene
Contynewallie, with kyng and quene,
And enterit to thy majestie   15
The day of thy natyvitie.
Quharethrow, my freindis bene eschamit
And with my fais I am defamit
(Seand that I am nocht regardit,
Nor with my brether in courte rewardit),   20
Blamand my sleuthfull neclygence
That seikis nocht sum recompence.
Quhen divers men dois me demand,
'Quhy gettis thow nocht sum peis of land,
Als weill as uther men hes gottin?'   25
Than wys I to be dede and rottin,
With sic extreme discomfortyng,
That I can mak no answeryng.

1   *beseik*: entreat
3   *dolent*: sorrowful; *constrane*: compel
4   *infortune*: misfortune
5   *Quhowbeit*: Although; *dowtance*:
    uncertainty
6   *Quhome*: Whom; *wyte*: blame;
    myschance: misfortune
7   *Quhidder*: Whether; *Saturnis*:
    Saturn's
8   *Ryngand*: Reigning
9   *Be*: By; *aspect*: phase [astrol.];
    quhilk: which; *wyrkis*: inflicts
10 *hevinlye*: of the heavens [astrol.]

11 *geve*: if; *predestinate*: fated
12 *infortunate*: unfortunate
14 *Contynewallie*: Continually
15 *enterit*: formally took up service
17 *bene*: are; *eschamit*: disgraced
18 *fais*: enemies; *defamit*: defamed
19 *Seand*: Seeing; *regardit*: esteemed
21 *Blamand*: Attributing [it] to;
    sleuthfull: slothful; *neclygence*:
    neglect   22 *seikis nocht*: seeks not
23 *divers*: various   24 *peis*: piece
26 *wys I*: I wish; *dede*: dead
27 *discomfortyng*: discouragement

41

I wald sum wyse man did me teche
Quhidder that I suld flatter or fleche. 30
I wyll nocht flyte, that I conclude,
For crabyng of thy celsitude
And to flatter, I am defamit:
Want I reward, than am I schamit.
Bot I hope thow sall do als weill 35
As did the father of fameill,
Of quhome Christ makis mentioun,
Quhilk, for ane certane pentioun,
Feit men to wyrk in his wyne yaird.
Bot quho come last gat first rewaird, 40
Quharethrow the first men wer displesit,
Bot he thame prudentlie amesit;
For thocht the last men first wer servit,
Yit gat the first that thay deservit.
So am I sure thy majestie 45
Sall anis rewarde me or I de,
And rube the ruste of my ingyne,
Quhilk bene for langour lyke to tyne.
Althocht I beir nocht lyke ane baird,
Lang servyce yarnis, ay, rewaird. 50
    I can nocht blame thyne excellence
That I so lang want recompance.
Had I solistit, lyke the laif,
My rewarde had nocht bene to craif.
Bot now I may weill understand: 55
Ane dum man yit wan never land,
And in the court men gettis na thyng
Withoute inopportune askyng.
Allace, my sleuth and schamefulnes

30 *fleche*: cajole
31 *flyte*: scold
32 *crabyng*: annoying; *celsitude*:
majesty   34 *schamit*: dishonoured
35 *als weill*: as well
36 *fameill*: [a] household
38 *pentioun*: regular payment
39 *Feit*: Hired; *wyne yaird*: vineyard
42 *amesit*: appeased
43 *servit*: provided for   44 *Yit*: Yet
46 *anis*: once; *or*: before; *de*: die
47 *rube*: remove; *ruste*: dullness;
ingyne: poetic ability
48 Which, for low spirits, is likely to be
lost
49 *beir*: behave; *baird*: common
minstrel
50 *yarnis*: deserves; *ay*: always
53 *solistit*: petitioned
54 *nocht...craif*: would not have
required asking
56 *dum*: silent; *wan*: gained
58 *inopportune*: untimely
59 *sleuth*: sloth

Debarrit fra me all gredynes. 60
Gredie men that ar delygent
Rycht oft obtenis thare intent,
And failyeis nocht to conqueis landis
And, namelye, at young prencis handis.
Bot I tuke never non uther cure 65
In speciall, bot for thy plesour.
Bot now I am na mair dispaird
Bot I sall get princely rewaird,
The quhilk, to me, sall be mair glore
Nor thame thow did reward afore. 70
Quhen men dois aske ocht at ane kyng
Sulde aske his grace ane nobyll thyng,
To his excellence honorabyll
And to the asker proffitabyll.
Thocht I be in my askyng lidder, 75
I praye thy grace for to considder:
Thow hes maid baith lordis and lairdis,
And hes gevin mony ryche rewardis
To thame that was full far to seik
Quhen I lay nychtlie be thy cheik. 80
  I tak the Quenis grace, thy mother,
My lord Chanclare and mony uther,
Thy nowreis, and thy auld maistres,
I tak thame all to beir wytnes.
Auld Wille Dile, wer he on lyve, 85
My lyfe full weill he could discryve,
Quhow, as ane chapman beris his pak,
I bure thy grace upon my bak
And sumtymes strydlingis on my nek,
Dansand with mony bend and bek. 90
The first sillabis that thow did mute
Was, 'Pa, Da Lyn'. Upon the lute

60 *Debarrit*: Excludes
61 *delygent*: persistent
64 *namelye*: in particular; *at...handis*:
  from   65 *cure*: charge
67 *dispaird*: in despair
69 *glore*: glory
71 *ocht*: anything; *at*: from
75 *lidder*: slow
77 *lairdis*: lesser barons or landowners
80 *cheik*: cheek   81 *Quenis*: Queen's

82 *Chanclare*: Chancellor
83 *nowreis*: nurse; *maistres*: governess
85 *on lyve*: alive
87 *chapman*: pedlar; *beris*: carries; *pak*:
  pack of wares
89 *strydlingis*: astride
90 *bend*: leaps; *bek*: bows
91 *sillabis*: syllables; *mute*: speak
92 *Pa*: ?Play; *Da Lyn*: David Lyndsay

Than playt I twenty spryngis perqueir,
Quhilk wos gret piete for to heir!
Fra play thow leit me never rest,   95
Bot *Gynkartoun* thow lufit, ay, best.
And ay, quhen thow come frome the scule,
Than I behuffit to play the fule,
As I, at lenth, in to my *Dreme*,
My sindry servyce did expreme.   100
Thocht it bene better, as sayis the wyse,
Hape to the court nor gude servyce,
I wate thow luffit me better, than,
Nor, now, sum wyfe dois hir gude man!
Than men tyll uther did recorde,   105
Said, 'Lyndsay wald be maid ane lorde'.
Thow hes maid lordis, schir, be Sanct Geill,
Of sum that hes nocht servit so weill.
To yow, my lordis, that standis by,
I sall yow schaw the causis quhy;   110
Geve ye lyst tary, I sall tell
Quhow my infortune first befell.
I prayit daylie on my knee
My young maister that I mycht see
Of eild, in his aistait royall,   115
Havand power imperyall.
Than traistit I, without demand,
To be promovit to sum land.
Bot my askyng I gat over soun,
Because ane clips fell in the mone   120
The quhilk all Scotland maid asteir.
Than did my purpose ryn arreir,
The quhilk war langsum to declare.

---

93 *spryngis*: dance tunes; *perqueir*: by
   heart
94 *gret piete*: [a cause for] great regret
95 *leit*: allowed
98 *behuffit*: was obliged
100 *sindry*: diverse; *expreme*: express
102 *Hape to*: To have good luck at; *nor*:
   than
103 *wate*: know; *luffit*: loved; *than*: then
104 *gude man*: husband
105 *tyll*: to; *uther*: [each] other; *recorde*:
   say   106 *wald*: would; *maid*: created

107 *Geill*: Giles   110 *quhy*: why
111 *Geve*: If; *lyst*: please to; *tary*: wait
115 *eild*: age [legal]; *aistait*: rank
117 *traistit*: expected
118 *promovit*: promoted
119 *askyng*: request; *over soun*: too soon
120 *clips...mone*: a lunar eclipse
   occurred
121 *maid asteir*: put in commotion
122 *ryn arreir*: retrogress
123 *langsum*: tedious

And als my hart is wounder sare
Quhen I have in remembrance
The suddand cheange, to my myschance.   125
The kyng was bot twelf yeris of aige
Quhen new rewlaris come in thare raige,
For commoun weill makand no cair,
Bot for thare proffeit singulair.   130
   Imprudentlie, lyk wytles fullis,
Thay tuke that young prince frome the sculis,
Quhare he, under Obedience,
Was lernand vertew and science,
And haistelie plat in his hand   135
The governance of all Scotland.
As quho wald, in ane stormye blast,
Quhen marinaris bene all agast
Throw dainger of the seis raige,
Wald tak ane chylde of tender aige   140
Quhilk never had bene on the sey,
And to his bidding al obey,
Gevying hym haill the governall
Of schip, marchand, and marinall?
For dreid of rockis and foreland,   145
To put the ruther in his hand
Without Godds grace is no refuge:
Geve thare be dainger, ye may juge.
I gyf thame to the devyll of hell
Quhilk first devysit that counsell!   150
I wyll nocht say that it was treassoun,
Bot, I dar sweir, it was no reassoun.
I pray God, lat me never se ryng
In to this realme so young ane kyng.

---

124 *als*: also; *wounder*: wonderfully;
   sare: sad
126 *cheange*: change
128 *raige*: passion [for power]
130 *proffeit singulair*: individual profit
131 *fullis*: fools   132 *sculis*: school
134 *vertew*: [moral] virtue; *science*:
   knowledge
135 *plat*: set
138 *marinaris*: sailors; *agast*: terrified

139 *seis*: sea's; *raige*: fury
140 *tender aige*: immature age
143 *haill*: all; *governal*: governing
144 *marchand*: merchant; *marinall*:
   seaman
145 *foreland*: headland
146 *ruther*: rudder 150 *devysit*: planned
152 *dar sweir*: venture to swear; *no
   reassoun*: not good or right
153 *ryng*: reign

I may nocht tary to desydit,   155
Quhow than the court ane quhyle was gydit
Be thame that peirtlye tuke on hand
To gyde the kyng and all Scotland;
And als, langsum for to declare,
Thare facound flattryng wordis fair: 160
'Schir', sum wald say, 'your majestie
Sall now go to your lybertie.
Ye sall to no man be coactit
Nor to the scule no more subjectit.
We thynk thame verray naturail fulis   165
That lernis ovir mekle at the sculis.
Schir, ye mon leir to ryn ane speir
And gyde yow lyke ane man of weir,
For we sall put sic men aboute yow
That all the warld, and mo, sall doute yow!'   170
Than to his grace thay put ane gaird,
Quhilk haistelie gat thare rewaird.
Ilke man, efter thare qualitie,
Thay did solyst his majestie.
Sum gart hym raiffell at the rakcat,   175
Sum harld hym to the hurly hakcat,
And sum, to schaw thare courtlie corsis,
Wald ryid to Leith and ryn thare horssis
And wychtlie wallope over the sandis;
Ye nother sparit spurris nor wandis,   180
Castand galmoundis with bendis and beckis;
For wantones, sum braik thare neckis.
Thare was no play bot cartis and dyce,

155 *tary*: tarry; *desydit*: decide it
156 *than*: then; *quhyle*: while; *gydit*:
    guided   157 *peirtlye*: boldly
160 *facound*: eloquent
163 *coactit*: coerced
164 *subjectit*: subjected
165 *naturail*: born
166 *ovir mekle*: too much
167 *mon*: must; *leir*: learn; *ryn*: thrust;
    speir: spear   168 *weir*: war
170 *mo*: more; *doute*: fear
171 *gaird*: guard
173 *qualitie*: character

175 *gart*: caused; *raiffell*: make merry;
    rakcat: [game of] rackets
176 Some dragged him on a sledge down
    a slope
177 *schaw*: reveal; *courtlie corsis*:
    refined bodies   178 *ryn*: race
179 *wychtlie*: vigorously; *wallope*: gallop
180 *nother*: neither; *sparit*: held back;
    spurris: [pricking with] spurs;
    wandis: straight, slender sticks
181 *Castand*: Casting; *galmoundis*: leaps
182 *wantones*: lack of restraint
183 *cartis and dyce*: cards and dicing

And ay, schir Flattre bure the pryce,
Roundand and rowkand, ane tyll uther: 185
'Tak thow my part,' quod he, 'my bruther,
And mak betwix us sicker bandis
(Quhen ocht sall vaik amangs our landis),
That ilk man stand to help his fallow.'
'I hald thareto, man, be Alhallow,   190
Swa thow fische nocht within my boundis!'
'That sall I nocht, be Godis woundis!'
Quod he. 'But erar tak thy part,
Swa sall I thyne, be Gods hart!
And geve the thesaureir be our freind,   195
Than sall we get baith tak and teind;
Tak he our part, than quha dar wrang us,
Bot we sall part the pelf amang us.
Bot haist us, quhill the kyng is young,
And lat ilk man keip weill ane toung,   200
And in ilk quarter have ane spye,
Us tyll adverteis haistelie
Quhen ony casualiteis
Sall happin in our countreis.
Lat us mak sure provissioun   205
Or he cum to discretioun;
No more he wate nor dois ane sancte
Quhat thyng it bene to have, or wante.
So, or he be of perfyte aige,
We sall be sicker of our waige,   210
And syne, lat ilk ane carle craif uther.'
'That mouth speik mair,' quod he, 'my brother,
For God nor I rax in ane raipe,

184 *Flattre*: Flattery; *bure the pryce*:
    was pre-eminent
185 *Roundand*: Whispering; *rowkand*:
    tale-bearing
187 *sicker*: certain; *bandis*: bonds
188 *ocht*: anything; *vaik*: fall vacant;
    amangs: among
189 *fallow*: associate
190 *hald*: adhere; *be Alhallow*: by all the
    saints
191 *Swa*: So; *boundis*: boundaries
192 *be...woundis*: by God's wounds
193 *But erar*: But sooner
194 *hart*: heart

195 *geve*: if; *thesaureir*: treasurer
196 *tak...teind*: leasehold farm and tithe
198 *part the pelf*: divide the spoil
199 *quhill*: while
202 *adverteis*: inform
203 *casualiteis*: casual payments [due
    from tenant or vassal]
205 *provissioun*: advance arrangements
206 *discretioun*: discernment
207 *wate*: knows; *sancte*: saint
209 *or*: before; *of perfyte aige*: legally
    mature
211 *carle*: fellow; *craif*: importune
213 *rax...raipe*: hang

Thow mycht geve counsale to the pape!'
Thus lauborit thay within few yeris   215
That thay become no pagis peris.
Swa haistelye thay maid ane hand,
Sum gadderit gold, sum conqueist land.
'Schir,' sum wald say, 'be Sanct Dinnyce,
Geve me sum fate benefyce,   220
And all the proffect ye sall have;
Geve me the name, tak yow the lave.'
Bot be his bowis war weill cumit hame,
To mak servyce he wald thynk schame;
Syne slyp awaye, withouttin more,   225
Quhen he had gottin that he sang fore.
Me thocht it was ane pieteous thyng
To se that fair young tender kyng,
Of quhome thir gallandis stude no awe,
To play with hym pluke at the crawe.   230
Thay become ryche, I yow assure,
Bot aye the prence remanit pure.
Thare wes few of that garisoun
That lernit hym ane gude lessoun,
Bot sum to crak and sum to clatter,   235
Sum maid the fule and sum did flatter.
Quod ane, 'The devyll stik me with ane knyfe,
Bot, schir, I knaw ane maid in Fyfe,
Ane of the lusteast wantoun lassis,
Quhare to, schir, be Gods blude scho passis!'   240
'Hald thy toung, brother,' quod ane uther,
'I knaw ane fairar, be fyftene futher!
Schir, quhen ye pleis to Leithgow pas,
Thare sall ye se ane lusty las!'

214 *geve*: give; *pape*: pope
216 *pagis peris*: equals of pages
219 *Dinnyce*: Denis   220 *fate*: rich
221 *proffect*: profit
222 *lave*: remainder
223 *be*: before; *bowis*: papal letters; *cumit hame*: received in Scotland
224 *mak servyse*: perform the duties
225 *Syne*: Then
227 *thocht*: thought
228 *tender*: youthful

229 *thir*: these; *gallandis*: fine young fellows; *stude...awe*: were not afraid
230 *pluke...crawe*: pluck at the crow
232 *pure*: poor   233 *garisoun*: company
234 *lernit*: taught; *gude*: beneficial
235 *crak*: boast; *clatter*: chatter
236 *maid*: played
237 Devil stab me with a knife!
238 *Fyfe*: Fife
239 *lusteast*: fairest; *wantoun*: wanton
240 *passis*: goes   242 *futher*: cart loads
243 *Leithgow*: Linlithgow

'Now trittyll, trattyll, trolylow,'   245
Quod the thrid man. 'Thow dois bot mow!
Quhen his grace cumis to fair Sterlyng,
Thair sall he se ane dayis derlyng!'
'Schir,' quod the fourt, 'tak my counsall,
And go, all, to the hie boirdall.   250
Thare may we lope at lybertie,
Withouttin ony gravitie.'
Thus every man said for hym self,
And did amangis thame part the pelf.
Bot I, allace, or ever I wyste,   255
Was trampit doun in to the douste,
With hevy charge, withouttin more,
Bot I wyste never yit quharefore.
And haistellie, before my face,
Ane uther slippit in my place,   260
Quhilk rychelie gat his rewaird
And stylit was the anscient laird.
That tyme I mycht mak no defence
Bot tuke perforce in pacience,
Prayand to send thame ane myschance   265
That had the court in governance,
The quhilkis aganis me did malyng
Contrar the plesour of the kyng.
For weill I knew his graces mynd
Was ever to me trew and kynd   270
And, contrar thare intentioun,
Gart pay me weill my pentioun.
Thocht I ane quhyle wantit presence,
He leit me have no indigence.
Quhen I durst nother peip nor luke,   275
Yit wald I hyde me in ane nuke

245 *trittyll...trolylow*: gossip, idle chatter,
     and lies   246 *mow*: jest
247 *Sterlyng*: Stirling
248 *dayis derlyng*: day's darling
250 *boirdall*: brothel
251 *lope*: spring upon [in sexual
     intercourse]
252 *gravitie*: grave behaviour
253 *said*: spoke   255 *wyste*: knew
256 *trampit*: trampled; *douste*: dust
257 *hevy*; serious; *charge*: imputation

258 *quharefore*: why
262 *stylit*: titled; *anscient laird*: present
     laird
267 *malyng*: speak disparagingly
268 *Contrar*: Contrary to
272 *Gart...me*: Had me paid
273 *presence*: admission to the king's
     presence
274 *leit*: allowed; *indigence*: poverty
275 *nother*: neither; *peip*: squeak
276 *hyde*: hide

To se those uncouth vaniteis,
Quhow thay, lyke ony beisy beis,
Did occupy thare goldin houris
With help of thare new governouris.   280
Bot, my complaynt for to compleit,
I gat the soure and thay the sweit,
Als Jhone Makerery, the kyngis fule,
Gat dowbyll garmoundis agane the Yule,
Yit, in his maist tryumphant glore,   285
For his rewarde gat the grand gore.
Now in the court seindell he gois
(In dreid men stramp upon his tois),
As I, that tyme, durst nocht be sene
In oppin court, for baith my eine.   290
Allace, I have no tyme to tary
To schaw yow all the fery fary,
Quhow those that had the governance
Amangis thame selfis raist variance,
And quho maist to my skaith consentit   295
Within few yeris full sore repentit
Quhen thay could mak me no remeid.
For thay war harlit out be the heid
And utheris tuke the governyng,
Weill wors than thay in alkin thyng.   300
Thay lordis tuke no more regaird
Bot quho mycht purches best rewaird.
Sum to thare freindis gat benefyceis
And uther sum gat byschopreis;
For every lord, as he thocht best,   305
Brocht in ane bird to fyll the nest,
To be ane wacheman to his marrow:
Thay gan to draw at the cat harrow.

277 *uncouth*: strange
283 *Als*: As; *Makerery*: McCrery
284 *Gat*: Obtained; *dowbyll*: double
   thick; *garmoundis*: garments; *again*:
   in anticipation of
286 *gat*: caught; *grand gore*: venereal
   disease   287 *seindell*: seldom
288 *dreid*: fear; *stramp*: tread; *tois*: toes
290 *baith*: both; *eine*: eyes
292 *yow*: you; *fery fary*: confusion
294 *raist*: caused; *variance*: dissension

295 *maist*: most; *skaith*: harm
297 *remeid*: redress
298 *harlit*: dragged forcibly; *heid*:
   principal mover
300 *alkin*: every kind of
301 *Thay*: Those
303 *benefyceis*: benefices
304 *byschopreis*: bishoprics
306 *fyll*: fill, befoul
307 *wacheman*: watchman; *marrow*:
   associate   308 *gan*: began

The proudest prelatis of the kirk
Was faine to hyde thame in the myrk   310
That tyme, so failyeit wes thare sycht.
Sen syne thay may nocht thole the lycht
Of Christis trew gospell to be sene,
So blyndit is thare corporall ene
With wardly lustis sensuall,   315
Takyng in realmes the governall,
Baith gyding court and cessioun
Contrar to thare professioun.
Quhareof I thynk thay sulde have schame
Of spirituall preistis to tak the name;   320
For Esayas, in to his wark,
Callis thame lyke doggis that can nocht bark,
That callit ar preistis and can nocht preche,
Nor Christis law to the peple teche.
Geve for to preche bene thare professioun,   325
Quhy sulde thay mell with court or cessioun
(Except it war in spirituall thyngis),
Referryng unto lordis and kyngis
Temporall causis to be desydit?
Geve thay thare spirituall office gydit,   330
Ilke man mycht say thay did thare partis;
Bot geve thay can play at the cairtis
And mollet moylie on ane mule,
Thocht thay had never sene the scule,
Yit, at this day, als weill as than,   335
Wyll be maid sic ane spirituall man.
Prencis that sic prelatis promofis,
Accompt thareof to geve behuffis,
Quhilk sall nocht pas but puneischement
Without thay mend and sore repent   340
And with dew ministratioun

310 *faine*: glad; *thame*: themselves;
    myrk: darkness
312 *Sen syne*: Since then; *thole*: allow
314 *corporall ene*: human eyes
315 *wardly*: worldly
316 *governall*: governing
317 *cessioun*: session
321 *Esayas*: Isaiah; *wark*: work
326 *sulde*: should; *mell*: be involved

331 *partis*: [appropriate] parts
332 *play...cairtis*: play card games
333 *mollet moylie*: ride using a curb
337 *promofis*: promote
338 *Accompt*: Account; *behuffis*: is
    necessary
339 *pas*: go; *but*: without
340 *Without*: Unless; *mend*: reform
341 *dew*: fitting; *ministratioun*: service

Wyrk efter thare vocatioun.
I wys that thyng quhilk wyll nocht be:
Thir perverst prelatis ar so hie!
Frome tyme that thay bene callit lordis   345
Thay ar occasioun of discordis,
And lairglie wyll propynis hecht
To gar ilk lord with uther fecht,
Geve, for thare part, it may availl.
Swa to the purpose of my taill.   350
That tyme in court rais gret debait,
And everilk lord did stryve for stait,
That all the realme mycht mak no reddyng,
Quhill, on ilk syde, thare was blude scheddyng
And feildit uther in land and burgh,   355
Att Lyithgow, Melros and Edinburgh.
Bot to deplore I thynk gret paine
Of nobyll men that thare was slane,
And als (langsum to be reportit)
Of thame quhilk to the court resortit   360
As tyrannis, tratouris and transgressouris,
And commoun publict plaine oppressouris,
Men murdresaris and commoun theiffis
In to that court gat, all, releiffis.
Thair was few lordis in all thir landis   365
Bot tyll new regentis maid thare bandis.
Than rais ane reik, or ever I wyste,
The quhilk gart all thare bandis bryste!
Than thay allone quhilk had the gyding,
Thay culde nocht keip thare feit frome slyding,   370
Bot of thare lyffis thay had sic dreid
That thay war faine tyll trott over Tweid.

343 *wys*: desire
344 *Thir*: These; *perverst*: wicked; *hie*:
    arrogant
346 *discordis*: dissension
347 *lairglie*: freely; *propynis*: gifts;
    hecht: promise
348 *fecht*: fight   349 *availl*: profit
352 *stait*: rank
353 *reddyng*: separation [of combatants]
354 *Quhill*: Until; *blude scheddyng*:
    bloodshed
355 *feildit*: encountered in battle
356 *Lyithgow*: Linlithgow

357 *deplore*: lament
359 *als*: also; *langsum*: tedious; *reportit*:
    written
360 *resortit*: went
361 *publict...oppressouris*: open
    oppressors
363 *Men murdresaris*: Lowly murderers
364 *releiffis*: payment
366 *bandis*: bonds [of allegiance]
367 *rais...reik*: arose a tumult; *or*: before
368 *bryste*: broke open   371 *dreid*: fear
372 *war*: were; *faine*: well-pleased;
    Tweid: [River] Tweed

Now, potent prince, I say to the,
I thank the haly Trinitie
That I have levit to se this daye   375
That all that warld is went awaye,
And thow to no man art subjectit,
Nor to sic counsalouris coactit.
The foure gret verteous cardinalis,
I see thame with the principalis.   380
For Justice haldis hir sweird on hie,
With hir ballance of equitie,
And in this realme hes maid sic ordour,
Baith throw the Heland and the Bordour,
That Oppressioun and all his fallowis   385
Ar hangit heych apon the gallous.
Dame Prudence hes the be the heid,
And Temperance dois thy brydill leid.
I se dame Force mak assistance,
Berand thy targe of assurance,   390
And lusty lady Chaistitie
Hes baneist Sensualitie.
Dame Ryches takis on the sic cure,
I pray God that scho lang indure,
That Povertie dar nocht be sene   395
In to thy hous, for baith hir ene,
Bot fra thy grace fled mony mylis,
Amangis the hountaris in the Ylis.
Dissimulance dar nocht schaw hir face,
Quhilk wount was to begyill thy grace.   400
Foly is fled out of the toun,
Quhilk ay was countrar to ressoun.
Polyce and Peace begynnis to plant,

373 *potent*: mighty
374 *haly*: holy   375 *levit*: lived
377 *subjectit*: subjected
378 *sic*: such; *coactit*: constrained
379 *verteous cardinalis*: cardinal virtues
380 *principalis*: leaders
381 *sweird*: sword
382 *ballance...equitie*: pair of scales
384 *Heland*: Highlands; *Bordour*:
    Border   385 *fallowis*: associates
386 *gallous*: gallows   387 *heid*: mind
388 *brydill*: bridle; *leid*: lead

389 *Force*: Strength; *mak assistance*:
    give help
390 *Berand*: Holding; *targe*: shield;
    assurance: security
394 *indure*: continue   397 *fra*: from
398 *hountaris*: hunters; *Ylis*: Western Isles
399 *Dissimulance*: Dissimulation
400 *wount*: accustomed; *begyill*: deceive
401 *Foly*: Folly
402 *ay*: always; *countrar*: antagonistic
403 *Polyce*: [Good] Government; *plant*:
    grow

That verteous men can no thyng want,   405
And as for sleuthfull idyll lownis,
Sall fetterit be in the gailyeownis!
Jhone Upeland bene full blyith, I trow,
Because the rysche bus kepis his kow.
Swa is thare nocht, I understand,   410
Withoute gude ordour in this land,
Except the Spiritualitie,
Prayand thy grace thareto have ee.
Cause thame mak ministratioun
Conforme to thare vocatioun,   415
To preche with unfenyeit intentis,
And trewly use the sacramentis
Efter Christis institutionis,
Levying thare vaine traditiounis
(Quhilkis dois the syllie scheip illude   420
Quhame for Christ Jesus sched his blude),
As superstitious pylgramagis,
Prayand to gravin imagis
Expres aganis the Lordis command.
I do thy grace tyll understand,   425
Geve thow to mennis lawis assent,
Aganis the Lordis commandiment
As Jeroboam and mony mo,
Prencis of Israell all so,
Assentaris to ydolatrie   430
Quhilkis puneist war, rycht pieteouslie,
And frome thare realmes wer rutit oute,
So sall thow be, withouttin doute,
Baith heir and hyne, withouttin more,

405 *lownis*: fellows
406 *fetterit*: secured with chains; *gailyeownis*: galleons [galleys]
407 *Jhone Upeland*: Country John
408 *rysche bus*: clump of rushes; *kepis*: retains; *kow*: cow
409 *nocht*: nothing
411 *Spiritualitie*: Ecclesiastical body
412 *Prayand*: Begging; *ee*: regard
413 *mak ministratioun*: execute the duties of a minister of religion
414 *Conforme*: Corresponding
415 *preche*: preach; *unfenyeit*: sincere
416 *use*: make use of
417 *Efter*: According to; *Christis institutionis*: Christ's doctrines, sacraments
418 *Levying*: Giving up; *vaine*: useless
419 *syllie*: simple; *illude*: delude
420 *Quhame*: Whom
422 *gravin*: carved
423 *Expres aganis*: Expressly contrary
430 *puneist*: punished
431 *rutit out*: removed completely
433 *heir...hyne*: here and from here

And want the everlestyng glore.
Bot geve thow wyll thy hart inclyne   435
And keip his blyssit law devyne,
As did the faithfull Patriarkis,
Boith in thare wordis and thare warkis,
And as did mony faithfull kyngis
Of Israell, duryng thare ryngis,   440
As kyng David and Salomone,
Quhilkis ymagis wald suffer none
In thare ryche tempillis for to stand,
Because it was nocht Goddis command,
Bot distroyit all ydolatrie   445
(As in the scripture thow may see),
Quhose ryche rewarde was hevinly blys,
Quhilk sall be thyne, thow doand this.
  Sen thow hes chosin sic ane gaird,
Now am I sure to get rewaird,   450
And sen thow art the rychest kyng
That ever in this realme did ryng,
Of gold and stonis precious
Maist prudent and ingenious,
And hes thy honour done avance,   455
In Scotland, Ingland, and in France,
Be merciall dedis honourabyll,
And art tyll every vertew abyll,
I wat thy grace wyll nocht misken me,
Bot thow wyll uther geve, or len me.   460
Wald thy grace len me, to ane day,
Of gold ane thousand pound or tway,
And I sall fix, with gude intent,
Thy grace ane daye of payment,
With selit oblygatioun,   465
Under this protestatioun:

434 *want*: be deprived of;
    everlestyng glore: salvation
437 *Patriarkis*: Founding Fathers
441 *Salomone*: Solomon
447 *blys*: bliss   448 *doand*: doing
449 *gaird*: guard
450 *rewaird*: recompense
455 *hes*: has; *done avance*: raised in
    repute   457 *merciall*: martial
458 *art tyll...abyll*: are qualified in
459 *wat*: know; *misken*: misunderstand
460 *Bot*: But that; *uther*: either; *len*: lend
461 *to ane day*: to a [specified] day
462 *tway*: two
465 *selit oblygatioun*: [legal] contract;
    promissory note with seals attached
466 *Under*: Below; *protestatioun*:
    [assertion of a] reservation

Quhen the Basse and the Yle of Maye
Beis sett upon the Mont Senaye;
Quhen the Lowmound besyde Falkland
Beis lyftit to Northhumberland;   470
Quhen kirkmen yairnis no dignitie,
Nor wyffis no soveranitie,
Wynter but frost, snaw, wynd, or rane,
Than sall I geve thy gold agane.
Or I sall mak the payment   475
Efter the daye of Jugement—
Within ane moneth, at the leist!
Quhen Sanct Peter sall mak ane feist
To all the fyscharis of Aberladye,
Swa thow have myne acquittance reddye.   480
Failyeand thareof, be Sanct Phillane,
Thy grace gettis never ane grote agane.
Geve thow be nocht content of this,
I man requeist the kyng of blys
That he to me have sum regaird,   485
And cause thy grace me to rewaird.
For David, kyng of Israell,
Quhilk was the gret propheit royall,
Sayis God hes haill at his command,
The hartis of prencis in his hand;   490
Evin as he lyste thame for to turne,
That mon thay do withoute sudgeorne;
Sum tyll exault to dignitie,
And sum to depryve, in povertie,
Sum tyme, of lawid men to mak lordis,   495
And sum tyme, lordis to bynd in cordis
And thame alutterlye distroye,

467 *Basse*: Bass Rock; *Yle..Maye*: Isle of
    May
468 *Beis*: Be (pl.); *sett*: placed; *Mont*
    Senaye: Mount Sinai
469 *Lowmound*: Lomond [Hills]
470 *lyftit*: taken up and removed
471 *yairnis*: desire; *dignitie*: high
    estate
472 *wyffis*: wives; *soveranitie*:
    supremacy   479 *fyscharis*: fishers
480 *acquittance*: formal discharge from
    debt

481 *Failyeand*: In the absence of;
    Phillane: Fillan
482 *grote*: groat
484 *man*: must   489 *haill*: the whole
491 *lyste*: chooses   492 *sudgeorne*: rest
493 *exault*: raise
494 *depryve*: dispossess
495 *lawid*: common
496 *bynd..cordis*: hang
497 *alutterlye*: completely

As plesis God, that ryall roye.
For thow art bot ane instrument
To that gret kyng omnipotent,   500
So, quhen plesis his excellence,
Thy grace sall mak me recompence,
Or he sall cause me stand content
Of quiet lyfe and sober rent,
And tak me, in my letter aige,   505
Unto my sempyll hermytage,
And spend it that my eldaris woun,
As did Matussalem in his toun.
Of this complaynt, with mynd full meik,
Thy graces answeir, schir, I beseik.   510

499 *instrument*: means
503 *stand*: abide
504 *sober*: moderate; *rent*: income
505 *letter*: last

506 *sempyll*: simple
507 *eldaris*: ancestors; *woun*: earned
508 *toun*: lands [of estate, farm]
509 *mynd*: disposition

THE TESTAMENT AND COMPLAYNT
OF OUR SOVERANE LORDIS
PAPYNGO

1

Suppose I had ingyne angelicall,
With sapience more than Salamonicall,
I not quhat mater put in memorie.
The poetis auld, in style heroycall,
In breve subtell termes rethorycall,   5
Of everilke mater, tragedie and storie,
So ornatlie, to thare heych laude and glorie,
Haith done indyte; quhose supreme sapience
Transcendith far the dull intellygence

2

Of poetis now, in tyll our vulgare toung.   10
For quhy? The bell of rethorick bene roung
Be Chawceir, Goweir, and Lidgate laureate.
Quho dar presume thir poetis tyll impung,
Quhose sweit sentence throuch Albione bene soung?
Or quho can, now, the workis cuntrafait   15
Of Kennedie, with termes aureait,
Or of Dunbar, quhilk language had at large,
As maye be sene in tyll his *Goldin Targe*?

3

Quintyng, Mersar, Rowle, Henderson, Hay, and Holland,
Thocht thay be ded, thar libells bene levand,   20
Quhilkis, to reheirs, makeith redaris to rejose.
Allace for one, quhilk lampe wes of this land!
Of eloquence the flowand balmy strand,
And, in our Inglis rethorick, the rose.
As, of rubeis, the charbunckle bene chose,   25

---

1   *Suppose*: Even if; *ingyne*: ability
2   *Salamonicall*: of Solomon
3   *I not*: I would not know
5   *breve*: short; *subtell*: clever
8   *indyte*: compose, write
10 *vulgare*: vernacular
11 *bell...roung*: arts of eloquence have been mastered
12 *laureate*: poet pre-eminent
13 *thir*: these; *tyll*: to; *impung*: attack
14 *Albione*: Britain; *bene*: is

15 *cuntrafait*: imitate
16 *aureait*: highly refined [lit. golden]
17 *at large*: with stylistic freedom and abundant vocabulary
18 *Targe*: 'Shield'
20 *libells*: little books; *levand*: living
21 *reheirs*: read aloud; *rejose*: rejoice
22 *lampe*: shining example
23 *balmy strand*: fragrant stream
25 *charbunckle*: carbuncle, ruby; *bene chose*: is chosen

58

And, as Phebus dois Synthia presell,
So Gawane Dowglas, byschope of Dunkell,

4

Had, quhen he wes in to this land on lyve,
Abufe vulgare poetis prerogatyve,
Boith in pratick and speculatioun. 30
I saye no more. Gude redaris may discryve
His worthy workis, in nowmer mo than fyve,
And speciallye the trew translatioun
Of Virgill, quhilk bene consolatioun
To cunnyng men, to knaw his gret ingyne 35
Als weill in naturall science as devyne.

5

And in the courte bene present, in thir dayis,
That ballattis brevis lustellie, and layis,
Quhilks tyll our prince daylie thay do present.
Quho can say more than schir James Inglis says, 40
In ballatts, farses, and in plesand playis?
Bot Culrose hes his pen maid impotent.
Kyde, in cunnyng and pratick rycht prudent,
And Stewarte, quhilk disyrith one staitly style,
Full ornate werkis daylie dois compyle. 45

6

Stewart of Lorne wyll carpe rycht curiouslie;
Galbreith, Kynlouch, quhen thay lyst tham applie
In to that art, ar craftie of ingyne.
Bot now, of lait, is starte upe haistelie
One cunnyng clerk quhilk wrytith craftelie, 50
One plant of poetis, callit Ballentyne,
Quhose ornat workis my wytt can nocht defyne.
Gett he in to the courte auctoritie
He wyll precell Quintyng and Kennetie.

---

26 *Phebus*: Phoebus; *Synthia*: Cynthia;
  presell: surpass
27 *Dunkell*: Dunkeld 28 *on lyve*: alive
29 *prerogatyve*: superiority
30 *pratick*: practical proficiency;
  speculatioun: [abstruse] theory
32 *nowmer*: number; *fyve*: five
34 *consolatioun*: comfort
35 *cunnyng*: learned 37 *bene*: are
38 *ballattis*: poems; *brevis*: compose;
  lustellie: eloquently; *layis*: songs

41 *farses*: short dramatic works
42 *Culrose*: Culross
44 *one*: a; *staitly*: dignified
46 *carpe*: speak; *curiouslie*: artfully
47 *quhen...applie*: when they care to
  apply themselves
48 *craftie*: skilful 51 *plant*: scion
53 *Gett he*: If he should get
54 *precell*: surpass

7

So thocht I had ingyne (as I have none),   55
I watt nocht quhat to wryt, be sweit Sanct Jhone.
For quhy? In all the garth of eloquence
Is no thyng left bot barrane stok and stone.
The poleit termes ar pullit, everilk one,
Be thir forenamit poetis of prudence.   60
And sen I fynd non uther new sentence,
I sall declare, or I depart yow fro,
The complaynt of ane woundit papingo.

8

Quharefor, because myne mater bene so rude
Of sentence, and of rethorike denude,   65
To rurall folke myne dyting bene directit,
Far flemit frome the sycht of men of gude.
For cunnyng men, I knaw, wyll soune conclude,
It dowe no thyng bot for to be dejectit.
And quhen I heir myne mater bene detractit,   70
Than sall I sweir I maid it bot in mowis,
To landwart lassis quhilks kepith kye and yowis.

Heir endis the Prolong. And followis
the Complaynt.

9

Quho clymmit to hycht, perforce his feit mon faill.
Expreme I sal that be experience,
Geve that yow pleis to heir one pieteous taill,   75
How one fair bird, be faitell violence,
Devorit was and mycht mak no defence
Contrare the deth, so failyeit naturall strenth,
As efter I sall schaw yow, at more lenth.

55 *thocht*: even if
56 *watt*: know; *Jhone*: John
57 *quhy*: why; *garth*: garden
58 *barrane*: barren; *stok*: stumps
59 *poleit*: polished; *pullit*: picked
61 *sen*: since; *sentence*: theme
62 *or*: before; *yow*: you
63 *papingo*: parrot
64 *rude*: unpolished
66 *rurall*: simple; *dyting*: composition
67 *flemit*: exiled; *gude*: importance

69 *dowe*: is worth; *bot for*: other than;
   dejectit: cast down
71 *sweir*: swear; *in mowis*: in jest
72 *landwart*: country; *kye*: cows; *yowis*:
   ewes
73 *hycht*: height; *mon*: must
74 *Expreme*: Express
75 *Geve*: If
77 *Devorit*: Destroyed; *mycht*: might
78 *failyeit*: failed

10

One papyngo, rycht plesand and perfyte,   80
Presentit was tyll our moist nobyll kyng,
Of quhome his grace one lang tyme had delyte.
More fair of forme, I wat, flew never on wyng!
This proper bird he gave in governyng
To me (quhilk wes his simpyll servetoure),   85
On quhome I did my delygence and cure

11

To lerne hir language artificiall,
To play *Platfute*, and quhissill *Fute before*.
Bot of hir inclynatioun naturall
Scho countrafaitit all fowlis, les and more.   90
Of hir curage, scho wald, without my lore,
Syng lyke the merle, and crawe lyke to the coke,
Pew lyke the gled, and chant lyke the laverock,

12

Bark lyk ane dog, and kekell lyke ane ka,
Blait lyk ane hog and buller lyke ane bull,   95
Gaill lyke ane goik and greit quhen scho wes wa,
Clym on ane corde, syne lauch and play the fule:
Scho mycht have bene ane menstrall agane Yule.
This blyssit bird wes to me so plesande,
Quhare ever I fure I bure hir on my hande.   100

13

And so befell, in tyll ane myrthfull morrow,
In to my garth I past me to repose,
This bird and I, as we wer wount aforrow,
Amang the flowris, fresche, fragrant and formose.
My vitale spretis dewlie did rejose   105
Quhen Phebus rose and rave the cloudis sabyll,
Throuch brychtnes of his beamys amyabyll.

---

80 *perfyte*: fully trained
81 *moist*: most   83 *wat*: know
84 *proper*: goodly; *governyng*:
   management
86 *cure*: care
87 *lerne*: teach; *artificiall*: invented
88 *Platfute*: 'Flat-foot'; *Fute before*:
   'Foot before [gossip]'
91 *curage*: disposition; *lore*: instruction
92 *merle*: blackbird; *crawe*: crow;
   coke: cock

93 *gled*: kite; *laverock*: skylark
94 *ka*: jackdaw
95 *Blait*: Bleat; *buller*: bellow
96 *Gaill*: Call; *goik*: cuckoo; *greit*:
   weep; *wa*: grieved
97 *syne*: next
98 *agane Yule*: near Christmas
100 *fure*: went; *bure*: bore
103 *wount aforrow*: accustomed
   previously   104 *formose*: beautiful
105 *spretis*: spirits   106 *rave*: pierced

14

Without vapour wes weill purificate
The temperat air, soft, sober and serene.
The erth, be Nature so edificate   110
With holsum herbis, blew, quhyte, reid, and grene,
Quhilk elevate my spretis frome the splene.
That day Saturne, nor Mars, durst not appeir,
Nor Eole, of his cove, he durst nocht steir.

15

That daye, perforce, behuffit to be fair,   115
Be influence and cours celestiall.
No planete presit for to perturbe the air,
For Mercurious, be movying naturall,
Exaultit wes, in to the throne tryumphall
Of his mantioun, unto the fyftene gre,   120
In his awin soverane signe of Virginee.

16

That day did Phebus plesandlie depart
Frome Geminie and enterit in Cancer.
That daye, Cupido did extend his dart.
Venus, that daye, conjunit with Jupiter.   125
That daye Neptunus hid hym, lyke one sker.
That daye dame Nature, with gret besynes,
Fortherit Flora to keyth hir craftynes,

17

And retrograde wes Mars in Capricorne,
And Synthea in Sagitter assesit.   130
That daye dame Ceres, goddes of the corne,
Full joyfullie Johane Upponland applesit;
The bad espect of Saturne wes appesit.
That daye, be Jono, of Jupiter the joye,
Perturband spretis causing to hauld coye.   135

---

108 *vapour*: mist; *purificate*: purified
110 *edificate*: built
112 *splene*: 'heart' [lit. spleen]
114 *Eole*: Aeolus; *cove*: cave; *steir*: stir
115 *behuffit*: was obliged
116 *influence*: planetary power
117 *presit*: pressed
118 *Mercurious*: Mercury
120 *mantioun*: zodiacal house;
   gre: degree

121 *soverane*: supreme; *Virginee*: Virgo
125 *conjunit*: united
126 *one sker*: a skerry
128 *Fortherit*: Helped; *keyth*: reveal
130 *Synthea*: Cynthia; *Sagitter*:
   Sagittarius; *assesit*: placed
132 *Johane Upponland*: John Ruralman;
   applesit: satisfied
133 *appesit*: appeased
134 *Jono*: Juno

18

The sound of birdis surmontit all the skyis
With melodie of notis musycall;
The balmy droppis of dew Tytane updryis
Hyngande upone the tender twystis small;
The hevinlie hew and sound angelicall   140
Sic perfyte plesoure prentit in myne hart
That with gret pyne frome thyne I mycht depart.

19

So, styll amang those herbis amyabyll,
I did remane one space for my pastance,
Bot wardlie plesour bene so variabyll,   145
Myxit with sorrow, dreid and inconstance,
That thare in tyll is no contyneuance.
So mycht I saye. My schorte solace, allace,
Was drevin in dolour in one lytill space.

20

For in that garth, amang those fragrant flouris   150
Walkyng allone, none bot my bird and I,
Onto the tyme that I had said myne houris,
This bird I sett upon one branche me bye.
Bot scho began to speill rycht spedalie,
And in that tree scho did so heych ascende,   155
That, be no waye, I mycht hir apprehende.

21

'Sweit bird,' said I, 'be war! Mont nocht over hie.
Returne in tyme! Perchance thy feit may failye!
Thou art rycht fat, and nocht weill usit to fle.
The gredie gled I dreid scho the assailye!'   160
'I wyll', said scho, 'ascend, vailye quod vailye.
It is my kynd to clym, aye, to the hycht:
Of fedther and bone I watt weill I am wycht.'

138 *Tytane*: Titan
139 *Hyngande*: Suspended; *twystis*: branches
140 *hew*: colour
141 *Sic*: Such; *prentit*: imprinted
142 *pyne*: effort
143 *amyabyll*: pleasant
144 *pastance*: recreation
146 *dreid*: dread
147 *contyneuance*: stability
149 *drevin in*: brought to
152 *houris*: [prescribed] prayers
154 *speill*: climb
156 *apprehende*: catch
157 *Mont*: Ascend
159 *fle*: fly
160 *assailye*: attack
161 *vailye...vailye*: come what may
162 *kynd*: nature
163 *wycht*: a creature

22

So, on the heychast lytill tender twyste,
With wyng displayit scho sat full wantounlie.   165
Bot Boreas blew one blast, or ever scho wyst,
Quhilk braik the branche, and blew hir, sodantlie,
Doun to the ground, with mony cairfull crye.
Upon ane stob scho lychtit on hir breist.
The blude ruschit out and scho cryit for a preist.   170

23

God wat gyff than my hart wes wo begone
To see that fowle flychter amang the flouris,
Quhilk, with gret murnyng, gan to mak hir mone:
'Now cumyng ar', said scho, 'the faitall houris.
Of bitter deth now mon I thole the schouris.   175
O dame Nature, I pray the of thy grace,
Len me layser to speik, one lytill space,

24

For to complene my fait infortunate,
And so dispone my geir or I depart,
Sen of all conforte I am desolate,   180
Allone, except the Deth, heir with his darte,
With aufull cheir, reddy to peirs myne hart.'
And with that word, scho tuke one passioun,
Syne flatlyngis fell and swappit in to swoun.

25

With sory hart, peirst with compassioun,   185
And salt teris distellyng frome myne eine,
To heir that birdis lamentatioun
I did aproche, onder ane hauthorne grene,
Quhare I mycht heir and se and be unsene.
And quhen this bird had swounit twyse or thryse,   190
Scho gan to speik, sayng on this wyse:

26

'O fals Fortune, quhy hes thou me begylit?
This day at morne, quho knew this cairfull cace?

---

164 *heychast*: highest
165 *displayit*: spread   166 *wyst*: knew
169 *stob*: stake; *lychtit*: landed
172 *flychter*: fly awkwardly
173 *murnyng*: lamentation
175 *thole*: suffer; *schouris*: pangs
177 *layser*: time

179 *dispone*: assign; *or*: before
182 *cheir*: countenance; *peirs*: pierce
183 *passioun*: sudden attack
184 *flatlyngis*: completely prostrate;
    swappit: sank; *swoun*: a faint
186 *distellyng*: falling in drops
191 *wyse*: manner 193 *cairfull*: distressing

Vaine hope in the my reasoun haith exilit,
Havyng sic traist in to thy fenyeit face. 195
That ever I wes brocht in to the court, allace!
Had I in forrest flowin amang my feris,
I mycht full weill have levit mony yeris.

27

Prudent counsell, allace, I did refuse,
Agane reassoun usyng myne appetyte. 200
Ambitioun did so myne hart abuse
That Eolus had me in gret dispyte.
Poetis, of me, haith mater to indyte,
Quhilk clam so heych, and wo is me thairfore,
Nocht doutyng that the deth durste me devore. 205

28

This daye, at morne, my forme and feddrem fair
Abufe the prude pacoke war precellande,
And nowe one catyve carioun, full of cair,
Baithand in blude doun from my hart distelland,
And in myne eir the bell of deith bene knelland. 210
O fals warld, fy on thy felicitie!
Thy pryde, avaryce and immundicitie!

29

In the I see no thyng bene permanent:
Of thy schort solace, sorrow is the ende.
Thy fals infortunate gyftis bene bot lent. 215
This day ful prude, the morne no thyng to spend.
O ye that doith pretende aye tyll ascend,
My fatale ende have in rememberance
And yow defende frome sic unhappy chance.'

30

Quhydder that I wes strickin in extasie, 220
Or throuch one stark imagynatioun,
Bot it apperit in myne fantasie

---

195 *fenyeit*: false
197 *flowin*: flown; *feris*: companions
198 *levit*: lived; *yeris*: years
203 *mater*: material
204 *clam*: climbed
205 *devore*: devour
206 *feddrem*: plumage
207 *prude*: proud; *pacoke*: peacock;
   precellande: superior

208 *catyve*: wretched
209 *Baithand*: Drenched
210 *knelland*: tolling
212 *immundicitie*: uncleanness
215 *infortunate*: unfortunate
216 *morne*: morrow
217 *pretende*: aspire; *tyll*: to
220 *Quhydder*: Whether
221 *stark*: strong 222 *apperit*: seemed

I hard this dolent lamentatioun.
Thus dullit in to desolatioun,
Me thocht this bird did breve, in hir maneir,   225
Hir counsale to the kyng, as ye sall heir.

Heir followis the first Epystill of the Papyngo
direct to Kyng James the Fyft.
31
'Prepotent prince, peirles of pulchritude,
Glore, honour, laude, tryumphe and victorie
Be to thy heych excellent celsitude,
With marciall dedis, dyng of memorie.   230
Sen Atropus consumit haith my glorie,
And dolente deith, allace, mon us depart,
I leif to the my trew unfenyeit hart,
32
To gydder with this cedull subsequent,
With moist reverent reconmendatioun.   235
I grant thy grace gettis mony one document
Be famous fatheris predicatioun,
With mony notabyll narratioun
Be plesande poetis, in style heroycall,
Quhou thow suld gyde thy seait imperiall.   240
33
Sum doith deplore the gret calamitieis
Of divers realmes transmutatioun;
Sum pieteouslie doith treat of tragedeis,
All for thy graces informatioun.
So I intend, but adullatioun,   245
In to my barbour rusticall indyte,
Amang the reste, schir, sum thyng for to wryte.

223 *dolent*: sorrowful
224 *dullit*: made dull
225 *breve*: compose
227 *Prepotent*: Very powerful; *peirles*:
     unequalled; *pulchritude*: beauty
229 *heych*: high; *celsitude*: majesty
230 *marciall*: valiant; *dyng*: worthy
232 *depart*: separate
233 *the*: thee
234 *To gydder*: Together; *cedull*:
     document

235 *reconmendatioun*: self
     commendation
236 *mony one document*: many a piece
     of instruction
237 *famous*: reputable; *fatheris*: fathers';
     predicatioun: preaching
240 *seait*: seat
242 *transmutatioun*: changed condition
245 *but*: without; *adullatioun*: adulation
246 *barbour*: barbarous; *rusticall*:
     unrefined; *indyte*: expression

34

Soverane, consave this simpyll similytude
Of officiaris servyng thy senyeorie:
Quho gydis thame weil gettis of thy grace gret gude;   250
Quho bene injuste, degradit ar of glorie
And cancillat out of thy memorie,
Providyng syne more plesand in thare place.
Beleve rycht so sall God do with thy grace.

35

Considder weill, thow bene bot officiare   255
And vassall to that kyng incomparabyll.
Preis thou to pleis that puissant prince preclare.
Thy ryche rewarde salbe inestimabyll,
Exaultit heych in glore interminabyll
Abone archangels, virtus, potestatis,   260
Plesandlie placit amang the principatis.

36

Of thy vertew, poetis perpetuallie
Sall mak mentioun unto the warld be endit;
So thou excers thyne office prudentlie,
In hevin and erth thy grace salbe commendit.   265
Quharefor, afeir that he be nocht offendit,
Quhilk hes exaultit the to sic honour,
Of his peple to be one gouvernour,

37

And in the erth haith maid sic ordinance.
Under thy feit, all thyng terrestryall   270
Ar subject to thy plesour and pastance,
Boith fowle and fysche and bestis pastorall.
Men to thy servyce, and wemen, thay bene thrall.
Halkyng, hountyng, armes, and leiffull amour
Preordinat ar, be God, for thy plesour;   275

38

Maisteris of museik, to recreat thy spreit,
With dantit voce and plesande instrument:

248 *consave*: comprehend; *similytude*: comparison
249 *senyeorie*: lordship
257 *Preis*: Strive; *puissant*: mighty; *preclare*: renowned
260 *virtus*: virtues; *potestatis*: powers
261 *principatis*: princes
264 *So*: If; *excers*: discharge
266 *afeir*: fear   269 *ordinance*: ruling
271 *pastance*: recreation
274 *leiffull*: lawful
276 *Maisteris*: Masters; *recreat*: refresh
277 *dantit*: subdued

Thus may thou be of all plesouris repleit,
So, in thyne office, thou be deligent.
Bot be thou found sleuthfull or negligent,   280
Or injuste in thyne exicutioun,
Thou sall nocht faill devine puneissioun.

39

Quharefor, sen thou hes sic capacitie
To lerne to playe so plesandlie and syng,
Ryde hors, ryn speris with gret audacitie,   285
Schute with hand bow, crosbow and culveryng,
Amang the rest, schir, lerne to be ane kyng.
Kyith on that craft thy pringnant fresche ingyne,
Grantit to the be influence divine.

40

And, sen the diffinitioun of ane kyng   290
Is for to have of peple governance,
Addres the first, abufe all uther thyng,
Tyll put thy bodye tyll sic ordinance
That thyne vertew thyne honour may avance;
For quhou suld prencis governe gret regionis,   295
That can nocht dewlie gyde thare awin personis?

41

And geve thy grace wald leif rycht plesandlie,
Call thy counsale, and cast on thame the cure,
Thare juste decretis defend and fortyfie.
But gude counsale may no prince lang indure;   300
Wyrk with counsale, than sall thy work be sure.
Cheis thy counsale of the moste sapient,
Without regarde to blude, ryches, or rent.

42

Amang all uther pastyme and plesour,
Now, in thy adolescent yeris yeing,   305
Wald thou, ilk day, studie bot half one hour
The regiment of princelie governyng,
To thy peple it war ane plesand thyng.

280 *sleuthfull*: slothful
285 *ryn*: thrust
286 *culveryng*: handgun
288 *Kyith*: Show; *pringnant*:
     promising   297 *leif*: live
298 *counsale*: body of advisers

299 *decretis*: decrees; *fortyfie*:
     strengthen
302 *Cheis*: Choose
305 *yeris yeing*: years young
306 *ilk*: each
307 *regiment*: rules

Thare mycht thou fynd thyne awin vocatioun,
Quhou thou suld use thy sceptour, swerd, and croun. 310

43

The cronecklis to knaw, I the exhorte,
Quhilk may be myrrour to thy majestie.
Thare sall thou fynd boith gude and evyll reporte
Of everilk prince efter his qualytie.
Thocht thay be dede, thare deidis sall nocht dee: 315
Traist weill thou salbe stylit, in that storie,
As thou deservis putt in memorie.

44

Request that roye quhilk rent wes on the rude,
The to defend frome dedis of defame,
That no poyte reporte of the bot gude. 320
For princes dayis induris bot ane drame:
Sen first kyng Fergus bure ane dyadame,
Thou art the last king, of fyve score and fyve,
And all ar dede, and none bot thou on lyve.

45

Of quhose number, fyftie and fyve bene slane, 325
And moist parte in thare awin misgovernance.
Quharefor, I the beseik my soverane,
Consydder of thare lyvis the circumstance.
And, quhen thou knawis the cause of thare mischance,
Of vertew than exault thy salis on hie, 330
Traistyng to chaip that faitale destanie.

46

Trait ilk trew barroun as he war thy brother,
Quhilk mon, at neid, the and thy realme defende.
Quhen suddantlie one doith oppresse one uther
Lat justice myxit with mercy thame amende. 335
Have thou thare hartis, thou hes yneuch to spend,
And be the contrar, thou arte bot Kyng of Bone,
Frome tyme thyne hereis hartis bene from the gone.

311 *cronecklis*: chronicles
314 *qualytie*: character
316 *stylit*: described
318 *rent*: lacerated; *rude*: cross
319 *defame*: infamy
320 *poyte*: poet   321 *drame*: dream
322 *dyadame*: crown

330 *exault...salis*: raise your sails
331 *chaip*: escape
332 *Trait*: Treat; *as*: as if
336 If you have their love you have sufficient
337 *Bone*: Bean
338 *hereis*: nobles'

47

I have no laser for to wryt at lenth,   340
Myne hole intent ontyll thyne excellence,
Decressit so I am in wytt and strenth.
My mortall wounde doith me sic violence,
Peple of me maye have experience:
Because, allace, I wes incounsolabyll,   345
Now mon I dee, on catyve myserabyll.'

Heir followis the secunde Epistyl of the
Papyngo, directit to hir Brether of Courte.

48

'Brether of court, with mynd precordial,
To the gret God, hartlie I commend yow.
Imprent my fall in your memoriall,
Togidder with this cedul that I send yow.
To preis over heych, I pray yow not pretend yow.   350
The vaine ascens of court quho wyll consydder:
Quho sittith moist hie sal fynd the sait most slidder.

49

So ye that now bene lansyng upe the ledder,
Tak tent in tyme, fassinnyng your fingaris faste.
Quho clymith moist heych moist dynt hes of the woder   355
And leist defence aganis the bitter blast
Of fals Fortune, quhilk takith never rest,
Bot moste redouttit daylie scho doun thryngis,
Nocht sparing papis, conquerours, nor kyngis.

50

Thocht ye be montit upe abone the skyis,   360
And hes boith kyng and court in governance,
Sum was als heych, quhilk now rycht lawly lyis,
Complanyng sore the courtis variance.
Thare preterit tyme may be experience,
Quhilk, throuch vaine hope of courte, did clym so hie,   365
Syne wantit wyngis quhen thay wend best to flie.

---

339 *laser*: breathing space
344 *incounsolabyll*: uncounsellable
345 *on*: a
346 *precordial*: sincere
348 *memoriall*: remembrance
352 *slidder*: slippery
353 *lansyng*: bounding; *ledder*: ladder

354 *Tak tent*: Beware; *fassinnyng*: fastening
355 *dynt*: blows; *woder*: turbulence
358 *doun thryngis*: throws down
362 *als heych*: as high
364 *preterit*: past
366 *wend*: thought

51

Sen ilke court bene untraist and transitorie,
Cheangyng als oft as woddercok in wynd,
Sum maikand glaid and uther sum rycht sorie,
Formaste this day, the morne may go behyind, 370
Lat not vaine hope of court your reasone blyind.
Traist weill, sum men wyll gyf you laud, as lordis,
Quhilk wald be glaid to se yow hang in cordis.

52

I durst declare the myserabilitie
Of divers curtis, war nocht my tyme bene schort. 375
The dreidfull cheange, vaine glore and vilitie,
The painfull plesour, as poetis doith reporte,
Sum tyme in hope, sum tyme in disconforte,
And how sum men dois spend thair youthed haill
In court, syne endis in the hospytaill. 380

53

Quhou sum in court bene quyet counsalouris,
Without regarde to commoun weill or kyngis,
Castyng thare cure for to be conquerouris,
And quhen thay bene heych rasit in thare ryngis,
How cheange of court tham dulfully doun thringis, 385
And quhen thay bene frome thair estait deposit,
Quhou mony, of thare fall, bene rycht rejosit.

54

And quhou fonde, fenyeit fulis and flatteraris
For small servyce optenith gret rewardis;
Pandaris, pykthankis, custronis, and clatteraris, 390
Loupis up frome laddis, sine lychtis amang lardis;
Blasphematours, beggaris and commoun bardis,
Sum tyme in court hes more auctoritie
Nor devote doctouris in divinitie.

368 *woddercok*: weathercock
370 *Formaste*: [He who is] foremost
373 *cordis*: [hangman's] ropes
375 *curtis*: courts
376 *vilitie*: vileness
379 *youthed*: youth; *haill*: healthy
380 *hospytaill*: alms-house
381 *quyet*: covert
383 *Castyng*: Directing; *cure*: attention
384 *rasit*: exalted; *ryngis*: reigns

385 *thringis*: throws
388 *fonde*: foolish; *feinyeit*: feigned
390 *Pandaris*: Pimps; *pykthankis*:
   sycophants; *custronis*: base fellows;
   clatteraris: idle talkers
391 *Loupis...lardis* Leap up from
   servants, then land among lords
392 *Blasphematours*: Blasphemers;
   commoun bardis: lesser bards
   [derog.]

55

Quhou in sum countre bene barnes of Baliall,	395
Full of dissimilit, payntit flatterrie,	
Provocande, be intoxicat counsall,	
Prencis tyll huredome and tyll hasardrie.	
Quho dois in prencis prent sic harlotrie,	
I saye for me, sic peirte provocatouris	400
Sulde puneist be, abufe all strang tratouris.	

56

Quhate travers, troubyll and calamitie	
Haith bene in courte, within thir houndreth yeris!	
Quhat mortall cheangis, quhat miseritie,	
Quhat nobyll men bene brocht upon thair beris!	405
Trast weil, my freinds, follow yow mon your feris.	
So sen in court bene no tranquillytie,	
Sett nocht on it your hole fielycite.	

57

The courte cheangeith, sumtyme with sic outrage,	
That few or none may makyng resistance,	410
And sparis nocht the prince more than the paige,	
As weill apperith be experience.	
The Duke of Rothasay mycht mak no defence,	
Quhilk wes pertenand roye of this regioun,	
Bot dulefully devorit in presoun.	415

58

Quhat dreid, quhat dolour, had that nobyll kyng,	
Robart the thride, frome tyme he knew the cace	
Of his two sonnis dolente departyng;	
Prince David deyid and James captyve, allace!	
Tyll trew Scottis men quhilk wes a cairful cace.	420
Thus may ye knaw the courte bene variand,	
Quhen blude ryall the cheang may not ganestand.	

59

Quho rang in court more hie and tryumphand	
Nor Duke Murdoke, quhil that his day indurit?	

---

395 *barnes...Baliall*: children of the
    Devil
397 *intoxicat*: poisoned
398 *hasardrie*: gambling
399 *prent*: impress; *harlotrie*: loose living
400 *peirte*: bold
402 *travers*: opposition

405 *beris*: funeral biers
409 *outrage*: violence
410 *Rothasay*: Rothesay
414 *pertenand*: claiming to be
417 *Robart...thride*: Robert III
423 *rang*: reigned
424 *Murdoke*: Murdoch; *quhil*: while

Was he nocht gret Protectour of Scotland? 425
Yit, of the court he was nocht weill assurit.
Itt cheangit so, his lang servyce wes smurit.
He and his sonne, fair Walter, but remede,
Forfaltit war, and put to dulefull dede.

60

Kyng James the first, the patroun of prudence, 430
Gem of ingyne and peirll of polycie,
Well of justice and flude of eloquence,
Quhose vertew doith transcende my fantasie
For tyll discryve, yit quhen he stude moste hie,
Be fals exhorbitant conspiratioun, 435
That prudent prince wes pieteouslie put doun.

61

Als, James the secunde, roye of gret renoun,
Beand in his superexcelland glore,
Throuch reakles schuttyng of one gret cannoun
The dolent deith, allace, did hym devore! 440
One thyng thair bene, of quhilk I marvell more:
That Fortune had at hym sic mortall feid,
Throuch fyftie thousand, to waill him by the heid.

62

My hart is peirst with panes for to pance
Or wrytt that courtis variatioun 445
Of James the thrid, quhen he had governance—
The dolour, dreid and desolatioun,
The cheange of court and conspiratioun—
And quhou that Cochrame, with his companye,
That tyme in courte clam so presumpteouslye. 450

63

It had bene gude tha beirnes had bene unborne,
Be quhome that nobyll prince wes so abusit.
Thay grew as did the weid abufe the corne,
That prudent lordis counsall wes refusit,
And held hym quyet, as he had bene inclusit. 455

---

427 *smurit*: smothered
429 *Forfaltit*: Forfeited
430 *patroun*: model
431 *polycie*: prudence
435 *exhorbitant*: flagrantly unfair;
    conspiratioun: conspiracy

439 *reakles*: reckless
442 *feid*: hostility
443 *waill*: choose 444 *pance*: reflect on
449 *Cochrame*: Cochrane
451 *beirnes*: men   452 *abusit*: misled
455 *inclusit*: imprisoned

Allace! That prince, be thare abusioun,
Was fynalie brocht to confusioun.

64

Thay clam so heych and gat sic audience
And with thare prince grew so familiar,
His germane brother mycht get no presence.   460
The Duke of Albanie, nor the Erle of Mar,
Lyke baneist men was haldin at the bar,
Tyll in the kyng thare grew sic mortall feid
He flemit the Duke and patt the Erle to dede.

65

Thus Cochrame, with his catyve companye,   465
Forsit thame to flee, bot yit thay wantit federis.
Abufe the heych cederis of Libanye
Thay clam so heych, tyll thay lape ovir thair ledderis;
On Lawder bryge syne keppit wer in tedderis.
Stranglit to deith, thay gat none uther grace,   470
Thair king captyve, quhilk wes ane cairful cace.

66

Tyl putt in forme that fait infortunat,
And mortall cheange, perturbith myne ingyne.
My wytt bene waik, my fyngaris faitegate
To dyte or wryte the rancour and rewyne,   475
The civyll weir, the battell intestyne;
How that the sonne, with baner braid displayit,
Agane the fader in battell come arrayit.

67

Wald God that prince had bene that day confortit
With sapience of the prudent Salomone,   480
And with the strenth of strang Sampsone supportit,
With the bauld oste of gret Agamenone!
Quhat suld I wys, remedie was thare none:
At morne, ane king, with sceptour, sweird and croun,
Att evin, ane dede, deformit carioun.   485

456 *abusioun*: wrong-doing
460 *germane*: own
462 *baneist*: banished; *haldin...bar*: held
    at the bar [of a law court]
465 *catyve*: base
466 *wantit*: lacked; *federis*: feathers
467 *cederis...Libanye*: cedars of Lebanon

469 *Lawder*: Lauder; *tedderis*: nooses
474 *faitegate*: fatigued
475 *rewyne*: destruction
476 *intestyne*: domestic
480 *Salomone*: Solomon
481 *Sampsone*: Samson
482 *oste*: host; *Agamenone*: Agamemnon
483 *wys*: wish

68

Allace! Quhare bene that rycht redoutit roye,
That potent prince, gentyll king James the feird?
I pray to Christe his saule for to convoye;
Ane greater nobyll rang nocht in to the eird.
O Atropus, warye we maye thy weird!　　　　　　　490
For he wes myrrour of humylitie,
Lode sterne, and lampe of libiralytie.

69

Duryng his tyme, so justice did prevaill,
The savage Iles trymblit for terrour.
Eskdale, Ewisdale, Liddisdale and Annerdale　　　495
Durste nocht rebell, doutyng his dyntis dour,
And of his lordis had sic perfyte favour.
So, for to schaw that he aferit no fone,
Out throuch his realme he wald ryde hym, alone.

70

And, of his courte, throuch Europe sprang the fame　　500
Of lustie lordis and lufesum ladyis ying,
Tryumphand tornayis, justyng and knychtly game,
With all pastyme accordyng for one kyng.
He wes the glore of princelie governyng
Quhilk, throuch the ardent lufe he had to France,　　505
Agane Ingland did move his ordinance.

71

Of Flodoun feilde the rewyne to rovolfe,
Or that moste dolent daye for tyll deplore,
I nyll, for dreid that dolour yow dissolfe,
Schaw how that prince, in his tryumphand glore,　　510
Distroyit was. Quhat nedeith proces more?
Nocht be the vertew of Inglis ordinance,
Bot be his awin wylfull mysgovernance.

---

487 *feird*: fourth
488 *convoye*: guide
490 *warye*: curse; *weird*: decree
492 *Lode sterne*: Guiding star
494 *savage Iles*: Western Isles
495 *Ewisdale*: Ewesdale; *Liddisdale*:
　　Liddesdale; *Annerdale*: Annandale
496 *dyntis dour*: hard blows

498 *aferit*: feared; *fone*: foe (pl.)
501 *lufesum*: lovely
503 *accordyng*: fitting
506 *ordinance*: military force
507 *Flodoun*: Flodden; *rovolfe*: consider
509 *I nyll*: I'm unwilling
513 *wylfull*: self-willed; *mysgovernance*:
　　misgovernment

72

Allace! That daye, had he bene counsalabyll,
He had obtenit laude, glore, and victorie,   515
Quhose pieteous proces bene so lamentabyll.
I nyll at lenth it put in memorie,
I never red, in tragidie nor storie,
At one jornaye, so mony nobyllis slane
For the defence and lufe of thare soverane.   520

73

Now brether, marke, in your remembrance,
Ane myrrour of those mutabiliteis.
So may ye knaw the courtis inconstance,
Quhen prencis bene thus pullit frome thair seis.
Efter quhose deith, quhat strainge adversiteis,   525
Quhat gret mysreule, in to this regioun rang
Quhen our yong prince could noder spek nor gang.

74

During his tender youthe and innocence
Quhat stouith, quhat raif, quhat murthur and myschance!
Thair wes not ellis bot wrakyng of vengeance.   530
In to that court thare rang sic variance,
Divers rewlaris maid divers ordinance:
Sum tyme our Quene rang in auctoritie,
Sum tyme the prudent Duke of Albanie;

75

Sum tyme the realme was reulit be regentis,   535
Sum tyme, lufetenentis, ledaris of the law.
Than rang so mony inobedientis,
That few, or none, stude of ane uther aw.
Oppressioun did so lowde his bugyll blaw
That none durst ryde, bot in to feir of weir;   540
Joke Uponeland that tyme did mys his meir.

76

Quho was more heycht in honour elevate
Nor was Margareit, our heych and mychtie princes?
Sic power was to hir appropriate:

---

519 *jornaye*: day of battle
521 *brether*: brothers
523 *knaw*: perceive   524 *seis*: thrones
529 *stouith*: violence; *raif*: spoliation
530 *wrakyng*: wreaking

536 *lufetenentis*: viceregents
538 *stude..aw*: was in fear of anyone else
540 *in...weir*: in warlike array
541 *Joke*: Jock; *meir*: mare
542 *elevate*: exalted

Of king and realme scho wes governores. 545
Yit, come one cheange, within ane schorte proces,
That peirle preclare, that lusty plesand quene,
Lang tyme durst nocht in to the court be sene.

77

The archebischop of Sanct Andrus, James Betoun,
Chancellare and primate in power pastorall, 550
Clam, nyxt the kyng, moste heych in this regioun.
The ledder schuke, he lape, and gat one fall.
Auctoritie, nor power spirituall,
Ryches, freindschip, mycht not that tyme prevail
Quhen dame Curia began to steir hir taill. 555

78

His heych prudence prevalit hym nocht ane myte,
That tyme the courte bair hym sic mortall feid.
As presoneir, thay keipt hym in dispyte,
And sum tyme wyst not quhare to hyde his heid,
Bot dissagysit lyke Jhone the Raif he raid. 560
Had nocht bene Hope bair hym sic companye,
He had been stranglit be malancolye.

79

Quhat cummer and cair wes in the court of France
Quhen kyng Francose wes takin presoneir?
The Duke of Burboun, amyd his ordinance, 565
Deit at ane straik, rycht bailfull brocht on beir;
The court of Rome, that tyme, rane all aureir
Quhen Pape Clement wes put in strang presoun,
The nobyll citie put to confusioun.

80

In Ingland, quho had greter governance 570
Nor thare tryumphand courtly cardinall?
The commoun weill, sum sayis, he did avance,
Be equale justice boith to gret and small.
Thare wes no prelate to hym paregall.
Inglismen sayis, 'Had he roung langer space, 575
He had deposit Sanct Peter of his place.'

---

545 *governores*: female governor
546 *proces*: lapse of time
547 *peirle*: pearl; *preclare*: lustrous
549 *Sanct Andrus*: St Andrews; *Betoun*:
   Beaton

552 *lape*: jumped   555 *steir*: stir
558 *presoneir*: prisoner
560 *Jhone...Raif*: John the Reeve
567 *rane...aureir*: retrogressed
574 *paregall*: equal

81

His princely pompe, nor papale gravitie,
His palyce ryall, ryche, and radious,
Nor yit the flude of superfluitie
Of his ryches, nor travell tedious,   580
Frome tyme dame Curia held hym odious,
Prevalit hym not, nor prudence moste profound.
The ledder braik and he fell to the ground.

82

Quhare bene the douchty Erlis of Dowglas
Quhilkis ryallie in to this regioun rang?   585
Forfalt and slane. Quhat nedith more proces?
The Erle of Marche wes merschellit tham amang;
Dame Curia thame dulefullie doun thrang.
And now, of lait, quho clam more heych amang us
Nor did Archebalde, umquhyle the Erle of Angous?   590

83

Quho with his prince wes more familiar,
Nor, of his grace, had more auctoritie?
Was he nocht gret wardane and chancellar?
Yit, quhen he stude upon the heychest gre,
Traistyng no thyng bot perpetuitie,   595
Was suddanlie deposit frome his place.
Forfalt and flemit, he gat non uther grace.

84

Quharefor, traist nocht in tyll auctoritie,
My deir brother, I praye yow hartfullie.
Presume nocht in your vaine prosperitie.   600
Conforme your traist in God alluterlie,
Syne serve your prince with enteir hart trewlie,
And quhen ye se the court bene at the best,
I counsall yow, than draw yow to your rest.

85

Quhare bene the heych tryumphant court of Troye?   605
Or Alexander, with his twelf prudent peris?
Or Julius, that rycht redoutit roye?
Agamenone, moste worthy in his weris?

---

579 *superfluitie*: immoderation   590 *umquhyle*: formerly; *Angous*: Angus
582 *Prevalit*: Profited   601 Put your complete trust in God
584 *Erlis...Dowglas*: Earls of Douglas   606 *peris*: peers
587 *merschellit*: ranked   608 *weris*: wars

To schaw thare fyne, my frayit hart aferis:
Sum murdreist war, sum poysonit pieteouslie,
Thare cairfull courtis dispersit dulefullie.

86

Traist weill, thare is no constant court bot one,
Quhar Christ bene kyng, quhose tyme interminabyll
And heych tryumphand glore beis nevir gone.
That quyet court, myrthfull and immutabyll,
But variance standith aye ferme and stabyll.
Dissimilance, flattry, nor fals reporte,
In to that court sall never get resorte.

87

Traist weill, my freindis, this is no fenyeit fare,
For quho that bene in the extreme of dede,
The veritie, but doute, thay sulde declare,
Without regarde to favour, or to fede.
Quhill ye have tyme, deir brother, mak remade.
Adew, for ever. Of me ye get no more,
Beseikand God to bryng yow to his glore.

88

Adew, Edinburgh, thow heych tryumphant toun,
Within quhose boundis rycht blythfull have I bene.
Of trew merchandis the rute of this regioun,
Moste reddy to resave court, king, and quene.
Thy polecye and justice may be sene.
War devotioun, wysedome, and honestie,
And credence tynt, thay mycht be found in the.

89

Adew, fair Snawdoun, with thy touris hie,
Thy Chapell Royall, park, and tabyll rounde.
May, June and July walde I dwell in the,
War I one man, to heir the birdis sounde,
Quhilk doith agane thy royall roche redounde.
Adew Lythquo, quhose palyce of plesance
Mycht be one patrone in Portingall or France.

610

615

620

625

630

635

---

609 *fyne*: end; *frayit*: frightened
619 *fenyeit fare*: feigned show
620 *in...dede*: on the point of death
623 *remade*: amends
626 *heych*: elevated; *tryumphant*: glorious
628 *merchandis*: merchants; *rute*: source

631 *War*: Were
632 *credence*: trust; *tynt*: lost
633 *Snawdoun*: Stirling
634 *Chapell Royall*: King's Chapel choir
637 *agane*: against; *redounde*: re-echo
638 *Lythquo*: Linlithgow
639 *patrone*: model; *Portingall*: Portugal

90

Fair weill, Falkland, the fortrace of Fyfe,   640
Thy polyte park, under the Lowmound law.
Sum tyme in the I led ane lustye lyfe;
The fallow deir, to see thame raik on rawe!
Courte men, to cum to the thay stand gret awe,
Saynd thy burgh bene of all burrowis baill,   645
Because in the thay never gat gude aill.'

Heir followis the Commonyng betuix the
Papingo and hir Holye Executouris.

91

The pye persavit the papingo in paine.
He lychtit doun and fenyeit him to greit.
'Sister,' said he, 'alace, quho hes yow slane?
I pray yow mak provisione for your spreit.   650
Dispone your geir and yow confes compleit.
I have power, be your contritioun,
Of all your mys to geve yow full remissioun.

92

'I am', said he, 'one channoun regulare,
And of my brether pryour principall.   655
My quhyte rocket my clene lyfe doith declare,
The blak bene of the deith memoriall.
Quharefor, I thynk your gudis naturall
Sulde be submyttit, hole, in to my cure:
Ye knaw I am ane holye creature.'   660

93

The revin come rolpand quhen he hard the rair.
So did the gled, with mony pieteous pew,
And fenyeitlye thay contrafait gret cair.
'Syster,' said thay, 'your raklesnes we rew.
Now best it is, our juste counsall ensew,   665

640 *fortrace*: fortress
641 *polyte*: beautified; *Lowmound law*:
    Lomond hill
643 *raik...rawe*: graze in file
644 *awe*: dread
645 *burrowis*: towns; *baill*: a misery
646 *aill*: ale
Subtitle: *commonyng*: talking together
647 *pye*: magpie; *persavit*: observed
650 *mak provisione*: provide for

651 *yow confes*: make your confession
653 *mys*: sins; *remissioun*: pardon
654 *channoun regulare*: canon regular
655 *pryour principall*: principal prior
656 *quhyte rocket*: white surplice
658 *gudis naturall*: physical attributes
661 *revin*: raven; *rolpand*: croaking;
    rair: noise   662 *gled*: kite
663 *contrafait*: imitate
665 *ensew*: follow

Sen we pretend to heych promotioun,
Religious men of gret devotioun.'

94

'I am ane blak monk', said the ruclande revin.
'So,' said the gled, 'I am ane holy freir,
And hes power to bryng yow quyke to hevin.   670
It is weill knawin my conscience bene full cleir.
The blak Bybill pronunce I sall, perqueir,
So tyll our brether ye wyll geve sum gude;
God wat geve we hes neid of lyves fude.'

95

The papyngo said, 'Father, be the rude,   675
Howbeit your rayment be religious lyke,
Your conscience, I suspect, be nocht gude.
I did persave quhen prevelye ye did pyke
Ane chekin frome ane hen, under ane dyke.'
'I grant', said he. 'That hen was my gude freind,   680
And I that chekin tuke, bot for my teind:

96

Ye knawe the faith be us mon be susteind.
So, be the Pope, it is preordinate
That spirituall men suld leve upon thair teind,
Bot weill wat I, ye bene predestinate,   685
In your extreme, to be so fortunate
To have sic holy consultatioun.
Quharefore, we mak yow exhortatioun:

97

Sen dame Nature hes grantit yow sic grace,
Layser to mak confessioun generall,   690
Schaw furth your syn, in haist quhil ye haif space,
Syne, of your geir mak one memoriall.
We thre sall mak your festis funerall,
And with gret blys, bury we sall your bonis,
Syne trentalls twenty trattyll, all at onis.   695

668 *blak*: black; *ruclande*: gurgling
672 *blak Bybill*: mass for the dead;
   perqueir: by heart
673 *So*: If
678 *prevelye*: surreptitiously; *pyke*: steal
681 *teind*: tithe

693 *festis*: feasts
694 *blys*: happiness
695 *trentalls twenty*: twenty sets of thirty
   requiem masses; *trattyll*: chatter;
   onis: once

98

The reukis sall rair, that men sall on thame rew,
And crye *Conmemoratio Animarum*.
We sall gar cheknis cheip, and geaslyngis pew,
Suppose the geis and hennis suld crye alarum.
And we sall serve *Secundum Usum Sarum*,   700
And mak yow saif (we fynd Sanct Blase to borgh),
Cryand for yow the cairfull corrynogh.

99

And we sall syng, about your sepulture,
Sanct Mongois matynis and the mekle creid,
And syne devotely saye, I yow assure,   705
The auld *Placebo* bakwart and the beid,
And we sall weir for yow the murnyng weid,
And thocht your spreit with Pluto war profest,
Devotelie sall your derigie be addrest.'

100

'Father,' said scho, 'your facunde wordis fair,   710
Full sore I dreid, be contrar to your dedis.
The wyffis of the village cryis with cair
Quhen thai persave your muow ovirthort thar medis.
Your fals consait boith duke and draik sore dreidis.
I marvell, suithlie, ye be nocht eschamit   715
For your defaltis, beyng so defamit.

101

It dois abhor my pure perturbit spreit
Tyll mak to yow ony confessioun.
I heir men saye ye bene one ypocrite,
Exemptit frome the senye and the sessioun.   720
To put my geir in your possessioun
That wyll I nocht, so help me dame Nature,
Nor of my corps I wyll yow geve no cure.

---

696 *reukis*: rooks; *rair*: cry; *rew*: pity
697 And cry 'Commemoration of Souls'
698 *gar*: make; *geaslyngis*: goslings
699 *Suppose*: Even if
700 *serve*: conduct
701 *saif*: [spiritually] safe; *fynd*: declare;
     Sanct...borgh; St Blaise as security
702 *corrynogh*: funeral lament (Gael.)
704 *Mongois matynis*: Mungo's matins;
     mekle creid: great [Apostles'] Creed

706 *Placebo*: Vespers; *beid*: bead
707 *weir*: wear; *murnyng*: mourning
708 *profest*: solemnly dedicated
709 *derigie*: religious service
710 *facunde*: eloquent
713 *muow*: mouth; *medis*: meadows
714 *consait*: stratagem; *duke*: duck
720 *senye*: consistory [eccles.] court;
     sessioun: civil court

102

But had I heir the nobyll nychtingall,
The gentyll ja, the merle, and turtur trew, 725
My obsequees and feistis funerall
Ordour thay wald, with notis of the new.
The plesand pown, moste angellyke of hew,
Wald God I wer this daye with hym confest,
And my devyse dewlie be hym addrest. 730

103

The myrthfull maveis, with the gay goldspink;
The lustye larke, wald God thay war present!
My infortune, forsuith, thay wald forthink,
And conforte me, that bene so impotent.
The swyft swallow, in prattick most prudent, 735
I wate scho wald my bledyng stem, belyve,
With hir moste verteous stone restringityve.'

104

'Compt me the cace, under confessioun,'
The gled said proudlye to the papingo,
'And we sall sweir, be our professioun, 740
Counsall to keip and schawit to no mo.
We the beseik, or thow depart us fro,
Declare to us sum causis reasonabyll
Quhy we bene haldin so abhominabyll.

105

Be thy travell, thow hes experience. 745
First beand bred in to the Orient,
Syne be thy gude servyce and delygence
To prencis maid, heir in the Occident,
Thow knawis the vulgare pepyllis jugement;
Quhare thow transcurrit the hote meridionall, 750
Syne nyxt the Poill, the plage septemtrionall.

106

So, be thyne heych ingyne superlatyve,
Of all countreis thow knawis the qualiteis.

---

725 *gentyll*: of good breeding; *ja*: jay;
  merle: blackbird; *turtur*: turtledove
728 *pown*: peacock
730 *devyse*: testament
731 *maveis*: song-thrush; *goldspink*:
  goldfinch 733 *forthink*: regret
734 *impotent*: helpless

737 *restringityve*: astringent
738 *Compt*: Give an account of
746 *Orient*: East 748 *Occident*: West
750 *transcurrit*: passed across; *hote
  meridionall*: Southern meridian
751 *Poill*: Pole; *plage septemtrionall*:
  Northern zone

Quharefore, I the conjure, be God of lyve,   755
The veritie declare, withouttin leis,
Quhat thow hes hard, be landis or be seis,
Of us kirkmen, boith gude and evyll reporte,
And quhou thay juge. Schaw us, we the exhorte.'
107
'Father,' said scho, 'I, catyve creature,   760
Dar nocht presume with sic mater to mell;
Of your caces, ye knaw I have no cure.
Demand thame quhilk in prudence doith precell.
I maye nocht pew, my panes bene so fell.
And als, perchance, ye wyll nocht stand content
To knaw the vulgare pepyllis jugement.   765
108
Yit wyll the deith alyte withdrawe his darte,
All that lyis in my memoryall
I sall declare, with trew unfenyeit hart.
And first I saye to yow, in generall,
The commoun peple sayith ye bene all   770
Degenerit frome your holy prematyvis,
As testyfeis the proces of your lyvis.
109
Of your peirles, prudent predicessouris,
The beginnyng, I grant, wes verray gude:
Apostolis, martyres, virgines, confessouris,   775
The sound of thair excellent sanctitude
Was hard over all the warld, be land and flude,
Plantyng the faith, be predicatioun,
As Christe had maid to thame narratioun.
110
To fortyfie the faith, thay tuke no feir,   780
Afore prencis precheing full prudentlie.
Of dolorus deith, thay doutit nocht the deir,
The veritie declaryng, ferventlie,
And martyrdome thay sufferit pacientlie.
Thay tuke no cure of land, ryches, nor rent;   785
Doctryne and deid war boith equevolent.

---

754 *conjure*: exhort; *lyve*: life
763 *fell*: severe   766 *alyte*: a little
771 *prematyvis*: predecessors
777 *flude*: sea

778 *predicatioun*: preaching
780 *tuke...feir*: were not afraid
782 *deir*: harm   786 *deid*: deed

111

To schaw at lenth thair workis wer gret wunder:
Thare myracklis, thay wer so manifest;
In name of Christe, thay halit mony hounder,
Rasyng the dede, and purgeing the possest,   790
With perverst spretis quhilks had bene opprest.
The crukit ran, the blynd men gat thare ene,
The deiff men hard, the lypper war maid clene.

112

The prelatis spowsit wer with Povertie,
Those dayis quhen so thay flurisit in fame;   795
And with hir generit lady Chaistitie,
And dame Devotioun, notabyll of name.
Humyll thay war, simpyll, and full of schame.
Thus, Chaistitie and dame Devotioun
War principall cause of thare promotioun.   800

113

Thus thay contynewit in this lyfe devyne
Aye tyll thare rang, in Romes gret cietie,
Ane potent prince, was namit Constantyne,
Persavit the kirk had spowsit povertie.
With gude intent and movit of pietie,   805
Cause of divors he fande betuix thame two,
And partit thame, withouttin wordis mo.

114

Syne, schortlie, with ane gret solempnitie,
Withouttin ony dispensatioun,
The kirk he spowsit with dame Propirtie,   810
Quhilk haistalye, be procliamatioun
To Povertie gart mak narratioun,
Under the pane of peirsyng of her eine,
That with the kirk scho sulde no more be seine.

115

Sanct Sylvester, that tyme, rang Pope in Rome,   815
Quhilk first consentit to the mariage
Of Propirtie, the quhilk began to blome,

---

789 *halit*: healed; *hounder*: hundred
791 *perverst*: evil
792 *crukit*: lame; *ene*: sight [lit. eyes]
793 *deiff*: deaf; *lypper*: lepers
796 *generit*: begat 798 *Humyll*: Humble

805 *movit of*: prompted by
809 *dispensatioun*: special licence
812 *gart...narratioun*: told
813 *peirsyng*: piercing
817 *blome*: bloom

Taking on hir the cure, with heych corrage.
Devotioun drew hir tyll one heremytage
Quhen scho considerit lady Propirtie   820
So heych exaultit in to dignitie.

116

O Sylvester, quhare was thy discretioun?
Quhilk Peter did renounce thow did resave.
Androw and Jhone did leif thare possessioun,
Thar schippis and nettis, lyinnes, and all the lave;   825
Of temporall substance no thing wald thay have
Contrarius to thare contemplatioun,
Bot, soberlye, thare sustentatioun.

117

Jhone the Baptist went to the wyldernes;
Lazarus, Martha and Marie Magdalane   830
Left heretage and guddis, more and les,
Prudent Sanct Paule thocht propertie prophane:
Frome toun to toun he ran in wynde and rane,
Upon his feit techeing the word of grace,
And never was subjectit to ryches.'   835

118

The gled said, 'Yit I heir no thyng bot gude.
Proceid schortlye, and thy mater avance.'
The papyngo said, 'Father, be the rude,
It wer to lang to schaw the circumstance
Quhow Propertie, with hir new alyance,   840
Grew gret with chylde, as trew men to me talde,
And bure two dochteris, gudlie to behalde.

119

The eldest dochter named was Ryches,
The secunde syster, Sensualytie,
Quhilks did incres, within one schorte proces   845
Preplesande to the spiritualytie,
In gret substance and excellent bewtie.
Thir ladyis two grew so within few yeris
That in the warld wer non mycht be thare peris.

---

819 *heremytage*: hermitage   842 *dochteris*: daughters
825 *lave*: rest   845 *incres*: grow
828 *soberlye*: in moderation   846 *Preplesande*: Exceedingly pleasing
831 *heretage*: inheritance   849 *peris*: equals

120

This royall Ryches and lady Sensuall,   850
Frome that tyme furth tuke hole the governance
Of the moste part of the stait spirituall.
And thay, agane with humyll observance,
Amorouslie thare wyttis did avance,
As trew luffaris, thare ladyis for to pleis.   855
God wate geve, than, thare hartis war at eis!

121

Soune thay foryet to study, praye, and preche;
Thay grew so subject to dame Sensuall,
And thocht bot paine pure pepyll for to teche.
Yit thay decretit, in thare gret counsall,   860
Thay wald no more to mariage be thrall,
Traistyng, surely, tyll observe chaistytie.
("And all begylit!" quod Sensualytie.)

122

Apperandlye, thay did expell thare wyffis,
That thay mycht leif at large, without thirlage,   865
At libertie to lede thare lustie lyffis,
Thynkand men thrall, that bene in mariage
(For new faces provokis new corrage).
Thus chaistytie thay turne in to delyte:
Wantyng of wyffis bene cause of appetyte.   870

123

Dame Chaistitie did steill away for schame,
Frome tyme scho did persave thare proviance;
Dame Sensuall one letter gart proclame,
And hir exilit Italy and France.
In Inglande couthe scho get none ordinance.   875
Than to the kyng and courte of Scotlande
Scho markit hir, withouttin more demande.

124

Traistyng in to that court to get conforte,
Scho maid hir humyll supplycatioun.
Schortlye, thay said, scho sulde get na supporte,   880

856 *at eis*: content
859 *paine*: labour   863 *quod*: said
865 *large*: liberty; *thirlage*: bondage
868 *corrage*: boldness
870 *Wantyng*: The lack

872 *proviance*: provision
873 *letter*: official writ; *gart*: had
  proclaimed
875 *ordinance*: maintenance provision
877 *markit*: betook

Bot bostit hir, with blasphematioun,
"To preistis go mak your protestatioun!
It is", said thay, "mony one houndreth yeir
Sen Chaistitie had ony entres heir."

125

Tyrit for travell, scho to the preistis past,   885
And to the rewlaris of religioun.
Of hir presens, schortlye, thay war agast,
Sayand thay thocht it bot abusioun
Hir to resave. So, with conclusioun,
With one avyce, decretit and gave dome: 890
Thay walde resset no rebell out of Rome.

126

"Sulde we resave that Romanis hes refusit
And baneist Inglande, Italye and France?
For your flattrye, than wer we weill abusit!
Passe hyne," said thay, "and fast your waye avance.   895
Amang the nonnis go seik your ordinance,
For we have maid aith of fidelytie
To dame Ryches and Sensualytie."

127

Than paciently scho maid progressioun
Towarde the nonnis, with hart syching ful sore.   900
Thay gaif hir presens, with processioun,
Ressavand hir with honour, laud, and glore,
Purposyng to preserve hir ever more.
Of that nowellis, come to dame Propertie,
To Ryches and to Sensualytie,   905

128

Quhilks sped thame at the post, rycht spedalye,
And sett ane seage, proudlye, about the place.
The sillye nonnis did yeild thame haistelye,
And humllye of that gylt askit grace,
Syne gave thair bandis of perpetuall peace.   910

---

881 *bostit*: threatened
885 *Tyrit for*: Weary of
888 *abusioun*: impropriety
890 *avyce*: opinion; *dome*: judgement
891 *resset*: shelter
895 *hyne*: from here 896 *nonnis*: nuns
897 *aith*: oath

901 *processioun*: [ceremonial] process
904 *nowellis*: news
906 *sped...post*: with all speed
907 *sett ane seage*: lay siege
908 *sillye*: defenceless
910 *bandis*: bonds

Ressavand thame, thay kest up wykketis wyde.
Than Chaistytie walde no langer abyde.

129

So, for refuge, fast to the freris scho fled,
Quhilks said thay wald of ladyis tak no cure.'
'Quhare bene scho now?' than said the gredy gled.   915
'Nocht amang yow,' said scho, 'I yow assure.
I traist scho bene upon the Borrow Mure
Besouth Edinburgh, and that rycht mony menis,
Profest amang the systeris of the Schenis.

130

Thare hes scho found hir mother, Povertie,   920
And Devotioun, hir awin syster carnall,
Thare hes scho found faith, hope and charitie,
Togidder with the verteous cardinall.
Thare hes scho found ane convent yit unthrall
To dame Sensuall, nor with ryches abusit,   925
So quietlye those ladyis bene inclusit.'

131

The pyote said, 'I dreid, be thay assailyeit,
Thay rander thame, as did the holy nonnis.'
'Doute nocht', said scho. 'For thay bene so artalyeit,
Thay purpose to defend thame with thair gounnis.   930
Reddy to schute, thay have sax gret cannounnis,
Perseverance, Constance, and Conscience,
Austerytie, Laubour, and Abstynance.

132

To resyste subtell Sensualytie
Strongly thay bene enarmit, feit and handis,   935
Be abstynence, and keipith povertie
Contrar Ryches, and all hir fals servandis.
Thay have ane boumbard, braissit up in bandis,
To keip thare porte in myddis of thare clois,
Quhilk is callit 'Domine custodi nos'.   940

---

911 *kest..wyde*: threw open the gates
917 *Borrow Mure*: Burgh Muir
918 *menis*: say
919 *Schenis*: Sciennes
923 *verteous cardinall*: chief virtues
926 *inclusit*: confined
927-28 'I'm afraid, if they're attacked, they will surrender, like the nuns.'

929 *artailyeit*: armed
930 *purpose*: intend; *gounnis*: guns
936 *Be*: By [means of]
938 *boumbard*: cannon; *braissit...bandis*: secured firmly
939 *clois*: enclosure
940 *Domine...nos*: 'Lord guard us'

133

Within quhose schote thare dar no enimeis
Approche thare place, for dreid of dyntis doure.
Boith nycht and daye thay wyrk lyke besye beis
For thare defence, reddye to stand in stoure,
And hes sic watcheis on thare utter toure   945
That dame Sensual with seage dar not assailye,
Nor cum within the schote of thare artailye.'

134

The pyote said, 'Quhareto sulde thay presume
For to resyste sweit Sensualytie,
Or dame Ryches, quhilkis reularis bene in Rome?   950
Ar thay more constant, in thare qualytie,
Nor the prencis of spiritualytie,
Quhilkis plesandlye, withouttin obstaikle,
Haith thame resavit in thare habitakle?

135

Quhow lang, traist ye, those ladyis sall remane   955
So solyter, in sic perfectioun?'
The papingo said, 'Brether, in certane,
So lang as thay obey Correctioun,
Cheisyng thare heddis be electioun
Unthrall to Ryches or to Povertie,   960
Bot as requyrith thare necessitie.

136

O prudent prelatis, quhare was your prescianis,
That tuke on hand tyll observe chaistytie
But austeir lyfe, laubour, and abstenance?
Persavit ye nocht the gret prosperitie,   965
Apperandlye, to cum of propertie?
Ye knaw gret cheir, gret eais, and idelnes,
To lychorie was mother and maistres.'

137

'Thow ravis unrockit,' the ravin said, 'be the rude,
So to reprove Ryches, or Propertie.   970
Abraham and Isaac war ryche and verry gude,
Jacobe and Josephe had prosperitie.'

944 *stoure*: battle   945 *utter*: outer
951 *qualytie*: character
954 *habitakle*: dwelling place
956 *solyter*: solitary

962 *prescianis*: foreknowledge
964 *But*: Without
968 *lychorie*: lechery
969 *raves unrockit*: talk nonsense

The papingo said, 'That is verytie.
Ryches, I grant, is nocht to be refusit,
Providyng, alwaye, it be nocht abusit.'   975
138
'Than,' said the ravin, 'one replycatioun.'
Syne said, 'Thy reasone is nocht worth ane myte,
As I sall preve, with protestatioun,
That no man tak my wordis in dispyte.
I saye the temporall prencis hes the wyte,   980
That in the kirk sic pastours dois provyde
To governe saulis, that not tham selfis can gyde.
139
Lang tyme efter the kirk tuke Propertie,
The prelatis levit in gret perfectioun,
Unthrall to Ryches or Sensualytie,   985
Under the Holy Spreitis protectioun,
Orderlye chosin, be electioun,
As Gregore, Jerome, Ambrose and Augustyne,
Benedic, Barnerd, Clement, Cleit and Lyne.
140
Sic pacient prelatis, enterit be the porte,   990
Plesand the peple be predicatioun.
Now, dyke lowparis dois in the kirk resort,
Be symonie, and supplycatioun
Of prencis be thare presentatioun;
So sillye saulis, that bene Christis scheip,   995
Ar gevin to hungre, gormande wolfis to keip.
141
No marvell is, thocht we religious men
Degenerit be, and in our lyfe confusit:
Bot sing and drynk, none uther craft we ken.
Our spirituall fatheris hes us so abusit.   1000
Agane our wyll, those treukouris bene intrusit:
Lawit men hes now religious men in curis:
Profest virgenis in keipyng of strong huris.

---

976 *replycatioun*: [legal] reply
979 *dispyte*: contempt   980 *wyte*: blame
989 Benedict, Bernard, Clement, Cletus
    and Linus   990 *porte*: gate
992 *dyke lowparis*: boundary wall
    jumpers
993 *symonie*: traffic in benefices

996 *gormande*: gluttonous
999 *Bot*: Except
1001 *treukouris*: pedlars; *intrusit*: pushed
    into office
1002 *Lawit*: Inferior; *in curis*: in charge
1003 *huris*: prostitutes

142

Prencis, prencis! Quhar bene your heych prudence
In dispositioun of your beneficeis?   1005
The guerdonyng of your courticience
Is sum cause of thir gret enormyteis.
Thare is one sorte, watand lyke houngre fleis
For spirituall cure (thocht thay be no thing abyll)
Quhose gredie thristis bene insaciabyll.   1010

143

Prencis, I pray yow be no more abusit,
To verteous men havyng so small regarde.
Quhy sulde vertew, throuch flattrye, be refusit,
That men for cunnyng can get no rewarde?
Allace, that ever one braggar, or ane barde,   1015
Ane hure maister, or commoun hasarture
Sulde, in the kirk, get ony kynde of cure!

144

War I one one man worthy to weir ane croun,
Aye quhen thare vakit ony beneficeis,
I suld gar call ane congregatioun: 1020
The principall of all the preliceis,
Moste counnyng clerkis of universiteis,
Moste famous fatheris of religioun,
With thare advyse, mak dispositioun.

145

I sulde dispone all offices pastorallis   1025
Tyll doctours of devynitie or jure,
And cause dame Vertew pull up all hir salis,
Quhen counnyng men had in the kirk moist cure;
Gar lordis send thare sonnes, I yow assure,
To seik science, and famous sculis frequent,   1030
Syne thame promove, that war moste sapient.

146

Gret plesour war to heir ane byschope preche:
One dane, or doctour in divinitie,

1006 *guerdonyng*: rewarding;
   courticience: courtiers
1008 *watand*: in attendance; *fleis*: flies
1010 *thristis*: thirsts
1011 *abusit*: deceived
1014 *cunnyng*: learning
1016 *hasarture*: gambler

1019 *vakit*: fell vacant
1020 *gar call*: cause to be called
1021 *preliceis*: benefices of prelates
1026 *jure*: law   1027 *pull up*: hoist
1031 *promove*: advance
1033 *dane*: dean

One abbote, quhilk could weill his convent teche;
One persoun, flowyng in phylosophie. 1035
I tyne my tyme, to wys quhilk wyll nocht be!
War nocht the precheing of the beggyng freris,
Tynt war the faith amang the seculeris.

147

As for thare precheing,' quod the papingo,
'I thame excuse. For quhy? Thay bene so thrall 1040
To Propertie, and hir ding dochteris two,
Dame Ryches and fair lady Sensuall,
Thay may nocht use no pastyme spirituall.
And in thare habitis thay take sic delyte,
Thay have renuncit russat and roploch quhyte, 1045

148

Cleikand to thame skarlote and crammosie,
With menever, martrik, grice and ryche armyne.
Thare lawe hartis exaultit ar so hie,
To se thare papale pompe it is ane pyne.
More ryche arraye is now, with frenyeis fyne, 1050
Upon the bardyng of ane byscheopis mule
Nor ever had Paule or Peter agane Yule.

149

Syne fair ladyis, thare chene may not eschape,
Dame Sensuall so sic seid haith in tham sawin.
Les skaith it war, with lycence of the Pape, 1055
That ilke prelate one wyfe had, of his awin,
Nor se thar bastardis ovirthort the cuntre blawin.
For now, be thay be weill cumin from the sculis,
Thay fall to work as thay war commoun bullis!'

150

'Pew', quod the gled. 'Thow prechis all in vaine. 1060
Ye seculare folkis hes of our cace no curis.'
'I grant', said scho. 'Yit men wyll speik agane

1035 *persoun*: parson
1036 *tyne*: lose; *wys*: desire
1038 *seculeris*: non-monastic clergy
1044 *habitis*: religious dress
1045 *russat...quhyte*: coarse undyed woollen cloth
1046 *cleikand*: snatching; *skarlote*: rich cloth, freq. red; *crammosie*: crimson cloth

1047 *menever*: miniver; *martrik*: marten; *grice*: grey fur; *armyne*: ermine
1049 *it...pyne*: it is distressing
1050 *frenyeis*: fringes
1051 *bardyng*: horse-armour
1053 *chene*: chain   1055 *skaith*: harm
1057 *blawin*: flaunted   1058 *be*: though

Quhow ye haif maid a hundreth thousand huris
Quhilkis nevir hade bene, war not your lychorus luris,
And geve I lee, hartlye I me repent;   1065
Was never bird, I watt, more penitent.'

151

Than scho hir schrave, with devote contynance,
To that fals gled, quhilk fenyeit hym one freir.
And quhen scho had fulfyllit hir pennance,
Full subtellye at hir he gan inqueir: 1070
'Cheis yow', said he, 'quhilk of us brether heir
Sall have of all your naturall geir the curis;
Ye knaw none bene more holye creaturis.'

152

'I am content', quod the pure papingo,
'That ye, freir gled, and corby monk, your brother,   1075
Have cure of all my guddis and no mo,
Sen at this tyme, freindschip I fynd non uther.'
'We salbe to yow trew, as tyll our mother,'
Quod thay and sweir tyll fulfyll hir intent.
'Of that', said scho, 'I tak ane instrument.'   1080

153

'The pyote said, 'Quhat sall myne office bee?'
'Ovirman', said scho, 'unto the tother two.'
The rowpand revin said, 'Sweit syster, lat se
Your holy intent, for it is tyme to go.'
The gredie gled said, 'Brother do nocht so.   1085
We wyll remane and haldin up hir hede
And never depart frome hir, tyll scho be dede.'

154

The papingo thame thankit tenderlye
And said, 'Sen ye have tane on yow this cure,
Depart myne naturall guddis equalye   1090
That ever I had, or hes of dame Nature.
First, to the howlet, indegent and pure,
Quhilk on the daye, for schame, dar nocht be sene,
Tyll hir I laif my gaye galbarte of grene.

1064 *luris*: enticements
1067 *hir schrave*: made her confession
1074 *pure*: hapless   1075 *corby*: raven
1080 *instrument*: formal legal document

1082 *Ovirman*: Chief executor
1090 *Depart*: Divide
1092 *howlet*: owl; *indegent*: needy
1094 *galbarte*: cloak

155

My brycht depurit ene, as christall cleir,   1095
On to the bak ye sall thame boith present
(In Phebus presens, quhilk dar nocht appeir),
Of naturall sycht scho bene so impotent.
My birneist beik I laif, with gude entent,
Onto the gentyll, pieteous pillycane,   1100
To helpe to peirs hir tender hart in twane.

156

I laif the goik, quhilk hes no sang bot one,
My musyke with my voce angelycall,
And to the guse, ye geve quhen I am gone,
My eloquence, and toung rethoricall.   1105
And tak and drye my bones, gret and small,
Syne close thame in one cais of ebure fyne,
And thame present onto the phenix, syne,

157

To birne with hir, quhen scho hir lyfe renewis.
In Arabye ye sall hir fynde, but weir,   1110
And sall knaw hir be hir moste hevinly hewis,
Gold, asure, gowles, purpour, and synopeir;
Hir dait is for to leif fyve houndreth yeir.
Mak to that bird my commendatioun.
And als, I mak yow supplycatioun,   1115

158

Sen of my corps I have yow gevin the cure,
Ye speid yow to the court, but tareyng,
And tak my hart, of perfyte portrature,
And it present onto my soverane kyng;
I wat he wyll it clois in to one ryng.   1120
Commande me to his grace, I yow exhorte,
And of my passioun mak hym trew reporte.

159

Ye thre my trypes sall have, for your travell,
With luffer and lowng, to part equale amang yow,

1096 *bak*: bat   1098 *impotent*: weak
1099 *birneist*: burnished
1100 *pieteous*: compassionate; *pillycane*:
    pelican   1102 *goik*: cuckoo
1107 *ebure*: ivory   1108 *phenix*: phoenix

1112 *asure*: azure; *gowles*: red;
    synopeir: green
1118 *portrature*: form
1122 *passioun*: suffering
1123 *trypes*: entrails
1124 *luffer*: liver; *lowng*: lung

Prayand Pluto, the potent prince of hell,   1125
Geve ye failye, that in his feit he fang yow.
Be to me trew, thocht I no thyng belang yow;
Sore I suspect your conscience be to large.'
'Doute nocht', said thay. 'We tak it with the charge.'

160

'Adew, brether', quod the pure papingo.   1130
'To talking more I have no tyme to tarye.
Bot sen my spreit mon fra my body go,
I recommend it to the quene of farye,
Eternallye in tyll hir court to carye,
In wyldernes, among the holtis hore.'   1135
Than scho inclynit hir hed and spak no more.

161

Plungit in tyll hir mortall passioun,
Full grevouslie scho gryppit to the ground.
It war to lang to mak narratioun
Of sychis sore, with mony stang and stound.   1140
Out of hir wound the blude did so abound,
One coumpas round was with hir blude maid reid.
Without remaid thare wes no thyng bot dede.

162

And be scho had 'In manus Tuas' said,
Extinctit wer hir naturall wyttis fyve.   1145
Hir hed full softlye on hir schulder laid,
Syne yaild the spreit, with panes pungityve.
The ravin began rudely to ruge and ryve
Full gormondlyke, his emptie throte to feid.
'Eait softlye, brother', said the gredy gled.   1150

163

'Quhill scho is hote, depart hir evin amang us.
Tak thow one half and reik to me ane uther;
In tyll our rycht, I wat, no wycht dar wrang us.'
The pyote said, 'The feinde resave the fouther!

1126 *feit*: feet, claws; *fang*: seize
1127 *belang*: concern
1128 *large*: free
1129 *charge*: commission
1133 *farye*: fairy-land
1134 *carye*: proceed
1135 *holtis hore*: frost-hoary woods
1138 *gryppit*: clutched

1140 *stang...stound*: sting and throb
1144 *be*: by the time; *In manus Tuas*: 'Into Thy hands'
1147 *yaild*: surrendered; *pungityve*: sharp
1148 *ruge...ryve*: tug and tear
1152 *reik*: give
1154 *feind...fouther*: devil receive the lot!

Quhy mak ye me stepbarne and I your brother?   1155
Ye do me wrang, schir gled, I schrew your harte.'
'Tak thare', said he, 'the puddyngis for thy parte!'
                    164
Than wyt ye weill, my hart wos wounder sair,
For to behalde that dolent departyng,
Hir angell fedderis fleyng in the air.   1160
Except the hart, was left of hir no thyng.
The pyote said, 'This pertenith to the kyng,
Quhilk, tyll his grace, I purpose to present.'
'Thow', quod the gled, 'sall faill of thy entent.'
                    165
The ravin said, 'God nor I rax in ane raipe   1165
And thow get this tyll other kyng or duke!'
The pyote said, 'Plene I nocht to the pape,
Than in ane smedie I be smorit with smuke!'
With that the gled the pece claucht in his cluke,
And fled his way; the lave, with all thare mycht,   1170
To cheace the gled, flew all out of my sycht.
                    166
Now have ye hard this lytill tragedie,
The sore complent, the testament and myschance
Of this pure bird, quhilk did ascend so hie;
Beseikand yow excuse myne ignorance   1175
And rude indyte, quhilk is nocht tyll avance.
And to the quair, I geve commandiment:
Mak no repair quhare poetis bene present.
                    167
Because thow bene but rethorike so rude,
Be never sene besyde none uther buke,   1180
With kyng nor quene, with lord, nor man of gude.
With coit unclene, clame kynrent to sum cuke:
Steil in ane nuke quhen thay lyste on the luke.
For smell of smuke, men wyll abhor to beir the.
Heir I mansweir the; quhairfor, to lurke go leir the!   1185

1156 *schrew*: curse 1157 *puddyngis*: guts   1168 *smedie*: smithy; *smorit*: smothered
1158 *sair*: sorry   1160 *fleyng*: flying   1169 *claucht...cluke*: caught in his claw
1165-66 ...God [grant that] I stretch in a   1177 *quair*: book
     rope if you get this to either...!   1185 *mansweir*: disown; *leir*: learn
1167 *Plene*: Complain

THE ANSWER
TO THE KINGIS FLYTING

1

Redoutit roy, your ragment I have red,
Quhilk dois perturb my dull intendement.
From your flyting, wald God that I wer fred!
Or ellis sum tygerris toung wer to me lent.
Schir, pardone me, thocht I be impacient,   5
Quhilk bene so with your prunyeand pen detractit,
And rude report, frome Venus court dejectit.

2

Lustie ladyis, that on your libellis lukis,
My cumpanie dois hald abhominable,
Commandand me beir cumpanie to the cukis.   10
Moist lyke ane devill, thay hald me detestable.
Thay banis me, sayand I am nocht able
Thame to compleis, or preis to thare presence.
Apon your pen, I cry ane loud vengeance!

3

Wer I ane poeit, I suld preis with my pen   15
To wreik me on your vennemous wryting,
Bot I man do as dog dois in his den,
Fald baith my feit, or fle fast frome your flyting.
The mekle Devil may nocht indure your dyting!
Quharefor, '*Cor mundum crea in me!*' I cry,   20
Proclamand yow, the prince of poetry.

4

Schir, with my prince pertenit me nocht to pley.
Bot sen your grace hes gevin me sic command,
To mak answer, it must neidis me obey.

---

1 *Redoutit*: Revered; *roy*: king; *ragment*: composition
2 *Quhilk*: Which; *perturb*: agitate; *dull*: slow; *intendement*: understanding
3 *flyting*: versified abuse; *wald*: would; *fred*: freed
5 *thocht*: although
6 *Quhilk bene*: Who is; *prunyeand*: sharp-pointed; *detractit*: disparaged
7 *rude*: offensive; *Venus court*: the court of love; *dejectit*: thrown out
8 *Lustie*: Fair; *libellis*: writing
10 *beir cumpanie*: associate with; *cukis*: cooks   11 *Moist*: Most
12 *banis*: banish
13 *compleis*: please; *preis*: advance
15 *preis*: strive   16 *wreik*: avenge
17 *man*: must
18 Kneel in acceptance of defeat; *fle*: flee
19 *mekle*: great; *indure*: bear; *dyting*: writing
20 'Create in me a clean heart'
22 *pertenit*: [it] befits; *pley*: contend
23 *sen*: since; *sic*: such

98

Thocht ye be now strang lyke ane elephand,   25
And in till Venus werkis maist vailyeand,
The day wyll cum, and that within few yeiris,
That ye wyll draw at laiser with your feiris.

                        5

Quhat can ye say forther, bot I am failyeit
In Venus werkis? I grant, schir, that is trew.   30
The tyme hes bene, I wes better artailyeit
Nor I am now. Bot yit full sair I rew
That ever I did mouth thankles so persew.
Quharefor, tak tent, and your fyne powder spair,
And waist it nocht, bot gyf ye wit weill quhair.   35

                        6

Thocht ye rin rudelie, lyke ane restles ram,
Schutand your bolt at mony sindrie schellis,
Beleif richt weill, it is ane bydand gam.
Quharefore, be war, with dowbling of the bellis
(For mony ane dois haist thair awin saule knellis),   40
And, speciallie, quhen that the well gois dry,
Syne can nocht get agane sic stufe to by.

                        7

I give your counsale to the feynd of hell,
That wald nocht of ane princes yow provide,
Tholand yow rin schutand frome schell to schell,   45
Waistand your corps, lettand the tyme overslyde.
For, lyke ane boisteous bull, ye rin and ryde
Royatouslie, lyke ane rude rubeatour,
Ay fukkand lyke ane furious fornicatour.

26 *till*: to; *Venus werkis*: amorous dalliance; *vailyeand*: bold
27 *yeiris*: years
28 *at laiser*: at leisure; *feiris*: companions
29 *forther*: further; *bot*: except; *failyeit*: impaired
31 *artailyeit*: provided with artillery
32 *Nor*: Than; *yit*: yet; *full sair*: bitterly; *rew*: regret
33 *mouth...persew*: chase [indiscriminate] sexual gratification
34 *tak tent*: take heed
35 *waist*: waste; *bot gyf*: unless; *wit*: know; *quhair*: where
36 *rin rudelie*: go about without restraint
37 Shooting your arrow at many diverse targets

38 *bydand gam*: game of waiting
39 *be war*: beware; *with dowbling... bellis*: the passing of time
40 *ane*: [a] one; *haist*: hasten; *saule knellis*: death peal
41 *well*: spring
42 *Syne*: Then; *stufe*: commodity; *to by*: for money
43 *counsale*: advisers; *feynd*: feind
44 That would not provide you with a princess   45 *Tholand*: Suffering
46 *Waistand*: Destroying; *corps*: body; *lettand*: allowing; *overslyde*: pass
47 *boisteous*: roaring; *ryde*: copulate
48 *Royatouslie*: Wildly; *rubeatour*: scoundrel
44 *fukkand*: copulating; *furious*: raging

8

On ladronis for to loip ye wyll nocht lat,   50
Howbeit the caribaldis cry the corinoch.
Remember how, besyde the masking fat,
Ye caist ane quene overthort ane stinking troch?
That feynd, with fuffilling of hir roistit hoch,
Caist doun the fat; quharthrow, drink, draf, and juggis   55
Come rudely rinnand doun about your luggis.

9

Wald God the lady that luffit yow best
Had sene yow thair, ly swetterand lyke twa swyne!
Bot to indyte how that duddroun wes drest
(Drowkit with dreggis, quhimperand with mony quhryne),   60
That proces to report it wer ane pyne.
On your behalf, I thank God tymes ten score
That yow preservit from gut and frome grandgore.

10

Now, schir, fairweill, because I can nocht flyte.
And thocht I could, I wer nocht tyll avance   65
Aganis your ornate meter to indyte.
Bot yit be war with lawbouring of your lance:
Sum sayis thare cummis ane bukler furth of France
Quhilk wyll indure your dintis, thocht thay be dour.
Fairweill, of flowand rethorik the flour.   70

Quod Lindesay in his flyting
Aganis the kingis dyting.

---

50 You won't abstain from coupling
    with loose women
51 *caribaldis*: monsters; *cry the*
    corinoch: make loud outcry
52 *masking fat*: [malt] mashing vat
53 You threw a wench across a stinking
    trough
54 *fuffilling*: jerking about; *roistit*:
    overheated; *hoch*: hock
55 *quharthrow*: with the result that;
    draf: dregs; *juggis*: swill
56 *rinnand*: flowing; *luggis*: ears
57 *Wald*: Would; *luffit*: loved

58 *ly*: lie; *swetterand*: wallowing
59 *indyte*: describe; *duddroun*: slut
60 *Drowkit*: Drenched; *dreggis*: lees;
    quhimperand: whimpering; *quhryne*:
    squeals
61 *wer...pyne*: would be an effort
63 *preservit*: [were] protected; *gut*: gout;
    grandgore: venereal disease
65 *wer...avance*: wouldn't proceed
67 *lawbouring*: using
68 *bukler*: small round shield
69 *dintis*: blows; *dour*: hard

THE DEPLORATIOUN
OF THE
DEITH OF QUENE MAGDALENE

1

O cruell Deith! To greit is thy puissance!
Devorar of all erthlie levyng thingis.
Adam, we may the wyit of this mischance!
In thy default this cruell tyrane ringis,
And spairis nother empryour nor kingis.   5
And now, allace, hes reft furth of this land,
The flour of France and confort of Scotland.

2

Father Adam, allace that thow abusit
Thy fre wyll, being inobedient!
Thow chesit deith, and lesting lyfe refusit.   10
Thy successioun, allace, that may repent,
That thow hes maid mankynd so impotent
That it may mak to Deith no resistance:
Exemple of our quene, the flour of France.

3

O dreidfull dragoun with thy dulefull dart,   15
Quhilk did nocht spair of feminine the flour,
Bot cruellie did pers hir throuch the hart,
And wald nocht give hir respite for ane hour,
To remane with hir prince and paramour,
That scho at laiser mycht have tane licence.   20
Scotland, on the, may cry ane loud vengeance!

4

Thow leit Mathusalem leif nine houndreth yeir
Thre score and nyne, bot, in thy furious rage,
Thow did devore this young princes but peir,

1 *To*: Too; *greit*: great; *puissance*: power	15 *dulefull*: painful; *dart*: light spear
2 *Devorar*: Devourer; *levyng*: living	16 *nocht*: not; *feminine*: womankind
3 *wyit*: blame; *mischance*: misfortune	17 *pers*: pierce; *hir*: her
4 *default*: offence; *tyrane*: tyrant; *ringis*: reigns 5 *nother*: neither	18 *wald*: would 19 *paramour*: lover
6 *reft*: stolen 7 *flour*: flower	20 *scho*: she; *laiser*: leisure; *tane licence*: leave to depart
8 *Father*: Forefather; *abusit*: misused	22 *leit*: allowed; *Mathusalem*: Methuselah; *leif*: live
10 *chesit*: chose; *lesting*: eternal	24 *devore*: devour; *but peir*: without equal
12 *impotent*: powerless	

Or scho was compleit sevintene yeir of age.   25
Gredie gorman! Quhy did thow nocht asswage
Thy furious rage contrair that lustie quene
Tyll we sum fruct had of hir bodie sene?

5

O dame Nature! Thow did no diligence
Contrair this theif, quhilk al the warld confoundis!   30
Had thow, with naturall targis, maid defence,
That brybour had nocht cummit within hir boundis,
And had bene savit frome sic mortall stoundis
This mony ane yeir. Bot quhair was thy discretion,
That leit hir pas til we had sene succession?   35

6

O Venus, with thy blynd sone, Cupido,
Fy on yow baith, that maid no resistance!
In to your court ye never had sic two,
So leill luffaris, without dissimulance,
As James the Fift and Magdalene of France,   40
Discending boith of blude imperiall,
To quhome in lufe I find no perigall.

7

For, as Leander swame outthrow the flude
To his fair lady Hero mony nichtis,
So did this prince, throw bulryng stremis wode,   45
With erlis, baronis, squyaris and with knichtis,
Contrair Neptune and Eol and thare michtis,
And left his realme in greit disesperance,
To seik his lufe, the first dochter of France.

8

And scho, lyke prudent quene Penelope,   50
Ful constantlie wald change hym for none uther.

---

25 *was compleit*: had completed;
  sevintene: seventeen; *yeir*: years
26 *gorman*: excessive eater
27 *contrair*: against; *lustie*: lovely
28 *fruct*: offspring
29 *did...diligence*: were not industrious
31 *naturall targis*: shields of nature
32 *brybour*: wretch; *boundis*: territory
33 *savit*: saved; *stoundis*: pains
34 *mony*: many; *quhair*: where
35 *leit...pas*: allowed her to die; *til*:
  before 36 *sone*: son; *Cupido*: Cupid

37 *yow*: you; *baith*: both
39 *leill*: faithful; *luffaris*: lovers;
  dissimulance: dissimulation
42 *perigall*: equal
43 *outthrow*: through; *flude*: sea
45 *bulryng...wode*: boiling seas furious
46 *squyaris*: squires
47 *Eol*: Aeolus; *michtis*: power
48 *disesperance*: despair
49 *dochter*: daughter

And, for his plesour, left hir awin countre,
Without regard to father or to mother,
Takyng no cure of sister, nor of brother;
Bot schortlie tuke hir leif, and left thame all,   55
For lufe of hym to quhome lufe maid hir thrall.

9

O dame Fortune! Quhare was thy greit confort
Till hir to quhome thow was so favorable?
Thy slyding gyftis maid hir no support—
Hir hie lynage, nor riches intellible.   60
I se thy puissance bene bot variable,
Quhen hir father, the most hie cristinit king,
Till his deir chyld mycht mak no supporting.

10

The potent prince, hir lustie lufe and knicht,
With his most hardie noblis of Scotland,   65
Contrair that bailfull bribour had no micht.
Thocht all the men had bene at his command
Of France, Flanderis, Italie, and Ingland,
With fiftie thousand millioun of tresour,
Mycht nocht prolong that ladyis lyfe ane hour.   70

11

O Paris! Of all citeis principall!
Quhilk did resave our prince with laud and glorie,
Solempnitlie, throw arkis triumphall
(Quhilk day bene digne to put in memorie),
For, as Pompey, efter his victorie,   75
Was in to Rome resavit with greit joy,
So thow resavit our richt redoutit roy.

12

Bot at his mariage maid upon the morne,
Sic solace and solempnizatioun
Was never sene afore, sen Christ was borne,   80

---

52 *awin*: own;   54 *cure*: care
55 *schortlie*: rapidly; *tuke...leif*: bade
   farewell
56 *thrall*: slave
58 *Till*: To; *favorable*: well disposed
60 *lynage*: ancestry; *intellible*:
   innumerable
62 *cristinit*: Christian
64 *potent*: powerful; *lustie*: gallant;
   knicht: champion

65 *hardie*: valiant; *noblis*: nobles
66 *bailfull*: destructive
69 *tresour*: wealth
72 *resave*: welcome formally
73 *arkis triumphall*: triumphal arches
74 *digne*: worthy
77 *richt redoutit roy*: right feared king
79 *solace*: delight; *solempnizatioun*:
   ceremonial celebration

Nor to Scotland sic consolatioun.
Thare selit was the confirmatioun
Of the weill keipit Ancient Alliance,
Maid betwix Scotland and the realme of France.

13

I never did se one day more glorious: 85
So mony, in so riche abilyementis
Of silk and gold, with stonis precious!
Sic banketting! Sic sound of instrumentis,
With sang, and dance, and martiall tornamentis!
Bot, lyke ane storme efter ane plesand morrow,   90
Sone was our solace changit in to sorrow.

14

O traytour Deith, quhom none may contramand,
Thow mycht have sene the preparatioun
Maid be the Thre Estaitis of Scotland,
With greit confort and consolatioun,   95
In everilk ciete, castell, toure, and town;
And how ilk nobill set his hole intent
To be excellent in habilyement.

15

Theif! Saw thow nocht the greit preparativis
Of Edinburgh, the nobill famous toun?   100
Thou saw the peple labouring for thare lyvis
To mak triumphe, with trump and clarioun.
Sic plesour was never in to this regioun
As suld have bene, the day of hir entrace,
With greit propynis gevin till hir grace.   105

16

Thow saw makand rycht costlie scaffalding,
Depayntit weill with gold and asure fyne,
Reddie preparit for the upsetting
With fontanis, flowing watter cleir, and wyne;

81 *consolatioun*: comfort
82 *selit*: sealed
86 *abilyementis*: apparel
88 *banketting*: holding of banquets
89 *martiall*: warlike; *tornamentis*: tournaments
92 *traytour*: traitor; *contramand*: countermand
96 *everilk*: every
101 *for...lyvis*: with all their might

102 *triumphe*: joyful celebration; *trump*: trumpet; *clarioun*: trumpet
104 *entrace*: [formal] entry
105 *propynis*: gifts; *gevin*: given
106 *makand*: being made; *scaffalding*: platform[s]
107 *Depayntit*: Decorated
108 *Reddie*: Completely; *upsetting*: setting up
109 *fontanis*: fountains

Disagysit folkis, lyke creaturis devyne,   110
On ilk scaffold to play ane syndrie storie:
Bot all in greiting turnit thow that glorie.

17

Thow saw mony ane lustie fresche galland
Weill ordourit for resaving of thair quene.
Ilk craftisman, with bent bow in his hand,   115
Full galyeartlie in schort clething of grene.
The honest burges cled, thow suld have sene,
Sum in scarlot and sum in claith of grane,
For till have met thare lady soverane.

18

Provest, baillies, and lordis of the toun;   120
The senatouris, in ordour consequent,
Cled in to silk, of purpure, blak, and brown;
Syne the greit lordis of the parliament,
With mony knychtlie barroun and baurent
In silk and gold, in colouris confortable: 125
Bot thow, allace, all turnit in to sable!

19

Syne, all the lordis of religioun,
And princes of the preistis venerable,
Full plesandlie in thare processioun,
With all the cunnyng clerkis honorable.   130
Bot thiftuouslie, thow tyrane tresonable,
All thare greit solace and solempniteis
Thow turnit in till dulefull dirigeis.

---

110 *Disagysit*: Costumed; *devyne*: divine
111 *scaffold*: temporary stage; *syndrie*: separate
112 *greiting*: weeping; *turnit*: turned
113 *lustie...galland*: handsome, finely dressed youth
114 *weill ordourit*: well prepared
116 *galyeartlie*: gaily; *clething*: clothing
117 *burges*: freemen of the burgh; *cled*: dressed
118 *claith of grane*: cloth of a fast dye, freq. scarlet
119 *soverane*: sovereign
120 *Provest*: Provost; *baillies*: town magistrates; *lordis...toun*: gentlemen of rank

121 *senatouris*: Court of Session judges; *in...consequent*: in sequence
124 *barroun*: barons; *baurent*: bannerets
125 *confortable*: giving comfort
126 *sable*: black
127 *lordis...religioun*: high-ranking churchmen
128 *princes...preistis*: higher-ranking churchmen
130 *cunnyng*: learned; *clerkis*: clerics
131 *thiftuouslie*: stealthily; *tresonable*: treacherous
132 *solempniteis*: ceremonies
133 *dulefull*: sorrowful; *dirigeis*: Offices of the Dead

20

Syne, nixt in ordour, passing throw the toun,
Thow suld have hard the din of instrumentis,   135
Of tabrone, trumpet, schalme, and clarioun,
With reird redoundand throw the elementis!
The herauldis with thare awfull vestimentis,
With maseris, upon ather of thare handis,
To rewle the preis with burneist silver wandis.   140

21

Syne, last of all, in ordour triumphall,
That most illuster princes honorable;
With hir, the lustie ladyis of Scotland,
Quhilk suld have bene ane sycht most delectable.
Hir rayment to rehers I am nocht able: 145
Of gold and perle, and precious stonis brycht,
Twynkling lyke sternis in ane frostie nycht.

22

Under ane pale of gold scho suld have past,
Be burgessis borne, clothit in silkis fyne.
The greit maister of houshold all thare last;   150
With hym, in ordour, all the kingis tryne,
Quhais ordinance war langsum to defyne.
On this maner, scho, passing throw the toun,
Suld have resavit mony benisoun

23

Of virginis, and of lustie burges wyiffis,   155
Quhilk suld have bene ane sycht celestiall,
'Vive la Royne!' cryand for thare lyiffis;
With ane harmonious sound angelicall,
In everilk corner myrthis musicall.

135 *hard*: heard
136 *tabrone*: tabor; *schalme*: shawm
137 *reird*: din; *redoundand*: resounding; *throw...elementis*: everywhere
138 *herauldis*: heralds; *awfull*: inspiring awe; *vestiments*: tabards of office
139 *maseris*: macers; *upon...handis*: on each side
140 *rewle*: rule; *preis*: crowd; *burneist*: polished; *wandis*: batons
141 *triumphall*: victorious
142 *illuster*: illustrious
144 *delectable*: delightful

145 *rehers*: describe
147 *sternis*: stars   148 *pale*: canopy
150 *maister...houshold*: master of [the royal] household; *all...last*: last of all
151 *tryne*: train
152 *ordinance*: order; *defyne*: state
154 *benisoun*: blessings
155 *virginis*: young girls
156 *sycht celestiall*: heavenly sight
157 *Vive...Royne!*: Long live the Queen!; *for...lyiffis*: with all their might   158 *angelicall*: angelic
159 *myrthis*: rejoicing

Bot thow, tyrane, in quhome is found no grace,   160
Our 'Alleluya!' hes turnit in 'Allace!'

24

Thow suld have hard the ornate oratouris
Makand hir hienes salutatioun,
Boith of the clergy, toun, and counsalouris,
With mony notable narratioun.   165
Thow suld have sene hir coronatioun,
In the fair abbay of Holy Rude,
In presence of ane myrthfull multitude.

25

Sic banketing, sic aufull tornamentis,
On hors and fute that tyme quhilk suld have bene!   170
Sic Chapell Royall, with sic instrumentis,
And craftie musick, singing frome the splene,
In this countre was never hard nor sene!
Bot all this greit solempnite and gam
Turnit thow hes, in Requiem æternam.   175

26

Inconstant warld, thy freindschip I defy,
Sen strenth, nor wisdome, riches, nor honour,
Vertew, nor bewtie, none may certefy
Within thy boundis for to remane ane hour.
Quhat valith to the king or empryour,   180
Sen pryncely puissance may nocht be exemit
From deith, quhose dolour can nocht be expremit?

27

Sen man in erth hes na place permanent,
Bot all mon passe be that horrible port,
Lat us pray to the Lord omnipotent,   185
That dulefull day, to be our greit comfort;
That in his realme we may with hym resort

---

161 Alleluya: 'Praise the Lord'
162 ornate oratouris: skilled orators
163 salutatioun: greeting
165 narratioun: factual part of an oration
167 abbay...Rude: Holyrood Abbey
169 banketing: sumptuous feasts
171 Chapell Royall: King's Chapel choir
172 craftie: skilfully composed or per-
     formed; splene: 'heart' [lit. spleen]
174 gam: sport

175 Requiem æternam: Rest forever
178 certefy: give assurance
179 boundis: territory
180 valith to: benefits
181 exemit: exempt
182 dolour: sorrow; expremit: expressed
184 mon...port: must go through that...
     door [die]
187 resort: stay

(Quhilkis from the hell with his blude ransonit bene),
With Magdalene, umquhyle of Scotland quene.

28

O Deith! Thocht thow the bodie may devore   190
Of every man, yit hes thow no puissance
Of thare vertew for to consume the glore;
As salbe sene of Magdalene of France,
Umquhyle our quene, quhom poetis sal avance
And put hir in perpetuall memorie: 195
So sall hir fame of the have victorie.

29

Thocht thou hes slane the hevinly flour of France,
Quhilk impit was in to the thrissill kene,
Quharein all Scotland saw thair hail plesance,
And maid the lyoun rejoysit frome the splene;   200
Thocht rute be pullit frome the levis grene,
The smell of it sall, in dispyte of the,
Keip, ay, twa realmes in peice and amite.

188 *blude*: blood ; *ransonit*: delivered
189 *umquhyle*: late
192 *consume*: destroy
194 *avance*: praise
196 *of*: over
198 *impit*: grafted; *thrissill*: thistle

200 *lyoun*: lion [of Scotland]; *rejoysit*:
        feel great joy
201 *rute*: [plant] root
202 *dispyte*: contempt
203 *twa*: two; *amite*: friendship

THE JUSTING
BETWIX
JAMES WATSOUN AND JHONE BARBOUR

In Sanct Androis on Witsoun Monnunday,
Twa campionis, thare manheid did assay,
Past to the barres, enarmit heid and handis
(Wes never sene sic justing in no landis),
In presence of the kingis grace and quene,   5
Quhare mony lustie lady mycht be sene.
Mony ane knight, barroun, and baurent
Come for to se that aufull tornament.
The ane of thame was gentill James Watsoun,
And Johne Barbour, the uther campioun.   10
Unto the king thay war familiaris
And of his chalmer boith cubicularis.
James was ane man of greit intelligence,
Ane medicinar, ful of experience.
And Johne Barbour, he was ane nobill leche;   15
Crukit carlingis he wald gar thame get speche.
Frome tyme thay enterit war in to the feild,
Full womanlie thay weildit speir and scheild
And wichtlie waiffit in the wynd thare heillis,
Hobland lyke cadgeris rydand on thare creillis.   20
Bot ather ran at uther with sic haist
That thay could never thair speir get in the reist!
Quhen gentil James trowit best with Johne to meit,
His speir did fald amang his horssis feit.
I am rycht sure gude James had bene undone,   25

Title *Justing*: Jousting
2 *twa*: two; *campionis*: champions; *manheid*: prowess; *assay*: test
3 *barres*: lists; *enarmit*: armed; *heid*: head 4 *sic*: such
7 *baurent*: banneret
8 *aufull*: inspiring awe
9 *The ane*: One; *gentill*: well-born
11 *familiaris*: confidential servants
12 *chalmer*: bedroom; *boith*: both; *cubicularis*: attendants
14 *medicinar*: physician
15 *nobill*: expert; *leche*: practitioner of medicine or surgery
16 *Crukit*: Crippled; *carlingis*: old women; *wald*: would; *gar...speche*: enable them to speak
17 *enterit*: entered; *war*: were; *feild*: place of tournament
18 *womanlie*: weakly [derog. of men]
19 *wichtlie*: valiantly; *waiffit*: moved to and fro; *heillis*: heels
20 *Hobland*: Moving unsteadily; *cadgeris*: itinerant dealers; *rydand*: riding; *creillis*: wicker panniers
21 *ather*: each   22 *reist*: [lance]rest
23 *trowit*: thought; *meit:* engage in battle
24 *fald*: bend

War not that Johne his mark tuke be the mone.
Quod Johne, 'Howbeit thou thinkis my leggis lyke rokkis,
My speir is gude; now keip the fra my knokkis!'
'Tary', quod James, 'ane quhyle, for, be my thrift,
The feind ane thing I can se bot the lift.'   30
'Nor more can I,' quod Johne, 'be Goddis breid!
I se no thing except the steipill heid!
Yit, thocht thy braunis be lyk twa barrow trammis,
Defend the, man!' Than ran thay to, lyk rammis.
At that rude rink, James had bene strykin doun,   35
Wer not that Johne, for feirsnes, fell in swoun.
And rychtso James to Johne had done gret deir,
Wer not amangis hors feit he brak his speir.
Quod James to Johne, 'Yit, for our ladyis saikis,
Lat us to gidder straik thre market straikis.'   40
'I had', quod Johne, 'that sall on the be wrokin!'
Bot or he spurrit his hors, his speir was brokin.
From tyme with speiris none could his marrow meit,
James drew ane sweird with ane rycht auful spreit
And ran til Johne til haif raucht him ane rout;   45
Johnis swerd was roustit and wald no way cum out.
Than James leit dryfe at Johne with boith his fystis;
He mist the man and dang upon the lystis.
And, with that straik, he trowit that Johne was slane,
His swerd stak fast and gat it never agane.   50
Be this, gude Johne had gottin furth his swerd,
And ran to James with mony aufull word:

26 *War*: Were [it]; *mark*: aim; *be...*
    mone: by...moon
27 *lyke rokkis*: like distaffs
28 *knokkis*: blows
29 *Tary*: Remain; *quhyle*: while;
    be...thrift: [I swear] by my luck
30 The devil a thing...but the sky.
31 *be Goddis breid*: by God's bread
32 *steipill heid*: steeple top
33 *Yit, thocht*: Yet, even if; *braunis*:
    rounded muscles [of arm, leg];
    barrow trammis: hand-barrow pole
    shafts
34 *ran...to*: rode swiftly...towards [each
    other]; *rammis*: male [horned] sheep
35 *rude rink*: rough onset
36 *feirsnes*: fierceness; *swoun*: swoon
37 *deir*: harm

40 *to gidder*: together; *straik*: strike;
    market: officially tallied; *straikis*:
    strokes
41 *I had*: I believe; *sall*: shall; *wrokin*:
    wreaked   42 *or*: before
43 *From tyme*: From [the] time [that];
    marrow: opponent
44 *sweird*: sword; *spreit*: spirit
45 *til*: to; *raucht*: dealt; *rout*: heavy blow
46 *roustit*: rusty; *wald...out*: could not be
    unsheathed
47 *leit dryfe*: drove; *fystis*: fists
48 *mist*: failed to hit; *dang*: dealt a
    blow; *lystis*: enclosure
49 *trowit*: believed
50 *stak*: stuck
51 *Be*: By; *gottin furth*: drawn

'My furiousnes, forsuith, now sall thow find!'
Straikand at James his swerd flew in the wind.
Than gentill James began to crak greit wordis: 55
'Allace', quod he, 'this day, for falt of swords!'
Than ather ran at uther with new raicis;
With gluifis of plait thay dang at utheris facis.
Quha wan this feild no creature could ken.
Till at the last, Johne cryit, 'Fy! Red the men!'   60
'Ye, red,' quod James, 'for that is my desyre.
It is ane hour sen I began to tyre.'
Sone be thay had endit that royall rink,
Into the feild mycht no man stand for stink.
Than every man that stude on far cryit, 'Fy!'   65
Sayand, 'Adew!'—for dirt partis cumpany.
Thare hors, harnes, and all geir was so gude,
Lovyng to God, that day was sched no blude.

55 *crak...words*: boast loudly
56 *falt*: defect
57 *raicis*: courses
58 *gluifis of plait*: gauntlets
59 *Quha*: Who; *wan*: won; *feild*: battle; *ken*: know
60 *Red*: Separate
61 *Ye*: Yes
63 *Sone be*: By the time that; *royall rink*: remarkable contest
65 *on far*: at a distance
66 *dirt*: excrement
67 *harnes*: harness; *geir*: arms and armour
68 *Lovyng to*: Praise

THE TRAGEDIE OF THE
CARDINALL

The Prolog.

1

Nocht lang ago, efter the hour of pryme,
Secreitly sittyng in myne oratorie,
I tuk ane buke, tyll occupye the tyme,
Quhare I fand mony tragedie and storie
Quhilk Jhone Bochas had put in memorie: 5
Quhow mony prencis, conquerouris and kingis
War dulfullie deposit frome thare ryngis.

2

Quhow Alexander, the potent conquerour,
In Babilone was poysonit pieteouslie,
And Julius, the mychtie emperiour,   10
Murdreist at Rome, causles and creuellie;
Prudent Pompey, in Egypt schamefullie
He murdreist was (quhat nedith proces more?)
Quhose tragideis war pietie tyll deplore.

3

I, sittyng so, upon my buke redyng,   15
Rycht suddantlie afore me did appeir
Ane woundit man, aboundantlie bledyng,
With vissage paill and with ane dedlye cheir,
Semand ane man of two and fyftie yeir;
In rayment reid, clothit full curiouslie   20
Of vellot and of saityng crammosie.

4

With febyll voce, as man opprest with paine,
Soiftlye he maid me supplycatioun,

1 *pryme*: first hour of the day
2 *Secreitly*: Privately; *oratorie*: study
3 *tuk*: took; *ane*: a; *tyll*: to
4 *Quhare*: Where; *fand*: found; *mony*:
   many
5 *Quhilk*: Which; *Bochas*: Boccaccio
6 *Quhow*: How
7 *dulfullie*: dolefully; *ryngis*: reigns
8 *potent*: mighty
9 *pieteouslie*: pitiably
13 *proces*: exposition

14 *pietie* [a cause for] pity; *deplore*:
   lament   16 *afore*: before
18 *vissage*: face; *dedlye*: death-like;
   cheir: expression
19 *Semand*: Appearing [to be]
20 *rayment reid*: red clothing;
   curiouslie: elaborately
21 *vellot*: velvet; *saityng crammosie*:
   crimson satin
22 *febyll*: weak; *voce*: voice
23 *Soiftlye*: Quietly

Sayand, 'My freind, go reid, and reid againe,
Geve thow can fynde, by trew narratioun,   25
Of ony paine lyke to my passioun.
Rycht sure I am, war Jhone Bochas on lyve,
My tragedie at lenth he wald discryve.

5

Sen he is gone, I pray the tyll indyte
Of my infortune sum remembrance,   30
Or at the leist my tragedie to wryte,
As I to the sall schaw the circumstance,
In teirmes breve, of my unhappy chance,
Sen my beginnyng tyll my faitell ende,
Quhilk I wald tyll all creature war kende.'   35

6

'I not', said I, 'mak sic memoriall,
Geve of thy name I had intelligence.'
'I am David, that cairfull cardinall,
Quhilk doith appeir', said he, 'to thy presens,
That umquhyle had so gret preeminens.'   40
Than he began his dedis tyll indyte
(As ye sall heir) and I began to wryte.

The Tragedie.
7

'I, David Betone, umquhyle cardinall,
Of nobyl blude be lyne I did discend.
Duryng my tyme I had no perigall,   45
Bot now is cum, allace, my faitell end.
Aye, gre by gre, upwarte I did ascende,
Swa that in to this realme did never ryng
So gret one man as I, under ane kyng.

---

24 *reid*: read
25 *Geve*: If; *trew*: truthful
26 *ony*: any; *passioun*: suffering
27 *war*: were; *on lyve*: alive
28 *wald*: would; *discryve*: give an
    account of
29 *the*: thee; *indyte*: compose
30 *infortune*: misfortune
32 *schaw*: show
33 *teirmes*: terms; *breve*: short
35 *kende*: known

36 I will not compile such a record
37 *Geve*: Unless; *intelligence*:
    information
38 *cairfull*: unhappy
40 *umquhyle*: formerly
41 *Than*: Then; *dedis*: deeds
45 *perigall*: equal
46 *faitell*: decreed by fate
47 *Aye*: Continually; *gre by gre*: step by
    step
48 *Swa*: So; *ryng*: rule

8

Quhen I was ane young joly gentyll man   50
Prencis to serve I sett my hole intent.
First tyll ascende, at Arbroith I began,
Ane abasie of gret ryches and rent.
Of that estait yit was I nocht contente;
To get more ryches, dignitie and glore,   55
My hart was set—allace! allace!—tharefore.

9

I maid sic servyce tyll our soverane kyng
He did promove me tyll more hie estait.
One prince abufe all preistis for tyll ryng,
Arschibyschope of Sanct Androus consecrat.   60
Tyll that honour, quhen I wes elevate,
My prydefull hart was nocht content at all,
Tyll that I create wes one cardinall.

10

Yit praist I tyll have more auctoritie,
And fynalie was chosin Chancelare.   65
And, for uphalding of my dignitie,
Was maid legate. Than had I no compare.
I purcheist, for my proffect singulare
(My boxsis and my threasure tyll avance),
The byschopreik of Merapose in France.   70

11

Of all Scotland I had the governall.
But my avyse concludit wes no thyng.
Abbot, byschope, archibyschope, cardinall:
In to this realme no hiear could I ryng
Bot I had bene pape, emperour, or kyng.   75
For schortnes of the tyme I am nocht abyll
At lenth to schaw my actis honorabyll.

50 *joly*: lighthearted
51 *hole*: whole
52 *Arbroith*: Arbroath
53 *abasie*: abbey
54 *estait*: rank [of Abbot]; *yit*: yet
55 *dignitie*: rank
57 *soverane*: sovereign
58 *promove*: promote
59 *One*: A   61 *elevate*: elevated
63 *create*: appointed
64 *praist*: pressed; *auctoritie*: authority

65 *Chancelare*: Chancellor
66 *uphalding*: upholding
68 *purcheist*: obtained by application;
     proffect singulare: private gain
69 *boxsis*: [document / money] boxes;
     avance: advance
70 *Merapose*: Mirepoix
71 *governall*: governing
72 *But*: Without; *avyse*: advise
75 *Bot*: Unless

12

For my moste princelye prodigalytie,
Amang prelatis in France I bure the pryse.
I schew my lordlye lyberalitie 80
In banketting, playng at cartis and dyse.
In to sic wysedome I was haldin wyse
And sparit nocht to playe, with kyng nor knycht,
Thre thousand crownis of gold upon ane nycht.

13

In France I made seir honest voyagis, 85
Quhare I did actis ding of remembrance.
Throuch me war maid tryumphand mariagis—
Tyll our soverane boith proffet and plesance.
Quene Magdalene, the first dochter of France,
With gret ryches was in to Scotland brocht: 90
That mariage throch my wysedome wes wrocht.

14

Efter quhose deith, in France I paste agane,
The secunde quene homwart I did convoye;
That lustye princes, Marie de Lorane,
Quhilk wes resavit with gret tryumphe and joye: 95
So servit I our rycht redouttit roye.
Sone efter that, Harye, of Ingland kyng,
Of our soverane desyrit ane commonyng.

15

Of that metyng our kyng wos weill content,
So that in Yorck was sett boith tyme and place. 100
Bot our prelatis, nor I, wald never consent
That he sulde se kyng Harye in the face.
Bot we wer weill content quhowbeit his grace
Had salit the sey to speik with ony uther
Except that kyng, quhilk was his mother brother! 105

78 *prodigalytie*: extravagance
79 *bure the pryse*: had pre-eminence
81 *banketting*: the holding of banquets;
cartis...dyse: cards...dice
82 *sic*: such
85 *seir*: various
86 *ding*: worthy
89 *dochter*: daughter
91 *wrocht*: wrought
93 *homwart*: homeward; *convoye*:
escort
94 *lustye*: fair
95 *resavit*: received; *tryumphe*:
triumphal pageant
96 *servit*: served; *redouttit*: respected;
roye: king
97 *Harye*: Henry [VIII]
98 *commonyng*: meeting
99 *weill*: well   100 *Yorck*: York
104 *salit...sey*: sailed...sea

16

Quhair throch thar rose gret weir and mortal stryfe,
Gret heirschippis, honnger, darth and desolatioun;
On ather syde did mony lose thare lyfe.
Geve I wald mak ane trew narratioun,
I causit all that trybulatioun: 110
For tyll tak peace I never wald consent
Without the kyng of France had bene content.

17

Duryng this weir war takin presoneris
Of nobyll men, fechtyng full furiouslie;
Mony one lorde, barrone, and bachileris.   115
Quhar throuch our king tuke sic melancolie
Quhilk drave hym to the dede, rycht dulefullie.
Extreme dolour ovirset did so his hart
That frome this lyfe, allace, he did depart.

18

Bot efter that boith strenth and speche wes lesit,   120
Ane paper blank his grace I gart subscryve,
In to the quhilk I wrait all that I plesit
Efter his deth, quhilk lang war tyll discryve.
Throuch that wrytting I purposit, belyve,
With supporte of sum lordis benevolens,   125
In this regioun tyll have preemynens.

19

As for my lord, our rychteous governour,
Geve I wald schortlie schaw the veritie,
Tyll hym I had no maner of favour.
Duryng that tyme I purposit that hee   130
Suld nevir cum to none auctoritie.
For his supporte tharefor he brocht amang us,
Furth of Ingland, the nobyll Erle of Angous.

---

106 *thar*: there; *weir*: war; *mortal*: fatal
107 *heirschippis*: plundering raids;
    honnger: hunger; *darth*: scarcity
108 *ather*: either
109 *Geve*: If   111 *tak*: take
114 *fechtyng*: fighting
115 *bachileris*: young knights
117 *drave*: drove
118 *ovirset*: overwhelm
120 *lesit*: lost
121 I had his grace sign a blank paper

122 *wrait*: wrote; *plesit*: pleased
124 *purposit*: resolved; *belyve*: with
    speed
125 *benevolens*: goodwill
126 *preemynens*: pre-eminence in
    authority
127 *rychteous*: rightful
128 *schortlie*: briefly
129 *maner*: kind   131 *none*: any
133 *Furth*: Out of; *Angous*: Angus

20

Than was I put abak frome my purpose
And suddantlie caste in captyvitie,   135
My prydefull hart to dant, as I suppose,
Devysit by the heych divinitie.
Yit in my hart sprang no humylitie.
Bot now the word of God full weill I knaw:
Quho dois exault hym self, God sall hym law.   140

21

In the meine tyme, quhen I wes so subjectit,
Ambassaldouris war sent in to Ingland,
Quhare thay boith peace and mariage contractit.
And, more surelie for tyll observe that band,
War promeist divers pleagis of Scotland.   145
Of that contract I wes no way content,
Nor nevir wald thare to geve my consent.

22

Tyll capytanis that kepit me in waird,
Gyftis of gold I gave thame gret plentie;
Rewlaris of court I rychelie did rewaird,   150
Quhare throuch I chapit frome captyvitie.
Bot quhen I was fre, at my libertie,
Than, lyke ane lyone lowsit of his caige,
Out throuch this realme I gan to reil and rage!

23

Contrare the governour and his companie,   155
Oft tymes maid I insurrextioun,
Purposyng for tyll have hym haistelie
Subdewit on to my correctioun,
Or put hym tyll extreme subjectioun.
Duryng this tyme, geve it war weill dissydit,   160
This realme by me was uterlie devydit.

---

134 *abak*: backwards 135 *caste*: thrown
136 *prydefull*: arrogant; *dant*: chastise
137 *Devysit*: Designed; *heych divinitie*:
    God
140 *law*: humble
141 *meine*: intervening; *subjectit*:
    subjugated
143 *contractit*: established formally
144 *band*: bond
145 *promeist*: promised; *divers*: various;

   pleagis: pledges
148 *capytanis*: captains; *waird*: custody
150 *Rewlaris*: Rulers
151 *chapit*: escaped
153 *lyone*: lion; *lowsit*: set free
154 *gan*: began; *reil*: run riot
157 *Purposyng*: Intending
158 *Subdewit*: Subdued
160 *weill dissydit*: properly decided
161 *uterlie*: completely; *devydit*: divided

24

The governour purposyng to subdew,
I rasit ane oyste of mony bald baroun
And maid ane raid quhilk Lythgow yit may rew,
For we distroyit ane myle about the town.   165
For that I gat mony blak malysoun!
Yit, contrare the governouris intent,
With our young princes we to Stervilyng went.

25

For heygh contemptioun of the governour,
I brocht the Erle of Lennox furth of France.   170
That lustie lord, levand in gret plesour,
Did loce that land and honest ordinance.
Bot he and I fell soune at variance
And, throch my counsall, was within schort space
Forfaltit and flemit. He gat none uther grace.   175

26

Than, throuch my prudens, pratyke and ingyne,
Our governour I causit to consent
Full quyetlie to my counsale inclyne.
Quhareof his nobyllis war nocht weill content.
For quhy? I gart dissolve, in plane parliament,   180
The band of peace contractit with Ingland,
Quharthroch com harme and heirschip to Scotland.

27

That peace brokin, arrose new mortall weris:
Be sey and land sic reif without releif!
Quhilk to report my frayit hart afferis.   185
The veritie to schaw, in termes breif,
I was the rute of all that gret myscheif.
The south countre may saye it had bene gude
That my noryce had smorde me in my cude!

163 *rasit*: gathered; *oyste*: armed
    company   164 *rew*: regret
166 *gat*: was given; *malysoun*: curses
168 *Stervilyng*: Stirling
169 *heygh*: extreme; *contemptioun*:
    contempt
171 *levand*: living
172 *did loce*: was deprived of
173 *soune*: soon
175 *Forfaltit*: forfeited; *flemit*: exiled
176 *prudens*: practical wisdom; *pratyke*:
    skilled dealing; *ingyne*: cleverness
178 *quyetlie*: privately; *inclyne*: yield
180 *gart dissolve*: caused to be annulled
182 *Quharthroch*: With the result that
183 *weris*: wars
184 *Be*: By; *reif*: robbery
185 *frayit*: frightened; *afferis*: is proper
187 *rute*: instigator
189 *noryce*: wet-nurse; *smorde*:
    suffocated; *cude*: chrism cloth

28

I wes the cause of mekle more myschance,   190
For uphald of my glore and dignitie
And plesour of the potent kyng of France.
With Ingland wald I have no unitie.
Bot quho consydder wald the veritie,
We mycht full weill have levit in peace and rest   195
Nyne or ten yeris, and than playit lowis or fast,

29

Had we with Ingland kepit our contrackis.
Our nobyll men had levit in peace and rest,
Our marchandis had nocht lost so mony packis,
Our commoun peple had nocht bene opprest;   200
On ather syde all wrangis had bene redrest.
Bot Edinburgh, sen syne, Leith and Kyngorne,
The day and hour may ban that I was borne.

30

Our governour, to mak hym to me sure,
With sweit and subtell wordis I did him syle,   205
Tyll I his sone and air gat in my cure.
To that effect I fand that crafty wyle
That he no maner of waye mycht me begyle.
Than leuch I quhen his liegis did allege
Quhow I his sone had gottin in to plege!   210

31

The Erle of Angus and his germane brother,
I purposit to gar thame lose thare lyfe.
Rycht so, tyll have distroyit mony uther
(Sum with the fyre, sum with the sword and knyfe),
In speciale, mony gentyll men of Fyfe,   215
And purposit tyll put to gret torment
All favoraris of the Auld and New Testament.

---

190 *mekle*: much; *myschance*: disaster
191 *uphald*: maintaining; *glore*: glory
192 *potent*: powerful
195 *levit*: lived
196 *than*: then; *playit...fast*: practised double dealing
199 *marchandis*: merchants; *packis*: packs of merchandise
200 *commoun peple*: community
201 *ather*: either

202 *sen syne*: since then; *Kyngorne*: Kinghorn
203 *ban*: curse   204 *sure*: loyal
205 *sweit*: sweet; *syle*: beguile
206 *air*: heir; *cure*: care
207 *fand*: devised
209 *leuch*: laughed; *liegis*: loyal subjects
210 *plege*: custody [as hostage]
211 *germane*: own
215 *speciale*: specifically; *Fyfe*: Fife
217 *favoraris*: supporters

32

Than every freik that tuke of me sic feir,
That tyme quhen I had so gret governans,
Gret lordis dreidyng I sulde do thame deir,   220
Thay durst nocht cum tyll court but assurans.
Sen syne thair hes nocht bene sic varians:
Now, tyll our prince, barronis obedientlie,
But assurance, thay cum full courteslie.

33

My hope was moste in to the kyng of France   225
(To gyddir with the Popis holynes)
More nor in God, my worschipe tyll avance.
I traistit so in to thare gentylnes
That no man durste presome me tyll oppres.
Bot quhen the day come of my faitell houre,   230
Far was frome me thare supporte and succoure!

34

Than, to preserve my ryches and my lyfe,
I maid one strynth of wallis heych and braid
(Sic ane fortres wes never found in Fyfe!),
Belevand thare durst no man me invaid.   235
Now fynd I trew the saw quhilk David said:
"Without God of ane hous be maister of wark,
He wyrkis in vaine, thocht it be never so stark."

35

For I was, throuch the hie power divine,
Rycht dulefulliye doung down amang the asse,   240
Quhilk culd not be throch mortal mannis ingyne,
Bot, as David did slay the gret Gollyasse,
Or Holopharne, be Judeth keillit wasse,

218 *freik*: man; *feir*: fear
219 *governans*: power to rule
220 *dreidyng*: apprehensive; *deir*: harm
221 *but assurans*: without a guarantee of safety   222 *varians*: instability
224 *courteslie*: courteously
226 *To gyddir*: Together
227 *nor*: than; *worschipe*: honour
228 *traistit*: trusted; *gentylnes*: [high] birth
229 *durste*: dared; *presome*: be so presumptuous as
230 *faitell houre*: time of death

233 *maid...strynth*: built a fortified place; *wallis*: walls; *braid*: broad
235 *invaid*: attack
236 *saw*: sententious saying
237 *maister of wark*: master of building operations
238 *stark*: strong
240 *doung*: beaten; *asse*: ashes
241 *ingyne*: contrivance
242 *Gollyasse*: Goliath
243 *Holopharne*: Holofernes; *Judeth*: Judith

In myd amang his tryumphant armye,
So was I slane, in to my cheiff cietie. 245

36

Quhen I had gretest dominatioun,
As Lucifer had in the hevin impyre,
Came suddantlyie my depryvatioun
Be thame quhilk did my dolent deith conspyre.
So creuell was thare furious byrnand yre, 250
I gat no tyme, layser, nor lybertie,
To saye, "*In manus Tuas, Domine*".

37

Behald my faitell infylicitie.
I beand in my strenth incomparabyll,
That dreidfull dungioun maid me no supple. 255
My gret ryches, nor rentis proffitabyll,
My sylver work, jowellis inestimabyll,
My papall pompe, of gold my ryche threasure,
My lyfe and all, I loste in half ane hour.

38

To the peple wes maid ane spectakle 260
Of my dede and deformit carioun.
Sum said it wes ane manifest myrakle,
Sum said it was divine punitioun
So to be slane, in to my strang dungeoun.
Quhen every man had jugit as hym lyste, 265
Thay saltit me, syne cloist me in ane kyste.

39

I laye unburyit—sevin monethtis and more
Or I was borne to closter, kirk, or queir!—
In ane mydding, quhilk paine bene tyll deplore,
Without suffrage of chanoun, monk, or freir. 270
All proude prelatis at me may lessonis leir,

247 *hevin impyre*: highest heaven
248 *depryvatioun*: deposition
251 *layser*: opportunity
252 *In...Domine*: 'Into Thy hands, O
　　Lord'　253 *infylicitie*: ill-fortune
254 *beand*: being
255 *dreidfull*: fear inspiring; *dungioun*:
　　castle keep; *supple*: assistance
257 *jowellis*: jewels
261 *dede*: dead; *deformit*: disfigured;
　　carioun: corpse

265 *jugit*: judged; *lyste*: pleased
266 *saltit*: preserved...in salt; *cloist*:
　　enclosed; *kyste*: chest
267 *unburyit*: unburied
268 *Or*: Before; *closter*: cloister; *queir*:
　　chancel
269 *myddyng*: midden; *quhilk...bene*:
　　which it is painful
270 *suffrage*: intercessory prayer;
　　chanoun: canon; *freir*: friar

Quhilk rang so lang and so tryumphantlie,
Syne in the dust doung doun so dulefullie.

To the Prelatis.
40

O ye my brether prencis of the preistis
I mak yow hartly supplycatioun: 275
Boith nycht and day revolfe in to your breistis
The proces of my deprivatioun.
Consydder quhat bene your vocatioun.
To follow me I pray yow nocht pretend yow,
Bot reid at lenth this sedull that I send yow.   280

41

Ye knaw quhow Jesu his disciplis sent,
Ambassaldouris, tyll every natioun,
To schaw his law and his commandiment
To all peple, by predycatioun.
Tharefor I mak to yow narratioun: 285
Sen ye to thame ar verray successouris,
Ye aucht tyll do as did your predicessouris.

42

Quhow dar ye be so bauld tyll tak on hand
For to be herraldis to so gret one kyng,
To beir his message boith to burgh and land,   290
Ye beand dum and can pronunce no thyng!
Lyke menstralis that can nocht play nor sing!
Or quhy suld men geve to sic hirdis hyre
Quhilk can not gyde thare scheip about the myre?

43
                                                             295
Schame ye nocht to be Christis servaturis
And for your fee hes gret temporall landis,
Syne of your office can nocht take the curis,
As cannone law and scripture yow commandis?
Ye wyll not want teind cheif, nor offrandis,

272 *rang*: wielded power
275 *hartly*: sincere
276 *breistis*: breasts [as seats of thought]
278 *bene*: is   280 *sedull*: document
284 *be predycatioun*: by public
    preaching   286 *verray*: true
288 *bauld*: bold   289 *herraldis*: heralds

293 *hirdis*: shepherds; *hyre*: employment
294 *about*: around; *myre*: mire
295 *servaturis*: servants
297 *curis*: spiritual charge
298 *cannone*: ecclesiastical
299 *want*: lack; *teind*: tithe; *cheif*:
    principal; *offrandis*: church dues

Teinde woll, teind lambe, teind calf, teind gryce and guse: 300
To mak servyce ye ar all out of use.

44

My deir brether, do nocht as ye war wount.
Amend your lyfe now, quhill your day induris.
Traist weill, ye sall be callit to your count
Of everilk thyng belanging to your curis.   305
Leif hasarttrie, your harlottrie and huris,
Remembring on my unprovisit dede;
For efter deith may no man mak remede.

45

Ye prelatis, quhilkis hes thousandis for to spende,
Ye send ane sempyll freir for yow to preche.   310
It is your craft, I mak it to yow kend,
Your selfis, in your templis, for to teche.
Bot farlye nocht, thocht syllie freris fleche,
For and thay planelie schaw the veritie,
Than wyll thay want the byschoppis charitie.   315

46

Quharefore bene gevin yow sic royall rent,
Bot for tyll fynd the peple spirituall fude,
Prechand to thame the Auld and New Testament?
The law of God doith planelye so conclude.
Put nocht your hope in to no wardly gude,   320
As I have done. Behauld, my gret threasoure
Maid me no helpe at my unhappye houre.

47

That day quhen I was byschope consecrat,
The gret Byble wes bound apon my bak.
Quhat wes tharein lytill I knew, God wat,   325
More than ane beist berand ane precious pak.
Bot haistelie my convenent I brak,

---

300 *woll*: wool; *gryce*: young pig; *guse*:
  goose   301 *mak*: provide
302 *wount*: accustomed [to do]
303 *quhill...induris*: while you are alive
304 *count*: account [before God]
306 *Leif*: Leave; *hasarttrie*: playing at
  dice; *harlottrie*: loose living; *huris*:
  whores
307 *unprovisit*: [spiritually] unprepared
  for; *dede*: death

308 *mak remede*: save his soul
310 *sempyll*: lowly
313 *farlye*: wonder; *thocht*: though;
  syllie: innocent; *fleche*: flatter
314 *For and*: Because if
323 *consecrat*: consecrated
326 *berand*: bearing
327 *convenent*: covenant

For I wes oblyste, with my awin consent,
The law of God to preche with gude intent.

48

Brether, rycht so quhen ye wer consecrat,   330
Ye oblyste yow all on the sammyn wyse.
Ye may be callit byschoppis countrafait,
As gallandis buskit for to mak ane gyse.
Now thynk I prencis ar no thyng to pryse,
Tyll geve ane famous office tyll ane fule;   335
As quho walde putt ane myter on ane mule?

49

Allace! And ye that sorrowfull sycht hade sene
(Quhow I laye bulrand, baithit in my blude),
To mend your lyfe it had occasioun bene,
And laif your auld corruptit conswetude.   340
Failyeing thare of, than schortlie I conclude,
Without ye frome your rebaldrye arryse,
Ye sall be servit on the sammyn wyse.

To the Prencis.
50

Imprudent prencis, but discretioun,
Havyng in erth power imperiall,   345
Ye bene the cause of this transgressioun.
I speik to yow all, in to generall,
Quhilk doith dispone all office spirituall,
Gevand the saulis quhilkis bene Chrystis scheip
To blynd pastouris, but conscience, to keip.   350

51

Quhen ye, prencis, doith laik ane officiar,
Ane baxster, browster, or ane maister cuke,
Ane trym tailyeour, ane counnyng cordonar,
Ovir all the land, at lenth, ye wyll gar luke

---

328 *oblyste*: bound
331 *on the sammym wyse*: similarly
332 *countrafait*: counterfeit
333 *gallandis*: young men; *buskit*: prepared; *gyse*: masquerade
334 *pryse*: hold in high regard
336 *myter*: mitre
338 *bulrand*: with blood issuing from the body

340 *laif*: leave; *conswetude*: custom
342 Unless you rise up from your debauched conduct
344 *but*: without   346 *bene*: are
348 *dispone*: distribute
349 *Gevand*: Giving   351 *laik*: lack
352 *baxster*: baker; *browster*: brewer
353 *counnyng*: highly skilled; *cordonar*: shoemaker

Most abyll men sic officis tyll bruke: 355
Ane browster quhilk can brew moste hoilsum aill,
Ane cunnyng cuke quhilk best can cessone caill,
52
Ane tailyeour quhilk hes fosterit bene in France,
That can mak garmentis on the gayest gyse.
Ye prencis bene the cause of this myschance,   360
That quhen thare doith vaik ony benefyse,
Ye aucht tyll do apone the sammyn wyse.
Gar sears and seik, baith in to burgh and lande,
The law of God quho best can understande.
53
Mak hym byschope that prudentlie can preche,   365
As dois pertene tyll his vocatioun;
Ane persone quhilk his parisone can teche.
Gar vicaris mak dew mynistratioun.
And als, I mak yow supplycatioun,
Mak your abbotis of rycht religious men,   370
Quhilk Christis law can to thare convent ken.
54
Bot not to rebaldis, new cum frome the roste,
Nor of ane stuffat, stollin out of ane stabyll,
The quhilk in to scule maid never na coste,
Nor never was tyll spirituall science abyll   375
(Except the cartis, the dyce, the ches and tabyll),
Of Rome rakaris, nor of rude ruffianis,
Of calsay paikaris, nor of publycanis,
55
Nor to fantastyke, fenyeit flaterraris,
Most meit to gather mussillis in to Maye;   380
Of cowhubeis nor yit of clatterraris,

355 *bruke*: have
356 *hoilsum*: wholesome
357 *cessone*: season; *caill*: [cabbage, colewort] broth
358 *fosterit*: trained
359 *gyse*: fashion
361 *vaik*: fall vacant; *benefyse*: church living   363 *sears*: search; *seik*: seek
366 *pertene*: pertain
367 *persone*: parson; *parisone*: parish
371 *ken*: make known
372 *rebaldis...roste*: rascals...feast
373 *stuffat*: ?groom; *stollin*: stolen
374 *scule*: school; *maid...cost*: incurred no cost
375 *science*: learning
376 *ches...tabyll*: chess...board games
377 *Rome rakaris*: travellers to Rome; *rude ruffianis*: ignorant rowdies
378 *calsay paikaris*: street pedlars; *publycanis*: reprobates
379 *fantastyke*: fanciful; *fenyeit*: false
380 *meit*: suitable; *mussillis*: mussels
381 *cowhubeis*: ?boobies; *clatterraris*: chatterers

That in the kirk can nother sing nor saye,
Thocht thay be clokit up in clerkis arraye,
Lyke doytit doctoris new cum out of Athenis
And mummyll over ane pair of maglit matenis.   385

56

Nocht qualyfeit to bruke ane benefyse,
Bot throuch schir Symonis solystatioun,
I was promovit on the sammyn wyse,
Allace, throuch prencis supplycatioun,
And maid in Rome, throuch fals narratioun,   390
Byschope, abbote, bot no religious man.
Quho me promovit, I now thare banis ban!

57

Quhowbeit I was legat and cardinall,
Lytill I knew tharein quhat sulde be done.
I understude no science spirituall   395
No more than did blynd Alane of the mone.
I dreid the kyng that syttith heych abone
On yow, prencis, sall mak sore punischement,
Rycht so, on us, throuch rychteous jugement;

58

On yow, prencis, for undescreit gevying   400
Tyll ignorantis, sic officis tyll use;
And we, for our inoportune askyng,
Quhilk sulde have done sic dignitie refuse.
Our ignorance hes done the warld abuse,
Throuch covatyce of ryches and of rent.   405
That ever I was ane prelate I repent.

59

O kyngis, mak ye no cair to geve in cure,
Virginis profest in to religioun,
In tyll the kepyng of ane commoun hure?
To mak—thynk ye nocht gret diresioun?—   410
Ane woman persone of ane parisoun

---

383 *clokit up*: disguised
384 *doytit*: stupid; *mummyll*: mumble;
  maglit: mangled; *matenis*: matins
386 *qualyfeit*: competent; *bruke*: enjoy
  the use of
387 *Symonis*: Simon's; *solystatioun*:
  petition 392 *banis*: bones; *ban*: curse
396 *blynd Alane*: blind Alan; *mone*: moon

397 *abone*: above   398 *sore*: painful
399 *rychteous*: just
400 *undescreit*: injudicious
401 *ignorantis*: ignorant people
402 *inoportune*: untimely
407 *mak...cair*: have you no concern?
410 *diresioun*: scorn 411 *parisoun*: parish

Quhare thare bene two thousand saulis to gyde,
That frome harlots can not hir hyppis hyde.

60

Quhat and Kyng David levit in thir dayis?
Or out of hevin quhat and he lukit down,   415
The quhilk did found so mony fair abbayis?
Seand the gret abhominatioun
In mony abayis of this natioun,
He wald repent that narrowit so his boundis
Of yeirly rent thre score of thousand poundis.   420

61

Quharefor I counsale everyilk christinit kyng
With in his realme mak reformatioun,
And suffer no mo rebaldis for to ryng
Abufe Christis trew congregatioun.
Failyeyng thareof, I mak narratioun   425
That ye prencis and prelatis, all at onis,
Sall bureit be in hell—saule, blude, and bonis!

62

That ever I brukit benefice I rew,
Or to sic hycht so proudely did pretend.
I man depart; tharefor, my freinds, adew.   430
Quhare ever it plesith God, now man I wend.
I praye the tyll my freindis me recommend,
And failye nocht at lenth to put in wryte
My tragedie, as I have done indyte.'

414 *Quhat and*: What if; *levit*: lived; *thir*: these
419 *narrowit*: reduced; *boundis*: boundaries
421 *christinit*: Christian
422 *reformatioun*: improvement, correction
424 *congregatioun*: Christian community
428 *brukit*: possessed
429 *pretend*: aspire
430 *man*: must
434 *done indyte*: put into words

SQUYER MELDRUM

Quho that antique stories reidis,
Considder may the famous deidis
Of our nobill progenitouris,
Quhilk suld to us be richt mirrouris,
Thair verteous deidis to ensew   5
And vicious leving to eschew.
Sic men bene put in memorie
That deith suld not confound thair glorie;
Howbeit thair bodie bene absent,
Thair verteous deidis bene present.   10
Poetis, thair honour to avance,
Hes put thame in rememberance.
Sum wryt of preclair conquerouris,
And sum of vailyeand empriouris,
And sum of nobill michtie kingis   15
That royallie did reull thair ringis;
And sum of campiounis and of knichtis
That bauldlie did defend thair richtis,
Quhilk vailyeandlie did stand in stour   20
For the defence of thair honour.
And sum, of squyeris douchtie deidis,
That wounders wrocht in weirlie weidis.
Sum wryt of deidis amorous,
As Chauceir wrait of Troilus
(How that he luiffit Cressida),   25
Of Jason and of Medea.
With help of Cleo, I intend,
Sa Minerve wald me sapience send,
Ane nobill squyer to discryfe,
Quhais douchtines during his lyfe   30
I knaw my self. Thairof I wryte,

---

1 *antique*: old
3 *progenitouris*: ancestors
5 *verteous*: virtuous; *ensew*: follow
6 *vicious*: wicked; *leving*: living
7 *Sic*: Such; *bene*: are
9 *Howbeit*: Although
11 *avance*: raise in repute
12 *put...rememberance*: commemorated
13 *preclair*: renowned
16 *ringis*: realms

17 *campiounis*: champions
18 *bauldlie*: boldly; *richtis*: rights
19 *stour*: battle
21 *douchtie*: courageously performed
22 *weirlie weidis*: armour
24 *wrait*: wrote
25 *luiffit*: loved   27 *Cleo*: Clio
28 *Sa*: If; *Minerve*: Minerva
29 *Ane*: A   30 *Quhais*: Whose

And all his deidis I dar indyte.
And secreitis that I did not knaw,
That nobill squyer did me schaw.
Sa I intend, the best I can,   35
Descryve the deidis and the man,
Quhais youth did occupie in lufe
Full plesantlie, without reprufe;
Quhilk did as monie douchtie deidis
As monie ane that men of reidis   40
Quhilkis poetis puttis in memorie
For the exalting of thair glorie.
Quhairfoir, I think, sa God me saif,
He suld have place amangis the laif,
That his hie honour suld not smure,   45
Considering quhat he did indure
Oft times for his ladeis sake.
I wait Sir Lancelote du Lake,
Quhen he did lufe king Arthuris wyfe,
Faucht never better with sword nor knyfe   50
For his ladie in no battell!
Nor had not half so just querrell.
The veritie, quha list declair,
His lufe was ane adulterair
And durst not cum into hir sicht   55
Bot lyke ane houlet on the nicht.
With this squyer it stude not so:
His ladie luifit him and no mo.
Husband nor lemman had scho none,
And so he had hir lufe alone.   60
I think it is no happie lyfe,
Ane man to jaip his maisteris wyfe,
As did Lancelote. This I conclude:
Of sic amour culd cum na gude.

---

32 *dar*: venture [to]; *indyte*: put into
  words   35 *Sa*: Thus
39 *Quhilk*: Who
40 *mony ane*: many [a] one
44 *amangis...laif*: among the rest
45 *smure*: be smothered
48 *wait*: know
50 *Faucht*: Fought
52 *querrell*: cause

53 *quha...declair*: who wishes [to] state
  openly
54 *adulterair*: adulteress
55 *And durst*: And [he] dare
56 *houlet*: owl
57 *stude...so*: circumstances were
  different   58 *mo*: more
59 *lemman*: lover   60 *hir*: her
62 *jaip*: seduce

Now to my purpois will I pas 65
And shaw yow how the squyer was
Ane gentilman of Scotland borne;
So was his father him beforne,
Of nobilnes lineallie discendit,
Quhilks thair gude fame hes ever defendit. 70
Gude Williame Meldrum he was namit,
Quhilk in his honour was never defamit.
Stalwart and stout in everie stryfe,
And borne within the schyre of Fyfe.
To Cleische and Bynnis richt heritour, 75
Quhilk stude for lufe in monie stour.
He was bot twentie yeiris of age
Quhen he began his vassalage.
Proportionat weill, of mid stature,
Feirie and wicht and micht indure. 80
Ovirset with travell both nicht and day;
Richt hardie, baith in ernist and play.
Blyith in countenance, richt fair of face,
And stude weill ay in his ladies grace,
For he was wounder amiabill 85
And in all deidis honorabill.
And ay his honour did avance
In Ingland, first, and syne in France
And thair his manheid did assaill,
Under the kingis greit admirall, 90
Quhen the greit navie of Scotland
Passit to the sey aganis Ingland.
And as thay passit be Ireland coist,
The admirall gart land his oist
And set Craigfergus into fyre 95
And saifit nouther barne nor byre.
It was greit pietie for to heir

73 *stout*: resolute   74 *schyre*: shire
75 *richt*: legally proper
78 *vassalage*: acts of prowess in battle
79 *weill*: well
80 *Feirie*: Vigorous; *wicht*: strong
81 *Ovirset with*: Pressed hard by;
   travell: labour
84 *stude*: stood; *grace*: favour
85 *wounder*: very

87 *avance*: raise in repute
88 *syne*: then
89 *manheid*: manliness; *assaill*: test
93 *be*: by; *coist*: coast
94 *gart...oist*: had his forces land
95 *Craigfergus*: Carrickfergus
96 *saifit*: saved; *nouther*: neither; *barne*:
   barn; *byre*: cow-house
97 *pietie*: cause for pity

Of the pepill the bailfull cheir,
And how the land folk wer spuilyeit:
Fair wemen under fute wer fuilyeit.   100
Bot this young squyer, bauld and wicht,
Savit all wemen quhair he micht;
All preistis and freiris he did save,
Till, at the last, he did persave,
Behind ane garding amiabill,   105
Ane womanis voce, richt lamentabill.
And on that voce he followit fast,
Till he did see hir, at the last.
Spuilyeit, naikit as scho was borne,
Twa men of weir wer hir beforne,   110
Quhilk wer richt cruell men and kene,
Partand the spuilyie thame betwene.
Ane fairer woman nor scho wes
He had not sene in onie place.
Befoir him, on hir kneis scho fell,   115
Sayand, 'For him that heryit Hell,
Help me, sweit sir! I am ane mayd'.
Than softlie to the men he said,
'I pray yow, give againe hir sark,
And tak to yow all uther wark'.   120
Hir kirtill was of scarlot reid,
Of gold ane garland on hir heid,
Decorit with enamelyne.
Belt and brochis of silver fyne;
Of yallow taftais wes hir sark,   125
Begaryit all with browderit wark
Richt craftelie, with gold and silk.

98 *bailfull*: wretched; *cheir*: grieving
99 *land folk*: country people; *spuilyeit*: robbed
100 *fuilyeit*: overcome
101 *bauld*: bold
102 *quhair*: where   103 *freiris*: friars
104 *persave*: become aware of
105 *garding*: garden; *amiabill*: attractive
106 *voce*: voice; *lamentabill*: full of sorrow
110 *men of weir*: soldiers; *beforne*: before
112 *Partand*: Parting; *spuilyie*: plunder

113 *nor*: than; *wes*: was
114 *onie*: any
116 *heryit*: harried   117 *mayd*: virgin
119 *sark*: chemise
120 And give up all your other work
121 *kirtill*: kirtle; *scarlot reid*: red scarlet   122 *heid*: head
123 *Decorit*: Adorned; *enamelyne*: enamelling   124 *brochis*: buckles
125 *yallow*: yellow; *taftais*: taffeta
126 *Begaryit*: Trimmed; *browderit*: embroidered
127 *craftelie*: skilfully

Than said the ladie, quhyte as milk,
'Except my sark, no thing I crave.
Let thame go hence, with all the lave.'   130
Quod thay to hir, 'Be Sanct Fillane,
Of this ye get nathing agane!'
Than said the squyer, courteslie,
'Gude freindis, I pray yow hartfullie,
Gif ye be worthie men of weir,   135
Restoir to hir agane hir geir,
Or, be greit God that all hes wrocht,
That spuilyie salbe full deir bocht'.
Quod thay to him, 'We the defy!'
And drew thair swordis haistely,   140
And straik at him with sa greit ire
That from his harnes flew the fyre,
With duntis sa darflie on him dang
That he was never in sic ane thrang.
Bot he him manfullie defendit,   145
And with ane bolt, on thame he bendit,
And hat the ane upon the heid
That to the ground he fell doun deid,
For to the teith he did him cleif.
Lat him ly thair, with ane mischeif.   150
Than, with the uther, hand for hand,
He beit him with his birneist brand.
The uther was baith stout and strang
And on the squyer darflie dang.
And than the squyer wrocht greit wonder,   155
Ay till his sword did shaik in sunder.
Than drew he furth ane sharp dagair,
And did him cleik be the collair

---

128 *quhyte*: white
129 *crave*: ask for   130 *lave*: rest
131 *Quod*: Said; *Be Sanct Fillane*: By
    Saint Fillan
133 *courteslie*: courteously
134 *hartfullie*: sincerely   135 *Gif*: If
136 *geir*: personal possessions
137 *wrocht*: wrought
138 *deir bocht*: bought with suffering
141 *straik*: struck; *sa*: such
142 *harnes*: defensive armour
143 *duntis*: heavy blows; *sa*: so; *darflie*:
    boldly; *dang*: beat

144 *thrang*: danger
146 *bolt*: sudden spring; *bendit*: leaped
147 *hat*: struck
149 *teith*: teeth; *cleif*: cleave
150 *with...mischeif*: brought to grief
151 *for*: to
152 *beit*: struck; *birneist brand*:
    burnished sword
156 *Ay till*: Ever until; *shaik in sunder*:
    break in pieces
157 *dagair*: dagger
158 *cleik...collar*: catch by the gorget

And evin in at the collerbane.
At the first straik he hes him slane! 160
He founderit fordward to the ground,
Yit was the squyer haill and sound.
For quhy? He was sa weill enarmit
He did escaip fra thame unharmit.
And quhen he saw thay wer baith slane, 165
He to that ladie past agane,
Quhair scho stude nakit on the bent,
And said, 'Tak your abulyement.'
And scho him thankit, full humillie,
And put hir claithis on spedilie. 170
Than kissit he that ladie fair
And tuik his leif at hir but mair.
Be that, the taburne and trumpet blew,
And everie man to shipburd drew.
That ladie was dolent in hart, 175
From tyme scho saw he wald depart
That hir relevit from hir harmes,
And hint the squyer in hir armes,
And said, 'Will ye byde in this land,
I sall yow tak to my husband. 180
Thocht I be cassin now in cair,
I am', quod scho, 'my fatheris air,
The quhilk may spend, of pennies round,
Of yeirlie rent ane thowsand pound.'
With that, hartlie scho did him kis. 185
'Ar ye', quod scho, 'content of this?'
'Of that', quod he, 'I wald be fane,
Gif I micht in this realme remane,
Bot I mon first pas into France.
Sa, quhen I cum agane, perchance, 190
And efter that the peice be maid,

159 *evin*: straight; *coller-
    bane*: collar bone 160 *straik*: blow
161 *founderit*: stumbled
163 *enarmit*: armed   164 *fra*: from
167 *bent*: open ground, coarsely grassed
168 *abulyement*: clothing
169 *humillie*: humbly
172 *but mair*: without delay

173 *Be that*: By that [time]; *taburne*:
    tabor [drum]   175 *dolent*: sad
177 *relevit*: rescued; *harmes*: distress
178 *hint*: clasped
179 *Will ye*: If you will; *byde*: remain
181 *cassin...in cair*: brought...to distress
182 *air*: heir
185 *hartlie*: sincerely
187 *fane*: well pleased

To marie yow I will be glaid.
Fair weill, I may no langer tarie,
I pray God keip yow, and sweit Sanct Marie.'
Than gaif scho him ane lufe taking,   195
Ane riche rubie, set in ane ring.
'I am', quod scho, 'at your command,
With yow to pas into Scotland.'
'I thank yow hartfullie', quod he.
'Ye ar ovir young to saill the see,   200
And speciallie with men of weir.'
'Of that', quod scho, 'tak ye na feir;
I sall me cleith in mennis clais,
And ga with yow quhair evir ye pleis.
Suld I not lufe him paramour,   205
That saifit my lyfe and my honour?'
'Ladie, I say yow in certane,
Ye sall have lufe for lufe agane,
Trewlie, unto my lyfis end.
Fair weill, to God I yow commend.'   210
With that, into his boit he past,
And to the ship he rowit fast.
Thay weyit thair ankeris and maid saill,
This navie with the admirall,
And landit in bauld Brytane.   215
This admirall was Erle of Arrane,
Quhilk was baith wyse and vailyeand,
Of the blude royall of Scotland,
Accompanyit with monie ane knicht,
Quhilk wer richt worthie men and wicht.   220
Amang the laif this young squyar
Was with him richt familiar.
And throw his verteous diligence,
Of that lord he gat sic credence,
That quhen he did his courage ken,   225
Gaif him cure of fyve hundreth men,
Quhilkis wer to him obedient,

195 *lufe taking*: love token
202 *tak...na feir*: don't be afraid
203 *cleith*: dress
205 *paramour*: as a lover
211 *boit*: boat   213 *maid saill*: set sail

215 *Brytane*: Brittany
222 *familiar*: closely associated
223 *verteous*: virtuous
224 *gat...credence*: obtained...standing
225 *ken*: know   226 *cure*: charge

Reddie at his commandement.
It wer to lang for to declair
The douchtie deidis that he did thair.   230
Becaus he was sa courageous,
Ladies of him wes amorous.
He was ane munyeoun for ane dame,
Meik in chalmer, lyk ane lame,
Bot in the feild, ane campioun,   235
Rampand lyke ane wyld lyoun.
Weill practikit with speir and scheild,
And with the formest in the feild.
No chiftane was amangis thame all
In expensis mair liberall.   240
In everilk play he wan the pryse;
With that, he was verteous and wyse.
And so, becaus he was weill pruifit,
With everie man he was weill luifit.

Hary the aucht, king of Ingland,   245
That tyme at Caleis wes lyand
With his triumphant ordinance,
Makand weir on the realme of France.
The king of France his greit armie
Lay neir hand by, in Picardie,   250
Quhair aither uther did assaill.
Howbeit thair was na set battaill,
Bot thair wes daylie skirmishing,
Quhair men of armis brak monie sting.
Quhen to the squyer Meldrum   255
Wer tauld thir novellis, all and sum,
He thocht he wald vesie the weiris,
And waillit furth ane hundreth speiris
And futemen quhilk wer bauld and stout,

233 *munyeoun*: lover; *dame*: lady
234 *chalmer*: bedroom; *lame*: lamb
236 *Rampand*: Rearing
238 *formest*: foremost
241 *wan...pryse*: was pre-eminent
243 *pruifit*: tried   244 *luifit*: loved
245 *Hary the aucht*: Henry VIII
246 *Caleis*: Calais; *lyand*: at anchor
247 *triumphant*: splendid; *ordinance*: military force

248 *weir*: war
251 *aither uther*: each other
252 *set*: fixed [as to day and place]
254 *brak...sting*: broke...pikeshafts
256 *thir*: these; *novellis*: recent events
257 *vesie*: see; *weiris*: wars
258 *waillit*: chose; *speiris*: lances
259 *futemen*: foot-soldiers

The maist worthie of all his rout.   260
   Quhen he come to the king of France,
He wes sone put in ordinance.
Richt so was all his companie,
That on him waitit continuallie.
Thair was into the Inglis oist   265
Ane campioun, that blew greit boist.
He was ane stout man, and ane strang,
Quhilk oist wald, with his conduct, gang
Outthrow the greit armie of France,
His valiantnes for to avance.   270
And maister Talbart was his name,
Of Scottis and Frenche quhilk spak disdane.
And on his bonnet usit to beir,
Of silver fyne, takinnis of weir.
And proclamatiounis he gart mak,   275
That he wald, for his ladies saik,
With any gentilman of France
To fecht with him, with speir or lance.
Bot no Frenche man in all that land
With him durst battell, hand for hand.   280
Than lyke ane weiriour vailyeand,
He enterit in the Scottis band,
And quhen the squyer Meldrum
Hard tell this campioun wes cum,
Richt haistelie he past him till,   285
Demanding him quhat was his will.
'Forsuith, I can find none', quod he,
'On hors, nor fute, dar fecht with me.'
'Than', said he, 'it wer greit schame
Without battell ye suld pas hame.   290
Thairfoir, to God I mak ane vow:
The morne, my self sall fecht with yow,
Outher on horsbak or on fute;

260 *rout*: contingent
262 *sone*: soon; *put...ordinance*:
    assigned to a military post
264 *waitit*: attended
266 *blew...boist*: spread...threats
268 *conduct*: leadership
269 *Outthrow*: Right through

273 *bonnet*: cap   274 *takinnis*: tokens
278 *fecht*: fight
280 *hand for hand*: one to one
282 *band*: company
284 *Hard tell*: Heard [it] said
285 *till*: to   292 *The morne*: Tomorrow
293 *Outher*: Either

Your crakkis I count thame not ane cute.
I sall be fund into the feild,
Armit on hors, with speir and scheild.'   295
Maister Talbart said, 'My gude chyld,
It wer maist lyk that thow wer wyld.
Thow ar to young, and hes no micht
To fecht with me, that is so wicht.   300
To speik to me thow suld have feir,
For I have sic practik in weir
That I wald not effeirit be
To mak debait aganis sic thre!
For I have stand in monie stour,   305
And ay defendit my honour.
Thairfoir, my barne, I counsell the,
Sic interprysis to let be.'
Than said this squyer to the knicht,
'I grant ye ar baith greit and wicht.   310
Young David was far les than I,
Quhen he, with Golias, manfullie,
Withouttin outher speir or scheild,
He faucht and slew him in the feild.
I traist that God salbe my gyde   315
And give me grace to stanche thy pryde.
Thocht thow be greit, like Gowmakmorne,
Traist weill, I sall yow meit the morne,
Beside Montruill, upon the grene.
Befoir ten houris I salbe sene.   320
And gif ye wyn me in the feild,
Baith hors and geir I sall yow yeild,
Sa that siclyke ye do to me.'
'That I sall do, be God,' quod he.
'And thairto I give the my hand.'   325
And swa betwene thame maid an band
That thay suld meit upon the morne.
Bot Talbart maid at him bot scorne,

---

294 *crakkis*: loud words; *cute*: jot
295 *fund*: found; *feild*: place of battle
297 *chyld*: lad [derog.]
299 *to*: too; *micht*: strength
302 *practik*: experience
303 *effeirit*: frightened 307 *barne*: child
308 *interprysis*: undertakings

312 *Golias*: Goliath
316 *stanche*: extinguish
317 *Gowmakmorne*: Goll Mac Morna
319 *Montruill*: Montreuil; *grene*: field
of combat   321 *wyn*: defeat
323 *Sa*: Provided; *siclyke*: the same
326 *band*: compact

Lychtlyand him with wordis of pryde,
Syne hamewart to his oist culd ryde,   330
And shew the brethren of his land
How ane young Scot had tane on hand
To fecht with him beside Montruill.
'Bot I traist he sall prufe the fuill!'
Quod thay, 'The morne that sall we ken;   335
The Scottis ar haldin hardie men.'
Quod he, 'I compt thame not ane cute!
He sall returne upon his fute,
And leif with me his armour bricht,
For weill I wait he hes no micht   340
On hors nor fute to fecht with me!'
Quod thay, 'The morne that sall we se.'
Quhan, to Monsour de Obenie,
Reportit was the veritie
(How that the squyer had tane on hand   345
To fecht with Talbart, hand for hand),
His greit courage he did commend,
Sine haistelie did for him send.
And quhen he come befoir the lord,
The veritie he did record: 350
How, for the honour of Scotland,
That battell he had tane on hand.
'And sen it givis me in my hart
(Get I ane hors to tak my part),
My traist is sa in Goddis grace   355
To leif him lyand in the place.
Howbeit he stalwart be and stout,
My lord, of him I have no dout.'
Than send the lord out throw the land
And gat ane hundreth hors fra hand.   360
To his presence he brocht in haist
And bad the squyer cheis him the best.
Of that the squyer was rejoisit

329 *Lychtlyand*: Disparaging   353 And since I desire it from the heart
332 *tane*: taken   335 *ken*: know 354 *Get*: [If I] get
336 *haldin*: regarded as   355 *traist*: trust; *sa*: therefore
337 *compt...cute*: count...not a jot   358 *of him*: of [defeating] him
343 *Monsour de Obenie*: Monsieur   359 *send*: sent
     d'Aubigny   360 *gat*: obtained; *fra hand*: forthwith
348 *haistelie*: speedily   362 *cheis*: choose

And cheisit the best, as he suppoisit,
And lap on him delyverlie:
Was never hors ran mair plesantlie, 365
With speir and sword at his command,
And was the best of all the land.
He tuik his leif and went to rest,
Syne airlie in the morne him drest, 370
Wantonlie, in his weirlyke weid,
All weill enarmit saif the heid.
He lap upon his cursour wicht
And straucht him in his stirroppis richt;
His speir and scheild and helme wes borne 375
With squyeris, that raid him beforne.
Ane velvot cap on heid he bair,
Ane quaif of gold to heild his hair.
This lord of him tuik sa greit joy
That he him self wald him convoy; 380
With him, ane hundreth men of armes,
That thair suld no man do him harmes.
The squyer buir, into his scheild,
Ane otter in ane silver feild.
His hors was bairdit full richelie, 385
Coverit with satyne cramesie.
Than fordward raid this campioun,
With sound of trumpet and clarioun.
And spedilie spurrit ovir the bent
Lyke Mars, the god armipotent. 390
Thus leif we rydand our squyar,
And speik of maister Talbart mair,
Quhilk gat up airlie in the morrow
And no maner of geir to borrow
(Hors, harnes, speir, nor scheild), 395
Bot was ay reddie for the feild.
And had sic practik into weir,

364 *suppoisit*: believed
365 *lap on*: mounted; *delyverlie*: nimbly
371 *Wantonlie*: Lightheartedly; *weirlyke
weid*: armour
373 *cursour*: large war horse
374 *straucht*: stretched
376 *raid*: rode; *beforne*: before, in front
378 *quaif*: skull cap; *heild*: cover

380 *convoy*: escort
382 *harmes*: injury
383 *buir*: bore; *into*: on
385 *bairdit*: protected by armour
386 *satyne cramesie*: crimson satin
388 *clarioun*: fanfare trumpet
390 *armipotent*: mighty in arms
392 *mair*: more

SIR DAVID LYNDSAY

Of our squyer he tuik na feir,
And said unto his companyeoun,
Or he come furth of his pavilyeoun: 400
'This nicht I saw into my dreame
(Quhilk to reheirs I think greit shame),
Me thocht I saw, cum fra the see,
Ane greit otter, rydand to me,
The quhilk was blak, with ane lang taill   405
And cruellie did me assaill,
And bait me, till he gart me bleid,
And drew me backwart fra my steid.
Quhat this suld mene I can nocht say,
Bot I was never in sic ane fray!'   410
His fellow said, 'Think ye not schame,
For to gif credence till ane dreame?
Ye knaw it is aganis our faith.
Thairfoir, go dres yow in your graith,
And think weill, throw your hie courage,   415
This day ye sall wyn vassalage.'
Than drest he him into his geir,
Wantounlie, like ane man of weir,
Quhilk had baith hardines and fors,
And lichtlie lap upon his hors.   420
His hors was bairdit full bravelie,
And coverit wes richt courtfullie
With browderit wark and velvot grene,
Sanct Georges croce thair micht be sene
On hors, harnes, and all his geir.   425
Than raid he furth withouttin weir,
Convoyit with his capitane
And with monie ane Inglisman,
Arrayit all with armes bricht.
Micht no man see ane fairer sicht!   430
    Than clariounis and trumpettis blew,
And weiriouris monie hither drew.

---

400 *Or*: Before; *of*: from; *pavilyeoun*:
    tent   402 *reheirs*: recount
407 *bait*: bit; *gart...bleid*: caused...to
    bleed
408 *steid*: horse   409 *suld*: should
410 *fray*: alarm   414 *graith*: armour
419 *hardines*: courage; *fors*: strength

420 *lichtlie*: with agility
421 *bravelie*: splendidly
422 *coverit*: covered; *courtfullie*:
    elegantly
423 *browderit wark*: embroidery
424 *croce*: cross
432 *weiriouris*: warriors

On everie side come monie man
To behald quha the battell wan.
The feild wes in the medow grene,   435
Quhair everie man micht weill be sene.
The heraldis put thame sa in ordour
That no man passit within the bordour,
Nor preissit to cum within the grene,
Bot heraldis and the campiounis kene.   440
The ordour and the circumstance
Wer lang to put in remembrance,
Quhen thir twa nobill men of weir
Wer weill accowterit in thair geir,
And in thair handis strang burdounis.   445
Than trumpotis blew and clariounis
And heraldis cryit hie on hicht,
'Now let thame go! God shaw the richt!'
Than spedilie thay spurrit thair hors,
And ran to uther with sic fors   450
That baith thair speiris in sindrie flaw.
Than said they all that stude on raw,
'Ane better cours than they twa ran
Was not sene sen the warld began!'
Than baith the parties wer rejoisit.   455
The campiounis ane quhyle repoisit,
Till thay had gottin speiris new,
Than, with triumph the trumpettis blew,
And they, with all the force thay can,
Wounder rudelie at aither ran,   460
And straik at uther with sa greit ire
That fra thair harnes flew the fyre!
Thair speiris war sa teuch and strang
That aither uther to eirth doun dang.
Baith hors and man, with speir and scheild,   465
Than flatlingis lay into the feild.
Than maister Talbart was eschamit.
'Forsuith, for ever I am defamit!'
And said this: 'I had rather die,

---

444 *accowterit*: equipped
451 *in sindrie flaw*: flew into many
    pieces
452 *stude on raw*: stood abreast

455 *wer rejoisit*: felt joy
456 *repoisit*: rested
463 *teuch*: tough
466 *flatlingis*: completely prostrate

Without that I revengit be.'   470
Our young squyer, sic was his hap,
Was first on fute, and on he lap
Upon his hors without support.
Of that the Scottis tuke gude comfort,
Quhen thay saw him, sa feirelie,   475
Loup on his hors, sa galyeardlie.
The squyer liftit his visair
Ane lytill space to take the air;
Thay bad him wyne, and he it drank,
And humillie he did thame thank.   480
Be that, Talbart on hors mountit,
And of our squyer lytill countit,
And cryit gif he durst undertak
To ryn anis for his ladies saik.
The squyer answerit hie on hicht,   485
'That sall I do, be Marie bricht.
I am content all day to ryn,
Till ane of us the honour wyn.'
Of that Talbart was weill content,
And ane greit speir in hand he hent.   490
The squyer in his hand he thrang
His speir, quhilk was baith greit and lang,
With ane sharp heid of grundin steill,
Of quhilk he was appleisit weill.
That plesand feild was lang and braid,   495
Quhair gay ordour and rowme was maid,
And everie man micht have gude sicht.
And thair was monie weirlyke knicht;
Sum man of everie natioun
Was in that congregatioun.   500
Than trumpettis blew triumphantlie,
And thay twa campiounis, egeirlie,
Thay spurrit thair hors, with speir on breist,
Pertlie to preif thair pith thay preist.

---

470 *Without that*: Unless
471 *hap*: luck   475 *feirelie*: vigorously
476 *galyeardlie*: gallantly
477 *visair*: visor   479 *bad*: bade
481 *Be that*: By that [time]
482 *countit*: regarded
484 *ryn*: ride a course; *anis*: once

486 *be Marie*: by Mary; *bricht*: bright
488 *ane*: one
490 *hent*: seized   491 *thrang*: thrust
493 *grundin*: sharpened
496 *rowme...maid*: space...cleared
504 *Pertlie*: Unflinchingly; *preif*:
     confirm; *pith*: mettle

That round rinkroume wes at utterance!　　　　　　505
Bot Talbartis hors, with ane mischance,
He outterit and to ryn was laith,
Quhairof Talbart was wonder wraith.
The squyer furth his rink he ran,
Commendit weill with everie man,　　　　　　510
And him dischargit of his speir,
Honestlie, lyke ane man of weir.
Becaus that rink thay ran in vane,
Than Talbart wald not ryn agane
Till he had gottin ane better steid,　　　　　　515
Quhilk was brocht to him with gude speid.
Quhairon he lap and tuik his speir,
As brym as he had bene ane beir!
And bowtit fordwart, with ane bend,
And ran on to the rinkis end,　　　　　　520
And saw his hors was at command;
Than wes he blyith, I understand,
Traistand na mair to ryn in vane.
Than all the trumpettis blew agane.
Be that, with all the force they can,　　　　　　525
Thay richt rudelie at uther ran.
Of that meiting ilk man thocht wounder,
Quhilk soundit lyke ane crak of thunder,
And nane of thame thair marrow mist.
Sir Talbartis speir in sunder brist,　　　　　　530
Bot the squyer, with his burdoun,
Sir Talbart to the eirth dang doun.
That straik was with sic micht and fors
That on the ground lay man and hors!
And throw the brydell-hand him bair,　　　　　　535
And in the breist, ane span and mair;
Throw curras, and throw gluifis of plait,

505 *rinkroume*: jousting space; *at*
　　utterance: [used] to the utmost
507 *outterit*: swerved aside; *laith*:
　　reluctant
508 *wraith*: angry
518 *brym*: fierce; *beir*: bear
519 *bowtit*: started; *bend*: spring
520 *ran...end*: completed the round

529 *nane*: none [neither]; *marrow*:
　　opponent
530 *in sunder brist*: broke asunder
531 *burdoun*: stout staff
535 *brydell-hand*: bridle [left] hand;
　　bair: pierced
536 *span*: [hand] span
537 *curras*: metal breastplate; *gluifis of*
　　plait: gauntlets

That Talbart micht mak na debait.
The trencheour of the squyeris speir
Stak still into Sir Talbart's geir.   540
Than everie man into that steid
Did all beleve that he was deid.
The squyer lap richt haistelie
From his cursour deliverlie
And to Sir Talbart maid support,   545
And humillie did him comfort.
Quhen Talbart saw, into his scheild,
Ane otter in an silver feild,
'This race', said he, 'I may fair rew,
For I see weill my dreame wes trew.   550
Me thocht yone otter gart me bleid
And buir me backwart from my steid,
Bot heir I vow to God soverane
That I sall never just agane.'
And sweitlie to the squyer said,   555
'Thow knawis the cunning that we maid:
Quhilk of us twa suld tyne the feild,
He suld baith hors and armour yeild
Till him that wan. Quhairfoir, I will
My hors and harnes geve the till.'   560
Than said the squyer courteouslie,
'Brother, I thank yow hartfullie.
Of yow, forsuith, nathing I crave,
For I have gottin that I wald have.'
With everie man he was commendit,   565
Sa vailyeandlie he him defendit.
The capitane of the Inglis band
Tuke the young squyer be the hand,
And led him to the pailyeoun,
And gart him mak collatioun.   570
Quhen Talbartis woundis wes bund up fast,
The Inglis capitane to him past
And prudentlie did him comfort,
Syne said, 'Brother, I yow exhort

538 *mak...debait*: not maintain combat   556 *cunning*: agreement
539 *trencheour*: cutting edge   559 *wan*: won   560 *till*: to
549 *race*: course   551 *yone*: that   570 *mak collatioun*: take refreshment
554 *just*: joust   555 *sweitlie*: graciously   571 *bund*: bound   574 *Syne*: Then

To tak the squyer be the hand.'   575
And sa he did at his command
And said, 'This bene bot chance of armes.'
With that he braisit him in his armes,
Sayand, 'Hartlie I yow forgeve.'
And than the squyer tuik his leve,   580
Commendit weill with everie man.
Than wichtlie on his hors he wan,
With monie ane nobill man convoyit.
Leve we thair Talbart, sair annoyit.
(Sum sayis, of that discomfitour,   585
He thocht sic schame and dishonour,
That he departit of that land
And never wes sene into Ingland.)
Bot our squyer did still remane,
Efter the weir, quhill peice was tane,   590
All capitanes of the kingis gairdis
Gaif to the squyer riche rewairdis
Becaus he had sa weill debaitit.
With everie nobill he wes weill traitit.
Efter the weir he tuke licence,   595
Syne did returne, with diligence,
From Pycardie to Normandie,
And thair ane space remanit he
Becaus the navie of Scotland
Wes still upon the coist lyand.   600
    Quhen he ane quhyle had sojornit,
He to the court of France returnit,
For to decore his vassalege.
From Bartanye tuke his veyage,
With aucht scoir in his companie   605
Of waillit wicht men and hardie,
Enarmit weill lyke men of weir
With hakbut, culvering, pik and speir.
And passit up throw Normandie,

---

582 *wan*: got   584 *sair*: sore
585 *discomfitour*: defeat
590 *quhill*: until; *tane*: taken
591 *gairdis*: guards 593 *debaitit*: fought
595 *tuke licence*: took leave to depart

603 *decore*: add distinction to
604 *Bartanye*: Brittany; *veyage*:
    voyage   606 *waillit*: best chosen
608 *hakbut*: portable guns; *culvering*:
    handguns; *pik*: pikestaffs

Till Ambiance in Pycardie,   610
Quhair nobill Lowes, the king of France,
Wes lyand with his ordinance,
With monie ane prince and worthie man.
And in the court of France wes than
Ane mervellous congregatioun   615
Of monie ane divers natioun:
Of Ingland monie ane prudent lord
Efter the weir makand record.
Thair wes, than, ane ambassadour,
Ane lord; ane man of greit honour   620
(With him was monie nobill knicht
Of Scotland to defend thair richt),
Quhilk guydit thame sa honestlie,
Inglismen had thame at invie,
And purposit to mak thame cummer   625
Becaus they wer of greiter number.
And sa, quhairever thay with thame met,
Upon the Scottis thay maid onset.
And lyke wyld lyounis furious
Thay layd ane seige about the hous,   630
Thame to destroy, sa thay intendit.
Our worthie Scottis thame weill defendit.
The sutheroun wes ay fyve for ane,
Sa on ilk syde thair wes men slane.
The Inglismen grew in greit ire   635
And cryit, 'Swyith! Set the hous in fyre!'
Be that, the squyer Meldrum
Into the market streit wes cum,
With his folkis in gude array,
And saw the toun wes in ane fray.   640
He did inquyre the occasioun.
Quod thay, 'The Scottis ar all put doun
Be Inglismen into thair innis.'
Quod he, 'I wald gif all the Bynnis

610 *Ambiance*: Amiens   633 *sutheroun*: English; *fyve for ane*:
611 *Lowes*: Louis   five to one
618 *makand record*: giving account 636 *Swyith*: Swiftly; *in*: on
624 *invie*: envy
625 *cummer*: trouble   643 *innis*: quarters

That I micht cum or thay departitit!'   645
With that, he grew sa cruell hartit
That he was like ane wyld lyoun,
And rudelie ran outthrow the toun
With all his companie weill arrayit
And with baner full braid displayit.   650
And quhen thay saw the Inglis rout,
Thay set upon thame, with ane schout,
With reird sa rudelie on thame ruschit
That fiftie to the eirth thay duschit!
Thair was nocht ellis bot tak and slay!   655
This squyer wounder did that day
And stoutlie stoppit in the stour
And dang on thame with dintis dour.
Wes never man buir better hand!
Thair micht na buckler byde his brand,   660
For it was weill sevin quarter lang.
With that sa derflie on thame dang,
That, lyke ane worthie campioun,
Ay at ane straik he dang ane doun.
Sum wes evill hurt, and sum wes slane,   665
Sum fell, quhilkis rais not yit agane.
Quhen that the sutheroun saw his micht,
Effrayitlie thay tuke the flicht
And wist not quhair to flie for haist:
Thus throw the toun he hes thame chaist!   670
Wer not Frenchemen come to the redding,
Thair had bene mekill mair blude shedding.
   Of this journey I mak ane end,
Quhilk everie nobill did commend.
Quhen to the king the cace wes knawin   675
And all the suith unto him shawin
(How this squyer sa manfullie
On sutheroun wan the victorie),

---

645 *or*: before   646 *cruell*: stern
649 *arrayit*: ordered [for battle]
650 *baner*: banner
653 *reird*: din of shouting
654 *duschit*: knocked down
655 *tak...slay*: take...slay
656 *wounder*: wonders

660 *buckler*: shield; *byde*: endure;
    brand: sword
661 *sevin quarter*: one and three-
    quarter ells
668 *Effrayitlie*: In alarm 669 *wist*: knew
671 *redding*: separating of combatants
673 *journey*: day's actions

He put him into ordinance.
And sa he did remane in France   680
Ane certane tyme, for his plesour;
Weill estemit in greit honour,
Quhair he did monie ane nobill deid;
With that, richt wantoun in his weid.
Quhen ladies knew his hie courage,   685
He was desyrit in mariage
Be ane ladie of greit rent.
Bot youth maid him sa insolent
That he in France wald not remane,
Bot come to Scotland hame agane.   690
Thocht Frenche ladies did for him murne,
The Scottis wer glaid of his returne.
At everie lord he tuke his leve,
Bot his departing did thame greive.
For he was luifit with all wichtis,   695
Quhilk had him sene defend his richtis.
Scottis capitanes did him convoy,
Thocht his departing did thame noy.
At Deip, he maid him for the saill,
Quhair he furnischit ane gay veschaill   700
For his self and his men of weir,
With artailyie, hakbut, bow, and speir;
And furneist hir with gude victuaill,
With the best wyne that he culd waill.
And quhen the ship was reddie maid,   705
He lay bot ane day in the raid,
Quhill he gat wind of the southeist.
Than thay thair ankeris weyit on haist
And syne maid saill, and fordwart past,
Ane day at morne, till at the last,   710
Of ane greit saill thay gat ane sicht
And Phoebus schew his bemis bricht
Into the morning richt airlie.

679 *into ordinance*: into battle
688 *insolent*: arrogant
691 *murne*: lament
695 *luifit with*: loved by; *wichtis*: people
698 *noy*: vex

699 *Deip*: Dieppe
700 *furnischit*: supplied; *veschaill*:
     vessel   704 *waill*: choose
706 *raid*: road
708 *weyit*: weighed; *on*: in

Than past the skipper richt spedelie
Up to the top, with richt greit feir,
And saw it wes ane man of weir,   715
And cryit, 'I see nocht ellis, perdie,
Bot we mon outher fecht or fle!'
The squyer wes in his bed lyand,
Quhen he hard tell this new tydand.
Be this, the Inglis artailye   720
Lyke hailschot maid on thame assailye,
And sloppit throw thair fechting saillis
And divers dang out ovir the waillis.
The Scottis agane, with all thair micht   725
Of gunnis, than thay leit fle ane flicht,
That thay micht weill see quhair they wair.
Heidis and armes flew in the air!
The Scottis schip, scho wes sa law,
That monie gunnis out ovir hir flaw,   730
Quhilk far beyond thame lichtit doun.
Bot the Inglis greit galyeoun
Fornent thame stude, lyke ane strang castell,
That the Scottish gunnis micht na way faill,
Bot hat hir, ay, on the richt syde   735
With monie ane slop, for all hir pryde,
That monie ane beft wer on thair bakkis.
Than rais the reik, with uglie crakkis,
Quhilk on the sey maid sic ane sound
That in the air it did redound,   740
That men micht weill wit, on the land,
That shippis wer on the sey fechtand.
Be this the gyder straik the shippis,
And ather on uther laid thair clippis.
And than began the strang battell: 745

715 *top*: top-castle; *feir*: dread
716 *man of weir*: warship
717 *perdie*: certainly
718 *outher*: either; *fecht*: fight
723 *sloppit*: made gaps
724 *divers*: a number; *dang*: struck;
   waillis: gunwales
726 *leit fle*: discharged speedily; *flicht*:
   flight [of shot]   727 *wair*: were
729 *sa law*: so low [in the water]
730 *ovir*: over; *flaw*: flew

732 *galyeoun*: galleon
733 *Fornent*: In front of
736 *slop*: breach
737 *beft*: beaten; *on...bakkis*: backwards
738 *rais...reik*: arose the smoke; *crakkis*:
   explosions   740 *redound*: resound
741 *wit*: know
743 *the gyder*: together; *straik*: struck,
   clashed
744 *clippis*: grappling hooks

Ilk man his marrow did assaill.
Sa rudelie thay did rushe togidder,
That nane micht hald thair feit for slidder;
Sum with halbert, and sum with speir,
Bot hakbuttis did the greitest deir.   750
Out of the top the grundin dartis
Did divers peirs outthrow the hartis.
Everie man did his diligence
Upon his fo to wirk vengence,
Ruschand on uther routtis rude,   755
That ovir the waillis ran the blude!
The Inglis capitane cryit hie,
'Swyith! Yeild, yow doggis, or ye sall die!
And do ye not, I mak ane vow
That Scotland salbe quyte of yow.'   760
Than peirtlie answerit the squyer,
And said, 'O tratour tavernar,
I lat the wit thow hes na micht
This day to put us to the flicht!'
Thay derflie ay at uther dang,   765
The squyer thristit throw the thrang,
And in the Inglis schip he lap,
And hat the capitane sic ane flap
Upon his heid, till he fell doun,
Welterand intill ane deidlie swoun.   770
And quhen the Scottis saw the squyer
Did strikkin doun that rank rever,
They left thair awin schip standand waist,
And in the Inglis schip in haist
They followit, all, thair capitane,   775
And sone wes all the sutheroun slane.
Howbeit thay wer of greiter number,
The Scottismen put thame in sic cummer
That thay wer fane to leif the feild,

---

748 *slidder*: slipperiness
749 *halbert*: halberd   750 *deir*: damage
751 *dartis*: arrows
752 *divers*: various [people]; *peirs*: pierce
755 Inflicting on others violent blows
757 *hie*: loudly   758 *Swyith*: Swiftly
760 *quyte*: rid   761 *peirtlye*: readily

762 *tavernar*: frequenter of taverns
763 *lat...wit*: let you know; *micht*: power
766 *thristit*: thrust; *thrang*: crowd
768 *hat*: hit; *flap*: blow
770 *Welterand*: Sinking
772 *rank rever*: gross pirate
773 *standand waist*: standing empty

Cryand, 'Mercie!' Than did thame yeild.   780
Yit wes the squyer straikand fast
At the capitane. Till, at the last,
Quhen he persavit no remeid
(Outher to yeild or to be deid),
He said, 'O gentill capitane,   785
Thoill me not for to be slane.
My lyfe to yow salbe mair pryse
Nor sall my deith, ane thowsand syse,
For ye may get, as I suppois,
Thrie thowsand nobillis of the rois   790
Of me and of my companie.
Thairfoir, I cry yow loud mercie.
Except my lyfe, nothing I craif;
Tak yow the schip and all the laif.
I yeild to yow baith sword and knyfe,   795
Thairfoir gude maister, save my lyfe.'
The squyer tuik him be the hand,
And on his feit he gart him stand,
And traittit him richt tenderly,
And syne unto his men did cry,   800
And gaif to thame richt strait command
To straik no moir, bot hald thair hand.
Than baith the capitanes ran and red
And so thair wes na mair blude shed.
Than all the laif thay did thame yeild   805
And to the Scottis gaif sword and sheild.
Ane nobill leiche the squyer had,
Quhairof the Inglismen wes full glaid,
To quhome the squyer gaif command
The woundit men to tak on hand.   810
And so he did, with diligence,
Quhairof he gat gude recompence.
Than, quhen the woundit men wer drest,
And all the deand men confest,
And deid men cassin in the see   815
(Quhilk to behold wes greit pietie),

---

786 *Thoill*: Suffer
787 *pryse*: valuable   788 *syse*: times
790 *nobillis...rois*: rose nobles

794 *laif*: rest   807 *leiche*: physician
814 *deand*: dying; *confest*: had made
        confessions   815 *cassin*: thrown

Thair was slane, of Inglis band,
Fyve scoir of men, I understand,
The quhilk wer cruell men and kene,
And of the Scottis wer slane fyftene.   820
And quhen the Inglis capitane
Saw how his men wer tane and slane,
And how the Scottis, sa few in number,
Had put thame in sa greit ane cummer,
He grew intill ane frenesy,   825
Sayand, 'Fals Fortoun, I the defy!
For I belevit, this day at morne,
That he was not in Scotland borne
That durst have met me, hand for hand,
Within the boundis of my brand.'   830
The squyer bad him mak gude cheir
And said, 'It wes bot chance of weir.
Greit conquerouris, I yow assure,
Hes hapnit siclike adventure.
Thairfoir mak mirrie, and go dyne,   835
And let us preif the michtie wyne.'
Sum drank wyne, and sum drank aill,
Syne put the shippis under saill,
And waillit furth of the Inglis band
Twa hundred men, and put on land,   840
Quyetlie, on the coist of Kent;
The laif in Scotland with him went.
The Inglis capitane, as I ges,
He wairdit him in the Blaknes,
And treitit him richt honestlie,   845
Togither with his companie,
And held thame in that garnisoun
Till thay had payit thair ransoun.
Out throw the land than sprang the fame
That squyer Meldrum wes cum hame.   850
    Quhen thay hard tell how he debaitit,

---

822 *tane*: taken   825 *frenesy*: frenzy
831 *mak...cheir*: be hopeful
834 Have experienced similar chance
839 *waillit furth of*: chose out of
843 *ges*: believe

844 *wairdit*: imprisoned; *Blaknes*:
    Blackness
847 *garnisoun*: garrisoned place
849 *fame*: report
851 *hard tell*: heard; *debaitit*: fought

With everie man he was sa treitit,
That quhen he travellit throw the land
Thay bankettit him, fra hand to hand,
With greit solace, till at the last,   855
Out throw Straitherne the squyer past,
And as it did approch the nicht,
Of ane castell he gat ane sicht,
Beside ane montane, in ane vaill,
And than, efter his greit travaill,   860
He purpoisit him to repois,
Quhair ilk man did of him rejois.
Of this triumphant plesand place,
Ane lustie ladie wes maistres,
Quhais lord was deid schort tyme befoir,   865
Quhairthrow hir dolour wes the moir.
Bot yit scho tuke sum comforting,
To heir the plesant, dulce talking
Of this young squyer, of his chance,
And how it fortunit him in France.   870
This squyer and the ladie gent
Did wesche, and then to supper went.
During that nicht thair was nocht ellis
Bot for to heir of his novellis.
Eneas, quhen he fled from Troy,   875
Did not quene Dido greiter joy
Quhen he in Carthage did arryve,
And did the seige of Troy discryve!
The wonderis that he did reheirs
Wer langsum for to put in vers,   880
Of quhilk this ladie did rejois.
Thay drank, and syne went to repois.
He fand his chalmer weill arrayit,
With dornik work on buird displayit.

852 *treitit*: treated
854 *bankettit*: entertained at banquets;
   fra...hand: from one person to
   another
856 *Out throw*: Across; *Straitherne*:
   Strathearn
861 *purpoisit*: decided; *repois*: rest
864 *lustie*: lovely   865 *Quhais*: Whose
866 *Quhairthrow*: Through which; *moir*:
   more   868 *dulce*: sweet

869 *chance*: fortune
870 *fortunit him*: fell out for him
871 *gent*: graceful
872 *wesche*: wash 874 *novellis*: news
876 *Did not*: Did not [give]
883 He found his chamber well adorned
884 *dornik work*: Tournai linen; *buird*:
   table; *displayit*: unfolded

Of venisoun he had his waill;   885
Gude aquavite, wyne, and aill,
With nobill confeittis, bran, and geill,
And swa the squyer fuir richt weill.
Sa, to heir mair of his narratioun,
This ladie come to his collatioun,   890
Sayand he was richt welcum hame.
'Grandmercie than,' quod he, 'madame.'
Thay past the time with ches and tabill,
For he to everie game was abill;
Than unto bed drew everie wicht.   895
To chalmer went this ladie bricht,
The quhilk this squyer did convoy,
Syne till his bed he went with joy.
That nicht he sleipit never ane wink,
Bot still did on the ladie think.   900
Cupido, with his fyrie dart,
Did peirs him so out throw the hart.
Sa, all that nicht, he did bot murnit:
Sum tyme sat up, and sumtyme turnit,
Sichand, with monie gant and grane,   905
To fair Venus makand his mane,
Sayand, 'Ladie, quhat may this mene?
I was ane fre man lait yistrene,
And now ane cative, bound and thrall,
For ane that I think flour of all.   910
  I pray God sen scho knew my mynd,
How, for hir saik, I am sa pynd.
Wald God I had bene yit in France,
Or I had hapnit sic mischance,
To be subject or serviture   915
Till ane quhilk takis of me na cure!'

886 *aquavite*: whisky
887 *nobill*: high quality; *confeittis*:
    sweetmeats; *bran...geill*: brawn
    [of boar]...jelly
888 *swa*: so; *fuir*: fared
890 *collatioun*: late evening refreshment
892 *Grandmercie*: Thank you
893 *ches*: chess; *tabill*: table games
901 *Cupido*: Cupid; *fyrie dart*: fiery
    arrow
903 *did...murnit*: lamented
905 *Sichand*: Sighing; *gant*: yawn;
    grane: groan
906 *makand...mane*: lamenting
908 *yistrene*: yesterday evening
909 *cative*: prisoner; *thrall*: enslaved
911 *sen*: grant
913 *Wald*: Would; *yit*: yet
914 Before I had suffered such
    misfortune
915 *serviture*: servant
916 To one who does not care for me

This ladie ludgit neirhand by
And hard the squyer prively,
With dreidfull hart, makand his mone,
With monie cairfull gant and grone.   920
Hir hart fulfillit with pietie,
Thocht scho wald haif of him mercie
And said, 'Howbeit I suld be slane,
He sall have lufe for lufe agane.
Wald God I micht, with my honour,   925
Have him to be my paramour!'
This wes the mirrie tyme of May,
Quhen this fair ladie, freshe and gay,
Start up to take the hailsum air,
With pantonis on hir feit ane pair,   930
Airlie into ane cleir morning,
Befoir fair Phoebus uprysing,
Kirtill alone, withouttin clok,
And saw the squyeris dure unlok.
Scho slippit in or ever he wist   935
And fenyeitlie past till ane kist,
And with hir keyis oppinnit the lokkis
And maid hir to take furth ane boxe.
Bot that was not hir erand thair.
With that, this lustie young squyar   940
Saw this ladie so plesantlie
Cum to his chalmer quyetlie,
In kyrtill of fyne damais broun,
Hir goldin traissis hingand doun.
Hir pappis wer hard, round and quhyte,   945
Quhome to behald wes greit delyte.
Lyke the quhyte lyllie wes hir lyre;
Hir hair was like the reid gold wyre.

---

917 *ludgit*: was accommodated;
    neirhand by: close by
918 *hard*: heard; *prively*: in private
919 *dreidfull*: fearful
920 *cairfull*: troubled
921 *fulfillit*: completely filled; *pietie*:
    compassion   922 *Thocht*: Thought
926 *paramour*: lover
929 *hailsum*: wholesome
930 *pantonis*: slippers
931 *Airlie*: Early

932 Before the fair sun's rising
933 *clok*: cloak
934 *dure*: door   935 *wist*: knew
936 *fenyeitlie*: in pretence; *kist*: chest
938 *maid hir*: made as if
939 *erand*: object
940 *lustie*: handsome
943 *damais*: damask
944 *traissis*: tresses, long locks; *hingand*:
    hanging   945 *pappis*: breasts
947 *lyre*: flesh

Hir schankis quhyte, withouttin hois,   950
Quhairat the squyer did rejois,
And said than, 'Now, vailye quod vailye,
Upon the ladie thow mak ane sailye!'
Hir courtlyke kirtill was unlaist
And sone into his armis hir braist,   955
And said to hir, 'Madame, gude morne.
Help me, your man that is forlorne.
Without ye mak me sum remeid,
Withouttin dout, I am bot deid!
Quhairfoir, ye mon releif my harmes.'   960
With that he hint hir in his armes
And talkit with hir on the flure,
Syne, quyetlie did bar the dure.
'Squyer,' quod scho, 'quhat is your will?
Think ye my womanheid to spill?   965
Na, God forbid, it wer greit syn;
My lord and ye wes neir of kyn.
Quhairfoir I mak yow supplicatioun:
Pas and seik ane dispensatioun.
Than sall I wed yow with ane ring.   970
Than may ye leif at your lyking,
For ye ar young, lustie, and fair,
And als, ye ar your fatheris air.
Thair is na ladie, in all this land,
May yow refuse to hir husband.   975
And gif ye lufe me as ye say,
Haist to dispens the best ye may.
And thair to yow I geve my hand:
I sall yow take to my husband.'
Quod he, 'Quhill that I may indure,

---

949 *schankis*: shins; *hois*: hose, stockings
951 *vailye...vailye*: come what may
952 *mak...sailye*: lay siege
953 *unlaist*: unlaced
954 *hir braist*: clasped her
956 *man*: lover; *forlorne*: utterly lost
957 *Without*: Unless; *mak...remeid*: devise for me a cure
958 *bot*: nothing but
959 *releif*: relieve; *harmes*: suffering
960 *hint*: clasped
961 *talkit*: talked, ?courted; *flure*: floor

962 *bar*: secure
964 *womanheid*: womanly virtue; *spill*: injure
966 *lord*: [late] husband; *neir...kyn*: close kin
968 *dispensatioun*: papal licence
970 *leif*: live; *at...lyking*: in contentment
971 *fair*: pleasing
972 *als*: also; *air*: heir
976 *Haist*: Make haste; *dispens*: [get the] dispensation
979 'While I live...'

I vow to be your serviture,   980
Bot I think greit vexatioun
To tarie upon dispensatioun.'
Than in his armis he did hir thrist
And aither uther sweitlie kist,
And wame for wame thay uther braissit;   985
With that hir kirtill wes unlaissit.
Than Cupido, with his fyrie dartis,
Inflammit sa thir luiferis hartis
Thay micht na maner of way dissever,
Nor ane micht not part fra ane uther,   990
Bot like wodbind thay wer baith wrappit.
Thair tenderlie he hes hir happit
Full softlie up intill his bed.
Judge ye gif he hir schankis shed.
'Allace!' quod scho, 'Quhat may this mene?'   995
And with hir hair scho dicht hir ene.
   I can not tell how thay did play,
Bot I beleve scho said not nay.
He pleisit hir sa, as I hard sane,
That he was welcum ay agane.   1000
Scho rais, and tendirlie him kist,
And on his hand ane ring scho thrist.
And he gaif hir ane lufe drowrie,
Ane ring set with ane riche rubie,
In takin that thair lufe for ever   1005
Suld never frome thir twa dissever.
And than scho passit unto hir chalmer
And fand hir madinnis, sweit as lammer,
Sleipand full sound and nothing wist
How that thair ladie past to the kist.   1010
Quod thay, 'Madame, quhair have ye bene?'
Quod scho, 'Into my gardine grene
To heir thir mirrie birdis sang.
I lat yow wit, I thocht not lang,

---

982 *tarie*: wait   983 *thrist*: thrust
985 *wame...wame*: belly to belly
988 *thir*: these; *luiferis*: lovers'
989 *dissever*: separate
991 *wodbind*: woodbind; *wrappit*:
    entwined   992 *happit*: covered
994 *shed*: parted

996 *dicht*: wiped; *ene*: eyes
999 *sane*: say
1001 *rais*: rose   1002 *thrist*: pressed
1003 *lufe drowrie*: love token
1008 *madinnis*: maidens; *lammer*: ?lambs
1013 *sang*: song
1014 *I lat yow wit*: I make known to you

Thocht I had taryit thair quhill none.'   1015
Quod thai, 'Quhair wes your hois and schone?
Quhy yeid ye with your bellie bair?'
Quod scho, 'The morning wes sa fair,
For, be him that deir Jesus sauld,
I felt na wayis ony maner of cauld.'   1020
Quod thay, 'Madame, me think ye sweit?'
Quod scho, 'Ye see, I sufferit heit;
The dew did sa on flouris fleit
That baith my lymmis ar maid weit.
Thairfoir ane quhyle I will heir ly,   1025
Till this dulce dew be fra me dry.
Ryse and gar mak our denner reddie.'
'That salbe done,' quod thay, 'my ladie.'
Efter that scho had tane hir rest,
Sho rais, and in hir chalmer hir drest,   1030
And efter mes to denner went;
Than wes the squyer diligent
To declair monie sindrie storie
Worthie to put in memorie.
    Quhat sall we of thir luiferis say?   1035
Bot all this tyme of lustie May
They past the tyme with joy and blis,
Full quyetlie, with monie ane kis.
Thair was na creature that knew
Yit of thir luiferis chalmer glew.   1040
And sa he levit plesandlie
Ane certane time with his ladie:
Sum time with halking and hunting,
Sum time with wantoun hors rinning,
And sum time like ane man of weir,   1045
Full galyardlie wald ryn ane speir.
He wan the pryse, abone thame all,
Baith at the buttis and the futeball.
Till everie solace he was abill

1015 *none*: noon
1016 *schone*: shoes
1017 *yeid*: went; *bair*: naked
1019 *sauld*: sold   1021 *sweit*: sweat
1022 *sufferit heit*: was affected by heat
1023 *fleit*: flow
1024 *lymmis*: legs; *weit*: wet

1027 *gar...reddie*: have our dinner
    prepared   1031 *mes*: mass
1040 *chalmer glew*: bedroom play
1044 *wantoun*: frisky; *rinning*: riding
1048 *buttis*: archery targets; *futeball*:
    football

(At cartis and dyce, at ches and tabill),   1050
And gif ye list, I sall yow tell,
How that he seigit ane castell.
Ane messinger come spedilie
From the Lennox to that ladie,
And schew how that Makfagon,   1055
And with him monie bauld baron,
Hir castell had tane perfors
And nouther left hir kow nor hors,
And heryit all that land about,
Quhairof the ladie had greit dout.   1060
Till hir squyer scho passit in haist
And schew him how scho wes opprest,
And how he waistit monie ane myle
Betwix Dunbartane and Argyle.
And quhen the squyer Meldrum   1065
Had hard thir novellis all and sum,
Intill his hart thair grew sic ire
That all his bodie brint in fyre,
And swoir it suld be full deir sald
Gif he micht find him in that hald!   1070
He and his men did them addres
Richt haistelie in thair harnes,
Sum with bow and sum with speir.
And he like Mars, the god of weir,
Come to the ladie, and tuke his leif.   1075
And scho gaif him hir richt hand gluif
The quhilk he on his basnet bure,
And said, 'Madame, I yow assure
That worthie Lancelot du Laik
Did never mair for his ladies saik   1080
Nor I sall do, or ellis de,
Without that ye revengit be.'
Than in hir armes scho him braist

1051 *list*: wish   1055 *schew*: revealed
1056 *bauld*: bold
1057 *perfors*: forcibly
1058 *nouther*: neither
1059 *heryit*: harried
1060 *dout*: [cause for] alarm
1063 *waistit*: had laid waste to
1064 *Dunbartane*: Dumbarton

1066 *all and sum*: in full
1068 *brint*: burned
1069 *swoir*: swore; *full deir*: most costly;
    sald: sold   1070 *hald*: place
1071 *addres*: dress
1076 *gluif*: glove   1077 *basnet*: steel
    headpiece

And he his leif did take in haist
And raid that day and all the nicht,   1085
Till on the morne he gat ane sicht
Of that castell, baith fair and strang.
Than in the middis his men amang
To michtie Mars his vow he maid,
That he suld never in hart be glaid,   1090
Nor yit returne furth of that land,
Quhill that strenth wer at his command.
All the tennentis of that ladie
Come to the squyer, haistelie,
And maid aith of fidelitie   1095
That thay suld never fra him flie.
Quhen to Makferland, wicht and bauld,
The veritie all haill wes tauld
(How the young squyer Meldrum
Wes now into the cuntrie cum   1100
Purpoisand to seige that place),
Than vittaillit he thar fortres
And swoir he suld that place defend
Bauldlie, untill his lyfis end.
Be this the squyer wes arrayit,   1105
With his baner bricht displayit,
With culvering, hakbut, bow and speir.
Of Makfarland he tuke na feir.
And like ane campioun courageous,
He cryit and said, 'Gif ovir the hous!'   1110
The capitane answerit heichly,
And said, 'Tratour, we the defy!
We sall remane this hous within
Into despyte of all thy kyn!'
With that the archeris, bauld and wicht,   1115
Of braid arrowis let fle ane flicht
Amang the squyeris companie,
And thay agane, richt manfullie,
With hakbute, bow, and culveryne,
Quhilk put Makferlandis men to pyne;   1120

1088 *middis*: middle   1108 *tuke na feir*: felt no fear
1092 *strenth*: stronghold   1110 *Gif ovir*: Surrender
1098 *all haill*: wholly   1111 *heichly*: scornfully
1102 *vittaillit*: provisioned   1120 *put...to pyne*: caused...to suffer

And on thair colleris laid full sikker.
And thair began ane bailfull bikker.
Thair was bot schot and schot agane,
Till, on ilk side, thair wes men slane.
Than cryit the squyer couragious,   1125
'Swyith, lay the ledderis to the hous!'
And sa thay did and clam belyfe,
As busie beis dois to thair hyfe.
Howbeit thair wes slane monie man,
Yit wichtlie ovir the wallis they wan.   1130
The squyer, formest of them all,
Plantit the baner ovir the wall.
And than began the mortall fray:
Thair wes not ellis bot tak and slay.
Than Makferland, that maid the prais,   1135
From time he saw the squyeris face
Upon his kneis he did him yeild,
Deliverand him baith speir and scheild.
The squyer hartlie him ressavit,
Commandand that he suld be savit.   1140
And sa did slaik that mortall feid,
Sa that na man wes put to deid.
In fre waird was Makferland seisit
And leit the laif gang quhair they pleisit.
And sa this squyer amorous   1145
Seigit and wan the ladies hous,
And left thairin ane capitane;
Syne to Stratherne returnit agane,
Quhair that he with his fair ladie
Ressavit wes full plesantlie   1150
And to tak rest did him convoy.
Judge ye gif thair wes mirth and joy!
Howbeit the chalmer dure wes cloisit,

1121 *colleris*: gorgets; *laid full
      sikker*: dealt blows vigorously
1122 *bailfull*: destructive; *bikker*:
      skirmish
1126 *lay the ledderis*: attach the ladders
1127 *belyfe*: with speed
1128 *busie beis*: busy bees; *dois*: do;
      hyfe: hive
1130 *wan*: won
1131 *formest*: in front

1132 *Plantit*: Placed in position
1135 *maid the prais*: initiated the
      sustained attack
1140 *savit*: spared
1141 *slaik*: abate; *mortall feid*: deadly
      enmity
1143 *in fre waird*: imprisoned without
      fetters
1147 *capitane*: military commander
1150 *Ressavit*: Received

They did bot kis, as I suppoisit.
Gif uther thing wes them betwene,   1155
Let them discover that luiferis bene,
For I am not in lufe expart
And never studyit in that art.
   Thus they remainit in merines,
Beleifand never to have distres.   1160
In that meine time this ladie fair
Ane douchter to the squyer bair;
Nane fund wes fairer of visage.
Than tuke the squyer sic courage,
Agane the mirrie time of May   1165
Threttie he put in his luferay,
In scarlot fyne and of hew grene,
Quhilk wes ane semelie sicht to sene.
   The gentilmen in all that land
Wer glaid with him to mak ane band,   1170
And he wald plainelie tak thair partis
And not desyring bot thair hartis.
Thus levit the squyer plesandlie,
With musick and with menstralie.
Of this ladie he wes sa glaid   1175
Thair micht na sorrow mak him sad;
Ilk ane did uther consolatioun,
Taryand upon dispensatioun.
Had it cum hame, he had hir bruikit;
Bot or it come, it wes miscuikit,   1180
And all this game he bocht full deir,
As ye at lenth sall efter heir.
   Of wardlie joy it wes weill kend
That sorrow bene the fatall end,
For jelousie and fals invie   1185
Did him persew richt cruellie.

1156 *discover*: disclose [it]
1157 *expart*: trained by experience
1160 *Beleifand*: Trusting
1162 *douchter*: daughter
1163 *Nane*: None; *fund*: found
1164 *tuk...courage*: took...heart
1165 *Agane*: In anticipation of
1166 *Threttie*: Thirty; *luferary*: livery
1167 *hew*: hue

1168 *semelie*: pleasing; *sene*: see
1170 *band*: compact of mutual interest
1171 *plainelie*: publicly
1174 *menstralie*: minstrelsy
1178 *Taryand*: Waiting
1179 *bruikit*: possessed
1180 *miscuikit*: mismanaged
1181 *game*: sport   1183 *kend*: known

I mervell not thocht it be so,
For they wer ever luiferis fo.
Quhairthrow he stude in monie ane stour
And ay defendit his honour.   1190
   Ane cruell knicht dwelt neir hand by
Quhilk at this squyer had invy,
Imaginand intill his hart
How he thir luiferis micht depart,
And wald have had hir maryand   1195
Ane gentilman within his land,
The quhilk to him wes not in blude.
Bot finallie, for to conclude,
Thairto scho wald never assent.
Quhairfoir the knicht set his intent   1200
This nobill squyer for to destroy,
And swore he suld never have joy
In till his hart, without remeid,
Till ane of thame wer left for deid.
This vailyeand squyer manfully   1205
In ernist or play did him defy,
Offerand himself for to assaill,
Bodie for bodie in battaill.
The knicht thairto not condiscendit,
Bot to betrais him ay intendit.   1210
   Sa it fell. Anis upon ane day
In Edinburgh, as I hard say,
This squyer and the ladie trew
Was thair, just matteris to persew.
That cruell knicht, full of invy,   1215
Gart hald on them ane secreit spy
Quhen thai suld pas furth of the toun,
For this squyeris confusioun,
Quhilk traistit no man suld him greive,
Nor of tressoun had no beleive,   1220
And tuik his licence from his oist

1187 I'm not surprised about it
1188 *fo*: enemies   1194 *depart*: separate
1195 *maryand*: marry
1197 *in blude*: related
1209 *not condiscendit*: did not agree
1210 *betrais*: deceive
1211 *fell*: happened

1214 *thair*: there; *just*: lawful
1216 *Gart hold*: Had [caused to be] kept
1218 *confusioun*: ruin
1219 *traistit*: believed; *greive*: harm
1220 *beleive*: expectation
1221 *tuik...licence*: took...leave;
   oist: armed company

And liberallie did pay his coist.
And sa departit, blyith and mirrie,
With purpois to pas ovir the Ferrie.
He wes bot aucht sum in his rout,   1225
For of danger he had no dout.
The spy come to the knicht anone
And him informit how they wer gone.
Than gadderit he his men in hy,
With thrie scoir in his company.   1230
Accowterit weill, in feir of weir,
Sum with bow, and sum with speir,
And on the squyer followit fast
Till thay did see him at the last,
With all his men richt weill arrayit,   1235
With cruell men nathing effrayit.
And quhen the ladie saw the rout
God wait gif scho stude in greit dout.
Quod scho, 'Your enemeis I see.
Thairfoir, sweit hart, I reid yow fle.   1240
In the cuntrey I will be kend;
Ye ar na partie to defend.
Ye knaw yone knichtis crueltie,
That in his hart hes no mercie.
It is bot ane that thay wald have;   1245
Thairfoir, deir hart, your self ye save.
Howbeit thay tak me with this trane,
I salbe sone at yow agane,
For ye war never sa hard staid.'
'Madame,' quod he, 'be ye not raid,   1250
For, be the halie Trinitie,
This day ane fute I will not fle.'
And be he had endit this word,
He drew his lang twa-handit sword,

1222 *pay his coist*: pay the price
1225 *bot*: only; *aucht sum*: eight together;
      rout: band
1226 *dout*: dread
1227 *come*: came; *anone*: forthwith
1229 *hy*: haste
1230 *thrie scoir*: three score
1231 *Accowterit*: Equipped; *in feir of
      war*: in warlike array
1235 *arrayit*: attired   1240 *reid*: advise

1242 *partie*: match; *defend*: to oppose
      [them]   1243 *yone*: that
1245 *bot ane*: only one [person]
1247 *trane*: deception
1248 *sone at*: soon in contact with
1249 *hard staid*: tightly beset
1250 *raid*: afraid
1253 *be*: by [the time that]
1254 *lang*: long; *twa-handit*: two-handed

And put his aucht men in array 1255
And bad that thay suld tak na fray.
Than to the squyer cryit the knicht
And said, 'Send me the ladie bricht!
Do ye not sa, be Goddis corce,
I sall hir tak away perforce.' 1260
The squyer said, 'Be thow ane knicht,
Cum furth to me and shaw the richt;
Bot hand for hand, without redding,
That thair be na mair blude shedding.
And gif thow winnis me in the feild, 1265
I sall my ladie to the yeild.'
The knicht durst not, for all his land,
Fecht with this squyer hand for hand.
The squyer than saw no remeid
Bot outher to fecht or to be deid. 1270
To hevin he liftit up his visage,
Cryand to God with hie courage,
'To the my querrell I do commend!'
Syne bowtit fordwart with ane bend.
With countenance baith bauld and stout, 1275
He rudelie rushit in that rout;
With him his litill companie,
Quhilk them defendit manfullie.
The squyer with his birneist brand
Amang his famen maid sic hand 1280
That Gaudefer, as sayis the letter,
At Gadderis Forray faucht no better.
His sword he swappit sa about
That he greit roum maid in the rout.
And, like ane man that was dispairit, 1285
His wapoun sa on thame he wairit,
Quhome ever he hit, as I hard say,
Thay did him na mair deir that day.
Quha ever come within his boundis

1255 *in array*: in battle order
1256 *bad*: ordered; *fray*: fear
1259 *Goddis corce*: God's body
1265 *winnis*: defeat
1278 *them defendit*: defended themselves
1280 *famen*: foemen; *maid sic
hand*: used such skill

1281 *letter*: literary composition
1282 *Gadderis Forray*: the Raid of Gaza
1283 *swappit*: struck   1284 *roum*: space
1285 *dispairit*: in despair
1286 *wapoun*: weapon; *wairit*: made war

He chaipit not but mortall woundis;   1290
Sum mutilate wer, and sum wer slane,
Sum fled and come not yit agane.
He hat the knicht abone the breis
That he fell fordwart on his kneis;
Wer not Thome Giffard did him save,   1295
The knicht had sone bene in his grave.
Bot than the squyer with his brand
Hat Thomas Giffard on the hand;
From that time furth during his lyfe,
He never weildit sword nor knyfe.   1300
Than come ane sort as brim as beiris
And in him festnit fyftene speiris
In purpois to have borne him doun,
Bot he, as forcie campioun,
Amang thai wicht men wrocht greit wounder,   1305
For all thai speiris he schure in sunder.
Nane durst cum neir him, hand for hand,
Within the boundis of his brand.
This worthie squyer courageous
Micht be compairit to Tydeus,   1310
Quhilk faucht for to defend his richtis
And slew of Thebes fyftie knichtis.
Rolland with Brandwell, his bricht brand,
Faucht never better, hand for hand;
Nor Gawin aganis Golibras,   1315
Nor Olyver with Pharambras.
I wait he faucht that day als weill
As did Sir Gryme aganis Graysteill,
And I dar say he was als abill
As onie knicht of the Round Tabill,   1320
And did his honour mair avance
Nor onie of thay knichtis, perchance.
The quhilk I offer me to preif
Gif that ye pleis, sirs, with your leif.

1290 *chaipit not*: did not escape
1293 *hat*: struck; *breis*: eyebrows
1295 *Wer not*: Were it not [that]
1301 *ane sort*: a group
1302 *festnit*: fastened
1304 *forcie*: very strong

1305 *thai*: those
1306 *schure*: cut; *in sunder*: asunder
1315 *Gawin*: Gawain; *Golibras*: Golagros
1316 *Pharambras*: Fierabras
1322 *Nor onie*: Than any
1323 *I offer...preif*: I am ready to prove

Amang thay knichtis wes maid ane band 1325
That they suld fecht bot hand for hand,
Assurit that thair suld cum no mo.
With this squyer it stude not so:
His stalwart stour quha wald discryfe,
Aganis ane man thair come ay fyfe. 1330
Quhen that this cruell tyrane knicht
Saw the squyer sa wounder wicht
And had no micht him to destroy,
Into his hart thair grew sic noy
That he was abill for to rage, 1335
That no man micht his ire asswage,
'Fy on us!' said he to his men,
'Ay aganis ane sen we ar ten,
Chaip he away, we ar eschamit;
Like cowartis we salbe defamit. 1340
I had rather be in hellis pane
Or he suld chaip fra us unslane!'
And callit thrie of his companie,
Said, 'Pas behind him, quyetlie.'
And sa thay did richt secreitlie 1345
And come behind him cowartlie,
And hackit on his hochis and theis
Till that he fell upon his kneis.
Yit, quhen his schankis wer schorne in sunder,
Upon his kneis he wrocht greit wounder, 1350
Sweipand his sword round about,
Not haifand of the deith na dout.
Durst nane approche within his boundis
Till that his cruell mortall woundis
Bled sa, that he did swap in swoun; 1355
Perforce behuifit him than fall doun
And, quhen he lay upon the ground,
They gaif him monie cruell wound

1330 *fyfe*: five
1334 *noy*: vexation   1337 *Fy*: Shame
1338 Since we are ever ten to one
1339 *Chaip...away*: [If] he [were to]
    escape; *eschamit*: shamed
1347 *hackit on*: hacked through; *hochis*:
    hamstrings; *theis*: thighs

1349 *schorne*: chopped in two
1352 Having no fear of death
1354 *Till that*: Until
1355 *sa*: so; *swap*: sink into
1356 *Perforce*: Of necessity; *behuifit
    him*: he had to

That men on far micht heir the knokkis,
Like boucheouris hakkand on thair stokkis.   1360
And finallie, without remeid,
They left him lyand thair for deid,
With ma woundis of sword and knyfe
Nor ever had man that keipit lyfe.
Quhat suld I of thir tratouris say?   1365
Quhen they had done, they fled away.
Bot than this lustie ladie fair
With dolent hart scho maid sic cair,
Quhilk wes greit pietie for to reheirs
And langsum for to put in vers.   1370
With teiris scho wuische his bludie face,
Sichand with manie loud 'allace!'
'Allace', quod scho, 'that I was borne!
In my querrell thow art forlorne.
Sall never man efter this hour   1375
Of my bodie have mair plesour.
For thow was gem of gentilnes
And verie well of worthines.'
Than to the eirth scho rushit doun
And lay intill ane deidlie swoun.   1380
Be that the regent of the land
Fra Edinburgh come fast rydand.
Sir Anthonie Darsie wes his name,
Ane knicht of France and man of fame,
Quhilk had the guiding haillilie   1385
Under Johne, Duke of Albanie,
Quhilk wes to our young king tutour
And of all Scotland governour.
(Our king was bot fyve yeiris of age
That time quhen done wes the outrage.)   1390
Quhen this gude knicht the squyer saw
Thus lyand in till his deid thraw,
'Wo is me,' quod he, 'to see this sicht
On the, quhilk worthie wes, and wicht!

1359 *knokkis*: blows
1360 *boucheouris*: butchers; *stokkis*:
  blocks
1364 *keipit*: preserved
1368 *cair*: lamentation

1371 *wuische*: washed
1374 Defending my cause you are lost
1385 *haillilie*: wholly
1387 *tutour*: guardian
1392 *deid thraw*: death-throe

Wald God that I had bene with the, 1395
As thow in France was anis with me
Into the land of Picardy,
Quhair Inglis men had greit invy
To have me slane, sa they intendit,
Bot manfullie thow me defendit 1400
And vailyeandlie did save my lyfe.
Was never man with sword nor knyfe,
Nocht Hercules, I dar weill say,
That ever faucht better for ane day.
Defendand me within ane stound, 1405
Thow dang seir sutheroun to the ground.
I may the mak no help, allace,
Bot I sall follow on the chace
Richt spedilie, baith day and nicht,
Till I may get that cruell knicht. 1410
I mak ane vow, gif I may get him,
In till ane presoun I sall set him,
And quhen I heir that thow beis deid,
Than sall my handis straik of his heid.'
With that he gave his hors the spurris 1415
And spedelie flaw ovir the furris.
He and his gaird, with all thair micht,
Thay ran till thai ovirtuik the knicht.
Quhen he approchit he lichtit doun
And, like ane vailyeand campioun, 1420
He tuik the tyrane presonar
And send him backward to Dumbar;
And thair remainit in presoun
Ane certane time in that dungeoun.
  Let him ly thair, with mekill cair, 1425
And speik we of our heynd squyar,
Of quhome we can not speik bot gude.
Quhen he lay bathand in his blude,
His freindis and his ladie fair

1405 *stound*: instant
1406 *seir*: many   1407 *mak*: render
1408 *chace*: pursuit
1412 *set*: put   1413 *beis*: are
1414 *of*: off

1416 *flaw*: flew; *furris*: furrows
1418 *ran*: hastened
1419 *lichtit*: dismounted
1422 *Dumbar*: Dunbar
1426 *heynd*: gentle

They maid for him sic dule and cair,   1430
Quhilk wer greit pietie to deploir.
Of that matter I speik no moir.
Thay send for leiches haistelie,
Syne buir his bodie tenderlie
To ludge into ane fair ludgyne,   1435
Quhair he ressavit medicyne.
The greitest leichis of the land
Come all to him, without command,
And all pratikis on him provit
Becaus he was sa weill belovit.   1440
Thay tuik on hand his life to save
And he thame gaif quhat they wald have;
Bot he sa lang lay into pane
He turnit to be ane chirurgiane,
And als, be his naturall ingyne,   1445
He lernit the art of medicyne.
He saw thame on his bodie wrocht,
Quhairfoir the science wes deir bocht;
Bot efterward, quhen he was haill,
He spairit na coist, nor yit travaill,   1450
To preif his practikis on the pure
And on thame previt monie ane cure
On his expensis, without rewaird;
Of money he tuik na regaird.

   Yit sum thing will we commoun mair   1455
Of this ladie, quhilk maid greit cair,
Quhilk to the squyer wes mair pane
Nor all his woundis, in certane.
And than hir freindis did conclude,
Becaus scho micht do him na gude,   1460
That scho suld take hir leif and go
Till hir cuntrie, and scho did so;

1430 *dule*: lamentation
1431 *deploir*: lament
1434 *buir*: carried
1435 *ludge*: be accommodated; *ludgyne*:
   dwelling
1439 *pratikis*: professional skills; *provit*:
   tested   1441 *on*: in
1444 *turnit*: grew; *chirurgiane*: surgeon
1445 *ingyne*: intelligence

1447 *thame*: i.e. medical arts
1449 *haill*: healed
1451 *preif*: prove; *pure*: poor
1455 *commoun*: talk about
1457 *wes...pane*: gave more suffering
1458 *in certane*: in truth
1459 *freindis*: kinsmen
1462 *hir cuntrie*: her own lands

Bot thir luiferis met never agane,
Quhilk wes to thame ane lestand pane,
For scho aganis hir will wes maryit,
Quhairthrow hir weird scho daylie waryit. 1465
Howbeit hir bodie wes absent,
Hir tender hart wes ay present
Baith nicht and day with hir squyar.
Wes never creature that maid sic cair:
Penelope for Ulisses, 1470
I wait, had never mair distres,
Nor Cresseid for trew Troylus
Wes not tent part sa dolorous.
I wait it wes aganis hir hart 1475
That scho did from hir lufe depart.
Helene had not sa mekill noy
Quhen scho perforce wes brocht to Troy.
I leif hir than with hart full sore
And speik now of this squyer more. 1480
   Quhen this squyer wes haill and sound
And softlie micht gang on the ground,
To the regent he did complane;
Bot he, allace, wes richt sone slane
Be David Hume of Wedderburne, 1485
The quhilk gart monie Frenche men murne,
For thair was nane mair nobill knicht,
Mair vailyeand, mair wyse, mair wicht.
And sone efter that crueltie,
The knicht was put to libertie, 1490
The quhilk the squyer had opprest.
Sa wes his matter left undrest:
Becaus the king was young of age,
Than tyrannis rang into thair rage.
Bot efterward, as I hard say, 1495
On Striviling brig upon ane day
This knicht wes slane, with crueltie,
And that day gat na mair mercie
Nor he gaif to the young squyer.

1464 *lestand*: enduring
1466 And so she daily cursed her fate
1474 *tent*: tenth
1482 *softlie*: with ease; *gang*: walk

1486 *murne*: grieve
1492 *undrest*: [legally] unresolved
1496 *Striviling brig*: Stirling bridge

I say na mair. Let him ly thair;   1500
For cruell men, ye may weill see,
They end ofttimes with crueltie.
For Christ to Peter said this word,
'Quha ever straikis with ane sword,
That man salbe with ane sword slane.'   1505
That saw is suith, I tell yow plane.
(He menis, quha straikis cruellie,
Aganis the law, without mercie.)
Bot this squyer to nane offendit,
Bot manfullie him self defendit.   1510
Wes never man with sword nor knyfe
Micht saif thair honour and thair lyfe
As did the squyer, all his dayis,
With monie terribill effrayis.
Wald I at lenth his lyfe declair   1515
I micht weill writ ane uther quair;
Bot at this time I may not mend it,
Bot shaw yow how the squyer endit.
   Thair dwelt in Fyfe ane agit lord,
That of this squyer hard record   1520
And did desire, richt hartfullie,
To have him in his companie,
And send for him with diligence,
And he come with obedience
And lang time did with him remane,   1525
Of quhome this agit lord was fane.
Wyse men desiris, commounlie,
Wyse men into thair companie.
For he had bene in monie ane land,
In Flanderis, France, and in Ingland,   1530
Quhairfoir the lord gaif him the cure
Of his houshald, I yow assure,
And in his hall, cheif merschall
And auditour of his comptis all.
He was ane richt courticiane   1535
And in the law ane practiciane,

1506 *saw*: adage   1507 *menis*: means   1533 *cheif merschall*: chief marshal
1514 *effrayis*: alarms 1516 *quair*: book   1534 *comptis*: accounts
1517 *mend*: right   1519 *agit*: elderly   1535 *courticiane*: court-man
1520 *hard record*: heard an account   1536 *practiciane*: practitioner

Quhairfoir, during this lordis lyfe,
Tchyref-depute he wes in Fyfe.
To everie man ane equall judge
And of the pure he wes refuge,   1540
And with justice did thame support
And curit thair sairis, with greit comfort.
For, as I did reheirs before,
Of medicine he tuke the lore
Quhen he saw the chirurgience   1545
Upon him do thair diligence.
Experience maid him perfyte
And of the science tuke sic delyte
That he did monie thriftie cure
And speciallie upon the pure,   1550
Without rewaird for his expensis,
Without regaird, or recompencis.
To gold, to silver, or to rent,
This nobill squyer tuke litill tent.
Of all this warld na mair he craifit   1555
Sa that his honour micht be saifit.
And ilk yeir, for his ladies saik,
Ane banket royall wald he maik
And that he maid on the Sonday
Precedand to Aschwednisday.   1560
With wyld foull, venisoun and wyne,
With tairt and flam, and frutage fyne;
Of bran and geill thair wes na skant,
And Ipocras he wald not want.
I have sene, sittand at his tabill,   1565
Lordis and lairdis honorabill,
With knichtis and monie ane gay squyar,
Quhilk wer to lang for to declair,
With mirth, musick, and menstrallie.
All this he did for his ladie   1570
And, for hir saik, during his lyfe
Wald never be weddit to ane wyfe.

1538 *Tchyref*: Sheriff
1539 *equall*: impartial
1542 *sairis*: injuries
1544 *tuke...lore*: took instruction
1554 *tuke little tent*: paid scant heed to

1555 *craifit*: desired
1556 *Sa that*: So long as; *saifit*: kept safe
1562 *tairt*: tart; *flam*: flawn; *frutage*:
    fruits   1564 *Ipocras*: Hippocras
1566 *lairdis*: lesser landowners

And quhen he did declyne to age
He faillit never, of his courage.
Of ancient storyis for to tell,   1575
Abone all uther he did precell,
Sa that everilk creature,
To heir him speik, thay tuke plesure.
Bot all his deidis honorabill
For to descryve I am not abill.   1580
Of everie man he was commendit
And as he leivit, sa he endit,
Plesandlie, till he micht indure,
Till dolent deith come to his dure
And cruellie, with his mortall dart,   1585
He straik the squyer throw the hart.
His saull, with joy angelicall,
Past to the hevin imperiall.
Thus, at the Struther, into Fyfe,
This nobill squyer loist his lyfe.   1590
I pray to Christ for to convoy
All sic trew luiferis to his joy.
Say ye, 'Amen', for cheritie.
Adew, ye sall get na mair of me.

1574 *courage*: spirit   1588 *imperiall*: empyrean
1583 *till*: while; *indure*: continue   1590 *loist*: lost

THE TESTAMENT
OF
SQUYER MELDRUM

1

The holie man, Job, ground of patience,
In his greit trubill trewlie did report,
Quilk I persave now be experience,
That mennis lyfe in eirth bene wounder short.
My youth is gane and eild now dois resort,   5
My time is gane. I think it but ane dreame.
Yit efter deith remane sall my gude fame.

1 *ground*: basis   3 *Quhilk*: Which   5 *gane*: gone; *eild*: age; *resort*: come

2

I persave shortlie that I man pay my det.
To me in eirth no place bene permanent.
My hart on it no mair now will I set,   10
Bot, with the help of God omnipotent,
With resolute mind go mak my testament,
And tak my leif at cuntriemen and kyn
And all the warld. And thus I will begyn.

3

Thrie lordis to me salbe executouris: 15
Lindesayis all thrie, in surname of renoun.
Of my testament thay sall have hail the cure
To put my mind till executioun.
That surname failyeit never to the croun;
Na mair will thay to me, I am richt sure,   20
Quhilk is the caus I give them the cure.

4

First, David, Erll of Craufuird, wise and wicht,
And Johne, Lord Lindesay, my maister speciall.
The thrid salbe ane nobill travellit knicht
Quhilk knawis the coistis of feistis funeral,   25
The wise Sir Walter Lindesay, they him cal,
Lord of S. Johne and knicht of Torfichane;
Be sey and land ane vailyeand capitane.

5

Thocht age hes maid my bodie impotent,
Yit in my hart hie courage doeth precell,   30
Quhairfoir I leif to God, with gude intent,
My spreit, the quhilk he hes maid immortall,
Intill his court perpetuallie to dwell
And nevir moir to steir furth of that steid
Till Christ discend, and judge baith quick and deid.   35

6

I yow beseik, my lordis executouris,
My geir geve till the nixt of my kynrent.
(It is weill kend I never tuik na cures

---

8   *shortlie*: soon   9 *bene*: is   27 *Torfichane*: Torphichen
11 *Bot*: But   13 *leif at*: leave of 30 *doeth precell*: is pre-eminent
17 *hail...cure*: the whole care   32 *spreit*: soul
19 *failyeit*: failed   34 *steir...steid*: move from that place
22 *Craufuird*: Crawford 25 *coistis*: costs 37 *geir*: property; *nixt*: next

Of conquessing of riches, nor of rent.)
Dispone as ye think maist expedient: 40
I never tuik cure of gold more than of glas;
Without honour, fy, fy, upon riches!

7

I yow requeist my freindis, ane and all,
And nobill men of quhome I am descendit,
Faill not to be at my feist funerall,   45
Quhilk throw the warld I traist salbe commendit.
Ye knaw how that my fame I have defendit
During my life unto this latter hour,
Quhilk suld to yow be infinit plesour.

8

First, of my bowellis, clenge my bodie clene,   50
Within and out, syne wesche it weill with wyne.
Bot honestie see that nothing be sene,
Syne clois it in ane coistlie carvit schryne
Of cedar treis, or of cyper fyne.
Anoynt my corps with balme delicious,   55
With cynamome and spycis precious.

9

In twa caissis, of gold and precious stanis,
Inclois my hart and toung richt craftelie.
My sepulture, syne, gar mak for my banis,
Into the tempill of Mars triumphandlie,   60
Of marbill stanis carvit richt curiouslie,
Quhairin my kist and banis ye sall clois
In that triumphand tempill to repois.

10

Mars, Venus and Mercurius: all thre
Gave me my natural inclinatiounis,   65
Quhilk rang the day of my nativitie,
And sa thair hevinlie constellatiounis
Did me support in monie natiounis.

---

39 *conquessing*: acquiring
41 *tuik...of*: had interest in
49 *suld*: should   51 *syne*: then
54 *cyper*: cypress
57 *caissis*: receptacles
58 *toung*: tongue; *craftelie*: skilfully
59 *sepulture*: tomb; *banis*: bones

60 *Into*: Within
61 *stanis*: stones; *curiouslie*: intricately
62 *kist*: coffin 64 *Mercurius*: Mercury
65 *natural inclinatiounis*: inherent
   human abilities
66 *rang*: held sway

Mars maid me hardie, like ane feirs lyoun,
Quhairthrow I conqueist honour and renoun.   70

11

Quho list to knaw the actis bellical,
Let thame go reid the legend of my life.
Thair sall thai find the deidis martiall,
How I have stand in monie stalwart strife
Victoriouslie, with speir, sheild, sword and knife.   75
Quhairfoir to Mars, the god armipotent,
My corps incloisit ye do till him present.

12

Mak offering of my toung rhetoricall
Till Mercurius, quhilk gaif me eloquence,
In his tempill to hing perpetuall.   80
I can mak him na better recompence,
For quhen I was brocht to the presence
Of kings, in Scotland, Ingland, and in France,
My ornate toung my honour did avance.

13

To fresche Venus, my hart ye sall present,   85
Quhilk hes to me bene ay comfortabill
And in my face sic grace scho did imprent
All creatures did think me amiabill.
Wemen to me scho maid sa favorabill,
Wes never ladie that luikit in my face   90
Bot, honestlie, I did obtene hir grace.

14

My freind, Sir David Lyndsay of the Mont,
Sall put in ordour my processioun.
I will that thair pas formest in the front,
To beir my penseil, ane wicht campioun.   95
With him, ane band of Mars his religioun
(That is to say, in steid of monkis and freiris),
In gude ordour ane thowsand hagbutteris.

---

70 *conqueist*: gained
71 *list*: pleases; *bellical*: warlike
72 *legend*: story
76 *armipotent*: mighty in arms
77 *till*: to
78 *rhetoricall*: persuasive
80 *hing*: hang

84 *ornate toung*: embellished speech
86 *comfortabill*: pleasant
87 *sic*: such; *imprent*: stamp
88 *creatures*: people
95 *penseil*: small pennon; *wicht*: valiant
98 *hagbutteris*: harquebusiers

15

Nixt them, ane thowsand futemen in ane rout,
With speir and sheild, with buckler, bow, and brand,   100
In ane luferay, young stalwart men and stout.
Thridlie in ordour, thair sall cum ane band
Of nobill men, abill to wraik thair harmes,
Thair capitane with my standart in his hand,
On bairdit hors ane hundreth men of armes.   105

16

Amang that band my baner salbe borne,
Of silver schene, thrie otteris into sabill,
With tabroun, trumpet, clarioun, and horne,
For men of armes verie convenabill.
Nixt efter them, ane campioun honorabill   110
Sall beir my basnet with my funerall.
Syne, efter him, in ordour triumphall,

17

My arming, sword, my gluifis of plait, and sheild,
Borne be ane forcie campioun or ane knicht
Quhilk did me serve in monie dangerous feild.   115
Nixt efter him, ane man in armour bricht,
Upon ane jonet, or ane cursour wicht,
The quhilk salbe ane man of greit honour,
Upon ane speir to beir my coit armour,

18

Syne, nixt my beir sall cum my corspresent   120
(My bairdit hors, my harnes and my speir,
With sum greit man of my awin kynrent),
As I wes wont on my bodie to beir
During my time quhen I went to the weir,
Quhilk salbe offerit with ane gay garment   125
To Mars his priest, at my interrement.

---

99 *futemen*: infantry; *rout*: contingent
100 *buckler*: small round shield; *brand*: sword
101 *luferay*: uniform
103 *wraik...harmes*: avenge their injuries   105 *bairdit*: armoured
108 *tabroun*: tabor [drum]
109 *convenabill*: appropriate
111 *basnet*: steel headpiece; *funerall*: funeral [procession]

113 *arming*: armour; *gluifis...plait*: gauntlets   114 *forcie*: strong
115 *feild*: battlefield
117 *jonet*: jennet; *wicht*: valiant
119 *speir*: lance; *beir*: carry; *coit*: coat
120 *beir*: bier; *corspresent*: corspresent
122 *kynrent*: kinsfolk
125 *gay*: handsome

19

Duill weidis I think hypocrisie and scorne,
With huidis heklit doun ovirthort thair ene.
With men of armes my bodie salbe borne.
Into that band see that no blak be sene.   130
My luferay salbe reid, blew and grene,
The reid for Mars, the grene for freshe Venus,
The blew for lufe of god, Mercurius.

20

About my beir sall ryde ane multitude,
All of ane luiferay of my cullouris thrie;   135
Erles and lords, knichtis, and men of gude,
Ilk barroun beirand in his hand on hie
Ane lawrer branche in signe of victorie,
Becaus I fled never out of the feild,
Nor yit as presoner unto my fois me yeild.   140

21

Agane that day, faill not to warne and call
All men of musick and of menstrallie
About my beir, with mirthis musicall,
To dance and sing with hevinlie harmonie,
Quhais plesant sound redound sall in the sky.   145
My spreit, I wait, salbe with mirth and joy,
Quhairfoir, with mirth my corps ye sal convoy.

22

This beand done and all thing reulit richt,
Than plesantlie mak your progressioun,
Quhilk I beleif salbe ane plesant sicht.   150
Se that ye thoill na preist in my processioun
Without he be of Venus professioun.
Quhairfoir, gar warne al Venus chapel clarks,
Quhilk hes bene most exercit in hir warkis.

23

With ane bischop of that religioun,   155
Solemnitlie gar thame sing my saull mes,

127 *Duill weidis*: Mourning clothes
128 *huidis heklit*: fringed hoods;
   ovirthort: across 132 *reid*: red
136 *gude*: substance 138 *lawrer*: laurel
141 *Agane*: In preparation for
142 *menstrallie*: minstrelsy

145 *Quhais*: Whose   146 *wait*: know
151 *thoill*: suffer
152 *of...professioun*: vowed to Venus
154 *exercit*: exercised
156 *saull mes*: mass for the soul

With organe, timpane, trumpet, and clarion;
To shaw thair musick, dewlie them addres.
I will that day be hard no hevines:
I will na service of the *Requiem*,   160
Bot *Alleluya*, with melodie and game.

24

Efter the evangell and the offertour,
Throw all the tempill gar proclame silence.
Than to the pulpet gar ane oratour
Pas up, and schaw in oppin audience,   165
Solempnitlie, with ornate eloquence,
At greit laser the legend of my life,
How I have stand in monie stalwart strife.

25

Quhen he hes red my buik fra end till end,
And of my life maid trew narratioun,   170
All creature, I wait, will me commend
And pray to God for my salvatioun.
Than efter this solempnizatioun
Of service, and all brocht to end,
With gravitie than with my bodie wend,   175

26

And clois it up into my sepulture,
Thair to repois till the greit Judgement,
The quhilk may not corrupt, I yow assure,
Be vertew of the precious oyntment
Of balme, and uther spyces redolent.   180
Let not be rung for me that day saull knellis,
Bot greit cannounis gar them crak for bellis.

27

Ane thousand hakbuttis gar schute, al at anis,
With swesche talburnis and trumpettis awfullie.
Lat never spair the poulder nor the stanis,   185
Quhais thundring sound redound sall in the sky,
That Mars may heir, quhair he triumphandlie
Abone Phebus is situate full evin,
Maist awfull god under the sternie hevin.

---

158 *schaw*: display   159 *hard*: heard
162 *evangell*: gospel; *offertour*: offertory
163 *gar...silence*: have silence called
165 *in...audience*: publicly

167 *At...laser*: With great deliberation
181 *saull knellis*: death peals
182 *crak*: explode
184 *swesche talburnis*: drums

28

And syne, hing up above my sepulture 190
My bricht harnes, my sheild, and als my speir,
Togidder with my courtlie coit armour
(Quhilk I wes wont upon my bodie beir
In France, in Ingland, being at the weir),
My baner, basnet, with my temperall, 195
As bene the use of feastis funerall.

29

This beand done, I pray yow, tak the pane
My epitaphe to writ, upon this wyis,
Abone my grave, in goldin letteris fyne:
'The maist invincibill weiriour heir lyis, 200
During his time quhilk wan sic laud and pryis,
That throw the hevinis sprang his nobil fame.
Victorious William Meldrum wes his name.'

30

Adew, my lordis, I may na langer tarie.
My Lord Lindesay, adew abone all uther. 205
I pray to God and to the Virgine Marie
With your lady to leif lang in the Struther.
Maister Patrik, with young Normand, your brother;
With my ladies, your sisteris, al adew.
My departing I wait weill ye will rew. 210

31

Bot maist of all, the fair ladies of France,
Quhen thai heir tell but dout that I am deid,
Extreme dolour wil change thair countenance
And for my saik will weir the murning weid.
Quhen thir novellis dois into Ingland spreide, 215
Of Londoun than the lustie ladies cleir
Will for my saik mak dule and drerie cheir.

32

Of Craigfergus, my dayis darling, adew.
In all Ireland of feminine the flour.
In your querrell twa men of weir I slew 220
Quhilk purposit to do yow dishonour.

---

188 *Abone*: Above; *full evin*: exactly   195 *temperall*: coat armour
189 *sternie*: starry   196 *use*: custom   216 *cleir*: beautiful

Ye suld have bene my spous and paramour,
With rent and riches for my recompence,
Quhilk I refusit throw youth and insolence.

33

Fair weill, ye lemant lampis of lustines   225
Of fair Scotland, adew my ladies all.
During my youth, with ardent besines,
Ye knaw how I was in your service thrall.
Ten thowsand times adew, abone thame all,
Sterne of Stratherne, my ladie soverane,   230
For quhom I sched my blud with mekill pane.

34

Yit wald my ladie luke, at evin and morrow,
On my legend at lenth, scho wald not mis
How for hir saik I sufferit mekill sorrow.
Yit give I micht at this time get my wis,   235
Of hir sweit mouth, deir God, I had ane kis.
I wis in vane. Allace, we will dissever.
I say na mair. Sweit hart, adew for ever.

35

Brether in armes, adew, in generall.
For me, I wait, your hartis bene full soir.   240
All trew companyeounis into speciall,
I say to yow, adew, for evermoir,
Till that we meit agane with God in gloir.
Sir curat now gif me, incontinent,
My crysme, with the holie sacrament.   245

36

My spreit hartlie I recommend,
In manus Tuas, Domine.
My hoip to the is till ascend,
Rex, quia redemisti me.
Fra syn *resurrexisti me,*   250
Or ellis my saull had bene forlorne.
With sapience *docuisti me.*
Blist be the hour that thow wes borne.

---

225 *lemant*: shining   230 *Sterne*: Star
232 *evin...morrow*: all times
235 *wis*: wish   237 *dissever*: separate
244 *incontinent*: without delay
245 *crysme*: chrism

247 *In...Domine*: Into thy hands, O Lord
249 King, because you have redeemed
me
250 *resurrexisti me*: you have raised me
252 *docuisti me*: you have taught me

ANE DIALOG
BETWIX
EXPERIENCE AND ANE COURTEOUR
(lines 1-684)

The Epistill

1

Thou, lytil quair, of mater miserabyll,
Weil auchtest thou coverit to be with sabyl,
Renunceand grene, the purpur, reid, and quhit.
To delicat men thou art nocht delectabyll,
Nor yit tyll amorous folkis amiabyll.   5
To reid on the thai wyl haif no delite.
Warldlye peple wyll have at the dispyte,
Quhilk fyxit hes thare hart and hole intentis
On sensuall luste, on dignitie, and rentis.

2

We have no kyng, the to present, allace!   10
Quhilk to this countre bene ane cairfull cace,
And als, our quene, of Scotland heretour,
Sche dwellith in France. I pray God saif her grace!
It war to lang for the to ryn that race
And far langar, or that young tender flour   15
Bryng home tyll us ane kyng and governour.
'Allace, tharefor!' we may with sorrow syng,
Quhilk moste so lang remane without one kyng.

3

I nott quhome to thy simpylnes to sende.
With cunnyng men, frome tyme that you be kende,   20
Thy vaniteis no waye thay wyll advance,
Thynkand the proude, sic thyngis to pretende.

---

1 *quair*: book; *miserabyll*: worthless, wretched
2 *Weil*: Well; *auchtest*: deserves; *sabyl*: black
3 *Renunceand*: rejecting; *purpur*: purple; *reid*: red; *quhit*: white
4 *delicat*: refined; *delectabyll*: agreeable
5 *yit*: yet; *tyll*: to; *amorous folkis*: those inclined to love
6 *reid on*: read; *haif*: have
7 *have...dispyte*: regard with contempt
8 *hole*: whole

9 *dignite*: high estate; *rentis*: wealth
10 *the*: thee
11 *Quhilk*: Which; *cairfull*: distressing; *cace*: state of things
12 *heretour*: heir   13 *saif*: save
14 *war*: were; *ryn...race*: follow... course   15 *or*: before; *flour*: flower
18 *moste*: must
19 *nott*: know not; *quhome to*: to whom; *simpylnes*: humble simplicity
20 *cunnyng*: learned; *kende*: known
21 *vaniteis*: self-conceit
22 *sic*: such; *pretende*: put forward

183

Nochtwithstanding, the straucht way sal thou wende
To thame quhilk hes the realme in governance.
Declare thy mynde to thame, with circumstance.   25
Go first tyll James, our prince and protectour,
And his brother, our spirituall governour

4

And prince of preistis in this natioun.
Efter reverend recommendatioun,
Under thare feit thow lawlye the submyt   30
And mak thame humyll supplicatioun:
Geve thay in the fynd wrang narratioun,
That thay wald pleis thy faltis to remyt.
And of thare grace, geve thay do the admyt,
Than go thy waye, quhare ever thow plesis best;   35
Be thay content, mak reverence to the rest.

5

To faithfull prudent pastouris spirituall,
To nobyll erlis, and lordis temporall,
Obedientlye tyll thame thow the addres,
Declaryng thame this schort memoriall,   40
Quhow mankynd bene to miserie maid thrall.
At lenth to thame the cause planelie confesse,
Beseikand thame all lawis to suppresse
Inventit be mennis traditioun,
Contrar to Christis institutioun.   45

6

And cause thame cleirlye for tyll understand
That, for the brekyng of the Lordis command,
His thrinfald wande of flagellatioun
Hes scurgit this pure realme of Scotland
Be mortall weris, baith be sey and land,   50
With mony terrabyll trybulatioun.   Re.xxiiii. and
Tharefore mak to thame trew narratioun   The.ii.

---

23 *straucht*: direct; *sal*: shall
24 *thame*: them
25 *with circumstance*: in detail
30 *lawlye*: humbly
32 *Geve*: If
33 *wald*: would; *pleis*: please; *remyt*: forgive
34 *grace*: favour; *admyt*: receive
36 *Be...content*: If they are satisfied; *mak reverence*: defer to
40 *memoriall*: account
41 *maid thrall*: enslaved
42 *planelie*: clearly
43 *Beseikand*: Entreating
45 *institutioun*: original practice
48 *thrinfald*: threefold; *wande*: rod
49 *pure*: poor   50 *weris*: wars

That al thir weris, this derth, hunger, and pest,
Was nocht bot for our synnis manefest.   i.Cor.iii.

7

Declare to thame quhow, in the tyme of Noye,   55
Alluterlye God did the warld distroye,   Gene.vii
As holy scripture maketh mentioun.
Sodom, Gomor, with thare regioun and roye
(God sparit nothir man, woman, nor boye),   Gene.xix
Bot all wer brynt for thare offentioun.   60
Jherusalem, that moste tryumphant town,
Distroyit wes for thare iniquytie,   Mathew.xxiii
As in the scripture, planelye thay may se.   Luc.xiii.

8

Declare to thame this mortall miserie:
Be sweird and fyre, derth, pest, and povertie,   65
Procedis of syn, gyf I can rycht discryve,   Jere.xv.
For laik of faith and for ydolatrye,
For fornicatioun, and for adultrye
Of princis, prelatis, with mony ane man and wyve.
Expell the cause, than the effect belyve   70
Sall cease, quhen that the peple doith repent.
Than God sall slak his bow quhilk yit is bent.

9

Mak thaim requeist, quhilk hes the governance,
The sinceir word of God for tyll avance
Conforme to Christis institutioun,   75
Without ypocrisie or dissimulance,
Causyng Justice hauld evinlye the ballance:
On publicanis makyng punyssioun,
Commendyng thame of gude conditioun.
That beyng done, I dout nocht bot the Lorde   80
Sall of this countre have misericorde.

10

Thoucht God, with mony terrabyll effrayis,
Hes done this cuntrie scurge by divers wayis

---

53 *thir*: these; *derth*: scarcity
55 *Noye*: Noah
56 *Alluterlye*: Completely
58 *Gomor*: Gomorrah
59 *nothir*: neither
60 *brynt*: burned; *offentioun*: offence
64 *mortall*: fatal   65 *sweird*: sword

70 *than*: then; *belyve*: at once
75 *Conforme to*: According to
76 *dissimulance*: feigning
77 *evinlye*: impartially
78 *publicanis*: sinners; *makyng
  punyssioun*: inflicting punishment
81 *misericorde*: compassion

Be juste jugement for our grevous offence,
Declare to thame thay sall have mery dayis 85
Efter this trubyll, as the propheit sayis.
Quhen God sall se our humyll repentence,
Tyll strange pepyll thoucht he hes gevin lycence
To be our scurge, induryng his desyre,
Wyll, quhen he lyste, that scurge cast in the fyre. 90

11

Pray thame that thay putt nocht thare esperance
In mortall men onelye, thame tyll advance,
Bot principallye in God omnipotent.   Psalme.
Than neid thai not to charge the realme of France   c.xvii.
With gounnis, galayis, nor uther ordinance,   95
So that thay be to God obedient.
In thir premyssis, be thay nocht negligent,
Displayand Christis banar hie on heycht,
Thare ennimeis of thame sall have no mycht.

12

Go hence, pure buke, quhilk I have done indyte 100
In rurall ryme, in maner of dispyte
Contrar the warldlis variatioun;
Of rethorick heir I proclame the quyte.
Idolatouris, I feir, sall with the flyte;
Because of thame thow makis narratioun. 105
Bot cure thow nocht the indignatioun
Of hypocritis and fals Pharisience,
Quhowbeit on the thay cry ane lowde vengence.

13

Requeist the gentyll redar that the redis,
Thocht ornat termes in to thy park not spredis, 110
As thay in the may have experience;

86 *propheit*: prophet
88 *strange*: foreign
90 *lyste*: chooses; *scurge*: whip
91 *Pray*: Entreat; *esperance*: hope
94 *charge*: burden
95 *gounnis*: guns; *galayis*: galleys; *ordinance*: munitions
96 *So that*: So long as
97 *premyssis*: foresaid [matters]
98 *Displayand*: Unfurling; *banar*: banner

100 *pure*: insignificant; *done indyte*: composed
101 *rurall*: unpolished; *dispyte*: contempt
102 *Contrar*: Against
103 *quyte*: destitute
104 *Idolatouris*: Idol worshippers; *flyte*: quarrel
106 *cure...not*: have no regard for
107 *Pharisience*: Pharisees
109 *gentyll*: well-born
110 *ornat*: highly ornamented

Thocht barran feildis beris nocht bot weidis,
Yit brutall beistis sweitlye on thame feidis.
Desyre of thame none uther recompance
Bot that thay wald reid the with pacience, 115
And geve thay be in ony way offendit,
Declare to thame it salbe weill amendit.

Finis.

Heir endis the Epistil and follouis the Prologe.

The Prologe
14

Musing and marvelling on the miserie
Frome day to day in erth quhilk dois incres,
And of ilk stait the instabilitie 120
Proceding of the restles besynes,
Quhare on the most part doith thair mynd addres
Inordinatlie, on houngrye covatyce,
Vaine glore, dissait, and uthir sensuall vyce,

15

Bot tumlyng in my bed I mycht nocht lye. 125
Quhairfore I fuir furth in ane Maye mornyng,
Conforte to gett of my malancolye,
Sumquhat affore fresche Phebus uperysing,
Quhare I mycht heir the birdis sweitlie syng.
Intyll ane park I past, for my plesure, 130
Decorit weill be craft of dame Nature.

16

Quhow I ressavit confort naturall
For tyll discryve at lenth, it war to lang;
Smelling the holsum herbis medicinall,
Quhare on the dulce and balmy dew down dang, 135
Lyke aurient peirles on the twistis hang,

---

112 *barran*: barren; *beris*: produces;
  nocht: nothing
113 *brutall beistis*: animals
119 *dois*: does; *incres*: increase
120 *ilk*: each; *stait*: estate
122 *addres*: direct
123 *Inordinatlie*: Excessively
124 *Vaine glore*: Vainglory
125 *tumlyng*: tossing; *lye*: settle
126 *fuir furth*: went abroad

128 *affore*: before; *Phebus uperysing*:
  sunrise
130 *Intyll*: Into   131 *Decorit*: Adorned
132 *Quhow*: How; *ressavit*: received;
  confort naturall: consolation from
  nature   134 *holsum*: health-giving
135 *dulce*: sweet-smelling; *balmy*:
  fragrant; *down dang*: beat down
136 *aurient*: eastern, finest; *twistis*:
  branches

Or quhow that the aromatik odouris
Did proceid frome the tender fragrant flouris.

17

Or quhow Phebus, that king etheriall,
Swyftlie sprang up in to the orient,   140
Ascending in his throne imperiall,
Quhose brycht and buriall bemes resplendent
Illumynit all on to the occident,
Confortand everye corporall creature
Quhilk formit war, in erth, be dame Nature.   145

18

Quhose donke impurpurit vestiment nocturnall,
With his imbroudit mantyll matutyne,
He lefte in tyll his regioun aurorall
(Quhilk on hym watit quhen he did declyne
Towarte his occident palyce vespertyne)   150
And rose in habyte gaye and glorious,
Brychtar nor gold, or stonis precious.

19

Bot Synthea, the hornit nychtis quene,
Scho loste hir lycht and lede ane lawar saill
Frome tyme hir soverane lorde that scho had sene,   155
And in his presens waxit dirk and paill
And over hir visage kest ane mistye vaill.
So did Venus, the goddes amorous,
With Jupiter, Mars, and Mercurius;

20

Rychtso the auld intoxicat Saturne,   160
Persavyng Phebus powir his beymes brycht,
Abufe the erth than maid he no sudgeourne,
Bot suddandlye did lose his borrowit lycht

---

139 *etheriall*: heavenly
140 *orient*: east
142 *buriall*: sparkling; *resplendent*:
   shining   143 *occident*: west
144 *corporall*: bodily
146 *donke*: moist; *impurpurit*:
   empurpled
147 *imbroudit*: embroidered; *mantyll*:
   loose cloak; *matutyne*: of the
   morning
148 *aurorall*: of the dawn
149 *on...watit*: awaited

150 *occident*: western; *vespertyne*: of
   the evening
151 *habyte*: dress
152 *nor*: than
153 *Synthea*: Cynthia; *hornit*: horned
155 *soverane*: supreme
156 *waxit*: grew [astrol.]; *dirk*: dark
157 *vaill*: veil   160 *intoxicat*: poisoned
161 *Persavyng*: Perceiving; *powir*: shed,
   send forth; *beymes*: rays
162 *maid...sudgeourne*: did not linger

(Quhilk he durst nevir schaw bot on the nycht).
The Pole Artick, Ursis and sterris all,   165
Quhilk situate ar in the septemtrionall,

21

(Tyll errand schyppis quhilks ar the sover gyde,
Convoyand thame upone the stromye nycht),
Within thare frostie circle did thame hyde.
Howbeit that sterris have none uthir lycht   170
Bot the reflex of Phebus bemes brycht,
That day durst none in to the hevin appeir
Tyll he had circuit all our hemispeir.

22

Me thocht it was ane sycht celestiall
To sene Phebus so angellyke ascend   175
In tyll his fyrie chariot tryumphall,
Quhose bewte brycht I culd nocht comprehend.
All warldlie cure anone did fro me wend
Quhen fresche Flora spred furth hir tapestrie,
Wrocht, be dame Nature, quent and curiouslie,   180

23

Depaynt with mony hundreth hevinlie hewis,
Glaid of the rysing of thare royall roye,
With blomes breckand on the tender bewis,
Quhilk did provoke myne hart tyl natural joye.
Neptune, that day, and Eoll, held thame coye,   185
That men on far mycht heir the birdis sounde,
Quhose noyis did to the sterrye hevin redounde.

24

The plesand powne, prunyeand his feddrem fair,
The myrthfull maves maid gret melodie,
The lustye lark ascending in the air,   190

165 *sterris*: stars
166 *septemtrionall*: [celestial] north
167 *errand*: wandering; *sover*: sure
168 *Convoyand*: guiding; *stromye*:
    stormy
170 *Howbeit*: Although; *lycht*: light
173 *circuit*: gone round
174 *sycht*: sight
175 *sene*: see   176 *In tyll*: In
178 *cure*: care; *wend*: go
181 *Depaynt*: Painted

182 *roye*: king
183 *blomes*: blossoms; *breckand*:
    opening up; *bewis*: boughs
184 *provoke*: arouse; *natural*: instinctive
185 *Eoll*: Aeolus; *held...coye*: kept quiet
186 *on far*: at a distance
187 *noyis*: rejoicing; *redounde*: resound
188 *powne*: peacock; *prunyeand*:
    preening; *feddrem*: plumage
189 *maves*: song-thrush

Numerand hir naturall notis craftelye;
The gay goldspink, the merll rycht myrralye,
The noyis of the nobyll nychtingalis
Redundit throuch the montans, meids, and valis.

25

Contempling this melodious armonye   195
(Quhow everilke bird drest thame for tyl advance
To saluss Nature with thare melodye),
That I stude gasing, halflingis in ane trance,
To heir thame mak thare naturall observance
So royallie that all the roches rang   200
Throuch repercussioun of thare suggurit sang.

26

I lose my tyme, allace, for to rehers
Sick unfrutful and vaine discriptioun;
Or wrytt, in to my raggit, rurall vers,
Mater without edificatioun,   205
Consydering quhow that myne intentioun
Bene tyll deplore the mortall misereis,
With continuall cairfull calamiteis,

27

Consisting in this wracheit vaill of sorrow.
Bot sad sentence sulde have ane sad indyte.   210
So termes brycht I lyste nocht for to borrow;
Of murnyng mater men hes no delyte.
With roustye termes tharefor wyl I wryte.
With sorrowful seychis ascending frome the splene
And bitter teris distellyng frome myne eine,   215

191 *Numerand*: measuring out
    proportionately
192 *goldspink*: goldfinch; *merll*: blackbird
194 *Redundit*: Resounded; *meids*:
    meadows
195 *Contempling*: Contemplating;
    armonye: harmony
196 *drest...advance*: prepared
    themselves to go forward
197 *saluss*: greet
198 *gasing*: staring; *halflingis*: half
201 *repercussioun*: reverberation;
    suggurit: sweet
202 *rehers*: recite formally
203 *Sick*: Such; *unfrutful*: unprofitable;
    vaine: useless
204 *raggit*: disordered; *rurall*: rustic
205 *Mater*: Material; *edificatioun*:
    instruction
207 *deplore*: lament; *mortall*: deadly
208 *cairfull*: sorrowful
209 *wracheit*: miserable
210 *sad*: serious; *sentence*: utterance;
    indyte: expression
211 *termes*: figures of speech; *brycht*:
    bright; *lyste*: choose
212 *murnyng*: distressing
213 *roustye*: unpolished
214 *seychis*: sighs; *splene*: 'heart' [lit.
    spleen]
215 *distellyng*: falling; *eine*: eyes

28

Withoute ony vaine invocatioun
To Minerva or to Melpominee,
Nor yitt wyll I mak supplicatioun
For help to Cleo, nor Caliopee—
Sick marde musis may mak me no supplee.   220
Proserpyne, I refuse, and Apollo,
And rycht so Euterp, Jupiter, and Juno,

29

Quhilkis bene to plesand poetis conforting.
Quharefor, because I am nocht one of tho,
I do desyre of thame no supporting.   225
For I did never sleip on Pernaso,
As did the poetis of lang tyme ago,
And speciallie the ornate Ennius;
Nor drank I never with Hysiodus,

30

Of Grece the perfyte poet soverane;   230
Of Hylicon, the sors of eloquence,
Of that mellifluus, famous, fresche fontane:
Quharefor, I awe to thame no reverence.
I purpose nocht to mak obedience
To sic mischeand musis, nor malmontrye   235
Afore tyme usit in to poetrye.

31

Raveand Rhammusia, goddes of dispyte,
Mycht be to me ane muse rycht convenabyll,
Gyff I desyrit sic help for tyll indyte
This murnyng mater, mad, and miserabyll.   240
I mon go seik ane muse more confortabyl
And sic vaine superstitioun to refuse,
Beseikand the gret God to be my muse,

---

216 *ony*: any   218 *yitt*: yet
219 *Cleo*: Clio; *Caliopee*: Calliope
220 *marde*: impaired; *supplee*:
   assistance
221 *Proserpyne*: Prosperpina
223 *conforting*: encouragement
224 *tho*: those   226 *Pernaso*: Parnassus
229 *Hysiodus*: Hesiod
230 *perfyte*: skilled
231 *Hylicon*: Helicon; *sors*: source

232 *mellifluus*: honeyed; *fontane*: natural
   spring   233 *awe*: owe
234 *purpose nocht*: do not intend; *mak
   obedience*: pay homage
235 *mischeand*: wicked; *malmontrye*:
   idols   236 *Afore tyme*: Formerly
237 *Raveand Rhammusia*: Raving
   Nemesis; *dispyte*: animosity
238 *convenabyll*: appropriate
240 *murnyng*: sorrowful; *mad*: distressing
241 *mon*: must; *confortabyl*: comforting

32

Be quhose wysdome al maner of thing bene wrocht   Genes.i.
(The heych hevinnis, with all thair ornamentis),   245
And without mater maid all thing of nocht,
Hell in myd centir of the elementis.   iii.Re.iii
That hevinlye muse, to seik my hole intent is,   Psalme.lxxxix
The quhilk gaif sapience to king Salomone,
To David grace, strenth to the strang Sampsone.   250

33

And of pure Peter maid ane prudent precheour,   Juges xiii.
And, be the power of his deitee,   Mat.iiii
Of creuell Paule he maid ane cunnyng techeour.   Actis.ix.
I mon beseik rycht lawly on my knee,
His heych superexcellent majestie,   255
That with his hevinlye spreit he me inspyre
To wrytt no thyng contrarye his disyre.

34

Beseikand als his soverane sonne, Jesu,   Luc.i.
Quhilk wes consavit be the Holy Spreit,
Incarnat of the purifyit Virgin trew,   260
In to the quhome the prophicie was compleit.
That prince of peace moist humyll and mansweit,
Quhilk onder Pylate sufferit passioun   Luc.xxiii
Upone the croce for our salvatioun.

35

And, be that creuell deith intollerabyll,   265
Lowsit we wer frome bandis of Balyall.
And mairattovir, it wes so proffitabyll
That, to this hour, come nevir man nor sall
To the tryumphant joye imperiall
Of lyfe, quhowbeit that thay war never sa gude,   270
Bot be the vertew of that precious blude.   Hebr.ix.

36

Quharefor, in steid of the Mont Pernaso,
Swyftlie I sall go seik my soverane.

---

245 *heych*: high; *ornamentis*: stars [fig.]
251 *pure*: unfortunate; *prudent*: wise
252 *be*: by   253 *cunnyng*: skilled
256 *spreit*: spirit
258 *als*: also   259 *consavit*: conceived
260 *Incarnat*: Made flesh
262 *mansweit*: meek

263 *onder*: on the authority of; *passioun*:
     pain of martyrdom   264 *croce*: cross
266 *Lowsit*: Released; *bandis...Balyall*:
     fetters of Belial
267 *mairattovir*: moreover; *proffitabyll*:
     beneficial   272 *steid*: place

To Mont Calvare the straucht waye mon I go,
To gett ane taist of that moist fresche fontane.   275
That sors to seik my hart may nocht refrane,
Of Hylicone, quhilk wes boith deip and wyde,
That Longeous did grave in tyll his syde.   Jho.xix.
                          37
From that fresche fontane sprang a famous flude,
Quhilk redolent rever throuch the warld yit rynnis,   280
As christall cleir and mixit bene with blude,
Quhose sound abufe the heyest hevinnis dinnis,
All faithfull peple purgeing frome thare synnis.
Quharefor, I sall beseik his excellence
To grant me grace, wysedome, and eloquence   285
                          38
And bayth me with those dulce and balmy strandis,
Quhilk on the croce did spedalie out spryng
Frome his moste tender feit, and hevinly handis,
And grant me grace to wrytt nor dyte no thyng
Bot tyll his heych honour, and loude lovyng;   290
But quhose support thare may na gude be wrocht
Tyll his plesure—gude workis, word, nor thocht.
                          39
Tharefor, O Lorde, I pray thy majestie,
As thou did schaw thy heych power divyne
First planelie in the Cane of Galelee,   295
Quhare thou convertit cauld watter in wyne,   Jhon.ii.
Convoye my mater tyll ane fructuous fyne
And save my sayingis baith frome schame and syn.
Tak tent, for now I purpose to begyn.
                    Finis.
              Heir endis the Prologe

              And beginnis the Mater.

274 *straucht*: direct, true
275 *taist*: taste; *moist*: most
278 *grave*: cut
280 *redolent*: fragrant
282 *dinnis*: resounds
286 *bayth*: bathe; *strandis*: streams
289 *dyte*: compose

290 *loude lovyng*: open praise
291 *wrocht*: wrought
295 *Cane...Galelee*: Cana of Galilee
297 *Convoye*: Guide; *fructuous*: fruitful; *fyne*: end
298 *save*: deliver
299 *Tak tent*: Pay attention

Into that park I sawe appeir   300
One ageit man, quhilk drew me neir,
Quhose beird wes weil thre quarteris lang.
His hair doun over his schulders hang,
The quhilk as ony snaw wes quhyte,
Quhome to behald I thocht delyte.   305
His habitt, angellyke of hew,
Of culloure lyke the sapheir blew.
Onder ane hollyng he reposit,
Of quhose presens I was rejosit.
I did hym saluss reverendlye,   310
So did he me rycht courteslye.
To sitt down he requeistit me,
Onder the schaddow of that tre
To saif me frome the sonnis heit,
Amangis the flowris, softe and sweit,   315
For I wes werye for walking.
Than we began to fall in talking.
I sperit his name with reverence.
    'I am', said he, 'Experience.'
    'Than schir,' said I, 'ye can nocht faill   320
To gyff ane desolate man counsaill.
Ye do appeir ane man of faime,
And, sen Experience bene your name,
I praye you, Father venerabyll,
Geve me sum counsell confortabyll.   325
    'Quhate bene', quod he, 'thy vocatioun,
Makand sic supplycatioun?'
    'I haif', quod I, 'bene to this hour
Sen I could ryde, one Courteour.
Bot now, Father, I thynk it best,   330
With your counsell, to leif in rest
And frome thynefurth to tak myne eais
And quyetlie my God to pleais

---

301 *One*: An; *ageit*: aged
302 *beird*: beard
306 *habitt*: dress; *hew*: appearance
307 *sapheir*: sapphire
308 *Onder*: Under; *hollyng*: holly tree
309 *rejosit*: gladdened
311 *courteslye*: courteously

316 *werye*: weary; *for*: because of
317 *fall*: engage   318 *sperit*: asked
322 *faime*: good repute   323 *sen*: since
329 *Courteour*: Courtier   331 *leif*: live
332 *thynefurth*: thenceforth; *tak...eais*: live in ease

And renunce curiositie,
Leveyng the court and lerne to de.   335
Oft have I salit over the strandis
And travalit throuch divers landis,
Boith south and north, and est and west;
Yitt can I never fynd quhare rest
Doith mak his habitatioun,   340
Withoute your supportatioun.
Quhen I beleif to be best easit,
Most suddantlye I am displeasit.
Frome trubbyll, quhen I fastast fle,
Than fynd I most adversate.   345
Schaw me, I pray yow hartfullye,
Quhow I may leif most plesandlye,
To serve my God, of kyngis kyng,
Sen I am tyrit for travellyng.
And lerne me for to be content   350
Of quyet lyfe and sobir rent,
That I may thank the kyng of glore
As thocht I had ane mylyeoun more.
Sen everilk court bene variant,
Full of invy, and inconstant,   355
Mycht I but trubbyll leif in rest,
Now in my aige I thynk it best.'
        'Thow art ane gret fuill, soune,' said he,
'Thyng to desyre quhilk may nocht be,
Yarnyng to have prerogatyve   360
Above all creature on lyfe.
Sen father Adam creat bene
In to the campe of Damassene,
Mycht no man say on to this hour
That ever he fand perfyte plesour,   365
Nor never sall, tyll that he se

334 *curiositie*: [undue] refinement
336 *strandis*: seas
337 *travalit*: travelled
341 *supportatioun*: support
345 *adversate*: adversity
346 *hartfullye*: sincerely
347 *leif*: live   349 *tyrit for*: weary of
351 *sobir*: moderate; *rent*: income
356 *but*: without

358 *fuill*: fool; *soune*: son
359 *Thyng*: Things
360 *Yarnyng*: Yearning; *prerogatyve*:
        precedence
361 *on lyfe*: alive
362 *creat bene*: was created
363 *campe*: field; *Damassene*: Damascus
365 *fand*: found

God in his divyne majestie.
Quharefore prepair the for travell,
Sen mennis lyfe bene bot battell.   Job.vii.
All men begynnis for tyll de   370
The day of thare nativite.
And journelly thay do proceid
Tyll Atrops cute the fatell threid
And in the breif tyme that thay have,
Betwix thare byrth on to thare grave,   375
Thow seis quhat mutabiliteis,
Quhat miserabyll calamiteis,
Quhat trubbyll, travell, and debait
Seis thow in evere mortall stait.
Begyn at pure lawe creaturis,   380
Ascending syne to synaturis,
To gret princis and potestatis,
Thow sall nocht fynd, in non estatis,
Sen the begynning, gennerallie,
Nor in our tyme now, speciallie,   385
Bot tiddious restles besynes
Bot ony maner of sickarnes.'
     'Prudent Father,' quod I, 'allace!
Ye tell to me one cairfull cace.
Ye say that no man, to this hour,   390
Hes found in erth perfyte plesour
Without infortunat variance.
Sen we bene thrall to sic myschance,
Quhy do we set so our intentis
On ryches, dignitie, and rentis,   395
Sen in the erth bene no man sure
One day but trubbyll tyll indure?
And, werst of all, quhen we leist wene,
The creuell deith we mon sustene.

368 *travell*: labour   386 *Bot*: Except; *tiddious*: tedious
372 *journelly*: daily   387 *sickarnes*: certainty
373 *Atrops*: Atropus; *cute*: cuts   389 *cairfull*: distressing
376 *mutabiliteis*: inconstancies   392 *infortunat*: unfortunate
377 *miserabyll*: lamentable   393 *bene thrall*: are in bondage
379 *stait*: condition   394 *intentis*: minds
380 *lawe*: low   395 *dignitie*: high estate
381 *synaturis*: senators   398 *wene*: expect
382 *potestatis*: magnates   399 *sustene*: endure

Geve I your fatherheid durste demand,   400
The cause I wald faine understand.
And als, Father, I yow implore,
Schaw me sum trubbyll gone afore,
That heryng utheris indigence
I may the more haif patience.   405
Marrowis in trybulatioun
Bene wracheis consolatioun.'
  Quod he, 'Efter my small cunnyng,
To the I sall mak answeryng,
Bot ordourlie for to begyn,   410
This misarie procedis of syn.
Bot it wer lang for to defyn it,
Quhow all men ar to syn inclynit.
Quhen syn aboundantlye doith ryng,
Justly, God makith punyssing.   415
Quharefore, gret God in to his handis
To dant the warld hes divers wandis.
Efter our evyll conditioun,
He makis on us punytioun,
With hunger, darth and indigens.   420
Sum tyme, gret plagis and pestilens,
And sum tyme, with his bludy wand
Throw creuell weir, be sey and land.
Concludyng, all our misarie
Proceidis of syn, alluterlie.'   425
  'Father,' quod I, 'declare to me
The cause of this fragyllitie,
That we bene all to syn inclynde,
In werk, in word, and in our mynde.
I wald the veritie wer schawin   430
Quho hes this seid amang us sawin,
And quhy we ar condampnit to dede
And quhow that we may get remede.'

---

400 *fatherheid*: fatherly authority
404 *heryng*: hearing; *indigence*:
   poverty
406 *Marrowis*: Companions
408 *cunnyng*: knowledge
410 *ordourlie*: in ordered fashion

412 *defyn*: describe
414 *ryng*: prevail
417 *dant*: chastise
427 *fragyllitie*: frailty   432 *dede*: death
433 *get remede*: make amends

Quod he, 'The scripture hes concludit:
Men frome felicitie wer denudit   435
Be Adam, our progenitour,   Gen.iii.
Umquhyle of Paradyse possessour;
Be quhose most wylfull arrogance
Wes mankynd brocht to this myschance,
Quhen he wes inobedient   440
In breking Godis commandiment.
Be solystatioun of his wyfe,
He loste that hevinlye plesand lyfe,
Etand of the forbiddin tre.
Thare began all our miserrie.   445
So Adam wes cause radicall   Rom.v.
That we bene fragyll synnaris all.
Adam brocht in this natioun
Syn, deith, and als dampnatioun.
Quho wyll say he is no synnar,   450
Christ sayis he is ane gret lear.   i.Joh.i
Mankynde sprang furth of Adamis loynis
And tuke of hym flesche, blude, and bonis,
And so, efter his qualytie,
All ar inclynit synnaris to be.   455
    Bot yit, my sonne, dispare thow nocht,
For God, that all the warld hes wrocht,
Hes maid ane soverane remede,
To saif us boith frome syn and dede
And frome etarne dampnatioun.   460
Tharefore tak consolatioun,
For God, as scripture doith recorde,
Haveyng of man misericorde,
Send doun his onelye sonne, Jesu,
Quhilk lychtit in one virgin trew,   465
And cled his heych divynitie
With our pure vyle humanytie.
Syne frome our synnis, to conclude,   Apoca.ii
He wysche us with his precious blude.

---

437 *Umquhyle*: Formerly
442 *solystatioun*: persistent pleading
446 *radicall*: primary
451 *lear*: liar   454 *qualytie*: nature

460 *etarne*: eternal
463 *misericorde*: compassion
465 *lychtit*: alighted
466 *cled*: clothed   469 *wysche*: washed

Quhowbeit, throw Adam, we mon dee,   470
Throuch that Lord we sall rasit bee,   Rom.v.
And everilk man he sall releve   Hebre.x
Quhilk in his blude dois ferme beleve,
And bryng us all unto his glore,
The quhilk throw Adam bene forlore,   475
Without that we, throw laik of faith,
Of his Godheid incur the wraith.
Bot quho in Christ fermely belevis   Joh.iii.v
Sall be relevit frome all myschevis.'
    'Quhat faith is that, that ye call ferme?   480
Schir, gar me understand that terme.'
    'Faith without hope and charitie   Hebr.xi.
Avalit nocht, my sonne,' said he.
    'Quhat charite bene? That wald I knaw.'
    Quod he, 'My sonne, that sall I schaw.   485
First, lufe thy God above all thyng   i.Corin.xiii.
And thy nychtbour but fenyeyng.
Do none injure, nor villanie,
Bot as thow wald wer done to the.
Quyk faith, but cheretabyll werkis,   490
Can never be, as wryttis clerkis,   Jaco.ii.
More than the fyre, in tyll his mycht,
Can be but heit, nor sonne but lycht.
Geve charitie in to the failis,
Thy faith, nor hope, no thyng availis.   495
The Devyll hes faith, and trymlis for dreid,
Bot he wantis hope, and lufe in deid.
Do all the gude that may be wrocht:
But charitie all availis nocht.
Quharefore, pray to the Trinite   500
For tyll support thy charite.
    Now have I schawin the, as I can,
Quhow father Adam, the first man,
Brocht in the warld boith syn and dede,
And quhow Christ Jesu maid remede,   505

---

470 *throw*: through
471 *rasit bee*: be raised [from the dead]
472 *releve*: free
475 *forlore*: lost   477 *wraith*: anger
480 *ferme*: firm

487 *nychtbour*: fellow creatures;
    fenyeyng: false pretence
488 *villanie*: evil   490 *Quyk*: Living
496 *trymlis*: trembles 497 *wantis*: lacks
500 *Trinite*: Trinity

Quhilk, on the day of Jugement,
Sall us delyver frome torment
And bryng us to his lestyng glore,
Quhilk sall indure for ever more.
Bot in this warld, thow gettis no rest,   510
I mak it to the manifest.
Tharefore, my sonne, be diligent
And lerne for to be patient
And in to God sett all thy traist.
All thyng sall than cum for the best.'   515
    'Father, I thank yow hartfullye
Of your conforte and cumpanye
And hevinlye consolatioun,
Makand yow supplicatioun
(Geve I durst put yow to sic pyne),   520
That ye wald pleis for to defyne
And gar me cleirlye understand,
Quhow Adam brak the Lordis command,
And quhow, throw his transgressioun,
Wer punyst his successioun.'   525
    'My sonne,' quod he, 'wald thow tak cure
To luke on the divyne scripture,
In to the buke of Genesis,
That storye thare thow sall nocht mis;
And alswa syndrie cunnyng clerkis   530
Hes done rehers, in to thare werkis,
Of Adamis fall, full ornatly,
Ane thousand tymes better nor I
Can wrytt of that unhappy man.
Bot I sall do the best I can,   535
Schortlie to schaw that cairfull cace,
With the support of Goddis grace.'

---

508 *lestyng*: everlasting   522 *gar*: make
514 *traist*: trust   526 *cure*: care
520 *pyne*: trouble   530 *clerkis*: scholars, theologians

Ane Exclamatioun to the Redar,
Tuycheyng the Wryttyng of Vulgare and Maternall Language

1

Gentyl redar, haif at me non dispyte,
Thynkand that I presumptuously pretend
In vulgair toung so heych mater to writ,   540
Bot quhair I mys, I pray the till amend.
Tyll unlernit I wald the cause wer kend
Of our most miserabyll travell and torment,
And quhow in erth no place bene parmanent.

2

Quhowbeit that divers devote cunnyng clerkis   545
In Latyne toung hes wryttin syndrie bukis,
Our unlernit knawis lytill of thare werkis
More than thay do the ravyng of the rukis.
Quharefore, to colyearis, cairtaris and to cukis,
To Jok and Thome my ryme sall be diractit,   550
With cunnyng men quhowbeit it wylbe lactit.

3

Thocht every commoun may nocht be one clerk,
Nor hes no leid except thare toung maternall,
Quhy suld of God the marvellous hevinly werk
Be hid frome thame? I thynk it nocht fraternall.   555
The father of hevin, quhilk wes and is eternall,
To Moyses gaif the law, on Mont Senay,   Exo.xx.
Nocht in to Greik, nor Latyne, I heir say.

4

He wrait the law, in tablis hard of stone,
In thare awin vulgare language of Hebrew,   560
That all the bairnis of Israell, every one,
Mycht knaw the law and so the sam ensew.
Had he done wryt in Latyne, or in Grew,

Subheading: *Exclamatioun*: Outcry
538 *haif...dispyte*: do not regard me with
    disdain
539 *pretend*: attempt
540 *vulgair*: vernacular; *heych*: weighty
541 *mys*: err
542 *unlernit*: the untaught; *kend*: known
545 *devote*: devout   548 *rukis*: rooks
549 *colyearis*: coal miners; *cairtaris*:
    carters; *cukis*: cooks

550 *diractit*: addressed
551 *lactit*: derided
552 *commoun*: common person
553 *leid*: language
557 *Mont Senay*: Mount Sinai
559 *wrait*: wrote   561 *bairnis*: children
562 *sam*: same; *ensew*: follow
563 *Grew*: Greek

It had to thame bene bot ane sawrles jest;
Ye may weill wytt God wrocht all for the best.   565
5

Arristotyll, nor Plato, I heir sane,
Wrait nocht thare hie philosophie naturall
In Duche, nor Dence, nor toung Italiane,
Bot in thare most ornate toung maternall,
Quhose fame and name doith ryng perpetuall.   570
Famous Virgill, the prince of poetrie,
Nor Cicero, the flour of oratrie,
6

Wrait nocht in Caldye language, nor in Grew,
Nor yit in to the language Sarayene,
Nor in the naturall language of Hebrew,   575
Bot in the Romane toung, as may be sene,
Quhilk wes thair proper language, as I wene.
Quhen Romanis rang dominatoris in deid,
The ornat Latyne wes thare propir leid.
7

In the mene tyme, quhen that thir bauld Romance   580
Over all the warld had the dominioun,
Maid Latyne scolis thare glore for tyll avance,
That thare language mycht be over all commoun,
To that intent, be my opinion,
Traistyng that thare impyre sulde ay indure,   585
Bot of fortune, alway, thay wer nocht sure.
8

Of languagis, the first diversytie   Gene.xx.
Wes maid be Goddis maledictioun,
Quhen Babilone wes beildit in Calde;
Those beildaris gat none uther afflictioun.   590
Affore the tyme of that punyssioun,
Wes bot one toung, quhilk Adam spak hym self,
Quhare now of toungis thare bene thre score and twelf.

---

564 *sawrles*: insipid   565 *wytt*: know
566 *Arristotyll*: Aristotle; *sane*: say
568 *Duche*: German; *Dence*: Danish
569 *ornate*: embellished
573 *Caldye*: Chaldean
574 *Sarayene*: Saracen
575 *naturall*: inborn   577 *proper*: native

578 *rang dominatoris*: wielded power; *in deid*: in act   580 *Romance*: Romans
582 *scolis*: schools
583 *over...commoun*: in general use
585 *sulde*: would; *ay*: always
589 *beildit*: built; *Calde*: Chaldea
590 *beildaris*: builders; *gat*: received
593 *thre...twelf*: i.e. seventy two

10

Nochtwithstandyng, I thynk it gret plesour,
Quhare cunnyng men hes languagis anew,   595
That in thare youth, be deligent laubour,
Hes leirnit Latyne, Greik, and ald Hebrew.
That I am nocht of that sorte, sore I rew,
Quharefore, I wald all bukis necessare
For our faith wer intyll our toung vulgare.   600

11

Christ, efter his glorious ascentioun,   Actis.ii.
Tyll his disciplis send the Holy Spreit
In toungis of fyre, to that intentioun,
Thay, beand of all languagis repleit,
Throuch all the warld, with wordis fair and sweit,   605
Tyll every man the faith thay suld furth schaw,
In thare awin leid delyverand thame the law.

12

Tharefore I thynk one gret dirisioun
To heir thir nunnis and systeris, nycht and day,
Syngand and sayand psalmes and orisoun,   610
Nocht understandyng quhat thay syng nor say,
Bot lyke one stirlyng, or ane papingay
(Quhilk leirnit ar to speik be lang usage),
Thame I compair to byrdis in ane cage.

13

Rycht so childreyng and ladyis of honouris   615
Prayis in Latyne, to thame ane uncuth leid,
Mumland thair matynis, evinsang and thare houris,
Thare *Pater Noster*, *Ave*, and thare *Creid*.
It wer als plesand to thare spreit in deid
(God have mercy on me for to say thus)   620
As to say *Miserere mei, Deus*.

14

Sanct Jerome, in his propir toung Romane,
The law of God he trewlie did translait

---

595 *anew*: sufficient   612 *stirlyng*: starling; *papingay*: parrot
598 *sorte*: company   613 *usage*: practice
601 *ascentioun*: ascension   615 *honouris*: good reputation
604 *repleit*: fully endowed   616 *uncuth leid*: unknown language
607 *law*: divine ordinances   617 *Mumland*: Mumbling
608 *one...dirisioun*: a [matter for] great
     scorn

Out of Hebrew, and Greik, in Latyne plane,
Quhilk hes bene hid frome us lang tyme—God wait,   625
Onto this tyme—bot, efter myne consait,
Had Sanct Jerome bene borne in tyll Argyle,
In to Irische toung his bukis had done compyle.

15

Prudent Sanct Paull doith mak narratioun   i.Cor.xiiii
Tuycheyng the divers leid of every land,   630
Sayand thare bene more edificatioun
In fyve wordis that folk doith understand,
Nor to pronunce of wordis ten thousand
In strange langage, sine wait not quhat it menis.
I thynk sic pattryng is not worth twa prenis.   635

16

Unlernit peple, on the holy day,
Solemnitlye thay heir the Evangell soung,
Nocht knawyng quhat the preist dois sing nor say,
Bot as ane bell, quhen that thay heir it roung.
Yit, wald the preistis in to thare mother toung,   640
Pas to the pulpitt, and that doctryne declare,
Tyll lawid pepyll it wer more necessare.

17

I wald prelattis and doctouris of the law
With us lawid peple wer nocht discontent,
Thocht we in to our vulgare toung did knaw   645
Of Christ Jesu, the lyfe and testament,
And quhow that we sulde keip commandiment,
Bot in our language lat us pray and reid
Our *Pater Noster, Ave*, and our *Creid*.

18

I wald sum prince of gret discretioun   650
In vulgare language planelye gart translait
The neidfull lawis of this regioun.

---

627 *Argyle*: Argyll
628 *Irische*: Irish [Gaelic]
630 *Tuycheyng*: Concerning
633 *Nor*: Than
634 *sine*: then; *wait*: knows
635 *pattryng*: rapid muttering of prayers;
    prenis: pins

637 *Evangell*: Gospel
642 *lawid*: untutored; *necessare*: useful
643 *wald*: wish
644 *discontent*: displeased
650 *discretioun*: discernment
651 *gart translait*: have translated
652 *neidfull*: necessary

Than wald thare nocht be half so gret debait
Amang us peple of the law estait;
Geve every man the veryte did knaw,   655
We nedit nocht to treit thir men of law.
19

Tyll do our nychtbour wrang we wald be war,
Gyf we did feir the lawis punysment.
Thare wald nocht be sic brawlyng at the bar,
Nor men of law loup to sic royall rent.   660
To keip the law, gyf all men war content,
And ilk man do as he wald be done to,
The jugis wald get lytill thyng ado.
20

The propheit David, kyng of Israell,
Compyld the plesand psalmes of the Psaltair   665
In his awin propir toung, as I heir tell;
And Salamone, quhilk wes his sone and air,
Did mak his buke in tyll his toung vulgare.
Quhy suld nocht thare sayng be tyll us schawin
In our language? I wald the cause wer knawin.   670
21

Lat doctoris wrytt thare curious questionis,
And argumentis sawin full of sophistrye,
Thare logick and thare heych opinionis,
Thare dirk jugementis of astronomye,
Thare medecyne and thare philosophye.   675
Latt poetis schaw thare glorious ingyne
As ever thay pleis, in Greik or in Latyne,
22

Bot lat us haif the bukis necessare
To commoun weill and our salvatioun,
Justlye translatit in our toung vulgare.   680
And als I mak the supplicatioun:
O gentyll redar, haif none indignatioun,
Thynkand I mell me with so hie matair.
Now to my purpose fordwart wyll I fair.

---

656 *treit*: deal with   657 *war*: cautious   667 *air*: heir   669 *sayng*: wise precepts
659 *brawlyng*: noisy contention   671 *curious*: expert   674 *dirk*: obscure
660 *loup*: jump; *royall*: splendid   680 *Justlye*: Accurately
665 *Psaltair*: Book of Psalms   683 *mell me*: involve myself

NOTES

The Dreme, c.1526

Text: The text is based on the earliest extant Scottish edition of 1559, printed by John Scot, in Edinburgh, *STC* 15675 (= Sc). Copies of this, with three other shorter poems, were bound with remaining copies of Scot's 1554 text of *Ane Dialog betwix Experience and ane Courteour* (*STC* 15672) to form a composite edition. Two extant earlier editions were printed in France during 1558, and are thought to be the work of Jean Petit of Rouen or his heirs, *STC* 15673 (= P); *STC* 15674 (= P(oct)). These suffer from the hands of compositors unfamiliar with Scots: where, for example, at 196 Sc has *deneris*, P and P(oct) have the meaningless *dinein*; at 498, Sc has *nynt*; P, P(oct) *mynt*; at 924, Sc's *malancolious* is altered to the contextually absurd *malicious* in P and P(oct); at 1026, similarly, Sc's *boltis* loses all logic in the *boitis* of P and P(oct). Nonetheless, P and P(oct) are important witnesses: it has been argued plausibly that they descend more directly from the first edition of *The Dreme*, now lost, than did the text that Scot has used (see Hamer 1931-36: III.2-9). P and P(oct) offer some preferable readings, which are noted. Sc, P and P(oct) were collated with the 1568 Edinburgh edition printed by Scot for Henry Charteris, *STC* 15658 (= C), also occasionally preferred.

Title: From Sc: *Heir followis the Dreme of Schir David Lyndesay of the mont, Familiar Servitour to our Soverane Lord Kyng James the Fyft.*

Form: The poem begins as a petition, at this time a well known and variable verse form: cf. Dunbar, *I thocht lang quhill* (B22) and *My lordis of chalker* (B36). Lyndsay's first stanzas enumerate his faithful services to the king during his youth, and emphasise the mutuality of good service and recompence. The main part of the poem is told as an allegorical dream (cf. 'visioun', 147), a literary form with classical antecedents (cf. Cicero's *Somnium Scipionis, De Re Publica*), and of great popularity from the late 14th to the late 16th c. (cf. de Lorris and de Meun, *The Romance of the Rose*; Chaucer, *HF, PF*; Lydgate, *Reson and Sensuallyte*; Douglas, *Pal. Honour*; Montgomerie, *Cherrie and the Slae*); see further, Spearing 1976.

Date: Following Chalmers (1806: I.54-56), Hamer sets 1528 as the date of composition, arguing that the title description of Lyndsay as 'Familiar Servitor' accords with that in the *Exchequer Rolls* for 1528-29 (1931-36: III.9). This should be treated with caution: extant texts of the poem postdate Lyndsay's death, so it is impossible to be certain that all details of the title are Lyndsay's own. For the grounds for a date of c.1526 see 992*n*, 1005-11*n*, and Edington 1994: 24-25.

Metre: Like Chaucer (*MLT, ClT*), Henryson (*Preaching of the Swallow*) and Douglas (*Eneados*, Prol. IV), Lyndsay uses the five-stress, seven-line rhyme royal stanza (*ababbcc*) for this serious, instructive verse; see Aitken 1983: 20-21. The 'Exhortatioun' (stanzas 149-58) signals its grander style partly by a change to a more formal five-stress nine-line stanza (*aabaabbab*); cf. Chaucer, *Anel*, 211-315. See also 1127-34*n*.

Subtitles: From Sc, with a few corrections of printer's errors (noted). Hamer (1931-36: III.5) considered the subtitles to be interpolations by Scot, adding in support that the 1558 text, the oldest extant, 'does not possess any of the subtitles'. This is not wholly correct, as is noted.

The Epistil] Sc; *The Epistil to the Kingis Grace* C; *om.* P, P(oct).

1 *imperial*: Cf. *Now fayre, fayrest* (Bawcutt 1998: I.19), 6.

3-24 *My servyce*: Lyndsay was described as 'ischar to the Prince' from 1512 (*TA*, IV.441). He was kept in this post after Flodden (*ER*, XIV.8-9, 127-28, 156-57; *TA*, V.37 and 112), until 1525. Though the offices Lyndsay mentions are not specifically associated with him in *TA* or *ER*, Lyndsay's duties, in the modest household of the king's early years, could plausibly have included them; some were among those listed as required for James's household in the 'Ordinance for the Keeping of King James the Fifth', HMC 1904: 11-12.

11 *sweitlie*] Sc, C; *softlye* P, P(oct). *lute in hand*: Cf. *Complaynt*, 92-96. A common skill for a king's personal servant; see Green 1980: 54-59; Stevens 1979: 265-95.

15 *transfegurate*: Cf. Douglas, *Pal. of Honour*, 740.

16 *gaist of Gye*: The ghost of Guido, or Guy, de Corvo, who returned from Purgatory to haunt his widow until, after a protracted theological debate with four Dominican friars, he was exorcised. There were many versions of this popular story, including Bower's (*Scotichronicon* 7, XIII, vi-ix), recorded in the 1440s. By the 16th c. there were allusions in Scottish literature; cf. Dunbar, *Flyting* (B65), 172; *Cupar Banns, Thrie Estaitis*, 251. The ghost's movement was said to be 'as if a broom was being swished across the floor' (*Scotichronicon* 7, XIII, vii.3-4), a detail lending itself to the kind of dramatic play that Lyndsay is recalling.

21 *seware...carvoure*: Offices given to noble youths in aristocratic or royal households as training for later life; see *Book of Keruynge* (1508).

23 *natyvitie*: James was born 10 April 1512; cf. *Complaynt*, 15-16.

24 *cheiffe cubiculare*: Cf. Holland, *Howlat*, 124-25; Douglas, *Pal. Honour*, 1799-1800.

28 *aggreabill*] P, P(oct); *agreable* C; *greabyll* Sc.

34-35 *Of Hectour...Pompeyus*: The first four were among those called the Nine Worthies, famous personages of ancient and medieval history and legend. *Hectour*: Eldest son of Priam and Hecuba; heroic leader of the Trojans in the War; killed by Achilles. *Arthour*: The mythical British king of the 5th or 6th c., believed to have ruled after the collapse of the Roman empire; cf. *Papyngo*, 364*n*. *Julyus*: Gaius Julius Caesar (c.102-44 BC), according to tradition, first emperor of Rome and a great general; *Tragedie*, 10-11*n*. He invaded Britain in 55-54 BC. *Alexander*: Alexander III, the Great, king of Macedonia, 336-323 BC. As commander in chief of the Greek states, he conquered Phoenicia, Palestine, Egypt, Tyre, Asia Minor, Persia and the Punjab. A pupil of Aristotle, Alexander was also a political and economic theorist of standing. Hay's *Buik of King Alexander the Conquerour* probably was known to Lyndsay, but Alexander's worth was a commonplace; cf. Chaucer, *MkT, CT,* VII 2631-70; Cary 1956; Bunt 1994. *Pompeyus*: Pompey the Great (106-48 BC); general and conqueror of Sicily and Africa; rival of Julius Caesar, who defeated him at Pharsalus, 48 BC; cf. Chaucer, *MkT, CT,* VII 2687-94; see *Tragedie,* 12-13*n.*

36 *Jasone...Media*: The legend of Jason's betrayal of Medea, who helped him win the Golden Fleece, was told by several late medieval poets, including Chaucer, *LGW,* 1580-1679; Gower, *Confessio Amantis,* 5.3227-4222, and was referred to by Douglas, *Pal. Honour,* 575, 1603-06.

37 *Hercules*: In Greek myth, Hercules, son of Jupiter and Alcmena. With the help of the gods, he accomplished twelve superhuman labours imposed by his brother, Eurysthenes, and finally was given the status of a god. The labours were often listed; see *Sex Werkdays,* 316-26, where they included the killing of Cacus, the 'horrible etyne'. See also *Meldrum,* 1403.

38 *Sampsone*, or Samson, was, in biblical story, a Jewish judge and also a strongman who destroyed the temple of Dagon; cf. Judg. 13-16. He was lover of Delilah, who betrayed him.

39 *leill luffaris*: Cf. Henryson, *Orpheus,* 207; *Deploratioun,* 39.

41 *Troylus*: Son of Hecuba and Priam of Troy. The source of the story of Troilus's love for Cressida was Benoît de Sainte-Maure's *Roman de Troie* (12th c.). Guido delle Colonne (*Historia destructionis Troiae*), Boccaccio (*Il Filostrato*), and Chaucer produced versions in the following centuries. *sorrow...joye*: Cf. Chaucer, *Tr,* I.400-27; III.814-33.

42 *seigis all*: *Tyir,* city on the Phoenician coast captured by Alexander the Great in a siege in 332 BC; see Cary 1956: 30-31. *Thebes,* capital of ancient Boetia, its siege commemorated in Statius, *Thebaid* and, among others, the late 12th c. *Roman de Thebes,* Chaucer, *KnT, CT,* Lydgate, *Troy Book. Troye,* possibly the capital of Troas, where in legend the Greeks sought to regain Helen, captured from Menelaus by the Trojan, Paris; cf. Douglas, *Pal. Honour,* 1615-18; see Benson 1980.

43 *Prophiseis...Marlyng*: Prophecy was a popular literary genre into the 17th c, though few examples survive; see Murray 1875; Jansen 1991: 62-90, 163-64. Lyndsay perhaps selected particular tales for the contribution each made to an educational scheme devised for James V; see Hadley Williams 1990: 155-66; Sutton and Visser-Fuchs 1997: 188-342.

45 *Reid Etin*: A tale named in *The Complaynt of Scotland,* fol. 50^v, but the earliest extant versions of the tale itself are from the 19th c.; see Fairley 1908: 143-47; Hadley Williams 1991: 165-66. *Gyir Carlyng*: An unascribed alliterative poem about 'ane grit gyre carling' is found in the *Bann. MS,* fols 136^v-137^r; see Hadley Williams 1991: 167-71.

48 *storye...new*: The emphasis implies that this work is Lyndsay's own; see Cairns 1985: 110-19; Hadley Williams 1996: 211-13.

54 *mynd*] Sc, C; *pen* P, P(oct).

57 *calendis*: At about this date, the sun entered Aquarius approximately ten days after the beginning of Jan., but Lyndsay seems to be using the word simply to mean 'beginning' (cf. Chaucer, *Tr*, II.7). The harsh season parallels past and still-present political conditions, and the imminence of change for the better, James V the warming 'sun' to his wintry kingdom. The date also suggests that the poem could have been, after common custom, a New Year gift to the king; cf. Dunbar's to James IV, *My prince in God* (B37), and Ferrerio's to abbot Chrystall, 1535, Stuart 1872: 63.

57-68 *In to the calendis...anone*: Cf. the opening and the sleepless dreamer, *Kingis Quair*, 1012. The linking of winter with a heightened awareness of worldly mutability was traditional; cf. 127-40.

58 *Phebus*: Phoebus, courtly term for the sun, cf. Dunbar, *Goldyn Targe* (B59), 7.

62 *Flora*: Cf. Lydgate, *Fall of Princes*, I.538; Douglas, *Pal. Honour*, 5. The reference to spring as the goddess Flora, like the astrological opening, marks the prologue as a formal, and wholly traditional piece.

63 *austeir Eolus*: Aeolus, god of winds; son of Menalippa and Jupiter; cf. Dunbar, *Goldyn Targe* (B59), 122-23.

64-68 *Efter...me anone*: The recounting of the sleepless perturbations of the narrator was a popular prelude to the dream vision, providing reason for (or explanation of) the narrative that followed; cf. Chaucer, *BD*, 1-47ff.

67 *Remembryng*] Sc, C; *Rememberyng* P, P(oct).

69 *Tytane*: Titan, god of the sun. He was often merged with Tithonus, lover of Aurora; cf. Chaucer, *Tr*, III.1464-68; Douglas, *Eneados*, XII, Prol. 13. *lemis lycht*: Cf. Henryson, *Fables*, 1324.

80 *stromes*] Sc; *stormis* C; *stormes* P, P(oct); cf. *Ane Dialog*, 168.

81 *Hir hevynlie...sabyll*: See 84n. Unlike Nature's gift to May of a gown 'Of eviry hew under the hevin', Dunbar, *Goldyn Targe* (B59), 89, Lyndsay describes its sombre absence, in similarly courtly terms. *sabyll*: A heraldic term, used in formal verse; cf. *Deploratioun*, 126.

84 *mantyll*: The reference is traditional, stemming from the 12th-c. vision by Alan of Lille, *Complaint of Nature*, Prose I, 85-86; cf. Chaucer, *PF*, 316; Dunbar, *Quhen Merche* (B52), 63ff; *Goldyn Targe* (B59), 48.

85-112 The formal complaint, and the role of the poet as auditor, are traditional devices; cf. *Papyngo*, 192-219 (to Fortune).

92 *Aurora*: Goddess of the dawn; see 69n; cf. Dunbar, *Goldyn Targe* (B59), 16-18. *syllie larke*: The lark was the herald of the day, in verse often associated with the dawn; cf. Chaucer, *Tr*, III.1191. See Bawcutt 1972: 5-12; Rowland 1978: 97-101.

93 *left*] Sc, C; *lost* P, P(oct). *balmy lyquour*: Cf. Dunbar, *In May as that Aurora* (B24), 10.

95 *sylver droppis*: Cf. Douglas, *Pal. Honour*, 16.

96 *O fair...hoilsum heit*: A traditional notion of Nature's beneficence (cf. Dunbar, *Goldyn Targe* (B59), 247-49), but here specifically associated with Phoebus, who is held up as a model of kingship later in the poem.

99 *May, with June, thy syster*: Cf. Dunbar, *Goldyn Targe* (B59), 82-83, but where Dunbar's narrator describes his first sight of these allegorised seasonal figures, Lyndsay's echo emphasises their absence.

102 *Enamilit*: cf. Dunbar, *Goldyn Targe* (B59), 12-13.

105 *Allace...indure*: Cf. Chaucer, *KnT, CT,* I(A), 1761; *LGW,* F503 (G491). Such expressions were popular in later courtly verse; cf. Dunbar, *My hartis tresure* (B34), 34 and Whiting H273, but Lyndsay also possibly refers tactfully to James V's difficult minority years.

116 *furth of]* P, P(oct), C; *furth out of* Sc.

128-29 *woltryng...instabilytie*: Cf. *Kingis Quair,* 162. Proverbial; cf. Whiting, S107; Whiting, 'Proverbs...Scottish', *Sea* (1).

129 *wardlis* Sc]; *warldis* C; *wakldis* P, P(oct).

133 *Quho...repent*: Cf. Whiting, 'Proverbs...Scottish', *Most.*

138 *skowland*: Cf. Douglas, *Eneados,* VII, xii.17-19.

140 *Morpheus*: Son and minister of Somnus, God of Sleep.

144 *Neptunus*: Son of Saturn and Ops; identified with Poseidon, God of the Sea. *route...rore*: Cf. Douglas, *Eneados,* I, ii.64.

Following 147 *Finis.]* Sc; *om.* P, P(oct), C.

Subtitle: *Heir endis the Prolonc. And Followis the Dreme.]* Sc; *The Dreme of Schir David Lyndesay.* C; *Heir endith the Prolog. And followith the dreme. Thessalon. v. Prophetias nolite spernere:omnia autem probate quod bonum est tenete* P, P(oct). The spelling of 'Prolonc' in Sc, probably a printer's error, is corrected. Hamer (1931-36: III.15-16) argues that the lines in P and P(oct), from I Thess. 5.20-21 ('Prove all things and hold fast to that which is good'), first appeared in a lost earlier edition of the poem and are thus likely to be authorial. His reason, Lyndsay's allusion to the same biblical lines, *Thrie Estaitis,* 269, is persuasive yet not conclusive; variations of these words were proverbial; cf. Whiting P429.

154 *Remembrance]* Sc, C; *rememberance* P, P(oct); also at 183, 785, 800 (C *remymbrance*), and 1040. *Dame Remembrance*: Lyndsay follows a well-established practice in introducing an allegorical figure to guide the dreamer (cf. Boethius's Lady Philosophy, widely known through Chaucer's translation, *Boece*). The specific choice of 'Remembrance', an aspect of the Cardinal Virtue, Prudence, is less common (contrast Bellenden's 'vertew' and 'delyt', *Proheme,* 81; 'varite' [verity], in *This hindir nycht, Bann. MS,* fols 87ᵛ-88ᵛ, 16; or Douglas's 'Nimphe' of Calliope, *Pal. Honour,* 1071). It is especially appropriate to this vision. Traditionally Prudence was depicted with three eyes, looking to the past, present and future; cf. Chaucer, *Tr,* V.744-49; see Seznec 1972: 120-21. Remembrance does just this, alluding to past melancholy, giving earlier princely examples and formal instruction in present-day kingship, and touching on James V's future role and policies; see Hadley Williams 1996: 212-13.

158-59 *malancolye*: In the manner of a physician, Remembrance has diagnosed the origin of the dreamer's state, alluding to the bodily humour or fluid of melancholy (black bile) that was associated with the earth, as cold and dry; with autumn, and with Saturn; cf. Dunbar, *Schir, ʒe haue mony seruitouris* (B67), 83-86. The passage foreshadows the reference to Saturn as 'cauld and drye' (477) and as a source of melancholy (482).

160 *Tharefor get up*: Cf. the admonitory tones of Dunbar's figure of authority in *Quhen Merche* (B52), 22-23.

161 *twynkling...ee*: Proverbial; cf. Whiting T547.

163ff *in to...hell*: For a 16th-c. description of Hell, with its 'placis', see Hamilton, *Catechism*, fols 107-109 (*STC* 12731).

164 *cairfull cove*: Cf. Chaucer, *BD*, 170-71, describing the 'cave' of Morpheus 'as derk / As helle-pit'.

165 *Yowtyng...yowlyng*: Cf. Chaucer, *NPT, CT*, VII, 3389; Holland, *Howlat*, 102; Douglas, *Eneados*, VII, Prol. 105-06.

166 *In flame of fyre*: The idea of Hell as a place of unquenchable fire was commonly accepted; cf. Chaucer, *ABC*, 95-96.

171 *wrangous conquerouris*: Cf. Henryson, *Orpheus* (of Alexander), 322. Lyndsay is familiar with Henryson's description of Hell (see further below), but unlike Henryson he emphasises Hell's clerical inhabitants.

175 *And archebischopis...pontificall*: Cf. Henryson, *Orpheus*, 340.

179 *Chartereris*] C; *Chartereirs* P, P(oct); *Chartarers* Sc. *Regulare channonis*, or canons regular, priests who were taking monastic vows and following the Rule of St Augustine; cf. *Papyngo*, 654. *Chartereris*: Monks of an uncompromisingly austere contemplative order inspired by the group of six led by St Bruno, who in the 11th c. settled as hermits in the mountains of La Grande Chartreuse (L. *Carthusia*, hence Carthusian). A Charterhouse was founded near Perth, 1429; cf. Holland, *Howlat*, 185.

182 *In haly...abusioun*] Cf. Henryson, *Orpheus*, 339.

1 8 6 *ambitioun*] P, P(oct), C; *ambusioun* Sc.

1 9 2 *wardlie*] Sc; *warldlie* C; *warldly* P, P(oct).

1 9 6 *deneris*] Sc; *deneiris* C; *dinein* P, P(oct). *for deneris...devotioun*: Proverbial-sounding; cf. Whiting, D220.

199-205 *Thay maid...the puris*: Lyndsay refers to the misuse of church income from 'teinds', tithes, or tenths of produce intended for the maintenance of the clergy, upkeep of church property, and relief of the poor; see McKay 1962: 86.

2 1 0 *rychelye rewlit*: *DOST*, citing this line, suggests tentatively the sense 'arrayed' (*Rewle*, v. III, 11.c). This sense of *rewlit* provides a telling contrast to *rewin* 'damaged' ('Thare kirkis' / 'thare ladyis'). *at burde and bed*: Cf. *Certane preceptis of gud counsale, Bann. MS*, fol. 72^r, 40. The use of a collocation common in secular settings deepens the irony.

211 *Thare bastarde barnis*: Many churchmen lived openly in relationships that were little different from marriage. In his *Papyngo* (1055-57) Lyndsay argues that prelates should be permitted to marry.

216 *capis of bras*] Sc; *tapis of bras* P, P(oct); *calpis of bras* C. Cf. Henryson, *Orpheus*, 318.

217 *Symone Magus*: A type of false Christ; he offered money to the Apostles (Acts 8.18-19); cf. Dunbar, *Lucina schynyng* (B29), 31-32.

217-18 *Cayphas...Judas*: Caiaphas and *Annas*, high priests, before whom Jesus was accused (John 18). *Judas*, betrayer of Christ.

218 *tratour*] P, P(oct), C; *treatour* Sc.

219 *Machomete*: Mohammed (Machomete, Mahoun) lived AD 570?-632, was founder of Islam and a prophet; cf. Chaucer, *MLT, CT*, II (B^1), 224. From a Christian perspective he advocated the worship of false idols; cf. *Ane Dialog*, 5784-85.

220 *Choro...Abirone*: Korah, Dathan and Abiram, with their followers, rebelled against the rule of Moses and Aaron. God's punishment, an earthquake, destroyed them (Num. 16.1-33); cf. *Sex Werkdays*, 483-84.

231 *wylfull*: Contrast Henryson, *Fables*, 1113-16.

232 *vocis lamentabyll*: Cf. Douglas, *Eneados*, VI, vii.5.

233 *Constantyne*: Constantine, c.AD 285-337, Emperor of Rome from 306. He was said to have granted Pope Sylvester spiritual supremacy over Rome, Italy, and the Western region (thus allowing the church to inherit property). This was disproved by Valla in the 15th c. but was still believed; it was, for instance, part of the pageantry of Charles V's coronation, 1529; see Strong 1973: 91.

253 *Nero*, Roman Emperor from AD 54-68, was remembered for the murders of his brother and mother, Agrippina; his incest with his sister; his passion for the arts, and for repressive, capricious acts (the burning of Rome in imitation of the sacking of Troy; the murders of leading Romans on treason charges, and the persecution of Christians); cf. Chaucer, *MkT*, *CT*, VII, 2463-550; Henryson, *Orpheus*, 326.

255 *Pharo*: Pharaoh, the oppressive ruler of ancient Egypt. See Henryson, *Orpheus*, 331-32; *Ane Dialog*, 3534-41, 4161-67 and 5744.

256 *barnis...Israell*: Figuratively, the 'chosen' people of Israel, led by Moses and Aaron; cf. I Pet. 2.9-10.

257 *Herode*: Either Herod the Great, who ordered the massacre of the Innocents, or Herod Antipas, who had John the Baptist beheaded (Mark 6.17-18); cf. Henryson, *Orpheus*, 325; *Ane Dialog*, 5746.

258 *Ponce Pylat*: Pontius Pilate, governor of Judaea, AD 26-36, who presided over the trial of Christ, but allowed others to declare the latter's guilt (Matt. 27.22-6); cf. Henryson, *Orpheus*, 327; *Ane Dialog*, 4070-78.

265 *wod lyonis*: A common collocation; cf. *Wallace*, XI.396-99; *Clariodus*, V.2035 ('als wode as lyoun in ane rage').

272-73 *thare pryde...lechorye*: Two of the Seven Deadly Sins; cf. Dunbar, *Off Februar* (B47), 16-30, 79-90.

282-84 *Overset...thare lyve*: Confession of sins at least once a year in Lent was an important part of the religious duties of every parishioner; see John Ireland's 'table' or form of confession, fols 33ᵛ-40ʳ, *Of penance*, *Asloan MS*; Dunbar, *To the, O marcifull saluiour* (B83).

284 *repentit never*: Cf. Henryson, *Fables*, 779-81.

285 *Quhairfor...thame ryve*: Cf. John Rowll, *Cursing vpoun the steilaris of his fowlis, Bann. MS*, fols 104ᵛ-107ʳ, 131-32, 'And ruffy ragmen with his taggis / Sall ryfe thair sinfull saule in raggis'.

290 *We mendit...space*, the sinner's fear that time to repent before death would be denied; cf. Dunbar, *To the, O marcifull saluiour* (B83), refrain.

303 *flichtrand*: Cf. Bellenden, *Chronicles*, II, bk 17, ch. x: 'his hart was...cassyn flichterand in the fyre'.

303-14 *Comoun peple...nummer*: Lyndsay depicts Hell as all-inclusive, mentioning here two further Deadly Sins, envy and ire.

310 *Hurdaris...occararis*: Cf. Dunbar, *Off Februar* (B47), 58-59.

320ff *That dully den...*: Cf. Henryson, *Orpheus*, 310ff.

324 *tadis and scorpionis*: Both were associated with the Seven Deadly Sins, the toad with anger, the scorpion with luxury (see Rowland 1971: 19); in verse, the scorpion, because of its poisoned dart, also was another name for death itself; cf. Dunbar, *I that in heill wes* (B21), 57.

325 *That myrke...stynk*: Cf. Chaucer's description of Aeolus's 'blake trumpe of bras', which emitted a sound like lead-coloured smoke that 'stank as the pit of helle', *HF*, 1654; *ABC*, 56, where Hell is described as 'stink eterne'; and Henryson, *Orpheus*, 311.

326 Sc's *horrayll* is corrected to *horrabyll* (cf. *horribill* P, P(oct), C).

330 *For melody...murnyng*: Cf. Dunbar, *Off Februar* (B47), 103.

331-33 *Thare is...with syte*: The image of Hell as a place of unending sorrow and weeping is also found in the Office for the Dead's responsory, 'Libera me...de morte aeterna', *Sarum Breviary*, II.280.

336 Sc's *plugeit* is corrected to *plungeit* (cf. *plungit* P, P(oct), C).

342 *Purgatorye*: Purgatory, place of temporary suffering, and of spiritual purging and purification after death; cf. Douglas, *Eneados*, VI, Prol. 43; see Duffy 1992: 338-78.

343 *Quhilk purgis...glorye*: Cf. Ireland, *Meroure*, fols 269ᵛ-275ᵛ.

348-50 *That the trew kirk...Cristis blud*: For Lyndsay this was the church unadorned by 'vaine traditiounis' (*Complaynt*, 418), such as the worship of images, or the immorality of the church hierarchy. Lyndsay's hint of reserve about Purgatory and his emphasis on the Passion stems from this; see Cameron 1990: 168-71; Edington 1994: 158-59.

351 *thrid presoun*: Limbo, the region believed to border Hell.

352 *ane place of perditione*: The 'Limbus Puerorum', the place of infants who had died unbaptised; see also Duffy 1992: 280-81.

360-61 *the Lymbe*: 'Limbus Patrum', abode of the just patriarchs who had died before Christ's coming; cf. Douglas, *Eneados*, VI, Prol. 92.

365-80 *Than throuch...fyre*: The four elements, each with its own nature, were earth (cold and dry), water (cold and moist), air (hot and moist), and fire (hot and dry); cf. Pliny, *Nat. Hist.*, II, iv.10-12.

375 *His regionis*: Air was thought to have three distinct regions: the highest, near the sphere of fire, was hot; the middle region was cold, that place where earth's vapours produced ice, hail and snow; the lowest was also thought hot, because of the reflection of the sun's rays from earth's surface; it produced clouds, rain and dew; see Heninger 1977: 32-33.

385 *Up throuch the speris*: The poet's ascent looks ultimately to the classical *Somnium Scipionis* and Macrobius's *Commentary* on it. Lyndsay reverses the order of Scipio and other earlier writers such as Pliny, *Nat. Hist.*, II, vi (who begin with the outermost sphere and end with the earth), so that the sight of the 'hevin impyre' (514), Christ 'sittand in to his sege royall' (548), is the climax. The descriptions of the seven planets (including the moon, believed to be one) are traditional; see Seznec 1972: 170-215. Lyndsay seems to have known Henryson's portraits (see below), but both poets were indebted to traditional motifs; see further, Fox 1981: 348-63 (135n-263n).

387 *Quene..see*: Cf. Douglas, *Eneados*, III, Prol. 4 ('Maistres of stremys'). Lyndsay depicts the moon as a monarch, ruler of the tides.

390 *reflex of Phebus*: Contrast Dunbar, *Goldyn Targe* (B59), 33, where the image of the sun's reflected light creates a scene dazzlingly bright, and Lyndsay's use of the image to show that a planet (by analogy, a monarch) dependent on reflected light is weak.

393-94 *Mercurious*: Lyndsay stresses the association with eloquence (cf. *Test. Meldrum*, 79), not Mercury's equally traditional role as physician noted in Henryson, *Test. Cresseid*, 250.

395 *termes delicious*: Cf. Henryson, *Test. Cresseid*, 241.

400 *cunnyng astrologis*: Astrologers were respected figures, often official members of royal courts; cf. Chaucer, *WBPro*, *CT*, III (D), 324: 'The wise astrologien, Daun Ptholome'; Dunbar, *Schir, ʒe haue mony seruitouris* (B67), 6.

404 *Venus*: Classical goddess of love, beauty and fertility, mother of Cupid, wife of Vulcan, but known also for her love affairs with gods (including Mars) and mortal men. Like Henryson, Lyndsay identifies Venus with Fortune, but her beneficent side, as 'that lustie luffis quene' (406), foil to Mars, is kept uppermost. For an earlier meeting of Venus, Mars, Jupiter and Saturn, in which traditional traits are displayed, see Chaucer, *KnT*, *CT*, I (A) 2437-78.

405 *set...sett*: Cf. Douglas, *Eneados*, XIII, Prol. 2.

407 *blenkis amorous*: A common collocation; cf. Henryson, *Test. Cresseid*, 226, *Orpheus*, 81; Stewart, *Croniclis*, 1041.

416 *provocatyve*: Cf. Henryson, *Test. Cresseid*, 226.

421 *Phebus*: Cf. Macrobius, *Commentary*, IV.2. Literally, 'bright', to describe Apollo, classical god of youth, often identified with the sun, and thus with the engendering of life; cf. Chaucer, *FranT*, *CT*, 1031-37; Douglas, *Pal. Honour*, 34-36. Lyndsay stresses his princeliness and virtue.

424 *principall*: Cf. *Ane Dialog*, 691.

425 *satt*] Sc; *set* P, P(oct); *sat* C.

426 *roye royall*: Cf. Henryson, *Test. Cresseid*, 204, 'king royall'.

438 *foure stedis*: Lyndsay briefly notes the four horses of the sun, but his traditional modest disclaimer and reference to 'poetis' shows an awareness of the detailed descriptions of others; see Henryson (*Test. Cresseid*, 212-16), who names them (Eoye, Ethios, Peros, Philogie), and alludes to traditional etymologies. On sources, see Fox 1981: 357-58 (212*n*-16*n*).

442 *Mars*, classical god of war and hunting, is presented here with some of his traditional attributes—fiery face, unrestrained rage, malicious looks—but his heavy armour is omitted (see Seznec 1972: 190-91). The mitigating role played by Venus (love) in preserving peace is emphasised for a second time, building the picture of what makes a good monarch.

443 *tunder*] P, P(oct); *tounder* Sc, C. Cf. Douglas, *Eneados*, I, iv.34; VII, iv.77-80.

445 *bost...brag*: Cf. *King Hart*, 393; Stewart, *Croniclis*, I, 19590. *thunder*] P, P(oct); *tounder* Sc, C; cf. Douglas, *Eneados*, III, viii.131, 142.

446 *in schonder*: Cf. Douglas, *Eneados*, V, x.67.

451 *sweir*] Sc, C; *suir* P, P(oct). *seditious*] P(oct), C; *seditiouns* P; *seditious* Sc.

455 *This...desolate*: How to achieve peace was being debated at this time by the Paris theologians; see further, Bense 1972.

458-69 *Jupiter...wyrk vengeance*: Jupiter, son of Saturn and Ops, was chief and most benign of the classical gods. His ability to govern well is stressed, but details are traditional; cf. Henryson, *Test. Cresseid*, 169-82.

464 *father principall...generall*: Douglas, *Eneados*, I, v.2n, explains that Jupiter, 'by the gentilis [Gentiles] was clepit the mast soueran god, fader of goddis and men, and all the otheris war bot haldyn as poweris dyuers of this Iupiter, callit "iuuans pater", the helply father'.

473 *hiest*] C; *heyest* P, P(oct); *hich* Sc.

474-88 *Tyll Saturnus...speir*: Saturn, the son of Coelus and Terra, married his own sister Rhea; Jupiter, Juno and Neptune were among their children. The enmity between Saturn and Jupiter was well known; cf. Henryson, *Test. Cresseid*, 182; see also Fox 1981: 355.

475 *paill as leid*: Cf. Chaucer, *CYT*, *CT*, VIII (G), 727-28; 828.

477 *And cauld and dry*: Note the link between the dreamer's state at 158-59 and the 'malancolious' Saturn.

478 *Foule...oule*: Cf. Whiting, 'Proverbs...Scottish', *Owl* (1), but the association had been made earlier; cf. Chaucer, *WBT*, *CT*, III (D), 1081-82; Holland, *Howlat*, 55.

480-81 *His intoxicat...perditioun*: Cf. Henryson, *Test. Cresseid*, 153-54 ('as ane busteous churle...crabitlie with auster luik and cheir').

485 *naturallie*] Sc, C; *naturall* P, P(oct).

486 *singis*: Cf. *King Hart*, 804.

490-91 *the firmament...sterris brycht*: The eighth sphere, or Firmament of Fixed Stars, according to Ptolemy, the Greek astronomer, geographer and writer of the second c. AD. His *Almageste* set out the earth-centred view of the universe that was still accepted during Lyndsay's day, although by 1543 Copernicus had put forward in detail his heliocentric view; see further Heninger 1977: 31-80. The stars were 'fixed' because, unlike the wandering planets, their relative positions remained unchanged.

498 *nynt*] Sc, C; *mynt* P, P(oct). *movare principall*: Lyndsay refers to Ptolemy's Primum Mobile, more usually the tenth not the ninth sphere. It was thought to move from E. to W., completing its revolution in twenty-four hours, in this diurnal movement distinct from the W. to E. 'natural' motions of the planets noted at 505-07.

502 *torne*] P, P(oct); *om.* Sc, C.

503 *houris*] P, P(oct); *yeiris* Sc, C.

504 *astronomouris*] P, P(oct); *austronomeris* Sc, C.

507 *kynde*] Sc; *kynd* C; *kyng* P, P(oct).

509-10 *Quhose motioun...sound*: A reference to the Platonic idea that the motion of the spheres caused a special celestial harmony of sound; see Macrobius, *Commentary*, V.5; cf. Henryson, *Orpheus*, 219-39.

513 *hevin...christallyne*: Derived from Gen. 1.6-8; more usually the ninth not the tenth sphere as here, the crystalline heaven was thought to be transparent, thus clear as crystal, and in some contemporary diagrams was depicted reflecting the signs of the zodiac; cf. Heninger 1977: 37-73 and fig. 28, reprinted from Apian's *Cosmographicus liber*, 1533. Cf. also *Complaynt of Scotland*, fol. 38ᵛ.

514 *hevin impyre*: For a near-contemporary visualisation, see Bosch's panel, *Ascent to the Empyrean*, Palazzo Ducale, Venice, reproduced in Pearsall and Salter 1973: pl. 27 and 74-75.

518-32 *angellis...In ordouris nyne*: Cf. *Sex Werkdays*, 29-33 and Douglas, *Pal. Honour*, 444. The chief source of this angelic scheme, which was widely accepted as a mean between God and man, was *De Hierarchia Celesti*, a 5th or 6th c. work attributed to pseudo-Denys the Areopagite. Lyndsay differs in some details of arrangement, but preserves the three internal hierarchies; see Lewis 1964: 70-72; Hamer 1931-36: III, 27-31; Sutton and Visser-Fuchs 1996: 230-32.

521 *lovyng*] Sc, C; *levyng* P; *le vyng* P(oct).

522 *'Sanctus!'*, 'Holy', is the first word of the 'angelic hymn' or 'Ter Sanctus' in the *Te Deum*; cf. Isa. 6.1-3.

531-32 *thronus...cherubin...seraphin*: The three species of angels closest to God.

545 *Creid*: Cf. Ireland, *Of penance, Asloan MS*, fol. 23ᵛ, 19-22.

548 *Christe...sege royall*: Christ as a monarch; cf. Douglas, *Eneados* I, xii.3-5.

550-52 *courte celestiall*: Cf. Douglas, *Eneados*, X, Prol. 166-68.

554 *Quene of quenis*: Cf. *Ane Dialog*, 5642.

556 *virginnis*: Cf. *Ane Dialog*, 5643.

560 *deite*] P, P(oct), C; *diete* Sc.

561 *Patriarkis*: The founding fathers of Israel. *prophetis*: Those who predicted Christ's coming (Isaiah, Jeremiah, Daniel, Ezekiel and Jonah).

563 *Evangellistis*: The writers of the four gospels (Matthew, Mark, Luke, John). *apostolis*: The first disciples of Christ (Andrew, Bartholomew, James the Great, Jude, Matthew, Paul, Peter, Philip, Thomas, Simon Zelotes, James the Less, John).

565 *Quhilk...the victorye*: The imagery is traditional; cf. Dunbar, *Done is a battell* (B10), 25, 38.

567 *Sanct Peter...generall*: Peter is traditionally depicted holding the keys of heaven given to him by Jesus, who singled him out as the rock upon which he would build his church; cf. Matt. 16.18-19. ('Peter' derives via Latin from Greek *petros*, stone or rock.)

574 *celsitude*] Sc, C; *sanctitude* P, P(oct).

581 *Innumirabyll*] Sc; *Innumerabill* P, P(oct); *Unmesurable* C.

589 *Thir*] Sc, C; *Thair* P, P(oct).

590 *arithmetik*] C, P, P(oct); *arthimatik* Sc.

590-92 *Be arithmetik...geomatre*: According to Pythagorean theory, arithmetic was one of the four mathematical disciplines (with music, geometry and astronomy). The Neoplatonist Proclus specified that 'Arithmetic contemplates multitude in itself'; Geometry, by contrast, contemplates 'unmoveable magnitude', that is, numbers with a spatial form (*Commentary on Euclid*, I, quoted by Stanley 1687: 522). Lyndsay's allusions reflect these widely-accepted assumptions. (Boethius's treatises on these four disciplines (*quadrivium*) had made them known to the late medieval reader; his *De Arithmetica* had been printed in 1488 and *De geometria* with other works in 1491-92.)

591 *palice*] P, P(oct), *place* Sc, C. P is preferable metrically and thematically; cf. 550 ('courte celestiall'); 554 ('throne').

593 *rethorike* was one of the disciplines that comprised the *trivium* (with grammar and dialectic), which with the *quadrivium* were called the Seven Liberal Arts. These formed the staple course of education, the *trivium* taught in the schools and the *quadrivium* at universities.

594 *none eiris*: Cf. 1 Cor. 2.9. Cf. also Whiting, E210 and Douglas, *Pal. Honour*, 1256-59.

595 *thair greit*] P, P(oct); *thare* Sc; *this thare* C. Both P and C are metrically apt; P is in keeping with the surrounding emphasis on size.

596-98 In these lines, as in this section on the 'hevin impyre' as a whole, Lyndsay heightens the style by professing his inability to describe (the 'inexpressibility' formula), and by the use of superlatives, hyperbole, and latinate and polysyllabic words.

597 *Sanct Paule*: Paul the Apostle, co-founder with St Peter of the Christian church. He was converted on the road to Damascus, and later undertook extensive missionary work, especially in the non-Jewish world. In Palestine he was arrested, but as a Roman citizen appealed for a trial before Nero. He was imprisoned in Rome, during which time, it is believed, he wrote the fourteen epistles. According to tradition Paul was beheaded in AD 65; see *Ane Dialog*, 251n, 253n.

604-16 *Geve I...dede*: Cf. Macrobius, *Commentary*, III.3-4.

609 *to ryng with hym in glore*] Sc, C (*regne*); *to dwell in to this gloir* P, P(oct).

624-26 *Quhare we...brycht*: Cf. Chaucer, *Tr*, V.1815-19.

Following 630 *The quantite of the Erth*] Sc, C; *om.* P, P(oct).

637 *quod scho, to the*] Sc, C; *to the quod sche* P, P(oct).

639 *auctour of the 'Speir'*: Sacrobosco (John of Holywood, ?1195-?1244), author of the *Sphæra Mundi*, a widely used textbook on geography and astronomy of the early Renaissance, first printed in Ferrara in 1492; see Thorndike 1949: 76-142.

642 *fyftie thousand liggis*: The calculations are based on those of Lyndsay's 'auctour', Sacrobosco. Although the 'quantytie' (50,750 leagues) is in error for 15,750, all extant texts of the *Dreme* quote it; cf. *Ane Dialog*, 1441-42. (The actual circumference of the earth is about 40,000 km or about 8,300 leagues.)

645 *stagis*: From *stadium*, a Greek and Roman measure commonly one-eighth of a Roman mile; cf. *OED*, *stadium*, 1; cf. Pliny, *Nat. Hist.*, II, cxii.247.

647 *than rycht*] Sc, C; *tham weil* P, P(oct).

Following 658 *Finis.*] Sc; *om.* P, P(oct), C.

Subtitle *The devisioun of the Eirth.*] Sc; *The divisioun of the Eirth.* C; *om.* P, P(oct).

659-756 The dreamer's geographical overview recalls others in late medieval poetry—cf. Chaucer, *HF*, 898-919; Douglas, *Pal. Honour*, 1081-1134—but Lyndsay's didactic and methodical presentation places this description at some remove from those journeys, in which various features, often classical, are marked out for cultural as well as geographical reasons (Bawcutt 1967: xlii-xliii). As he notes (665), Lyndsay has sought his information from the 'warldlis discriptouris'. He names two, Pliny and Ptolemy (748), but it is less likely that Lyndsay drew on them directly (or on others such as the Latin fathers Eusebius, Isidore and Honorius of Autun), than that he used one or more of the universal histories, very popular during the medieval period, which cited such authorities or drew on them without acknowledgement. Manuscripts of Wyntoun's *Original Chronicle*, in verse, and of Bower's prose *Scotichronicon*, for example, were in circulation by the 1500s, and both included geographical overviews. Among other available works were *The Sex Werkdays and Agis*, a prose treatise on history and typology that included a geographical description of the world. On early geographical authorities see Kish 1978.

664 *cosmographouris*: Those, such as Pliny and Ptolemy, who describe or map the general features of the universe (see 748*n*).

673-75 This follows the *mappae mundi*, the medieval maps of the world shaped by Christian theology and contemporary travellers' reports (see Shirley 1987: xix-xxi, 1, 7, 10, 13; MacDonald 1987: 379-81). Jerusalem was at their centre; Asia, to the E., occupied the top half of the circle (orient), with a terrestrial paradise at the very top; Europe and Africa, to the W., occupied the two quarters of the bottom half (occident).

684 *Penthapolis*: There was a Pentapolis on the N. African coast, but this refers to that region bordering on Arabia noted by Honorius, *De Imagine Mundi*, I.xvii, comprising the five cities of biblical renown for their wickedness, Sodom, Gomorrah, Adama, Seboin and Segor; cf. Bower, *Scotichronicon*, 1, I, iv.49; *Sex Werkdays*, 208.

685 *Capadocia*: A region in Asia Minor; see Ptolemy, *Geographia* (1540): 89 and Tabula Asiae I. Cf. Bower, *Scotichronicon*, 1, I, iv.47. *Seres*: A town in the E. of Syria; see Honorius, *De Imagine Mundi*, I.xix: 'Seres est oppidum Orientis, quo Serica regio, et restis, et gens est dicta', and Ptolemy, Tabula Asiae VIII. Cf. also Wyntoun, *Original Chronicle*, II, xi.995-97. *Armenye*: A region N. of Cilicia and Syria; see Honorius, I.xix and Ptolemy, 91, 97 and Tabula Asiae I. Cf. Bower, *Scotichronicon*, 1, I, iv.47.

686 *Babilone*: A region in S. Mesopotamia, its chief city Babylon; see Honorius, *De Imagine Mundi*, I, xv; Ptolemy, *Geographia* (1540): 106 and Tabula Asiae IIII. *Caldia*: A region in S. Babylonia; see Ptolemy, 106-07 and Tabula Asia IIII. *Perth*: Parthia, a region S. of ancient Hyrcania; see Honorius, I.xiv and Ptolemy, 112 and Tabula Asiae V; cf. Bower, *Scotichronicon*, 1, I, iv.46. *Arabye*: See Ptolemy, 112 and Tabula Asiae VI; cf. *Sex Werkdays*, 157.

687 *Sedone*: A coastal region (city) of the province of Phoenicia, Palestine; see Honorius, *De Imagine Mundi*, I.xvi and Ptolemy, *Geographia* (1540), Tabula Asiae IIII (Sidon). *Judea*: In S. Palestine. See Ptolemy, 103 and Tabula Asiae IIII. *Palestina*: See Honorius, I.xvii.

688 *Ever*] Sc, P, P(oct); *Upper* C. *Ever*: Probably an error for 'Over' = upper or outer; cf. Wyntoun, *Original Chronicle*, I.xiii.1190, 'Owir Sithi'.

Sethea: The regions within and without the Imavus Mountains; see Ptolemy, *Geographia* (1540): 120-21 and Tabulae Asiae VII and VIII. Cf. *Sex Werkdays*, 198 ('Sithia'). *Tyir*: Coastal city in Palestine; see Ptolemy, Tabula Asiae IIII. *Galelie*: Galilaea, region of N. Palestine near Lake Tiberias (Sea of Galilee); see Ptolemy, Tabula Asiae IIII. Cf. *Sex Werkdays*, 163.

689 *Hiberia*: Region in the Caucasus; see Honorius, *De Imagine Mundi*, I.xix and Ptolemy, *Geographia* (1540): Tabula Asiae III; cf. *Sex Werkdays*, 198. *Bactria*: Region (chief city Bactra) to the E. of *Hircanea* (690); for both see Honorius, I.xix and Ptolemy, Tabula Asiae VII; cf. *Sex Werkdays*, 197 ('Baitry', 'Hircanyca'). *Phelestina*: Possibly the place also known as Ascalon; see Honorius, I.xvi: 'Est in ea quoque Palæstina, a civitate Palæstin, quae nunc Ascalon vocatur, dicta'; cf. Wyntoun, *Original Chronicle*, II, x.905-06; *Sex Werkdays*, 160 ('Phalestyne').

690 *Compagena*: Comagen, a region N. of Syria, S. of Armenia and E. of Cilicia; see Honorius, *De Imagine Mundi*, I.xvi; cf. *Sex Werkdays*, 159. *Samarie*: Samaria was S. of Galilee and N. of Judea; cf. *Sex Werkdays*, 163. For both see Ptolemy, *Geographia* (1540): Tabula Asiae IIII.

691 Sc's *tytill* has been corrected; cf. *lytill* P, P(oct); *litle* C. *Galathie*: Galatia, once called Gallo-Greece, a region in central Asia Minor, W. of Cappadocia; see Honorius, *De Imagine Mundi*, I.xxi and Ptolemy, *Geographia* (1540): Tabula Asiae I. Cf. *Sex Werkdays*, 199.

692 *Pamphilia*: Maritime district between Lycia and Silicia (Ptolemy, *Geographia* (1540): 88 and Tabula Asiae I); cf. *Sex Werkdays*, 201. *Isaria...Leid*: See Honorius, *De Imagine Mundi*, I.xxi; cf. *Sex Werkdays*, 200 ('Lydea', 'Ysawrea'). All are in Anatolia; see Ptolemy, Tabula Asiae I.

693 *Regia...Meid*: These are all regions in the S. of modern Afghanistan. Honorius mentions all but Regia in *De Imagine Mundi*, I.xiv ('De Parthia'). *Regia* possibly is Rhagæa, a city in Parthia (Ptolemy, *Geographia* (1540): Tabula Asiae V); *Arathusa* possibly is Arachosia (cf. Douglas, *Eneados*, III, x.80), which, with *Assiria* and *Meid* or Media, is mapped by Ptolemy on Tabula Asiae VII.

694 Sc's *Secuudlie* has been corrected; cf. *Secundlie*, C; *Secundly* P; *Secundlye* P(oct). *Africa*: Cf. Orosius, *Historiarum*, I.8-11; *Sex Werkdays*, 207-16.

696-701 *Ethiope*: In SW Africa; see Honorius, *De Imagine Mundi*, I.xxxiii. *Tripolitana*: Perhaps Tripoli, the N. African city, but probably Tripolitania, a region on the N. African coast. It and *Cartage* (698), *Nadabar*, *Libia* (699), *Getulia*, *Maritania* (700), *Numidie* and *Thingetane* (701) are mentioned together by Honorius, I.xxxii ('De Africa'). *Zeuges* (697) was originally a province, but became the name of the district surrounding Carthage; cf. Orosius, *Historiarum*, II.91-92. See also Ptolemy, *Geographia* (1540): Aphricae Tabulae I, II and III. Cf. Bower, *Scotichronicon*, 1, I, iv.49.

698 *Cartage*: This brief additional description was traditional; see Honorius, *De Imagine Mundi*, I.xxxii.

699 *Garamantes*: Honorius, *De Imagine Mundi*, I.xxxiii, lists Garamantes as within Ethiopia; see Ptolemy, *Geographia* (1540): Tabula

Africae IIII, where it is S. of 'Cyrene'. *Nadabar*: Possibly the 'Nababurum' mentioned by Ptolemy (Aphricae Tabula I) in his list of cities in Caesarensis, a region of *Maritania* (700). *Libia*: See 696-701*n*; cf. Douglas, *Eneados*, IV, i.88.

700 *Getulia*: See 696-701*n*; cf. Douglas, *Eneados*, V, ii.20. *Maritania*: See 696-701*n*.

701 *Futhensis* in Sc is in C, before modernisation, *Feʒensis*, lending support to the possibility that this is Fez, Morocco, in NW Africa (see Hamer 1931-36: III.37), but Ptolemy does not record it under that name. *Numedie...Thingetane*: Also in NW Africa; see Honorius, *De Imagine Mundi*, I.xxxii and Ptolemy, Aphricae Tabula I (which also maps 'Tingis', capital of Tingitana). Cf. *Sex Werkdays*, 210 ('Singitana').

703 *Than Europe*: Europe was considered to begin at the Riphaean Mountains, the Tanais (Don) river acting as a boundary; see Orosius, *Historiarum*, I.7-8 and Honorius, *De Imagine Mundi*, I.xxii. Cf. Wyntoun, *Original Chronicle*, I, xiii.1181-86; Bower, *Scotichronicon*, 1, I, v.5-10 and *Sex Werkdays*, 218-20; Douglas, *Pal. Honour*, 1116.

705 *Foure principallis*: Lyndsay speaks of four main regions but lists only three (706). Hamer (1931-36: III.37) suggests that the fourth could be 'the braid Yle of Bertane' mentioned later in the poem (791). Alternatively, Cairns (1985: 112) suggests Germany, arguing that this country is 'missing altogether' from the poem (but see 708*n*), and suggesting that a stanza on Germany (707ff) has been lost. Lyndsay lists the ancient sub-German regions (cf. Honorius, *De Imagine Mundi*, I.xxiv-xxv), followed by those of Italy, Greece, France and Spain.

708 *Nether Scithia*: See Honorius, *De Imagine Mundi*, I.xxiii: 'A Thanai est Scythia inferior'; cf. Wyntoun, *Original Chronicle*, I.xiii.1189. Ptolemy, 120-21 and Tabula Asiae II, notes the relationship to the Caucasus as in Douglas, *Pal. Honour*, 1125. *Trace*: Thrace, bounded by the Gulf of Propontis and the city of Byzantium (Constantinople) in the E. and the Aegean Sea on the S.; see Orosius, *Historiarum*, I.56; Ptolemy, Tabula Europae IX. Cf. Wyntoun, *Original Chronicle*, I, xiii.1241. *Garmanie*] Sc; *Germanie* P, P(oct); *Carmanie* C. Chalmers (1806: I.225) argued that 'Carmanie' was correct, but it is S. of Parthia and thus in Asia; see Ptolemy, *Geographia* (1540): Tabula Asiae V. Although *DOST* lists *Almaine* or *Almane* as the common Scots word for Germany (cf. Lyndsay, *Ane Satyre*, 896), 'Garmanie' is also used; cf. Douglas, *Pal. Honour*, 1090 (1553 edn; 'Germanie', 1579 edn). Douglas subsequently refers (1087) to 'Almanie', region of N. Switzerland and S. Germany; cf. *Dreme*, 710.

709 *Thusia*: Perhaps Thusis, E. Switzerland. *Histria...Panonia*: Honorius, *De Imagine Mundi*, I.xxviii, notes both as part of Greece. See Ptolemy, *Geographia* (1540): Tabula Europae VI.

710 *Gotland*: Island in the Baltic Sea E. of Sweden; cf. Wyntoun, *Original Chronicle*, I, xiii, 1197; *Sex Werkdayis*, 223-24, wherein it is called a 'kingdome'. *Grunland*: Land joining N. Scandinavia to Russia (Hamer 1931-36: III.37); if so, modern Lapland. *Almanie*: See 708*n*. See also Wyntoun, *Original Chronicle*, I, xiii.1209-11.

711 *Boeme*: Bohemia, as in Douglas, *Eneados*, I, v.29n; *Sex Werkdays*, 236 ('Boyem'). *Norica, Rethia*: Cf. Orosius, *Historiarum*, I.60; see Ptolemy, *Geographia* (1540): Tabula Europae V, where they are N. of the Poenean Alps and S. of the Danube.

712 Sc's *Tentonia* has been corrected; cf. *Teutonia* P, P(oct), C. *Teutonia*: Region near modern Hamburg; see Ptolemy, *Geographia* (1540): Tabula Europae IIII.

713-17 *And was...Janewayis*: See Honorius, *De Imagine Mundi*, I.xxviii. *Tuskane*, cf. Douglas, *Pal. Honour*, 1086; *Ethuria*, region between the Tiber and Arno rivers; *Champanye*, region of S. Italy; *Calaber*, cf. *Sex Werkdays*, 281; *Janewayis*, cf. *Sex Werkdays*, 261 ('Iane'). See Ptolemy, *Geographia* (1540): Tabulae Europae IIII ('Langobardi'/Lombardy) and VI (for all other regions).

718-21 *In Grece...Lacedone*: See Honorius, *De Imagine Mundi*, I.xxvii and Ptolemy, *Geographia* (1540): Tabula Europae X, except *Illeria*, for which see V; cf. Wyntoun, *Original Chronicle*, I, xiii.1271. Stewart, *Croniclis*, 170, refers to 'Achchaya'.

722-26 *And France...in certane*: A traditional view; see Honorius, *De Imagine Mundi*, I.xxix: 'De Gallia—Gallia Belgica, Francia, Francus rex. Gallia Lugdunensis [region of Lyons], Comaga, Togata. Gallia Narbonensis. Aquitania.' *Rethia* appears to be out of place; see 711.

723 *Rethia*] Sc, P(oct); *rethia* P; *Celtica* C.

729-30 *In Spanye...Garnat*: Of this group, Castile (or more strictly, Leon and Castile), Aragon, Navarre (that part on the Spanish side of the Pyrenees), and Granada, were under the same ruler, the Emperor Charles V (Carlos I). Cf. Bower, *Scotichronicon*, 1, I, vi.1-8 and *Sex Werkdays*, 286-88. See Ptolemy, *Geographia* (1540): Hispania III, Nova Tabula.

737 *Madagascar*: Ptolemy mentions it in his commentary on Africa, *Geographia* (1540): 80, but does not map it; it became known to the Portuguese only in 1500. *Gardes*: Cf. Orosius, *Historiarum*, I.72, 'Tertius angulus [spectans ad orientem] eius est qua Gades insulae intentae in africum, Athlantem montem interiecto sinu oceani prospiciunt'. See also Pliny, *Nat. Hist.*, VI, xxxiv.175 ('Gadis'); Ptolemy's Tabula Europae II ('Gadira'), and *Sex Werkdays*, 323 (an allusion to the 'gold in the occiane at Gaddis, Sibillis Strichtis [Straits of Gibraltar]'). *Taprobane*: An ancient name for Ceylon, now Sri Lanka (cf. Pliny, *Nat. Hist.*, VI, xxiv.81), but distinguished from Ceylon ('Zaylon') by Ptolemy, who identifies it with modern Sumatra; see Tabula Asiae XII and India Extrema XIX. Nova Tabula.

740 *Syper*: See Honorius, *De Imagine Mundi*, I.xxxiv and Ptolemy, *Geographia* (1540): Tabula Asiae IIII. *Candie*: Possibly Cauda, an island in the Mediterranean Sea, close to Crete (but it also was used as an alternative name for Crete itself); cf. the references to both Candy and Crete in *Sex Werkdays*, 246 and note. *Sardane*: See 741n.

741 *Abidos*: See Honorius, *De Imagine Mundi*, I.xxxiv; Ptolemy, *Geographia* (1540): Tabula Europae IX; cf. Douglas, *Eneados*, IV, Prol. 79. *Thoes*: In the Aegean Sea; see Pliny, *Nat. Hist.*, V, xxxviii.136 and Ptolemy, Tabula Asiae I. *Cecilia*: Sicily and *Sardane* (740), islands in the

Mediterranean Sea SW of Italy mapped by Ptolemy, Tabula Europae VII; see also Honorius, I.xxxv and xxxvi.

742 *Tapsone*: Island near Sicily; cf. Douglas, *Eneados*, III, x.66 ('Tapsum'). *Eolie*: A group of islands, also known as Lipari, N. of Sicily; see Ptolemy, *Geographia* (1540): Tabula Europa VI.

748 *Plenius*: Gaius Plinius (Pliny the Elder), AD 24-79, the cavalry officer, naval commander and scholar. His *Natural History* is an encyclopaedic work of facts and myths connected with all aspects of man and the world about him; Books III-VI give details of world geography. Published in 1469, it was among the first books to be printed in Italy, and was well known in later centuries. *Tholomie*: See 490-91*n*.

Subtitle following 756 *Of Paradice*.] Sc, C; *om*. P, P(oct).

757ff *Paradyce*: Although it reverses the order of Honorius and those others following him, who introduce it before all other terrestrial places (see *De Imagine Mundi*, I.viii; Higden, *Polychronicon*, I.x), the description itself is traditional: the dreamer's Paradise is in the E. or 'Orient' (758), has an abundance of flowers and fruit, a temperate climate, wholesome perfumes and four rivers flowing from a spring; cf. Gen. 2.8-14. See further Pearsall and Salter 1973: 56-75.

760 *lillyis...rosis*: Symbols of purity, both also associated with the Virgin Mary; see Pearsall and Salter 1973: 108-10, 114-15.

761 *fructis, indeficient*: The trees of the Earthly Paradise were believed to bear fruit continuously; cf. Hay, *Buik of King Alexander the Conquerour*, III.16274.

763 *temperat air*: Cf. Chaucer, *PF*, 204-05.

771 *hie in situatioun*: The Earthly Paradise was believed to be located on a high mountain, thus evading the Flood and air turbulence at lower levels; cf. Hay, *Buik of King Alexander the Conquerour*, III.16199-210.

775 *Four fludis*: See Gen. 2.10-14: Pison (= Ganges), Gihon, Nile and Hiddekel (= Tigris); cf. Honorius, *De Imagine Mundi*, I.xix; Wyntoun, *Original Chronicle*, I, iii.117-34; Hay, *Buik of King Alexander the Conquerour*, III.16267-71; *Sex Werkdays*, 146-47.

778-84 *The countre...successioun*: Cf. Gen. 3.23-24.

780 *straitly kepit*: Cherubim and a turning, flaming sword guarded the garden of Eden after the expulsion; cf. Gen. 3.24; Wyntoun, *Original Chronicle*, I, xiii.121-26.

782 *his cryme*: Against God's command, Adam ate the apple from the tree of knowledge; cf. Gen. 2.17; 3.3-23.

791 *braid yle of Bertane*: Cf. *Colkelbie Sow*, 436.

792 *in the occiane see*: Cf. Douglas, *Eneados*, VII, iv.72-75.

Subtitle following 798 *Of the realme of Scotland*.] C; *Of the realne of Scotlamd*. Sc; *om*. P, P(oct). Sc's compositor's errors are corrected in C.

808 *lytill*] P, P(oct); *tytill* Sc; *litle* C.

814ff *Of Scotland...properteis*: Cf. Bellenden, noting Scotland's 'sindry commoditeis', *Chronicles* (?1540), fol. Bii^r, preliminaries.

820 *ryveris*] Sc, C; *revaris* P, P(oct).

823 *da, ra, hartis, and hyndis*:   Animals of the hunt often grouped together in verse; cf. Henryson, *Fables*, 900; Hay, *Ordre of Knychthede*, 91^r, iii.159-60; Bellenden, *Chronicles* (?1540), fol. Cii^r, prelims.

824 *strandis*] Sc, C; *strinds* P, P(oct) = very small streams, trickles.

825 *fair flureist*] P, P(oct); *fluriste* Sc; *flurischit* C.

833 *Quhilkis ellis*] C; *Quhilkis als* Sc; *Than als* P, P(oct); eye skip from 831 is a possible source of error in Sc. *mapamound*, from the *mappae mundi*; see 673-75n.

843 *under confessioun*:   'Under the seal of confession (as a religious duty), if I lie or mislead'; cf. Dunbar, *Ane murelandis man* (B2), 5.

847 *governyng*] P, P(oct); *governing* C; *gorvernyng* Sc. *laubour...governyng*: Bellenden (*Chronicles* (?1540), fol. Bii^r, prelims), also notes that Scotland's commodities would be more than sufficient 'gyf our peple had perfite craft and industrye'.

849 *Quod*] P, P(oct), C; *Quhod* Sc.

853-54 *So plesand...on hand*:   A more positive observation, but cf. *Doverrit with dreme* (B11), as in, for instance, 'So few to wend this mischeif to amend', 34.

860-68   Traditional arguments; cf., for example, *Contemplacioun of synnaris*, *Asloan MS*, fol. 265^v, 145-52.

877 *mendis*] Sc, *a mendis* C; *amendis* P, P(oct).   Alliteration emphasises the question about proper leadership of Scotland.

880 *rute and grund*:   A common phrase; cf. Hay, *Gouernaunce of Princis*, fol. 108^r, iii.45-46.

881 *heddis*:   The idea of the monarch as the body politic (comprising the head or kingly office of government and the bodily members as the subjects), was long known. John of Salisbury put forward a formulation in the 12th-c. *Policraticus*, as did Giraldus Cambrensis (*De Principis Instructione*, i, 19) and Thomas Aquinas (*De Regimine Principum*, 12) in the 13th c. Such 15th-c. French commentators as Jean Juvenal des Ursins and Jean Gerson in turn influenced the Scots writers on kingship, including John Ireland.

890 *sloug*] Sc, C; *lunge* P, P(oct).

890-903   The analogy of the good shepherd and the spiritual guide or pastor had biblical precedent (see John 10) and was frequently used in literature; cf. *Thre Prestis*, 413; Henryson, *Fables*, 2707-76 and Lauder, *Office and Dewtie of Kyngis*, 287-88, 303-14, 350-52.

895 *Lowrance*:   A Scottish nickname for the fox; cf. Henryson, *Fables*, 429, 469; Dunbar, *This hindir nycht in Dumfermeling* (B76), 16.

897 *Bot the*] Sc, C; *Bot be the* P, P(oct).

898 *that all his flokis ar rewlit rycht*] Sc, C (*flockis, richt*); *than ar his flokis rewlit all at rycht* P, P(oct).

902 *slane*] Sc, C; *flane* P, P(oct); the latter may not be a printer's error; see *DOST*, *flayne*, flayed [p.p. of 'Fla', v.] and cf. Henryson, *Fables*, 2058-59 (the cadger's plan to make mittens of the fox's flayed skin).

909 *Havand small ee*:   A common expression; cf. Henryson, *Fables*, 384; *Wallace*, IX.500.

909-10 *Havand small...everilk deill*: An opposition often expressed by Lyndsay, but also found in earlier verse; cf. Dunbar, *Quhy will 3e, merchantis* (B55), 71-72.

915 The line seems defective in all three witnesses: *That ryches mycht be polices incres* P, P(oct); *That ryches mycht be and policey incres* Sc, C (*policie*). If 'be' is taken to mean 'by means of', 'by the use of' (as in Purfoote's 1566 English text of the poem), then P gives the better reading. If so, P's 'polices' must be regarded as a printer's error for 'policey' (good government), as in Sc.

Subtitle following 917 *The Complaynt of the Comoun Weill of Scotland.*] Sc, C; *om.* P, P(oct).

919 *boustius berne*: John the Commonweal represents the weal (health and wealth) of the kingdom, and the ideal of common good before 'singular proffeit'. As an allegorical figure, he should not be confused with John 'Upeland', representative of the countryman; cf. Lyndsay's *Complaynt*, 407, and *Papyngo*, 540.

928 *quhat wer*] Sc, C; *quhar is* P, P(oct). Sc's *wer* helps to suggest that the figure, though now rough and landless, once had a name and place; cf. 932 ('disgysit').

938 *happinnis now, your*] Sc, C; *happynnis this* P, P(oct).

945 *raggit, revin, and rent*: The alliteration stresses the point: cf. *Buik of Alexander*, IV.9494; *Ane Dialog*, 5105.

946ff *tender freindis*: The personification allegory was traditional; cf. Dunbar, *Quhom to sall I compleine* (B54), 'Oft Falsett rydis...Quhone Treuthe gois on his fute', 11-12. The coupling of the figure of 'Polacey' with the reference to France may also be a more explicit allusion to Albany, regent 1514-24. His arrival in Scotland from his native France in 1515 initiated a period of firm government, which did not continue after his departure in 1517. His second and third terms of personal rule (1521-22, 1523-24) reintroduced relative stability, but there was mixed support for his war against England. When he left in 1524 Albany gave assurances of an early return, but his involvement in Francis I's disastrous Italian campaign prevented it. The absence permitted Arran formally to end both the regency and James V's minority; at the age of twelve, the prince was invested with the symbols of office on 26 July 1524.

950 *clene*] P, P(oct); *plane* Sc, C. *clene*: Cf. the alliterative use of 'clene' in *Ane Dialog*, 2532 ('nocht ellis bot clene confusioun').

955 *Mers...Lowmabane*: The Merse, in the E., was the wide valley of the lower Tweed or Border plain, bounded by the Lammermuirs. Lochmaben and its castle, on the river Annan, were of great strategic importance in Scotland's defence against English attack.

956 *I culde...be ane theif*: Proverbial sounding; contextually, 'be' has the sense 'from'.

958 *vecious workis*] Sc; *vicious workis* C; *vicionsnes* P, P(oct).

960 *could fynd no remeid*] Sc; *could find no remeid* C; *cowth fint no resort* P, P(oct). *Hieland*: The N. and NW mountainous country of Scotland, where most inhabitants spoke Gaelic only; see further, Maclean 1981.

961 *put to*] Sc, C; *put in* P, P(oct).

962 *thay tuke of me non heid*] Sc, C; *warld mak me no support* P, P(oct). *sweir swyngeoris*: The common Lowland perception; see Bawcutt 1992: 228, 238, 252-56. For the Highland view: MacInnes 1989: 94.

964 *Syklykin to*] P, P(oct); *Als in* Sc, C. P is preferable on metrical grounds (see Hamer 1931-36: III.42). *Oute Ylis...Argyle*: The 'Outer' or Western Isles of Scotland; Argyle, SW Highland region.

974 *debait*] P, P(oct), C; *bebait* Sc.

975 *quhome to I suld me mene*] Sc, C; *quham to to mak my mane* P, P(oct). A common expression, used in legal as well as literary contexts; cf. *Bagsche*, 3; *Meldrum*, 906n, and see Basing 1994: 73.

976 *socht throw all the spirituall stait*] Sc, C; *Goweht throw all the spirituall flait* P, *Gowecht* P(oct).

979 *rewlit all*] P, P(oct); *rewlis up all* Sc, C.

981 *chaist frome*] Sc, C; *chaist far from* P, P(oct).

985 *tellyng...deneris*: Cf. *Dreme*, 196. *Tell*, to count, is a common usage; cf. Chaucer, *BD*, 439-40; Dunbar, *Schir, ʒe haue mony seruitouris* (B67), 27.

991 *brag...boste*: A popular alliterative collocation; cf. *King Hart*, 393; Stewart, *Croniclis*, 19590.

992 *everylk*] P, P(oct); *everilk* C; *ever* Sc. *oist*] Sc, C; *cost* P, P(oct). *The civele weir...oist*: Internal dissension prevents any effective military opposition to threats from without; cf. 1018-28n and see further, *Complaynt*, 356n.

993 *ilk...self*: Proverbial; cf. Whiting M63 and M73; Tilley M112.

994 *lyke ane elf*: Cf. Henryson, *Orpheus*, 359. Eurydice is thus described because of her extreme pallor, caused by her 'banishment' to Pluto's hell-like spirit world. John the Commonweal's state ('visage leyne', 'rycht malancolious', exiled) bears passing comparison.

9 9 6 *St Jhone...borrow*: A familiar leavetaking phrase; cf. *Kingis Quair*, 159-61; *Wallace*, IX.170. The saint is called upon to act as guarantor that the addressee will 'fare weill' (= travel safely).

999 *efter...glaid morrow*: Proverbial; cf. Whiting N108; Whiting, 'Proverbs...Scottish', *Night* (4).

1005-11 *ane gude auld prudent kyng*: Scotland had not had a king who had lived to old age since the earliest Stewarts, Robert II (1316-90) and Robert III (c.1337-1406); see *Papyngo*, 417n, 436n, 437n, 446n, 487n. When, in 1524, after Albany's return to France, James V was declared of age to govern, he had not even reached his majority, or 'perfyte aige'; see *Complaynt*, 209n. John the Commonweal's lamenting prediction of c.1526, expressed at the end of the period of instability that followed, must have seemed all too accurate.

1010-11 *that proverbe*: The ultimate source was biblical: Eccles. 10.16; cf. Whiting, W436 and Tilley W600.

1018-28 *one schip did...approche*: A partial contrast to Dunbar's *Goldyn Targe* (B59), 230-45, in which the sound of Aeolus's bugle signals to the dream figures to board and sail away, awakening the dreamer by firing 'gunnis with powder violent' as they do so. Lyndsay's ship of attacking 'marenaris', however, approaches Scotland's shore with fierce fire and prepares to stay ('doun thar ankeris fell'). The episode awakens the dreamer to action, the recording of the vision for the king. The linked sudden noises, resultant awakening, and the desire to record are familiar concluding devices (cf. Chaucer, *BD*, 1330-33), but Lyndsay also uses convention to draw attention to a real threat—attack from without—should Scotland's condition remain without 'remeid'.

1027 *youte and yell*: Cf. *Dreme*, 165; a possibly intentional echo, likening the fulfilment of the present political threat from without Scotland to 'the lawest hell'.

1028 *drame*] P, P(oct); *dreme* Sc, C.

1030 *with lyste and*] Sc, C; *and lest with* P, P(oct).

1031 *oritore*: A room for study, writing and reflection; cf. Henryson, *Test. Cresseid*, 8; *Tragedie*, 2-3.

1034 *thou gettis*] Sc, C; *I hef* P, P(oct).

Subtitle following 1037 *Heir endis the Dreme. And begynnis the Exhortatioun to the Kyngis Grace.*] Sc; *The Exhortatioun to the Kingis Grace.* C; *And exhortatioun to the Kyngis grace.* P, P(oct). *Exhortatioun*: Cf., in content, *Papyngo*, first 'Epystill' (227-345), but the Exhortatioun's more formal stanza and austere tone differ from the former's more fluent rhyme royal and gracefully instructive tone.

1040 *remembrance*: An important concept in the earlier sections of the poem, 'remembrance', or the idea of keeping in mind, is also central here; (cf. 'dres the', 'prent the', 'tak tent'): Lyndsay lists the traditional precepts that the king must remember to be a successful adult ruler.

1041 *That*] Sc, C; *Quhow* P, P(oct).

1043 *uther thyng*] Sc, C; *erthly thing* P, P(oct).

1047 *prent*: The sense underlines the reciprocal nature of the relationship between God and the king; cf. 1037-40.

1052 *thow...sawin*: Cf. II Cor. 9.6 and Gal. 6.7-9; Whiting, S542.

1058 *weill wyt*] Sc; *weill wit* C; *weill heir* P, P(oct).

1064-67 *Tak manlie...Temporance*: The four Cardinal Virtues: Strength (or courage), Prudence, Justice and Temperance; see further, Lyall 1976.

1079-80 *Kyngis...nocht lyberall*: The concept was traditional; cf. Hay, *Gouernaunce of Princis*, fol. 106ʳ, ii.29-49.

1081 *Was never yit na wrache*] Sc, C; *Without fredome is none* P, P(oct).

1083 *Mydas of Trace*] Sc, C (*Thrace*); *Cresus of Pers* P, P(oct). *Mydas of Trace*: Legendary king of Phrygia, to whom Dionysius granted the request that everything he touched be turned to gold. When his food and drink were transformed, Midas realised his error. In some versions he was able to cure himself by bathing in the river Pactolus, but Lyndsay depicts him dying for want of ungilded food. King Croesus's wealth (P, P(oct)), was also proverbial, but not his death from starvation.

1086 *tuycheit*] Sc; *uycheit* P, P(oct); *tuichit* C.

1092 *Frome lychorie*: Traditional advice; cf. Hay, *Gouernaunce of Princis*, fol. 108ʳ, iv.1-30.

1094 *sensuall syn*] Sc, C; *lusty thy self* P, P(oct).

1097 *Tarquyne*: Tarquinius Sextius or Sextus, son of Tarquinius Superbus, the last king of Rome (539-510 BC). He came to notoriety by feigning allegiance to the Galbi rebels, then destroying them, and by raping Lucretia (wife of Tarquinius Collatinus), for which his family was banished from Rome.

1104 *gane on*] Sc; *gan on* C; *gan over* P; *han over* P(oct).

1105 *chosin of Romanis*] Sc, C; *chosin Romes* P, P(oct).

1107 *That vicious...endyng*: Proverbial; cf. Whiting, E91, 93, 94.

1110-13 *Use counsall*: Cf. the more abstract rendering at 1065. Lyndsay could be referring to the process of seeking advice, to the body so-called, or the advice itself; cf. *Complaynt*, 150 or 249; *Papyngo*, 297-303; *Answer*, 43.

1112 *perticulare*] Sc; *particular* C; *perculiar* P, P(oct). *Thy awin perticulare weill*: Possibly a more specific allusion to the self-serving policies of those in power during the minority, but perhaps also to a youthful royal egoism known to Lyndsay.

1113 *so sall*] Sc, C; *than sal* P, P(oct).

1114 *Remember*] Sc, C; *Rememberyng* P, P(oct).

1118 *remember...dee*: A classical topic common in late medieval literature; see Curtius 1953: 80-82.

1121 *sentence*] C, P, P(oct); *scentence* Sc.

1122 Sc's *kyucht* is corrected to *knycht*; cf. *knyt* P, P(oct); *knicht* C.

1123 *of deith...schouris*: Cf. Lydgate, *Timor mortis*, 75-76: 'Deth... /...with his dedly mortal shours'; Dunbar, *I that in heill wes* (B21): Death's 'schour of mortall haill', 70. (The analogy is also behind the traditional 'rain' of arrows loosed at once, as in *The Goldyn Targe* (B59), 178 and 195.) The idea of death as bitter was proverbial; cf. Whiting D79.

1124 *Quhar bene*: A popular rhetorical formula (*ubi sunt*); cf. *Papyngo*, 605-11, 323-24n.

1125 *fair on*] Sc, C; *far of* P, P(oct). *DOST, fare*, v., 3, however, gives some support for P's reading.

Following 1126 *Finis.*] Sc; *om.* P, P(oct), C.

1127-34 *And so*: The brisk concluding two-stress stanza (*aaabaaab*) is a sharp contrast to the sombre and elevated nine-line pentameter of the 'Exhortatioun'. It has been called doggerel (Hamer 1931-36: III.46); rather, Lyndsay takes up a poetic fashion of the period; cf. *Bann. MS*, fol. 74, and see Hamer 1931-36: IV.lvi-lvii. The stanza's brief remembrance (of man's sin and the saving grace of the crucifixion) creates a short prayer. Its hopeful complicity—'Mak *our* provisioun'; 'Confirmand *our* peace'—draws ruled and ruler together before God.

1132 *scorne*] P, P(oct), C; *scrone* Sc.

The Complaynt, c.1530

Text: The text is based on the earliest extant, John Scot's, printed in Edinburgh in 1559, *STC* 15675 (= Sc). This, with other shorter poems by Lyndsay, was appended to remaining copies of the 1554 edition of *Ane Dialog* (*STC* 15672). Sc was collated with two later editions, Scot's for Henry Charteris, 1568, *STC* 15658 (= C) and Bassandyne's of 1574, *STC* 15660 (= Bs). Important variants are noted.

Title: In Sc: *Heir beginnis the Complaynt of Schir David Lindesay.*

Form: The late-medieval verse *complaynt* (Fr. *complaint*) expressed, in a variety of styles, grief, lament, or outcry at wrong suffered. Love was a frequent theme (cf. Criseyde's embedded lament, *Tr* IV.743-98), but there were also petitions (cf. Dunbar, *Complane I wald*, B9); formal allegations (cf. Dunbar, *Schir, I complane off iniuris*, B64); devotional pieces (cf. Greene 1977: 333, *Cryste made mane*); and attacks on the current standards or professions (cf. *Doverrit with dreme*, B11). Lyndsay's *Complaynt* has a petitionary thread but is also concerned with the corruptions of the times, the latter sharpened by a localised setting and allusions to actual events.

Date: Lyndsay refers to his earlier *Dreme*, c.1526 (99). He also mentions datable political events (including those that affected him personally, 258-60*n*) during 1525-26, 1528, and, at the latest, 1529-30 (see 120-21*n*, 156-58*n*, 171*n*, 299-300*n*, 356*n*; 195-96*n*, 262*n*, 372*n*; and 85*n*, 383-34*n*, 457*n*). These argue for a c.1530 date.

Metre: There is no single 'complaint' metre, but a great variety; cf. Chaucer's elaborate lament, *Anel*, 211-341, or the subtle simplicity of Dunbar's four-stress stanza (*aabB*) in *This waverand warldis wretchidnes* (B79). Lyndsay's four-stress couplets, used also in *Meldrum* and *Ane Dialog*, help to establish a conversational tone, and allow the easy switching between several levels of diction; cf. 186-214.

1-6 *Schir, I beseik*: Cf. Dunbar, *Schir, 3it remember* (B68), 46-50.

6 Cf. Dunbar, *Complane I wald* (B9), 1.

7-9 *Quidder Saturnis creueltie...vengeance*: Lyndsay wonders if Saturn, considered a malefic planet, was in a position of influence at the time of his birth. The astrological interpretation of a person's birthdate or character was common in medieval literature; cf. Chaucer, *SqT*, *CT*, V (F), 45-51; Dunbar, *Ballade of...Barnard Stewart* (B56), 73-80. Hamer 1931-36: III.49, 7*n*, argues with caution that the lines may be used to calculate the poet's own birthdate; Eade 1984: 157 considers, however, that 'Lyndsay's invocation of astrology here is merely token'. The approach is likely to have been attractive to the poem's addressee, James V, who had an interest in astrological forecasting; see Durkan 1981: 181-94.

9 *aspect*, or angular separation (in celestial longitude) of one planetary body from another (latitude not being taken into account): Eade 1984: 61.

18 *fais*] Sc, C; *face* Bs.

27 *discomfortyng*: Cf. Barbour, *Bruce*, III.193-98.

30 *flatter or fleche*: A common alliterative pair; cf. Dunbar, *Schir, 3e haue mony seruitouris* (B67), 39.

36-39 *As did...wyne yaird*: As did the biblical father / householder in the parable of the labourers in the vineyard, Matt. 20.1-16.

43-44 *the last...deservit*: In the parable, the shortest-serving workers were paid first, and received the same amount as the longest-serving. Lyndsay, contrasting his own long service and unpaid position to the shorter service of newcomers at court who are already paid, looks to the king for just reward; see Burrow 1986: 60-66; cf. Dunbar, *Schir, ʒit remember* (B68), 31-35.

49 *beir nocht lyke ane baird*: Cf. Dunbar, *Schir, ʒe haue mony seruitouris* (B67), 43, 'Inopportoun askaris of Yrland kynd'. A *baird* was a poet or minstrel, often itinerant (thus seen as scurrilous). With beggars and sorners [scroungers] they had long been officially condemned (*APS*, II.36, 51). Lyndsay associates flyting invective with the bard (see 31); cf. Dunbar, *Flyting* (B65), 17-23. (These vagabonds were at some remove from the Gaelic professional bards and poet-genealogists also sometimes at court, although the two are merged in Holland, *Howlat*, 795-806.)

50 *Lang servyce...rewaird*: Proverbial; cf. Whiting S168.

51 The line begins with a Roman capital (cf. 81, 131 and 449), represented here as a new paragraph.

56 *Ane dum...land*: Proverbial; cf. Dunbar, *Off every asking* (B44), 26-27 and Whiting M276 (cf. A211 and A212).

77 *Thow hes...and lairdis*: Lyndsay speaks in general; cf. *Rolling in my remembrance, Bann. MS*, fol. 94. James V created only one title, Lord Methven. He did grant land to loyal servants, but those who became heritable proprietors as a result of the Douglas forfeiture did not remain so to the reign's end; see Kelley 1978: 79-92. See also *Meldrum*, 1566n.

80 *lay...cheik*: Cf. HMC 1904: 11-12, which states that Lyndsay and others were to 'ly in the king's chalmer'. Lyndsay sets his loyal personal service at this difficult time beside its absence in others, now rewarded.

81-83 *Quenis grace...Chanclare...nowreis...maistres*: All were members of the inner court circle during the minority: Margaret Tudor; Gavin Dunbar, the king's early tutor and chancellor from 1528; Marion Douglas, nurse, *ER*, XIV.350; XVII.289; Elizabeth Douglas, governess, *ER*, XIV.287, XV.546; *TA*, V.146.

85 *Wille Dile*: William Dillye (Dille or Duly), at court in 1506 (*TA*, III.354), was first mentioned as a liveried servant of James V in 1516 (*TA*, V.96); explicitly, as groom, in 1522-23 (*TA*, V.197). In 1525 he was one of the 'verletis camere exteriores' (*ER* XV.201) and a crossbowman, 1526-29 (*TA* V.310, 383; *RSS*, II, no. 324). The reference to his death helps to date the poem to late 1529 or 1530.

92 *'Pa, Da Lyn'*: *DOST* defines *Pa* as a child's attempt to pronounce 'Play', thus 'Da Lyn' as an attempt at 'David Lyndsay'. A possible alternative sense for *Pa* is 'kiss'; cf. Chaucer, *MilT, CT*, I (A) 3709, where it is quoted as part of a song title, *Com pa me*; see Nicolson 1981: 98-102.

96 *DOST* defines *Gynkartoun* tentatively as 'some boyish game' possibly derived from the verb *jink*. *Gynkartoun* seems to have been the title of an early song, a stanza of which was recorded in the now-lost Constable's Cantus (1680), and quoted in Leyden 1801: 283 ('I would go twentie mile,/

I would go twentie mile on my bair foot,/ Ginkertoune...till hear him, Ginkertoune,/ Play on a lute').

99-100 See *Dreme*, opening stanzas.

102 *Hape...gude servyce*: Proverbial; cf. Whiting, 'Proverbs...Scottish', *Hap* (2), and *Rolling in my Remembrance, Bann. MS*, fol. 94, refrain.

103-04 *I wate...gude man*: A humorous aside of the kind made earlier by Dunbar; cf. *Schir, for ʒour grace* (B63), refrain.

107 *Sanct Geill*: Giles, patron saint of beggars (also cripples and blacksmiths), and dedicatee of Edinburgh's High Kirk.

120-21 *Because ane clips...asteir*: A continuation of the astrological theme (cf. *Dreme*, 385-92), the darkness a metaphor for the turn of political events after 1524, when Albany returned to France and Margaret declared her son (then aged 12) of age to govern; see *Dreme*, 1005-11n.

130 *proffeit singulair*: Cf. *Dreme*, 910. The opposition of singular profit and communal benefit was a longstanding social and political concern, mentioned in a parliamentary act of 1399, and still recurrent in the work of Lyndsay and others; cf. Dunbar, *Quhy will ʒe* (B55), 71-72.

132-34 *Thay tuke...vertew and science*: Gavin Dunbar's post as king's 'maister' ended with the ascendancy of Angus, 1525-26 (*TA*, V.129).

137-48 *As quho wald...ye may juge*: The ship of state metaphor (cf. *Kingis Quair*, 101-105) exposes the king's youth and inexperience, thus highlights the irresponsibility of those who were advisers at the time.

138 *agast*: Cf. *Buke of the Chess*, fol. 74ᵛ, 1919.

140 *tender aige*: Cf. *King Hart*, 922.

142 *bidding al*] C; *bidding all* Bs; *biddyng of* Sc.

147 *Godds*] Sc, C; *Goddis* Bs.

156-58 *Quhow than...Scotland*: Margaret's second period as regent (mid 1524 to Feb. 1525), in which appointments were made favouring the Stewarts of Avandale, the Hamiltons, Maxwells and Kennedys.

160 *facound flattryng wordis fair*: A familiar alliterative collocation; cf. Douglas, *Eneados*, 'Heir the translatour direkkis', 93; *Papyngo*, 710.

171 *gaird*: During 1524-25, Robert, Lord Maxwell, served as captain and James Stewart as principal lieutenant of the king's guard (*RSS*, I, no. 3283), its two hundred soldiers paid for by England (see *SPHenry VIII*, IV, pt iv, 85-92 (91), Wolsey to Norfolk).

176 *harld hym*: The line plays with literal and metaphorical senses.

177 *courtlie*: Cf. Dunbar, *Tretis* (B3), 268, 369, 419. Both Lyndsay and Dunbar use this word with an ironic edge.

178 *Leith*: The sea port near Edinburgh where many foreign goods entered Scotland. Its sands were long-used for horse races and other outdoor pursuits; cf. Dunbar, *This hinder nycht halff sleiping* (B75), 111-14.

181 *Castand galmoundis*: Cf. Dunbar, *Schir, lat it neuer* (B66), 51-52.

184 *Flattre*: A traditional personification; cf. Dunbar, *To dwell in court* (B81), 26; *Thrie Estaitis*, 904-17, 984-1009.

185 *Roundand*: Cf. Dunbar's *Quhom to sall I compleine* (B54), 37 ('rovn') and *To dwell in court* (B81), 33 ('ane roundar in the nwke').

186-214 The exchanges create a mini drama (cf. 237-54), in which the lowering of diction level (by colloquial language and blasphemous oaths,

190, 192, 194, 213) is effective both as entertainment and moral lesson; cf. Douglas, *Eneados*, XII, Prol. 211-24.

188 *landis*: All exemplars have 'handis', but this seems to be textually corrupt; cf. 'landis', *Thrie Estaitis*, 985-88.

194 *Gods*] Sc; *Goddis* C, Bs.

195-96 *thesaureir...teind*: The alliteration ('thesaureir', 'tak', 'teind') establishes the mercenary emphasis; cf. 197-98's 'our part', 'part', 'pelf'. The treasurers during the minority were: John Campbell (of Thornton, then Lundy, 1516/17-26); William, Master of Glencairn (son of the Earl of Angus's brother-in-law and appointee of Angus, 1526); Archibald Douglas of Kilspindie (uncle and appointee of Angus, 1526-27). For beneficiaries in lands, property, and offices in this period, see Kelley 1973: 381-90.

198 *part the pelf*: Cf. Dunbar, *Off benefice* (B43), 5, 10, 25; *Thrie Estaitis*, 1553-54. Cf. 254.

199-214 *Bot haist us...the pape!*: Cf. *Thrie Estaitis*, 994-1009.

200 *toung*] C, Bs; *toun* Sc. *And lat...ane toung*: Cf. *Thrie Estaitis*, 76-77, where it is expanded as a gibe to both men and women.

203 *ony*] C, Bs; *On* Sc. *Quhen ony casualiteis*: These incidental dues (of wardship, non-entry) were collected by sheriffs and other royal officers who, after deducting their expenses, rendered them to the treasurer, the securing of whose 'freindschip' thus was vital; cf. 195ff.

204 *in*] Sc; *in tyll* C; *in till* Bs.

207 *nor dois ane sancte*: James V's innocence and almost-martyrdom at the hands of his corrupters are stressed; his present personal rule thus separated from the instability of his minority.

209 *So, or he be of perfyte aige*: 'Before he attains his legal competence, or maturity'; cf. *Rolling in my remembrance, Bann. MS*, fol. 94, especially the final stanza. Once James attained his majority (usually fourteen for a boy), the acts of his minority could be revoked.

213-14 Cf. *Papyngo*, 1165; *Thrie Estaitis*, 1008-09.

215 *within*] C, Bs; *withtin* Sc.

216 *pagis peris*: Cf. Whiting, 'Proverbs...Scottish', *Page*.

217 *maid ane hand*: Though 'band' seems more likely, all exemplars use 'hand'. The text is not necessarily corrupt: the hand was given as a pledge (see *DOST, hand*, n., sense 1e); cf. *Meldrum*, 977.

219 *Sanct Dinnyce*: St Denis was confused with those figures called Dionysius; C and Bs indeed print 'Dionis'. Possibly a pointed reference, as this saint, patron of France, was invoked against frenzy and strife.

223 *be his bowis war weill cumit hame*: 'Before he received papal grant or confirmation of presentation to a benefice'.

230 *pluke at the crawe*: In *DOST (pluk, v.)* a name of a game in which the *craw* [crow] was an object of sport to other players, who tugged his clothes or hair; cf. Douglas, *Pal. Honour*, 648-52; Skelton, *Speke, Parrott*, 396.

235 *to clatter*: Cf. Dunbar, *Be diuers wyis* (B5), 10.

237-54 The sexual corruption of the king is presented as a mini-drama (cf. 186-214), in which he has a passive, trusting part.

237 *devyll...knyfe*: Blasphemy of this kind was the subject of a 1551 act against 'blasphematioun of the name of God sweirand...be...Deuill stik, cummer, gor...and vthers vgsume aithis' (*APS*, II.485); cf. Dunbar, *This nycht in my sleip* (B78), in which the Devil tempts the population to swear 'aithis of crewaltie', 3. See also Woolf 1968: 305-400.

238 *Fyfe*, region defined by the peninsular between the Firths of Tay and Forth in the North Sea, and within which was Falkland palace.

240 *Gods*] Sc; *Goddis* C, Bs.

243 *Leithgow*: Linlithgow, a royal burgh, about midway between Edinburgh and Stirling; its palace had been James V's birthplace.

245 *trittyl, trattyll, trolylow*: Dunbar speaks of the 'tratlar', in *Be 3e ane luvar* (B7), 10; of 'leis and trattillis', *Flyting* (B65), 313; of 'tratling tungis' in *Musing allone* (B33), 39. Cf. also *Thrie Estaitis*, 4366.

247 *fair Sterlyng*: Stirling, a royal burgh (on the highest navigable point on the Forth) of great strategic importance, its heavily fortified royal castle guarding the principal N-S and E-W routes across Scotland; cf. *Papyngo*, 633-36.

248 *dayis derlyng*: Cf. Henryson, *Fables*, 497.

250 *the hie boirdall*: Perhaps an oblique reference to the royal burgh of Edinburgh (cf. *Papyngo*, 626), since the previous lines list all other major royal centres (Fife/Falkland, Linlithgow, Stirling).

251 *lope*: Cf. *Answer to the Kingis Flyting*, 50.

254 *And did...the pelf*: Cf. 198n.

255 *or ever I wyste*: A common collocation: cf. Henryson, *Fables*, 2898; Douglas, *Eneados*, III, x.61.

256 *trampit*: Cf. Henryson, *Orpheus*, 105 and 124.

258-72 *Bot...my pentioun*: Exchequer records bear out Lyndsay's claim. For 1525-26 (possibly 1527 for which no record survives), he was described 'quondam hostiario domini regis [formerly usher to the king]'. Lyndsay asserts that he knew not 'quharefor' he was put from office. During Margaret's second regency, she bestowed great favour upon Andrew Stewart, Lord Avandale, and his brothers James, Henry and William (of whom Henry later became the Queen's third husband). Avandale was appointed Master Usher; Henry became Master Carver. James and William Stewart, as 'gentilmen in the kingis hous', also served daily (*RSS* XV, nos. 3268, 3273, 3275, 3278-79, 3285, 3287-89, 3291, 3295, 3320). From 1525 (when under Angus some positions, including that of carver, changed hands again), the precise post that Lyndsay had held before the king was declared of age to govern seems to have ceased to exist.

262 *anscient laird*: A play on two senses of these words (cf. *DOST*, *larde*, n.[1], 3a and 3b): 'auld laird' was both the title given to the present laird (cf. '3oung laird' or heir-apparent), and a mock-title or nickname. Lyndsay thus comments dryly on the inappropriateness of the name given to the newcomer who, he alleges, usurped his long-held position. See 258-72n.

273 *presence*: Cf. *Papyngo*, 460; Stewart, *Croniclis*, 1551.

274 *He...indigence*: There are few clues to Lyndsay's activities during this period; Hamer 1931-36: IV.xiv suggests that he 'may have been a pursuivant', but surviving Treasury records are unrevealing.

275 *peip*: *DOST* suggests tentatively an alteration from or resemblance to *keke*, 'glance', citing this line, but the usual sense of 'squeak' or 'cheep' also is apt.

283 *Makerery*: Payments of fees and livery, though not 'dowbyll garmoundis', were made to McCrery from 1525 until 1540 (irregularly after 1533). A payment in 1531-32, 'quhen he lay seik at sindry tymez' (*TA*, VI.39), could allude to the 'grandgore [syphilis]' mentioned at 286.

284 *dowbyll garmoundis*: Cf. *Dreme*, 72; *Ane Dialog*, 4675.

288 *In dreid...his tois*: Cf. *Bagsche*, 174-76; Dunbar, *Tretis*, (B3), 493.

290 *For...eine*: Proverbial; cf. Whiting E215.

299-300 *utheris...Weill wors*: The allusion is probably to the period of the sixth Earl of Angus's assumption of power (2 Nov. 1525 to 4 Sept. 1526), after his legitimate authority to have custody of the king (the three-month rotation approved by council) had expired. He was supported by some fellow councillors, including Glencairn, Gavin Dunbar, Cassilis (who later allied himself with Lennox to free the king) and, in earlier months, David Beaton. All saw Angus's strong links with England—especially his marriage to Henry VIII's sister—as assisting the interests of peace. Angus was opposed by the Queen, by now desiring divorce; various other lords (including James, Earl of Moray, who saw his authority as king's lieutenant in the N. under threat); the borderers, Scott of Buccleuch, Home, Kerr and others (who opposed Arran's increased power in SE Scotland); and Arran (with Eglinton), who sought to re-establish his claim to power by taking the leading role in a council as planned in 1525.

304 *byschopreis*: Cf. *Thrie Estaitis*, 3045-46.

306 *ane bird...nest*: A play on the proverb, 'It is a foul bird that fouls its own nest'; see Whiting B306. (It was applied more often to those wishing to condemn women; cf. Dunbar, *Now of wemen* (B40), 21-24.)

308 *draw...cat harrow*: To draw in different ways, as in the game, in which crossing loops of thread are pulled (see *OED*, *cat-harrow*); to thwart each other.

309 *proudest prelatis*: Lyndsay's specific targets were probably James Beaton, Archbishop of Glasgow (1509-23) and St Andrews (1523-39) and his nephew, David, who by 1524 was Arbroath's commendator (cf. *Tragedie*, 53n); both supported Scotland's continuing alliance with France. From 1513, James Beaton was also Chancellor, until in 1526 Angus forced him to give up the Great Seal. It was then that Beaton is said to have 'kept away from the capital, even resorting to disguise...in order to avoid Angus's spies': Sanderson 1986: 46; cf. *Papyngo*, 549, 556-60.

309-15 *The proudest...sensuall*: Imagery associated with the bat (cf. *Papyngo*, 1095-98; 1096n) is transferred to these 'blind' and corrupt prelates.

314 *blyndit...ene*: Cf. *Ane Dialog*, 5362-63.

315 *wardly*] Sc; *warldlie* C, Bs. *wardly*: Cf. Dunbar, *Complane I wald* (B9), 7.

317 *court and cessioun*: The secular courts of justice.

318 *Contrar...professioun*: Against their commitment to spiritual matters as opposed to secular.

321-24 *Esayas...the peple teche*: A reference to Isa. 56.10-11; cf. *Ane Dialog*, 5366-67.

333 'And, through some minimal skill with the bridle bit, ride on a mule'.

337-39 *Prencis...but puneischement*: Cf. *Tragedie*, 398.

344 *perverst prelatis*: Cf. *Dreme*, 176.

356 *Att Lyithgow, Melros...Edinburgh*: These references to three places of particular and eventually bloody significance in the struggle for power are shorthand for a series of attempts to remove the king from Angus's charge. On 17 Jan. 1526, Angus (with the king) met opponents led by Arran (and to be joined by Moray and his northern supporters) near Linlithgow. This encounter was checked because of Arran's unwillingness to risk the king's person, and led Moray to offer his support to Angus.

On 26 July 1526, Angus, with James V, visited Melrose to hold a justice-ayre at Jedburgh. The border lord, Walter Scott of Buccleuch, and his supporters, attempted to remove the king during their return journey to Melrose, engaging with the Kerrs only, and causing the death of Andrew Kerr of Cessford.

The third major conspiracy differed in that James V himself appears to have been involved. It was led by Lennox and the Master of Glencairn (previously Angus supporters). They first tried to help the king escape from Holyrood Palace in Edinburgh; when the outcome was unsuccessful he was kept in closer confinement. On 4 Sept. 1526 an armed battle between Lennox and Angus led to Lennox's death. The combatants disengaged and the active opposition to Angus was firmly quashed, the parties ostensibly reconciled, until Dec. 1528; see Emond 1988: 486-573.

361-63 *As tyrannis...commoun theiffis*: Alliteration gives added force to Lyndsay's list; cf. Dunbar, *Complane I wald* (B9), 15-27.

367 *or ever I wyste*: See 255n. The use of the phrase lends authenticity to Lyndsay's claims of his ignorance of the king's escape plans.

372 *That thay...Tweid*: The Earl, his brother, George, his uncle, Archibald of Kilspindie, and Alexander Drummond of Carnock were summonsed for treason on 13 July 1528. Angus was found guilty and his goods were forfeited, but he was permitted to go into exile in England, since the Treaty of Berwick (Dec. 1528) seemed to have assured stable relations with that country.

373 *Now, potent prince*: A more formal style of address begins a passage of kingly admonition (373-448).

379 *The foure...cardinalis*: A traditional allegorisation of the four Cardinal Virtues, Justice, Prudence, Strength, Temperance, cf. Dunbar, *To the, O marcifull saluiour* (B83), 73-80; *Papyngo*, 923.

383-84 *ordour...the bordour*: In May and June 1529, James and his council held justice-ayres in the border towns (between Scotland and England) 'for pacifying of the samin' (*ADCP*, 306, 311, General bond). In June 1530, James summoned a second muster at Peebles and Dumfries, at which thieves and pledges were taken, and the border leader, Armstrong of Gilnockie, was hanged (*ADCP*, 327-28, where it is noted, 'his hienes sall pas in propir persone to put gude reule outthrow all his bordouris...').

At the same time, James moved to pursue opponents in the Western Isles (see 398), directing his lieutenant, Colin, Earl of Argyll, to carry this out (*ADCP*, 313-14; see also 19 Oct. 1529, 317; 22 Apr. 1530, 326-27; 19 May 1530, 327-29).

386 *hangit...apon the gallous*: Cf. *Thrie Estaitis*, 3990-97.

388 *Temporance...brydill leid*: A traditional association (cf. Douglas, *Eneados*, VI, ii.45-46), but recalling also the earlier references to the poor advisers of the king who, in opposition to temperance, had made reckless rides to Leith (178).

391-92 *Chaistitie...baneist Sensualitie*: Common imagery; cf. *Dreme*, 983; *Thrie Estaitis*, 1661-1752.

395-98 *Povertie...Amangis the hountaris in the Ylis*: 'Poverty has fled the court for the savage Western Isles'; contrast *Dreme*, 964-65.

396 *baith hir ene*: Proverbial; see 290*n*.

399 *Dissimulance...hir face*: Cf. Dunbar's allegory, *Goldyn Targe* (B59), 217.

403 *Polyce*: Cf. *Dreme*, 862-65.

407 *Jhone Upeland*: John Upland, the countryman. A traditional figure; cf. the 15th c. *Jack Upland, Friar Daw's Reply* and *Upland's Rejoinder* (Heyworth 1968: 54-72); *Now is our king in tendir aige, Bann. MS*, fols 93^v-94^r, refrain. *Jhone* (or *Jok*) *Upeland* (or *Uponeland*), is distinct from John the Commonweal, who represents, rather, the weal—welfare and wealth—of all Scotland; cf. *Dreme*, 917-1015, *Papyngo*, 541, *Thrie Estaitis*, 2436-66.

408 *rysche bus kepis his kow*: Proverbial; cf. Whiting, 'Proverbs...from Scottish', *bush* (6). The sense, that the grazing cattle remain undisturbed, is here applied, more particularly, to James V's stern measures against cattle raids; see 383-84*n*.

413 *mak minstratioun*: Cf. *Tragedie*, 368.

418 *vaine*: Cf. Dunbar, *To speik of science* (B82), refrain.

421 *superstitious*] C, Bs; *superstitionis* Sc.

423 *Expres aganis...*: Cf. *Bagsche*, 188.

427 *As Jeroboam*, king of Israel, who set up two calves of gold at Beth-el and Dan (within his own realm), and ordered his subjects to worship them (I Kings 12.20-33).

441 *David and Salomone*: Father and son, kings of Israel. David destroyed images (II Sam. 5.21); Solomon built a magnificent temple to God (I Kings 5-8); see further, 487-88*n*, *Papyngo*, 2*n*.

450 *get rewaird*: Cf. 67-70, but here the tone is jocular.

457 *Be merciall dedis*: In the early days of his personal reign, James used military force to resist Angus, in Oct. 1528 laying unsuccessful siege to Tantallon, principal seat of the Douglases.

458 *art...abyll*: Cf. the easy, though complimentary question-begging in the *Papyngo*, 283-94.

467 *Basse...Maye*: Islands in the Firth of Forth. In Lyndsay's day, May was owned by the Augustinian Priory of St Andrews.

467-79 Such 'impossibilities' belonged to a literary tradition of 'lying' poems that was especially popular in Scotland; see further, *Bann. MS*, fols 265^r-267^r; Utley 1944: 133-34.

468 *Mont Senaye*: This was the biblical Mt Horeb (Sinai) where, during forty days and nights, Moses spoke with God and received the two tablets of God's law (Exod. 34).

469 *Lowmound...Falkland*: The Lomond Hills, the twin volcanic mounds dominating central and NW Fife; cf. *Papyngo*, 641.

471 *kirkmen...dignitie*: Cf. *Duncan Laideus' Testament*, 330.

478-79 *Quhen Sanct Peter... fyscharis of Aberladye*: St Peter, one of the disciples who had been a fisherman, was sometimes depicted holding a fish, to denote both his calling and his Christian work as a fisher of souls, but his 'feist' for all the fishermen of Aberlady (a coastal village near Haddington, East Lothian) was unlikely to occur, the vast Aberlady Bay, waterless at low tide, being almost unfishable.

481 *Sanct Phillane*: Fillan, an 8th c. saint long identified with the Perthshire region; see *Butler's Lives*, I, 120.

482 *grote*: The silver groat of 1526 was worth 18 pence, the silver used in its striking, ten deniers fine, being the lowest standard any silver groat had held; see Stewart 1955: 75-76; Bateson 1987: 11.

483 Lyndsay's tone and message again become more sober.

487-88 *David...propheit royall*: David, slayer of Goliath, champion of the Philistines (I Sam. 17), was king of Israel for forty years (I Kings 2.11). He was seen as a prophet because his triumphant entry into Jerusalem, after his recapture of the Ark of God from the Philistines, was considered to foretell Christ's entry into the same city prior to the events of the Passion.

489-500 *God hes haill...omnipotent*: For a longer version of this traditional, but personalised advice, cf. *Papyngo*, 248-82.

495 *Sum*] C, Bs; *Dum* Sc.   *lawid*] Sc; *layit* C, Bs.

501 *quhen*] Sc; *quhen it* C, Bs.

503-04 *Or he sall...sober rent*: A common theme of the medieval period; cf. Dunbar, *Quho thinkis that he hes sufficence* (B53).

507 *woun*] Sc; *wun* C, Bs.

508 *Matussalem*] Sc; *Diogenes* C, Bs.   *toun*] Sc, Bs; *tun* C. Methuselah's great age was proverbial (cf. Whiting M526), but Diogenes' austere, self-sustained life in a barrel was a commonplace perhaps more appropriate to Lyndsay's wry allusion to an old age lived away from court in contented poverty (cf. Chaucer, *Form Age*; 35; Lydgate, *Fall*, I.6224-300). In the want of Lyndsay's own manuscript, or the postulated first printed edition of c.1530, however, there is insufficient extant evidence to justify a change to the 1568 reading.

510 *Thy graces answeir*: Not necessarily simply a petition for a financial response, but a possible request for a poetic answer; cf. the eight-line *Respontio regis*, perhaps by James IV, of Dunbar's *Schir, lat it neuer in toune be tald* (B66); see Bawcutt 1992: 126-27. James V purportedly wrote at least one poem to Lyndsay, who responded with the *Answer to the Kingis Flyting*.

The Testament of the Papyngo, 1530

Text: The text is based on John Scot's Edinburgh edition of 1559, *STC* 15675 (= Sc), which was appended to the 1554 edition of *Ane Dialog* (*STC* 15672). Sc was collated with two 1558 editions thought to be by the Rouen printer, Jean Petit or his heirs: the quarto, *STC* 15673 (= P) and the octavo, *STC* 15674 (= P(oct)). Sc was also collated with John Byddell's earlier London edition, 1538, *STC* 15671 (= B). Both B and P appear to have used the same (now lost) exemplar, being closely similar in layout. B, although early, is an anglicised text, and thus less useful here. P's Scots occasionally suffers from its French? compositors' unfamiliarity with the language: *cove* (114) becomes *cofe*; *Baliall* (395) becomes *valiale*; *feid* (463) becomes *feit*, for instance. References here to P include those to P(oct) unless noted otherwise, since differences usually are slight. A further Scottish witness, the Elphinstone MS, Edinburgh University Library, MS Dk.7.49 (= E), was examined. Portions of E were copied in 1527, the Lyndsay poems (including the *Papyngo*) in c.1566. E's transposition of lines 755 and 756 of the *Papyngo* suggests that the scribe copied from P(oct) or a text in some way related to it—a page break occurs between these lines only in P(oct)—but the poem-title in E is closer, in spelling and punctuation, to Sc. The 1568 Edinburgh edition, also produced by Scot, for Henry Charteris, *STC* 15658 (= C), is based upon that of 1559, but has some useful revisions. A later London edition, by T. Purfoote for W. Pickering, 1566, *STC* 15676 (= PP), is of some literary, linguistic and historical interest, replacing the name of the Scottish poet, *Kennedie* (16), with that of *Skelton*, for instance.

Title: As in Sc: *Heir follouis the Testament, and Complaynt of our Soverane Lordis Papyngo. King James the Fyft. Quhilk lyith sore woundit, and maye not dee. Tyll every man have hard quhat he sayis. Quharefor gentyll redaris haist yow that he wer out of paine.*

Form: The poem combines, for both serious and comic effects, features from several genres. The parrot's fall perhaps had a basis in fact (see 81*n*), but the poem is also a bird fable, an amplified *exemplum* demonstrating the result of refusing, through ambition and pride, prudent counsel (199-219), cf. Holland, *Howlat*. The parrot's case, presented formally, also becomes an illustration of Fortune's mutability, linking the poem to works in the *de casibus* tradition, such as Lydgate's *Fall of Princes*. To set the scene for the parrot's downfall, Lyndsay borrows from the *chanson d'aventure* the idealised garden setting and, later, the traditional eavesdropper role for the poet. In the 'Commonyng' of the parrot and her avian executors, moreover, there are links to bird-assembly poems, such as Chaucer's *Parliament of Fowls* and, especially, Skelton's *Phyllyp Sparowe*, 387-587. By its title, the *Papyngo* is both complaint (see Lyndsay's *Complaynt*, note on 'Form') and literary testament. Based on the legal testament, the literary testament, often satiric in its bequests, had great popularity in 15th and 16th c. France, England and Scotland; see Perrow 1913; Rice 1941; Boffey 1992; Wilson 1994. Among Scottish examples are *King Hart* (concluding stanzas); Dunbar, *I maister Andro Kennedy* (B19), Lyndsay, *Test. Meldrum*; and *Duncan Laideus' Testament*.

Date: B's double colophon dates the poem by quoting from the lost exemplar, '...and finysshed the .xiiij day of Decembre...1530'. This is supported by internal evidence; see 571*n*.

Metre: The poem's opening is in a 'Chaucerian' five-stress nine-line stanza (*aabaabbcc*) used also, with different rhyme schemes, in Lyndsay's formal 'Exhortatioun', *Dreme*, 1037-1126, and Douglas's *Palice of Honour*. The rhyme royal, or five-stress seven-line stanza (*ababbcc*) of the remaining verses, also associated with Chaucer, was widely used for formal narrative verse, *The Kingis Quair* the first known Scottish work to do so.

1 Cf. Douglas, *Pal. Honour*, 411.

2 *sapience...Salamonicall*: Cf. Douglas, *Pal. Honour*, 250. The wisdom of Solomon, king of Israel, 974-c.937 BC, was a feature of biblical narratives (see I Kings, 3.16-27), and was proverbial; cf. Whiting S460; Douglas, *Pal. Honour*, 1540-41. The books of the Bible, Ecclesiastes and The Song of Solomon, were attributed to him; cf. *Ane Dialog*, 668*n*.

4 *The poetis...heroycall*: Cf Douglas, *Eneados*, IX, Prol. 21-21; *Papyngo*, 239.

8 *Haith done indyte*: A form of the infinitive often used in MSc. verse; cf. Dunbar, *Quhen Merche* (B52), 56; *Goldyn Targe* (B59), 159.

9-10 *dull intellygence / Of poetis now*: The traditional modest dismissal of the poet's work here covers contemporary writing in general.

12 *Chawceir, Goweir, and Lidgate*: A traditional eulogistic linking of the three pre-eminent 15th-c. English poets writing in the vulgar tongue; cf. *Kingis Quair* (of Chaucer and Gower), 1374-75; Dunbar, *Goldyn Targe* (B59), 253-70; Douglas, *Pal. Honour*, 919-21.

13 Sc's *Quhoo* is corrected to *Quho*, as in C.

14 *Albione*: cf. Douglas, *Pal. Honour*, 918.

16 *Kennedie*: A contemporary of Dunbar, Walter Kennedy died c.1518. He called himself James IV's 'trew speciall clerk' (*Flyting*, B65, 417); see Baxter 1952: 62-63; Bawcutt 1998: II.427. Although Douglas also called him 'Greit' (*Pal. Honour*, 923), the evidence for Kennedy's high reputation as a poet of 'termes aureait' is now meagre—his *Flyting* with Dunbar; *The Passion of Crist* (B.L. Arundel MS 285, fols 6ʳ - 46ᵛ, ed. Bennett 1955); and a few poems in the Asloan, Bannatyne and Maitland Fol. MSS (*Ane ageit man*; *At matine hour, Closter of crist, Leiff luff my luif*).

17 *Dunbar*: William Dunbar (c.1460-?1513), cleric and poet at James IV's court; see Baxter 1952; on his 'language...at large', Bawcutt 1992: 347-82.

18 *Goldin*] Sc, B, P, E, C, not *golden* as in Hamer 1931-36: I.56. *Goldin Targe*: A reference to Dunbar's allegorical dream vision, composed in the 1490s and referred to by this title in the c.1508 Chepman and Myllar print; see also *Goldyn Targe* (B59), 151. The poem's intricate structure, highly-patterned *Anelida* stanza, mix of the 'aureate' with a plainer style, and imagery of decorated surfaces reacting to light of various kinds, greatly influenced both contemporary and later poets.

19 *Quintyng*: None of Quintyng's poems are known to survive, but they were highly regarded: Lyndsay links him with Kennedy (54); so, too, do Dunbar, *Flyting* (B65), 2, and Kennedy himself, *Flyting*, 34. Douglas groups him with both Kennedy and Dunbar (*Pal. Honour*, 922-24). In *Now lythis off ane gentill knycht* (B39), Dunbar refers again to 'Quenetyne' (37) and to his remarks about Sir Thomas Norny (probably a fool at James IV's court) as 'ane full plum iurdane [plump chamber pot]', 34, hinting that Quenetyne also had written on the same topic; see Kinsley 1979: 302. *Mersar*: Dunbar praises him (*I that in heill wes*, B21, 74-75) as one 'That did in luf so lifly write,/ So schort, so quyk, of sentence hie'. Surviving poems are among Bannatyne's 'Ballatis of Luve' (*Off luve*, fol. 213; *Allace so sober*, fol. 269ʳ; *Thir billis are brevit*, fol. 278). A version of the long-popular, *Erthe upon Erthe*, is attributed to Mersar (*Maitl. Fol. MS*, no. clxiii). *Rowle*: A 'Rowlis' is said to be the author of a poem of considerable flyting ingenuity, *The Cursing...vpoun the steilaris of his fowlis*, *Bann. MS*, fols 104ᵛ-107ʳ (and, with some significant differences, *Maitl. Fol. MS*, no. xlvi). Dunbar notes two men called 'Roull' (of 'Aberdene' and 'Corstorphin'), *I that in heill wes* (B21), 77-78, but he does not describe or distinguish their work—unless the 'gentill' before Roull of Corstorphine can be taken as a tongue-in-cheek reference to the blistering *Cursing*. *Henderson*: Probably Robert Henryson (c.1425-a.1505), notary public and Dunfermline schoolmaster; author of the *Fables*, *Testament of Cresseid*, *Orpheus and Eurydice* and other shorter poems; see Fox 1981: xiii-xxv. *Hay*: Sir Gilbert Hay (fl.1450-60) is mentioned in *I that in heill wes* (B21), 68, grouped with Clerk of Tranent, author of the 'anteris [adventures] of Gawane' (66). This suggests that it was Hay's poetic *Buik of King Alexander the Conquerour* (based on a French Alexander narrative) that Dunbar (and Lyndsay) had in mind. Hay also translated, in prose, the *Buke of the Law of Armys*, *Buke of the Ordre of Knychthede*, and *Buke of the Gouernaunce of Princis*. *Holland*: Notary, cleric, and by 1450 secretary to Archibald Douglas, the Earl of Moray, Richard Holland was author of a poem in thirteen-line alliterative stanzas with wheel, the *Buke of the Howlat*, which he composed for the Countess of Moray between 1445 and 1452; see Stewart 1972. For a recent edition see Bawcutt and Riddy 1987: 43-84.

21 *Quhilkis*] P, C; *Quhilk is* E; *Quhikis*, Sc.

24 'Inglis' and 'Scottis' were used interchangeably of the language of Scottish texts; see McClure 1997: 5-8.

26 *Phebus*: The sun; see *Dreme*, 58*n*; *Synthia*: Cynthia, the moon. In verse, the pair were often related; cf. Douglas, *Eneados*, VII, Prol. 113-26.

27 *Gawane Dowglas*: Gavin Douglas (c.1475-1522), son of Archibald 'Bell the Cat' (fifth Earl of Angus) and Elizabeth Boyd, and uncle of Archibald, sixth Earl. He was provost of the collegiate church of St Giles, 1503-1516; made free burgess of Edinburgh, 1513; a Lord of Council, 1513; and bishop of Dunkeld, 1516. He wrote the *Palice of Honour* (1501); a translation of Virgil's *Aeneid* (1513); the short *Conscience* and, according to Bale's *Scriptorum Illustrium* and Lyndsay's poem, at least three other works; see Bawcutt 1976: 47-49; Bawcutt 1994: 95-106. His political fortunes fluctuated with those of his nephew, Archibald (second husband of Margaret Tudor), and his brother, Archibald of Kilspindie, but his reputation as poet was high during James V's reign, when Thomas Davidson printed the *Palice*, c.1530-40; see Bawcutt 1967: xv-xvi.

37 The subject here is understood: 'And in the court [those] are present'.

40-42 *Inglis*: Priest, poet-servitor, and clerk of the closet to James IV. His service as chaplain to the young James V and his brother, and participation in theatrical court entertainments would have brought him into close contact with Lyndsay; see *TA*, IV.321; V.9-10, 65-66. A Sir James Inglis was 'chancellar of the Kingis chapell' in 1526 (*TA*, 268, V.310) and 'maister of werk' in 1527 (*TA*, V.325-28), but it is uncertain whether these are the same man. By 1530 Lyndsay's Inglis was at Culross where, Lyndsay implies, he no longer composed. It is just possible that Lyndsay refers to Inglis's murder, committed before Mar. 1531 (when provision for apprehending his murderers was made, *TA*, V.442-43 and lxx). *Doverrit in dreme* is attributed to 'Schir Iames inglis' in the *Maitl. Fol. MS*, no. lxii, but to Dunbar by Bannatyne, in both draft and main MSS. The dating of several words in the poem argues for its composition during James V's reign or later, and supports the authorship of Inglis, but the poem's alliterative end-rhyme stanza and theme of 'general satire' had many precedents; see Kratzmann 1980: 165-67; Bawcutt 1998: II.311-13.

4 3 *Kyde*: A poem of stern advice to the prince, *The rich fontane of hailfull sapience*, is attributed to a 'mr aleix^r kid', *Bann. MS*, fols 92^r-93^r. An Alexander Kyd was prebendary and canon of the Chapel Royal, Stirling, in the early 1530s (*RSS*, II, 'Index of Offices'), but no direct link between poem and man as yet has been found.

4 4 *Stewarte*: A 'Maister William Stewart' was among liveried servants of the late 1520s and 1530s (*TA*, VI.39, 92, 95, 97, 205), possibly the William Stewart who was author of the metrical translation (1535) of Boece's Latin history of Scotland, but no contemporary confirmation is known. Several poems with ascriptions to 'William Stewart', 'W Stewart' and 'Stewarte' survive in the Bannatyne and Maitland Fol. MSS. Of these, *Sir sen of men* (ascribed 'q Stewart to the Kingis Grace', *Bann. MS*, fol. 96^v), *Precellend prince*, and *Rolling in my remembrance,* in content appear to belong to the late 1520s. Topical allusions in the wry carol, *First lerges* (ascribed 'q stewart', *Bann. MS*, fols. 95^v-96^r), show that this poem also belongs to James V's reign; see MacDonald 1996: 195-96; Hadley Williams, 'Dunbar and His Immediate Heirs', forthcoming.

4 6 *Stewart of Lorne*: An Alan Stewart of Lorne was Captain of the King's Guard in 1528 (*ER*, XV.158) and listed as 'servitor regis' in 1538 (*RMS*, III, no. 1866), but is not known to have been a poet. Lorne, in the W. of Scotland, was Gaelic-speaking. *carpe...curiouslie*: Both terms had a musical sense, and often described harp playing; see *DOST*, carp, 1.c.; Sanger and Kinnaird 1992: 41-52.

47 *Galbreith*: Poems by Galbraith are not known to survive, but Galbraiths, perhaps from the hereditary Mac a' Bhreatnaich harping family, provided several royal servitors during James V's reign. A William Galbraith is closely identified with both court entertainment and the king's favour in the early 1530s, when he received from the king a lute and strings and, on a separate occasion, a 'godbarn' [godchild] gift (*TA*, VI.18; *TA*, VI.22). A possible alternative is Robert Galbraith of Ester Winschellis, the lawyer-author of the work on logic, *Quadrupertitum*. He was treasurer of the Chapel Royal 1528-32, but his extant verses are in Latin, not Scots; see Menzies 1929: 205-13. (Thomas Galbraith, illuminator and clerk of the Chapel Royal during James IV's reign, has been considered by Edington (1994: 97) the 'more plausible candidate', but references to him do not continue into James V's reign; see Apted and Hannabuss 1978: 40-41.) *Kynlouch*: His poetry is not known to survive, but the family of the name, like the Galbraiths, provided royal servitors over several generations. In 1527 a Kinloch was 'court stewart to the kingis grace of his houshald' (*RSS*, I, No. 3757), and, in the accounts, he was listed among liveried servants, 1529-34.

5 1 *Ballentyne*: John Bellenden (c.1495-c.1548), clerk of the exchequer (1515-22), archdeacon of Moray (1533-38), and precentor of Glasgow (1537-47), whose prose translation of Boece, probably in progress when Lyndsay was composing his *Papyngo*, was completed by Oct. 1531 (*TA*, VI.37) and published by Davidson, c.1538-40; see also Royan 1998. By Nov. 1533, Bellenden had also translated Livy for the king (*TA*, VI.97, 206). Little of his poetry survives, that mostly attached as Prologues to his prose works; see Bellenden, *Chronicles*, II, 411-61).

55-72 *So thocht...kye and yowis*: Lyndsay focuses the earlier general declaration of inadequacy (9-10) upon his own lack of talent; cf. 246.

59 *termes...pullit*: Cf. Douglas, *Pal. Honour*, 2065-67.

63 *papingo*: The parrot was an emblem of pride and of self-indulgent pampering; cf. Whiting, 'Proverbs...Scottish', *papingo*; Chaucer, *PF*, 359. From the early 12th c., it was singled out in bestiaries and heraldic treatises for its bright plumage and ability to speak; see Pliny, *Nat. Hist.*, X, lviii; *Deidis of Armorie*, fol. 26, 1442-72; Yapp 1982: 484. Poetic allusions often stressed the bird's eloquence and erotic associations (cf. Ovid, *Amores* II, vi; Chaucer, *RvPro, CT*, 3878; Jean Lemaire de Belges, *L'Amant Vert*, Skelton, *Speke, Parrott*); others, such as Boccaccio's *De Genealogia Deorum*, IV.xlix, noted the bird's association with wisdom.

73 *Quho clymmit...faill*: Proverbial; cf. Whiting, 'Proverbs...Scottish', *Climb* (1).

8 1 *Presentit...kyng*: In extant records, James V's ownership of a parrot dates from 1538, when 'Thomas Kellis' is called 'kepar of the King[is] parrocatis' (*TA*, VI.390) and 'keeper of the parrot' (429).

88 *The Complaynt of Scotland*, fol. 53^r, 52 refers to both dance and tune. *Platfute* appears in *Was nevir in scotland, Bann. MS*, fols 99^r-101^r, 48; *Fut before gossep* ['Foot before partner'] is noted in Leyden 1801: 280.

103 *aforrow*: Courtly poetic native Scots; cf. *taforrow* (or *toforowe*): *Kingis Quair*, 339; Dunbar, *Quhen Merche* (B52), 188.

106 *sabyll*: A heraldic and courtly term.

108 *vapour*: Cf. Dunbar, *Goldyn Targe* (B59), 247.

112 *frome...splene*: A loosely used, common expression ('from the heart'); cf. Dunbar, *Goldyn Targe* (B59), 106. (The spleen was known to be a separate organ; cf. Henryson, *Ressoning*, 54.)

113-14 *That...steir*: Cf. Douglas, *Pal. Honour*, 49-50. For the traditional intemperateness of Saturn and Mars, see *Dreme*, 474-88n and 442n. *Eole*, Aeolus, god of winds, was associated with unfavourable conditions; see *Ane Dialog*, 185n.

113-42 The references to the planetary gods have many precedents (see Seznec: 1972, and cf. Chaucer, *KnT, CT*, (A) 2210-2478, Henryson, *Test. Cresseid*, 147-263, Dunbar, *Goldyn Targe* (B59), 64-66), but Lyndsay stresses these planets' astrological significance; for instance, that the inauspicious planets, Saturn and Mars, are cowed; see *Ane Dialog*, 185.

118 Mercury's prominence in the astrological scheme, 'Exaultit...in to the throne tryumphall' (119), is a reminder of this god's associations with eloquence and thus with loquacious parrots; see Eade 1984: 157-59.

124 *Cupido*: Cupid, god of love; see Chaucer, *KnT, CT*, I (A) 1963-66.

125 *Venus*, goddess of erotic love and beauty, was mother of Cupid, in some versions of the myth by Jupiter, chief and most benign of the gods. *Conjunit* perhaps has both this and the astrological sense.

126 *lyke one sker*: Early editors argue plausibly that, in describing Neptune thus, Lyndsay refers to a sea rock covered at high tide, cf. skerry (from ON *sker*), with *one* being the indefinite article in the simile.

132 Cf. 'Iohne vponland', speaker of *Now is our king in tendir aige*, *Bann. MS*, fols 93^v-94^r.

136-37 *The sound...musycall*: Cf. Douglas, *Pal. Honour*, 21-24.

138 *balmy droppis*: Cf. Douglas, *Pal. Honour*, 58. *Tytane*: Titan, god of the sun; see *Dreme*, 69n.

151 Sc's *annd* has been corrected; cf. P, C.

152 Sc's *Onto to*, omitted in all other witnesses, is corrected.

154 *Bot scho began to speill*: A hint of how the 'part' of the parrot might have been performed; cf. James IV's household 'spelar' boy and his master, climbers or acrobats; see Mill 1927: 39.

161 *vailye quod vailye*: A French phrase (*quod* a corruption of *que*) also used by Douglas; cf. *Eneados*, VI, Prol. 167; IX, Prol. 186.

165 *displayit*: Cf. Holland, *Howlat*, 354.

166 *Boreas*: The northern wind, associated with the cold and dry element, and the melancholy complexion. The allusion is in keeping with the disaster to follow; cf. Henryson, *Test. Cresseid*, 1-2, 17-21.

173 *Quhilk...mak hir mone*: Cf. Henryson, *Test. Cresseid*, 406.

174 *Now...faitall houris*: Cf. *Wallace*, IV.293-94.

175 *Of bitter deth...schouris*: Cf. *Dreme*, 1123n.

181 *deth...with his darte*: A common collocation; cf. *Papyngo*, 766, *Deploratioun*, 15.

188 *onder ane hauthorne grene*: Cf. Henryson, *Fables*, 1729, 1781-82.

192-219 Formal complaints against Fortune were popular set pieces in verse; cf. Henryson, *Test. Cresseid*, 407-69; *Pal. Honour*, 627-36; Hay, *Buik of King Alexander the Conquerour*, 3576-94.

195 *fenyeit*: Cf. Stewart, *Croniclis*, 16411.

207 *prude pacoke*: Proverbial; cf. Whiting P71, P73; Dunbar, *Tretis* (B3), 379: 'pako, proudest of fedderis'.

217 *pretende*] P; *pretend* E, C; *prentende* Sc.

224 Sc's *desolationn* is corrected to *desolatioun*; cf. P, E, C. *dullit*: Cf. Douglas, *Pal. Honour*, 393.

227 *Prepotent prince*: A common formal address; cf. Stewart, *Croniclis*, 5754.

228 *victorie*] P, C; *victore* Sc, E.

231 *Atropus*: Oldest sister of the three Fates, Atropos is represented blind or black-veiled, with a pair of scissors, with which she cuts the thread of life her sisters spin; cf. Chaucer, *Tr*, IV, 1546; *Ane Dialog*, 373.

233 Sc's *unfeuyeit* is corrected to *unfenyeit*; cf. P, E, C.

236 *mony one document*: Cf. *Ane Dialog*, 4382.

236-44 *thy grace...graces informatioun*: An allusion to a well-established court practice of offering the king poems of advice, narrative (romance, tragedy), or petition, in the hope of guiding the monarch's actions, providing entertainment (cf. *Dreme*, 32-46), and / or winning personal advancement. Few such works addressed explicitly to James V have survived; see 43n, 44n, 51n, and Lyndsay's *Dreme* and *Complaynt*.

239 *style heroycall*: Verse in tetrameter or pentameter ('heroic') couplets, often of 'dedis martial' (*Dreme*, 31); see Aitken 1983: 18-49 (19); cf. Douglas, *Eneados*, IX, Prol. 21, 90.

246 *my barbour...indyte*: See 55-72n.

248 *simpyll similytude*: A popular device of comparison; cf. Bellenden, *Quhen siluer diane, Bann. MS*, fols 4r-8v, 217-43; *Tragedie*, 351-64.

248-338 The papyngo offers the king traditional advice (see Lyall 1976: 5-29), deftly including some possibly personalised allusions—to James V's musical ability (284), and his practice of the martial arts (285-86), for example; see Hadley Williams 1996: 204-05.

260-61 *Abone archangels...principatis*: Above some levels of the celestial hierarchy; cf. *Dreme*, 518-32.

307 *regiment*: A reference to the rules of governing, or perhaps to Hay's expression of them, *Buik of King Alexander the Conquerour*, 9355-10107.

310 *sceptour...croun*: Instruments of kingly office: the sceptre for justice, sword for authority, and crown (the closed arch of *imperium*), for divine wisdom in rule; cf. *Be gratious ground, Bann. MS*, fol. 86, 33-56.

311 *The cronecklis*: Perhaps a general reference to the Latin histories (such as Major's *Historia Maioris Britanniae tam Angliae quam Scotiae* (1521) and Boece's *Scotorum Historiae* (1527), both dedicated to James V); or a more specific reference to the Scots translations of the chronicles, perhaps then underway or commissioned, by Bellenden and Stewart.

315-17 *Thocht thay...in memorie*: 'A good or bad ruler's reputation after death depends upon the written record of his deeds.'

320 *That no poyte*: Cf. *Wallace*, I.1-4; *Meldrum*, 11-20.

322 *Fergus*: In legend, and repeated by Boece and Bellenden, Fergus was the first king of the Scots in Scotland, 330 BC. (He was distinct from the historical Fergus, who reigned in Dalriada in the early 6th c. AD.)

323-24 *Thou art...on lyve*: The theme of the instability of earthly life here introduced is developed, in the bird's following address to her 'brether', into an *ubi sunt* set-piece strikingly particularised by the use of English and Scottish examples from the last hundred years.

336-37 *Have thou...Kyng of Bone*: Traditional advice (cf. Hay, *Buik of King Alexander the Conquerour*, 7319-336), refashioned as a metaphor of the play King of Bean; see 337n, and cf. Durkan 1959: 420.

337 *Kyng of Bone*: The King of Bean, a mock king, for one day of festival only, being that man in whose portion of the Twelfth Night cake the bean was found; see Billington 1986: 104-05.

352 Proverbial; cf. Whiting, 'Proverbs...Scottish', *high* (1).

353-59 *So ye...nor kyngis*: Cf. Henryson, *Fables*, 2609-15.

354 *Tak tent in tyme*: Cf. Whiting, 'Proverbs...Scottish', *tent*, and variations, *time* (7), (8).

355 *Quho clymith...the woder*: Proverbial; cf. Whiting, 'Proverbs ...Scottish', *Climb* (1).

358 *Bot moste...doun thryngis*: 'But those [who are] most feared daily she [Fortune] throws down'.

368 Proverbial; cf. Whiting, 'Proverbs...Scottish', *weathercock* (3).

377 *painfull plesour*: An oxymoron; cf. Chaucer, *Tr*, I, 402-20.

379 An apparently extraneous 'L.' appearing before 'youthed' in Sc, P and E, is omitted. Its appearance in three texts helps to confirm the existence of a now-lost exemplar that probably also contained it.

381 Sc's *cousalouris*, lacking the abbreviation mark, is corrected.

388 *fonde...flatteraris*: Cf. the clerk who 'fenyeit him ane fule' to ingratiate himself with the king in *Thre Prestis*, 470.

390-92 Cf. the alliterative list of servitor-scoundrels in Dunbar, *Schir, ȝe haue mony seruitouris* (B67), 39-43. See *Complaynt*, 49n.

395 *barnes of Baliall*: Cf. *Contemplacioun of synnaris*, *Asloan MS*, fol. 283ʳ, 1166-68; on *Baliall*, see *Ane Dialog*, 266n.

397 *intoxicat*] P, C; *intoxitat* Sc, E.

402 *travers*: Cf. *OED*, *traverse*, n., 7.

409 Sc's *cheageith*, lacking the abbreviation mark, is corrected to *cheangeith*.

409-625 *The court cheangeith*: Cf. Lydgate's more recent examples in *Of the Sodein Fal of Princes in Oure Dayes*, *Minor Poems*, I. 660-61.

413 *Rothasay*] Sc, P; *rothasay* E; *Rothesay* C. *Rothasay*: Hamer (1931-36: III.64 and 86) amends to *Rothesay*, reminding that the word is not trisyllabic. *Duke of Rothasay*: David (1378-1402), eldest son of Annabella Drummond and Robert III, and the latter's Lieutenant from 1399. He was confined to Falkland on the advice of his uncle, the Duke of Albany, and the fourth Earl of Douglas, in part for his unkept promises of marriage to the daughters of the Earls of Crawford and March, and for his unfaithfulness to his wife, sister of the Earl of Douglas. Albany was implicated in his death there (26 Mar. 1402); see Boardman 1996.

417 *Robart the thride* (c.1337-1406). His disabling accident caused Robert's younger brother, also Robert, Duke of Albany, to rule as governor until the Duke of Rothesay became regent (see 413n).

419 *Prince David*: See 413*n*. *James*: See 430*n*.

424 *Duke Murdoke*: Murdoch Stewart (c.1362-1425) succeeded his father as Duke of Albany in 1420 and was governor until 1424 when he successfully ransomed James I. Murdoch was willing to support the king, but he, his son, Walter, and family members were executed, May 1425.

430 *James the first* (1394-1437), second son of Annabella Drummond and Robert III. Captured en route to France by the English, he returned to Scotland as King (James I) in 1424: Brown 1994; Wormald 1985: 270-76.

431-32 *Gem...flude of eloquence*: Cf. Douglas, of Virgil, *Eneados*, I, Prol. 4. Possibly a reference to James I's literary activities: the *Kingis Quair* is usually attributed to him, but no contemporary references explicitly link the two. (Oxford, Bodleian Library MS Arch. Selden. B.24, the earliest surviving copy of the poem, is a late 15th c. production.) Bower, however, notes that James 'applied himself with eagerness...to the art of literary composition and writing' (*Scotichronicon*, 8, XVI, xxx.309); see also Boffey and Edwards 1997: 19-20 and fol. 191[v].

433 *fantasie*] E, C; *fantasy* P; *fantansie* Sc.

436 *put doun*: James I's policies, especially the subjugation of the Stewart nobles, led to his murder at Perth, 21 Feb. 1437: see Brown 1994: 172-211; Connolly 1992: 46-69.

437 *James the secunde* (1430-60) succeeded as a minor and assumed personal authority upon his marriage to Mary of Gueldres (1449). He then put down the Livingstones, who had earlier held him in custody and taken important offices of state. James conducted a long and finally successful campaign to overthrow William, Earl of Douglas, but he was killed by an exploding cannon during the siege of Roxburgh; see McGladdery 1990.

446 *James the thrid* (1452-88) succeeded as a minor and was held captive by the powerful Boyds in Edinburgh Castle, 1466-1469, until his marriage to Margaret of Denmark and Norway, when he took personal control. His foreign policy (especially rapprochement with England) was unpopular, as was his replacement of the first archbishop of St Andrews by his favourite, the physician, William Schevez (1478). His brothers, Albany and Mar, drew wide support; James had them arrested in 1475. Mar died soon after in mysterious circumstances; Albany escaped to France and then England, from which he invaded Scotland with an English force in 1482. The Scottish army assembled at Lauder, where a group of Scots nobles seized the king and killed some of his attendants (this incident forming the basis for later references to James's 'catyve company', *Papyngo*, 465). A reconciliation between James and Albany was attempted, but had failed by 1488; a group of lords with individual grievances against James attracted the future James IV to their cause, and finally defeated James's army at Sauchieburn, where the king himself was killed; see Macdougall 1982.

449 *Cochrame*: In later legend, Robert (or Thomas) Cochrane was principal favourite of James III and architect of the Great Hall, Stirling Castle (actually built during James IV's reign). In the 1530s, the Observant Franciscan, Adam Abell, chronicled the Lauder hangings (NLS MS 1746, fols 110[v]-112[r]). Other historians—Lesley, Ferrerio, and Lindsay of Pitscottie—add to the legend; see Macdougall 1992: 28-49.

453 *Thay grew...corne*: Proverbial; cf. Whiting C429, 174. Cf. also *This hindir nycht neir by the hour of nine, Bann. MS*, fols 87ᵛ-88ᵛ, 86 (and *Maitl. Fol. MS*, no. cxxviii.86, attributed to William Stewart).

461 *Albanie...Mar*: Brothers of James III; see 446*n*.

469 *Lawder*: Lauder Bridge; see 446*n* and 449*n*.

477 *baner...displayit*: A common expression in verse; in general, an indication of readiness for battle (cf. *Bruce*, VIII, 47-48), here also stressing the self-destructive nature of a war between a king and his heir, both perhaps unfurling a banner of the saltire cross of Scotland.

480 *Salomone*: See 2*n*.

481 *Sampsone*. The biblical figure, Samson (Judges 13-16), whose strength was proverbial; cf. Whiting, S52; *Ane Dialog*, 957.

482 *Agamenone*: Agamemnon, leader of the Greeks in the Trojan War, his valiance in the field a literary commonplace; cf. Dunbar, *Ballade of ...Barnard Stewart* (B56), 60.

484-85 *At morne...carioun*: Proverbial; cf. Whiting M688, Tilley M1174; an echo of the papyngo's earlier words at 193, 206-08, 216.

486 *Quhare bene*: Cf. 323-24*n*, 584, 605.

487 *James the feird* (1473-1513) assumed personal power immediately after James III's death, soon improving civil and criminal justice and 'pacification' of the Highlands. A 'Treaty of Perpetual Peace' was concluded with England (1502) as part of negotiations for his marriage to Margaret Tudor in 1503. At his court James IV gathered scientists (medical and alchemical), artists, musicians and writers, and, for political purposes, encouraged printing (royal patent to Chepman and Myllar, 1508). He was not scholarly, but was notably interested in jousting, hawking, and hunting. James IV's commitment to the traditional alliance with France led to the battle of Flodden (see 507-13*n*) and the end of the reign in 1513; see Macdougall 1989. In his last years his servitors included Lyndsay.

494 *savage Iles*: From 1493 on, James made several attempts to subdue the Western Isles (forfeiting the Lordship and holding in custody Donald Owre, natural son of the last Lord of the Isles), but the daunting was usually temporary only; for an overview, see Mackie 1958: 188-99.

495 *Eskdale...Annerdale*: Regions of the West March, along the Anglo-Scottish border; see Rae 1966: 1-20; McNeill and MacQueen 1996: 79-80.

499 On official business, pilgrimage, and hawking and hunting, James IV travelled with only a few retainers; see Macdougall 1989: 308.

500-03 James IV staged several tournaments; that of the Black Lady, of June 1507, was repeated May 1508 at the time of Barnard Stewart's visit: *TA*, III.257-61; IV.22, 119; Fradenburg 1991: 225-64.

505-06 See 487*n*.

507-13 *Of Flodoun...misgovernaunce*: James IV was killed at this decisive battle against English forces led by the Earl of Surrey; see Laing 1867: 141-52; Macdougall 1989: 247-81.

511 *Quhat...more?* A common rhetorical device; cf. Douglas, *Eneados*, XII, xiv.110.

519 *so mony nobyllis slane*: The king, three bishops, eleven earls, and fifteen lords were killed; see further Emond 1988: App. A, 633-36.

525-36 *Efter...of the law*: James V's minority, a fifteen-year period of instability in which the Queen, the Earl of Angus, Governor Albany, and the Earl of Arran, with their supporters, fought for power. Angus finally achieved it by gaining custody of the king (1526-28).

533 *Quene*: Margaret Tudor (1489-1541), daughter of Henry VII and Elizabeth of York, married James IV in 1503. The future James V was her fourth and only child of five to survive to adulthood. James IV's will gave Margaret the role of regent (although traditionally it was given to the next in succession), also naming her guardian of the young king, but by 1515 she was forced to give way to Albany, her re-marriage to the Earl of Angus having weakened her position.

534 *Albanie*: John Stewart (c.1484-1536), Duke of Albany, French-born cousin to James IV, being the son of Alexander, brother of James III, and thus next-in-succession to the Scottish throne. In 1513 he was called by the Scottish lords to be Governor of Scotland, and was so 1515-24, although intermittently in residence.

540 *in...weir*: Cf. Douglas, *Eneados*, XII, iv, 13; a common expression: see Legge 1956: 21-25.

541 *Joke Uponeland*: Cf. *Complaynt*, 407n. *mys his meir*: Cf. *Duncan Laideus' Testament*, 132-34.

542-48 *Quho...be sene*: See 533n.

543 *mychtie*] E; *mychty* P; *michtie* C; *mychie* Sc.

547 *That peirle*: A common pun on the Latin word for pearl, *margarita*. The pearl was a symbol of the pure and the precious; cf. Matt. 13.45-46; *Deidis of Armorie*, fol. 33^r, 1835-51; the anonymous *Pearl*; Chaucer, *ProLGW*, F, 221-22.

549 *James Betoun* (c.1480-1539), Archbishop of Glasgow (1509) and St Andrews (1522); Chancellor (1513-26), and a leading supporter of the French 'party' during the minority. Angus deprived Beaton of his office as Chancellor in 1526; James V did not reinstate him after 1528.

555 *dame Curia*: A personified allusion to the royal court.

558 Beaton was imprisoned in 1524 when, after the 'erection' of the young king by Margaret and Arran, he would not renounce his allegiance to Albany.

559 *And...hyde his heid*: The line could refer ironically to Beaton's undeclared political allegiances after his release, and to the greater favour that Gavin Dunbar, Archbishop of Glasgow, and now Chancellor, was receiving (regarding his See's exemption from the primatial and legatine jurisdiction of St Andrews).

560 *lyke Jhone the Raif*: Beaton is compared with John the Reeve, chief character in a late 14th-c. English tale about a low-born hero who is knighted by the king; see Furrow 1985: 177-85. Cf. Dunbar, *Schir, ȝit remember* (B68), 32-33; *Pal. Honour*, 1712; cf. also *Complaynt*, 309-10n.

564 *Francose*: Francis I, King of France (1494-1547), captured at Pavia by imperial forces, Feb. 1525, and released at Madrid in Mar. 1526.

565 *Duke of Burboun*: Charles III (1490-1527), Duke of Bourbon (1503-27), constable of France (1513), but later supporter of the Emperor and

Henry VIII. He was killed as he led his troops over the city wall during the sack of Rome (6 May 1527).

568 *Clement*: Clement VII, Pope (1523-34). He was imprisoned in the castle of Sant'Angelo during the sack of Rome, his truce with the Emperor's viceroy unheeded, and his support to Henry VIII and Francis I repledged too late. He escaped 7 Dec. 1527.

571 *cardinall*: Thomas Wolsey (1475-1530), Cardinal, Archbishop of York (1513-30), Lord Chancellor (1515-29), who had immense influence over England's domestic and foreign policy until, failing to secure the dispensation for Henry's divorce from Katherine of Aragon, he lost favour. He was arrested for treason, Nov. 1530, dying on his way to trial. Lyndsay's unspecific reference (583) to Wolsey's fall (rather than his death) helps to date the poem to late 1530.

578 *palyce ryall*: Possibly a reference to Hampton Court, or to York Place, Westminster, both sumptuous Wolsey palaces; cf. Skelton, *Why Come Ye Nat to Court?*, 402-19.

584-86 *Erlis of Dowglas*: The Douglas earldom had become extinct with the forfeiture of James, the ninth Earl, in 1452, on his withdrawal of support for the king. The Earl took part, with Alexander, Duke of Albany, in the English invasions of Scotland in 1482 and 1484, and died after his capture at Lindores, 1488.

587 *Erle of Marche*: George Dunbar (died c.1455) whose father, also George, was forfeited after he joined the English at Homildon Hill and Shrewsbury (1400). The Dunbars were restored to Scotland in 1409, but forfeited again by James I in 1435.

590-97 *Erle of Angous*: Archibald Douglas (c.1489-1557), sixth Earl; married James IV's widow, Margaret Tudor (1514), his rise alienating many of his peers; see *Complaynt*, 299-300n. On James's escape (1528), Douglas and his close kin were forfeited and forbidden to approach the king's person; see *Complaynt*, 356n, 372n.

605-25 *Quhare bene*: See 323-24n. To some chiefly northern examples Lyndsay adds universalising classical instances; cf. *Contemplacioun of synnaris, Asloan MS*, fol. 273ʳ, 561-68.

606 *twelf...peris*: King Alexander's twelve 'peers', appointed to lead the battalions of his army; cf. *Buik of Alexander*, III.7929-34.

606-07 *Alexander...Julius*: See *Dreme*, 34-35n.

608 *Agamenone*: See 482n.

618 *resorte*] P; *resort* B, E, PP, C; *resore* Sc.

619 *fenyeit fare*: A popular expression; cf. *This warld is all bot fenȝeit fair, Bann. MS*, fols 80ᵛ-81ᵛ; Stewart, *Croniclis*, II, 39493.

626 Edinburgh was *heych* as principal burgh, seat of government, and site of two royal residences, Holyrood Palace and the Castle (which stood high on a long ridge). It dominated trade (see 628n), and its population was large (by 1560, c.10,000-12,500 lived within its walls). The city's main thoroughfare, Lawnmarket and High Street, was lined with multi-storeyed structures; see Robinson 1984: 52-64; Lynch 1988: 261-86.

626-46 The papyngo's amusing and touching farewells to her haunts (also James V's) contemporise the *ubi sunt* theme; they also allude to an elegiac tradition in Irish and Scots Gaelic verse; see Gillies 1978: 75-76.

628 Merchants of various kinds accounted for forty-five per cent of known occupations in 16th-c. Edinburgh, and thus were indeed the 'rute' (629) or source of the region's wealth; see Lynch 1988: 262.

631-32 *War devotioun...in the*: The fulsome praise is strikingly at odds with Dunbar's attack on the city's noise, stink, squalor, and corruption in *Quhy will 3e, merchantis* (B55).

633 *touris hie*: Perhaps a traditional epithet (cf. Lydgate, *Troy Book*, IV, 7051), but Stirling's 'touris hie', erected 1500-10, would have dominated the SE approach to Castle Hill, the Prince's Tower on the W., the Elphinstone Tower on the E., with two round towers flanking the entrance gateway and, on either side of them, a D-shaped tower; cf. Cavers 1993: 22-24; see RCAHMS 1963: 179-84.

634 *Chapell Royall*: The Chapels Royal, at Stirling, Restalrig, and St Mary on the Rock, St Andrews, provided fine sacred music for the royal household. Stirling, founded by James IV, ultimately supported a thirty-two voice choir, and numbered among its personnel Robert Carver, John Fethy, and Alexander Scott. It was reduced during James V's minority, but continued to be important, despite reforming pressures, once James assumed personal leadership; see Easson 1938: 198-99, 204, 209; van Heijnsbergen 1995: 299-313. *park, and tabyll rounde*: At about this time there was interest in Stirling's park (*TA*, V.436; *Works Accounts I*, 109-10), which contained elaborate formal gardens; see Hynd 1984: 270. If 'tabyll rounde' is to be associated closely with 'park', then it could be an allusion to a (round) plot of ground for planting (cf. *OED*, *table*, sb. sense 13), but the chivalric connotations of the words were well established; cf. Hay, *Ordre of Knychthede*, fol. 91^r, iii.156-59: 'knychtis suld...haunt justis and tournaymentis - to hald table round'; *Golagros*, 14: 'the royale [Arthur]...with his Round Tabill'. Leslie (*Historie*, ed. Cody, II.128*n*) notes that one of James IV's pageants was 'The counterfutting of the round tabill of King Arthour'.

637 *redounde*: Cf. *Deploratioun*, 137, *Ane Dialog*, 201*n*; see *DOST*, *redound*, v. 3*n*.

638 *Lythquo*: Building of Linlithgow palace began during James I's reign; improvements and extensions were made during the reigns of James III and IV. It thus was an imposing structure at the time Lyndsay wrote, but (though it has been assumed otherwise) James V's own distinctive changes—the addition of the outer gate with its carvings of the king's four orders of chivalry, the re-siting of the main entrance to the S., and the building of both the central-court fountain and the tennis court—were yet to come; RCAHMS 1929: 220-30; Campbell 1994: 1-20; Campbell 1995: 312, 314-19.

639 *one patrone in Portingall or France*: The perspective remains that of the well-travelled parrot (cf. 745-51). (Lyndsay first visited France in 1532 (*TA* VI.44), and Portugal in 1542: *James V Letters*, 430-31; 437; Burnett 1996: 299, 44*n*).

640 *Falkland*: A palace from the time of James II, it was extended under James III and IV, who added the E. range. The work there that was to result in the erection of some of the earliest fully-developed Renaissance façades in Britain, however, was done in the late 1530s (RCAHMS 1933: 134-38), the poem (in its combination of elements from established genres with a fresh emphasis on vernacular poetry, for instance) thus foreshadowing, rather than echoing, James V's re-invigorating policies.

641 *Lowmound law*: See *Complaynt*, 469n.

643 *raik...rawe*: A common alliterative phrase; cf. Henryson, *Robene and Makyne*, 12.

646 *never...aill*: A traditional insult; cf. *My guddame wes ane gay wife*, Bann. MS, fols 135^v-136^r, 30; *Thrie Estaitis* (1554), 4135-40.

[647-53] PP adds a moralising stanza: 'Trust well my friendes this is no fayned fare,/ For who that is in the extremitie of death/ The veritie without doubt they declare./ Without regarde to favour or to birth/ While ye have time seeke remedy:/ Adew for ever with hart right sory,/ Beseching God to bring you to his glory'.

647 *pye*: The unattractive, untrustworthy nature of the bird is the basis of its heraldic symbolism; cf. *Deidis of Armorie*, fols 26^v-27^r, 1502-03, 1509-11: 'The pye is...rycht full of gosouyll [twittering] and tharfor thai ler hir to spek as men dois...And signifies that he that bur that first in armes...couth spek of al materis and til al purpos...'.

653 *yow*] E, C; *you* P; *your* Sc.

654 *channoun regulare*: See *Dreme*, 179n.

656-57 *My quhyte rocket...memoriall*: The magpie claims, on the basis of dress, that he is an Augustinian canon of unimpeachable morals.

661 *The revin come rolpand*: A popular alliterative pair; cf. Holland, *Howlat*, 215; Dunbar, *Off Februar* (B47), 117. In bestiary lore, the raven, like the pye, was condemned as treacherous; see White 1954: 141.

663 *And fenyeitlye*: The irony already suggested by the roles taken by these birds of prey is here made more explicit (cf. 666, 'pretend').

668 *one blak monk*: The raven claims he is a Benedictine.

669 *gled*: To assign to the gled (kite) the profession of a 'holy freir' is a strong indictment of the latter: in literary sources, from antiquity, this bird was despised, a symbol of greed, thievery, cowardice, death and envy: see Rowland 1978: 93-96; Yapp 1981: 33, 158; cf. Chaucer, *PF*, 349; Holland, *Howlat*, 642-46; Douglas, *Eneados*, XIII, ii.119-22.

672 *The blak...perqueir*: The sense is ambiguous; the gled appears to value his feat of memory above the provision of Christian comfort.

680-81 *I grant...my teind*: The gled-friar, referring to the annual tax to which the church was entitled (see *Dreme*, 199-205n), ironically also shows how the privilege is abused; see also 683-84. The quick wit recalls Tod Lowrie's response when accused of killing a lamb, Henryson, *Fables*, 1078-82.

693 *We thre...funerall*: The double sense of the allusion—the church Office of the Dead and a meal of the deceased—is confirmed at 1148-57.

695 *trentalls twenty*: A disproportionate number of such masses; one trental was said 'for the Kingis grace in Quithorne' in 1533 (*TA*, VI.90).

696 *The reukis*: Flesh-eating birds, disliked for their cry and ragged feathers; cf. Holland, *Howlat*, 794; Dunbar, *A Ballat of the Abbot of Tungland* (B4), 70; Dunbar, *Flyting* (B65), 57.

697 *And crye 'Conmemoratio'*: Masses for the parrot's soul.

698-99 *We sall...crye alarum*: The theatrical (and comically threatening) tactics call into question the sincerity of the funeral rites.

700 *Secundum...Sarum*: 'According to Sarum or Salisbury use', the usual order of divine service; cf. McRoberts 1957: 39; *Sarum Missal*, 571-76.

701 *saif*: cf. Dunbar, *To the, O marcifull saluiour* (B83), 69. *Blase*: A 3rd c. Cappadocian bishop, physician, hermit and martyr, invoked against sore throats; cf. *Thrie Estaitis*, 1382, 1550.

704 *Sanct Mongois matynis*: Alliteration adds to an impression of clerical learning. St Mungo (or Kentigern) was patron saint of Glasgow and, traditionally, founder-bishop (from 573) of Glasgow Cathedral; see Galbraith 1984: 23-33; Purser 1992: 48. None of the traditional stories associated with Mungo (on which see MacQuarrie 1997: 117-44) are invoked by the raven and gled.

706 *Placebo*, the opening word of the Latin liturgy for the evening Office of the Dead, recited the night before the funeral. *Beid*, the set of devotions that used the rosary beads; see McRoberts 1972: 81-83.

708 *Pluto*: Ruler of the underworld in classical, pagan times; in late medieval literature also associated with Hell; cf. Chaucer, *HF*, 1511-12, Henryson, *Orpheus*, 345, 392-93.

709 *Devotelie...be addrest*: The 'derigie' or 'dirige' was part of the Matins Office of the Dead, forming, with Lauds, the night service. It was said before the corpse in church and at remembrance services; Duffy 1992: 368-69; *Prymer*, I.56-70.

720 *Exemptit...sessioun*: The papyngo points out that churchmen escape every jurisdiction; cf. *Thrie Estaitis*, 3633-42.

724 *nychtingall*: The bird was traditionally a harbinger of spring and symbol of amorous love (cf. *Kingis Quair*, 372-431), but was, conversely, sometimes associated with Christian love (cf. Dunbar, *In May as that Aurora*, B24).

725 *ja*: Traditionally the jay was described as 'jangling' (chattering and noisy); cf. Whiting J17-21. To describe it as 'gentyll' preserves the alliteration but jars in sense (as does the description of the pown as 'plesand'). The point is perhaps that those outside the Church are no less a mix of hypocrisy and sincerity than those within. *merle*: The blackbird was associated traditionally with May and for its song at that season; cf. Henryson, *Test. Cresseid*, 430-31. *turtur*: The turtle dove (as opposed to the dove) symbolised faithfulness, especially to a dead mate; see Rowland 1978: 46-48. In *Deidis of Armorie*, fol. 26[v], 1491-1501, the bird's 'suet sang' is also among her attributes.

728 *pown*: The bird was often described as 'plesant' (cf. Holland, *Howlat*, 81, 614), but was proverbially a symbol of pride, cf. Whiting, P73. Here, as in some bestiaries, the peacock's tail feathers are associated with angels' wings. The 'eyes' in these tail feathers were linked to the many-eyed Argus Panoptes of classical myth (cf. Douglas, *Eneados*, XII,

Prol. 161-64), but were also associated, in Christian settings, with the all-seeing Church; cf. Holland's peacock pope (*Howlat*, 79-91).

728-32 Cf. *Ane Dialog*, 188-90.

730 *devyse*: Not the heraldic 'device' (cf. Hamer (1931-36: III.106). The papyngo wishes the peacock to receive, or set in order, her testament.

731 *maveis*: The song-thrush was associated with May, lovers and spring, cf. Henryson, *Test. Cresseid*, 425-30. *goldspink*: A bird often kept caged for its bright plumage and song (see Yapp 1982: 480-84), it was frequently depicted in Madonna and Child scenes, thought to represent either the soul (that Christ would save), grace, or the earthly paradise.

732 *larke*: The lark, whose song heralds the beginning of the day, was often associated with the Virgin Mary; cf. Holland, *Howlat*, 714; Douglas, *Eneados*, XII, Prol. 246-50; Dunbar, *Quhen Merche* (B52), 12-14. See further, Bawcutt 1972: 5-12.

733 *forthink*] P, C; *forthing* Sc, E.

735 *swallow*: The bird's swiftness was proverbial; cf. Whiting, 'Proverbs... Scottish', *Swallow*; Tilley S1023. It was also noted for its wisdom and parental care. In Christian contexts, it was a symbol of rebirth and hope for mankind; see Rowland 1978: 163-69.

737 *With hir...stone restringityve*: The swallow's medical skill was mentioned in the bestiaries; cf. White 1954: 148.

746 *bred in to the Orient*: The gled's reference to the parrot's Eastern origin suggests that the bird is an Indian rose-ringed parakeet (*Psittacula krameri*), the type (mostly green with red bill, feet, and collar) depicted in early European manuscripts, tapestries and bestiaries: see Clark 1977: 108, pl. 53; Paris B.N., MS Lat. 18014, fol. 40^v (Petites Heures de Jean de Berry); Unicorn Tapestry ('Le Goût'), Paris, Museé de Thermes et de l'Hôtel de Cluny.

748 Sc's *oecident* has been corrected; cf. *Occident* E, C; *Occedent* P.

751 *septemtrionall*: A technical term for 'northern', used frequently as a qualifier and applied to either the heavens or the earth; cf. Douglas, *Pal. Honour*, 195 (the 'plague Septemptrionall'); *Complaynt of Scotland*, fol. 39^r ('the pole artick boreal or septemtrional'); *Ane Dialog*, 166.

764-65 *And als...jugement*: Cf. *Ane Dialog*, 643-44.

778 *predicatioun*: Cf. *Tragedie*, 281-91, where Beaton's ghost stresses to his brother prelates the need to return to preaching.

786 *Doctryne...equevolent*: This had a biblical source, Matt. 23.3, but was also proverbial (Whiting P359, P361); cf. *Papyngo*, 710-11.

792-93 *The crukit...clene*: Cf. *Thre Prestis*, 368-69 (Charteris ed.).

794-1003 The allegory depicts the church's long struggle to retain its ideals, and its ultimate corruption by way of 'marriage' to Property, and 'offspring', Riches and Sensuality. The method was traditional, but is here developed dramatically; cf. Lydgate, *Testament*, 269-75); Dunbar, *This hinder nycht, halff sleiping* (B75); *King Hart*.

803 *Constantyne*: See *Dreme*, 233n.

815 *Sanct Sylvester*: Pope, AD 314-35. His pontificate, like Constantine's, was noted for the richness of his gifts to the Church; see *Liber Pontificalis*, 41-72.

823 Sc's *renounc* has been corrected; cf. *renounce* P, E.

823-25 *Quhilk Peter...the lave*: The apostles Peter, Andrew and John formerly were fishermen; cf. *Ane Dialog*, 4750-91.

830 *Lazarus, Martha and Marie Magdalane*: This adheres to the then-common belief that the three were brother and sisters, disciples of Jesus who, in Biblical accounts, had raised Lazarus from the dead. In legend, Martha and Mary went to France, where Martha converted the people of Aix and delivered them from a dragon.

832 *Paule*: See *Dreme*, 597n; cf. *Ane Dialog*, 253, 629.

838 *be the rude*: A common expression, originally invoked because of the central role of the crucifixion in the Christian story of man's salvation.

862 Sc's *chiastytie*, also in E, is corrected; cf. 796, 799, 871.

863 *Sensualytie*] P, E; *Sensualite* C; *Sesualytie* Sc. *And all begylit*: Cf. Henryson, *Fables*, 1263.

868 *For...corrage*: Cf. Whiting, 'Proverbs...Scottish', *Face* (2).

907 *sett...seage*: The martial phrasing is ironic in this setting; cf. *Buik of Alexander*, II.275; *In Tiberus tyme*, Bann. *MS*, fols 136^v-137^r, 15.

917 *Borrow Mure*: An open common, S. of Edinburgh, site of the nunnery mentioned at 919.

919 *Schenis*: Sciennes, a Dominican convent in Edinburgh in which James V took a personal interest. It was founded by Scottish noblewomen in 1517 in honour of St Catherine of Siena; see Bryce 1918: 96-131; *TA*, V.306 and 430.

923 *verteous cardinall*: The Cardinal Virtues: Justice, Prudence, Temperance and Strength; cf. *Dreme*, 1064-67; *Complaynt*, 379-90.

927-40 The battle between the chaste sisters of Sciennes and the corrupt Sensualitie and Ryches, representatives of the earthly church, adds a topical edge to the traditional allegory; see Loomis 1919: 264-66.

952 *the*] P, E, C; *om.* Sc.

957 *in certane*] E, C; *incertane* Sc, P; cf. *Meldrum*, 207-08.

967-68 Proverbial; cf. Whiting I16; 'Proverbs...Scottish', *idleness*.

969 *ravis unrockit*: Cf. Henryson, *Fables*, 2346, where the words are spoken by the similarly unscrupulous fox.

971 *Abraham and Isaac*: Abraham, descendant of Noah and leader in Canaan, whose faith was tested by God's request that he sacrifice his son, Isaac (prefiguring the Passion); see Gen. 20.1-12.

972 *Jacobe*: Isaac's son, Jacob, who dreamed of the ladder between earth and heaven, and to whom God gave the land of Bethel; see Gen. 28.12-13; 35.1. *Josephe*, the son of Jacob and Rachel, was favoured over his brothers, who sold him into slavery (prefiguring the betrayal of Christ), but he later became governor of Egypt; see Gen. 37-50.

988 *As Gregore...and Augustyne*: These were known as the four Doctors of the Church.

989 *Benedic*: 6th-c. founder of the Benedictine Order. *Barnerd*: 12th-c. Cistercian abbot of Clairvaux. *Clement*: Apostolic father and 2nd-c. bishop of Rome. *Cleit*: Pope between c.79 and c.90. *Lyne*: Pope between c.67-c.79.

990-92 *Sic pacient prelatis...resort*: Those properly appointed, who have entered 'by the gate', are contrasted to the irregular appointees, who have 'climbed the boundary wall' by using underhand practices.

1004 Sc's *preucis* is corrected; cf. E's *prencis*.

1027 *pull...salis*: A common expression; cf. Dunbar, *Be mery, man* (B6), 15.

1037 *beggyng freris*: The Carmelite, Dominican, Observant and Conventual Franciscan orders all had such friars; see Donaldson 1960: 9; Ross 1962; *Ane Dialog*, note under 'Title-page'.

1045 *roploch quhyte*: A cloth associated with humble status, as opposed to the fabrics of the wealthy (*skarlote, crammosie*, 1046); cf. Lyndsay, *Syde Taillis*, 62: 'Pure claggokis cled in roiploch quhyte'.

1050-53 *More ryche arraye...agane Yule*: The papyngo contrasts Christian poverty and contemporary Church excess in terms her courtly 'brether' will understand—the customary royal bestowal of clothing at this season. The pointed contrast satirically extends the joke of the *Respontio regis* of Dunbar's *Schir, lat it neuer* (B66), wherein the king promises Dunbar clothing as rich as a bishop's mule's (74); see also *Tragedie*, 336*n*.

1061 *folkis*] C; *folks* E; *floks* Sc; *florhs* P.

1067-1136 The papyngo reluctantly appoints her executors and makes her testament and funeral arrangements, drawing on both legal practice and literary tradition; see note on 'Form'.

1092 *howlet*: The owl was associated from antiquity with evil and darkness; cf. Chaucer, *PF*, 343, 'The oule...that of deth the bode bryngeth'; Holland, *Howlat*, 55-70; *Dreme*, 478.

1096 *bak*: In the bestiaries the owl was associated with day blindness (cf. White 1954: 133-34), but the bat and the owl, both creatures of the night and of ill omen, were often mentioned together, and blindness is here associated with the bat; cf. Rowland 1978: 7.

1100-01 *pillycane*: In the bestiaries, the pelican was said to nourish her young by piercing her breast; she thus became a type of Christ; cf. Ps. 102.6 ('I am like a pelican in the wilderness'); *Deidis of Armorie*, fol. 24ʳ, 1325-31; White 1954: 132-33.

1102 *goik*: The cuckoo's repetitive song was proverbial; cf. Whiting C600; cf. Rowland 1978: 38-41; Hatto 1965: 800-08.

1104-05 *guse*: For Chaucer the goose was synonymous with the fool (cf. *Tr*, III, 584), but it is the bird's unembellished cackling to which the parrot seems to refer here.

1105 *My eloquence...rethoricall*: Contrast *Test. Meldrum*, 78-80, where Mercury is the legatee.

1108 *phenix*: In bestiary lore, the phoenix, having reached its life span, was thought to burn itself on a funeral pyre and rise, restored, from its own ashes (cf. White 1954: 125-27), thus symbolising the Resurrection, faith and constancy.

1112 *Gold, asure...synopeir*: The elevating, heraldic terms for these colours; see *Deidis of Armorie*, fols 10ᵛ-12ʳ, 374-483.

1124 Sc's *amag*, lacking the abbreviation mark, is expanded to *amang*; cf. E, C, P.

1126 *feit*: Previous editors have changed this word to 'seit', against the unanimous evidence of the witnesses and the alliteration of the line. The parrot, alluding to the stories of Pluto's abduction of Proserpina, and to his re-seizure of Eurydice from Orpheus (when the latter broke his word not to look back upon her as they made their way out of Hell), portrays Pluto like a greater bird of rapine, seizing his prey in his claws; see 1169n.

1127 *I no thyng belang yow*: The parrot is not a bird of rapine, nor a corrupt cleric; and her soul is of no matter to them.

1133 *quene of farye*: See 1126n. Proserpina was associated with the classical underworld, darkness and death, but also identified with 'fary'; cf. Henryson, *Orpheus*, 119, 125-26; see Allen 1964.

1134 *Eternallye in tyll hir court*: The parrot's wish that her spirit be received at Proserpina's court casts further doubt on her belief in the promises of the pye, raven, and gled; see Rowland 1978: xiii-xv.

1135 *among the holtis hore*: A frequently-used collocation in verse; cf. Lydgate, *Floure of Curtesye*, 47; Henryson, *Robene and Makyne*, 128; *Still vndir the levis grene, Maitl. Fol. MS*, no. cxxx.26-27; see Parkinson 1991: 309-18.

1140 *Of sychis...stound*: Cf. Henryson, *Test. Cresseid*, 540-42.

1144 *'In manus Tuas'*: The beginning of the formula (said in compline, the last office of the liturgical day, and in the private prayer of and for the devout near death), which refers to Christ's words from the Cross (Luke 23.46), which in turn allude to Ps. 30.5: *In manus tuas, commendo spiritum meum; redemisti me, Domine, Deus veritatis* ['Into Thy hands, O Lord, I commend my spirit. You have redeemed me, O Lord, Thou God of truth']; cf. *Test. Meldrum*, 247.

1148 *ruge and ryve*: A common alliterative coupling; cf. Douglas, *Eneados*, VI, ix.140.

1150 *gredy gled*: Proverbial; cf. Whiting, G136.

1160 *angell*: The allusion to the 'angellike' feathers had many precedents (cf. Chaucer, *PF*, 356; Dunbar, *In May as that Aurora* (B24), 14), but the link between the papyngo—with her warnings to king and court—and the angelic hierarchy of divine messengers, is delicately and aptly made.

1169 *claucht...cluke*: An alliterative pair also used by Douglas, *Eneados*, IX, ix.82.

1172-85 The author's disclaimer and address to his book were traditional; cf. Chaucer, *Tr*, V, 1786-92; Dunbar, *Goldyn Targe* (B59), 271-79; Douglas, *Pal. Honour*, 2161-69.

1179-85 The internal rhyme of these lines belies the poet's words.

1182 *unclene*] P, C; *one unclene* Sc, E.

The Answer to the Kingis Flyting, c.1535-1536

Text: The text is based on the earliest extant edition of 1568, printed in Edinburgh by John Scot for Henry Charteris, *STC* 15658 (= C). C was collated with the unique copy of a possible reissue of 1569, *STC* 15658.5 (= C(StJ)), and with the surviving first 18 lines of Scot's reissue (again for Charteris) of 1571, *STC* 15659 (= Ch). Thomas Bassandyne's 1574 edition, *STC* 15660 (= Bs), also examined, differs little (*gif* is substituted for C's *gyf*, 35, for example).

Title: From C: *The Answer quhilk schir David Lindesay maid to the Kingis Flyting*.

Form: The literary flyting, a verse contest in mutual abuse of a scurrilous, yet highly inventive and controlled nature, was popular in Scotland during the late 15th and 16th centuries; see Lampe 1979, Bawcutt 1983, Gray 1984. It reached a high point during the reign of James IV, in a four-part exchange between William Dunbar and Walter Kennedy (B65), which was printed by Chepman and Myllar, c.1508; see Bawcutt 1992: 220-56; MacDonald 1994: 276-77.

According to Lyndsay's description of it, the king's challenge seems to have been a literary flyting: it was insulting to the addressee (6-7), poetically highly skilled (21), and demanding of a response in kind (23-24). Lyndsay never admits that his poem is, similarly, a flyting; with self-mockery, he frequently denies it, noting that his wits are not sharp but 'dull' (2), that he is not a poet (15), that the king (his status unmatchable, 22) without doubt has won the contest (20-21), and that he, Lyndsay, 'can nocht flyte' (64). The poem is also carefully modulated. Although its direct opening line foreshadows the aggressive stance of a flyting response, and word-play is a notable feature throughout, the poem changes rapidly into defensive capitulation highly flattering to the opponent. It changes again to a mix of sober counsel against promiscuity (some of it offered in the alliterative style identified with the flyting), then to compliments on the king's 'ornate meter' (66), and finally to lighthearted warning, that James V may yet find a worthy opponent; see 67-68*n*.

Date: Internal evidence suggests a composition date of c.1535-1536. Lyndsay alludes to royal behaviour that matches that of James V's unmarried years (1529-1536), during which he fathered four known illegitimate children; see 36-37, 45-49; Hamer 1931-35: III.45. Lyndsay condemns the king's council for its as yet inconclusive marriage negotiations (43), and seems to allude (68) to the imminent fulfilment of the Franco-Scots agreement that James marry a French princess (see 43*n*).

Metre: Lyndsay uses the seven-line rhyme royal stanza (*ababbcc*) (cf. *Dreme*), thereby hinting that this is a poem of instruction, thus unsuitable for the metrical virtuosity expected of a literary flyting.

1 *your ragment*: The king's insulting poetic challenge does not survive, but it seems likely that he wrote it; in c.1533 Bellenden also noted that James V was one who 'writis in ornate stile poeticall / Qwik flowand vers of rhetorik cullouris' (*Livy*, prol. 17-18).

4 *tygerris toung...lent*: The identification of the tiger's tongue with its ferocity is an extension of its proverbial reputation (cf. Whiting T287, T289), but it might have had an ironic twist in this context: the line, 'Als terne as tygir of tung vntollerable' appears in a contemporary poem, *O wicket wemen, Bann. MS*, fols 263ʳ, 15, in which the poet is describing female characteristics.

7 *Venus court dejectit*: James V's insulting remarks, Lyndsay argues, have been the cause of his ejection from the court at which Venus, goddess of love, presides; that is, he protests that his prowess in love has been disparaged; cf. *Kingis Quair*, 538-679; Douglas, *Pal. Honour*, 401-08; 481-89; *Deploratioun*, 36-40. See also Neilson 1899.

8 The sense and metre are defective: 'on' has been added after 'that'.

20 In full, *Cor mundum crea in me, Deus, et spiritum rectum innova in visceribus meis* ['Create in me a clean heart, O God, and renew a right spirit within me'], from the penitential Ps. 51.10, said at lauds on the first Sunday in Lent; also quoted in other flytings, but usually as a taunt to the opponent; cf. *Flyting of Dumbar and Kennedie* (65), 394; *Flyting Betwixt Montgomerie and Polwart*, 79, 222.

21 *prince of poetry*: An epithet more often given to Virgil; cf. Douglas, *Eneados*, IX, Prol. 75; *Ane Dialog*, 571.

22 *pley*: Several senses are implied: to toy with; to flatter; to contend with in debate; to make a formal allegation (recalling 'Venus court'); see *DOST, play*, v.ᴵ, IV.10, VI.19b and *Pley*, v., 3 and 4.

25 *strang...elephand*: Proverbial; cf. Whiting E65, but this complimentary simile had an ironic edge: in the bestiaries, the elephant was noted for its chaste virtue; cf. *Deidis of Armorie*, fol. 19ᵛ; Douglas, *Pal. Honour*, 330-32; see Druce 1919: 5-7.

30 *Venus werkis*: Cf. Douglas, *Eneados*, IV, Prol. 168.

33 *mouth thankles*: A term for the female external genital organs; the pursuit of, or service to, 'mouth thankles' was proverbial; cf. Whiting M763; Whiting, 'Proverbs...Scottish', *mouth* (3), and Kennedy, *Ane aigit man, Bann. MS*, fol. 268, refrain.

34-35 *fyne powder spair...weill quhair*: The sense is deliberately ambiguous: as an allusion to the misuse of gunpowder, the expression continues the martial imagery, but the underlying subject is the proper disposal of the royal semen.

36 *restles ram*: A common expression for promiscuous behaviour; cf. Dunbar, *This hindir nycht in Dumfermeling* (B76), 6; *Madame, ʒour men said* (B30), 16; Whiting R28.

37 *Schutand...sindrie schellis*: The expression and its martial imagery have a factual basis—James V was practised in these arts (cf. *TA*, V.252, 258, 265, 276, 407, 415, 421)—but in verse they also had an established sexual connotation; cf. Dunbar, *He that hes gold* (B17), 13; Balnevis, *O gallandis all, Bann. MS*, 138ᵛ-139ᵛ, 57-58.

38 *ane bydand gam*: Cf. *O gallandis all, Bann. MS*, fols 138ᵛ-139ᵛ, 49, 61, 109.

39 *dowbling...bellis*: There is a creative ambiguity in the allusion, which encompasses both funeral bells and bells of canonical hours. Each were used as markers of the passing of time—in Christian observance, and of human life, here the Scottish king's in particular.

40 *saule knellis*: The solemn, slow peal of bells rung to announce a person's death or at a funeral; see also Mackay 1962: 104.

41-42 *the well...stufe to by*: Cf. *O gallandis all, Bann. MS*, fols 138^v-139^v, 55-56.

43 *your counsale*: As early as 1517, a suggested provision of the Franco-Scottish military alliance known as the Treaty of Rouen had been the offer of a (then hypothetical) French princess as bride for the Scottish king. This was ratified in Scotland in 1521 and in France in 1522. In the following years, before James's marriage to the French princess Madeleine in 1537, approaches were made in other quarters on James V's behalf (among them those for Catherine de Medici and Mary of Hungary), as were also various counter offers (for a Danish princess, or for Marie de Vendôme), in line with the changing political alliances between France, the Empire of Charles V, the Papacy, England, and Scotland.

47 *lyke ane boisteous bull*: Proverbial ; cf. Whiting B590, B591. Like that at 36, this comparison offers the king superficial flattery, but is also indicative of a lack of self control. *rin...ryde*: A common alliterative collocation; cf. Henryson, *Fables*, 946; Dunbar, *This hindir nycht in Dumfermeling* (B767), 6 ('riddin').

48 Cf. *Ze blindit luveris, Bann. MS*, fol. 290^r, 83-84.

50 *Ladronis*, perhaps related to *ladry*, one sense of which is 'persons of low rank or conduct, collectively'; Lyndsay applies it to women only.

51 *corinoch*: Cf. Gaelic *corranach*; Dunbar, *Off Februar* (B47), 112-16.

54 *fuffilling...hoch*: See *DOST*, *Fuffiling*, n., for which Lyndsay's is the only citation. The line possibly is defective (under alliterative influence), originally perhaps, 'That feynd, with the ruffilling of hir roistit hoch'; cf. *DOST, Ruf(f)le*, v., 1, to throw into disarray. See also *OED, Roist*, v., to play the roister; b., to roist it (out), and *roister*, sb. I.b, a romp. Various forms of *Ruffle* and *Roist* were used together to indicate noisy revelling frequently of a sexual nature; cf. *OED, Roisterkin, Roisterous, Roisting*. A play on *roy*, king, is also possible. Cf. *Thrie Estaitis*, 690-94.

57 *lady...best*: Possibly a tactfully reticent reference to the Scottish noblewoman, Margaret Erskine, who was at about this time James V's own preferred marriage partner (*James V Letters*, 320).

59 *duddroun*: Cf. Dunbar, *Off Februar* (B47), 71.

62-63 *On your...frome grandgore*: Cf. Dunbar, *He that hes gold* (B17), a comparable allusion to one who 'schuttis syne at ane vncow schell' (13) and suffers syphilis (referred to as 'the fleis of Spenȝie' (14)) as a result.

63 C's *gtandgore* is corrected; cf. *grandgore* C(StJ), Bs.

67-69 *Bot yit...be dour*: The ambiguous use of jousting imagery (cf. *O gallandis all, Bann. MS*, fols 138^v-139^v, 13-16, 37-44) allows Lyndsay to hint that the hoped-for French royal alliance will bring James V an equal opponent—but whether in martial, amatory, or literary spheres is, with teasing wit, left unclear.

Text: The text is based on the earliest surviving Scottish edition, John Scot's for Henry Charteris, printed in Edinburgh in 1568, *STC* 15658 (= C). C was collated with two French editions of Lyndsay's works, probably printed by Jean Petit or his heirs in 1558; in quarto, *STC* 15673 (= P) and octavo, *STC* 15674 (= P(oct)). Errors in both showed that the typesetters had difficulties understanding Scots. These included inadvertent coinages (*resput* for *respite*, 18, *trium* for *triumph*, 102); unfortunate substitutions (*rest* for *reft*, 6, *sit* for *sic*, 33, *blud* for *blynd*, 36); and French 'replacements' (*Soleil* for *So leill*, 39). Scot's 1571 edition for Charteris, *STC* 15659 (= Ch) and Bassandyne's 1574 edition, *STC* 15660 (= Bs), also collated with C, did not contain substantive differences.

Title: As in C: *The Deploratioun of the Deith of Quene Magdalene*. See *DOST*, *Deploratioun*, where the citations listed suggest that the printed use of the word in Scotland dates from the 1530s. As a French literary title, however, *Deploration* (from F. *déplorer*, L. *deplorare*, to bewail, lament for) had been used frequently; see McFarlane 1974: 33-34; Hamer 1931-36: III.126 and 129-30. Lyndsay's choice of title was a diplomatic acknowledgement of the two countries' unity in sorrow.

Form: The formal lament for the dead is a genre of longstanding. In the early 13th c. it was included by Geoffrey de Vinsauf in his *Poetria Nova* (29-31); Chaucer also used it (*MkT*, *LGW*), as did Lydgate (*Fall of Princes*, III.3655-82, for instance). In late medieval Scottish literature there are many examples, including the *Playnt* for Margaret, daughter of James I (*Liber Pluscardensis*, XI, ch. viii, 383-88; Bawcutt 1988), Dunbar, *Illuster Lodouick* (B23) and, within longer narrative poems, Hay, *Buik of King Alexander the Conquerour*, 18592-625 and Henryson, *Orpheus*, 134-83.

Lyndsay's poem employs the rhetorical figures common to the form, such as apostrophes (to Death, the gods), superlatives, and stock phrases ('dreidfull dragoun', 15; 'of feminine the flour', 16). It also includes the usual final prayer (cf. Dunbar, *Illuster Lodouick* (B23), 25-32), but adds after it a less expected defiant address to Death. This, and other aspects (the praise of the Paris reception, 71-77; the stress on the marriage as evidence of the strength of the Auld Alliance, 78-79, the enumeration of the details of Edinburgh's planned reception, 99-173) show an acute awareness of the larger political implications.

Date: James and Madeleine arrived in Scotland in May 1537, but the queen, never robust in health, died on 7 July, before her Edinburgh entry could take place. The poem thus was completed soon after, in late 1537.

Metre: The poem is in the seven-line, five-stress rhyme royal stanza (*ababbcc*); see *Papyngo*, note on 'Metre'.

1 *cruell Deith*: Apostrophes were frequent features of funeral laments; cf. Dunbar, *Illuster Lodouick* (B23) 17, and the French epitaph to Madeleine, *Et fratres Helenæ et poli nitentes*, 7-9, Desmontiers 1538: fol. xxx.

2 *Devorar*: Cf. Douglas, *Eneados*, IV, Prol. 243.

4 *default*: See *Dreme*, 782n.

7 *flour of France*: A reference (cf. 14) to the princess Madeleine, fifth child, third and eldest surviving daughter of Francis I, King of France, and his first wife, Claude de France. The flower emblem, reappearing in the last stanza, is among the many stylistic symmetries of the poem. *confort of Scotland*: Madeleine was a source of comfort as the expected provider of a long-awaited legitimate heir.

8 *Father*: Adam, the first man created by God, thus 'Father' in the sense 'progenitor' (Gen. 2.7); cf. Douglas, *Pal. Honour*, 1500; *Ane Dialog*, 941-43.

15-17 *O dreidfull...the hart*: See *Papyngo*, 181*n;* cf. Dunbar, *Illuster Lodouick* (B23), 17. Alliteration heightens the formality throughout (cf. 24, 64, 78-79).

18 *respite*: Cf. Ireland, *Of penance, Asloan MS*, fol. 3ʳ, 16-21.

22-23 In Gen. 5.21-32, the long-lived Methuselah is named son of Enoch and grandfather of Noah; see *Complaynt*, 508*n*.

25 *Or scho...sevintene*: Madeleine, born 10 Aug. 1520, was dead by 7 July 1537; see Knecht 1994: 116, 339; Bentley-Cranch and Marshall 1996: 273-88 and figs. 1-7.

25-27 Internal rhyme (*age, asswage, rage*) further elevates the style.

26 *Gredie gorman*: Death is personified as a glutton.

29 *O dame Nature*: Nature is chastised for not giving Madeleine sustained good health.

30 *this theif*: A common epithet for Death; cf. Chaucer, *PardT, CT*, VI (C), 675.

31 *with naturall targis*: The image of Death with his attacking dart (15-17) is matched here by that of Nature and her defensive shields.

36 *Venus, with...Cupido*: Their association with blindness was proverbial; cf. Whiting, C634; cf. also Chaucer, *KnT, CT*, I (A), 1955-66; Douglas, *Pal. Honour*, 475-83.

38 *your court*: Venus's court; see *Answer*, 7*n*.

43-44 *as Leander*: The story of Hero and Leander, derived from Ovid's *Heroides*, 18, was well known in this period; cf. Chaucer, *MLPro, CT*, II, (B¹) 69; Douglas, *Eneados*, IV, Prol. 72-84. Leander from Abydos loved Hero, the priestess of Venus at Sestos. To meet her, Leander escaped his family's guard at night, swimming across the Hellespont with the help of Hero's guiding torch, shone from her tower. A stormy night put out the torch, Leander drowned, and Hero, in her grief, followed suit.

45 *bulryng stremis wode*: A vivid but common literary collocation; cf. Douglas, *Eneados*, I, iii.25-26 and 50-51.

46 *erlis, baronis, squyaris...knichtis*: Lyndsay carefully ranks James V's noble retinue, which, besides David Beaton, Abbot of Arbroath, household officers, and several hundred soldiers, included the Earls of Argyll, Arran and Rothes, and the Lords Fleming and Maxwell; see *L&P Henry VIII*, XI.400.

47 *Contrair Neptune and Eol*: See *Ane Dialog*, 185*n*. James V had attempted to sail to France on 23 July 1536, but ill winds had forced a landing at Whithorn; see *L&P Henry VIII*, XI.396.

48 *disesperance*: This in part is an idealising statement, to emphasise that James V is beloved by his people as their knightly defender, but it also had an element of truth: in 1513, a similar large party had left Scotland for Flodden, where monarch and many nobles had been lost.

49 *first dochter of France*: Thus, as Francis I's eldest surviving daughter; cf. *Tragedie*, 89, and Marot's title, *Chant nuptial du Roy d'Escoce & de Madame Magdelene Premiere Fille de France*, Epithalame II, Mayer 1958-80: III, no. LXXXVI, 314-18.

50-56 *lyke...Penelope*: In classical myth Penelope was wife of Ulysses, king of Ithaca, in whose twenty-year absence at the Trojan wars she remained faithful. In the medieval-Renaissance period she was a symbol of wifely virtue. This is perhaps a delicate reference to the twenty years of negotiations between France and Scotland preceding the marriage; see *Answer*, 43n. Like the classical pair, James and Madeleine had had obstacles to overcome before they could be united. During negotiations, various substitutes had been offered to or considered by James, as political alliances changed. (After the battle of Pavia (1525) at which Francis was taken prisoner, for example, Henry VIII offered James V the princess Mary.) The classical allusion also exploits the fact that, for Ulysses, Penelope had left her native Sparta as, for James V, Madeleine had left France; see 52-55n.

52-55 Cf. Marot, *Chant nuptial*, 51-53, and Ps. 45.10-11.

54 *Takyng no cure*: When she sailed for Scotland, Madeleine left behind a younger sister, Marguerite de France, later duchess of Savoy (1523-74), and two brothers (her elder brother François having died suddenly on 10 Aug. 1536), the Dauphin, Henri, later Henri II (1519-59) and Charles, duc d'Orléans (1522-45).

57ff *O dame Fortune*: Complaints to Fortune were frequent in medieval verse; cf. *Kingis Quair*, 645-51; 1105-55; Douglas, *Pal. Honour*, 165-92.

59-60 *Thy slyding gyftis*: Madeleine received gifts of high lineage and wealth (her dowry alone worth 100,000 gold crowns of the sun), yet they were no proof against a third, death. The collocation alludes to the popular image of Fortune's turning wheel; cf. Henryson, *Fables*, 2418-19.

62-63 *hir father...mycht mak no supporting*: Lyndsay alludes, with diplomatic precision, to Francis I's formal title, 'Rex Christianissimus', in doing so adroitly refuting any suspicion that the frail princess did not receive proper care in Scotland.

64 *hir lustie lufe and knicht*: James is Madeleine's knight or champion in the chivalric sense; cf. *Clariodus*, 4.1457.

71-72 *O Paris!*: There were many precedents for this laudatory address to a city receiving a monarch; cf. *To London*, Mackenzie 1960: 177-78; Dunbar, *Blyth Aberdeane* (B8). James V made his ceremonial entry into Paris on 31 Dec. 1536: Teulet 1852-60: I.122-23; Bentley-Cranch and Marshall 1996: 278-81.

73-87 *arkis triumphall*: Such entries were important statements of power, which in Francis I's reign incorporated many classical elements. Lyndsay reflects this in his references to Pompey (75) and, later, to the 'ornate oratouris' (162); cf. Knecht 1994: 47-49, 71, 104, 130-31; Dolan 1994: 87-109.

74 *digne...in memorie*: Cf. *Papyngo*, 230.

75 *Pompey*: See *Dreme*, 34-35*n*.

78 *mariage...the morne*: Cf. Marot, *Chant nuptial*, 1. The marriage took place on New Year's Day morning, 1537, followed by the solemnisation on a raised platform before Notre-Dame. Largess was distributed, then Mass celebrated within by the Cardinal of Bourbon.

83-84 *Ancient Alliance*: France and Scotland had been political allies since 1295, when Philip IV of France and John Balliol of Scotland had drafted a treaty (Archives Nationales, Paris, J 677/U) promising mutual military assistance against their common enemy, England. Though this treaty was short-lived, every later Scottish and French monarch (except Louis XI) renewed what was known as the 'Auld Alliance'; cf. *Papyngo*, 505; Marot, *Chant nuptial*, 45-48; see Bonner 1999.

85 *I never did se*: This adds to the sense of vivid authenticity, but is more than a poetic device: as senior herald, Lyndsay attended the ceremonies in France (see *TA*, VI.455, 456; VII.16), returning to Scotland in late Jan., presumably to prepare for the state reception.

88-89 *Sic banketting!*: A dinner followed the wedding ceremonies, then supper, with musical entertainments, and at which gold and silver serving vessels were used; cf. Guiffrey 1860: 200-205; Teulet 1852-60: I.124.

89 *martiall tornamentis*: Following the wedding ceremonies, James participated in fifteen days of jousting, his elaborate feathers, horse caparisons, riding coats, and tunics (for wearing over armour) suggestive of the display and richness these events demanded; cf. *TA*, VII.16, 17, 53. Pitscottie, who states in his Preface that Lyndsay was among his sources, gives a description of the ceremonies that echoes but also adds to that of Lyndsay's poem; cf. *Historie*, I.xlii-xliii, 2 and 363-67.

90-91 *lyke ane storme...to sorrow*: The expression was proverbial; cf. Whiting, 'Proverbs...Scottish', *storm* (2).

92 *O traytour Deith*: The epithet had greater impact in this period; cf. Dunbar, *In vice most vicius* (B27); see also 93*n*.

93 *mycht have*: The use of the indirect tense forms a contrast to Marot's use of it, *Chant nuptial*, 5 ('Vous eussiez [You would have]'), where it helps to convey to a wider interested audience the experience of those who were present in the streets to see Madeleine. Lyndsay uses the tense ostensibly to censure Death for his treachery to Scotland—'thow mycht have sene the preparatioun'—but thereby also provides reason for the striking description, emphasising the country's deep grief, of events 'As suld have bene', 104.

94 *Thre Estaitis of Scotland*: The reference to the Lords, Clergy, and Burgesses recalls the prominence of the French Parliament in James's formal reception in Paris; cf. Teulet 1852-60: I.123-24.

100 *the nobill famous toun*: The reference to Edinburgh's fame balances that to Paris (71).

101 *peple labouring*: The whole of Scotland, the 'peple' and the parliament, it is stressed, were involved; cf. Dunbar, *Illuster Lodouick* (B23), 29; Marot, *Chant nuptial*, 5.

102 *mak triumphe*: Trump and clarioun were the sounds of chivalric or royal ceremony; cf. *Meldrum*, 388, where they open the young squire's joust with Talbart. Cf. also Marot, *Chant nuptial*, 60.

104 *As suld have bene*: A sharp return to the indirect after the joyfully direct 'sic pleasour was never...' (103).

105 *greit propynis*: At a cost of £1,000, which was met by 'ane universall taxt and stent', the new queen was to receive from Edinburgh 'fourty tunnis of wyne in propyne', Marwick 1869-82: II.74; cf. Dunbar, *Blyth Aberdeane* (B8), 61-63.

107 *Depayntit*: A term used only in verse; cf. *Clariodus*, 900.

109 *fontanis*: Fountains of clear water or wine were a frequent feature of state celebrations; Aberdeen's Cross 'aboundantlie rane wyne' at the 1511 entry of Queen Margaret (Dunbar, *Blyth Aberdeane* (B8), 58); a pageant at Charles V's 1522 London entry featured leaves that 'dropped swete water': Anglo 1969: 194.

110 *Disagysit folkis*: Cf. the use of 'dissagysit', *Dreme*, 18. *creaturis devyne*: Perhaps a hint that the actors' roles were those of classical gods and goddesses.

111 *On ilk scaffold*: Lyndsay implies that several separate pageant scenes had been prepared; cf. Dunbar's descriptions of the Aberdeen welcome, where there were representations of the Three Kings, the expulsion of Adam and Eve, Robert the Bruce, and a ?Stewart genealogical tree, *Blyth Aberdeane*, (B8), 25-40, and see Mill 1927: 78-85; Kipling 1998: 120, 263, 316-18.

114 *Weill ordourit*: Surviving records concerning Madeleine's Edinburgh reception are meagre, but for the 1538 entry of Marie de Guise careful thought was given to dress; see Marwick 1869-82: II.89-91.

115-16 *Ilk craftisman...in grene*: The craft is unspecified, but green clothing was associated with woods and hunting; cf. Douglas, *Pal. Honour*, 479 (where it is the dress of Cupid). In heraldry, the colour represented 'blithnes and vertu' (*Deidis of Armorie*, fol. 11ᵛ, 451). It was long linked to May, lovers, and youthful festivities; cf. *Kingis Quair*, 211-38; Dunbar, *Blyth Aberdeane* (B8), 42; *Test. Meldrum*, 132.

118 *scarlot*: This was a rich cloth of various colours, frequently bright red; cf. *Papyngo*, 1047; *Meldrum*, 1167. *claith of grane* was cloth of good quality, used for royal garments; cf. *TA*, VI.183.

120-25 *Provest, baillies...confortable*: The carefully ordered Edinburgh spectacle would have equalled, it is stressed, the Paris entry; cf. 'Ordre dans lequel le Parlement s'est rendu en grand solennité au devant du roi d'Ecosse'; Teulet 1852-60: I.123-24. Contrast the emphasis on the whole colourful spectacle (before order) in Lydgate's *King Henry VI's Triumphal Entry*, 29-42, *Minor Poems*, II.630-48.

122 *silk, of purpure, blak, and brown*: A similar colour scheme greeted Marie de Guise, though in that case the gowns were of velvet; see Marwick 1869-82: II.89.

123 *lordis of the parliament*: These officers were the Constable, Marischal, Serjeant and Dempster; see Hannay 1932: 125-38.

124 *knychtlie barroun and baurent*: For their formal dress, see Innes 1944-45. On *baurent*, the rank just below the baron, see *Justing*, 7n.

126 *sable*: The term adds courtly formality, but this rapid change was fact: records for 8 July 1536 note, in connection with cloth price-fixing, that 'the lords vnderstands that the kings grace and all the lieges of his realme hes instantlie ado with...all sorts of blak clayth'; Marwick 1869-82: II.77.

137 *reird redoundand*: Cf. Hay, *Buik of King Alexander the Conquerour*, 941-42 and *Papyngo*, 637.

138-40 *herauldis*: The heraldic aspect of a similar public procession is illustrated in Burnett and Tabraham 1993: 42.

139-40 *maseris...silver wandis*: As officers of arms, macers carried a slender rod as a symbol of authority. They made public proclamations and served as ushers, keeping order in law courts or, as here, in public ceremony. *the preis*: Cf. Douglas, *Pal. Honour*, 1142.

141-42 *ordour triumphall*: The royal entry, especially in Europe, had been gradually transformed to resemble the Roman imperial triumph, in which the victorious leader appeared in the final chariot; see Strong 1973: 25-37 and pl. 33; see also 73-87n.

142 *illuster princes*: Cf. Dunbar, *Illuster Lodouick* (B23), 1.

147 *Twynkling lyke sternis...nycht*: Cf. the proverbial similes in Whiting (S673, S674, S685 and S686), in which either stones/pebbles or eyes are said to resemble stars on a winter night. Lyndsay extends the comparison to describe the sparkle of the precious 'stonis' on Madeleine's clothing; cf. Marot of her diamond-studded hair, *Chant nuptial*, 29-32.

148 *Under ane pale*: No record of Madeleine's golden pall survives; cf. the 1538 entry into St Andrews of Marie de Guise, for which she was provided with a canopy of 'blew velvet' (*TA*, VI.410).

149 *Be burgessis borne*: They appear to have been the traditional pall bearers; cf. Dunbar, *Blyth Aberdeane* (B8), 9-14.

150 *greit maister of houshold*: Patrick Wemys held the position in 1537 (*TA*, VI.354).

155 *virginis*: Cf. Dunbar, *Goldyn Targe* (B59), 154, 'Syne tender Youth...wyth hir virgyns ying'; Marot, *Chant nuptial*, 61, 'les Nymphes Escossoises'.

157 *'Vive la Royne'*: An appropriately French greeting, cf. Marot, *Chant nuptial*, 63-64; Knecht 1994: 46.

158 *sound angelicall*: Cf. *Papyngo*, 140.

162 *ornate oratouris*: A transferred epithet in which the embellished language of those skilled in rhetoric has been used to describe the speakers; cf. Stewart, *For to declair*, *Bann. MS*, fol. 277ᵛ, 59. Formal oratory was part of the official welcome to James V in Paris (see Teulet 1852-60: I.124), and of Marie de Guise's entry into Edinburgh in 1538, Lyndsay himself involved in the latter (see Marwick 1869-82: II.91).

167 *abbay of Holy Rude*: Holyrood was an Augustinian abbey founded by David I in 1128. Close to Edinburgh Castle, it also provided a royal palace, which James IV rebuilt in 1501-05, and to which James V added, 1528-32. Lyndsay states that Madeleine would have been crowned at Holyrood, as was her successor, Marie de Guise, 22 Feb. 1540.

169-70 *aufull tornamentis*: The reference recalls events at Charles V's court, witnessed and similarly described by Lyndsay in 1531; see Hadley Williams, 'Of officiaris', in press.

170 *On hors and fute*: The three main activities of the chivalric tournament were the tilt (on horseback with lances across a barrier), the tourney (on horseback with swords), and the barriers (exchanged blows on foot across a barrier).

171-73 *Sic Chapell Royall*: See *Papyngo*, 634n; see also Easson 1938: 193-215 and 1939: 30-47; Ross 1993: 1-111.

172 *frome the splene*: See *Papyngo*, 112n.

173 *In this countre was never hard nor sene*: A common emphatic collocation; cf. *Was nevir in scotland hard, Bann. MS*, fols 99^r-101^r (here also referring to musical entertainment), and *Doverrit with dreme* (B11), (where it is the refrain). See further, *Bann. Facsimile*, xxviii (164).

175 *In 'Requiem æternam'*: C, P and P(oct) italicise 'In', but only the words *Requiem æternam* (referring to eternal rest after death), begin the Introit in the Mass for the Dead.

188 *Quhilkis*: The subject of this aside is 'we' of the previous line.

190ff *O Deith!*: The apostrophe, in its assertions of the continuing strength of the alliance, prepares the ground for a second French marriage.

191-92 *yit hes thow no puissance...the glore*: 'yet you have no power to destroy the glory of their virtue'.

193-94 *Magdalene...poetis sal avance*: The immortality of the dead through literary praise was a familiar elegiac theme; cf. *Meldrum*, 11-12.

197-98 Though 'flour of France' and the 'thrissill' refer to Madeleine and James (and James again, as 'lyoun' at 200), the use of emblems allows the quiet replacement of specifics with consolatory (and politically expedient) generalities. In Christian symbolism the fleur de lys was long associated with the Virgin as a symbol of purity; in heraldry, uppermost here, it was an emblem of France, first borne on a seal of Louis VII. The thistle was a heraldic emblem of Scotland from the reigns of James III and James IV. The lion was a familiar heraldic beast across Europe, symbol of strength, courage and magnanimity, but was also linked early with Scotland in particular (see Bower, *Scotichronicon* I, ii, 12.7-18; also Bawcutt 1986: 83-97, and *Deidis of Armorie*, fols 15^v-16^v, 761-77; fol. 36, 2144-64).

198 *Quhilk impit...thrissill kene*: Cf. Henryson's metaphorical use of the practice of grafting (or not) onto good stock, in *Against Hasty Credence*, 1-2. In this heraldic setting, the word could also have acquired the sense, 'impaled'; see *OED*, *impalement*, sense 3.

201-03 With the mention of an indestructible heavenly fragrance issuing from the roots, the image of the grafted plants incorporates Christian symbolism; cf. *Pearl*, 46 and *Dreme*, 764-67.

The Justing betwix James Watsoun and Jhone Barbour, c.1538-40

Text: The text is based on the earliest extant, John Scot's for Henry Charteris, Edinburgh, 1568, *STC* 15658 (= C). Checked against Thomas Bassandyne's Edinburgh 1574 edition, *STC* 15660 (= B), C showed greater use of anglicised forms (*no* for B's Scots form *na* (4, 68); *wer* for B's *war* (36, 38), *boith* for B's *baith* (12)), but there are no important variants. Both texts show some corruption in transmission, noted below.

Title: The full title, as in C, is: *The Justing betwix James Watsoun and Jhone Barbour, Servitouris to King James the Fyft.*

Form: *The Justing* belongs to the mock-tournament genre popular in Scotland during the late 15th and 16th centuries; cf. *Was nevir in scotland* [*Christis Kirk*], *Bann. MS*, fols 99ʳ-101ʳ; Dunbar, *Off Februar* (B47), 121-216, *Sym and his bruder*, *Bann. MS*, fols 145ᵛ-147ʳ; Scott, *Justing and Debait*. Lyndsay's jousters, Watsoun and Barbour, are the king's personal servants (see 5n, 9n, 10n, 14-15n), thus unlike the opponents of these other burlesques who are craftsmen, tradesmen, idle youths or charlatans.

Date: The court was at St Andrews for jousting, in the period including Whitsun, in 1538, during celebrations marking the arrival from France of James V's second wife, Marie de Guise. Jousting also took place there in 1539 and 1540; see *TA*, VI.412-13; VII.164-66, 317.

Metre: The *Justing* is in the flexible five-stress couplets used often for narrative verse, whether formal or comic; cf. *Wallace*; Douglas, *Eneados*; Lichtoun, *Quha douttis dremis, Bann. MS*, fols 101ʳ-102ʳ.

1 Sanct Androis: An ecclesiastical centre from the 11th c., St Andrews was a metropolitan see by 1472, its priory one of Scotland's wealthiest. **Witsoun Monnunday**: Whitmonday, following Whitsunday (Pentecost), seventh after Easter.

2 Twa campionis: A seeming high seriousness is quickly established; cf. *Wallace*, XII.149.

3 heid and handis: The alliterating sequence of the heroic romance.

4 Wes never...landis: A common expression, often, as here, with a double negative for alliterative emphasis; cf. *Was nevir in scotland, Bann. MS*, fols 99ʳ-101ʳ, 1.

5 In presence...quene: Lyndsay's poem may have been a fictional entertainment, in keeping with, yet comically undercutting, the court's formal recreation at St Andrews, but it could also tell of a joust enacted; cf. a joust at Nuremberg, 1491, during a serious tournament, at which the armour was of straw and weapons were blunt; see Jones 1951: 1125-28.

7 knight, barroun...baurent: The expensive equipment needed for jousting made it a sport limited to bannerets and above; see Barber 1970: 170. **baurent**: This spelling is in all extant texts; cf. *Deploratioun*, 124. *DOST*, s.v. *banrent*, and *OED*, s.v. *banneret*, incorrectly cite these two examples from Lyndsay as *banrent*.

8 aufull tornament: Cf. *Deploratioun*, 169.

9 James Watsoun: Watsoun appears as a barber ('barbitonsori') and yeoman in the king's chamber, 1538-1542; see *ER* XVII.280; *TA*, VII.143, 303, 332, 475. For his good service 'in arte chirurgia impenso',

he was granted, 3 Mar. 1539-40, 'duas partes terrarum de Balbunno, cum 2
acris ex prato de langforgund, in baronia de L., vic. Perth'.
10 *Johne Barbour*: Barbour is described as a groom of the wardrobe, not
'leche', during the years 1538-42 (*ER* XVII.166, 281; *TA*, VII.116, 126,
158, 264, 276, 281, 314-15, 324, 333, 424, 476). Apart from those to do
with the royal wardrobe, his duties included the purchase of a lute and two
dozen strings, skins for hawk hoods, and 'curches [kerchiefs, caps worn at
night]'. Accounts also record that Watsoun dried and purchased cloth for
these curches (which strongly suggests that the two men knew each other).
In Apr. 1540 Barbour was given £6 12s 'at the kingis gracis command
to...by hyme ane horse wyth', but it is not known whether the gift
preceded or followed Lyndsay's jocular poem about the joust with
Watsoun; see Murray 1965: 41.
14-15 *Ane medicinar...ane nobill leche*: An incongruous choice of
combatants; such men were needed after a battle or joust; cf. *Golagros*,
882-83: 'Thai hynt of [removed] his harnese, to helyn his wound;/ Lechis
war noght to [too] lait, with sawis [salves] sa sle'.
15 *nobill leche*: Cf. *Meldrum*, 807. See also 10*n*.
16 *Crukit carlingis...speche*: The line throws retrospective doubt on
'nobill' (15)—since it seems that Barbour's 'skill' did not heal the
womens' lameness—and suggests that the women's 'speche' was probably
the strong language of complaint; cf. Dunbar, *Flyting* (B65), 136.
18 *Full...scheild*: Contrast Stewart, *Croniclis*, 39367: 'Thir beirnis bald
that waponis weill culd weild'. *speir*, a weapon in its own right, could also
refer to the 'lance', and seems to do so here; cf. 22; *Meldrum*, 451*n*.
19 *And wichtlie...heillis*: The pair energetically, but uselessly, flung out
their feet (from their horses' flanks); see Gillmor 1992: 14-15.
20 *cadgeris...creillis*: A common alliterative association; cf. Dunbar,
Flyting (B65), 229; Henryson, *Fables*, 2028.
21 *ather...uther*: Cf. Barbour, *Bruce*, XVI.164.
22 *speir...in reist*: Contrast the skilled handling in *Wallace*, V.260.
27 *leggis lyke rokkis*: Cf. Dunbar, *Madam, ȝour men said thai wald ryde*
(B30), 23: 'With schinnis scharp and small lyk rockis'.
29 *be my thrift*: Cf. Chaucer, *RvT, CT*, I (A) 4049.
29-32 James's spear is bent by the earlier entanglement with his horse's
hoofs and he finds it difficult to aim. Apparently leaning back in the saddle
(rather than in the correct forward position), James can see only sky. John
has not managed to keep his spear horizontal and (through his visor) sees
only the steeple top; see Keen 1984: 206.
31 *be Goddis breid!*: A blasphemous oath on the sacramental bread
(symbol of the body of Christ), used also by Dissait and Pauper in *Thrie
Estaitis*, 932, 2289, 2943; see *Complaynt*, 237*n*.
33-34 *Yit...Defend the, man!*: The strong shafts were also used as
weapons, it would seem; cf. Dunbar, *O gracious princes* (B73), 19; *Was
nevir in scotland, Bann. MS*, fols 99ʳ-101ʳ, 166. Barbour is saying that
even if Watsoun's limbs are as tough as barrow poles, he should beware:
the joust in earnest is about to begin. (Contrast Hamer 1931-36: III.141.)
34 *lyk rammis*: Cf. *Was nevir in scotland, Bann. MS*, fols 99ʳ-101ʳ, 164.

35-36 *At that...in swoun*: Cf. *Sym and his bruder, Bann. MS*, fols 145ᵛ-147ʳ, 115-16.

38 *Wer not...speir*: C and B have the six-stressed: 'Wer not amangis his hors feit he brak his speir', possibly a compositor's eye-skip (cf. the part-similar 24); 'his' has been excluded, for better metrical sense.

39 *our ladyis saikis*: A common knightly vow, in this case remaining unfulfilled; contrast *Meldrum*, 484.

40 *market straikis*: See *DOST, Markit*, (c). Each jouster aimed to use his lance to unhorse, or to land blows (preferably thereby breaking the lance) on head or body. These strokes, and the number of courses (or charges) run to accomplish them, were noted by a herald on a score cheque. Surviving cheques show that many riders did not score at all, for the exercise required great skill and strength. The ribaldry therefore derives from the pair's belief that they can attempt three such strokes; cf. the even more unlikely challenge in *Cupar Banns, Thrie Estaitis*, 119-21. See also Starkey 1991: 46-48 and Hay, *Law of Armys*, fol. 75ᵛ (Stevenson 269).

42 *Bot...brokin*: James's spear is already broken (38) and John's similar loss ends the combat with lances.

44-45 *James drew...rout*: The use of swords (on horseback or foot) usually followed combat with lances, but was normally introduced because the latter had shattered on impact (or jousters had been unhorsed); cf. *Golagros*, 615-29.

45 *raucht...rout*: Cf. Barbour, *Bruce*, V.634.

47-48 *Than James...lystis*: Although it seems at first as if James has begun punching John, the reference to his sword (50) suggests instead that, unlike the practised jouster, James drove at John grasping his sword with two hands.

48 *dang upon the lystis*: This was considered a principal fault in a jouster's performance; see Anglo 1961: 155.

55 *crack greit wordis*: A sign of inadequacy; cf. *Cupar Banns, Thrie Estaitis*, 136-37.

56 *falt of swordis*: Watsoun notes this point because, if accepted, it would allow the pair to continue with honour; cf. Hay, *Law of Armys*, fol. 75ᵛ (Stevenson 268-69): 'For gif the suerd...failis, or fallis fra him, or that his party advers takis it fra him...throu his foly or misgovernaunce, it war na resoun he had ane othir. Bot, and suerd for sum alde fault, or new beand, in the self wapin, nocht in his default, war brokin in the felde fechtand...it war wele accordand to resoun that he had ane othir...'.

58 *With gluifis...facis*: These gloves, of thin pieces of metal over leather, were not weapons, but worn for protection during jousting swordplay; cf. James V's requirements for his wedding jousts in France; *TA*, VII.13: '...for ane gluiff of plait to fecht witht the suerd'.

59 *this feild*: Cf. Douglas, *Eneados*, V, x.72.

60-62 *Till at the last...tyre*: If events had not already decided a victor, the decision to end the combat, in battle or joust, rested with the king or judges, not the participants; cf. Stewart, *Croniclis*, 39369-371. James's admission of tiredness also was unacceptable; enduring the physical effects of a long contest was part of the test; cf. *Golagros*, 973-74; 999.

63 *royall*: Cf. Hay, *Buik of King Alexander the Conquerour*, 857-58.

64 *Into...stink*: A side-effect of fear becomes apparent; cf. Dunbar, *Off Februar* (B47), 205-07.

66 *dirt partis cumpany*: A proverbial expression; cf. Whiting, 'Proverbs...Scottish', *Dirt*.

67-68 *Thare hors...no blude*: Some agile reasoning ends the poem lightheartedly. Since the 'geir' that has been in evidence has bent, proven rusty, or broken prematurely, the inferences must be, first, that 'gude' is used with irony (albeit alliteratively) and, secondly, that the very inadequacy of the 'geir' paradoxically has made it 'gude', since, as a result, no blood has been spilled.

The Tragedie of the Cardinall, 1547

Text: The text is based on the earliest extant Scottish edition, John Scot's of 1559, *STC* 15675 (= Sc), which was appended with other Lyndsay poems to the 1554 edition of *Ane Dialog* (*STC* 15672). Sc was collated with the two 1558 French editions thought to be the work of the Rouen printer, Jean Petit or his heirs: the quarto, *STC* 15673 (= P) and the octavo, *STC* 15674 (= P(oct)). These provide a few (noted) emendations, but because of their compositors' evident unfamiliarity with Scots, neither has been chosen as copy text. With other prose works on the reformer, George Wishart, *The Tragedie* was also printed in London, c.1548, by the printers, John Day and William Seres. This, *STC* 15683 (= D), is an anglicised and, in places, a significantly different text. The changes (noted selectively) provide clues to the extent of English understanding of Scots at this period (as perceived by the printers, or the probable English editor, Robert Burrant). They also throw light on contemporary English political and religious attitudes, during the minority of Edward VI, to the deaths of Wishart (who, at Beaton's orders, had been arrested, sentenced as a heretic, and burned, Mar. 1546), and of Beaton himself.

Title: In Sc: *Heir follouis the Tragedie of the Umquhyle maist Reverend Father David, be the Mercy of God, Cardinall and Archibyschope of Sanct Androus. &c.* Where Sc's title may be compared with those of P, P(oct) and D, it is superior (*Umquhyle* to P's *unquhyle*; *maist* to *maister*, for instance). Sc's *&c.*, implying a longer original title, is wanting in P, P(oct) and D; all have instead similarly-worded lists of further honours. Those in P read: *And of the haill Realme of Scotlande Primate, Legate, and Chancelare. And Administrator of the Byschoprik of Merapoys in France. And Commendator perpetuall of the Abay of Aberbrothok.* Such details of high rank are in line with the tragic theme, and are less unusual than might be presumed; cf. Dunbar's *Ballade of...Barnard Stewart* (B56), and the Latin work by Beaton's nephew, Archibald Hay: *Ad illustrissimum tituli S. Stephani in monte Coelio Cardinalem, D. Davidem Betoun, Primatem Scotiae, Archiepiscopum S. Andreae, Episcopum Meripocensem, De Poel-*

*ici accessione dignitatis Cardinalitiae, gratulatorius panegyricus
Archibaldi Hay* (Paris, 1540). While Dunbar's poem is a panegyric, Hay's
prose work, which mixes extravagant eulogy of Beaton with comment on
his duty, as cardinal, to reform the degeneracies of the church (see Murison
1938: 188-200), offered a partial precedent to Lyndsay, whose similarly
laudatory title ultimately has a satiric intent.

Form: In his prologue, Lyndsay connects the poem to John Boccaccio's
14th-c. work of 'tragedie and storie' (4), *De Casibus Virorum Illustrium*.
Written in Latin prose, with a combined moral and historical purpose that
had great appeal in the later medieval period, it took the vicissitudes of
Fortune as its theme, using material from Biblical, Patristic, and classical
sources to exemplify it in a series of lives of famous men and women, from
Adam and Eve to the French king, Jean le Bon. The *De Casibus* was
Lydgate's ultimate source for his *Fall of Princes* (c.1438), but he worked
from Laurent de Premierfait's second, free and amplified, French prose
translation of the early 15th c. Lydgate made additions in turn, in
particular his moralising envoys, which became popular excerptions. The
Fall of Princes, however, was strongly identified with the *De Casibus*, and
it is probable that Lyndsay, in referring to the book by 'Jhone Bochas',
was in fact alluding to Lydgate's *Fall*; see Edwards 1977: 424-39; Pearsall
1970: 230-54. *The Tragedie* is distinctive in its satiric use of the
discrepancy between the fictional Beaton's words and the known facts;
see, for instance, note under 'Title', 26*n*, 78-80*n*, 82*n*, 176*n*, 311*n*, 351*n*.

Date: Beaton was assassinated 2 May 1546; at 267 Lyndsay refers to the
seven-month delay before Beaton was buried. The poem thus was
composed after Dec. 1546, but before the London edition appeared,
c.1548, the earliest known year of the Day and Seres partnership.

Metre: *The Tragedie* is in the formal but flexible five-foot rhyme royal
stanza (*ababbcc*), also used by Lydgate, *Fall of Princes*, and favoured by
Lyndsay; cf. *Dreme*, 1-1036; *Papyngo*, 73-1185.

1 *pryme*: In general, the term for early morning, it also had a specifically
religious sense, as the first canonical hour and its office.

4-7 *tragedie*: The word is used in the medieval sense; see Chaucer,
MkTPro CT, VII, 1973-77; Chaucer, *Bo*, II, pr. 2.70-73; Lydgate, *Fall*,
V.3120-22 ('For tragedie, as poetes spesephie, Gynneth with joie, endith
with adversite: From hih estate men cast in low degre'); see also Farnham
1936: 69-172; Chambers 1903: II.209-11; Axton 1992.

5 *Jhone Bochas*: Giovanni Boccaccio, 14th c. Italian author, whose
works include the *Filostrato, Decameron, De Casibus Virorum Illustrium,
De Genealogia Deorum* and *De Claris Mulieribus*; see note under 'Form'.

7 *deposit*] P, P(oct); *deposed* D; *depsosit* Sc.

8-9 *Alexander*: Alexander III (The Great); see *Dreme*, 34-35*n*; cf. *Ane
Dialog*, 3650. His death by poisoning (as in Diodorus Siculus, 17.118)
was generally accepted by medieval writers; cf. Chaucer, *MkT*, *CT*,
VII.2669; Hay, *Buik of King Alexander the Conquerour*, 17888-997.

10-11 *And Julius...creuellie*: Gaius Julius Caesar; see *Dreme*, 34-35*n*. He
was murdered by a conspiracy led by Brutus and Cassius; cf. Lydgate, *Fall*,
VI.2819-919.

12-13 *Pompey...murdreist was*: Pompey the Great; see *Dreme*, 34-35n. Chaucer (*MkT, CT*, VII, 2690-94), refers to his murder, but Lyndsay refers to the role of Egypt in that event; cf. Lydgate, *Fall*, VI.2436-57.

13 *quhat nedith proces more?*: A common stylistic device (*interrogatio*); cf. Douglas, *Eneados*, XII, xiv.110; *Papyngo*, 586.

14 Sc's *depolre* is corrected; cf. *deplore* D, P, P(oct).

20-21 *In rayment reid...of saityng crammosie*: The dress of a cardinal; cf. Holland, *Howlat*, 161-64.

21 D substitutes: *wyth fyne velvet, and satten richely.*

26 *my passioun*: The word's primary sense associated it with events of the passion of Christ, or of a saint or martyr; cf. Chaucer, *SNPro, CT*, VIII.26; *Ane Dialog*, 262-63; see *DOST, Passio(u)n*, 1, and Strohm 1975-76: 63-67, 154-58. Its use by Beaton's wraith is deeply ironic.

28 *My tragedie*: See 4-7n. The words place the narrative of the events of the cardinal's life beside earlier Boccaccian examples.

29-31 *Sen he is gone*: Additions to Boccaccio were common, especially in the later 16th c. Lyndsay's poem was followed by George Cavendish's c.1555 *Metrical Visions* (London, BL, Egerton 2402) of Wolsey, Anne Boleyn, Henry VIII and others; followed shortly afterwards by the first edition and additions to The *Mirror for Magistrates*. Sempill's c.1571 *Bischoppis Lyfe and Testament* is among Scottish examples; see Fisher 1968; Campbell 1938 and *Satirical Poems*, I.193-200, II.129-40.

30 Sc's *remembrace* lacks the abbreviation mark, and is corrected.

32 *As I to the sall schaw*: Beaton takes the position of author / authority; the poet, by pointed contrast, is presented as mere recipient and amanuensis; see 42n and cf. Strohm 1982: 293-98.

38 *David*: David Beaton, c.1494-1546. Son of John Beaton of Balfour, Fife, and Isobel Monypenny. The request for Beaton's name (37) is an effective separation of Lyndsay the man from his poet-persona; almost certainly Beaton was personally known to Lyndsay, as near neighbour and court colleague. See Sanderson 1986; Herkless 1891.

42 *I began to wryte*: Cf. [Lydgate], *In may quhen Flora the fresche lusty quene* (*CM*), 180-82: 'as doth a scryuenere / That can nemore bot that he schal write / Ryght as his maister beside hym dotth endite'.

43ff The fictional Beaton is sole narrator, without the poet-commentator used by Lydgate in *The Fall*.

44 *Of nobyl blude*: 14th- and 15th-c. Beaton ancestors had married into families related to the royal house of Stewart; see Sanderson 1986: 8.

49 *under ane kyng*: The hierarchical pattern of authority is acknowledged—kings are above cardinals—but the ironic emphasis is on the first half of the line: 'So gret one man as I'.

51 *Prencis to serve*: Beaton studied at St Andrews university (1508), and Glasgow (c.1512). According to his cousin, Archibald Hay, Beaton also studied in Paris; at Orleans in 1519 he received training in civil law (a recognised preparation for a legal career or royal administrative service). He served at the French court under the patronage of the governor of Scotland, John, Duke of Albany, with whom he returned to Scotland in 1521. Beaton thereby was introduced to the court during James V's minority, serving it as a diplomat. See Sanderson 1986: 11-15; Kirkpatrick 1904: 85.

52 *at Arbroith I began*: On his translation from Glasgow to the St Andrews archbishopric (1521, effective 1523), James Beaton resigned the abbacy of Arbroath to his nephew; see *James V Letters*: 95-97.

53 *Ane abasie*: Arbroath Abbey, founded by William I in the 12th c., was an important religious house, in the 14th c. second only to St Andrews in the size of its revenues. By the 15th c. it attracted secular clerics, such as Beaton, rather than monks, as its abbots. Hamer (1931-36: III.154) notes, however, that Beaton was not entitled to all Arbroath's revenues, and that his lavish style of living brought him into financial difficulties; see also Sanderson 1986: 21-23; Mackie and others 1982: 21-30.

56 *allace! allace!*: The exclamations, foreshadowing Beaton's end, reinforce the poem's *Fall of Princes* structure.

57 *servyce tyll our...kyng*: Beaton's service, begun under Albany, continued into James V's personal reign: by 1529 he was Keeper of the Privy Seal, and also acted as auditor of the Treasurer's accounts (*RSS*, I.4019; Sanderson 1986: 51-53; *ER*, XVI.402, 447; XVII.70; *TA*, VI.239). His most successful service was the negotiation of the French marriages in the 1530s; see 85-88*n*; Lang 1909: 150-58.

58 *He did promove me*: Cf. *Tragedie*, 388. The stress on each step by which Beaton's ascent was achieved creates a cumulative tension characteristic of the *De Casibus* mode; cf. Lydgate's story of Alcibiades, *Fall*, III.3334, 3382, 3405, 3578-85, where, as in other lives, Fortune's role in the downfall is emphasised. Lyndsay, notably, looks also to human agency; see 346*n*.

59 *One prince...for tyll ryng*: Beaton presents his promotion not in terms of increased responsibilities for the spiritual welfare of his flock, but as an achievement of additional worldly power.

60 *Arschibyschope of Sanct Androus*: During 1537 Beaton was coadjutor of St Andrews, administering the see for his uncle and effectively its archbishop, formally becoming so on James Beaton's death in Feb. 1539. See Dowden 1912: 41 and Sanderson 1986: 67.

63 *one cardinall*: Beaton was created cardinal on 20 Dec. 1538; see *James V Letters*: 360-61, 366-68.

64 *auctoritie*] P, P(oct); *authoritie* D; *auctorie* Sc.

65 *chosin Chancelare*: Beaton became Chancellor on 10 Jan. 1543 after James V's death (*RSS*, III, no. 21).

67 *maid legate*: As legate *a latere* from 1544, Beaton had papal authority in Scotland; see Sanderson 1986: 195.

68 *I purcheist*: Beaton appears to be saying that he obtained his French bishopric in the normal way, by application to the ecclesiastical authorities, but the word has multiple senses (see *DOST*, *purchas(e*, v.), some linked to soliciting or bribery. These acquire potent force in a setting where *proffect singular* and *threasure* are stressed. *proffect singulare*: A recurring topic in late medieval verse, it is often explicitly contrasted to the common good; cf. Dunbar, *Quhy will 3e, merchantis* (B55), 71-72; *Dreme*, 904-10, 969-73.

69 *My boxsis and my threasure*: Lyndsay follows Lydgate's stress on the dangers of worldly riches (cf. *Fall*, III.3718-80, for example), but Beaton's wealth was real; cf. a list of goods stolen from him in 1544: 'a great cross of silver, silver basins, lavers, trenchers, salt-fats, plates, dishes, candlesticks, a mitre, spoons, napery etc, valued on the Cardinal's oath at £2,800...' (*ADCP*, 539).

70 *Merapose*: On 5 Dec. 1537, Beaton was provided to the bishopric of Mirepoix in the Languedoc, to which he had been nominated by Francis I. His consecration followed in late July or Aug. 1538; see Sanderson 1986: 57. In Boccaccian style, Lyndsay lists Beaton's honours in order of their importance, not chronologically. That Lyndsay shapes the poem as a 'fall of princes' piece is confirmed by his omission of one honour, Francis I's grant of French naturalisation, Nov. 1537 (Archives Nationales, Reg., Chancellerie de Paris, JJ 250, No. 190, fol. 53ᵛ; Bonner 1997a: 1106-07. This was well known in 1547, but the Mirepoix bishopric is allowed to represent all Beaton's French links, and to provide the reason for his support of that country (and his own and the church's interests) before those, as interpreted here, of the Scottish king and realm.

75 *emperour*] D; *empriour* P, P(oct); *emperous* Sc.

78-80 *princelye prodigalytie...lordlye lyberalitie*: The moral ambiguity (and verbal irony) of the previous lines (that there is not enough time to describe Beaton's 'actis honorabyll') is extended here. Of the two seemingly laudable qualities, *Prodigalytie* was used, chiefly in secular contexts, to describe 'fule largess', the opposite of the largess proper to princes (cf. Hay, *Gouernaunce of Princes*, fol. 106ʳ, i.29-35). *Liberalitie*, akin to Hay's 'resonable largess' (*Gouernaunce*, fol. 106ʳ, i.34; cf. *Papyngo*, 491-92), is a subtler criticism, since it could be used legitimately by Beaton, whose estates and great household made him a lord; see Sanderson 1986: 96-145. The alliteration, adding plain, yet carefully-weighted secular modifiers, reinforces the impression of Beaton's misjudged stress on worldly riches and high estate.

81 *banketting...dyse*: These activities, unless taken to excess, were not considered inappropriate for those with court duties, as Beaton had, but they were a 'solace' more appropriate to kings or secular lords; cf. *Thrie Estaitis* [1554], 1833-38; *Meldrum*, 1050. See Sanderson 1986: 140-41.

82 *Into sic wysedome...wyse*: The word *sic* qualifies *wysedome*, and admits a doubt about how wise Beaton actually was; cf. Ireland, *Meroure*, I, 12.21-24.

84 *crownis of gold*: The French écu or crown of the sun, was worth about 22 shillings Scots; see *TA*, VIII.253, 365. The foreign currency stresses the French source of part of Beaton's wealth; see 70.

85-88 *In France...plesance*: Throughout the 1530s, Beaton was James V's indispensable ambassador to France, trusted also by Francis I and the Pope. His fluent French and familiarity with the French court were real assets to the Scottish government. By his skilled negotiation of the successive marriages with Madeleine de Valois and Marie de Guise-Lorraine, Beaton brought James prestige and considerable wealth in dowries; see *L&P Henry VIII*, XI.1173, 1194; Bentley-Cranch and Marshall 1996: 273-88; *TA*, VII.xv-xvi ('1436-7' should read '1536-7').

89 *first dochter of France*: Cf. *Deploratioun*, 49n.

95 *resavit with gret tryumphe*: See *Deploratioun*, 141-42n. Pitscottie notes the 'trieumphant frais [farce]', devised by Lyndsay, that was part of Marie's reception at St Andrews in 1538 (*Historie*, I.379).

99 *our kyng wos weill content*: Very similar words are used later in the same stanza: 'Bot we wer weill content' (103). The repetition opposes 'our kyng' and 'we', so that James V's moves to meet (and potentially to embrace the anti-papal policies of) his uncle, Henry VIII, and thereby (it is implied) ensure peace, are set against the militant, self-preserving policy of Beaton and the church hierarchy, to pursue a European alliance. The latter policy, moreover, is presented as encouragement of the king to oppose his own kin (Henry VIII is described as 'his mother brother', 105).

100-105 *So that in Yorck*: Henry had tried unsuccessfully to arrange a meeting at York in 1536 (see *James V Letters*: 316-19). He tried again in 1541, although by then the meeting was even less attractive, since Scotland's ties with France and the papacy (through Beaton's cardinalate) were greatly strengthened. Henry journeyed to York with pomp, despite the fact (or perhaps because) he knew, through his spy network, that before Beaton had sailed to France, James had promised him he would not go into England (see *Hamilton Papers*, I, (85)). Through Beaton, now in France, Francis I assured James that if necessary he would send 'succurris and supple' (although he was in fact slow to act, being on the brink of war with Charles V); see Lang 1909: 152, 154; *James V Letters*: 316-19; Bonner 1997b: 36-53; Lamb, *Ane Resonyng*, 34-43.

104 *Had salit...to speik with ony uther*: A meeting with either Francis I, the Pope, or Charles V, is implied.

106 *gret weir*: An allusion to the armed hostility between Scotland and England that began with border skirmishes in late 1541, and culminated in the disastrous defeat at Solway Moss, Nov. 1542; see *L&P Henry VIII*, XVII.1052, 1060, 1086, 1100 and 1110.

108 *ather*] Sc, P, P(oct); *the other* D (the opposite viewpoint).

110 *I causit all*: Beaton saw Anglo-Scots armed conflict as essential, since it would ensure that 'the King will not revolt from the holy see and take part against the French king'; see *L&P Henry VIII*, XVII.1072.

113-15 *war takin presoneris*: Among the c.1200 taken prisoner were two earls, five barons and several hundred lairds; see *SPHenry VIII*, V, pt. iv.234-35 and *L&P Henry VIII*, XVII.1143.

119 *he did depart*: James V died 14 Dec. 1542, the humiliation of both defeat and, according to English opinion, the unfaithfulness of his lords, seemingly unrelieved by the news of his daughter's birth, 8 Dec. 1542.

121-23 *Ane paper blank*: The allegation, never formalised, that the cardinal had forged the king's will, was first made four months after the king's death, by governor Arran, in an exchange with Ralph Sadler, the English ambassador then at Holyrood, who reported it to Henry, 12 Apr. 1543 (*SP Sadler*, I.138; see also Lang 1906: 410-22). The preservation among Hamilton muniments of an unsigned notarial instrument (drawn up allegedly in James V's presence by Henry Balfour, afterwards servant of Beaton), which names Beaton and the Earls of Moray, Huntly and Argyll as chief governors, is possible evidence, Sanderson argues (1986: 153-58), that the instrument had a role in a compromise agreed between Beaton and Arran after the latter became governor in Jan. 1543: specifically, that Beaton be made Chancellor in exchange for the document of the king's supposed last wishes, in which Arran's name did not appear. (Contention about a king's last wishes was not uncommon; five years later, on Henry VIII's death, William Paget's word came under scrutiny; see Miller 1978.)

125 *sum lordis benevolens*: A probable allusion to the lords who, just after the king's death, were named with Beaton as chief governors: James Stewart, Earl of Moray; Alexander Gordon, Earl of Huntly, and Archibald Campbell, Earl of Argyll.

127 *rychteous governour*: James Hamilton (c.1516-1575), second Earl of Arran and Duke of Châtelherault, is presented as the legitimate candidate. He was heir presumptive to the throne through his grandfather's marriage to James II's daughter, Mary, in 1474. A child of his father's second marriage, the first being annulled, the Earl's legitimacy was controversial; see Finnie 1985: 18-19; *Ane Dialog*, 26n.

131 *nevir...none*: A double negative stresses ill-judged resolve.

133 *Erle of Angous*: Archibald Douglas, sixth Earl of Angus (c.1489-1557), in exile in England since the first days of James V's personal reign (1528); see *Complaynt*, 299-300n, 356n, 372n; *Papyngo*, 590.

135 *caste in captyvitie*: Beaton was arrested in Council, in the governor's presence (27 Jan. 1543), the pretext his willingness to allow French intervention in Scotland; see *Hamilton Papers*, I, (289).

136 *dant*] Sc, P, P(oct); *breake* D.

136-37 *My prydefull...divinitie*: The brief but formally patterned moralisation (*dant, devysit, divinitie*), attributing Beaton's imprisonment to divine chastisement of pride, fits the Lydgatean model, less so the historical evidence (see 135n); cf. *Fall*, II.218-24.

139-40 *Bot now...law*: Cf. Luke 14.11; Prov. 16.18; Whiting P393.

141-42 *quhen I...to Ingland*: During Mar. 1543, parliament appointed three commissioners to negotiate a marriage treaty with England, but, despite the reference here, Beaton had gained his freedom by the time the Scots travelled to London; see 148-50n; Sanderson 1986: 161-65.

143 *peace and mariage contractit*: An allusion to the proposal that the young queen, Mary, should marry Henry VIII's son, Edward, thus ensuring peace between the realms; see *APS*, II.411-13.

145 *divers pleagis*: The Scots agreed to the treaties but in fact promised little, refusing to allow Mary to be sent to England, or to cancel existing alliances with France; see *SP Sadler*, I.146-50; Sanderson 1986: 165.

148-50 *capytanis...did rewaird*: Beaton is said to have bribed George Douglas with 400 crowns, thereby securing his transfer from Dalkeith Castle (a Douglas property) to the house of a supporter, Lord Seton. Beaton was taken by Seton to Blackness state prison in Mar., but by the end of the month he had returned to his own castle in St Andrews; see *SP Sadler*, I.130-31, 136-37; Sanderson 1986: 162-63.

153-54 *lyke ane lyone lowsit*: An alliterative simile often used of the vehemence with which knights pursued their cause in battle (cf. Stewart, *Croniclis*, 19646-47). Its use by a religious leader is strikingly inappropriate (cf. 'reil and rage', 154).

156-59 *maid I insurrextioun*: At this time Beaton's public alliance with Arran gave constitutionality to his actions. He sent his hopes for peace between Scotland and England to the English ambassador, but did so in the midst, first, of growing fears of Douglas power backed by Henry VIII's plans for wholesale intervention in Scotland; of the outward solidarity of the church hierarchy in the face of Arran's agreement to allow the Scriptures in English to circulate; and of the temporising diplomacy of Marie de Guise, who assured the ambassador of Beaton's wisdom and support for the English marriage alliance; see Sanderson 1986: 164-65.

163 *I rasit ane oyste*: By mid-year, Beaton had gathered promises of armed support from within Scotland and from France (the French fleet appeared along the E. coast in early July). He strengthened the promises of Lennox, Huntly, Bothwell and Montrose by taking their sons into his household: *Hamilton Papers*, I, (390), (392), (414), (416), (418); (397).

164 *ane raid quhilk Lythgow yit may rew*: On 21 July, Beaton and a force of more than 6,000 arrived in Linlithgow to demand the removal of Mary and her mother to Stirling. Arran had fortified the palace, and Beaton was forced to negotiate. Yet the outcome, the Linlithgow bond, wherein custody of the queen was to be rotated at any one time between four lords, two nominated by Beaton, two by the governor, must have satisfied the cardinal; see Sanderson 1986: 167-68; Wormald 1988: 50-51.

165 *we distroyit*: There was no warfare (see 164*n*); Beaton alludes to the demands of a large army on local resources; cf. Pitscottie: 'thair oist in linlythgow...lay thair so lang that thay distroyit the haill cornis about the towne...the space of ane myll round about' (*Historie*, II.13).

166 *blak malysoun*: Cf. *Thrie Estaitis*, 2846.

168 *With...went*: Mary was taken to the more secure Stirling in late July.

170 *I brocht...Lennox*: Matthew Stewart, fourth Earl of Lennox (1516-71), was a rival to Arran as governor (since both were descended from the marriage of Mary, daughter of James II, and James, Lord Hamilton). Lennox had been living in France; his arrival in Scotland, which had been encouraged by Beaton, threatened to re-ignite the issue of Arran's legitimacy (cf. 127*n*); see *Hamilton Papers*, I (295), (400).

172 *Did loce that land*: Lennox had reacted to Arran's change of heart by taking England's part and seeking marriage to Margaret Douglas (daughter of Margaret Tudor and the Earl of Angus) to strengthen his claim to the throne still further. He drew support not only from those keen for Anglo-Scottish peace, from church reformers, and from those opposing the Hamilton leadership, but also from those formerly of Beaton's Francophile party, who had become disaffected because of his alliance with Arran. After the siege of Glasgow castle, Lennox sailed to England; his return on military raids later in the year was openly with English backing. In Oct. 1545 parliament found Lennox guilty of treason, forfeiting his lands and goods; see *Hamilton Papers*, I, (392), (406); *APS*, II.456-58; Sanderson 1986: 200-12.

175 *Forfaltit and flemit*: Cf. *Papyngo*, 597. By their close association here, Lennox's flaws and Beaton's faulty 'counsall' (174) are equally exposed. *gat none uther grace*: A common expression in Lyndsay's works; cf. *Papyngo*, 470, 597; in D *flemit* becomes *banished*.

176 *my prudens...ingyne*: The word choice is ambiguous, lending itself to satiric interpretation; cf. 77-84.

178 *my counsale*: In a context of downfalls, the repetition (cf. 174) continues to question the quality of Beaton's advice.

180 *For quhy?*: Cf. *Papyngo*, 11 and Douglas, *Eneados*, V, Prol. 33; VI, Prol. 164. *plane parliament*: This term, strictly defined, described the most formal meeting of the King's Council in parliament, summoned upon forty days' notice; cf. *Thre Prestis*, 65.

180-81 *I gart dissolve*: The Dec. 1543 parliament annulled the peace treaty on the pretext of an English attack on Scottish merchant ships (though this attack pre-dated the treaty); *APS*, II.431-32.

181 Sc's *contratit* omits the abbreviation mark, and is emended.

183 *new...weris*: Cf. 106. In May 1544 English forces invaded. Many Scots were either unwilling to fight or, as 'assured' Scots (disaffected and bribed by England), had reason not to; see Merriman 1968: 10-34; Sanderson 1986: 181-82.

184 *Be sey and land*: While Wharton's men attacked in the Borders, Hertford's came by sea. Landing near Leith, which they captured, the army marched on Edinburgh. After formal parley with the provost, Hertford attacked, burned and pillaged, damaging Holyrood Abbey and Palace, then turned S. to Berwick, destroying as he went; see Hertford, *Late expedition*, 39-51; Balfour 1911: 113-31. Internal rhyme ('reif without releif') adds emphasis to the fictional Beaton's belated admission of his role as initiator of the devastation (187).

185 'Which to report my frightened heart is fitting, proper'; see *DOST*, *Affer(e*, v. D replaces with the adverb, *farre*: 'it frayeth my herte farre'.

189 *in my cude*: Cf. Holland, *Howlat*, 978; *Thrie Estaitis*, 2070-73. This cloth, a symbol of innocence, covered the face at baptism; see *OED*, *chrism*, 4 and *chrisom*, 2.

190 *cause*] P, P(oct), D; *canse* Sc.

191 *my glore and dignitie*: Cf. 66.

193 *With Ingland...unitie*: See 180-81n.

196 *playit lowis or fast*: From the name of a cheating game (see *OED*, *fast and loose*).

201 *ather*] Sc, P, P(oct); *thother* D (the opposing viewpoint).

202 *Edinburgh...Leith...Kyngorne*: Hertford attacked all three; see 184n.

205 *With sweit...him syle*: Cf. Dunbar, *Goldyn Targe* (B59), 217: 'Dissymulance was besy me to sile'.

206 *sone and air*: It was a frequent practice for sons of noblemen to be placed within a great household to learn the tasks and codes of behaviour that would be required later; Arran's oldest son had joined Beaton's household in 1543, after Beaton and Arran had become reconciled. Whether or not Beaton also had a political motive for the action, the presence of James Hamilton within his household was interpreted as Arran's pledge of continuing commitment. Once Beaton was murdered, Arran's son became hostage of the slayers, his presence delaying the resolution of the castle siege; see Bonner 1996b: 595-98.

209 *Than leuch I*: Cf. Henryson, *Fables*, 446, 684, 1741 and 1762; where the word also indicates a lack of wisdom, or deceitfulness.

211 *his germane brother*: Sir George Douglas of Pittendreich; see 133*n*. Initially agents for Henry VIII, the Douglases played a wily game, co-operating also with Arran, Beaton, and Marie de Guise as necessary, often accepting financial inducements; see *Hamilton Papers*, I, (397): Parr's note that the Scots describe George Douglas as one who 'cane shifte the tyme for his comoditie, though it never come to effecte that whiche he promysethe'.

213-14 *distroyit mony uther*: Probably an allusion to the inquisition, arrests, imprisonments, and executions of heretics in Angus and the Mearns (1543) and Perth (1544), and perhaps also to the death of Wishart, whose burning before St Andrews Castle was witnessed by the cardinal; see Sanderson 1986: 214-20.

215 *gentyll men of Fyfe*: The Fife landholders were tenants, relatives, or former servants of Beaton; all had Anglophile-reformist opinions. The chief conspirators to Beaton's murder were among them: Norman Leslie (eldest son of George, fourth Earl of Rothes), William Kirkcaldy (son of James Kirkcaldy of Grange), John Leslie of Parkhill (uncle of Norman), Peter Carmichael of Balmaddie, James Melville of Carnbee; see Bardgett 1989: 19-41; Sanderson 1986: 222-28; Christensen 1983: 60-70.

217 *All favoraris...Testament*: A shorthand allusion to those who favoured reform and the free availability of the Bible in the vernacular. In the *Thrie Estaitis*, Lyndsay draws a satiric contrasting picture, of Spiritualitie boastfully answering Gude Counsall's query with: 'I red never the New testament nor auld: / Nor ever thinks to do sir be the Rude. / I heir freiris say that reiding dois na gude', 2918-22.

225-26 *My hope...Popis holynes*: Francis I and Pope Paul III promised Beaton support because, as representative of the Francophile party in Scotland, he also preserved the Church's authority. In 1543 France sent financial assistance and arms, but during 1544 France was occupied with wars against imperial and English forces. Limited French forces (less than 5,000) arrived in May 1545 under de Lorges, captain of the Scots Guard, but were defeated by the English; see Sanderson 1986: 200-04.

230 *houre*] P, P(oct), D; *hure* Sc. (*DOST* lists *hure* as a variant of *houre*, but also as a head-word, meaning 'harlot'.)

234 *Sic ane fortres*: St Andrews Castle, in existence in some form from at least the 12th c., was the main residence of the bishops and later archbishops of St Andrews, serving also as a prison for local and state offenders. Mindful of the open Anglo-Scottish conflict after Flodden, and of the growing support for church reform, James Beaton improved its defences to withstand an attack by heavy artillery. This continued under his nephew: a second stone curtain wall was being added on the S. front at the time of the murder (Fawcett 1992: 8-9).

236-38 *the saw quhilk David said*: An allusion to Ps. 127.1: 'Except the Lord build the house, they labour in vain that build it'.

237 *maister of wark* generally was used in secular contexts, but the offical involved could be a cleric; see Paton 1958: xvi-xviii.

240 *doung down...asse*: Ashes were a symbol of penitence (as at Ash Wednesday, the first of Lent, when ashes from the Palm Sunday crosses were placed on the forehead). They were also identified with the shortness of human life; cf. Dunbar, '*Memento homo*' (B32), 2; Job 30.19 and Gen. 3.19. A veiled allusion to the burning of Wishart is also possible.

242 *Bot, as David*: A reference to the biblical heroic battle between the shepherd, David, and Goliath, champion of the Philistines, in which David used a stone sling to fell the well-armed warrior; I Sam. 17. The fictional Beaton's portrayal of himself as mighty and powerful, elaborately costumed and scornful of his opposition, is in pointed parallel to the biblical warrior, even to the now little-known detail that the cardinal latterly wore armour under his robes as he moved about Scotland with his large retinue; Sanderson 1986: 232-34.

243 *Or Holopharne*: The story (in Old Testament Apocrypha) of Judith, a widow in the city of Bethulia, and Holofernes, chief military captain of Nebuchadnezzar, king of Babylonia. When Holofernes cut off Bethulia's water supply rather than begin a long assault on the city, Judith told him that the city might be taken more quickly. Remaining in his camp for three days, each night praying outside, she beheaded Holofernes with his own sword on the fourth night, after he became drunk at a banquet (Jth 13.7). His death demoralised the Babylonian army, which was defeated. Cf. *Ane Dialog*, where Holofernes is called 'Gret oppressour of Israell' (5760).

245 *my chieff cietie*: Beaton refers to St Andrews, which had been a metropolitan see from 1472.

247 *As Lucifer*: The fallen archangel, sometimes identified with Satan. His boast, 'I will exalt my throne above the stars of God' (Isa.14.13), made him a type of the overambitious and proud; cf. Whiting L586, L587.

249 *Be thame quhilk...conspyre*: See 215n.

252 '*In manus Tuas, Domine*': See *Papyngo*, 1144n.

253-59 *Behald...ane hour*: The heightened formality of the stanza, with its alliterative patterns (*faitell infylicitie, papall pompe*); *repetitio* (*My*); and use of superlatives, places it within the long tradition of admonitions on man's mutability, such as Dunbar's *O wreche, be war* (B42).

255 *dreidfull dungioun*: Beaton's fortified castle, afterwards place of the assassination (264); cf. the terms frequently used of Hell; cf. Dunbar, *Off Februar* (B47); *Dreme*, 337; see also *DOST, dungeoun*, 1 and 2.

260 *To the peple*: According to Knox (*History*, I.178), at the news of Beaton's death, a crowd gathered at the castle, demanding proof. The body was brought to the eastern blockhouse and displayed.

261 Cf. Douglas, *Eneados*, VIII, iv.176.

262-64 *Sum said*: The continuing alliterative patterns, and the use of *repetitio* (*sum*) to present the division of opinion, increases the impact of *saltit* (266).

266-69 *Thay saltit...deplore*: The murderers, who had been put to the horn, held the castle in the expectation of the arrival of English support. After some delay the castle was attacked ineffectively by an army under the governor. Beaton's body meanwhile was preserved in a salt-filled chest and, according to Pitscottie (*Historie*, II.84), was buried in a midden for seven months or more before it could be given a church burial. See also Bonner 1996: 596-97. *In ane mydding*: Such a fate was that of criminals and excommunicants.

282-94 *Ambassaldouris...the myre*: The fictional Beaton's choice of secular offices (*herraldis, menstralis, hirdis*) to explain his point to fellow prelates stresses both his own worldliness and that of the church itself.

291 *pronunce*] P, P(oct); *pronounce* D; *pronunc* Sc.

296 *temporall landis*: As high-ranking churchman, Beaton himself had lands in Fife, the Lothians, Kincardineshire and Aberdeenshire and a secular barony in Angus; see *Rentale Sancti Andree* 1913; Sanderson 1986: 131-45.

299-301 *teind cheif...out of use*: The church was entitled to a tenth of the fruits of the parish, but this system was open to abuse; see Mackay 1962: 86; *DOST*, *schef(e*, n^2, sense 1c. Repetition of *teind* exposes the pervasive acquisitiveness of the church; cf. *Thrie Estaitis*, 2002-22, 2822-24; see 317n.

306 *hasarttrie*] Sc, P; *hasartrie* P(oct); *idolatrie* D.

307 *my unprovisit dede*: According to Knox (*History*, I.176-78), Beaton, with a servant, barricaded himself in his bed chamber, but opened his door to the attackers when they threatened to set fire to it. He was murdered by their sword thrusts, and given no time for confession, the slayers leaving him 'without *Requiem æternam*, and *Requiescant in pace*, song for his saule'.

310 *Ye send...to preche*: Cf. *Papyngo* 1032-38; see Donaldson 1960: 9-10; Edington 1993: 22-42.

311 *I mak it...kend*: Apparently innocuous, but sharply satiric in its implication that the prelates did not know what were their proper duties.

315 *byschoppis*] P, P(oct); *bishoppes* D; *byschope* Sc. 'Then will they lack the bishop's favour [if they tell the truth]'; cf. *Thrie Estaitis*, 750-52.

316-18 *royall rent...Testament*: Prelatial fees of office were on a kingly scale; the return for them (the preaching and interpreting of God's word), it is implied, should be of equivalent generosity.

317 *spirituall fude*: Contrast 299-301n. The fictional Beaton asserts that the church fails to provide, in its turn, 'fude' for the salvation of souls, seeking only to accumulate 'threasure' (321).

323-24 *That day...my bak*: Cf. *Thrie Estaitis*, 2924-25. A rite in the episcopal consecration ceremony, symbolising the acceptance of an obligation to go out and preach to those under care; cf. 328-29.

325 *tharein lytill I knew*: Beaton's training had been in civil law; see 51*n*. The admission also could refer ironically to the extent of the cardinal's knowledge of Christian precepts.

336 *ane myter on ane mule*: The mule was proverbially a symbol of obstinacy and stupidity; to give it a 'mitre', or the high ecclesiastic office that the tall, two-pointed headdress of popes, cardinals, and archbishops symbolised, was a mockery. The seemingly innocent query has a double edge: the sight of a bishop riding on a mule was familiar in late medieval Scotland, the sumptuous trappings a frequent subject for attack; cf. Dunbar, *Schir, lat it neuer*, (B66), 74; *Complaynt*, 330-36; *Papyngo*, 1050-52. Erasmus (*Praise of Folly*, 1517) also notes that high-ranking churchmen ignore the symbolism of clerical vestments; see Dolan 1964: 156-57.

337 *sene*] P, P(oct), D; *syne* Sc.

338 *bulrand*] Sc; *bulrande* P, P(oct); *blentheryng* D.

340 *corruptit conswetude*: The church used the argument of established custom to defend its less defensible actions, such as the exaction of excessive mortuary dues; cf. *Thrie Estaitis*, 2789-99.

346 *Ye bene the cause*: A contrast to Boccaccio's and Lydgate's stress on the various forms of Fortune as the agent of destruction. Lyndsay's poem provides a precedent for the greater emphasis in the *Mirror* tragedies on contemporary politico-religious agents as causal.

351 *Quhen ye...officiar*: This sequence had a particular irony for contemporary readers: Beaton employed many merchants and craftsmen also engaged by the crown, among them the royal baker and cordiner. He also employed a French tailor (cf. 358) and a French muleteer; see Sanderson 1986: 135-36; *Rentale Sancti Andree* 1913: 110. The contrast between these well-qualified, handpicked secular officers and the unskilled spirituality is also drawn in *Thrie Estaitis*, 3147-51.

354 *ye wyll gar luke*: 'you will cause [your searcher] look'.

363 *Ga sears*: Cf. *Thrie Estaitis*, 3323-26.

372 *rebaldis*: Cf. Dunbar, *Flyting* (B65), 27.

373 *stuffat*: Cf. Dunbar, *Complane I wald* (B9), 17.

376 *cartis...tabyll*: See 81*n*; the newly-promoted clergy's proficiency in these recreational activities of a noble life stresses their ignorance of the proper skills, those required to minister to a parish.

377 *Rome rakaris*: The compound describes those who, seeking rich ecclesiastical benefices, went (or sent representatives) to Rome to lobby; cf. *Peder Coffeis, Bann. MS*, fol. 162ʳ, 21; see *James V Letters*: 353-55.

378 *calsay paikaris*: Cf. *Thrie Estaitis*, 2202.

379 *flaterraris*] P, P(oct); *flatterars* D; *flattaris*, Sc. *fenyeit flatteraris*: Cf. Dunbar, *Schir, ȝe haue mony seruitouris* (B67), 39.

380 *Most meit...Maye*: A foolish activity, since May (N. hemisphere) is within the period when mussels spawn, and are unfit for eating; cf. *May is the moneth, Bann. MS*, fol. 156ᵛ-157ᵛ, 33.

381 *Of cowhubeis*] Sc, P, P(oct); *To lacke lattins* D. Cf. Dunbar, *In secreit place*, (B25), 58; *Papyngo*, 388-90.

382 *kirk*] Sc, P, P(oct); *churche* D.

384 *doytit*] Sc, P, P(oct); *doughtie* D. *doctoris new cum out of Athenis*:
For the remark's basis, cf. Hay, *Buik of King Alexander the Conquerour*,
398-99, but the reference is scathingly directed at those churchmen highly
educated at continental universities, yet untrained in spiritual guidance and
intelligible preaching. See *OED*, *Greek*, sense 8, 'unintelligible speech'.
(Its earliest citation is 1600, but cf. 385.)

387 *schir Symonis solystatioun*: A personified reference to the practice
of simony (the buying or selling of ecclesiastical preferments, benefices
and emoluments), derived from Simon Magus, the sorcerer (see Acts 8.9);
cf. Chaucer, *ParsT*, *CT*, X (1), 780-84.

389 *throuch prencis supplycatioun*: Beaton was nominated to the
bishopric of Mirepoix in France by Francis I in 1537, and to the
cardinalate and legatine faculty by James V in 1538 (although until 1544
only the former was granted by the Pope).

396 *blynd Alane*: Perhaps proverbial; cf. Whiting, 'Proverbs...
Scottish', but he may have existed; Lyndsay's and Dunbar's (*I maister
Andro Kennedy* (B19), 12) are the only references known.

402 *inoportune*] Sc, P, P(oct); *importune* D. *inoportune askyng*: Cf.
Dunbar, *Schir, ʒe haue mony seruitouris* (B67), 43.

404 *warld*] Sc, P, P(oct); *worldly* D.

409 *In tyll...hure*: 'In the keeping of a promiscuous abbess.'

414-16 *Kyng David...abbayis?*: King of Scots 1124-53, David was the
youngest son of Malcolm III and Margaret, later St Margaret. Her influence
is reflected in his interest in reformed monasticism. He founded many
monasteries (including Holyrood, Jedburgh and Kinloss). At his death,
Glasgow, St Andrews, Dunkeld, Brechin and Aberdeen, and the provinces
of Strathearn, Moray, Ross and Caithness were recognised episcopal sees.

419 *narrowit...boundis*: Cf. *Thrie Estaitis*, 2952-61. David's grants of
land and revenue to the church were afterwards seen as overgenerous, the
cause of the crown's financial difficulties; cf. Bellenden, *Chronicles*, II, bk
xii, ch. xvi.

421 *everyilk*] Sc; *everylk* P, P(oct); *every* D.

430-31 *I man...wend*: Cf. *Duncan Laideus' Testament*, 372-74.

434 *done*] Sc, P, P(oct); *nowe* D.

Squyer Meldrum, c.1550

Text: There was at least one earlier edition of the poem (noted in
bookbinder Robert Gourlaw's 1585 inventory of stock (*Bann. Misc.*,
2.214), but the earliest extant edition, upon which the present text is
based, is that of 1594, by Henry Charteris, Edinburgh, *STC* 15679 (=
Cha). This was collated with the Edinburgh edition of [T. Finlayson for]
Richard Lawson, 1610, *STC* 15680 (= L), the few preferences for which are
noted. Significant variants are also listed. (Many lesser variants are
orthographic: L is more anglicised than Cha, hence Cha's *deidis* becomes
deeds in L (5); *defendit* becomes *defended* (70), *battaill* becomes *battell*
(252)). Both texts are occasionally corrupt, as noted.

Title: From Cha: *The Historie of Ane Nobil and Vailyeand Squyer, William Meldrum, umquhyle Laird of Cleische and Bynnis.*

In the late medieval period the word *Squyer*, from the ML word for an armour bearer, was given to a young man of good birth who attended upon a knight; cf. *OED, squire*, sb, 1a.

Epigraphs: Also on the titlepage is the title of the appended *Testament*, then two classical epigraphs, not entirely accurately reproduced, from Cicero, *Philippic XIV*, xi.30 and Ovid, *Fasti*, II.379-80. Both are on the theme with which Lyndsay opens his poem: the lasting fame of heroic deeds, especially those attempted for the sake of national honour. There is no certainty that the epigraphs appeared in the now-lost authorial manuscript, yet both Cicero ('Tullius') and Ovid were familiar mentors at this time. Cicero was respected as a model of rhetoric (cf. Dunbar, *Goldyn Targe* (B59), 67-72); Ovid, although associated with poetry of love, was also linked to heroic poetry (cf. Douglas, *Pal. Honour*, 1187). Lyndsay likewise may have followed this association. On the other hand, it is plausible that the epigraphs were added by Charteris: the growth in interest in the concept of civic humanism during the mid to late 16th c. provided a sympathetic context for the use of these quotations in later editions (see Williamson 1993; Edington 1994: 208-09; Ringler 1988: 14).

Form: In order to celebrate Meldrum's 'glorie' (42) (as modern chivalric example equal to any from the distant past), and to commemorate with affection the life of a much-admired friend, the exploits of Meldrum are set down as a heroic romance, with the metre, formulae, alliteration, and embedded passages of heightened diction typical of the genre of Barbour's *Bruce* and the *Buik of Alexander*. In this late poem the facts and the generic conventions are used selectively, and with mixed success, but a disarming humour leavens formal passages or otherwise highly conventional scenes.

Date: Lyndsay writes after Meldrum's death (see 1582-86). Meldrum is last mentioned as witness to a charter recording the sale of land by James Spens of Lathalland to Norman, third son of John, Lord Lindsay of the Byres, 25 July 1550, confirmed 31 July 1550 (*RMS*, IV, no. 490).

Metre: For its ease, and fast pace, Lyndsay uses the four-stress couplets of earlier narrative histories; cf. Barbour's *Bruce*.

1 *antique stories*: Cf. *Dreme*, 31-42. The sense of 'storie', in the late medieval period, was close to that of 'history', considered to be a narrative of events, true or presumed to be true; see Morse 1982.

3-6 *Of our...to eschew*: The traditional allusion to 'progenitouris' can be taken in general terms (cf. the use of 'elderris', *Florimond*, 5), but can also be used of particular heroes of old, or of those pertaining specifically to Scotland, as Boece refers to Gathelus and others in his chronicles. Similarly, in his preface to the translation of Boece, Bellenden draws the attention of his dedicatee, James V, to the models these ancestors provide, quoting Cicero: 'He that is ignorant of sik thingis as bene done afoir his tyme, for lak of experience, is bot ane barne', *Chronicles*, I.16.

7-10 *Sic men...present*: A popular theme, often linked, as here at 11-12, to the writer's role as preserver of reputations; cf. Barbour, *Bruce*, I.11-20.

13-21 *preclair conquerouris...douchtie deidis*: The catalogue is carefully ordered. A descending scale of power and social status both introduces the squire at his proper level and places him in illustrious company.

19 *stand in stour*: Cf. *Wallace*, V.64; *Golagros*, 353.

21 *douchtie deidis*: Cf. Barbour, *Bruce*, I.532; *Golagros*, 184.

22 *wounders*] Cha; *wonderouslie* L. *in weirlie*] Cha; *into their* L.

24-26 *As Chauceir...Medea*: Allusions to Chaucer's *Troilus* and *LGW*, 1580-1679. See *Dreme*, 36n.

27 *Cleo*: Lyndsay invokes Clio, muse of history, associated with fame and eloquence; cf. Chaucer (himself following Statius), *Tr*, II.8; 47-49.

28 *Sa Minerve...send*: Minerva, goddess of wisdom; cf. Chaucer, *Tr*, II.1062-03; Douglas, *Pal. Honour*, 199-264.

31-34 *I knaw myself...schaw*: In drawing attention to his own firsthand knowledge, and then to the squire's contribution to the descriptions of events, Lyndsay helps to establish the truth and reliability of his following account. Both were, however, common rhetorical ploys, as were allusions to a supposed source or sources, and to specific authors (cf. Chaucer, *Tr*, II.14-18; Barbour, *Bruce*, IX.580-81; Malory, *Morte Arthur*, XX, 674.37), but the various legal dealings involving Lyndsay and Meldrum prove that they knew each other (see, for instance, *RMS*, III. no. 2529). The blend of the real with literary convention allows Meldrum's history to be both detached from and connected to those of earlier heroic figures; see Riddy 1974: 26-36; Morse 1985: 257-68.

36 *Descryve the deidis and the man*: A plain statement, but with a literary echo of Douglas, *Eneados*, I.1, 'The batalis and the man I wil discrive'.

45 *That his...smure*: Cf. *Wallace*, XII.1434: 'Gret harm, I thocht, his [Wallace's] gud deid suld be smord'; *Papyngo*, 427.

46-60 *Considering...lufe alone*: Like the earlier allusions to *Troilus*, those here (cf. 61-64) to Lancelot's adulterous love of Guinevere, wife of King Arthur, provide a scaffolding on which Lyndsay can introduce and defend Meldrum's love out of wedlock for Marjorie Lawson, widow of the Sir John Haldane killed at Flodden in 1513. Meldrum, Lyndsay asserts, fought for his lady's cause with just as much skill as Lancelot and, in contrast to the latter, had both a just complaint (52) and the love of a woman who was free to give it (59).

55-56 *And durst...the nicht*: The subject, 'he', is understood from 48. The owl, well known as a creature of the dark, was often connected with evil or sin; cf. *Wallace*, XI.146-48.

61-64 *I think...na gude*: This pointed interpolation views Lancelot's story from the moral perspective of the 1550s. It suggests that Lyndsay wanted his audience to compare Meldrum to other great heroes of the romances only so far as the process might add to the squire's stature as similarly valorous and skilled in warfare.

65-88 *Now to...in France*: The description of Meldrum the man follows a traditional ordering and uses the various set topics of *effictio* (of physical appearance) and *notatio* (of character), beginning with Meldrum's ancestry and birth (67-75); the auspicious early start to his career (76-78); his pleasing physical appearance (79-84) and disposition (85-86); and his achievements in military service abroad (87-90); see Morse 1985: 260-61; Kinsley 1959: 75.

69 *nobilnes*] Cha; *nobles* L.

71 *Williame Meldrum*: Born c.1486, Meldrum inherited his estates of Cleish and Binns from his father, Archibald Meldrum, who died c.1508. The beginning of Meldrum's military service in France is dated by his part in the raid of Carrickfergus, en route, in early August 1513. From the events of the poem, Meldrum returned to Scotland in the early months of 1515. (Neither the death of Louis XII, 1 Jan. 1515, nor the accession of Francis I, are mentioned.) Given the reference to spring, Meldrum's leisurely progress home apparently saw him in the vale of Strathearn by May (927); this is perhaps poetic licence, but nothing is known to dispute it. Meldrum was Sheriff-Depute of Fife from 1522 (Dickinson 1928: 226, 234, 255, 259, 265, 269), by which time he was closely associated with the Lyndsays of the Byres. He lived with and served them until his death c.July 1550. (For relevant documents see Hamer 1931-36: III.177-81.)

77-80 *He was...indure*: Cf. Chaucer's portrait of the 'yong squier', *GP*, *CT*, 79-88, or Wallace as a youth, *Wallace*, I.184, 190-92.

78 *his vassalage*: Cf. *Buik of Alexander*, I.2835.

79 *Proportionat weill, of mid stature*: The ideal physique; cf. Hay, *Buik of King Alexander the Conquerour*, 10419-21,'In mydlin way...In all proportioun...Nor hie nor law, nor fatt nor lene alsua'.

90 *kingis...admirall*: James IV's cousin, James Hamilton, second Earl of Arran, commanded the fleet during the expedition to France.

91 *greit navie of Scotland*: Those Scottish ships sent to France in July 1513 were led by James IV's 1000-ton *Michael* (with 300 crew and 1000 soldiers) and about 11 other ships, including the *Margaret, James, Mary,* and *Crown*, with others hired from owner-captains such as Robert and John Barton; see *TA*, IV, App. I (449-504).

95 *Craigfergus*: Carrickfergus, County Antrim, Ireland. It was the port nearest Kintyre, and its castle was principal stronghold of the English in Ulster. For a brief account of the attack, see Pitscottie, *Croniclis*, I.255-56. See also McDiarmid 1971 and Macdougall 1991 (its pl. 2 reproduces a near-contemporary plan of Carrickfergus).

96 *barne nor byre*: A common alliterative collocation; cf. *Golagros*, 32.

102-03 *Savit all wemen...and freiris*: Meldrum is the ideal knight in defending those unable to protect themselves; cf. Hay, *Ordre of Knychthede*, fol. 92ʳ, iii.280-83, fol. 98ᵛ, vii.34; *Wallace*, IX.647-52.

105-30 *Behind...the lave*: A specific scene and young woman, but traditional literary motifs (such as the 'gardyng amiabill'; cf. Douglas, *Pal. Honour*, 7-8, and the portrayal of the lady as 'quhyte as milk'; cf. Henryson, *Thre Deid Pollis*, 25-27).

111 *richt cruell...kene*: A common alliterative formula; cf. *Wallace*, II.58, VII.998; *Golagros*, 846; Stewart, *Croniclis*, 19452.

120 *And tak...wark*: Meldrum is not allowing the men to make off with their spoils (as Hamer 1931-36: III.192). Rather, he orders them to withdraw from all intended deeds, presumably including the maiden's rape and the plundering of her possessions; cf. Henryson, *Annunciation*, 66-67; Dunbar, *To the, O marcifull saluiour* (B83), 6.

121 *Hir kirtill...scarlot reid*: The kirtle was the skirt and bodice worn either as an undergarment or, as in this case, as a gown worn over a petticoat or sark, here, of a rich cloth, red in colour.

122 *on*] L; *of* Cha.

131 *Sanct Fillane*: An appropriate saint for the oaths of these attackers, whether they were Scottish or Irish soldiers. Fillan, whose mother was the Irish St Kentigerna, was included in the calendars and martyrologies of both countries; see *Butler's Lives*, I.120.

133 *Than said...courteslie*: Courtesy was an important aspect of knightly behaviour; cf. Hay, *Ordre of Knychthede*, fol. 102r, vii.420-21; *Clariodus*, I.607.

134-38 *Gude freindis...deir bocht*: The quiet warning of serious intent illustrates Meldrum's previously noted 'hie honour' and, in their response, his opponents' contrasting lack of chivalrous scruples.

138 *deir bocht*: A common (regretful or threatening) warning: cf. Dunbar, *Goldyn Targe* (B59), 135; Kennedy, *Flyting* (B65), 408.

141-43 The attack begins in familiar literary (frequently alliterative) terms; cf. *Golagros*, 680, 711, 758; *Wallace*, VII.310, XI.30, XI.286.

144 *in...thrang*: Cf. Douglas, *Pal. Honour*, 1625, where the expression is used in the description of the Trojan war, in particular of the 'douchtie deidis' (1626) of Achilles, Hector, and Troilus.

147-49 *And hat...him cleif*: Cf. Barbour, *Bruce*, III.137-40; *Buik of Alexander*, I.1489-91. Such feats of strength typified the ideal knight: North 1986: 112-16.

152 *He beit...brand*: Common alliterative associations; cf. *Buik of Alexander*, IV.10254; *Wallace*, II.130; *Golagros*, 626.

154 *darflie dang*: Cf. *Wallace*, V.837; *Golagros*, 711.

156 *Ay till...sunder*: The emphasis again is on Meldrum's heroic martial skills; cf. *Buik of Alexander*, I.3206; IV.9739.

171 *Than kissit he*: Another courteous gesture (as at 178); cf. *Wallace*, VIII.1234-35.

173 *taburne and trumpet blew*: The signal adds dramatic urgency to Meldrum's choice.

179-92 *And said...be glaid*: The exchange blends with the features of the romance world those of contemporary necessity, where prudent alliances were sought by noblewomen of wealth and landed property. The lady recognises in Meldrum's chivalrous behaviour a well-born and suitably doughty match.

182 *fathrris* in Cha has been corrected to *fatheris*; cf. L's *fathers*.

195-96 *Than gaif...ane ring*: The maiden's practical proposal is softened and stylised by a gesture familiar in earlier literature; cf. Chaucer, *Tr*, III.1368; Henryson, *Test. Cresseid*, 582-83. The squire's similar traditional vows follow (207-09) but, as he later admits (*Test. Meldrum*, 224), he was at this time too young and 'insolent' [arrogant] to wish to make a real commitment.

197-98 *I am...into Scotland*:   The remarks follow literary tradition; cf. Chaucer, *LGW*, 1666; *Deploratioun*, 50-56n. (The maiden could not have known that the Scottish fleet would return to Ayr (Aug. 1513) before continuing to France.) The courtly motifs, idealising the rescue, suggest that this incident in Meldrum's early life was retold many times. Yet the various courtly conventions it incorporates are deftly recalled later, to balance those in the encounter with the lady of Gleneagles, and to chart the squire's development as man and chivalric hero.

205 *him*] Cha; *my* L.

205-06 *Suld...my honour*:   A literary, and impetuous, solution, which, again, forms an instructive contrast to the more astute words of the lady of Gleneagles, who seeks first to formalise the arrangement, 967-69; cf. *Aganis mariage of evill wyvis*, *Bann. MS*, fols 263ᵛ-264ʳ, 33-34.

215 *And landit...Brytane*:   The fleet landed at Brest, proceeding to Honfleur, in early Sept. 1513; see Loades 1992: 65. *Brytane* was the French duchy of Brittany, also called Little Britain (*OED*, *Britain*, 2).

233-35 *He was...campioun*:   A traditional, and proverbial, contrast; cf. Whiting L38.

236 *Rampand...lyoun*:   A common simile; cf. Hay, *Ordre of Knychthede*, fol. 93ᵛ, iii.468-70; Stewart, *Croniclis*, 19646-47 ('Syne furiouslie wnto the feild thai fuir, /As rampand lyounis'), but the comparison in the singular suggests also the heraldic lion of the royal Scottish arms, identifying Meldrum as Scotland's champion.

239-40 *No chiftane...liberall*:   Proper behaviour for a prince or leader; cf. Hay, *Ordre of Knychthede*, fol. 100ᵛ, vii.209-22.

243 Cha's *pruift* has been corrected to *pruifit*; cf. L's *proved*.

245-54 *Hary...monie sting*:   To set this new French scene, Lyndsay interrupts the natural sequence of events, returning to June 1513 when Henry VIII, then an ally of the Emperor, invaded France. This shift in time, a device also used later in the poem (the simultaneous armings and apprehensions of Meldrum and his opponent before their joust), is a stratagem also used in earlier heroic works to maintain tension and fast pace; cf. Barbour's endings and beginnings in *Bruce*, III, IV, XV, XVI.

253 *skirmishing*] L; *skirmshing* Cha.

254 *monie sting*:   The *sting* or staff was an established weapon of warfare; see Jackson 1986: 60; cf. Douglas, *Eneados*, III, ix.87-88.

256 *thir novellis*:   At the time the Scottish fleet arrived, France was very hard pressed. Swiss forces had defeated La Tremoïlle's army at Novara in N. Italy; the forces of Henry VIII and the Emperor Maximilian had invaded Picardy and were besieging Thérouanne. On 16 Aug. a French relieving force had been routed at nearby Guinegatte (forced to retreat so urgently that the action became known as 'The Battle of the Spurs'); in Sept. the Swiss had invaded Burgundy and were besieging Dijon; see Knecht 1994: 15-16. Meldrum's instant desire to participate is a sign of his courage.

266 *blew greit boist*:   A common collocation; cf. *Rauf Coilȝear*, 369; *King Hart*, 220.

271 *maister Talbart*:   Hamer (1931-36: III.195) suggests plausibly that this could be Sir Humphrey Talbot, eldest son of the lieutenant of Calais,

Sir Gilbert Talbot. He adds, without giving his source, that Sir Humphrey was called 'the giant'. If so, the depiction of Talbart as an opponent of the fearsome calibre of 'Golias' (312) or 'Gowmakmorne' (317) perhaps has a factual basis, but the knight's encounter with a giant was also a common episode in the medieval romance; cf. *Eger and Gryme*, a work well known in the 16th c., in which Gryme slays the giant, Graysteel; see 1318*n*.

273-74 *And on his bonnet...takinnis of weir*: The bonnet or cap could be worn as protection under a helmet—James IV had one in 1496 (*TA*, I.298)—but here the reference to 'takinnis of weir' suggests that Talbart's was a fashionable bonnet decorated with jewels or Italian-inspired cap badges. Talbart's tokens possibly were spoils of war, or badges appropriate to his martial calling; see Starkey 1991: 59 for contemporary examples. (Medals commemorating specific battles were struck at this time, mostly in Europe, but these, on elaborate chains and straps, were worn as neck pendants.)

276 *for his ladies saik*: Traditional literary knightly behaviour; cf. *Buik of Alexander*, II.1357-74; also in fact; see Keen 1984: 212-16.

280 *hand for hand*: Single combat was dangerous, but its display of the skill of only two could bring the victor the greatest honour and fame; see Barber 1970: 163-64; Keen 1984: 267.

295-96 *I sall...and scheild*: Cf. Dunbar, *Off Februar* (B47), 127-28.

299 *to*] Cha; *sa* L.

304 *aganis sic thre*: The ideal knight of the romances took on contests where the odds were against him, or in which he was outnumbered (cf. Barbour, *Bruce*, VI.128-31; *Wallace*, IV.240-41), but Talbart, boasting of his ability to fight three such as the young Meldrum, emphasises the squire's courage rather than his own.

307 *my barne*: Cf. Hay, *Buik of King Alexander the Conquerour*, 4284 (said by Darius, also unwisely, of Alexander).

311-14 *Young David...the feild*: See *Tragedie*, 242*n*.

316 *stanche thy pryde*: Cf. Douglas, *Eneados*, III, iv.107.

317 *greit, like Gowmakmorne*: A comparison with the hero of Gaelic legend who slew the father of another legendary hero, Finn Mac Coul. There were other allusions to him in Scottish literature; cf. Barbour, *Bruce*, III.67-75; Douglas, *Pal. Honour*, 1715-16; *Hiry hary hubbilschow, Bann. MS*, fol. 118ᵛ-120ʳ, 73.

319 *Montruill*: Montreuil-sur-Mer, S. of Calais.

320 *ten*] Cha; *nine* L.

322 *Baith hors...yeild*: Such forfeitures or ransoms are recorded from the 12th c. on; see Barber 1970: 158, 163, 166.

323-24 *Sa that...quod he*: Meldrum offers, and Talbart accepts, the usual contract between jousters, but its expression here has proverbial echoes (cf. Whiting D274), and an ultimately biblical origin (cf. Luke 6.31).

329 *Lychtlyand...pryde*: Cf. Dunbar, *Tretis* (B3), 328.

335-36 *Quod thay...hardie men*: Cf. 342. The comments by Talbart's compatriots heighten dramatic tension: the very similar lines are almost refrain- or chorus-like; the tone is ambivalent.

343 *Monsour de Obenie*:   Robert Stewart (c.1470-1543), cousin to Francis I; fourth Seigneur d'Aubigny; see Bonner 1997: 1104. He served under his uncle, the distinguished military commander and diplomat Barnard Stewart (third seigneur d'Aubigny until his death in 1508). He became lieutenant in the Scots Guard and Marshal of France (1515). At the time of the joust, d'Aubigny was making his name in the Italian wars.

351 *for the honour of Scotland*:   In the setting of Anglo-French wars, the joust represents not only the testing of one man's skill against another's 'for his ladies saik' (276). Meldrum upholds the 'Auld Alliance' of France and Scotland; cf. *Wallace*, IX.359.

353 *And sen it givis me in my hart*:   Not 'I have a foreboding' (Kinsley 1959: 81), but an action that is wholehearted; cf. Barbour, *Bruce*, XIX.97-98 and 107-10.

354 *Get I ane hors*:   The sense is not that Meldrum did not have a horse (Hamer 1931-36: III.196), but that he saw the reliability of his mount under intense attack as necessary for a victory otherwise assured.

357 *stalwart...stout*:   Cf. the alliterative formula in *Wallace*, VI.156.

365 *And lap...delyverlie*:   Frequent in chivalric verse; cf. Barbour, *Bruce*, II.141-42; *Buik of Alexander*, I.2663.

371 *Wantonlie*:   Cf. 418; see *OED*, *Wantonly*, 1b; Riddy 1974: 31. A consciously lighthearted manner; cf. *Buik of Alexander*, I.83-84.

373 *his cursour wicht*:   A frequent literary collocation; cf. Douglas, *Eneados*, IX, v.105; Stewart, *Croniclis*, 59445; *Test. Meldrum*, 117.

375-90 *His speir...armipotent*:   The formal details of the squire's entry, in which the support of France is stressed (379-81), both balance and form a contrast to the details of Talbart's entry (for instance in the borrowing, as against ownership, of the necessary arms); see 411-13n; cf. *Clariodus*, I.9-43.

378 *heild*] Cha; *hide* L. *Ane quaif of gold*:   See 273-74n. Meldrum's cap of velvet overlain with gold is unusually fine (a sign of French support); the coif was often of mail or leather; cf. *Buik of Alexander*, III.6024-25.

384 *Ane otter...silver feild*:   As was the custom (cf. *Buik of Alexander*, II.4096-98; *Wallace*, IX.236-41), Meldrum bore his arms on his shield as a form of instant identification. The single otter, but not the tincture of the field, is close to Lyndsay's record of the Meldrum of Fyvie arms in his armorial MS (NLS Adv. MS 31.4.3), in which no other Meldrum is recorded (Laing 1822: 111). There, the first and fourth quarters depict a demi-otter, Sable, issuant from a fess wavy Azure. (These arms are impaled with those of Preston.) Talbart's description (403-04) also recalls Lyndsay's MS record, the phrase, 'fra the see' (403) implying an Azure rather than a Silver (Argent) tincture. At 548 and *Testament*, 106-07 (which gives the most precise description heraldically), however, the squire's arms again are differenced by their 'silver feild' from the Lyndsay MS's Meldrum of Fyvie. Later heraldists recorded the Meldrum of Fyvie arms, like those described in the squire's *Testament*, as three otters, again with a silver field. See also Hamer 1931-36: III.197.

385 *His hors was bairdit*: Horse armour, at first simply protective, had become by this time also richly decorative and of a high standard of design and craftsmanship; see Starkey 1991: 43-44.

388 *With sound...clarioun*: The music of outdoor ceremony; cf. 173; *Deploratioun*, 102.

390 *Lyke Mars, the god armipotent*: A familiar epithet for Mars; cf. Chaucer, *KnT, CT*, I (A), 1982, 2441; Dunbar, *Ballade of...Barnard Stewart* (B56), 73; *Test. Meldrum*, 76.

393 *in*] Cha; *on* L.

400 *he*] Cha; *we* L.   *his*] Cha; *this* L.

403-08 *Me thocht...steid*: The use of the dream to reveal both mental and physical states was a familiar device with an ultimately biblical origin (cf. Chaucer, *NPT, CT*; Hay, *Buik of King Alexander the Conquerour*, 17881-88); see Spearing 1976. Talbart's dream increases the dramatic tension—since the squire's arms are known—and it also stylises and elevates the encounter.

407 *bait*] Cha; *beat* L.

411-13 *His fellow...aganis our faith*: This advice, ostensibly spoken to banish Talbart's doubt, recalls Meldrum's earlier, contrasting words, 'My traist is sa in Goddis grace' (355) and foreshadows the outcome; cf. the heralds' traditional cry, 'God shaw the richt!' (448).

414 *your graith*: For details of the knight's dress and personal equipment, see *Buke of the Chess*, fol. 59, 830-37.

419 *baith hardines and fors*: Talbart is drawn as a worthy foe, potentially not lacking in the qualities of the ideal knight; cf. Hay, *Ordre of Knychthede*, fol. 100ʳ, vii.157-162.

424 *Sanct Georges croce*: A red cross on a white background. From the crusades, St George was associated particularly with England. A patron saint of the Order of the Garter (adopted c.1348), George was also patron of soldiers, armourers, and archers. The St George's Cross on Talbart's 'geir' thus made a patriotic and professional statement. Talbart's personal arms, if 'Talbart' may be identified with 'Talbot' and thus relate him to the Earls of Shrewsbury, probably would have included the *talbot*, or dog, (represented heraldically as a mastiff with a hound's head and long, drooping ears): the Talbot crest was originally such a beast; see Brooke-Little 1985: 201; Fox-Davies 1969: 256; Scattergood 1971: 184-86.

437-48 *The heraldis...God schaw the richt*: Several of the heralds' professional duties are mentioned: the designation of the area to become the 'feild' or lists; the ordering and exclusion of the onlookers from entering the lists (437-40); the ritual cry (that God would give the victory to the man with the just cause) to open the combat. Heralds also inspected the arms of opponents to ensure equality and lack of visible flaws; kept careful score sheets of blows; recorded the names, and feats of prowess of participants (Anglo 1961; Anglo 1962); see Jackson 1986: 61-66.

444 Cha's *accownterit* (cf. L's *accountered*) is corrected to *accowterit*; see *DOST, Accouterit*.

451 *sindrie*] Cha; *sunder* L. *thair speiris in sindrie flaw*: Cf. *Buik of Alexander*, II.1225-30; *speiris* is used here to mean lances; cf. *Justing*, 18.

(They were long wooden shafts with iron or steel heads, sometimes painted decoratively.) Each man has shattered his lance and the score is even; see Keen 1985: pl. 53; Wright 1973: pl. 1 (BL Harley 4205, fol. 14); Dürer 1990: 208-09.

461-62 *And straik...fyre*: Cf. 141-42. A familiar literary description of the knight in action; cf. *Buik of Alexander*, IV.8441-42.

464 *aither uther...doun dang*: The score remains even, a shameful position for the experienced Talbart.

471-73 *Our young squyer...without support*: The youthful Meldrum, in no way dishonored by the equal score, is the quicker to recover, his leap (in full armour) onto his horse a knightly feat also mentioned in earlier romances; cf. *Lancelot of the Laik*, 3130-34.

475 *feirelie*] Cha; *fiercelie* L.

476 *his*] L; *hois* Cha.

477 *his*] Cha; *the* L.

479 *Thay bad him wyne*: *Bad*, preterite of *bid*, to ask, command; 'They bade him [take, drink] wine'.

484 *for his ladies saik*: Cf. 276n.

485 *answerit*] Cha; *cryed* L.

486 *be Marie bricht*: Meldrum's choice of the Virgin Mary again draws attention to his faith in God's justice.

492 *greit*] Cha; *stif* L.

492-93 *His speir...grundin steill*: Cf. Douglas, *Eneados*, II, ix.40-41. Meldrum has matched Talbart's change from the blunted weapon of *armes courtois* to the sharpened lance denoting *armes à outrance* ('to the bitter end'); cf. *trencheour*, or cutting edge (539). Such weapons were used only by experts, and for hostile combats; Barber 1970: 165.

493 *gtundin* in Cha is corrected to *grundin*; cf. L's *grunden*.

496 *Quhair...rowme was maid*: Cf. *Clariodus*, V.3006.

504 *Pertlie...preist*: Alliteration stresses and stylises the strenuous effort; cf. *Golagros*, 926-27.

507 *He outterit*: Cf. Pitscottie, *Historie*, I.234: '[They] gat new speiris and recounterit freschlie againe. Bot Schir Patrickis horse wtterit witht him and wald on nowayis reconter his marrow'. See Gillmor 1992: 15.

509-11 *The squyer...dischargit of his speir*: From his place at the western end (as the defender), Meldrum ran his charge successfully.

518 *As brym...beir*: The boar [*bair*] is the usual subject of this simile (cf. Holland, *Howlat*, 775; Hay, *Buik of King Alexander the Conquerour*, 3636), but the spelling here (influenced by the 'speir' rhyme), is that for bear; see *DOST*, *Bere*, *Beir*, n.; Scheibe 1996: 252, 262.

528 *lyke ane crak of thunder*: A familiar simile in battle descriptions, it was proverbial from at least the 13th c.; cf. Whiting T269-71, T276-77.

529 *nane...thair marrow mist*: This took skill and strength; see Anglo 1961: 155-57.

537 *gluifis of plait*: See *Justing*, 58n.

549 *This race...rew*: Talbart regrets not simply the jousting encounter but the whole course of events; cf. *Bagsche*, 17.

556 *cunning*: A solemn covenant (see *DOST*, *cunnand*, n.), a word used frequently in the chivalric histories; cf. *Buik of Alexander*, III.6508-11; Barbour, *Bruce*, III.753-57.

557 *tyne*] Cha; *win* L.

570 *mak*] Cha; *take* L.

577 *bot chance of armes*: The injured Talbart shows generosity in defeat, indicating that he considers the enmity at an end.

588 *And never...Ingland*: The shame of the knight's loss of personal and national honour is stressed, whether or not the basis is factual.

590 *Efter...was tane*: On 7 Aug. 1514, Henry VIII signed two treaties with Louis XII: a formal peace settlement and a marriage alliance between Louis and Henry's sister, Mary; Knecht 1994: 17.

591 *All capitanes...kingis gairdis*: The French king's bodyguard, or Garde Écossaise du Corps du Roi, of 100 men-at-arms and 200 archers, in existence from the early 15th c. Robert Stewart, Sieur d'Aubigny, was its captain, 1512-1543; see Bonner 1996a: 8-9; Bonner 1997: 1086-91.

608 *With hakbut...speir*: Field weapons; see further, Caldwell 1981.

613 *worthie*] Cha; *noble* L.

619-22 *Thair wes, than, ane ambassadour*: The withholding of the lord's name keeps the focus on Meldrum, yet potentially is confusing. The official Scottish ambassador of the time was Andrew Forman, bishop of Moray, but the lord is revealed (at 1381-1400) as the famed knight and acting regent of Scotland (1513-14), Antoine d'Arces, Sieur de la Bastie.

629 *lyke wyld lyounis furious*: A common simile, here without the secondary heraldic sense present at 236; cf. *Wallace*, III.173.

635 *grew*] Cha; *cryed* L.

644 *all the Bynnis*: Meldrum puts the chance to save his fellow Scots before his own estate, presumably his most valued possession.

647 *like ane wyld lyoun*: Cf. 236, 629.

650 *with baner...displayit*: See *Papyngo*, 477n; Meldrum could have displayed either Scotland's saltire or his own arms; see Innes 1978: 20-21; cf. *Wallace*, XI.206-07, 968. See also *Test. Meldrum*, 106n.

654 *That fiftie...duschit*: Cf. Barbour, *Bruce*, XVI.163-65.

657-62 *And stoutlie...dang*: The alliterating sequences quicken the pace; cf. Barbour, *Bruce*, XVI.169-75.

660-61 *his brand...sevin quarter lang*: A fearsome weapon, longer than average at about 1.65m; see Norman 1972: 19 (no. 21).

664 *Ay at ane straik*: Meldrum's feats of strength mark him out as a 'campioun'; see North 1986: 112-16; cf. Barbour, *Bruce*, XIII.139-51; *Wallace*, V.1117-19.

667 *his micht*] Cha; *that sicht* L.

685 *his hie courage*: An attribute necessary to the knight; see North 1986: 120; cf. *Buik of Alexander* I, 3171-73; Hay, *Ordre of Knychthede*, fol. 98ᵛ, vii.1-45.

688 *Bot youth...insolent*: Cf. *Test. Meldrum*, 224.

691-96 *Frenche ladies did for him murne...his richtis*: Cf. Wallace's leavetaking of France, *Wallace*, XII.312-19.

702 *bow*: Possibly crossbows (noted in use in 1540; *TA*, VII.356).

712-13 *And Phoebus...airlie*: See *Dreme*, 421n. A formal literary reference to the sun; cf. *Wallace*, IX.137-38.

715 *Up to the top*: The platform at the head of a ship's masts, used for surveillance and missile attacks; see 751, and *Wallace*, XI.879-80.

721-22 *Inglis artailye...assailye*: The warship's national affiliation and intention are evident as the vessel draws near enough to fire. (England was still at war with France until late 1514; see Loades 1992: 66-67.)

724 *And divers...waillis*: 'Some dealt out blows over the uppermost planking of the ship's starboard (right) side' (cf. 735). This implies that the ship did not have gun ports.

729-35 *The Scottis schip...syde*: The ammunition fired from the fixed guns on the menacingly large man of war, which was much higher in the water, missed the Scottish ship, to land beyond. The latter, being smaller, sat low, and its guns, by contrast, had an easy target.

736 *With...ane slop*: Cf. Barbour, *Bruce*, VIII.179-82.

737 *That monie...thair bakkis*: Cf. Barbour, *Bruce*, XV.508, 'To put yar fayis on bak agayn'.

738-40 *Than...redound*: Cf. Dunbar, *Goldyn Targe* (B59), 238-40.

743 *the gyder straik the shippis*: Editors have glossed *gyder* as steersman or pilot. Rather, *the gyder* is a variant spelling; see *CSD*, *thegither* and *thegidder*; *OED*, *together*, adv., variants list; *MED*, *striken*, v, 1a, '... ~togeder (togederes)...crash or clash together'.

748 *That nane...slidder*: The men rush to the near sides of the vessels to begin the attack, thus causing both ships to list and all feet to slide. Cf. Douglas, *Pal. Honour*, 1776 and *n*.

749 *halbert*: A combined spear and battle-axe on a handle approx. 1.5-2m long.

755 *Ruschand...rude*: Again, the alliteration adds intensity; cf. Barbour, *Bruce*, II.355-59.

762 *tratour tavernar*: An insult in the form of a proverbial allusion; cf. Whiting T49: 'Those are stout and stern at the Tavern that turn their heels when strokes begin'. The alliterative *tratour* adds the trait of falseness to that of cowardice; cf. Dunbar, *In vice most vicius* (B27), 19-20.

772 *rever*] Cha; *river* L. *that rank rever*: Cf. Stewart, *Croniclis*, 1545-46 ('he that is ane traitour or ane theif, Ane rank revar reddie till all mischeif').

776 *slane*: The sense seems to be 'defeated', given following events.

785 *capitane*: The English captain speaks submissively to Meldrum.

787 *My lyfe...mair pryse*: The Englishman, his outlook mercenary, offers Meldrum ransom payments in return for sparing his life and those of his men. He thus provides a striking contrast to the heroic solution Meldrum proposes, when he, in turn, is faced with certain defeat (1261ff).

790 *nobillis of the rois*: English currency of the 15th and 16th c.; a gold coin with the figure of a rose stamped on it and worth about 53s Scots in 1539-40. See Gilbert 1977: 139; Murray 1965: 31.

797-802 *The squyer...hald thair hand*: The generous behaviour fitting to the victor; cf. Wallace and the 'Rede Reffayr', *Wallace*, IX.273-300.

808 *Inglismen wes full*] Cha; *English hoast was* L.

814 *deand men confest*: Confession before death gave hope of salvation; contrast *Bagsche*, 64; *Tragedie*, 251-52.

826-30 *'Fals Fortoun...my brand'*: A traditional outburst (see *Papyngo*, 192-219n), but here used to underline Meldrum's prowess.

832 *bot chance of weir*: Cf. Talbart's magnanimity, 577.

843-44 *I ges...in the Blaknes*: A traditional qualifier (cf. Holland, *Howlat*, 397; *Wallace*, VIII.323), implying that this is information about which Lyndsay is uncertain (and thus also suggesting that the rest is firm fact). If Meldrum did not continue on land from Blackness (a castle, on the S. side of the Firth of Forth, used as a state prison), then his ship must have travelled up the Firth of Tay, from which Meldrum could have journeyed on land across Strathearn (856).

849 *Out throw...fame*: Cf. Barbour, *Bruce*, II.78.

850 *cum hame*: Meldrum is no longer a private citizen but a national hero; cf. *Wallace*, XII.359 (from the enemy's perspective).

856 *Out throw Straitherne...past*: See 843-44n. Meldrum's route recalls Wallace's (*Wallace*, XII.326-30). Strathearn, the Perthshire region SE of Loch Earn, bounded on the S. by the Ochil Hills.

858 *Of ane castell*: Gleneagles, which stood on the hill behind the present Gleneagles House (built in 1624), about 5.2km SW of Auchterarder; see Hamer 1931-36: III.203.

864-65 *Ane lustie ladie...Quhais lord was deid*: See 46-60n.

867-70 *Bot yit...France*: The widowed lady of Gleneagles' role parallels that of the widowed Dido, queen of Carthage, a comparison later made explicitly; cf. Douglas, *Eneados*, I, xi.109-24; see 875-81n.

870 *fortunit*] Cha; *hapned* L.

871-72 *This squyer...Did wesche*: A public ritual of formal dining; cf. Douglas, *Eneados*, I, xi.15-17; see also Caldwell 1982: 94-95.

875-81 Cf. Chaucer, *LGW*, 1150-59; Douglas, *Eneados*, II and III.

885-87 *Of venisoun...geill*: The dishes of a kingly repast; cf. Murray 1965: 36-37 (payments to the servants of those who sent James V 'venasone and aquavite', and 'ane fed bare').

887 *bran*: Cf. *Rauf Coilȝear*, 185. *geill*: Cf. Henryson, *Fables*, 285. Probably the jellied stock made from marrow bones.

890 *This ladie come to his collatioun*: The lady's presence at this more intimate late-evening meal marks her hospitality and perhaps her growing interest in the squire: the collation was linked with amorous dalliance; cf. Henryson, *Test. Cresseid*, 416-21; Dunbar, *Thir ladeis fair* (B74), 13-14.

893-94 *ches and tabill...abill*: These activities were features of the noble life from at least the 12th c. Meldrum's familiarity with them shows his fitness to partner the lady; see *Buke of the Chess*, xcv-cix; Eales 1986. Murray (1941: 58) explains that table games were called so because played with pieces or discs (ML *tabula*) on a board (ML *tabularum*) identical with the modern backgammon board. For an example of the discourse of innuendo that chess games allowed, see *Buik of Alexander* (II.3711-3920); for an illustration of a set of tables, see Caldwell and Marshall 1987: 23.

898-916 *Syne till his bed...na cure*: The description of Meldrum as courtly lover incorporates both literary conventions (noted below) and some more realistic details and stylistic omissions. Although, for instance, Meldrum expresses his attraction to the lady much as Palamon or Troilus do, he does not use their oxymorons ('quike deth', 'swete harm', *Tr*, I.411). Similarly, there is a strong sense of actuality when, with an undisguised eagerness born of physical attraction, he seizes the opportunity provided by the lady. Yet, like Chaucer's portrayal of Criseyde assessing her position before committing herself to Troilus ('It were honour...with swich a lord to deele, For myn estat, and also for his heele', II.705-07), Meldrum and the lady make a practical, if speedy, assessment of the good and difficult aspects of such a liaison, 965-76.

901 *Cupido...dart*: A traditional literary association; see Seznec 1972: 110, 196, 248. Cf. Chaucer, *KnT, CT*, I (A), 1564-65; *Kingis Quair*, 653-63; Dunbar, *Goldyn Targe* (B59), 110-11; *Papyngo*, 124.

903-16 *Sa, all...na cure*: Meldrum's distress as new lover, his complaint to Venus, goddess of love, and his prayerful cogitations, are familiar set pieces; cf. Chaucer, *Tr*, I.358-61, 400-34; *Kingis Quair*, 292-308, 358-64.

906 *makand his mane*: A common expression, denoting something more formal than a passing complaint; cf. *Kingis Quair*, 309; *Wallace* V.238.

908-10 *I was ane fre man...flour of all*: Cf. *Kingis Quair*, 285-87.

911 *God sen*: Cf. Henryson, *Fables*, 556-57.

913-15 *Wald God...serviture*: Cf. Chaucer, *KnT, CT*, I(A), 1227-29.

914 *Or I...mischance*: Cf. *Clariodus*, I.1240.

915 *To be...serviture*: A common literary description of the lover's position; cf. *The bewty of Hir amorus ene, Bann. MS*, fol. 217ᵛ-218ʳ, 17; *To ȝow that is the harbre, Bann. MS*, fol. 218ᵛ, refrain.

918 *hard the squyer*: The overheard lover's complaint was a familiar device; cf. [Lydgate], *In may quhen Flora, (CM)*, 127-40.

924 *lufe for lufe agane*: Proverbial; cf. Whiting L506, 514.

927-33 *This wes...withouttin clok*: The lady's enjoyment of the May morning was a favourite literary set piece; cf. Chaucer, *KnT, CT*, I(A), 1034-55; *Kingis Quair*, 337-43.

935 *Scho slippit in*: Cf. the stealth of the equally self-possessed lady in *Sir Gawain and the Green Knight*, 1183, 1187-88. *Or ever he wist*: A common expression; cf. *King Hart*, 507; *Complaynt*, 255. The handling of a part-similar episode in *Syr Eglamoure* (*CM*), 489-505, forms a striking contrast to the deftly presented love scene here, where factual details are presented, with gentle humour, in an elevated style.

943 *damais*, or damask, a rich silk fabric, often figured, was originally imported from Damascus (later from France, Spain, and Italy), and within the means of only the wealthy.

944 *Hir goldin traissis*: A traditional detail in literary portraits of the courtly lady; cf. Chaucer, *BD*, 855-58; Dunbar, *In May as that Aurora* (B24), 77; *Thrie Estaitis*, 342; see Brewer 1955.

947 *Lyke the...lyre*: A proverbial comparison; cf. Whiting L281 and *In may in a morning, Bann. MS*, fol. 225ᵛ, 14.

948 *Hir hair...wyre*: The lady's *traissis* have been noted (944). This slightly differing, yet still traditional, reference may mark the growing intensity of Meldrum's response as the lady bends over the chest.

Alternatively, since the portrait moves conventionally from the lady's head down to her feet, the allusion is to pubic hair, which, like her breasts (and, in the following line, her legs), is semi-visible; cf. the more reticent Geoffrey de Vinsauf, *Poetria Nova*, 37 (594-96).

952 *Upon the ladie...ane sailye*: The transferred use of the language of military tactics indicates Meldrum's profession, but also, lightly, his trepidation before a rather different 'opponent'.

953 Cha's *Courlyke* is emended to *courtlyke*; cf. *curtlike* in L. *Hir courtlyke kirtill was unlaist*: *Courtlyke* suggests the modishness of the lady's kirtle, being akin, in material or style, to such garments at the royal court (cf. *TA*, VII.114, listing kirtles for court ladies, of red damask, and white silk taffeta; *Meldrum*, 121n.) The bodice of the kirtle was closed by lacing (cf. *TA*, V.230), but here, the unlaced state of the garment is a motif of deliberate enticement; cf. Henryson, *Garmont of Gud Ladeis*, 13-14; Scott, *3e lusty ladyis*, Bann. *MS*, fol. 128^v-129^v, 41-42.

956 *Help me, your man*: A popular expression, depicting the lover as the lady's vassal; cf. Chaucer, *Tr*, I.427; *Kingis Quair*, 435-36.

958 *I am bot deid*: Such expressions were common in late medieval love poetry; cf. Robbins 1955: 138.51; 140.28; 199.38.

961 *And talkit*: Cf. *Freiris of Berwick*, Bann. *MS*, fol. 350^v, 169 (173 in Furrow 1985), 'Than in hett luve thay talkit vderis till [to each other]'.

964 *womanheid*] Cha; *Maidenheid* L. *my womanheid*: Cf. Henryson, *Test. Cresseid*, 88.

966-68 *My lord...dispensatioun*: Lyndsay implies that the pair were too closely related to be permitted to marry (according to canon law), and had to seek papal permission; see Scanlan 1958: 77-78; Ireland 1958: 90-92; Barry 1951: 98-99.

971 *For ye ar...fair*: Cf. Barbour, *Bruce*, I.361-62.

972 *your fatheris air*: Meldrum had inherited the family estate by about 1508: in 1506 he is described as Archibald's Meldrum's 'son and heir apparent' (*RMS*, II, no. 2996). The lady's comment provides an amusing counterbalance to the Carrickfergus maiden's attempt to keep Meldrum by declaring her own status as an heiress (183). Here, it is the lady who considers Meldrum himself in the same way.

977 *thair to yow I geve*] Cha; *thereto I give you* L. L is possibly preferable; cf. 325. The formal betrothal pledge; handfasting.

991 *like wodbind*: Like the climbing, twining plant, honeysuckle; Grigson 1955: 355-56; cf. Chaucer, *Tr*, III.1230-32.

992 *tenderlie...happit*: Cf. *Dreme*, 10, 134.

994 *Judge ye...shed*: Cf. *I saw me thocht*, Bann. *MS*, fol. 143^v-144^r, 7. Here (cf. 998-1000), Lyndsay follows rhetorical tradition, professing an ignorance that is full of innuendo yet seemingly tactful; cf. Chaucer, *Tr*, III.1310-16; *Wallace*, IV.738-40.

995-96 *'Allace!'...dicht hir ene*: The lady's question, 'What may this mene?' matches Meldrum's (907), indicating in familiar terms that she, too, has become love's willing prisoner (cf. *Quhat meneth this*, Bann. *MS*, fols 281^r-283^r; Wyatt, *What meaneth this?*). The very conventionality hints at a lighter undertone, which seems confirmed by the lady's teasing pretence of tears and her manner of wiping them away. The courtly forms are observed, but both parties, not innocents, act as real people, thus continuing the blend of romance and engaging candour.

997-1000: *I can not tell*: See 994n.

999 *her sa as*] Cha; *her as* L.

1001 *Scho rais*: Cf. *In somer quhen flouris, Bann. MS*, fol. 141, 56.

1002-04 *And on...rich rubie*: The exchange of rings affirmed the betrothal promises in both legal practice and literature (notably in Chaucer, *Tr*, III.1368). In literary examples, moreover, the ruby ring was a common gift from the lover (cf. Henryson, *Test. Cresseid*, 582-83; *Thrie Estaitis*, 426). Presumably, Meldrum had in his possession the ruby ring given to him by the Carrickfergus maiden (196). If he used it again here, then the gesture could be taken as an extension of the convention—as a knowing displacement of the youthful, semi-forced promise, with that of a more happily mutual mature commitment.

1008 *sweit as lammer*: *Lammer*, usually glossed as 'amber or perhaps ambergris' (see *DOST, Lammer*, n., 1b), is here possibly the OE plural for 'lambs'; see Bawcutt and Riddy 1987: 397. The context supports the latter reading (as does Hay, *Gouernaunce of Princes*, fol. 127ᵛ, xxxvii.20, 'suete as a lam', *sweit* meaning 'sweet', 'gentle', but perhaps also 'chaste', 'innocent'); cf. Whiting L27-28, L31, L33.

1014-15 *I thocht...quhill none*: The subject, 'it' (the time elapsed), is understood.

1019 *be him...sauld*: An oath to the aptly untrustworthy figure of Judas, who betrayed Jesus to the servants of the high priest, Caiaphas (Mark 14.10-11, 43-46).

1023 *The dew...fleit*: An evasive answer, but in keeping with springtime love; cf. Dunbar, *Goldyn Targe* (B59), 15; *Quhen Merche* (B52), 49.

1041-42 *And sa...his ladie*: Even as he describes it, Lyndsay's reference to 'ane certane time' foreshadows the end of Meldrum's happiness; cf. *Wallace*, VI.49-62.

1043-50 *Sum time...tabill*: Pursuits of a gentleman in time of peace, except football, banned by law for its uselessness as training for war (*APS* II.5, 226; cf Ireland, *Meroure*, fol. 337ᵛ, 14-18, 25-31), but this is qualified by the fact that James IV himself, aged twenty-four, owned footballs (*TA*, I.330); see 893-94n.

1051 *And gif ye...tell*: The opening of a new section of the poem resembles a romance in tone and address; cf. *King Horn*, 1-3.

1054 *the Lennox*: The region of Dumbartonshire and W. Stirlingshire; see McNeill and MacQueen 1996: 206.

1055 *Makfagon*, subsequently *Makfarland* (1097, 1108, 1135) in both Cha and L. This first use is possibly an editorial confusion of Meldrum's opponent with Wallace's Highland enemy, 'Makfadȝan'; *Wallace*, VII. 626; cf. also Dunbar, *Off Februar* (B47), 110. The Macfarlanes were descended from the rulers of the province of Lennox, who had given them the lands of Arrochar on the W. shore of Loch Lomond in the 13th c. Andrew Macfarlane of that Ilk, tenth clan chief, 1513-c.1544 (whose son had been killed at Flodden), opposes Meldrum (Moncrieffe 1982: 138-39).

1057 *Hir castell*: As well as other lands in the Lennox, and a quarter part fishing right to Loch Lomond, Marjorie Lawson owned Boturich ('Boturchis') Castle, granted by Matthew, tenth Earl of Lennox, to the lady's first husband, 29 July 1498 (*RMS*, I, no. 2436).

1066 *all and sum*: A popular tag in verse; cf. Chaucer, *PF*, 650; *Thre Prestis*, *Asloan MS*, fol. 261ʳ, 264.

1069 *it suld...deir sald*: Proverbial; cf. Whiting B42.

1074-75 *And he like Mars...leif*: The classical reference elevates both Meldrum and his task. (By inference, his lady has the status of Venus.) Cf. Chaucer, *Tr*, II.628-32; *Mars*, 75-77, 92-97 (in which, by impermanent astrological conjunction, Venus is his love).

1075-92 *Come to the ladie...command*: The details of Meldrum's leavetaking—the wearing of the lady's glove as favour, the solemn vows to equal Lancelot in his effort to avenge her, and to fight until victory is achieved—recall similar chivalric acts in literature, but were also aspects of actual practice; cf. Barbour, *Bruce*, VIII.488-98; *Buik of Alexander*, I.3202-04; III.7056-65 and Keen 1984: 91, 212-16.

1079 *Lancelot du Laik*: See 46-60*n*. Lancelot's prowess as a knight and his secret love of Guinevere were popular literary subjects from the late 12th c. The Scottish *Lancelot of the Laik*, derived from the Vulgate cycle, was produced in the late 15th c. Lyndsay possibly knew it—see the contemporary *Complaynt of Scotland*, fol. 50ᵛ—but it has survived, incomplete, in only one MS (CUL Kk.1.5); ed. Lupack 1994.

1085 *And raid...the nicht*: On horseback, Meldrum had to skirt the Ochils to reach Dunblane, cross the Forth W. of Stirling (and later possibly other rivers and tributaries), from Kippen veer S. around the end of the Campsie Fells and on to Loch Lomond. The distance would not have been great, c.63km, but the stated length of time is realistic for a journey mostly undertaken at night through hilly terrain.

1093-96 *All the tennentis...flie*: The lady's tenants swore a bond of manrent, whereby they undertook to warn their lord, offer him the best possible counsel, to 'ride and gang' with him in peace or war, and to take his part (Wormald 1985: 52-75). That they were willing to give allegiance to Meldrum implies that his position in the lady's household, or his kinship to her, had been recognised and approved.

1097 *wicht and bauld*: A verse tag; cf. *Buik of Alexander*, IV.8437-38.

1103-04 *And swoir...lyfis end*: Like Meldrum's previous encounters, this clash with Macfarlane portrays Meldrum's opponent as a worthy foe.

1106 *his baner*] Cha; *his braid baner* L. *baner bricht displayit*: A common alliterative expression, denoting readiness for battle; see 650*n*.

1107 *With culvering...speir*: The artillery of warfare; cf. 702, 749-50, 1073, 1119.

1121 *And on...laid*: Cf. *Ane Schort Memoriale*, *Asloan MS*, fol. 114ᵛ, 27-28 ('straik him in at the colere and down in the body').

1122 *bikker*: This form of fighting was damaging and wearying, but not full-scale battle; cf. Barbour, *Bruce*, IX.152-60.

1126 *lay the ledderis*: Ladders of hemp or wood were the means by which besiegers entered enemy strongholds; cf. Barbour, *Bruce*, IX.315-19.

1131 *formest of them all*: Cf. 238.

1143 *In fre waird...seisit*: Meldrum's treatment of his opponent is in keeping with the knightly code; cf. Hay, *Law of Armys*, fols 50ᵛ-51ʳ (Stevenson 175-76). Macfarlane was certainly in ward before 21 July 1518 (when the Lords of Council noted the imprisonment of the 'lardis of Bucquhannane and McFerlane' for 'gret misreul maid be thaim in the cuntre', and suggested that thought be given to the lairds' future guidance, so that the west country and the Lennox 'may be putt to peax', *ADCP*, 126.

1152-58 *Judge ye...that art*: Cf. 994n; Chaucer, *Tr*, III.1331-36.

1159-63 *Thus they remainit...of visage*: 'Beleifand' hints at the temporary nature of Meldrum's happiness; cf. *Wallace*, VI.89-92.

1167 *In scarlot fyne, and of hew grene*] Cha; *In scarlot grene and that richt fine* L. *scarlot fyne*: See 121n; *Deploratioun*, 118n. *hew grene*: See *Deploratioun*, 115-16n.

1170 *ane band*: See 1093-96n.

1172 *And not desyring bot thair hartis*: Cf. *Papyngo*, 336n.

1180 *it wes miscuikit*: Cf. Dunbar, *Tretis* (B3), 455.

1183-84 *Of warldlie...end*: Proverbial; cf. Whiting J58, J61, J64; Douglas, *Eneados*, II, Prol. 20-21.

1189 *monie ane stour*: These unspecified conflicts may refer to the armed opposition to Meldrum by the lady's brother, Patrick Lawson, in 1517; see *TA*, V.107-08.

1191 *Ane cruell knicht*: This person is nowhere identified by name. As at 619ff., the suppression keeps the focus on Meldrum, while allowing the factually-based savage attack to be stylised and elevated. The distancing process begins in the lines immediately before, where it is noted in general that Meldrum's happy position as the lady of Gleneagles' lover and lord was challenged on several earlier occasions. The episode now detailed thus becomes another such attack—if much more serious in effects—also rooted in envy of the lovers. Lyndsay shapes the narrative accordingly: although the part played by territorial issues is not ignored (see 1195-96), the chivalric aspects of the encounter are emphasised. The details of the narrative, however, are sufficient to identify the knight as Sir John Stirling of Keir: Lyndsay refers to his murder, probably near Stirling in 1539, at 1496-97, and this is supported by official record (*RSS*, II, no. 4968). In his differing account, Pitscottie (*Historie*, I.299) says that Sir John was acting on behalf of his uncle, Luke Stirling, who later married the lady; but the fact of the marriage may simply have inspired Pitscottie's comment; see further, Hamer 1931-36: III.205.

1206-08 *In ernist...battaill*: Maintaining the knightly virtue of temperance (cf. Hay, *Ordre of Knychthede*, fol. 101ᵛ, vii.333-42), Meldrum deflects evil attempts to destroy him, and offers the just, open and courteously chivalrous alternative of single combat.

1209-10 *The knicht...ay intendit*: The knight's behaviour—ungenerous, proud yet furtive—forms a clear contrast to Meldrum's, cf. Hay, *Ordre of Knychthede*, fol. 93ᵛ, iii.462-65.

1211 *Sa it fell*: Cf. Barbour, *Bruce*, I.587.

1212 *as I hard say*: A common expression; cf. *Colkelbie Sow*, 498.

1224 *the Ferrie*: The crossing over the Firth of Forth at Queensferry, near Edinburgh.

1225 *aucht sum*] Cha; *aucht men* L. *He was bot aucht sum*: Not 'one of eight', but nine including Meldrum; cf. 1255.

1231 *in feir of weir*: A common legal and literary phrase; cf. Dickinson 1928: 231; Douglas, *Eneados*, XII, iv.13.

1245 *It is bot ane*: The lady refers to herself, not Meldrum, as she confirms at 1247, and the knight at 1258.

1254 *his lang twa-handit sword*: Cf. 660-61; these weapons were very popular in 16th c. Lowland Scotland; Caldwell 1979: 24-25.

1258 *ladie bricht*: Cf. Chaucer, *Tr*, III.1485, V.1241, 1247.

1259 *Goddis corce*] Cha; *God's croce* L. *be Goddis corce*, a blasphemous oath, fitting to such a treacherous opponent; cf. *Complaynt*, 237n; 240.

1261 *Be thow ane knicht*: An appeal in chivalric terms, but also in those that might sting his opponent's proud arrogance; cf. 1209.

1262 *shaw the richt*: Cf. 448 and 437-48n.

1267 *for all his land*: Land as property; see *DOST, Land*, n¹, 6.

1270 *fecht or to be deid*: A familiar literary expression; cf. Hay, *Buik of King Alexander the Conquerour*, 3423.

1274 *Syne bowtit...bend*: Cf. 519.

1279 *The squyer...burneist brand*: Cf. 153.

1281 *as sayis the letter*: The source of the written account to which Lyndsay alludes was the OF *Fuerre de Gadres*, stemming from the 12th c. *Roman d'Alexandre*, itself derived from a work by an otherwise unknown writer, Eustache of Kent. A Scots translation of this popular French romance, made in c.1438, formed the first part of *The Buik of Alexander*. The earliest extant text of this work is Alexander Arbuthnet's print of c.1580. Lyndsay possibly saw an earlier print of it, or knew the account in Hay's *Buik of King Alexander the Conquerour*, where it is separately titled (fol. 45ᵛ), *Off the forraye of Gadderis*.

1281-82 *That Gaudefer...no better*: Gaudefeir de Larris, follower of the Duke of Gadres [Gaza], and participant in the attack on a foraging or raiding party associated with King Alexander's siege of Tyre. Lyndsay alludes to Gaudefeir's courageous death defending the Duke's retreat, and the fact that the odds were so clearly against him. Gaudefeir's exploits were well known; cf. Barbour, *Bruce*, III.71-88; *Buik of Alexander*, 2615-3235; Hay, *Buik of King Alexander the Conquerour*, 3652-3928.

1282 *Ferrie*, found in both Cha and L, is probably a textual corruption (not an initial error by Lyndsay, as argued by Hamer 1931-36: III.216), deriving from the fact that the attack on Meldrum, and his heroic defence, occurred near Queensferry—the Firth of Forth crossing called 'the Ferrie' at 1224. By association, the place of Gaudefeir's courageous defence became 'Gadderis Ferrie' at some stage in the poem's textual history. (The word *forray* was in common use in Scotland; see 1281-82n; cf. Barbour, *Bruce*, II.284, 308.) *Ferrie* therefore has been replaced by *Forray*.

1283 *His sword he swappit*: His sword he so struck about; see *OED*, *swap*, v, 1a; cf. Barbour, *Bruce*, VI.231 (the story of Tydeus).

1284 *greit roum maid*: A common expression in battle descriptions; cf. *Buik of Alexander*, I.1547-8.

1293 *He hat...the breis*: Cf. *Wallace*, X.1235; *Rauf Coilȝear*, 858-60. The blow to the temple evidently is dizzying and not simply forceful—the knight falls forward, not back (1294)—and it must be assumed that, even if they began on horseback, the combatants by now are fighting on foot.

1295 *Wer not*: An abbreviated form ('were it not that'), which, by allowing the alternative possibility to stand until the last possible moment, increases the tension; cf. *Justing*, 38. *Thome Giffard*: An otherwise unidentified participant; one of Stirling of Keir's force.

1301 *brim as beiris*: Cf. 518*n*.

1302 *festnit*: Cf. Bellenden's use of the term to describe the penetration of a spear into the body; *Livy*, II, bk 4, ch. ix.8-9 (p.79).

1304 *as forcie campioun*: Cf. *Buik of Alexander*, II.3315-16

1310 *compairit to Tydeus*: Tydeus, the exiled king of Caledon. His heroic exploits to the death during the siege of Thebes were recorded in the 12th c. OF *Roman de Thèbes* and in subsequent French prose redactions, one of which was the basis for Lydgate's *Siege of Thebes* (Pearsall 1970: 151-56). The comparison, specifically with Tydeus' single-handed defence during an ambush by fifty of Eteocles' men, also was made of Bruce; cf. Barbour, *Bruce*, VI.181-293.

1311 *to defend his richtis*: Tydeus in fact is representing Eteocles' brother, Polyneices, exiled king of Thebes, but the rights to which Lyndsay alludes may be simply those of just conditions of combat.

1313 *Rolland with Brandwell*: Roland was nephew and one of the legendary 'douzeperis' of the Emperor Charlemagne. He was hero of the epic, *La Chanson de Roland* (late 11th or early 12th c., ed. and trans. Sayers 1957), in which he dies with Oliver, fighting the Saracens at Roncevaux. Roland's exploits are told in many versions of the OF chronicles, and in many languages beside French, including an episode in the Scottish *Rauf Coilȝear*. 'Durendal' was Roland's sword, 'Brandwell' perhaps a loose translation, made necessary by the metre.

1315 *Gawin aganis Golibras*: Gawain was one of King Arthur's best knights; Golagros a knight who at first refused to acknowledge any overlord, but eventually paid homage to Arthur after Gawain won their lengthy, hard-fought combat. The story's source was Chrétien de Troyes' *Perceval* (early 13th c.), but it was well known in Scotland by Lyndsay's day. An alliterative version in Scots was published by Chepman and Myllar in 1508 and it was also in MS circulation, the title appearing among others in a contents list (alluding to a now missing section) of the Asloan MS; cf. *Thrie Estaitis*, *Cupar Banns*, 240-41, 246-47.

1316 *Nor Olyver with Pharambras*: Charlemagne's knight, Oliver, who answered the Saracen Fierabras' challenge to single combat. Oliver wounded Fierabras almost to the death in a drawn-out battle; Fierabras' resultant request to be baptised as a Christian ultimately ended the conflict. The story derives from the OF *Fierabras* (late 12th c.), but several late ME versions were known, including *Sir Ferumbras*, and *The Sowdane of*

Babylone. The story of Oliver and Ferumbras was known in Scotland from the late 14th c.; cf. Barbour, *Bruce*, III.435-39; *Rauf Coilȝear*, 791-959.

1318 *Sir Gryme aganis Graysteill*: Knightly opponents in the Scottish romance (late 15th c. or earlier), in which Sir Gryme, armed with his magic sword, seeks out the red knight, Graysteill, to avenge the latter's defeat of Sir Eger, Gryme's sworn brother-knight. The fierce fight is eventually won by Gryme; ed. Caldwell 1933. The story was sung at James IV's court in 1497; see *TA*, I.330; *Graysteil*, Dorian, DIS-80141, track 12.

1320 *As onie knicht of the Round Tabill*: 'As any of King Arthur's principal knights'; see *Papyngo*, 634n.

1325 *thay knichtis*: The meaning is unclear. Possibly a reference to all of the knights just cited—in each case the fight was at close quarters—but the vows of the Round Table knights in particular could be the subject; cf. *Golagros*, 734, in which Arthur's knights compare their combats with those of Golagros, 'We sal evin that is od, or end in the pane!'; or Malory, *Quest of the Holy Grail*, XIII, 522.11-22.

1334-36 *Into his...ire asswage*: The knight again shows his shortcomings: contrast Hay, *Ordre of Knychthede*, fol. 101ᵛ, vii.320-23 (advising the knight to control 'the vnresonable passiouns of ire'); cf. Barbour, *Bruce*, VI.155-59 (the ire of Bruce's opponents).

1344-46 Since Meldrum is so heavily outnumbered, the use of a battle tactic requiring silence (1344) and stealth (1345) is just as shaming to the knight as would be the squire's escape he fears.

1347-48 *And hackit...kneis*: Heroism with a significant literary precedent in *Wallace*, I.320-26. Both the tactic and response also figured in several ballads (Hamer 1931-36: III.221).

1355 *swap in swoun*: A common alliterative collocation; cf. Chaucer, *ClT*, *CT*, IV (E), 1099-1100; *Papyngo*, 184.

1360 Cha's *stokks* (L *stocks*) is emended to *stokkis*, cf. *knokkis*, 1359.

1366 *they fled away*: The flight implies that, after all, fear of reprisal prevented the knight from capturing the lady.

1371 *With teiris*: A stark contrast to the tears of playful pleasure at 996.

1373-78 *Allace!...of worthines*: Meldrum is honoured by his lady in a short traditional panegyric; cf. the lament of Alexander's queen: Hay, *Buik of King Alexander the Conquerour*, 18267-97.

1383-84 *Sir Anthonie Darsie...of fame*: Antoine d'Arces, Sieur de la Bastie. He was in Scotland at the time of the battle of Flodden, and in early days afterwards became the representative of the Duke of Albany at the Scottish court (*James V Letters*, 2-3). D'Arces acted as warden and lieutenant of the E. March in late 1516 (*TA*, V.96) and in May 1517, now as a regent's commissioner during Albany's absence, also oversaw the Merse and Lothian. It was at about this time that the attack on Meldrum must have occurred. D'Arces was well known in Scotland for his joust with Lord Hamilton (later Earl of Arran) in 1506 (*TA*, III.xli-xlv, 354), for his part in the tournament of 1508 (*James IV Letters*, 178), as well as for his exploits in the Franco-Italian wars, during which, Lyndsay notes, he was aided by Meldrum's own fighting skills.

1386 *Johne, Duke of Albanie*:   John Stewart (c.1485-1536); see *Dreme*, 946*n*. He was in France at the time of this incident.

1387 *our young king*:   James V, born 10 April 1512.

1393-1406 *Wo is me...ground*:   The lament and eulogy by Meldrum's leader (a renowned military champion) establishes the squire's stature, and the necessity to avenge the act; cf. *Wallace*, XI.566-82.

1397 *Into...Picardy*:   Cf. 610.

1403 *Nocht Hercules*:   See *Dreme*, 37*n*; cf. Chaucer, *MkT*, *CT*, VII.2095-2142; Bellenden, *Proheme of the Cosmographe*, *Chronicles* (?1540), A5ᵛ, v.3; Wells 1975: 22 (82), and Knecht 1994: 441-42.

1405 *ane stound*:   The word conveys Meldrum's courageous readiness within an instant; see *OED*, *stound*, sb¹; cf. *Buik of Alexander*, III.5471-72; Douglas, *Eneados*, II, x.80.

1421 *the tyrane*:   For anecdotal evidence that Stirling of Keir was, if not tyrannous, aggressive and unscrupulous in at least one of his land dealings; see Buchanan of Auchmar 1984: 68.

1422 *to Dumbar*:   Dunbar Castle, used as a prison: *ADCP*, 99, 358.

1423-44 *remainit in presoun*:   Pitscottie (*Historie*, I.299-300) notes that 'the laird of Keir' was caught at Linlithgow, convicted, and imprisoned in Edinburgh castle; extant official records do not refer to this.

1425 L's indentation at this line, not made in Cha, marks a change of scene and has been preferred.

1426 *heynd*] Cha; *kynd* L. *heynd squyar*:   Common in verse; cf. *Golagros*, 126, 'The heynd knight'.

1430 *dule and cair*:   Cf. Barbour, *Bruce*, XX.596.

1444 *He turnit...chirurgiane*:   The change from the active to the more contemplative life had precedents in the romances; see Riddy 1974: 36, where she also notes that Meldrum's social responsibility in later life 'delineates in the contemporary man of affairs the same kind of ideals, in an unheroic mode, as those which sustained knighthood'.

1463 *met never agane*:   On 20 June 1517, the Lords of Council passed an act (unpublished; see Hamer 1931-36: III.205), decreeing (without giving a reason) that the lady 'be put at freedom and have her free will to pas quher scho plesis best', and that neither Meldrum nor her brothers, James and Patrick Lawson, 'mak hir na trouble nor impediment thairintill'.

1465 *For scho...maryit*:   The lady is known to have married Sir John Stirling of Keir's uncle, Luke Stirling (Hamer 1931-36: III.205).

1467-68 *Howbeit...ay present*:   Cf. Chaucer, *Tr*, IV.697-98.

1471 *Penelope for Ulisses*:   See *Deploratioun*, 50-56*n*.

1472 *never mair*] Cha; *no greater* L.

1473 *Nor Cresseid for...Troylus*:   In Chaucer's *Troilus*, Criseyde's distress at separation from Troilus is expressed as a memorable 'heigh compleynte' (IV.743-98, 805). (Meldrum, it is implied, might be compared with 'trew Troylus'. The subsequent lives of the squire and the lady—the one remaining faithful, the other remarrying—seemingly extend and bear out this parallel.)

1475 *it*] L; *is* Cha.

1477-78 *Helene...to Troy*: In myth, Helen, daughter of Zeus and Nemesis (in some versions, Leda), married Menelaus, king of Sparta, but was abducted by Paris, son of king Priam of Troy. The story of the attempt to recover her, was well known (cf. Chaucer, *Tr*, I.57-63), as was, in some versions, Helen's own sorrow at separation from Menelaus (cf. Chaucer, *ProMLT*, *CT*, II (B[1]), 70. Here, cf. 1465, the underlying sense is that the lady's subsequent actions were not wholly within her own control.

1484 *Bot he...sone slane*: In Sept. 1517, the acting regent, Antoine d'Arces, was murdered near Dunbar Castle by Hume of Wedderburn and his company, who were taking revenge for Albany's execution the year before of Alexander, Lord Hume, and his brother.

1486-89 *The quhilk...that crueltie*: The impact of the regent's death is evident in the unusual note of it in the treasurer's accounts (*TA*, V.149). Hume and his associates were charged with treason and forfeited.

1491 *had*] Cha; *sore* L.

1493-94 *Becaus...thair rage*: Cf. *Complaynt*, 127-28.

1497 *This knicht wes slane*: See 1191*n*.

1501-02 *For cruell...crueltie*: Cf. *Dreme*, 1107. Proverbial; cf. Whiting, L250.

1503-05 *For Christ...slane*: The source is Matt. 26.52.

1507-08 *He menis...mercie*: The aside emphasises that the morality and the legality of the swordsman's act are both crucial.

1515-16 *Wald I...uther quair*: Lyndsay points out that his account of Meldrum's early life has been selective, though the order of chosen incidents is clearly chronological; see further, Riddy 1974: 28-29.

1519 *Thair...agit lord*: The Fife location, and the precise reference at 1589 to 'the Struther', seat of the Lindsays of the Byres, identifies this elderly nobleman as Patrick, fourth Lord Lindsay of the Byres, Sheriff of Fife from 1514 (Dickinson 1928: 205), who died in 1526.

1527-28 *Wyse men...companie*: Proverbial; cf. Whiting, 'Proverbs...Scottish', *wise man*, (2).

1533 *cheif merschall*: In a household such as Lord Lindsay's, the chief marshal would superintend all arrangements for banquets and ceremonies; cf. also *King Hart*, 307-08. A more settled existence for the knight, often achieved through advantageous marriage, or, like Meldrum, by acquiring other offices, was a common end to the literary romance; cf. *Gamelyn*, 891-92, 'the king made Gamelyn...Chef justice of all his free forest'.

1535 *ane richt courticiane*: The opposite of the knightly man of arms; cf. Dunbar, *Musing allone* (B33), 21.

1536 *And in the law ane practiciane*: See 71*n*.

1552 Cha's *regaitd* is corrected; cf. L's *regarde*.

1559-60 *the Sonday / Precedand to Aschwednisday*: Quinquagesima, the last Sunday before Lent.

1562 *tairt...flam...frutage*: Meldrum serves delicacies: tarts, with base and cover of dough, filled with a mixture of soft cheese, eggs, and cream (Hodgett and Smith 1972: 27); flawns, or round cakes with similar ingredients, and a selection of spring fruits; cf. Hay, *Gouernaunce of Princis*, fol. 119[v], ch. xxiv.25.

1564 *And Ipocras*: See *Book of Keruynge* (1508), fols A2ᵛ-A3ʳ and Black 1992: 120 for the steps in its production, which included filtering the wine through a bag called 'Hippocrates' sleeve' (cf. 'Ipocras'). The extra effort required to make the wine made it highly prized; cf. Douglas, *Eneados*, I, xi.65-70, where Dido puts 'the rych Ypocras' into a weighty gold cup set with precious stones.

1566 *Lordis and lairdis*: Both terms, having the same root, denoted noblemen. By the mid-15th c. the titles of lords were honorific and personal, rather than territorial; lairds, or lesser nobles, were so by virtue of their landed estates; see Wormald 1986: 187.

1582 *And as...he endit*: Proverbial; cf. Whiting L408.

1585 *mortall dart*: Cf. *Deploratioun*, 15.

1586 *He straik the*] Cha; *Strake this kynd* L.

1588 *the hevin imperiall*: See *Dreme*, 385n; 514n.

1589 *Struther*: See *Meldrum*, 1519n; *Test. Meldrum*, 207.

The Testament of Squyer Meldrum, c.1550

Text: See *Meldrum*, note on 'Text'.

Title: From Cha: *The Testament of the nobill and vailyeand Squyer Williame Meldrum of the Bynnis*. In essential form, the full title follows the beginning of the legal testament, where full name, territorial association(s) and social status commonly were given; cf. *Bann. Misc.* III, 107. See also the title discussion, *Meldrum*.

Form: The poem is a literary testament; see *Papyngo*, note on 'Form'. This example is not satiric, in contrast to Dunbar's *I maister Andro Kennedy* (B19), or the anonymous *Duncan Laideus' Testament*, but its tone is not wholly solemn. Its mixture of the customary legal appointments and requests with those more fanciful is in keeping with the blend of fact and chivalric romance in *Squyer Meldrum*.

Date: The composition date logically is c.1550. Both the narrative poem and the poetic testament must have been written before Lyndsay's own death in 1555. Marjorie Lawson, who died in 1553, is addressed as one still living (230). On the other hand, so, too, is 'Walter Lindesay' (26), although elsewhere he is said to have died in 1546 (Cowan et al 1983: lii), but the evidence is unclear: Sir Walter's resignation from his preceptorship (of Torphichen, property of the Knights of St John) had been anticipated as early as 1540, but Sandilands, his successor, did not take formal possession of Torphichen until the summer of 1550 (Hamer 1931-36: III.227-28; Cowan et al 1983: l-liii). Meldrum himself is last mentioned as a witness to a charter in late July 1550 (*RMS*, IV, no. 490).

Metre: Except for the final stanza, *The Testament* is in the seven-line (*ababbcc*) rhyme royal verse used frequently by Lyndsay. Here, however, after the four-stress couplets of *Squyer Meldrum*, the change marks a fitting increase in formality without loss of all flexibility.

The final, more highly-patterned stanza of eight lines (*ababbcbc*) is used only once elsewhere by Lyndsay (*Ane Dialog*, 'Exclamatioun aganis Idolatrie', 2397-708), but it is not uncommon in late medieval verse: Dunbar used it, for example, in many poems (all with refrains), including *Done is a battell* (B10) and *Blyth Aberdeane* (B8). Hamer (1931-36: III.231) calls the stanza's mix of Scots and Latin 'Macaronic'. The stanza has no elements of burlesque, or of the language jumble often associated with such verse, and only fleetingly recalls the artful bilingualism of Dunbar's *I maister Andro Kennedy* (B19); see Bawcutt 1992: 350-53. Rather, Lyndsay's stanza seems to be quoting lines from the traditional Latin prayer (cf. *Papyngo*, 1144*n*) and, at 246 and 248, offering a simple part-paraphrase of it in Scots (as opposed to a continuous carrying forward of the sense in Scots and Latin; see Greene 1977: lxxxii). Lines 246, 248, 251 and 253 of the stanza (all those without a Latin component) also may be read as a self-contained poem, in the much simpler scheme, *aabb*; similarly, all lines in Latin or part-Latin (247, 249, 250, 252) may also stand as an independent quatrain, with the rhyme scheme, *aaaa*.

1 *Job*: This biblical figure's patience was proverbial; cf. Whiting J45.

4 *That mennis...short*: Cf. Job 7.6 or 9.25: 'Now my days are swifter than a post, they flee away'.

5 *My youth is gane and eild now dois resort*] Cha; *My by past time was spent in weir and sport* L.

5-6 *My youth...ane dreame*: Cf. Job 17.11: 'My days are past'.

6 *time*] Cha; *youth* L.

7 *Yit efter...gude fame*: Cf. *Meldrum*, 7-10.

8 *my*] Cha; *the* L.

12 *With resolute mind*: This follows in general the form of the legal testament, where the word more often found is *hail* [sound] in mind; cf. *Bann. Misc.* III.96. For the many literary precedents, see Perrow 1913; Boffey 1992: 43.

13 *And tak...and kyn*: A frequent element in literary testaments; cf. Hay, *Buik of King Alexander the Conquerour*, 18330; herein 204*n*.

15 *Thrie lordis...executouris*: Meldrum nominates three people to administer his property, again in keeping with legal practice; cf. *Bann. Misc.* III.100; *Selkirk Prot.*, 9, (46).

22 *David, Erll of Craufuird*: Probably an allusion to the ninth earl of Crawford (succeeded 1517; died 1558), son of Walter, of Edzell, who had been killed at Flodden in 1513; see Lindsay 1849: I.192, 196.

23 *Johne, Lord Lindesay*: Grandson of the 'agit lord', Patrick, fourth Lord Lindsay of the Byres (on whom see *Meldrum*, 1519*n*), John succeeded him in 1526; see Lindsay 1849: I.190.

26-28 *Sir Walter Lindesay...vailyeand capitane*: An allusion to Sir Walter's position (as senior Knight of St John in Scotland) as preceptor of Torphichen priory, and to his parts in the siege of Rhodes (1522) and at Solway Moss (1542); see Cowan et al 1983: l-lii. After James V's death, Sir Walter was named, in letters from Mary Queen of Scots to Queen Mary of Hungary, and to the Lord of Veere, as the bearer of the king's insignia of the Golden Fleece, for return to the Emperor. The poet and Lyon King, Sir David, a relative of Sir Walter's, also was commissioned for the task, but it is unknown whether Sir Walter replaced him, or whether both accomplished the task; see *L&P Henry VIII*, XIX, i.434, 435, 436.

31-32 *I leif to God...My spreit*: Cf. the wording of Archbishop Robert Blackadder's (Latin) testament, 1508 (Durkan 1972: 146); Sir David Synclar's 1506 testament (translated 1525), 'I leif and commendis my saule to God Almychte' (*Bann. Misc*, III.107); and that of the literary bequest of Alexander, 'I leave my saull into my Godis handis', Hay, *Buik of King Alexander the Conquerour*, 18341.

36-37 *I yow beseik...my kynrent*: Executors at this time dealt only with movable property.

42 *Without honour...riches*: Proverbial; cf. Whiting H447; R122.

50-52 *First, of my bowellis...be sene*: Cf. the embalming process in Barbour, *Bruce*, XX.295-96, and see Gittings 1984: 166-67.

54 *Of cedar treis, or of cyper*: Fragrant woods, of reddish colour and long lasting. The cypress often was associated with death and mourning (cf. Douglas, *Eneados*, III, i.120-22), the cedar with Christ's majesty (cf. Ezek. 17.22-24; Lydgate, *On Kissing at Verbum Caro Factum Est, Minor Poems*, I, 116.9-10).

55-56 *Anoynt my corps...precious*: Cf. Hay, *Buik of King Alexander the Conquerour*, 18532-34.

57-58 *In twa caissis...Inclois my hart and toung*: The separate burial, and/or bestowal as legacies, of bodily organs is a frequent feature of literary testaments; cf. Barbour, *Bruce*, XX.195-96; *Papyngo*, 1104-05 and 1118-20. In *King Hart* bequests are extended to many bodily parts; 909-10, 915, 925, 928, 953. Cf. contemporary French examples, in which the lover leaves his heart to his mistress; Perrow 1913: 722.

59-60 *My sepulture...tempill of Mars*: Chaucer (*KnT, CT* I (A), 1969, 2050) provides a well known precedent for the allusion to Mars' temple.

64-68 *Mars, Venus...in monie natiounis*: Meldrum's birth date is interpreted astrologically; cf. Dunbar's imaginary horoscope for Barnard Stewart in *Ballade* (B56), 73-78, in which the planets, Mars, Venus and Mercury, also are said to have been in positions of propitious combined influence, with Mars, as Roman god of war and patron of soldiers, dominant among them; cf. *Dreme*, 448. See also *Complaynt*, 7-9n.

72 *the legend of my life*: The term, *legend*, had the primary sense of a story (often biographical or of notable deeds), and probably refers here specifically to *Squyer Meldrum* (cf. Riddy 1974: 28). The word was also used in clerical settings of saints' lives (especially of Jacobus de Voragine's *Legenda aurea*), or of exemplary lives from the scriptures read aloud within divine service. Chaucer's influential uses of *legend* vary, from the traditional (*SNPro, CT*, VIII (G), 25-28), to the mocking (*MilPro, CT*, I, (A), 3136-43). Dunbar, in the widow's misuse of the word to describe her own less-than-saintly life, follows suit (*Tretis* (B3), 504). Here, Lyndsay's *legend* is both story and 'exemplary' life, but also, in its hint that there are more saints outside the church than within, perhaps provides another notable variation; see Strohm 1975-76: 70-72, 161-64.

76 *the god armipotent* A common epithet for Mars; see *Meldrum*, 390n.

79-80 *Till Mercurius...In his tempill:* The allusion to Mercury's temple balances that to Mars' (and later Venus's 'chapel', 153). There is here, however, no precise literary precedent, although there are several part-similar instances (cf. *Colyn Blowbol's Testament*, 132-34, where the corpse is bequeathed to Bacchus, the sepulchre to be contained in his temple). The association of Mercury with eloquence (often also closely allied with poetic ability) is traditional; cf. Henryson, *Test. Cresseid*, 239-45, 252; *Dreme*, 393-98.

92 *My freind, Sir David:* Aside from the call on him as friend, Lyndsay, as an officer of arms, was the appropriate person to organise the funeral of an armigerous person; see Burnett 1986: 474.

95 *To beir my penseil, ane wicht campioun:* Meldrum probably refers to the carrying of the pennon or pennoncel, a small triangular flag, which was not without actual precedents; see Gittings 1984: 171-72.

96 *ane band of Mars his religioun:* In keeping with his vocation, Meldrum requests that soldiers rather than churchmen be placed at the beginning of his funeral procession.

98 *ane thowsand hagbutteris:* This (and the following references to many military followers) perhaps is generous to Meldrum's rank, but is not without foundation: funerals of the nobility were notable public spectacles, with large numbers of ranked mourners in the processions; see Burnett 1986: 474-76.

100 *With speir...brand:* The alliterative grouping associates the procession with the world of the heroic romance, where such terms as 'brand' are frequent; cf. *Buik of Alexander*, I.1714; *Golagros*, 688.

103 *abill]* Cha; *readie* L.

104 *with my standart:* A flag, often swallow-tailed, which probably bore the saltire of Scotland on the hoist (section nearest the staff) and Meldrum's badge on the remainder of the flag (fly); see Innes 1978: 21-23; Campbell n.d.: 12-20.

105 *On bairdit hors:* See *Meldrum*, 385n.

106 *my baner:* The banner was permitted to knights-bannerets and ranks above. This flag, as Meldrum notes, displayed the arms as on the shield; see Innes 1978: 20-21; Campbell n.d.: 8-11.

107 *Of silver...into sabill:* The change to the black background is not alliterative licence, but based on actual practice; see Burnett 1986: 490, 492 and, for illustrations, 496-553; see also *Meldrum*, 384n.

108 *With tabroun...horne:* The instruments of war and of ceremony, often played by heralds; cf. Henryson, *Fables*, 842-44; *Deploratioun*, 102, 136; *Meldrum*, 173, 388, 446-48.

112 *in ordour triumphall:* As a 'triumph', or solemn procession through the city (originally ancient Rome), in celebration of a military victory.

113-14 *My arming...Borne be ane forcie campioun:* The inclusion of Meldrum's accoutrements and the valiant knight as bearer marks the high

formality of the procession; see Gittings 1984: 174. *my gluifis of plait*:
See *Justing*, 58n.

117 *ane jonet...cursour wicht*: The small Spanish horse and the large
powerful war horse were prized; they were, for instance, gifts for James V
from Francis I in 1540: Wood 1923: 55-56. In literary contexts, coursers
often were 'wicht'; cf. *Wallace*, V.825; Douglas, *Eneados*, IX, v.105.

119 *Upon ane speir...coit armour*: A reference to the tabard or coat of
arms, most often associated with heraldic office, but also worn over
conventional armour; cf. Stewart, *Croniclis*, I.19617-20. As here, in
actual funeral processions of the nobility it was borne aloft on a pole:
Innes 1943: 160 and pl. XVIII.3.

120 *my corspresent*: This was a mortuary due, normally paid to the
clergy, which was drawn from the goods of a deceased householder at his
burial. (Its exaction, which caused great hardship to the poor, was
condemned explicitly by Lyndsay (*Thrie Estaitis*, 1973-2000); Meldrum's
offering of this due to the priest of Mars rather than to the parish priest
thus has a satiric edge.)

125 *ane gay garment*: A popular alliterative grouping; cf. Henryson,
Garmont of Gud Ladeis, 37; *Thre Prestis*, 213.

127-28 *Duill weidis...thair ene*: A scene frequently illustrated in
psalters, breviaries and books of hours; see Boase 1972: 111, 114-15.

132 *grene for freshe Venus*: Cf. *Meldrum*, 1167n.

133 *blew for...Mercury*: Mercury's association with the colour blue,
traditionally a symbol of loyalty, possibly alludes to Meldrum's own
constancy in love and in national allegiance; see Saunders 1974: 243,
245, 247-49. The colour was also a symbol of heaven and heavenly love;
cf. *Ane Dialog*, 307n.

138-40 *Ane lawrer...me yeild*: The laurel reference (cf. 112) alludes to an
aspect of the secular (Roman) triumph. The c.1494 treatise, *The Seven
Deeds of Honour* (written in, or possibly translated into Scots, by Adam
Loutfut, Kintyre Pursuivant), notes that the 'murall' crown 'of greyn
lawrye' is awarded to the commander who, 'throu his grett manhed and
cheualrye enteris first apon the wall and fechtis thair befor his fallowis',
and that the crown is 'callit the signe of victory and honour', Houwen
1993: 160.

151 *na priest*: Cf. Dunbar's *I maister Andro Kennedy* (B19), 105.

160 *I will na...'Requiem'*: The 'be hard' of the previous line also serves
this one. The word, *Requiem* (from the L. word for 'rest'), opens the Introit
in the Mass for the Dead.

161 *'Alleluya'*: The song of praise presumably is to Venus.

162 *the evangell and the offertour*: Familiar religious forms again are
given pagan or secular senses: the portion of the gospel or *evangell* which
was read or sung as part of the church service is here, by inference, a poem
or song of love; the *offertour* thus possibly similar to Palamon's to Venus;
Chaucer, *KnT, CT*, I (A), 2251-53.

164-67 *Than to the pulpet...legend of my life*: This follows, and
elaborates upon, real practice, where at this point in ceremonies, the

deceased's 'style' (titles) was solemnly proclaimed by the senior herald; see Gittings 1984: 178.

167 *the legend*: See 72*n*.

175 *than with*] Cha; *see yee* L.

177 *the greit Judgement*: With Death, Heaven, and Hell, Judgement was believed to be one of the four last things, on which day Christ would return from glory to judge both the living and the dead; see Matt. 25.31-46; cf. Dunbar, *To the, O marcifull saluiour* (B83), 62.

181 *Let not...saull knellis*: Meldrum forbids the use of this solemn peal of bells; cf. *Answer*, 40*n*. Such a request is also found in other literary testaments; cf. Dunbar, *I maister Andro Kennedy* (B19), 107-09; *Le Testament du gentil cossoys*, st. 7.

188 *Abone Phebus*: Mars, in the fifth planetary sphere, is above Phebus in the fourth; cf. *Dreme*, 421-57.

190-96 *And syne...feastis funerall*: These were usual practices for funerals of knights; see Mackay 1962: 111; Gittings 1984: 177.

195 *temperall*: The word does not refer to worldly possessions (Kinsley 1959: 119), but has a French derivation; see Cotgrave 1611, '*temporalles*. coat-armors; or Heraulds coats'. Meldrum thus refers to the 'coit armour' (192) already hung up above his tomb.

198 *My epitaphe*: Cf. *Le Testament du gentil cossoys*, st. 15-18.

204ff *Adew*: Meldrum takes formal leave of his friends and relatives in traditional (literary) fashion; cf. *Le Testament du gentil cossoys*, st. 13-14; *Duncan Laideus Testament*, 372-421.

205-09 *My Lord Lindesay...al adew*: On John, fifth Lord, of the Byres, see 23*n*. His *lady* was Helen Stuart (daughter of John, second Earl of Atholl). *Maister Patrik*, the eldest son, became sixth Lord in 1563; *Normand* or Norman, was the third son (the second having died by 1526), and *your sisteris* were Isabel, Janet, Margaret, Marie, Helen, Catherine, and Elizabeth; see Hamer 1931-36: III.230; Edington 1994: 12.

210 *My departing I wait weill ye will rew*] Cha; *And sa fairwel I may not tary now* L.

215-17 *Quhen thir novellis...drerie cheir*: Meldrum's early service in England is noted but undescribed in *Meldrum*, 88.

218-24 *Of Craigfergus...and insolence*: Cf. *Meldrum*, 93-210.

225 *lemant lampis*: A popular alliterative collocation, especially in figurative contexts; cf. Douglas on Hector, *Eneados*, II, v.59.

227 *youth*] Cha; *time* L.

231 *quhom*] Cha; *you* L.

244-45 *Sir curat...sacrament*: Meldrum asks to be anointed with oil and balm, the sacrament of extreme unction.

246-52 *My spreit...wes borne*: See *Papyngo*, 1144*n*; *Prymer*, I, 58 (Psalm 7); I, 60 (leccio iii[a]); I, 66-67 (Psalm 41). Cf. *Duncan Laideus Testament*, 435-39. The stanza's alliterative groups have a thematic bearing: *hartlie* (246) and *hoip* (248) lighten the sombre dignity of the Latin and encapsulate Meldrum's outlook; *spreit* (246), *syn* (250), *saull* (250) and *sapience* (252) point to the obstacle (sin), and the way (learning from God's word) to salvation. See note on 'Metre'.

Ane Dialog betwix Experience and ane Courteour, 1553
(lines 1-684)

Text: The text is based on the first edition, of 1554, probably printed by John Scot (Edinburgh or St Andrews), *STC* 15672 (= S). S was collated with London, Lambeth Palace MS 332, of 1556 (= La). This (being early) is an important but more anglicised text. A few significant variants (noted) may indicate a source separate from that used for S, or that the MS was prepared especially for an English audience; see Hamer 1931-36: IV.233-37. S was also collated with the quarto and octavo 1558 editions thought to be printed in Rouen by Jean Petit or his heirs, *STC* 15673 (= P) and *STC* 15674 (= P(oct)). Both vary little from S and are almost certainly based on the Scottish edition; some small errors in S are corrected therein, but independent errors also appear; see further, Hamer 1931-36: IV.27.

Title: In S, amended, *and ane*] La, P, P(oct); *and an* S: *Ane Dialog betwix Experience and ane Courteour, Of the Miserabyll Estait of the Warld.*

    The poem is also known as the *Monarche*. As a title this is not used in any of the early witnesses; rather, it is derived from the running headlines, thus probably added by the printer; see further, Keiser 1995: 207-26, on the printer's role. The use of the *Monarche* title (by editors of Lyndsay, and some later critics and historians) nevertheless is of note. It reflects less a desire to distinguish Lyndsay's poem from the many other dialogues of the period, than it does a resurgence of interest in the nature of royal authority, in both the 16th and 20th centuries; see Burns 1996; Mason 1998. Lyndsay's use of the term within the text, however, is based on a different understanding of *Monarchie* (or *Monarche*). He and near-contemporaries (cf. Ireland, *Meroure*, fol. 11ʳ, 19-21) closely relate it to the idea of Empire:

> Monarchie bene one terme of Grew,
> As, quhen one province principall
> Had hole power imperiall,
> During thare dominationis,
> Abufe all kyngis and nationis.   (1974-78)

Title-page: Other features of the title-pages of S, P, and P(oct) suggest that *Ane Dialog* was a somewhat controversial publication. In S, both Scot's name and the location of his press at this time were omitted; the ambiguous imprint reads: *And Imprentit at the Conmand and Expensis of Doctor Machabeus, In Copmanhouin*. The reference probably is to Dr John Macalpine, a Scottish Protestant reformer, to whom Melanchthon is thought to have given the Latinised name, 'Macchabæus'; see Bredahl-Petersen 1937: 66-68, Durkan 1959: 388 and 404-11; and see Lucas 1982: 238 on patrons' roles. Macalpine, rector of the University of Copenhagen at the time of Lyndsay's diplomatic mission to Denmark in 1548, possibly met the fellow Scot, though this is not documented (Bredahl-Petersen 1937: 122, 173-76). They had common interests: Macalpine's involvement in the publication of a Danish translation of the Bible may have inspired Lyndsay's work, which draws attention to the need for translations into Scots of 'the bukis necessare / To commoun weill and our salvatioun' (678-79); see Hadley Williams 1992: 101-03.

The imprints of P and P(oct) allude to the financial patronage of 'Maister Sammuel Jascuy, in Paris'. Jascuy's identity has been discussed: Dickson and Edmond 1975: 195 suggest it is a deception; Watry 1992: 25 also implies this. Hamer 1929: 30 argues that the name is an anagram for *Cujas*, but cannot adequately support the thesis. Durkan 1959: 426-27 puts forward the as yet most plausible suggestion, that Jascuy was related to the Dauphiné family of Jacquy, the Genevan refugees and book-sellers.

Title-pages of S, P, and P(oct), though not that of La, also include an excerpt from the New Testament Pauline epistle, Gal. 6.14: *Absit Gloriari Nisi in Cruce Domini nostri Iesu Christi* ['But God forbid that I should glory, save in the cross of our Lord Jesus Christ']. Since Lyndsay was alive at the time S was printed, this biblical epigraph could have been approved, if not chosen by the poet himself. Yet the possibility that this is an independent contribution by Scot cannot be ruled out; the Latin form is surprising in a work focusing on the vernacular, and Galatians is not cited again within a text notable for its biblical references and translations. Too little is known, however, of the printer Scot's religious inclinations. Hamer 1931-36: III.248 states that the epigraph is taken from the motto of the Franciscans, but the association is difficult to verify. Such a link would be in keeping with Lyndsay's earlier approval of the Observant Franciscans, 'the beggyng freris' who continued to preach (cf. *Papyngo*, 1037-38), which theme is taken up again within *Ane Dialog*. (On the Observants in the 16th century: see Galbraith 1984: 27; Lynch 1994: 122; Durkan 1984; Krailsheimer 1963: 11-60; 288-304.) Luther's commentary on Galatians, of which five editions appeared between 1535-46, was known in Scotland, despite import restrictions; see Watt 1935: 35-39.

Form: The dialogue, or conversation between two or more persons, was a form long popular in both prose and poetry; see Burke 1989: 1-12; Cox 1992: 1-21; cf. Rolland, *Seuin Seages*, Prol. 38-43. For its usefulness in argument, and the opportunities it provided for authorial 'detachment', it was favoured by the 16th c. religious and political reformist poets, such as Davidson, in his *Ane Dialog or Mutual talking betuix a Clerk and ane Courteour, Satirical Poems*, I.296-324; see also Lyall 1985: xxiv-xxvi. Lyndsay's *Dialog* is of the student-teacher type, unlike his dramatic and lively 'Commonyng', *Papyngo*, 647-1185. There is little attempt to individualise the speakers. The stress is not on disputation, but on the exposition and explication of a single point of view. The two speakers, 'Courteour' and 'Experience' are fictional stereotypes, their roles delineated by the characterising names. Courteour's questions (such as 'Quhat wes the cause schir...Ydolatrye did so lang indure?', 2191-92, or 'Quhen sall that dreidfull day appeir / Quhilk ye call Jugement?', 5257-58), and Experience's didactic replies, organise and divide the mass of information into suitable portions for private study, or for reading (or singing) aloud, as the contemporary diarist, Melvill, notes (1842: 18-19).

Date: The poem was begun in late 1548: to the inferences drawn from the imprint (see under 'Text') may be added the allusion to the infant Mary's residence in France ('Epistill', 12-13). She had been taken there for safekeeping in Aug. 1548, after Scotland, breaking earlier understandings with England (see 13*n*), had renewed its alliance with France. Similarly, S refers (94-95) to the assistance of France (1548 and 1549) with 'gounnis, galayis [and] uther ordinance'. (The fact that La refers more generally, to 'the gret outtrance / Of innemyis with aufull ordinance', may indicate that the poem was begun at a yet earlier date (see Hamer 1931-36: IV.5-7), but the differences also could be scribal-editorial, or authorial in origin, since La (with its low accession number) possibly was acquired very early by an English owner; see further James 1959; Bill 1966; Pearson 1992: 235.)

  Other details indicate that the poem was completed by 1553. James Hamilton is called 'our prince and protectour' ('Epistill', 26), a reference to his post as regent, which he held from Dec. 1542 until Apr. 1554. At 5286-301 Lyndsay alludes to the scheme of the world's three ages (lasting 6,000 years in total). This was a commonplace of the time, set out, for instance, in the histories of Paulus Orosius (whose work was translated into French by Seyssel) or of Johann Carion (whose *Chronica* was translated into English by Walter Lynne in 1550 (*STC* 4626); on Carion, see Stewart 1972). Lyndsay notes that the periods from the Creation to Abraham, and from Abraham to Christ's incarnation, were each 2,000 years; that 2,000 remain, that 5,553 are 'by gone', with 447 yet to come. This establishes the date at which he writes as late 1553 (or possibly early 1554; see Hamer 1931-36: III.237-38).

Metre: The bulk of the poem is in the 4-stress couplets used for longer narratives; cf. *Buik of Alexander*; *Buke of the Sevyne Sagis*; *Squyer Meldrum*.

  The opening 'Epistill' is in the elaborate 9-line stanza (*aabaabbcc*) of Lyndsay's most courtly manner (as is the closing 'Exhortatioun', 6267-338); see *Papyngo*, note on 'Metre'.

  Ane Dialog's 'Prologe' (118-299) and 'Exclamatioun' on the written use of the native language (538-684) are, by contrast, in the rhyme royal 5-stress stanza (*ababbcc*) frequently used by Lyndsay; see *Dreme*, note on 'Metre'. This form, and the 8-line 5-stress stanza (*ababbcbc*), are used for semi-discrete pieces throughout the work. The metrical changes give concentrated attention to the various themes expounded in the narrative (such as the dangers of idolatry; the world's instability and degeneration; the need for reformation in the lives of Christendom's leaders).

  The metrical changes also distinguish the discursive sections in four-stress couplets. It was lines from these sections that were popular excerptions: the passage on the date of the Last Judgement (*Ane Dialog*, 5254-309) was copied into the protocol book of Alexander Ramsay (SRO GD 83/1092, pp. 23-25), for instance. The ballad by John Barker, *Of the the horyble and wofull destruccion of Ierusalem*, London, Thomas Colwell, 1568 (*STC* 1420), drew on *Ane Dialog*'s narrative of the siege of Jerusalem (3953-4125). Sir Richard Maitland recast the passage on the Creation (685-1122) for his *Ballat of the Creatioun of the Warld* (*Bann. MS*, fols 12^r-14^r). Row 1842: 6 also speaks of the work as one 'wherein many other treatises are conteined'.

Marginal Material: All early witnesses have biblical marginal glosses (those in La begin at 369). Only books, not also verses, of the bible are cited, as was early practice; numbered verses appeared in English bibles in 1557 and 1560 (in the Geneva New Testament and Geneva Bible). In S, P, and P(oct) the names of Experience and Courteour also appear in the margins opposite their speeches. Since the text does not require these markers, it is likely that they are an aid introduced by the printer, an assessment supported by La's lack of them. They therefore have been omitted here.

Sub-heading: *The Epistill*] La; *The Epistil to the Redar* S, P, P(oct), the latter three as running headline.

1-117 The poet's dismissive address to the work was a frequent device in the late-medieval period; cf. Dunbar, *Goldyn Targe* (B59), 271-79; *Papyngo*, 1172-85; see Curtius 1953: 83-85; 411-12. Such addresses were more often envoys, but all early witnesses give Lyndsay's a prefacing position. This is appropriate, since the epistle is also a dedicatory piece, which makes use of the modesty conventions to survey in detail the unstable politico-religious position of contemporary Scotland; see discussion under 'Date' and below. Lyndsay's epistle not only follows the traditional 'inadequacy' precedent, but deliberately adds to it, in that the address includes moral condemnation of those (the *delicat*, 4, *amorous*, 5, *Warldlye*, 7, and *idolatouris*, 105) who will not like the work.

2 *sabyl*: A courtly and heraldic term; cf. *Deploratioun*, 126.

2-3 A reference to the 'colours' (embellishments in style or diction) of rhetoric, but also a hint of the sober nature of the subject, directly announced only at 41 ('Quhow mankynd bene to miserie maid thrall').

7 *Warldlye peple*: Those pre-occupied with the ephemeral things of this world (as opposed to those of the hereafter).

10 *no kyng*: James V died on 14 Dec. 1542. Lyndsay alludes to a frequent practice; cf. Douglas, *Pal. Honour*, 2143-69, 'The Author directis his buik to the richt Nobill and Illuster Prince Iames the Feird King of Scottis'.

12 *our quene...heretour*: Mary, born to James V and Marie de Guise on 8 Dec. 1542, was, strictly, *heretrice* or *heretrix*, *heretour* being the masculine form, used here because of the following rhymes (15, 16).

13 *dwellith in France*: In the autumn of 1547, the Scots had been defeated at Pinkie by a large English army led by the Duke of Somerset (regent during the minority of Edward VI). English forces were again active in the following spring. The Treaty of Haddington, 6 July 1548, which formalised Franco-Scots agreement to the marriage of Mary and the Dauphin, Francis, secured French military assistance. Against this background, Mary was sent to France for greater safety, in Aug. 1548.

15 *tender flour*: An allusion to Mary; such imagery was common in both religious and secular verse; cf. Dunbar, *Hale, sterne superne* (B16), 10.

19 *I nott*: Cf. Douglas, *Pal. Honour*, 382. *thy simpylnes*: Such a term continues the modesty declaration (cf. Dunbar, *Be diuers wyis* (B5), 21-24, where the poet speaks of himself thus), but it also draws attention to the poem's art; cf. Dunbar, *Goldyn Targe* (B59), 272.

20 *cunnyng*] La, P(oct); *cunnyg* S, P.

24 *hes*] La; *wes* S, P, P(oct).

26 *James, our prince*: James Hamilton; see *Tragedie*, 127*n*. As royal heir presumptive he was governor of Scotland during Mary's minority (Dec. 1542-Apr. 1554). In his early administration, Arran concluded peace and marriage treaties with England (1 July 1543), and introduced legislation permitting the reading of the scriptures in the vernacular (Mar. 1543), but these policies were soon undermined; see *Tragedie*, 170*n* and 172*n*.

27 *his brother*: John Hamilton (1512-1571), the illegitimate son of the first Earl of Arran. He was made keeper of the Privy Seal and Treasurer after his brother became governor, as well as bishop of Dunkeld (1546) and archbishop of St Andrews (1547). At first he did not advocate church reform, but Lyndsay's hopes of his sympathy were ultimately well-founded: Hamilton presided over several reforming councils (1549-59) and in 1552 authorised the publication (by John Scot's press) of a concessionary *Catechism*, which did not refer, for example, to the papacy.

28 *prince of preistis*: Hamilton was created papal legate a latere in 1547 at the time he became archbishop of St Andrews.

29 *Efter...recommendatioun*: Cf. *Papyngo*, 235.

30 *Under...the submyt*: 'Prostrate yourself'.

37-38 *To...lordis temporall*: The poem's hoped-for readership is delineated further.

41 An allusion to Gen. 2-3, the temptation of Adam and Eve, and their expulsion from the garden of Eden. *maid thrall*: A common poetic expression; cf. Henryson, *Allone as I went vp and doun*, 38.

43-45 *Beseikand...Christis institutioun*: Advocating a return to the original practices and doctrines of the church and rejection of the later corrupt accretions; cf. *Complaynt*, 413-23; *Papyngo*, 738-1066.

46-90 *And cause...in the fyre*: A well-established view (found, for example, in the popular books of consolation), which argued that tribulations were God's preparation of man for his ultimate receipt of grace; see Gray 1986: 209-21.

48 *thrinfald*] La; *thrynfall* S, P, P(oct).

48-51 *His thrinfald wande...trybulatioun*: The standard medieval view that God, by virtue of the princely authority that the 'wand' or sceptre symbolised, would chastise the disobedient by inflicting war, famine and pestilence upon them. Such threats were very real: war, and the famine it brought, had been constant features of Scottish life since 1542, outbreaks of plague frequent throughout the century; cf. Henryson, *Fables*, 1314-16.

50-52 S, P and P(oct) have biblical marginal glosses near these lines. 'Re.xxiiii.', if it refers to Revelations (which has 22 chapters), is inappropriate, possibly a misprint. 'The.ii.' probably refers to Paul's second epistle to the Thessalonians; cf. 2 Thess. 1.4-5.

54 The marginal reference to 'i.Cor.iii.' is an error for 1 John 3 (as Hamer 1931-36: III.252 points out), wherein verse 5 begins, 'And ye know that he was manifested to take away our sins', cf. *Ane Dialog*, 90.

55 The marginal gloss, Gen. 7 (S, P, P(oct)), refers to God's punishment for earthly wickedness, excepting Noah. The ark, carrying his family and every kind of male and female bird and beast, endures the great rains and ensuing floods; for a lively recounting, see *Ane Dialog*, 1393-1470.

57-59 The Gen. 19 marginal gloss (S, P, P(oct)) is to God's intervention to save Lot and his family from death during the following destruction of Sodom and Gomorrah; see *Dreme*, 684n; *Ane Dialog*, 3391-407.

61-62 The marginal glosses (S, P, and probably P(oct)), which is cropped at the fore-edge) refer to the prophecy of Jerusalem's destruction; cf. *Ane Dialog*, 3826-4125, wherein Lyndsay cites Josephus (3952), as well as biblical sources, for his account. The English poem on the destruction of Jerusalem was well known in Scotland; see Hadley Williams 1990: 160-61. (*Mathew* is the gloss spelling in both S and P.) Jerusalem was *tryumphant* (61) because it received Christ as a hero; cf. Mark 11.8-10.

66 The marginal gloss (S, P, P(oct)) refers to Jer. 15.2; cf. also Jer. 14.11-12.

70 *than*: Cf. Douglas, *Pal. Honour*, 197.

72 *God...his bow*: The image has biblical sources; cf. Ps. 64.7, 'But God shall shoot at them [the wicked] with an arrow', and Ps. 7.12, in which God is pictured with bow 'bent', ready to punish; cf. also Ps. 45.5.

75 *Conforme...Christis institutioun*: 'In conformity to the customs and instructions of Christ'; cf. 43-45n.

77-78 *Causyng Justice...punyssioun*: Allusions to the cardinal virtues were common in advice-to-princes literature; cf. Ireland, *Meroure*, fol. 234ᵛ, 15; *Complaynt*, 379-406. Here, the figure of Justice highlights the role of princes in the correction of present spiritual abuses.

80 *I dout nocht bot*: 'I don't doubt that.'

83-84 *Hes done...offence*: Cf. Heb. 12.6, 'For whom the Lord loveth he chasteneth, and scourgeth every son whom he receiveth'.

85-86 *thay sall...as the propheit sayis*: Possibly a reference to Isa. 52.9, 'Break forth into joy, sing together, ye waste places of Jerusalem: for the Lord hath comforted his people, he hath redeemed Jerusalem'.

88 *Tyll strange pepyll*: An allusion to the biblical narrative of the oppression of the Jews by the Egyptians and Assyrians (cf. Isa. 30-31), but containing a parallel to the contemporary oppression of Scotland by England of the late 1540s and perhaps also to the later presence of the French troops and administrators, who remained in Scotland in the 1550s.

93-94 S, P, and P(oct) all contain the marginal gloss to Ps. 117.

94-95 La reads: 'Than neid thai nocht to dreid the gret outtrance / Of innemyis with aufull ordinance'. (For its possible significance, see previous discussion under 'Date'.) The French had given military aid to Scotland during the English attacks of 1548-49. By early 1550, England had agreed to withdraw (Treaty of Boulogne, 24 Mar.), but the French remained dominant in Scotland (led by the Queen dowager, and the French ambassador, Henry Cleutin), the regent Arran the nominal ruler only.

97 *premyssis* in S, P, P(oct) and La, not *promyssis* as in Hamer 1931-36: II.201.

98 *Displayand Christis banar*: An indication, as in secular contexts, of readiness for battle (cf. *Papyngo*, 477n; *Meldrum*, 650). Lyndsay's precise meaning is unclear. His support for a return to 'Christis institutioun' (45,

75) is tantamount, at the least, to advocating church reform from within.
The 'ennimeis' to which he now refers (99) could thus be those who
oppose this, but Scotland's political position complicated the message,
since those who most strongly opposed such reform, the French, had
provided Scotland with military assistance.

101 *rurall ryme*: Such expressions were part of the modesty declaration;
cf. *Wallace*, XII.1429 ('this rurall dyt').

103 *Of rethorick...quyte*: Cf. Douglas, *Pal. Honour*, 2161.

104 Lyndsay singles out, as the particular opponents of his work, those
who worship the man-made (and thus false) images of the unreformed
church; see also, 2397-708 ('One Exclamatioun aganis idolatrie').

107 *fals Pharisience*: Those pretending to be strict observers of
traditional and written law, with pretensions thereby to possess a superior
sanctity; see Luke 7.36-50; *OED*, *Pharisee*, sb. 1.

109 *the gentyll redar*: See 37-38n; cf. Douglas, *Eneados*, XIII, 'Ane
exclamatioun aganyst detractouris', 43 ('Now salt thou with euery gentill
Scot be kend').

110 *park* is used figuratively, as the 'enclosed land' of the poem.

110-13 *Thocht ornat...feidis*: As in stanza one, Lyndsay extends the
disclaimer of the poem's worth to make a moral, proverbial-sounding
point, strongly recalling Henryson, *Fables*, 1398-1404.

112 *barran*: A word often used in disclaimers of rhetorical skill; cf.
Douglas, *Pal. Honour*, 2164; *Papyngo*, 58.

113 *brutall beistis*: See 110-13n.

123 *houngrye covatyce*: The vice of covetousness (one of the Seven
Deadly Sins) is traditionally associated with insatiable appetites; cf.
Chaucer, *ParsT, CT*, X (1), 336-44; Dunbar, *Off Februar* (B47), 55-66.

125 Accounts of the poet's restless inability to sleep were popular
openings to medieval dream-visions and complaints on Fortune's
variability; cf. Dunbar, *Lucina schynyng* (B29), 1-10; *Dreme*, 64-68.

126 *Maye mornyng*: The spring setting is traditional in verse, often
linked to renewal and to lovers; cf. Chaucer, *Tr*, II.50-58.

127 *malancolye*: See *Dreme*, 158-59n.

128 *Phebus*: Phœbus, the sun; see *Dreme*, 58n and 421n.

130 *Intyll ane park I past*: This setting, removing the speaker from
everyday concerns, was a traditional device; cf. [Lydgate], *In may quhen
Flora*, (*CM*), 42-43; Douglas, *Pal. Honour*, 7.

131-45 *be craft...dame Nature*: Cf. *Dreme*, 84; Dunbar, *Quhen Merche*
(B52), 64-77. The idea of Nature as engenderer (as well as embellisher) is
traditional, its source Alan of Lille's *Complaint of Nature*, Prose 3, 118.

133-201 The courtly style, language and matter of this spring sunrise
had many precedents (see Pearsall and Salter 1973: 229-43; 119-204), but
Lyndsay seems occasionally to allude to Dunbar and Douglas in particular.

134 *holsum herbis*: Cf. Dunbar, *Sweit rois of vertew* (B71), 9.

135 *balmy dew*: Cf. [Lydgate], *In may quhen Flora*, (*CM*), 26-27;
Dunbar, *Goldyn Targe* (B59), 15; Douglas, *Pal. Honour*, 58.

137-38 *Or quhow...fragrant flouris*: Cf. Douglas, *Pal. Honour*, 15, 19;
Bellenden, *Chronicles*, I, bk 5, ch. 13 ('aromatik odouris').

139 *Phebus*: See 128*n*; cf. Douglas, *Eneados*, XII, Prol. 35-43.

140 *orient*: A courtly term, common in verse, for the East; cf. Dunbar, *Goldyn Targe* (B59), 38.

141 *Ascending...throne*: Cf. Douglas, *Eneados*, XII, Prol. 41.

142 *buriall bemes resplendent*: Cf. Dunbar, *Goldyn Targe* (B59), 39, 44.

143 *occident*: The complementary term to 'orient' (140); cf. Douglas, *Eneados*, VII, Prol. 25.

144 'Every living thing'; cf. Hay, *Ordre of Knychthede*, fol. 85ʳ, prologus, 12.

146 *impurpurit vestiment nocturnall*: The dark 'clothing' of the night; cf. Dunbar, *Goldyn Targe* (B59), 7, which has a similar ecclesiastical undertone. Note also at 151, the similarly ambivalent 'habyte'.

146-47 *Quhose*: The subject is not dame Nature but Phœbus. *Matutyne* and other Latinate and poetic terms such as 'vespertyne', 'buriall', and 'impurpurit' (Lyndsay's coinage) were frequent features of courtly verse; see Aitken 1983: 33-38.

150 *palyce vespertyne*: The palace of the evening star, Vesper; cf. Dunbar, *Goldyn Targe* (B59), 2; Douglas, *Eneados*, I, vi.119.

153-56 *Synthea...waxit dirk and paill*: Cynthia, goddess of the moon, traditionally 'hornit' in reference to the two pointed ends of her scimitar shape when waning; cf. Henryson, *Test. Cresseid*, 253-59; Douglas, *Eneados*, III, Prol. 1-4; *Complaynt of Scotland*, fol. 43ᵛ.

154 *lede ane lawar saill*: 'Showed herself less prominently'. (The moon was believed to be one of the planets; cf. *Dreme*, 386-92.)

155 *soverane lorde*: Phoebus, the sun.

158-64 *So did Venus...on the nycht*: The planets, here seen as stars; cf. Douglas, *Eneados*, XII, Prol. 4-12 (referring to the fading of Venus, Mars, Saturn and Jupiter).

160-66 P(oct) omits this stanza.

160 *auld intoxicat Saturne*: Cf. *Dreme*, 480-81*n*.

162 *no sudgeourne*: Cf. *Dreme*, 456, 470.

164 *Quhilk...on the nycht*: A collocation that links Saturn to the devil and ill-omen associated with night creatures such as the owl and the bat; cf. *Wallace*, XI, 145-48; *Papyngo*, 1092-98.

165 *Pole Artick*: The Pole Star (*Polaris*), of the constellation, Ursa Minor, found close to the northern celestial Pole; cf. Douglas, *Pal. Honour*, 1844; *Complaynt of Scotland*, fol. 39ʳ. *Ursis*, or Ursa Major (the Great Bear), a seven-star constellation close to the Pole Star; cf. Douglas, *Eneados*, XIII, Prol. 67.

166 *septemtrionall*: See *Papyngo*, 751*n*.

167 *quhilks*] S, P, P(oct); *quhilkis* La.

167-68 *Tyll errand...stromye nycht*: Douglas, *Eneados*, III, Prol. 4-5, refers to the moon as reverenced by 'Schipmen and pilgrymys'.

169 *thare frostie circle*: The Arctic Circle; cf. *Complaynt of Scotland*, fol. 40ᵛ.

170-73 The disappearance of the stars during the hours of daylight is reinterpreted here as an act of reverential homage to the sun's power, paralleling the (incorrect) reason given at 155 for the moon's weakened light. Courteour's words foreshadow the passing of a whole day spent in conversation with Experience.

171 *reflex of Phebus bemes*: Light and its effects are described frequently in late medieval courtly verse; cf. Douglas, *Eneados*, XII, Prol. 61-62; Dunbar, *Goldyn Targe* (B59), 32-33.

173 *hemispeir*] S, P, P(oct); *hevin speir* La.

174 *sycht*] S, P, P(oct); *thing* La.

176 *his fyrie chariot*: The 'goldin cairt' or 'fyrie chariot' of Phoebus, drawn by four horses, was a commonplace deriving in part from Ovid's *Metamorphoses* (ii.153-54); see Fox 1981: 357; cf. Henryson, *Test. Cresseid*, 204-10; *Dreme*, 437-38.

177 *nocht*] La; *notht* S, P, P(oct).

179-81 *fresche Flora...hevinlie hewis*: A traditional image; cf. Chaucer, *LGW*, F. 171-74; Dunbar, *Goldyn Targe* (B59), 40-42, 48; Douglas, *Pal. Honour*, 10-12.

181 *Depaynt*: A term used only in verse; cf. Dunbar, *Goldyn Targe* (B59), 65-66; Douglas, *Pal. Honour*, 8; *Intill ane morning, Maitl. Quarto MS*, no. lxix.9.

183 *blomes breckand*: Cf. Henryson, *Fables*, 1339.

185 Neptune (god of the sea and all water), and Aeolus (god of winds), possessed powers potentially harmful to nature; in late medieval Scottish verse, mention of their absence or abeyance denoted fair prospects; cf. Dunbar, *Quhen Merche* (B52), 64-68; Douglas, *Pal. Honour*, 49-52; *Eneados*, XII, Prol. 73; *Papyngo*, 113-17, 126.

186-201 The emphasis on echoing bird song and the inclusion of a particularised catalogue of birds were common features of late medieval verse, often placed within May-morning descriptions; cf. Chaucer, *PF*, 190-91, 323-64; Holland, *Howlat* (in which the catalogued birds take the principal roles); Douglas, *Eneados*, XII, Prol. 234-66. An early source was Alan of Lille, *Complaint of Nature*, Prose 1, 86-94.

188 *plesand pown*: Cf. *Papyngo*, 728n.

189-90 *myrthfull maves...lustye lark*: See *Papyngo*, 731n, 732n.

192 *gay goldspink*: Cf. *Papyngo*, 731n. *merll*: Cf. *Papyngo*, 725n.

193 *The noyis...nychtingalis*: Cf. Dunbar, *In May as that Aurora* (B24), 25-26, 'Nevir suetar noys...Na maid this mirry gentill nychtingaill'.

194 *Redundit*: See 186-201n; cf. also [Lydgate], *In may quhen Flora*, (*CM*), 45-46.

197 *To saluss Nature*: Cf. Dunbar, *In May as that Aurora* (B24), 17-18.

198 In early verse the term *gasing* was used perjoratively; cf. Chaucer, *ClT*, *CT*, IV (E), 1003-05. *halflingis in ane trance*: Cf. Dunbar, *Quhen Merche* (B52), 187; Douglas, *Pal. Honour*, 1870-72.

201 *Throuch repercussioun...sang*: The repetition (cf. 186-87, 193-94) perhaps enacts the idea of the reverberating sound. The term was also used by Douglas, *Pal. Honour*, 25 and, later, Montgomerie, *Cherrie and the Slae*, 89. *suggurit sang*: Cf. Lydgate, *Churl and the Bird, Minor Poems*, II.71-75, but the words often described the highest rhetorical skills; cf. Douglas, *Pal. Honour*, 406; Dunbar, *Goldyn Targe* (B59), 263-64.

202 *I lose my tyme*: An abrupt change of mood, but not of the style, which continues to be courtly (note the alliterative patterning, the modesty formula, and the attention to proper decorum (210)). Lyndsay's dismissal on Christian grounds of an invocation to the Muses (via a lengthy catalogue of them) is traditional; see Curtius 1953: 232-46. His immediate inspiration possibly was Douglas, *Eneados*, X, Prol. 151-60; see also *Eneados*, VI, Prol. and Bawcutt 1976: 69-78.

204 *my raggit...vers*: Cf. Douglas, *Pal. Honour*, 2150-51 ('this Roustie rurall Rebaldrie').

206-09 *Consydering...vaill of sorrow*: The stated purpose of the poem is lamentation, but Lyndsay's rejection of 'Mater without edificatioun' (205) and his earlier summary of his poem's subject (41-43) imply that he wishes also to offer moral and / or religious instruction.

210 *Bot sad sentence...indyte*: Cf. Henryson, *Fables*, 1099-1103. The word *sad* had a moral undertone (as 'steadfast', 'constant') for Chaucer and later poets; see *OED*, *sad*, a. and adv., sense 2. For his sense of decorum (of the aptness of style for subject), cf. Henryson, *Test. Cresseid*, 1-2.

211 *termes brycht*: An allusion to the kind of aureate language and idealising imagery that Dunbar's *Goldyn Targe* exemplifies.

213 *roustye termes*: Cf. 101, 110 and 204.

214 *With sorrowful seychis*: Cf. Henryson, *Test. Cresseid*, 450; *Papyngo*, 1140. *from the splene*: See *Papyngo*, 112n.

215 *And bitter...myne eine*: Cf. Dunbar, *To the, O marcifull saluiour* (B83), 15; *Papyngo*, 186.

217 *Minerva*: Roman goddess of wisdom; see *Meldrum*, 28n. *Melpominee*: Melpomene, muse of tragedy; cf. Douglas, *Pal. Honour*, 860-61. Lyndsay adds further ornamentation to his rejection of the muses here; cf. 219, 221 and 222, by his alliterative groupings.

219 *Cleo*: Clio, muse of history; see *Meldrum*, 27n. *Caliopee*: Calliope, muse of epic poetry; cf. Douglas, *Pal. Honour*, 871-79.

221 *Proserpyne*: Proserpina, queen of the underworld, wife of Pluto; see also *Papyngo*, 1133n. *Apollo*: Classical god of the sun; cf. Dunbar, *Goldyn Targe* (B59), 75.

222 *Euterp*: Euterpe, muse of music and lyric poetry; cf. Douglas, *Pal. Honour*, 856-57. *Jupiter, and Juno*: Chief and most benign god of the heavens (Jove, Zeus), and his wife (Hera), goddess of women; cf. *Dreme*, 458-72 (Jupiter); *Papyngo*, 134-35.

223 *plesand poetis*: Classical writers, and those for whom the use of agreeable words and sounds was important; cf. Kennedy, *Closter of crist*, *Asloan MS*, fol. 302^r, 29 ('plesand pennis'); *Papyngo*, 239.

224-33 *I am nocht...no reverence*: Lyndsay uses the modesty formula to draw attention to his different poetic purpose.

226 *Pernaso*: Mt Parnassus, sacred to the muses; contrast the invocation of Chaucer, *HF*, 520-22.

228 *Ennius*: Quintus Ennius (239-169 BC), the Roman playwright and epic poet of the *Annales* (of Rome's history), who was highly regarded by Virgil and Cicero.

229 *Hysiodus*: Hesiod, c.8th c. BC, the Greek author of the *Theogony* (a history of the Greek deities), and *Works and Days* (a poem of moral counsel).

231 *Hylicon*: Helicon, the highest mountain of the range in W. Boetia, NW of Athens, but Lyndsay follows earlier poets in describing it as a well or spring; cf. Chaucer, *HF*, 522 and Douglas, *Pal. Honour*, 840.

237 *Rhammusia*: Nemesis, goddess of fate and retribution.

244-50 There is an appropriate marginal gloss, near the beginning of the stanza in S, P, and P(oct), to the creation of the world.

245 *all*] S, P, P(oct); *om.* La. *ornamentis* is used in a figurative sense; cf. *Ze rychteous reioyis, Gude and Godlie Ballatis*, 93, [15-16].

246 *And...of nocht*: Cf. *Thrie Estaitis*, 3456. The marginal gloss (S, P, P(oct)), alluding to 249, derives from the Vulgate's 'Regum' or 'Kings', hence is 1 Kings 3.12; see Hamer 1931-36: III.260-61; cf. *Tyndale's Old Testament*, 460 ('The Third Book of the Kings after the reckoning of the Latinists, which after the Hebrews is called, the first of the Kings').

247 *Hell in myd centir*: Cf. *Dreme*, 162-63.

248 The marginal gloss (S, P, P(oct)) alludes especially to Ps. 89.19-37, 49 (the references to David).

249 *Salomone*: Solomon, king of Israel after his father, David; see *Papyngo*, 2n and *Ane Dialog*, 667-68.

250 *Sampsone*: Samson; see *Papyngo*, 481n.

251ff The marginal gloss (S, P, and P(oct)) alludes to Judg. 13.24, noting the birth of Samson to Manoah and his previously barren wife. The following gloss (S, P, P(oct)) refers to Matt. 4.18-20, in which Peter and his brother, Andrew, are called away from their livelihood as fishermen to become disciples. The third gloss (S, P, P(oct)), is to Acts 9, which describes Saul's conversion and baptism as Paul. See also below, 253n.

253 *Paule*: See *Dreme*, 597n; cf. *Papyngo*, 832, *Ane Dialog*, 629.

258 The marginal gloss (S, P, P(oct)) at the stanza's beginning refers to the birth of John to Zacharias and the previously barren Elisabeth, and the conception of Jesus to Joseph and Elisabeth's cousin, Mary, a virgin.

258-64 *Beseikand...our salvatioun*: These were orthodoxies frequently expressed (within, for instance, the twelve articles of truth); cf. Ireland, *Of penance, Asloan MS*, fol. 38^v, 7-11; Dunbar, *To the, O marcifull saluiour* (B83), 59-60.

261 *the prophicie*: The birth, death, and resurrection of Christ.

262 *humyll and mansweit*: A common collocation; cf. Stewart, *Croniclis*, 55876; *Quhen tayis bank, Bann. MS*, fol. 229, 81.

263 *Pylate*: Pontius Pilate; see *Dreme*, 258n. The marginal gloss (S, P, P(oct)) alludes to the narrative of Christ's crucifixion, death, and burial, Luke 23.

264 *the croce*: The Latin cross (with a longer upright than crossbar) to which Christ was nailed. It had long been a symbol of Christ and the Christian religion, atonement, and salvation.

266 *bandis...Balyall*: Literally, 'bonds of worthlessness, destruction'; by the 16th c., however, *Balyall* was understood as an alternative name for the Devil; cf. 2 Cor. 6.15.

267 The subject ('it') is Christ's death and resurrection.

268-71 In paraphrase, Christ's suffering and triumph over death have enabled man to achieve the joy 'imperiall' of heavenly salvation; cf. *Dreme*, 514 ('the hevin impyre'); 516-81.

271 The text suggests that the marginal gloss (S, P, P(oct)) is Hebr. 9.12, 'Neither by the blood of goats and calves, but by his own blood he [Christ] entered in once into the holy place, having obtained eternal redemption for us'.

274 *Mont Calvare*: Mt Calvary (L. *Golgotha*), where Jesus was crucified. *straucht waye*: Cf. Dunbar, *Hale, sterne superne* (B16), 35, and *Quhat is this lyfe bot ane straucht way to deid* (B51).

275-78 *To gett...his syde*: The image of the springs of Helicon as source of poetic inspiration is transformed, transferred to Calvary, where the 'fontane' becomes the blood issuing from Christ's crucifixion wound, result of the spear-thrust of the centurion, Longinus; cf. Chaucer, *ABC*, 163-64 (his source Jacobus de Voragine's *Legenda aurea*, ch. 47). John 19, the marginal gloss in S, P, P(oct), does not name Longinus, referring simply to 'one of the soldiers' (19.34).

281 *As christall...with blude*: An allusion to John 19.34 ('forthwith came there out [of his side] blood and water)', and also to symbols of the major sacraments, baptism and the eucharist.

282 *Quhose sound...dinnis*: The image of a strange and powerful torrent is allied to the idea that all other 'hevinnis', however high, are subject to the ringing sounds of God's.

291 *may*] S, P, P(oct); *can* La.

291-92 *But quhose support...nor thocht*: Lyndsay stresses the central importance of God's support, but does not appear to endorse the view held by some reformers that penance and good works are unnecessary; see 470-79*n*.

295-96 The marginal gloss (S, P, P(oct)) directs the reader to John 2.1-11, of the wedding in Cana of Galilee attended by Mary, Jesus and his disciples, at which Jesus miraculously turned the water into good wine.

Subheading: *Prologe*] P; *Prolog*, La, P(oct); *Ploge* S.

Running headline: *om.*] La; *The First Buke of the Monarche*, S, P, P(oct).

300 *Into*] La, P(oct); *Imto* S, P. *that park*: An allusion to line 130.

301-09 *One ageit...was rejosit*: A figure of authority who imparts advice was a frequent feature of the *chanson d'aventure* and the dream vision (see Spearing 1976: 10-11). Details of his physical appearance mark this man as a possessor of spiritual wisdom (see below).

302 *quarteris*] La; *quarter* S; *quart* P, P(oct). *thre quarteris lang*: A beard three-quarters of an ell in length, or approximately 71 cm.

303-04 *His hair...wes quhyte*: Cf. Henryson, *Fables*, 1354-55.

307 *Of culloure...blew*: Blue was a symbol of heaven and heavenly love, associated with truth. Blue mantles often featured in iconography of Christ and Mary. In the *Deidis of Armorie*, fol. 11, 425-27, blue was likened to the precious sapphire, which 'exedis of hir beaulte and subtilite mony diuers thingis inuisiblis' and 'signifie₃ in blasoun of vertu loiaulte'; see also *Test. Meldrum*, 133*n*.

308 *Onder ane hollyng*: Christian tradition identifies the evergreen, thorny-leaved holly as a symbol of Christ's crown of thorns, and the wood of the tree, sometimes believed to have been used for the cross, as an instrument of the Passion. Earlier poets also allude to the heavenly association: *Quhen tayis bank, Bann. MS*, fol. 229, 11-12 ('ane holene hevinly hewit grene'); Dunbar, *The Tretis* (B3), 11.

329 *Courteour*] La; *Courtiour* S, P, P(oct).

336 *salit over the strandis*: Cf. Douglas, *Eneados*, I, iv.5-7.

341 *your supportatioun*: Cf. Henryson, *Fables*, 1671-72.

349 *tyrit for travellyng*: Cf. *Papyngo*, 885.

350-51 *And lerne...sobir rent*: Cf. *Complaynt*, 503-04.

358 *soune*: A further delineation of the relationship between Courteour and Experience; cf. 324, 388, 456 etc.

359 *Thyng*, in all witnesses; cf. Henryson, *Fables*, 90, 387-88. (*Thynk* as in Hamer 1931-36: I.209 is incorrect.)

363 *campe of Damassene*: Plain of Damascus, on which Adam was believed to have been created; cf. *Sex Werkdayis*, 174; 808-09.

366-67 *Nor never sall...majestie*: That is, no man will [find perfect pleasure] until after death; cf. *Dreme*, 603-16.

369 The marginal gloss to Job 7 (S, P, P(oct), La) shows that Lyndsay follows the Vulgate ('Militia est vita hominis super terram').

370-87 Earthly mutability was a common medieval theme; cf. Dunbar, '*Memento, homo*' (B32); Lichtoun, *O mortall man, Bann. MS*, fol. 48ʳ.

373 *Tyll Atrops...threid*: See *Papyngo*, 231*n*.

406-07 *Marrowis in trybulatioun...consolatioun*: Proverbial; see Tilley C571 and Whiting, 'Proverbs...Scottish', *marrowis*.

411-25 Cf. *Ane Dialog*, 47-72.

412 All witnesses have merged the last two words (influenced by the following rhyme, *inclynit*). For better sense, *defyn it* replaces *defynit*.

435 *felicitie*] La, P, P(oct); *felicitite* S.

436 The marginal gloss (S, P, P(oct), La) refers, as the poem does, to the serpent's deception of Adam and Eve, and their fall from innocence; cf. *Deploratioun*, 8-11.

446 The marginal gloss (S, P, P(oct), La) is to Rom. 5.12-21, again alluding to Adam's role in introducing sin into the world and Christ's role as redeemer.

450-51 The marginal gloss (S, P, P(oct), La) is to 1 John 1.10, 'If we say that we have not sinned, we make him [God] a liar'.

468 and **469** are omitted in La.

468-69 The marginal gloss in S, P, P(oct) and La (at 467), 'Apoca.ii', refers to Rev. 1.5. Following glosses also refer to the same lines of the poem; cf. Rom. 5.9 and Heb. 10.10-11.

470-79: *Quhowbeit...all myschevis*: The argument of those who believed that man could be 'justified' (made righteous) by faith alone; see Knox, *History*, III, 3-28; 403-542 (Henry Balnaves' 'On Justification by

Faith'). This is qualified at 490-91, with the reference to the place of 'cheretabyll werkis'.

478-79 The marginal gloss (S, P, P(oct) and La) is incorrect (see Hamer 1931-36: 268). It should be John 3.15, 'That whosoever believeth in him should not perish, but have eternal life'.

482-83 The marginal gloss to Heb. 11.1 (S, P, P(oct), La) provides a definition of faith as 'the substance of things hoped for, the evidence of things not seen'. Following verses list examples of faith, such as those of Noah and Abraham. 'Charitie' is unmentioned in them, but Lyndsay possibly has the following gloss (at 486) in mind.

486 Lyndsay's lines provide a very loose paraphrase of the marginal gloss (S, P, P(oct), La) to 1 Cor. 13.

488-89 *Do none injure...to the*: Cf. Luke 6.31 ('And as ye would that men should do to you, do ye also to them likewise'); also Matt. 7.12.

490 S's marginal gloss is to Jas. 2.14, 'What doth it profit, my brethren, though a man say he hath faith, and have not works? can faith save him?' (P, P(oct) and La have 'Iaco.i' in error).

496 *The Devyll...for dreid*: The alliterative line also has a biblical source (noted by Hamer 1931-36: III.269), Jas. 2.19, '...the devils also believe, and tremble'.

514-15 *And in to...the best*: Lyndsay paraphrases Rom. 8.28, '...all things work together for good to them that love God, to them who are the called according to his purpose'.

530-31 *cunnyng clerkis / Hes done rehers*: Hamer (1931-36: III.269) suggests that Lyndsay could refer here to Orosius (*Le Premier...Volume de Orose*); cf. also Wyntoun, *Original Chronicle*, I, iii, 'Off manis first generatioune'.

Following 537 *Exclamatioun*] S, P, P(oct); *Excusatioun* La. This subheading is more likely to be authorial (unlike the running headlines), for there was a notable precedent in Douglas's 'Ane exclamatioun aganyst detractouris and oncurtass redaris...', *Eneados*, following XIII. Douglas's purpose for his translation (stated within his 'exclamatioun') was that Virgil should 'with euery gentill Scot be kend, / And to onletterit folk be read' (43-44). Lyndsay seems to draw on this attitude, but his focus is Douglas's second category, 'Our unlernit' (547), and his intention is not to translate a pre-Christian literary work from Latin into Scots, but, more pragmatically (and in line with current international thinking; see Higman, 1993), to translate the Latin Scriptures into the vernacular for the use of the unlettered. Thus he advocates also the translation of the instruments of basic Christian instruction and belief (649), and the civil laws, for those Scots who have only 'thare toung maternall' (553). (Note that Lyndsay speaks here in his authorial voice, not in the role of Experience or Courteour; cf. the opening dedicatory epistle.)

541 *Bot quhair...till amend*: Earlier poets also expressed similar wishes (as envoys); cf. Douglas, *Pal. Honour*, 2168 ('pray Ilk man til amend the'); *Eneados*, 'Ane exclamatioun', 39.

548 *ravyng...rukis*: A succinct, alliterative description of meaningless sound, but also a borrowing from the similar term of general abuse, 'revand ruke'; cf. Dunbar, *Flyting* (B65), 57; Stewart, *Croniclis*, 36697.

551 *lactit*] S, P, P(oct); *lakit* La.

556-57 *The father...on Mont Senay*: The marginal gloss (S, P, P(oct), La) refers to Exod. 20, which lists the Ten Commandments given on Mount Sinai to Moses, leader of the Israelites driven out of Egypt.

559 *in   tablis...stone*:   Cf. Exod. 31.18, 'And he gave unto Moses...tables of stone, written with the finger of God'.

560 *In thare awin...Hebrew*: Unstated in Exodus, but a common assumption of the time; cf. *Sex Werkdayis*, 512-14. Cf. also (and 566-79) with Chaucer, *Astr.*, Prol. 30-40.

567 *philosophie naturall*: The scientific study of natural phenomena; cf. Hay, *Gouernaunce of Princes*, fol. 113ᵛ, ch. xv.49-65; see 672-76n.

571 *Virgill...prince of poetrie*: Cf. Douglas, *Eneados*, IX, Prol. 75.

574 *language   Sarayene*:   Lyndsay is attempting to convey comprehensiveness; the Saracens were the nomadic peoples of the Syro-Arabian desert, thus, later, were Arabs and Muslims.

580 *Romance*] S, P, P(oct); *Romanis* La. This variant (a pl. form of *Romane*) is also found in London, BL Harley MS 6149 (Loutfut MS), copied c.1494, fol. 124ᵛ; see Houwen 1993: 158.

582 *Latyne scolis*: An alternative term for the grammar schools of Lyndsay's time, at which Latin was taught; see Durkan 1962: 151-54.

587-88 *Of languagis...maledictioun*: The marginal gloss alludes to God's punishment for the arrogant building of the tower of Babel; cf. Gen. 11.7-9; see also Wyntoun's account, *Original Chronicle*, I, xv.

589 *Babilone*: A common confusion with 'Babel' (Gen. 11.9); cf. Wyntoun, *Original Chronicle*, I, x.876-79; *Sex Werkdayis*, 363; *Ane Dialog*, 1628, 1669-1806.

593 *thre score...twelf*: The commonly accepted number; cf. *Ane Dialog*, 1774 ('Gode send thame languagis three schore').

598 *That I am nocht...rew*: Both a continuation of the modesty formula and a strengthening of the theme that every Scot should have access to the 'bukis necessare / For our faith' (599-600).

601-04 *Christ...languagis repleit*: The marginal gloss (S, P, P(oct), *om* La) alludes to Acts 2.3-11 in which, through the appearance of 'tongues like as of fire', the disciples acquired the ability to speak many languages.

607 *delyverand thame the law*: Cf. *Complaynt*, 436.

612-13 *Bot lyke...be lang usage*: The abilities of the starling as a mimic were noted from Pliny's time (cf. *Nat. Hist.* X, lix.122-26) to Shakespeare's (cf. *King Henry IV, Part I*, Act I, Sc. iii, 224-25); for those of the parrot see *Papyngo*, 86-98 and 63n.

617 *Mumland...thare houris*: The similar, but more reprehensible shortcomings of churchmen who do this are censured in the *Tragedie*, 385. *matynis*: One of the canonical hours; properly a midnight office, but recited at dawn. *evinsang*: The sixth of the canonical hours; a service just before sunset. *houris*: The prayers or offices said at the seven times allotted during the day to this purpose.

618 *Thare 'Pater Noster'*: Their recital of the Lord's Prayer, the first words of which are 'Our Father'; cf. Dunbar, *Amang thir freiris* (B1), 3. *'Ave'*: An allusion, in shortened form, to the Marian prayer, *Ave Maria gratia plena*, derived from Luke 1.28. *'Creid'*: The Creed, the statement of essential beliefs of the Christian.

620-21 *God have mercy...'Deus'*: The assertion is that children and ladies, ignorant of Latin, will not know the difference between the *Pater Noster* and the penitential Psalm 51 quoted ('Have mercy upon me, O God'), but the poet's use of the same words (in Scots), 620, to ask God's mercy for his own outspokenness, adds a twist both modest and amusing.

622-24 *Jerome*: One of the four Latin Doctors of the Church (AD c.340-420); cf. *Papyngo*, 988. Jerome was best known for his knowledge of Hebrew, Latin and Greek, his revision of the Latin version of the Bible to create a student text (which by the 13th c. was known as the Vulgate version), and his encouragement of a group of Christian women to study the Scriptures.

627 *Argyle*: Argyll (*Earra-Ghàidheal* = the coastland of the Gael), region on the SW coast of Scotland, which (with Tarbert) was originally Scottish Dalriada. At this time its inhabitants spoke Gaelic, or, in contemporary Lowland usage, 'Yrische', 'Ersche', or 'Erse'; cf. Dunbar, 'Off Februar' (B47), 116.

629-34 *Prudent Sanct Paull...it menis*: The marginal gloss (S, P, P(oct); *om* La) is to 1 Cor. 14.19; note also the concern of the whole 'Exclamatioun' to distinguish between the uses of scholarly and divinely inspired learning, and the needs of those without education.

635 *not worth twa prenis*: Proverbial; see Whiting, 'Proverbs... Scottish', *preen*; cf. *Thrie Estaitis*, 4169-70.

637 *the Evangell*: Contextually, an allusion to the portion of a gospel sung as part of the church service.

638-39 *Nocht knawyng...it roung*: Worshippers were unable to see the elevation of the host (performed within screened choirs and chancels), and thus had to respond blindly to the bell, which the priest rang to signify that they should kneel; see Hamer 1931-36: III.275.

662 *And ilk man...done to*: Cf. 488-89n.

664 *David*: A shepherd who became king of Israel (cf. 1 Sam. 17 to 2 Sam. 5.4; *Tragedie*, 242), often represented playing the harp; cf. 1 Sam. 16.23.

667 *Salamone*: See *Ane Dialog*, 249n.

668 *his buke*: Probably Ecclesiastes, of which there were many paraphrases during the period, especially in France; cf. the 15th c. Scots prose paraphrase, *Dicta Salomonis, Ratis Raving*, App. 6, 177-92.

672-76 *And argumentis sawin...ingyne*: Cf. Dunbar, *To speik of science* (B82), 9-13. Both Lyndsay and Dunbar are alluding to the subjects of the university curriculum, including logic, astronomy and philosophy. (Dunbar's theme, however, is the uselessness of all learning without its association with moral virtue.)

ABBREVIATIONS AND BIBLIOGRAPHY

This Bibliography lists, in one alphabetical sequence, full details of both primary and secondary works cited in the Introduction and Notes.

Abbreviations

ADCP	*Acts of the Lords of Council in Public Affairs, 1501-1554*, ed. R.K. Hannay. Edinburgh, 1932.
APS	*The Acts of the Parliaments of Scotland*, ed. T. Thomson and C. Innes. 12 vols, Edinburgh, 1814-75.
Asloan MS	*The Asloan Manuscript*, ed. W.A. Craigie. 2 vols, STS, 1923-25.
Bann. Facsimile	*The Bannatyne Manuscript, National Library of Scotland Advocates' MS. 1.1.6*, intro. D. Fox and W. Ringler. London, 1980.
Bann. MS	*The Bannatyne Manuscript*, ed. W. Tod Ritchie. 4 vols, STS, 1928-34.
Bann Misc.	*The Bannatyne Miscellany; containing original papers and tracts, chiefly relating to the history of Scotland*, eds W. Scott, D. Laing, and T. Thomson. 3 vols, Bannatyne Club, Edinburgh, 1827-55.
CM	*Pieces from The Makculloch and the Gray MSS. together with The Chepman and Myllar Prints*, ed. G. Stevenson. STS, 1918.
CSD	*The Concise Scots Dictionary.*
DOST	*A Dictionary of the Older Scottish Tongue.*
ER	*The Exchequer Rolls of Scotland*, ed. J. Stuart and others. 23 vols, Edinburgh, 1878-1908.
EETS	Early English Text Society. (London.)
EHR	*English Historical Review.*
ES	*English Studies.*
Hamilton Papers	*The Hamilton Papers*, ed. J. Bain. 2 vols, Edinburgh, 1890-92.
HMC	Historical Manuscripts Commission.
IR	*Innes Review.*
L&P Henry VIII	*Letters and Papers, Foreign and Domestic, of the Reign of King Henry VIII*, eds J. Brewer and J. Gairdner. 21 vols, London, 1862-1910. (Cited by document number.)
Maitl. Fol. MS	*The Maitland Folio Manuscript*, ed. W.A. Craigie. 2 vols, STS, 1919-27.

Maitl. Quarto MS	*The Maitland Quarto Manuscript*, ed. W.A. Craigie. STS, 1920.
MÆ	*Medieum Ævum.*
MED	*Middle English Dictionary.*
MLR	*Modern Language Review.*
MS; MSS	Manuscript; Manuscripts.
OED	*The Oxford English Dictionary.*
PMLA	*Publications of the Modern Language Association.*
PSAS	*Proceedings of the Society of Antiquaries of Scotland.*
RCAHMS	*Royal Commission on Ancient and Historical Monuments...of Scotland.*
RMS	*Registrum Magni Sigilli Regum Scotorum*, ed. J. Balfour Paul and others. 12 vols, Edinburgh and London, 1882-1912.
RSCHS	*Records of the Scottish Church History Society.*
RSS	*Registrum Secreti Sigilli Regum Scotorum*, ed. M. Livingstone and others. 8 vols, Edinburgh, 1908.
SBRS	Scottish Burgh Record Society.
SHR	*Scottish Historical Review.*
SHS	Scottish History Society.
SLJ	*Scottish Literary Journal.*
SP Henry VIII	*State Papers of Henry VIII.* 11 vols, London, 1830-52.
SP Sadler	*State Papers and Letters of Sir Ralph Sadler*, ed A. Clifford. 2 vols, Edinburgh and London, 1809.
SRS	Scottish Record Society.
SSL	*Studies in Scottish Literature.*
STC	*A Short-Title Catalogue of Books Printed in England, Scotland and Ireland and of English Books Printed Abroad 1475-1640*, comp. A.W. Pollard, G.R. Redgrave, W.A. Jackson, F.S. Ferguson, and K.F. Pantzer. London, 1976-91.
STS	Scottish Text Society. (Edinburgh and London.)
TA	*Accounts of the Lord High Treasurer of Scotland*, ed. T. Dickson and J. Balfour Paul. 12 vols, Edinburgh, 1877-1916.

Bibliography

Aitken, A. J. 1983. 'The Language of Older Scots Poetry', in J.D. McClure, ed., *Scotland and the Lowland Tongue*. Aberdeen, 1983, pp. 18-49.

— 1985. 'A History of Scots', in *CSD*, pp. ix-xvi.

— 1997. 'The Pioneers of Anglicised Speech in Scotland; a second look', *Scottish Language*, 1-36.

Alan of Lille, *Complaint of Nature*, trans. J.L. Sheridan. Toronto, 1980.

Allen, D. 1964. 'Orpheus and Orfeo: The Dead and the Taken', *MÆ*, 33, 102-11.

Anderson, J.M., ed. 1926. *Early Records of the University of St Andrews*. SHS, Edinburgh.

Anglo, S. 1961. 'Archives of the English Tournament: Score Cheques and Lists', *Journal of the Society of Archivists*, 2.4, 153-62.

— 1962. 'Financial and Heraldic Records of the English Tournament', *Journal of the Society of Archivists*, 2.5, 183-95.

— 1969. *Spectacle Pageantry, and Early Tudor Policy*. Oxford.

Apted, M.R. and Hannabuss, S. 1978. *Painters in Scotland 1301-1700: A Biographical Dictionary*. Edinburgh.

Axton, R. 1992. 'Chaucer and "Tragedy"', in T. Takamiya and R. Beadle, eds, *Chaucer to Shakespeare: Essays in Honour of Shinsuke Ando*. Cambridge, 1992, pp. 33-43.

Baird Smith, D. 1920. '*Le Testament du Gentil Cossoys*', *SHR*, 17.67, 190-98.

Balfour, J.H. 'Edinburgh in 1544 and Hertford's Invasion', *SHR*, 8.30, 113-31.

Bapst, E. 1889. *Les Mariages de Jacques V*. Paris.

Barber, R. 1970. *The Knight and Chivalry*. London.

Barbour, John, *Barbour's Bruce*, ed. M.P. McDiarmid and J.A.C. Stevenson. 3 vols, STS, 1980-85.

Barclay, Alexander, *The Eclogues of Alexander Barclay*, ed. B. White. EETS, 1928.

Bardgett, F.D. 1989. *Scotland Reformed: The Reformation in Angus and the Mearns*. Edinburgh.

Barry, J.C. 1951. 'William Hay of Aberdeen: A Sixteenth-Century Scottish Theologian and Canonist', *IR*, 2, 83-99.

Basing, P. 1994. 'Robert Beale and the Queen of Scots', *British Library Journal*, 20.1, 65-82.

Bateson, D. 1987. *Scottish Coins*. Aylesbury.

Bawcutt 1967 *see* Douglas, *Shorter Poems*.

Bawcutt, P. 1972. 'The Lark in Chaucer and Some Later Poets', *YES*, 2, 5-12.

— 1976. *Gavin Douglas: A Critical Study*. Edinburgh.

— 1983. 'The Art of Flyting', *SLJ*, 10.2, 5-24.

— 1986. 'Dunbar's Use of the Symbolic Lion and Thistle', *Cosmos*, 2, 83-97.

— 1988. 'A Medieval Scottish Elegy and its French Original', *SLJ*, 15.1, 5-13.

— 1992. *Dunbar the Makar*. Oxford.

— 1994. 'New Light on Gavin Douglas', in MacDonald and others, eds, 1994, pp. 95-106.

— 1996 *see* Dunbar, *Selected Poems*.

— 1998 *see* Dunbar, *The Poems*.

— and Riddy, eds. 1987. *Longer Scottish Poems I: 1375-1650*. Edinburgh.

Baxter, J.W. 1952. *William Dunbar: a Biographical Study*. Edinburgh.

Bellenden, John, *The Chronicles of Scotland Compiled by Hector Boece, Translated into Scots by John Bellenden*, ed. R.W. Chambers, E.C. Batho and H.W. Husbands. 2 vols, STS, 1938-41. (Cited by volume, book, and chapter; preface by volume and page.)

— *Chronicles* (?1540). *Hector Boethius. Chronicle of Scotland Edinburgh (1540?)*. Amsterdam, 1977. [A composite facsimile of STC 3203.] (Cited by chapter and folio.)

— *Livy. Livy's History of Rome. The First Five Books, Translated into Scots by John Bellenden*, ed. W.A. Craigie. 2 vols, STS, 1901-03. (Cited by volume, book, chapter and line.)

— *Proheme* see *Bann. MS*, fols 4^r-8^v.

Bennett, J.A.W., ed. 1955. *Devotional Pieces in Verse and Prose from MS. Arundel 285 and MS. Harleian 6919*. STS.

Bense, W.F. 1972. 'Paris Theologians on War and Peace, 1521-1529', *Church History*, 41.2, 168-85.

Benson, C.D. 1980. *The History of Troy in Middle English Literature*. Woodbridge.

Bentley-Cranch, D. and R.K. Marshall. 1996. 'Iconography and Literature in the Service of Diplomacy: The Franco-Scottish Alliance, James V and Scotland's two French Queens, Madeleine of France and Marie de Guise', in Hadley Williams, ed., 1996a, pp. 273-88, figs. 1-7.

Béroul, *The Romance of Tristan*, ed. A.S. Fedrick. Harmondsworth, 1970.

Bill, G. 1966. 'Lambeth Palace Library', *The Library*, 21, 192-206.

Billington, S. 1986. 'The Lord of Misrule in Late Medieval Renaissance England, *Cosmos*, 2, 98-110.

Black, M. 1992. *The Medieval Cookbook*. New York.

Blanchot, J.-J. and C. Graf, eds. 1978. *Actes du 2e Colloque de Langue et de Littérature Écossaises (Moyen Age et Renaissance)*. Strasbourg.

Boardman, S.I. 1996. *The Early Stewart Kings: Robert II and Robert III 1371-1406*. East Linton.

Boase, T.S.R. 1972. *Death in the Middle Ages: Mortality, Judgement and Remembrance*. London.

Boece, *History* (MLT). *The Mar Lodge Translation of the History of Scotland by Hector Boece*, ed. G. Watson. STS, 1946.

Boffey, J. 1992. 'Lydgate, Henryson, and the Literary Testament', *Modern Language Quarterly*, 53, 41-56.

— and Edwards. 1997. *The Works of Geoffrey Chaucer and 'The Kingis Quair': A Facsimile of Bodleian Library, Oxford, MS Arch. Selden. B. 24*, intro. J. Boffey and A.S.G. Edwards; app. B.C. Barker-Benfield. Woodbridge.

Bonner, E. 1996a. 'The "Auld Alliance" and the Betrothal of Mary Queen of Scots: Fact and Fable', *Journal of the Sydney Society for Scottish History*, 4, 3-22.

— 1996b. 'The Recovery of St Andrews Castle in 1547: French Naval Policy and Diplomacy in the British Isles', *EHR*, 111.442, 578-98.

— 1997a. 'French Naturalization of the Scots in the Fifteenth and Sixteenth Centuries', *The Historical Journal*, 40.4, 1085-1115.

— 1997b. 'The Genesis of Henry VIII's "Rough Wooing" of the Scots', *Northern History*, 33, 36-53.

— 1999. 'Scotland's "Auld Alliance" with France, 1295-1560', *History*, 84.273, 5-30.

Book of Keruynge. London 1508, The. Amsterdam, 1971.

Bower, Walter. *Scotichronicon in Latin and English*, ed. D.E.R. Watt and others. 9 vols, Aberdeen and Edinburgh, 1987-98. (Cited by volume, book, chapter, and line.)

Bredahl Petersen, F. 1937. 'Dr. Johannes Macchabæus: John MacAlpin: Scotland's Contribution to the Reformation in Denmark', D. Phil. Diss. Edinburgh.

Brewer, D.S. 1955. 'The Ideal of Feminine Beauty in Medieval Literature, especially "Harley Lyrics", Chaucer, and Some Elizabethans', *MLR*, 50.3, 17-269.

Brooke-Little, J.P. 1985. *An Heraldic Alphabet*. London.

Brown, M. 1994. *James I*. Edinburgh.

Bryce, W.M. 1918. 'The Convent of St Catherine of Siena', *Book of the Old Edinburgh Club*, 10, 96-131.

Buchanan of Auchmar, W. 1984. *An Historical and Genealogical Essay upon The Family and Surname of Buchanan*. [1732]. Morgantown.

Buik of Alexander, The, ed. R.L.G. Ritchie. 4 vols, STS, 1921-29. (Cited by volume and line.)

Buke of the Chess, The, ed. C. van Buuren. STS, 1997.

Buke of the Sevyne Sagis, The, ed. C. van Buuren. Leiden, 1982.

Bunt, G.H.V. 1994. *Alexander the Great in the Literature of Medieval Britain*. Groningen.

Burke, P. 1989. 'The Renaissance Dialogue', *Renaissance Studies*, 3.2, 1-12.

Burnett, C.J. 1981. 'The Court of the Lord Lyon', *The Scottish Genealogist*, 28, 181-84.

— 1986. 'Funeral Heraldry in Scotland with particular reference to hatchments', *PSAS*, 116, 473-559.

— 1996 'Outward Signs of Majesty 1535-1540', in Hadley Williams, ed., 1996a, pp. 289-302.

— and Bennet, H. 1987. *The Green Mantle*. Edinburgh.

Burns, J.H. 1996. *The True Law of Kingship: Concepts of Monarchy in Early-Modern Scotland*. Oxford.

Burrow, J.A. 1986. *The Ages of Man*. Oxford.

Butler's Lives of the Saints, ed. and rev., H. Thurston and D. Attwater. 4 vols, London, 1926-38; 1956.

Cairns, S. 1985. 'Sir David Lindsay's *Dreme*: Poetry, Propaganda, and Encomium in the Scottish Court', in G.S. Burgess and R.A. Taylor, eds, *The Spirit of the Court*. Cambridge, 1985, pp. 110-19.

Caldwell, D.H. 1979. *The Scottish Armoury*. Edinburgh.

— 1981. 'Royal Patronage of Arms and Armour Making in Fifteenth and Sixteenth-Century Scotland', in D.H. Caldwell, ed., *Scottish Weapons and Fortifications 1100-1800*. Edinburgh, 1981, pp. 73-93.

— 1982. *Angels Nobles and Unicorns: Art and Patronage in Medieval Scotland*. Edinburgh.

— and Marshall, R.K. 1987. *The Queen's World*. Edinburgh.

Caldwell, J.R., ed. 1933. *Eger and Grime. A parallel text edition of the Percy and Huntington-Laing versions of the romance, Harvard Studies in Comparative Literature*, 9. Cambridge, Mass.

Cameron, J.K. 1990. 'Humanism and Religious Life', in J. MacQueen, ed., *Humanism in Renaissance Scotland*. Edinburgh, 1990, pp. 161-71.

Campbell, C. n.d. *Medieval Flags*. Heraldry Society of Scotland, Edinburgh.

Campbell, I. 1994. 'Linlithgow's "Princely Palace" and its Influence in Europe', *Architectural Heritage*, V, 1-20.

— 1995. 'A Romanesque Revival and the Early Renaissance in Scotland, c.1380-1513', *Journal of the Society of Architectural Historians*, 54.3, 302-25.

Campbell, L.B., ed. 1938. *The Mirror for Magistrates*. New York.

Cant, R.G. 1970. *The University of St Andrews. A Short History*. Edinburgh and London.

Carion, John, *The thre bokes of Cronicles, whyche John Carion...Gathered with great diligence*, trans. W. Lynne. London, 1550.

Cary, G. 1956. *The Medieval Alexander*, ed. D.J.A. Ross. Cambridge.

Cavers, K. 1993. *A Vision of Scotland: The Nation Observed by John Slezer 1671-1717*. Edinburgh.

Chalmers 1806. *The Poetical Works of Sir David Lyndsay of the Mount*, ed. G. Chalmers. 3 vols, London, 1806.

Chambers, E.K. 1901-03. *The Medieval Stage*. 2 vols, Oxford.

Chanson de Roland. The Song of Roland, ed. and trans. D. Sayers. Harmondsworth, 1957.

Chaucer, Geoffrey. *The Riverside Chaucer*, ed. L.D. Benson. Oxford, 1988.

Christensen, T.L. 1983. 'The Earl of Rothes in Denmark', in Cowan and Shaw, eds, 1983, pp. 60-70.

Clariodus: A Metrical Romance, [ed. D. Irving]. Maitland Club, Edinburgh, 1830.

Clark, K. 1977. *Animals and Men: Their Relationship as Reflected in Western Art*. London.

Colkelbie Sow and the Talis of the Fyve Bestes, ed. G. Kratzmann. New York, 1983.

Colyn Blowbol's Testament, ed. W.C. Hazlitt, *Remains of the Early Popular Poetry of England*. Vol. I, London, 1864, 91-109.

Complaynt of Scotland, The, ed. A.M. Stewart. STS, 1979.

Connolly, M. 1992. '"The Dethe of the Kynge of Scotis": A New Edition', *SHR*, 71, 46-69.

Contemplacioun of synnaris, [William of Touris], *Asloan MS*, fols 263^r-290^r.

Cotgrave, R. 1611. *A Dictionarie of the French and English Tongues* [*STC* 5830]. Menston, 1968.

Cowan, I.B. 1995. *The Medieval Church in Scotland*, ed. J. Kirk. Edinburgh.

— and Shaw, D., eds. 1983. *The Renaissance and Reformation in Scotland.* Edinburgh.

— Mackay, P.H.R., and Macquarrie, A., eds. 1983. *The Knights of St John of Jerusalem in Scotland.* SHS, Edinburgh.

Cox, V. 1992. *The Renaissance dialogue: Literary dialogue in its social and political contexts, Castiglione to Galileo.* Cambridge.

Cranstoun, J., ed. 1891-93. *Satirical Poems of the time of the Reformation.* 2 vols, STS. (Cited by poem number.)

Cupar Banns see Hamer 1931-36.

Curtius, E.R. 1953. *European Literature in the Latin Middle Ages*, trans. W.R. Trask. Princeton.

Darwin, T. 1996. *The Scots Herbal: The Plant Lore of Scotland.* Edinburgh.

Deidis of Armorie, ed. L.A.J.R. Houwen. 2 vols, STS, 1994. (Cited by folio and line.)

Desmontiers, J. 1538. *La sommaire des antiquitez et merveilles d'Ecosse.* Paris.

Dickinson, W.C., ed. 1928. *The Sheriff Court Book of Fife 1515-1522.* SHS, Edinburgh.

Dickson, R. and Edmond, J. Ph. 1975. *Annals of Scottish Printing.* Cambridge, 1890; 1975.

Dolan, C. 1994. 'Liturgies urbaines et rapports sociaux en France au XVe siècle', *Journal of the Canadian Historical Association*, New Ser. 5, 87-109.

Dolan, J.P. 1964. *The Essential Erasmus*, ed. and trans. J.P. Dolan. New York.

Donaldson, G. 1960. *The Scottish Reformation.* Cambridge.

Douglas, Gavin, *Eneados. Virgil's 'Aeneid' Translated into Scottish Verse by Gavin Douglas*, ed. D.F.C. Coldwell. 4 vols, STS, 1957-64.

— *The Shorter Poems*, ed. P. Bawcutt. STS, 1967. [*Palice of Honour, Conscience*; Anon., *King Hart.*]

Dowden, J. 1912. *The Bishops of Scotland.* Glasgow.

Drijvers, J.W. and MacDonald, A.A., eds. 1995. *Centres of Learning.* Leiden.

Druce, G.C. 1919. 'The Elephant in Medieval Legend and Art', *The Archaeological Journal*, 76, 1-73.

Duffy, E. 1992. *The Stripping of the Altars.* London and New Haven.

Dunbar, William, *Selected Poems*, ed. P. Bawcutt. London and New York, 1996.

— *The Poems*, ed. P. Bawcutt. 2 vols. Glasgow, 1998.

Duncan Laideus' Testament. In *The Black Book of Taymouth with other Papers from the Breadalbane Charter Room*, [ed. C. Innes]. Bannatyne Club, Edinburgh, 1855, pp. 149-73.

Durkan, J. 1959. 'The Cultural Background in Sixteenth-Century Scotland', *IR*, 10.2, 382-439.

— 1962. 'Education in the Century of the Reformation', in D. McRoberts, ed., 1962, pp. 145-68.

— 1972. 'Archbishop Robert Blackadder's Will', *IR*, 23.1, 138-48.
— 1981. 'Giovanni Ferrerio, Humanist: His Influence in Sixteenth-Century Scotland', in K. Robbins, ed., *Religion and Humanism*. Oxford, pp. 181-94.
— 1982. 'Scottish "Evangelicals" in the Patronage of Thomas Cromwell', *RSCHS*, 21.3, 127-56.
— 1984. 'The Observant Franciscan Province in Scotland', *IR*, 35.2, 51-57.
— 1990. 'Education: The Laying of Fresh Foundations', in J. MacQueen, ed., *Humanism in Renaissance Scotland*. Edinburgh, pp. 123-60.
— and Ross, A. 1961. *Early Scottish Libraries*. Glasgow.
Eade, J.C. 1984. *The Forgotten Sky. A Guide to Astrology in English Literature*. Oxford.
Eales, R. 1986. 'The Game of Chess. An Aspect of Knightly Culture', in C. Harper-Bill and R. Harvey, eds, 1986, pp. 12-34.
Easson, D.E. 1938. 'The Collegiate Churches of Scotland: Part I—Their characteristics', *RSCHS*, 6.3, 193-215.
— 1939. 'The Collegiate Churches of Scotland: Part II—Their significance', *RSCHS*, 7.1, 30-47.
— 1947. *Gavin Dunbar: Chancellor of Scotland. Archbishop of Glasgow*. Edinburgh and London.
Edington, C. 1993. '"To speik of Preistis be sure it is na bourds": discussing the priesthood in pre-Reformation Scotland', in A. Pettegree, ed., *The Reformation in the Parishes*. Manchester, 1993, pp. 22-42.
— 1994. *Court and Culture in Renaissance Scotland. Sir David Lindsay of the Mount*. Amherst, Mass.
Edwards, A.S.G. 1977. 'The Influence of Lydgate's *Fall of Princes* c.1440-1559: A Survey', *Mediaeval Studies*, 39, 424-39.
Emond, W.K. 1988. 'The Minority of James V 1513-1528', D. Phil. Diss. St Andrews.
Fairley, J.S., ed. 1908. 'Ancient Scottish Tales: An Unpublished Collection made by Peter Buchan', *Transactions of the Buchan Field Club*, 9, 143-47.
Farnham, W. 1936. *The Medieval Heritage of Elizabethan Tragedy*. Oxford.
Fawcett, R. 1992. *St Andrews Castle*. Edinburgh.
Ferguson, G. 1954. *Signs and Symbols in Christian Art*. Oxford.
Fergusson's Scottish Proverbs from the Original Print of 1641, ed. E. Beveridge. STS, 1924.
Finnie, E. 1985. 'The House of Hamilton: Patronage, Politics and the Church in the Reformation Period', *IR*, 36.1, 3-28.
Fisher, M.R. 1968. 'George Cavendish's Metrical Visions', D. Phil. Diss. Columbia.
Florimond see McClure 1979.
[Foulis]. *Strena*. IJsewijn, J. and Thomson, D.F.S. 1975. 'The Latin Poems of Jacobus Follisius or James Foullis of Edinburgh', *Humanistica Lovaniensia*, 24, 103-52.

Fox 1981 *see* Henryson.

Fox-Davies, A.C. 1969. *A Complete Guide to Heraldry*, rev. J.P. Brooke-Little. London.

Fradenburg, L.O. 1991. *City Marriage Tournament: Arts of Rule in Late Medieval Scotland*. Madison, Wis.

Freiris of Berwick see Furrow, ed., 1985.

Furrow, M., ed. 1985. *Ten Fifteenth-Century Comic Poems*. New York and London. [Includes *John the Reeve* and *The Friars of Berwick*.]

Galbraith, J. 1984. 'The Middle Ages', in D.B. Forrester and D.M. Murray, eds, *Studies in the History of Worship in Scotland*. Edinburgh, 1984, pp. 17-32.

Gamelyn, see Sands, ed., 1966.

Geoffrey de Vinsauf, *Poetria Nova*, trans. M.F. Nims. Toronto, 1967.

Geddie, W. 1912. *A Bibliography of Middle Scots Poets, With an Introduction on the History of their Reputations*. STS.

Gilbert, J.M. 1977. 'The Usual Money of Scotland and Exchange Rates Against Foreign Coin', in D.M. Metcalf, ed., *Coinage in Medieval Scotland (1100-1600)*. Oxford, 1977.

Gilbert, J.M. 1979. *Hunting and Hunting Reserves in Medieval Scotland*. Edinburgh.

Gillies, W. 1978. 'Gaelic and Scots Literature down to the Reformation', in Blanchot and Graf, eds., 1978, pp. 63-79.

Gillmor, C. 1992. 'Practical Chivalry: The Training of Horses for Tournaments and Warfare', *Studies in Medieval and Renaissance History XIII*, pp. 7-29.

Gittings, C. 1984. *Death, Burial and the Individual in Early Modern England*. London and Sydney.

Golagros. The Knightly Tale of Golagros and Gawane, in *Scottish Alliterative Poems in Rhyming Stanzas*, ed. F.J. Amours. STS, 1897.

Gower, John, *The English Works*, ed. G.C. Macaulay. 2 vols, EETS, Oxford, 1900-1901.

Gray, D. 1972. *Themes and Images in the Medieval English Religious Lyric*. London.

— 1984. 'Rough Music: Some Early Invectives and Flytings', *YES*, 14, 21-43.

— 1986. 'Books of Comfort', in G.C. Kratzmann and J. Simpson, eds, *Medieval English Religious and Ethical Literature*. Cambridge, 1986, pp. 209-21.

Green, R.F. 1980. *Poets and Princepleasers. Literature and the English Court in the Late Middle Ages*. Toronto.

Greene, R.L. 1977. *The Early English Carols*. Oxford.

Grene Knight see Speed, ed., 1989.

Grigson, G. 1955. *The Englishman's Flora*. London.

Gude and Godlie Ballatis. A Compendious Book of Godly and Spiritual Songs commonly known as 'The Gude and Godlie Ballatis', ed. A.F. Mitchell. STS, 1897.

Guiffrey, G. 1860. *La Cronique du Roy François Ier*. Paris.

HMC. 1891. *Report on the Manuscripts of the Earl of Hume*. London.

— 1904. *Report on the Manuscripts of the Earl of Mar and Kellie.* London.

H[adley] Williams, J. 1981. 'The Lyon and the Hound: Sir David Lyndsay's *Complaint and...Confessioun of...Bagsche*', *Parergon*, No. 31, 3-11.

— 1989. '"Thus Euery Man Said for Hym Self": The Voices of Sir David Lyndsay's Poems', in McClure and Spiller, eds, 1989, pp. 258-72.

— 1990. 'David Lyndsay's "Antique" and "Plesand" Storeis', in A. Gardner-Medwin and J. Hadley Williams, eds, *A Day Estivall.* Aberdeen, pp. 156-66.

— 1991. 'James V, David Lyndsay, and the Bannatyne Manuscript Poem of the Gyre Carling', *SSL*, 26, 164-71.

— 1992. 'Shady Publishing in Sixteenth-Century Scotland: The Case of David Lyndsay's Poems', *Bulletin of the Bibliographical Society of Australia and New Zealand*, 16.3, 97-105.

— ed. 1996a. *Stewart Style 1513-1542: Essays on the Court of James V.* East Linton.

— 1996b. 'David Lyndsay and the Making of King James V', in Hadley Williams, ed., 1996a, pp. 201-26.

— in press. '"Of officiaris serving thy senyeorie": David Lyndsay's diplomatic letter of 1531', in L.A.J.R. Houwen, A.A. MacDonald, and S.L. Mapstone, eds, *A Palace in the Wild: Essays on Vernacular Culture in Late-Medieval and Renaissance Scotland.*

— in press. 'Lyndsay and Europe: Politics, Patronage, Printing', in G. Caie, R. Lyall and K. Simpson, eds, *The European Sun.*

— forthcoming. 'Dunbar and His Immediate Heirs', in S.L. Mapstone, ed., *William Dunbar: the nobill poyet.*

Hamer, D. 1929. 'The Bibliography of Sir David Lindsay (1490-1555)', *The Library*, 10.1, 1-42.

— 1931-36. *The Works of Sir David Lindsay of the Mount 1490-1555*, ed. D. Hamer. 4 vols, STS.

Hamilton, John. *The catechism.* St Andrews, 1552 [*STC* 12731].

Hamilton Papers, The. Letters and Papers Illustrating the Political Relations of England and Scotland in the XVIth century, ed. J. Bain. 2 vols, Edinburgh, 1890-92.

Hannay, R.K. 1932. 'Observations on the Officers of the Scottish Parliament', *Juridical Review*, 44, 125-38.

Harper-Bill, C. and Harvey, R. eds. 1986. *The Ideals and Practice of Medieval Knighthood.* Woodbridge.

Hary's Wallace, ed. M.P. McDiarmid. 2 vols, STS, 1968-69.

Hatto, A.T. 1965. *Eos.* The Hague.

Hay, Gilbert. *The Buik Of King Alexander the Conquerour*, ed. J. Cartwright. 2 vols, STS, 1986-90.

— *Gilbert of the Haye's Prose Manuscript (A.D.1456)*, I. ed. J.H. Stevenson. STS, 1901. [*The Buke of the Law of Armys.*]

— *The Prose Works of Sir Gilbert Hay*, III, ed. J.A. Glenn. STS, 1993. [*The Buke of the Ordre of Knychthede* and *The Buke of the Gouernaunce of Princis.*]

Heijnsbergen, T. van. 1994. 'The Interaction between Literature and History in Queen Mary's Edinburgh: The Bannatyne Manuscript and its Prosopographical Context', in MacDonald and others, eds, 1994, pp. 183-225.

— 1995. 'The Scottish Chapel Royal as a Cultural Intermediary between Town and Court', in Drijvers and MacDonald, eds, 1995, pp. 299-313.

Heninger, S.K. 1977. *The Cosmographical Glass: Renaissance Diagrams of the Universe.* San Marino.

Henryson, Robert. *The Poems,* ed. D. Fox. Oxford, 1981.

Herkless, J. 1891. *Cardinal Beaton: Priest and Politician.* Edinburgh and London.

Hertford, *Late Expedition. The late expedition in Scotland, made by...the Earl of Hertford...1544,* in *Tudor Tracts 1532-1588,* ed. T. Seccombe and A.F. Pollard [rpt from *An English Garner,* 8 vols, ed. E. Arber, 1877-90]. London, 1903, pp. 39-51.

Heyworth, P.L., ed. 1968. *Jack Upland, Friar Daw's Reply* and *Upland's Rejoinder.* Oxford.

Higden, Ranulf, *Polychronicon,* ed. C. Babington and J.R. Lumby. Rolls Series, 9 vols, London, 1865-86.

Higman, F.M. 1993. 'Ideas for Export: Translations in the Early Reformation', in J.R. Brink and W.F. Gentrup, eds, *Renaissance Culture in Context.* Aldershot, 1993, pp. 100-13.

Hodgett, G.A.J. and Smith, D., eds. 1972. *Stere Htt Well.* [Facsimile with modern transcription of Cambridge, Pepys 1047.] London.

Holland, Richard. *The Buke of the Howlat* see Bawcutt and Riddy, eds. 1987.

Honorius, *De imagine mundi.* Honorius, Augustodunensis. *Opera Omnia,* J.P. Migne. *Patrologiae Cursus Completus Series Latina.* Vol. 172, Paris, 1895.

Houwen 1990 *see Sex Werkdays and Agis.*

Houwen, L.A.J.R. 1993. 'The Seven Deeds of Honour and Their Crowns: Lydgate and a Late Fifteenth-Century Scots Chivalric Treatise', *SSL,* 28, 150-64.

— and MacDonald, A.A., eds. 1994. *Loyal Letters: Studies on Mediaeval Alliterative Poetry and Prose.* Groningen.

Hynd, N. 1984. 'Towards a Study of Gardening in Scotland from the 16th to the 18th Centuries', in D.J. Breeze, ed., *Studies in Scottish Antiquity Presented to Stewart Cruden.* Edinburgh, 1984, pp. 269-84.

Innes, T., of Learney. 1932. 'The Scottish Parliament; its Symbolism and its Ceremonial', *IR,* 44, 87-124.

— 1935. 'Sir David Lindsay of the Mount. Lord Lyon King of Arms, 1538-1555', *Scottish Notes and Queries,* 13, 145-48, 170-73, 180-83.

— 1936. 'Heraldic Law', in H. McKechnie, ed., *An Introductory Survey of the Sources and Literature of Scots Law.* Edinburgh, 1936, pp. 379-95.

— 1944-45. 'The Robes of the Feudal Baronage of Scotland', *PSAS,* 79, 111-63, pl. I-XIII.

— 1934; 1978. *Scots Heraldry.* London and Edinburgh.

Ireland, John. *The Meroure of Wyssdome*, ed. C. Macpherson, F. Quinn and C. McDonald. 3 vols, STS, 1926-1990. (Cited by volume, page and line.)

— *Of penance* see *Asloan MS*, fols 1ʳ-40ᵛ.

Ireland, R.D. 1958. 'Husband and Wife. Divorce, Nullity of Marriage and Separation', in Paton and others, eds, 1958, pp. 90-98.

Jackson, W.H. 1986. 'The Tournament in German Tournament Books of the Sixteenth Century and in the Literary Works of Emperor Maximilian I', in C. Harper-Bill and R. Harvey, eds, Woodbridge, 1986, pp. 49-73.

James, M.R. 1959. 'The History of Lambeth Palace Library', *Transactions of the Cambridge Bibliographical Society*, 3.1, 1-31.

James IV Letters. The Letters of James IV 1505-1513. ed. R.L. Mackie. SHS, Edinburgh, 1953.

James V Letters. The Letters of James V, eds R.K. Hannay and D. Hay. Edinburgh, 1954.

Jansen, S.L. 1991. *Political Protest and Prophecy under Henry VIII*. Woodbridge.

John the Reeve see Furrow, ed., 1985.

Jones, G.F. 1951. 'The Tournaments of Tottenham and Lappenhausen', *PMLA*, 66, 1123-40.

Kantrowitz, J.S. 1975. *Dramatic Allegory: Lindsay's 'Ane Satyre of the Thrie Estaitis*. Lincoln, Nebraska.

Keen, M. 1984a. *Chivalry*. New Haven and London.

— 1984b. 'Heralds in the Age of Chivalry', *History Today*, 34, 33-39.

Keiser, G.R. 1995. 'Serving the needs of readers: textual division in some late-medieval English texts', in R. Beadle and A.J. Piper, eds, *New Science Out of Old Books: Studies in Manuscripts and Early Printed Books in Honour of A.I. Doyle*. Aldershot, 1995, pp. 207-26.

Kelley, M.G. 1973. 'The Douglas Earls of Angus', D. Phil. Diss. Edinburgh.

— 1978. 'Land Tenure and Forfeiture: A Sixteenth-Century Scottish Example', *Sixteenth Century Journal*, 9.3, 79-92.

King Hart see Douglas, *Shorter Poems*.

King Horn see Sands, ed., 1966.

Kinghorn, A.M., ed. 1970. *The Middle Scots Poets*. London.

Kingis Quair, The. ed. J. Norton-Smith. Oxford, 1971.

Kinsley 1959. *Sir David Lindsay. 'Squyer Meldrum'*, ed. J. Kinsley. London and Edinburgh, 1959.

— 1979. *The Poems of William Dunbar*. Oxford, 1979.

Kipling, G. 1998. *Enter the King: Theatre, Liturgy, and Ritual in the Medieval Civic Triumph*. Oxford.

Kirkpatrick, J., ed. 1904. 'The Scottish Nation in the University of Orleans 1336-1538', *Miscellany of the Scottish History Society II*. Edinburgh, 47-102.

Kish, G. 1978. *A Source Book in Geography*. Cambridge, Mass. and London.

Knecht, R.J. 1994. *Renaissance Warrior and Patron: The Reign of Francis I*. Cambridge.

Knox, John. *The History of the Reformation in Scotland*, ed. D. Laing. 6 vols, Edinburgh, 1845-64.

Kratzmann, G.C. 1980. *Anglo-Scottish Literary Relations 1430-1550*. Cambridge.

Krailsheimer, A.J. 1963. *Rabelais and the Franciscans*. Oxford.

Laing, D., ed. 1822. *Facsimile of an Ancient Heraldic Manuscript Emblazoned by Sir David Lyndsay of the Mount Lyon King of Arms 1542*. Edinburgh.

— 1867. 'A contemporary account of the Battle of Flodden, 9 September 1513', *PSAS*, 7, 141-52.

— ed. 1871. *The Poetical Works of Sir David Lyndsay of the Mount*. 2 vols. Edinburgh.

— and Hazlitt, W.C., eds. 1895. *Early Popular Poetry of Scotland and the Northern Border*. 2 vols. London.

Lamb, W. *Ane Resonyng of ane Scottish and Inglis Merchand betuix Rowand and Lionis*, ed. R.J. Lyall. Aberdeen, 1985.

Lampe, D. 1979. '"Flyting no reason hath": The Inverted Rhetoric of Abuse', in A.S. Bernardo, ed., *The Early Renaissance*. Binghampton, 1979, pp. 101-120.

Lancelot of the Laik and *Sir Tristrem*, ed. A. Lupack. Kalamazoo, 1994.

Lang, A. 1906. 'The Cardinal and the King's Will', *SHR*, 3.12, 410-22.

— 1909. 'Letters of Cardinal Beaton 1537-1541', *SHR*, 6.22, 150-58.

Lauder, William, *Ane Compendious and Breve Tractate concernyng the Office and Dewtie of Kyngis*, ed. F. Hall. EETS, 1869.

Legge, M.D. 1956. 'In fere of werre', *SHR*, 35.119, 21-25.

Leland, John. 1774. *De rebus Britannicis collectanea*. 6 vols, London.

Lemaire, de Belges, Jean. *Les Épitres de l'Amant Vert*, ed. J. Frappier. Lille and Geneva, 1948.

Leslie, John, *The Historie of Scotland wrytten first in Latin by...Jhone Leslie...and translated into Scottish by Father James Dalrymple*, ed. E.G. Cody and W. Murison. 2 vols, STS, 1888-1895.

Lewis, C.S. 1964. *The Discarded Image*. Cambridge.

Leyden, J., ed. 1801. *The Complaynt of Scotland*. Edinburgh.

Liber Pontificalis: The Book of the Popes, trans. L.R. Loomis. New York, 1916.

Lindesay *see* Pitscottie.

Lindsay, [A.]. 1849. *Lives of the Lindsays; a memoir of the houses of Crawford and Balcarres*. 3 vols, London.

Lindsay, J. 1938. 'The Lindsays of the Mount', *Publications of the Clan Lindsay Society*, 5.17, 9-82.

Loades, D. 1992. *The Tudor Navy: An administrative, political and military history*. Aldershot.

Loomis, R.S. 1919. 'The Allegorical Siege in the Art of the Middle Ages', *American Journal of Archaeology*, 23.3, 255-69.

Lucas, P.J. 1982. 'The Growth and Development of English Literary Patronage in the Later Middle Ages and Early Renaissance', *The Library*, 4.3, 219-48.

Lupack 1994 *see Lancelot of the Laik.*

Lyall, R.J. 1976. 'Politics and Poetry in Fifteenth and Sixteenth Century Scotland', *SLJ*, 3.2, 5-29.

— 1978. 'The Linlithgow Interlude of 1540', in Blanchot and Graf, eds, 1978, pp. 409-21.

— ed. 1985 *see* Lamb, *Ane Resonyng.*

— ed. 1989. *Sir David Lindsay of the Mount: 'Ane Satyre of the Thrie Estaitis'.* Edinburgh.

Lydgate, John. *Lydgate's Fall of Princes*, ed. H. Bergen. 4 vols, EETS, 1924-27.

— *Minor Poems*, ed. H.N. MacCracken. Parts I and II, EETS, 1911-34.

— *Troy Book*, ed. H. Bergen. 4 vols, EETS, 1906-35.

Lynch, M. 1988. 'The Social and Economic Structure of the Larger Towns, 1450-1600', in M. Lynch, M. Spearman and G. Stell, eds, *The Scottish Medieval Town.* Edinburgh, 1988, pp. 261-86.

— 1994. 'Religious Life in Scotland', in S. Gilley and W.J. Shiels, eds, *A History of Religion in Britain: Practice and Belief from Pre-Roman Times to the Present.* Oxford, pp. 99-124.

McClure, J.D., ed. 1983. *Scotland and the Lowland Tongue.* Aberdeen.

— and Spiller, M.R.G., eds. 1989. *Bryght Lanternis: Essays on the Language and Literature of Medieval and Renaissance Scotland.* Aberdeen.

— 1997. *Why Scots Matters.* Edinburgh.

McDiarmid, M.P. 1971. 'Sir David Lindsay's Report of the Sack of Carrickfergus 1513', *Studies in Scottish Literature*, 9.1, 40-47.

MacDonald, A.A. 1987. 'William Dunbar, Medieval Cosmography, and the Alleged first reference to the New World in English Literature', *English Studies*, 68-5, 377-91.

— 1994. 'Alliterative Poetry and its Context: The Case of William Dunbar', in L.A.J.R. Houwen and A.A. MacDonald, eds, 1994, pp. 261-79.

— Lynch, M. and Cowan, I.B., eds. 1994. *The Renaissance in Scotland: Studies in Literature, History and Culture offered to John Durkan.* Leiden.

— 1996. 'William Stewart and the Court Poetry of the Reign of James V of Scots', in Hadley Williams, ed., 1996a, pp. 179-200.

Macdougall, N. 1989. *James IV.* Edinburgh.

— 1991. '"The greattest scheip that ewer saillit in Ingland or France": James IV's "Great Michael"', in Macdougall, ed. *Scotland and War AD 79-1918.* Savage, Maryland, 1989.

— 1992. '"It is I, the Earl of Mar": In Search of Thomas Cochrane', in R. Mason and N. Macdougall, eds, *People and Power in Scotland.* Edinburgh, 1992, pp. 28-49.

Macfarlane, L.J. 1985. *William Elphinstone and The Kingdom of Scotland 1431-1514.* Aberdeen.

McFarlane, I.D. 1974. *A Literary History of France: Renaissance France 1470-1589*. London.

McGavin, J.J. 1993. 'The Dramatic Prosody of Sir David Lindsay', in R.D.S. Jack and K. McGinley, eds, *Of Lion and Of Unicorn*. Edinburgh, 1993, pp. 39-66.

McGladdery, C. 1990. *James II*. Edinburgh,

MacInnes, J. 1989. 'The Gaelic Perception of the Lowlands', in W. Gillies, ed., *Gaelic and Scotland: Alba Agus A' Ghàidhlig*. Edinburgh, 1989, pp. 89-100.

McIntosh, A. 1989. 'Some Notes on the Language and Textual Transmission of *The Scottish Troy Book*', in M. Laing, ed., *Middle English Dialectology*. Aberdeen, 1989, pp. 237-55.

McKay, D. 1962. 'Parish Life in Scotland', in McRoberts, ed., 1962, pp. 85-115.

Mackenzie, W.M., ed. 1932; 1960. *The Poems of William Dunbar*. London.

Mackie, R.L., Cruden, S. and and Fawcett, R., eds. 1982. *Arbroath Abbey*. Edinburgh.

MacLaine, A.H., ed. 1996. *The Christis Kirk Tradition: Scots Poems of Folk Festivity*. Glasgow.

Maclean, L., ed. 1981. *The Middle Ages in the Highlands*. Inverness.

McNeill, P.G. and MacQueen, H.L., eds. 1996. *Atlas of Scottish History to 1707*. Edinburgh.

Macquarrie, A. 1997. *The Saints of Scotland: Essays in Scottish Church History AD 450-1093*. Edinburgh.

McRoberts, D. 1957. 'The Medieval Scottish Liturgy illustrated by surviving documents', *Transactions of the Scottish Ecclesiological Society*, 15.1, 24-40.

— ed. 1962. *Essays on the Scottish Reformation 1513-1625*. Glasgow.

— 1972. 'The Rosary in Scotland', *IR*, 23.1, 81-86.

Macrobius, A.T. *Commentary on the Dream of Scipio*, trans. W.H. Stahl. New York, 1952.

Malory, Thomas. *Works*, ed. E. Vinaver. London, 1971.

Mapstone, S. 1994. 'The Scots *Buke of Phisnomy* and Sir Gilbert Hay', in MacDonald and others, eds, 1994, pp. 1-44.

— and Wood, J., eds. 1998. *The Rose and the Thistle: Essays on the Culture of Late Medieval and Renaissance Scotland*. East Linton.

Marwick, J.D., ed. 1869-82. *Extracts from the Records of the Burgh of Edinburgh, 1403-1589*. 4 vols, SBRS, Edinburgh.

Mason, R. 1998. *Kingship and the Commonweal: Political Thought in Renaissance and Reformation Scotland*. East Linton.

Mather, J.Y. and Speital, H.H., eds. 1975-86. *The Linguistic Atlas of Scotland*. 3 vols, London.

Mayer, C.A., ed. 1958-80. *Clément Marot: Œuvres Complètes*. 6 vols, London.

Melvill, James, *The Autobiography and Diary of Mr James Melvill*, ed. R. Pitcairn. Wodrow Society, Edinburgh, 1842.

Menzies, W. 1929. 'Robert Galbraith, 148--1543', *Aberdeen University Library Bulletin*, 7.39, 205-13.

Merriman, M.H. 'The Assured Scots: Scottish Collaborators with England During the Rough Wooing', *SHR*, 47.143, 10-34.

Mill, A.J. 1927. *Medieval Plays in Scotland*. Edinburgh.

Millar, A.H. 'Scotland Described for Queen Magdalene: A Curious Volume', *SHR*, 1.1, 27-38.

Miller, H. 1978. 'Henry VIII's Unwritten Will: Grants of Lands and Honours in 1547', in E.W. Ives, R.J. Knecht and J.J. Scarisbrick, eds, *Wealth and Power in Tudor England*. London, 1978, pp. 87-105.

Moncrieffe, I. 1982. *The Highland Clans*. London.

— and Pottinger, D. 1953; 1978. *Simple Heraldry*. Edinburgh.

Montgomerie, Alexander, *The Cherrie and the Slae*, ed. H. Harvey Wood. London, 1937.

— *The Poems*, ed. J. Cranstoun. STS, 1887.

Morse, R. 1982. '"This Vague Relation": Historical Fiction and Historical Veracity in the Later Middle Ages', *Leeds Studies in English*, 13, 85-103.

— 1985. 'Medieval Biography: History as a branch of Literature', *MLR*, 80, 257-68.

Murison, W. 1938. *Sir David Lindsay, Poet and Satirist of the Old Church in Scotland*. Cambridge.

Murray, A.L., ed. 1965. 'Accounts of the King's Pursemaster, 1539-40', *Miscellany X*, SHS, 13-51.

— 1983. 'Financing the Royal Household: James V and his Comptrollers 1513-43', in Cowan and Shaw, eds, 1983, pp. 41-59.

Murray, H.J.R. 1941. 'The Mediæval Games of Tables, *MÆ*, 10.2, 57-69.

Murray, J.A.H., ed. 1871. *The Minor Poems of Lyndesay*. Part V, EETS.

— ed. 1875. *The Romance and Prophecies of Thomas of Erceldoune*. EETS.

Neilson, W.A. 1899. *The Origins and Sources of the 'Court of Love'*, *Harvard Studies and Notes in Philology and Literature*, 6. Boston.

Nicholson, L.E. 1981. 'Chaucer's "Com Pa Me": A Famous Crux Re-examined', *English Language Notes*, 19, 98-102.

Nisbet, Murdoch. *The New Testament in Scots...by Murdoch Nisbet c. 1520*, ed. T.G. Law. 2 vols, STS, 1901-1905.

Norman, A.V.B. 1972. *Arms and Armour in the Royal Scottish Museum*. Edinburgh.

North, S. 1986. 'The Ideal Knight as presented in some French Narrative Poems, c.1090-c.1240: An Outline Sketch', in Harper-Bill and R. Harvey, eds, 1986, pp. 111-32.

Orme, N. 1984. *From Childhood to Chivalry: The Education of the English Kings and Aristocracy 1066-1530*. London and New York.

Orosius, Paulus, *Histoires (Contre les Païens)*, ed. and trans. M.-P. Arnaud-Lindet. 3 vols, Paris, 1990.

— *The Seven Books of History Against the Pagans*, ed. and trans. R.J. Deferrari. Washington, 1964.

Ortiz, A.D., Carretero, C.H. and Godoy, J.A. 1991. *Resplendence of the Spanish Monarchy: Renaissance Tapestries and Armour from the Patrimonio Nacional.* New York.

Panofsky, E. 1939; 1962. *Studies in Iconology: Humanistic Themes in the Art of the Renaissance.* New York.

Parkinson, D. 1991. '"Holtis Hair": Tracking a Phrase Through Middle Scots Poetry', *SSL*, 26, 309-18.

Paton, G.C.H., ed. 1958. *An Introduction to Scottish Legal History.* Edinburgh.

Pearl, ed. E.V. Gordon. Oxford, 1953.

Pearsall, D. 1970. *John Lydgate.* London.

— and Salter, E. 1973. *Landscapes and Seasons of the Medieval World.* London.

Pearson, D. 1992. 'The Libraries of English Bishops, 1600-40', *The Library*, 14, 221-57.

Perrow, E.C. 1913. 'The Last Will and Testament as a Form of Literature', *Wisconsin Academy of Sciences, Arts, and Letters, 17*, 682-753.

Pitscottie, Robert Lindesay of, *The Historie and Cronicles of Scotland*, ed. Æ.J.G. Mackay. 3 vols, STS, 1899-1911.

Pliny [the Elder], *Natural History*, ed. H. Rackham, W.H.S. Jones and D.E. Eichholz. 10 vols, London, 1938-63.

Prymer, or Lay Folks Prayer Book, The, ed. H. Littlehales. 2 vols, EETS, 1895-97.

Ptolemy, Claudius, ed. Sebastian Münster, *Geographia*, Basle, 1540. Ed. R.A. Skelton. Amsterdam, 1966.

Purser, J. 1992. *Scotland's Music.* Edinburgh and London.

— 1996. '*Graysteil*', in Hadley Williams, ed., 1996a, pp. 142-52.

RCAHMS. 1929. *Tenth Report with Inventory of Monuments and Constructions in the Counties of Midlothian and West Lothian.* Edinburgh.

— 1933. *Eleventh Report...in the Counties of Fife, Kinross, and Clackmannan.* Edinburgh.

— 1963. *Stirlingshire. An Inventory of Ancient Monuments.* Edinburgh.

Ratis Raving and Other Early Scots Poems on Morals, ed. R. Girvan. STS, 1939.

Rauf Coilȝear see Speed, ed., 1989.

Rentale Sancti Andree, being the chamberlain and granitar accounts of the archbishopric in the time of Cardinal Betoun, 1538-1546, ed. R.K. Hannay. SHS, Edinburgh, 1913.

Rice, W.H. 1941. *The European Ancestry of Villon's Satirical Testaments.* New York.

Richmond, V.B. 1966. *Laments for the Dead in Medieval Narrative.* Pittsburgh.

Riddy, F. 1974. '*Squyer Meldrum* and the Romance of Chivalry', *YES*, 14, 26-36.

Ringler, W.A. 1992. *Bibliography and Index of English Verse Printed 1476-1558.* London and New York.

Robbins, R.H., ed. 1955. *Secular Lyrics of the XIVth and XVth Centuries*, Oxford.

Robinson, P. 1984. 'Tenements: A Pre-Industrial Urban Tradition', *Review of Scottish Culture*, 1, 52-64.

Rolland, John, *The seuin Seages*, ed. G.F. Black. STS, 1932.

Ross, A. 1962. 'Some notes on the Religious Orders in Pre-Reformation Scotland', in McRoberts, ed., 1962, pp. 185-233.

Ross, D.J. 1993. *Musick Fyne: Robert Carver and the Art of Music in Sixteenth Century Scotland*. Edinburgh.

Row, John, *The History of the Kirk of Scotland, from the year 1558 to August 1637*, [ed. D. Laing]. Wodrow Society, Edinburgh, 1842.

Rowland, B. 1971. *Blind Beasts. Chaucer's Animal World*. Chatham.

— 1978. *Birds with Human Souls*. Knoxville.

Royan, N. 1998. 'The Relationship between the *Scotorum Historia* of Hector Boece and John Bellenden's *Chronicles of Scotland*', in Mapstone and Wood, eds, 1998, pp. 136-57.

Russell, J.G. 1992. *Diplomats at Work*. Stroud.

Sacrobosco *see* Thorndike, 1949.

Sanderson, M.H.B. 1986. *Cardinal of Scotland: David Beaton c.1494-1546*. Edinburgh.

Sands, D.B., ed. 1966. *Middle English Verse Romances*. New York.

Sanger, K. and Kinnaird, A. 1992. *Tree of Strings: crann nan teud: a history of the harp in Scotland*. Temple.

Sarum Breviary, ed. F. Proctor and C. Wordsworth. 3 vols, Cambridge, 1879-86.

Sarum Missal, done into English, The, ed. A. Harford Pearson. London, 1868; 1884.

Satirical Poems of the Time of the Reformation see Cranstoun, ed., 1891-93.

Saunders, A.M. 1974. 'Symbolism in Colour: Colours and their symbolic values in literature of the fifteenth and sixteenth centuries in France', *Aberdeen University Review*, 45.3, No. 151, 242-53.

Scanlan, J.D. 1958. 'Husband and Wife. Pre-Reformation Canon Law of Marriage of the Officials' Courts', in Paton, ed., 1958, pp. 69-89.

Scattergood, V.J. 1971. *Politics and Poetry in the Fifteenth Century*. London.

Scheibe, R. 1996. *A Catalogue of Amphibians and Reptiles in Older Scots Literature*. Frankfurt am Main.

Scott, Alexander, *Justing and Debait* see Bawcutt and Riddy, eds, 1987.

Selkirk Protocol Books 1511-1547, eds. T. Malley and W. Elliott. Stair Society, Edinburgh, 1993.

Sex Werkdays and Agis: An Edition of a Late Medieval Scots Universal History from the Asloan Manuscript, ed. L.A.J.R. Houwen. Groningen, 1990.

Seznec, J. 1972. *The Survival of the Pagan Gods*, trans. B.F. Sessions. Princeton, 1953; 1972.

Shire, H.M. 1969. *Song, Dance and Poetry of the Court of Scotland Under King James VI*. Cambridge.

Shirley, R.W. 1987. *The Mapping of the World: Printed World Maps 1472-1700*. London.

Simpson, G.G. 1977. *Scottish Handwriting 1150-1650. An Introduction to the Reading of Documents*. Aberdeen.

Sir Cleges see Speed, ed., 1989.

Sir Gawain and the Green Knight, ed. J.R.R. Tolkien and E.V. Gordon. Oxford, 1925; 1967.

Skelton, John, *The Complete English Poems*, ed. J. Scattergood. Harmondsworth, 1983.

Spearing, A.C. 1976. *Medieval Dream-Poetry*. Cambridge.

Speed, D., ed. 1987; 1989. *Medieval English Romances*. 2 Parts, Sydney. [Includes *Sir Cleges, Rauf Coilȝear, The Grene Knight*.]

Stanley, T. 1687. *The History of Philosophy*. London.

Starkey, D., ed. 1991. *Henry VIII: A European Court in England*. London.

Stevenson, J.H. 1914. *Heraldry in Scotland*. 2 vols, Glasgow.

Stewart, A.M. 1972. 'Carion, Wedderburn, Lindsay', *Aberdeen University Review*, No. 147, 271-74.

Stewart, I.H. 1955. *The Scottish Coinage*. London.

Stewart, M.M. 1972. 'Holland of the *Howlat*', *IR*, 23.1, 3-15.

Stewart, *Croniclis*. William Stewart, *The Buik of the Croniclis of Scotland; A Metrical Version of the History of Hector Boece*, ed. W.B. Turnbull. 3 vols, London, 1858.

Strohm, P. 1975-76. '*Passion, Lyf, Miracle, Legende*: Some Generic Terms in Hagiographical Narrative', *Chaucer Review*, 10, 1975-76, 63-75 and 154-171.

— 1982. 'A Note on Gower's Persona', in M.J. Carruthers and E.D. Kirk, eds, *Acts of Interpretation*. Norman, Oklahoma, 1982, pp. 293-98.

Strong, R. 1973. *Splendour at Court: Renaissance Spectacle and Illusion*. London.

Stuart, J., ed. 1872. *Record of the Monastery of Kinloss*. Edinburgh.

Sutton A.F. and Visser-Fuchs, L. 1996. 'The Cult of Angels in Late Fifteenth-Century England: An Hours of the Guardian Angel presented to Queen Elizabeth Woodville', in J.H.M. Taylor and L. Smith, eds, *Women and the Book*. London, 1996, pp. 230-65.

— 1997. *Richard III's Books*. Stroud.

Syr Eglamour see *CM*.

Testament du Gentil Cossoys, see Baird Smith, 1920.

Teulet, A. ed., 1852-60. *Papiers d'état: pièces et documents inédits...à l'histoire de l'Ecosse au XVIème siècle*. 3 vols, Bannatyne Club, Paris.

Thorndike, L. 1949. *The 'Sphere' of Sacrobosco and its Commentators*. Chicago.

Thre Prestis of Peblis, The, ed. T.D. Robb. STS, 1920.

Thrie Estaitis, see Hamer 1931-36.

Tilley, M.P. 1950. *A Dictionary of the Proverbs in England in the Sixteenth and Seventeenth Centuries*. Ann Arbor.

Tyndale, William, *Tyndale's Old Testament being the Pentateuch of 1530, Joshua to 2 Chronicles of 1537, and Jonah, translated by William Tyndale*, ed. D. Daniell. New Haven and London, 1992.

Utley, F.L. 1944. *The Crooked Rib: An Analytic Index to the Argument about Women in English and Scots Literature to...1568*. New York.

Vulgate. Biblia Vulgata, ed. A. Colunga and L. Turrado. Madrid, 1965.

Wallace see Hary.

Warton, T. 1824. *The History of English Poetry*. 4 vols. London.

Watry, P.B. 1992. 'Sixteenth Century Printing Types and Ornaments of Scotland with an Introductory Survey of the Scottish Book Trade', D. Phil. Diss. Oxford.

Watt, H. 1935. 'Henry Balnaves and the Scottish Reformation', *RSCHS*, 5, 23-39.

Wedderburn, *see Complaynt of Scotland*, ed. Stewart, 1979.

White, T.H., ed. 1954. *The Book of Beasts, being a translation from a Latin Bestiary of the Twelfth Century*. London.

Whiting, B.J. 1949-51. 'Proverbs and Proverbial Sayings from Scottish Writings Before 1600', *Mediaeval Studies*, 11, 123-205 and 13, 87-164.

— and Whiting, H.W. 1968. *Proverbs, Sentences, and Proverbial Phrases from English Writings Mainly before 1500*. Cambridge, Mass.

Williams, A.M. 1915. 'Sir David Lindsay: 1490-1555', *SHR*, 12, 166-73.

Williams, J.H. *see* Hadley Williams, J.

Williamson, A.H. 1993. 'A Patriot Nobility? Calvinism, Kin-Ties and Civic Humanism', *SHR*, 72.1: No. 193, 1-21.

Wilson, E. 1994. 'The *Testament of the Buck* and the Sociology of the Text', *Review of English Studies*, 45.178, 157-84.

Wood, M., ed. 1923. *Foreign Correspondence with Marie de Lorraine...1537-1548*. SHS, Edinburgh.

— ed. 1941. *Protocol Book of John Foular*. Vol. I., pt ii, SRS, Edinburgh.

Woolf, R. 1968. *The English Religious Lyric in the Middle Ages*. Oxford.

Works Accounts I. Accounts of the Masters of Works for Building and Repairing of Royal Palaces and Castles, 1529-1615. Vol. I, ed. H.M. Paton. Edinburgh, 1957.

Wormald, J. 1985a. *Lords and Men in Scotland: Bonds of Manrent 1442-1603*. Edinburgh.

— 1985b. 'Taming the Magnates?' in K. J. Stringer, ed., *Essays on the Nobility of Medieval Scotland. Edinburgh*, 1985, pp. 270-80.

— 1986. 'Lords and Lairds in Fifteenth-Century Scotland: Nobles and Gentry?', in M. Jones, ed., *Gentry and Lesser Nobility in Late Medieval Europe*. New York, 1986, pp. 181-200.

— 1988. *Mary Queen of Scots*. London.

Wright, C.E. 1973. *English Heraldic Manuscripts in the British Museum*. London.

Wyatt, Thomas, *Collected Poems*, ed. J. Daalder. Oxford, 1975.

Wyntoun, Andrew, *The Original Chronicle*, ed. F.J. Amours. 6 vols, STS, 1902-1914.

Yapp, B. 1981. *Birds in Medieval Manuscripts*. London.

— 1982. 'Birds in captivity in the Middle Ages', *Archives of Natural History*, 10.3, 479-500.

THE ASSOCIATION FOR SCOTTISH LITERARY STUDIES

ANNUAL VOLUMES

Volumes marked * are still available from the address given opposite the title page of this book.

1971 James Hogg, *The Three Perils of Man*, ed. Douglas Gifford.

1972 *The Poems of John Davidson*, vol. I, ed. Andrew Turnbull.

1973 *The Poems of John Davidson*, vol. II, ed. Andrew Turnbull.

1974 Allan Ramsay and Robert Fergusson, *Poems*, ed. Alexander M. Kinghorn and Alexander Law.

1975 John Galt, *The Member*, ed. Ian A. Gordon.

1976 William Drummond of Hawthornden, *Poems and Prose*, ed. Robert H. MacDonald.

1977 John G. Lockhart, *Peter's Letters to his Kinsfolk*, ed. William Ruddick.

1978 John Galt, *Selected Short Stories*, ed. Ian A. Gordon.

1979 Andrew Fletcher of Saltoun, *Selected Political Writings and Speeches*, ed. David Daiches.

1980 *Scott on Himself*, ed. David Hewitt.

1981 *The Party-Coloured Mind*, ed. David Reid.

1982 James Hogg, *Selected Stories and Sketches*, ed. Douglas S. Mack.

1983 Sir Thomas Urquhart of Cromarty, *The Jewel*, ed. R.D.S. Jack and R.J. Lyall.

1984 John Galt, *Ringan Gilhaize*, ed. Patricia J. Wilson.

1985 Margaret Oliphant, *Selected Short Stories of the Supernatural*, ed. Margaret K. Gray.

1986 James Hogg, *Selected Poems and Songs*, ed. David Groves.

1987* Hugh MacDiarmid, *A Drunk Man Looks at the Thistle*, ed. Kenneth Buthlay.

1988 *The Book of Sandy Stewart*, ed. Roger Leitch.

1989* *The Comic Poems of William Tennant*, ed. Alexander Scott and Maurice Lindsay.

1990* Thomas Hamilton, *The Youth and Manhood of Cyril Thornton*, ed. Maurice Lindsay.

1991* *The Complete Poems of Edwin Muir*, ed. Peter Butter.

1992* *The Tavern Sages: Selections from the 'Noctes Ambrosianae'*, ed. J.H. Alexander.

1993* *Gaelic Poetry in the Eighteenth Century*, ed. D.S. Thomson.

1994* Violet Jacob, *Flemington*, ed. Carol Anderson.

1995* *'Scotland's Ruine': Lockhart of Carnwath's Memoirs of the Union*, ed. Daniel Szechi, with a foreword by Paul Scott.

1996* *The Christis Kirk Tradition: Scots Poems of Folk Festivity*, ed. Allan H. MacLaine.

1997-8* *The Poems of William Dunbar* (two vols.), ed. Priscilla Bawcutt.

1999* *The Scotswoman at Home and Abroad*, ed. Dorothy McMillan.